# Contents

*List of Figures*                                                   *page* ix
*Acknowledgements*                                                        xii
*Note on Names, Terms, and Abbreviations*                                xiv

Introduction: History as Performance History                               1

1    Forms and Increments of Performance                                  11
     Meetings as Cultural Form                                            16
     Meetings with Mobbings                                               30
     In Judgement at Meetings                                             38
     Perceptible Dramaturgies                                            54
     Advocacy, Judgement, and Play                                       57

2    Change Making: Incrementalism                                       72
     A Change Came O'er the Spirit of Our Dream                          72
     Give Me the Hurricane                                                77
     Sowing the Seeds of a New Truth                                      87
     The Case against the Company                                         99
     Race: Principles and Performance Strategies                        115
     George Thompson, MP                                                 128
     Grant Me Life, and I Will Solve the Problem                         134

3    *Bildung*: Leveraging Critique to Propel the Precarious
     into Political Life                                                  161
     Recirculation                                                        162
     Networked Self-cultivation                                           175
     Into the Fray                                                        180
     Ties That Bind                                                       184
     Activism                                                             192
     Activism across Distance                                            197
     Advocating Activism                                                 208
     Observational Citizenship                                           213

4   Combative Pens                                                     232
    Cable Knit                                                         234
    Quotidian Activism                                                 242
    The Jamaica Affair                                                 250
    Crime Scenes: 'Doing' Activism, Conceiving Human Rights            261
    Reputations                                                        274

5   Experiments in Becoming                                            287
    Great Exhibitions                                                  288
    Great Inhibitions                                                  297
    Work: Relationalist Subjecthood                                    306
    Sociability: The Power of Weak Publics                             322
    Domestic Life: 'But still the house-affairs would draw her thence' 328

*Bibliography*                                                         345
*Index*                                                                370

# LIBERAL LIVES AND ACTIVIST REPERTOIRES

This ambitious study traces the strategies of human rights activists to show how world-changing reform movements were shaped by women and men from modest backgrounds who were deeply attuned to the power of performance. Tracy C. Davis explores nineteenth-century reform campaigns through the pioneering work of a family of activists – prominent anti-slavery lecturer George Thompson, his daughter Amelia (the first female theatre and music critic for a British daily newspaper), and her husband, the political organiser Frederick Chesson. Engaging in some of the most important social struggles of the late Georgian and Victorian periods – including abolition, enfranchisement, and anti-genocide – this book reveals how two generations' insights into performance consolidated into activist tactics that persist today. Characterised by a skilful deployment of performance theory alongside deep and wide-ranging historical knowledge, this ground-breaking work demonstrates what 'dramaturgy' can teach us about 'history'.

TRACY C. DAVIS is Barber Professor of Performing Arts and Professor of Theatre and English at Northwestern University. She has published books on nineteenth-century theatre, the economics and business history of theatre, performance theory, and gender and theatre. Her latest book combines these interests in a study of two generations of Victorian activists.

# LIBERAL LIVES AND ACTIVIST REPERTOIRES

*Political Performance and Victorian Social Reform*

TRACY C. DAVIS

*Northwestern University, Illinois*

CAMBRIDGE
UNIVERSITY PRESS

Shaftesbury Road, Cambridge CB2 8EA, United Kingdom

One Liberty Plaza, 20th Floor, New York, NY 10006, USA

477 Williamstown Road, Port Melbourne, VIC 3207, Australia

314–321, 3rd Floor, Plot 3, Splendor Forum, Jasola District Centre,
New Delhi – 110025, India

103 Penang Road, #05–06/07, Visioncrest Commercial, Singapore 238467

Cambridge University Press is part of Cambridge University Press & Assessment,
a department of the University of Cambridge.

We share the University's mission to contribute to society through the pursuit of
education, learning and research at the highest international levels of excellence.

www.cambridge.org
Information on this title: www.cambridge.org/9781009297530

DOI: 10.1017/9781009297554

First published 2023

Printed in the United Kingdom by TJ Books Limited, Padstow, Cornwall

*A catalogue record for this publication is available from the British Library.*

*Library of Congress Cataloging-in-Publication Data*
NAMES: Davis, Tracy C., 1960– author.
TITLE: Liberal lives and activist repertoires : political performance and
Victorian social reform / Tracy C. Davis, Northwestern University, Illinois.
DESCRIPTION: Cambridge, United Kingdom ; New York : Cambridge University
Press, 2023. | Includes bibliographical references and index.
IDENTIFIERS: LCCN 2022049033 (print) | LCCN 2022049034 (ebook) |
ISBN 9781009297530 (hardback) | ISBN 9781009297554 (ebook)
SUBJECTS: LCSH: Great Britain – Politics and government – 19th century. |
Political participation – Great Britain – History – 19th century. | Protest
movements – Great Britain – History – 19th century. | Theater – Political
aspects – Great Britain – History – 19th century. | Social movements – Great
Britain – History – 19th century.
CLASSIFICATION: LCC DA530 .D335 2023 (print) | LCC DA530 (ebook) |
DDC 941.081–dc23/eng/20230213
LC record available at https://lccn.loc.gov/2022049033
LC ebook record available at https://lccn.loc.gov/2022049034

ISBN 978-1-009-29753-0 Hardback

*In ever-loving memory*
*of*
*Thora and Ernie Davis*

*Dedicated*
*to reconciliation,*
*the process and aspiration*

Some people have an idea that reforms consist of one great spasmodic effort; but, to succeed, we must be willing to work slowly, by patient and often unheralded endeavour. Read the history of the reforms of the world. What patient persistence! What endeavour to build better!

(Gough, Orations, 3)

# *Figures*

1.1 George Thompson (by Charles Turner after George
Evans), mezzotint, 1842. NPG D4367, National Portrait
Gallery, London.                                                    *page* 24

1.2 A meeting at Exeter Hall on the abolition of the slave trade,
engraving by H. Melville after T. H. Shepherd, ca. 1841.
578856i, Wellcome Collection.                                              31

1.3 Poster dated 30 October 1835, Thompson Extract Books, LC
3449.S43. Library of Congress.                                             36

1.4 Frederick Chesson, Portraits of US Abolitionists, 81.137,
Massachusetts Historical Society, 81.                                      39

1.5 Presentation of testimonial plate to Charles Kean at
St James's Hall, London. *Illustrated London News*,
29 March 1862, 319.                                                        44

1.6 Charles Spurgeon preaching at Surrey Music Hall, Kennington
(Spurgeon, *Sermons Preached and Revised*, frontispiece, 1859),
University of Virginia Library.                                            47

2.1 Peter Borthwick. *Illustrated London News*, 7 January 1843, 8.
Getty Images.                                                             82

2.2 East India Court of Proprietors. *Illustrated London News*, 4
May 1844, 289. Getty Images.                                             104

2.3 Dwarkanath Tagore (1846), steel mezzotint engraved by
George Raphael Ward after a painting by Frederick Richard
Say, 1846, 1110.1. British Museum.                                       108

2.4 Shah of Delhi's Elephant, Sir Thomas Metcalfe (1795–1853),
Add.Or.5475, fol.59c-B. British Library.                                 115

2.5 Tower Hamlets election, showing the hustings at Stepney
Green during George Thompson's bid for re-election.
*Illustrated London News*, 10 July 1852, 24. Getty Images.               130

3.1   *Voyage Round the Globe*, Haymarket Theatre, Playbill, 29
      April 1854. *British Library Volume Playbills* 146 (1). Creative
      Commons licence.                                                    162
3.2   Mr Albert Smith's *Ascent of Mont Blanc* at the Egyptian Hall,
      Piccadilly. *Illustrated London News*, 25 December 1852, 565.
      Getty Images.                                                       164
3.3   Abolition meeting held at Willis's Rooms in honour of Harriet
      Beecher Stowe, 1853, William Henry Fisk, watercolour. Getty
      Images.                                                             164
3.4   Feat of Mr Sands, the 'air walker', Drury Lane Theatre.
      *Illustrated London News*, 2 April 1853, 253. Getty Images.        165
3.5   'Mr Wyld's Model of the Earth', Leicester Square. *Illustrated
      London News*, 7 June 1851, 511. Getty Images.                      166
3.6   Scene from the tragedy of *Sardanapalus*, the Hall of Nimrod,
      Princess's Theatre. *Illustrated London News*, 18 June 1853, 493.  168
3.7   George Cruickshank, 'Passing Events, or The Tail of the
      Comet of 1853', etching, *Cruikshank's Magazine*, January 1854.
      2017JW5484, Theaterwissenschaftliche Sammlung, University
      of Cologne.                                                        170
3.8   The Volunteer Review in Hyde Park, return of volunteer corps
      down Constitution Hill. *Illustrated London News*, 30 July 1860,
      617. Getty Images.                                                 215
3.9   'Great Anti-Slavery Demonstration at Exeter Hall.' *Illustrated
      London News*, 7 February 1863, 154. Getty Images.                  216
4.1   John Tenniel, 'A word to the mermaids.' *Punch*, 5 August 1865,
      49. Getty Images.                                                  238
4.2   'Amateur dramatic entertainment on board the Great Eastern
      steam-ship at sea'. *Illustrated London News*, 28 July 1866, 80.
      Getty Images.                                                      239
4.3   Robert Charles Dudley, 'Awaiting the reply', oil painting,
      ca. 1866, Metropolitan Museum of Art, Accession number
      92.10.43.                                                          240
4.4   Motto of the Aborigines' Protection Society, 'Ab uno sanguine'
      [from one blood], cover of *The Colonial Intelligencer; or,
      Aborigines' Friend*, 1852. University of Wisconsin Library,
      (public domain).                                                   244
4.5   'Execution of rebels at the ruins of the court house, Morant
      Bay.' Alexander Dudgeon Gulland, compiler, photography
      album, albumen print of pen and ink drawing. Special
      Collections, Princeton University Library.                         255

4.6 Open-air meeting at Blackheath to hear Mr Gladstone on
the Turkish atrocities. *Illustrated London News*, 16 September
1876, 173. 271

5.1 The US exhibits, including Hiram Powers' sculpture *The Greek
Slave*, Great Exhibition, 1851. From *Recollections of the Great
Exhibition*, Library of Congress. 291

5.2 John Tenneil, 'The Virginian Slave: Intended as a companion
to Power's "Greek Slave."' *Punch*, 7 June 1851, 236. 293

5.3 'The abolition of the slave trade' (a.k.a. 'The Anti-Slavery
Society Convention', lithograph by John Alfred Vinter, after
Benjamin Robert Haydon, 1840), lithograph, ca. 1846–64.
D20516, National Portrait Gallery. 298

5.4 'Key to the Anti-Slavery Society Convention, 1840' (list of
sitters in the picture by Benjamin Robert Haydon), letterpress,
1880, PG D23547. National Portrait Gallery. 299

5.5 'Looking eastward from Fleet Street (1857).' This was Amelia
Chesson's route to the *Star* office. Blanchard, *Bradshaw's
Guide*, 15. Oxford University Press. 310

5.6 Camille Pisarro, *Crystal Palace Sydenham*, 1871. Art Institute of
Chicago. 314

5.7 'The Great Handel Festival.' *Illustrated London News*, 27 June
1857, 640. 315

5.8 Amelia Chesson: Maternal age at parturition and children's
longevity. 321

# Acknowledgements

This project was incubated during a fellowship from Queen Mary University of London. Periods of study at the Centre for Advanced Studies at Ludwig Maximilian University of Munich, New College Oxford, and the John Rylands Library (JRL) were augmented with stupendous generosity from the Alexander von Humboldt Foundation, which enabled several residencies at the Theaterwissenschaftliche Sammlung and the Institute for Media Culture and Theatre at Cologne University. There, Peter W. Marx was the resident genie who listened with endless patience, encouragement, and wisdom as I tried out ideas. Additional primary research at the British Library, Library of Congress, University of Michigan Clements Library, and Bodleian Library undergirds the book. This long labour ended with a faculty fellowship from the Kaplan Institute for the Humanities, where I wrote most of the book during trying months of the Covid-19 pandemic. What a port during a year of storms.

Little could happen until the Chessons' diaries were scanned, transcribed, and annotated. My thanks to the JRL for the scans, to Josh Honn who guided the digital humanities facet of this work at Northwestern University, and to all the kindly souls at Northwestern University Library and the Hathi Trust. The Provost's Undergraduate Research Program (URAP) enabled me to train undergraduates to transcribe the holographs. Some were impressively good at it, and it was always fun to tell twenty year olds that the busy days and stunning productivity of Frederick Chesson came from a man near their own age with half their education. Thanks to Rudy Russe Eiland, Alexander Kurland, and Benjamin David Ratskoff, and to Kayla Hammersmith for genealogical research with lasting benefits. Dana Pepowski lent her exacting eye and discretion to the citations. Numerous doctoral students brought additional skills – such as project management, bibliography, and database construction – and I hope that working on this was even a fraction as useful to them as it has been to me. Here, at last, is the fruit of your labours: Lauren Beck, David Calder, John

Carnwath, Shane Clauser, Lia Dewey, Laura Ferdinand, Gillian Hemme, Elizabeth Hunter, Alex Knapp, Liz Laurie, Aileen Robinson, Holly Dayton Swenson, Keary Watts, and Elynne Whaley, I salute you.

Colleagues at Northwestern have commented on portions of the work, given encouragement, and in many ways populated the echo chamber of my study and my mind. Special thanks to Deborah Anne Cohen, Gary Fine, Christopher Herbert, D. Soyini Madison, Tessie Liu, Angela Ray, Liz Son, and David Zarefsky. Prateek provided valuable advice while on his Fulbright Post-doc. Department chairs have animated possibilities through clever administrative acumen so my appreciation goes to Rives Collins, Henry Godinez, Ramón Rivera-Servera, and Harvey Young. Beverley Wright listened to all kinds of mutterings and exclamations as I wrote the book, offering gentle questions that always probed the heart of the matter. The unsparingly smart Evanston Workshop members – Jordana Cox, Marcy Dinius, Lisa Freeman, Laura MacDonald, Stefka Mihaylova, Noémie Ndiaye, Aileen Robinson, Marlis Schweitzer, and Ann Folino White – were also wonderful interlocutors.

I am indebted to numerous scholarly organisations and colleagues who invited me to share work in progress. Special appreciation is due to Josh Abrams, Christopher Balme, Marin Blažević, Simona Brunetti, Michael Burden, Vicki Ann Cremona, Jim Davis, Kate Dorney, Bishnupriya Dutt, Lade Čale Feldman, Tony Fisher, John Fletcher, Maggie Gale, Jonathan Hicks, Stefan Hulfeld, Sonja Kuftinec, Nic Leonhardt, Charlotte McIvor, Michael McKinnie, David Levin, Martin Puchner, and Nick Ridout.

There are so many people who made research a pleasure. Susan Bennett, Jacky Bratton, Gilli Bush-Bailey, Penny Farfan, and Heather Nathans talked with me when they had a great deal of other things to do, but are just the kind of people who make academia worth the bother. Helen and David Mayer have offered Mancunian hospitality too many times to count. In Cologne, Kerstin Schorner and Friederike Heuck facilitated many things, always with kindness and good results. The incomparable Katharina Görgen taught me German with valiant optimism. Marie Franck, Sabine Päsler, Alexandra Portmann, Sofie Taubert, Christine Vollmert, Elena Weber, and the peerless Sascha Förster were the leading lights of Cologne, all helpful, generous, creative, brilliant people.

Max Shapey welcomed George, Fred, and Millie into our house for over a decade, but even when I took the trio abroad he kept the home fires burning. Thanks for everything. Now we give the eviction notice to our long-dead tenants.

# Note on Names, Terms, and Abbreviations

Whenever possible, the first appearance of a name includes inclusive dates. This emphasizes how individuals align with George Thompson's (b. 1804) and Amelia and Frederick Chesson's (b. 1833) lives. Respectively, they were the last Georgian and first Victorian generations. Later critics, historians, and theorists are not accorded dates.

For readers unfamiliar with the terminology of British Protestant sects, designations can be confusing. In England, the state-supported Established Church was styled the Church of England, or the Episcopal Church (thus, the Anglican Church in British colonies). Anglicanism was the Established Church in Ireland, styled the Church of Ireland despite the Catholic majority. In Scotland, the Established Church was Presbyterian. Any Protestant outside these congregations was a Nonconformist; most prominently, during the nineteenth century, this designated Congregationalists, Baptists, Methodists, and Quakers. If, additionally, a Nonconformist also disagreed with the principle of national or state churches they could be styled a Dissenter.

The Reform Movement – a constellation of efforts to enfranchise Britons, revise parliamentary seat selection and district definition, and alter voting methods – is indicated through capitalization, true to its contemporaneous usage. Allied causes, such as disestablishment of the Churches of England and Ireland, Nonconformists' access to university education, universal primary education, abolition of slavery, and labour rights – all fuelled by liberal critiques – are reform causes (lower-case). Liberal Members of Parliament (MPs) adhered more or less to Reform and reform – sometimes as Radicals (a semi-organized faction) or radicals (believers in liberalism's more extreme ideas, atheism, and/or republicanism). Not strictly a party in the later sense, Liberals nevertheless rallied to vote pro-reform as liberals (lower-case). Chartism (active 1836–48) was a working-class movement that arose in reaction to the limitation of the 1832 Reform Act's granting of suffrage only to men of the property-owning middle classes. Named after the People's Charter, Chartists advocated for universal suffrage for men aged twenty-one and older, a secret ballot, no property qualifications for MPs, salaries for MPs, equally proportioned electoral districts, and annual parliamentary elections.

A few frequently occurring organisations are abbreviated:

| | |
|---|---|
| ACLL | Anti-Corn Law League |
| APS | Aborigines' Protection Society |
| AASS | American Anti-Slavery Society |
| BFASS | British and Foreign Anti-Slavery Society |
| The Company | British East India Company |
| HBC | Hudson's Bay Company |
| JRL | John Rylands Library |
| MP | Member of Parliament |

# *History as Performance History*

What does acuity to dramaturgy bring to the study of history, and vice versa?

This close examination of two generations of a nineteenth-century British family shows how people from modest backgrounds, with little formal education, could have a great impact on the implementation of liberal policy in Britain. This was achieved through a particular kind of cultural knowledge. Letters and diaries, private and professional correspondence, journalism, lecture transcripts, pamphlets, tracts, and other ephemeral publications demonstrate precocious and consistent use of observation and critique of performances. (Here, performance is broadly defined, encompassing the spectrum from opera to orations; platform speaking to pantomimes; technical demonstrations to parades and rallies; and quotidian acts of attestation and empathy.) They utilised this habit of scrutinising performance to improve the efficacy of reform work on behalf of the key liberal tenets of the late Georgian and Victorian period, inclusive of domestic and foreign, legislative and extra-parliamentary change. Their activity and discourse, tracked over time, shows growing perceptivity, sophistication, and variety. Insights consolidated into tactics that gradually changed the world and persist until today in impetus, impact, and form. Through the optic of this family, history *is* performance history.

Given that so many nineteenth-century populations suffered under liberalism's imperial and capitalist manifestations, a 'progress narrative' of political theory yoked to performance is unjustifiable. Nevertheless, among liberals there were also trenchant critics of colonisation, rapacious enslavement and labour practices, and the consequences of open markets, and thus liberalism warrants attention as a history of advocacy that engaged rhetorics of reform. Together with their national and international networks of collaborators, the reformers central to this book sustained numerous single-issue campaigns, starting with the abolition of slavery in British Caribbean colonies during the early 1830s. Linking the liberal causes of abolition and human rights to free trade as the key to British prosperity and international amity, and championing universal suffrage and parliamentary reform (reorganisation of seats and voting methods, and separation of church and state), they began agitating through *meetings, lectures,* and *debates* in halls and the open air, then broadened to *bazaars* and *trade fairs.* In the 1840s, the Anti-Corn Law League (ACLL, advocates of a free market, notably repeal of tariffs on imported grain) and the Reform League (champions of expanded male suffrage) extensively *petitioned* as a performance tactic. Just as vociferous participation at meetings performatively indicated public opinion, petitions performed political dramaturgy: beginning with each individual's act to *affix a signature or mark,* petitions grew into bulky documents that were *exhibited* at meetings, *paraded* through the streets, and ceremoniously *delivered* to Parliament. Theatrical flair was inherent to how each phase of a petition's creation and deployment transpired. With the emergence of coordinated *letter-writing campaigns,* a new repertoire for liberal reform emerged that extended the act of affixing a signature to composing a document (a durational act of conscience); this was followed by small-group in-person *depositions* and *lobbying,* then participation in *mass meetings* where arguments were tested, points of view enacted, and both individual and public resolve reaffirmed. These tactical performances utilised the dramaturgical tools of 'timing, surprise, strong visuals, compelling characters, dynamic tension, specificity, discipline, and rehearsal' to optimise outcomes.[1] Leadership came from prominent organisers such as John Bright, Richard Cobden, Lord Brougham, and Edmond Beales, bolstered by the influential liberal theorists John Stuart Mill, John Elliott Cairnes, and Herbert Spencer. Working alongside them were the chief figures of this book: George Thompson, his daughter Amelia Chesson, and her husband, Frederick Chesson. Their acts consolidated into a legible repertoire manipulated by dedicated reformers as well as the wider public and maintained to the present day. Though there was no unifying concept for it at the time, the umbrella term for what they did is now called activism.

Activism is a set of techniques, and like all human endeavours these techniques have a history. Reform, protest, and agitation are populist tactics dating back to the 1400s to the 1700s. During the nineteenth century, lobbying and demonstrating were added to the English lexicon. Such acts promoted the conception and dissemination of alternative ways of knowing by advocating for those whose lives under capitalism and/or colonialism were precarious and whose ability to register politically was (at best) notional. In addition to national issues, activism aimed to counter some of the most deleterious practices of nineteenth-century globalisation – land appropriation, human trafficking, and territorial warfare exacerbated by imperialism, 'colour prejudice', sexism, and jingoism – on behalf of those with limited or no power (the enslaved, exploited, and low-waged or unemployed, peoples at risk of extinction, and women, who could not elect their parliamentary or local representatives). Complementing the backroom performative tactics of persuading men of power to implement liberal ideas, *marches*, *rallies*, and *mass meetings* were public shows of conviction that enabled peoples experiencing precarity to also 'do' activism in new ways. Cooperatives and trades unions added to the repertoire, and innovators including the suffragettes and Mahatma Gandhi showed how to leverage *personal sacrifices* such as hunger strikes and *coordinated acts* such as the 1930 Salt March to accrue power for the powerless. After 1950, as *occupations* began to be emphasised, forms of *personal testimonial* that involved privation, self-restraint, or even immolation – allied with the new modes of *performance art* such as entertaining *zaps* – augmented the repertoire to focus more explicitly on performing. Our contemporary concept of activism draws on the entire legacy, including the use of polemical rhetoric and personal (usually bodily) *demonstrations of solidarity and commitment to a cause*. Across the world, women, the poor, and marginalised and disenfranchised minorities and majorities draw upon Victorian tactics. Once this repertoire gained the unifying name of activism, it became a playbook used with equal aptitude by progressivists and their foes alike.[2]

Analysing performances' dramaturgy – spatial arrangements, casting of roles, authorisation of speech, oratorical techniques, styles of movement, conventions of behaviour, and audience reactions – shows how nineteenth-century activists connected performative forms to critical content. Studying this exceeds mere rhetorical analysis to encompass an examination of the totality of the mise-en-scène of any event. Across the continuum of theatre and the performances of nineteenth-century life, the makers, observers, and interpreters of events understood how mise-en-scène drew upon social intelligence to consolidate performative modes as a constitutive facet of reform politics.

By the end of the Georgian period, antitheatricalism held sway only among a tiny minority of religious fanatics. For everyone else in Britain, and increasingly for spheres of British influence around the globe, theatre was constitutive of and indispensable to public life. Liberalisation, secularisation, and Romanticism cleared away lingering pejorative connotations about the theatre being predicated on deception in favour of it being a technology for inquisitive interpellation of the contours of contemporaneous social life, scientific discovery, cultures distant in time and place, and the joie de vivre of playful fantasy. Theatre and theatrical entertainments thrived as mass media throughout Britain, growing in exponents, spawning new subgenres, and absorbing new topics. Both the popularity and the multifarious forms demonstrate theatre's centrality to nineteenth-century life. Theatre and performance entrained, and reflected, norms for how people calibrated empathy – as well as sanctioned standing-aside – to negotiate their lives (and contrived representations of lives like theirs) to connect across difference and determine responsibilities within real or imagined communities. This made performance an indispensable political tool of dissensus – distinctly experiencing a sensorial experience and its signified meaning – as well as a ubiquitous part of the cultural landscape.[3]

Activists appealed to their auditors' better selves not merely on ideological, moral, or theological grounds but also on the basis of how well performances registered. As persuasion prompted action, *performing* facilitated *reforming*, whether the objective was to convince a Member of Parliament (whom one might not be allowed to elect) to vote a particular way, to reach out to fellow workers and women to demand rights they theretofore had not known, or to forge a new aesthetic to express emerging sensibilities. Citizenship movements focused on gaining full rights overlapped with post-citizen movements (taken up by people already integrated into the social fabric by criteria such as race, gender, and class) to advocate for protections and benefits for others.[4] Performance is the increment and the communicative affordance wielded in mises-en-scène and accumulated as the repertoires to advance these politics. This book demonstrates how this was done in small committee rooms, in vast halls, and even across oceans. Whenever discursive description was translated into vivid accounts of envisioned actions, it was *performed* via language, bodies, and spaces to enable spectators, auditors, and readers to enhance their symbolic, subtextual, cognitive, and affective understanding accordingly.[5]

By aggregating insights from discourse analysis and dramaturgical analysis, inclusive of live and mediated forms of communicative repertoire, this study explains how and why tactics combined, tropes recurred, and recombinant elements evolved into new tactics that persisted as repertoires. Within repertoires, skills of vocalisation, physicalisation, and rhetorical deployment facilitated what was understood. Liberal activists and the general public shared this knowledge. Across two generations, the Thompson-Chesson family illustrates how individuals from modest backgrounds grasped and contributed to this systemic understanding. Their specific careers are unique to them, yet *Liberal Lives and Activist Repertoires: Political Performance and Victorian Social Reform* demonstrates how others – including African Americans fleeing enslavement by embarking on the British lecture circuit, Bengalis forging institutions for mutual training and empowerment, Black and mixed-race Jamaicans protesting economic disadvantage and extra-judicial murder, newly enfranchised British voters gathered at the hustings, women protesting state-sanctioned gynaecological assaults, and activists who decried the conjoined atrocities of massacres and cultural genocides in Australia, North America, the Transvaal, and the Balkans – also understood and manipulated the affordances of performance within critique.

During the early phases of George Thompson's career, international activism necessitated international travel, as when he undertook journeys to the United States and India or when delegates from the United States, the Caribbean, and Sierra Leone came to London for the 1840 Anti-Slavery Convention or the 1846 Evangelical Alliance. This is the first period in human history when (outside conquest or diplomacy) international connections were sought in order to radically revise understandings of a connected community of humanity. To an important extent, this newly invented tradition of travel-based networking is linked to other activisms: the in-person testimonial-based lectures of freedom-seeking African Americans who sought refuge and support in Europe – Moses Grandy (1786?–1843?), William Wells Brown (1814?–84), John S. Jacobs (1815?–73), Frederick Douglass (1818–95), William Craft (1824–1900), and Ellen Craft (1826–91) – and the petitioning and lobbying tactics of Indians such as Raja Rammohun Roy (1772/74–1833) and Dwarkanath Tagore (1794–1846), who ventured to Britain in order to promote liberalisation of foreign policy and advance business enterprises.

Steamships and efficient postal networks linked activist communities, yet for the next generation of activists, efficiency and efficacy were exponentially advanced by two revolutions in communication: cheap newspapers and globalised telegraphy. During the 1830s and 1840s, reporters at meetings took down speeches verbatim, including speakers' inflections and auditors' reactions, and published them in newspapers. Other newspapers reprinted the accounts, amplifying their effect to other cities, nations, and colonies. Thus, what were essentially performance scripts swiftly circulated and facilitated 'intentionality and purpose', what Homi Bhabha credits as 'the signs of agency' that 'emerge from [a] "time-lag"'.[6] Thompson invested in two newspapers that respectively advanced Anglo-Indian issues and the Peace Movement for exactly this reason. During the mid-1850s, after repeal of the Stamp Acts substantially reduced the costs of daily newspapers in Britain, the modern idea of a press corps developed, with journalists travelling far beyond their municipal ambits to report on events first hand. William Howard Russell (1820–1907), who sent dispatches back from the Crimean War, is the most famous example, however Frederick Chesson (who mainly covered the politics beat) and Amelia Chesson (who joined the press corps as a book, theatre, and music critic) contributed too. Concurrently, postal systems increasingly interconnected the British Empire, and letters allowed eyewitnesses to share information about all facets of human life. As secretary to the Aborigines' Protection Society (APS) from the mid-1850s to 1888, Frederick Chesson was the receiving point – centralised in London but with a global compass – for epistolary information that he used to inform reformist lobbying efforts and journalism. Thus connected to events worldwide, the Thompson-Chesson family functioned as a 'multiplier effect' even when at home.[7] They utilised epistolary accounts of transgressions and newspaper reports of abuses to forge a cogent concept of human rights, expressed in speeches (Thompson) and journalism (Thompson and both Chessons), outreach to Members of Parliament (MPs) and cabinet ministers (Frederick Chesson), connections with activists abroad (Thompson and Frederick Chesson), and leadership of successive reform campaigns (Thompson and both Chessons). Additionally, from the 1860s, transcontinental telegraphy increased the speed of the transmission of news as well as the responsivity to concerns expressed by and to the many arms of colonial administration. Together, these communication media and technologies were feedback loops for liberal reform, incrementally pursued and enhanced by performative means. By the period of the 1860s to the 1880s (the heyday of the Chessons' careers), much of what had necessitated person-to-person transmission in the early 1830s (at the outset of Thompson's career) could be done remotely and sometimes with great rapidity. Yet meetings (amplified by printed accounts) remained the lynchpin of reform work, constitutive of performance and bolstered by performance know-how, to interrelate activism of all kinds.

Apart from studies of the women's suffrage movement, women are rarely the agential protagonists in studies of liberalism. They warrant being recentred: not just as the childbearers and homemakers who were, as Emma Rothschild puts it, 'a site for a moralised order that could balance market forces', but as full participants in liberal politics whose contributions fundamentally upset differentiation of household and public sites and concerns over domestic and foreign welfare.[8] Close study of the contributions of Amelia Chesson and other women in her circles who were networked across familial and social spheres shows reformers recreating together, enhancing bonds, jointly attending performances, and linking networks that campaigned on a myriad of issues. Orthodoxy about the Habermasian divide between bourgeois and governmental publics fails to reflect how Amelia Chesson came to be a multifaceted critic and activist, write performance reviews, attend political meetings, serve on the Women's Suffrage Committee during the 1870s, and collaborate with her father, mother, sister, and husband on domestic and transnational campaigns. Her unsung efforts show that there was no definitive divide between homes and workplaces, no truly separate spheres for women and men, and no retreat from the performance of politics. Recuperating her history is not the integration of someone marginal into a centre, for though women like Amelia Chesson could be kept out of some corridors of power, this did not constrain her knowledge or her understanding, her ability to innovate or her perseverance to engage. How she and her family spent their time doing various kinds of things (speaking, writing, editing, organising, and advocating contiguously with engaging in social life, leisure, and private time) shows the collapse of the administrative and regulatory concerns of the governmental public sphere fully into family and social life. There is no objective line between 'the private and public, the civil and the familial', as Bhabha puts it, and through 'performative discourse' community 'enacts the impossibility of drawing an objective line between the two'.[9] For committed activists, public life (steeped in consciousness about the dramaturgy of performance) dominated experience *and* permeated private interactions.

Thompson and the Chessons were vibrant, complex human beings who dedicated themselves to reform, almost exclusively outside what is called public service. For a brief period, George Thompson was an MP, but while in office he conducted himself with little alteration from before. As the family members were citizens of Britain, their imaginations, erudition, and actions embraced the globe, touching on the challenges present on every inhabited continent and the question of what was wrought by trafficking people and goods between regions and nations. Thompson and the Chessons stand apart from many of their compatriots for their prescient abilities to envision how to intervene in globalised markets (Chapter 2), protest the deleterious effects of colonialism (Chapter 3), name genocides and their imperialist and racialised causes (Chapter 4), and perceive and call out intersectional racism and sexism (Chapter 5). At the same time, the entire family stands in for how people in their circles consistently analysed performance and utilised these insights to become more effective advocates. There is much to admire in them, even if history judges the outcomes of the turn to liberal principles with a jaundiced eye. Working with the theory available to them and the tactics they engineered, they were indefatigable advocates for greater equity, self-determination, and the imperative to care.

Chapter 1 outlines the liberal causes and indicative approaches undertaken by the three principal figures, and argues for the primacy of how dramaturgy was recognised and manipulated. The next chapter analyses George Thompson's career as a lecturer and debater, with techniques grounded in the campaign to repeal slavery in the West Indies and Thompson's subsequent role in creating a transatlantic abolitionist movement. While the basic contours of these facets of Thompson's career have been lightly addressed elsewhere, neither his efforts on behalf of free trade (especially his call to change Britain's economic and administrative approaches to India and the United States) nor his instrumentality in encouraging a rising class of Indian reformers have been systematically studied. This comes together vividly through his embedded activism at meetings of the proprietors of the East India Company (The Company) in London as well as his eyewitness account of the survivors of the siege of Lucknow arriving in Calcutta, both scathing indictments of British misrule.

Two successive chapters take up phases of Frederick Chesson's career in conjunction with developments in mass communication. This brings Chesson into scholarly focus for the very first time. Witnessing a man taken into custody under the Fugitive Slave Law of 1850 radicalised Chesson, and by the age of eighteen he had already built relationships that enabled his future career as an organiser, journalist, and social critic. He leveraged passion and energy with carefully honed and operationalised knowledge about performance. Like others of his time, Chesson understood that Victorian performance (theatre, circus, music hall, street entertainments, ethnographic displays, etc.) repurposed and recirculated social rites, political events, archaeological heritage, and scientific discovery in ways instrumental to mid-Victorians' *Bildung*. Chesson's diaries demonstrate how his own *Bildung* – maturation within conscious and unconscious practices of self-cultivation constitutive of active citizenship – built upon his critical practices of consuming performance, as well as reading, to become an activist. Diverging from Thompson's stunt activism against the British East India Company and the Free Church of Scotland, Chesson and his allies utilised placarding to protest against imperialist war, allying this populist activism to speechifying and mass meetings. Over a longer period, with subtler rhetoric, he spearheaded lobbying to disband the monopoly of the Hudson's Bay Company, a chartered corporation that held in its thrall the fate of Indigenous peoples who dwelt on 11.7 million square kilometres (4.5 million square miles) of North America. Chesson's work typifies the capacity to activate the British public's empathy across great distances and rhetoricise cultural difference on behalf of subject peoples throughout Britain's vast empire.

Chapter 4 documents how Chesson's journalism on the laying of the first transoceanic cable demonstrates his understanding of telegraphy's capacity for distant yet rapid communication. This development revolutionised journalism as well as commerce, and thus bore on how politics were monitored and reported by men such as Chesson in newspapers, public meetings, and cabinet ministers' offices. Through the medium of newspapers, each of which uniquely embodied a politically inflected persona and 'combative pens', the work of advocating for emancipated African Americans as well as tortured and murdered Jamaicans occurred on one side of the temporal threshold of the telegraphic revolution, while addressing genocides in Bulgaria and the western Balkans occurred on the other. In all cases, the full repertoire of liberal activism was deployed and documented by Chesson and his colleagues.

While the first four chapters draw on a plethora of evidence from newspapers, pamphlets, letters, and speeches (almost all examined for the first time), as well as Frederick Chesson's diaries, the final chapter embraces a historiographic and evidentiary challenge of a different kind. Whereas her father gave thousands of speeches and her husband likely wrote upwards of seven million words of unsigned journalism plus voluminous correspondence, Amelia Chesson has left few overt traces. The fact that she is the first documentable female theatre and music critic for the daily press was hitherto unknown. Research based on diaries, other manuscripts, and newspapers has surfaced her career both as a professional evaluator of social and aesthetic performance and as an activist in a succession of campaigns. Whereas it could be argued that she was constrained by her gender, in fact she made strategic alliances with African American abolitionists, utilising innovative and subtle performative tactics that rely upon affordances of racialisation and gender. And whereas it could be argued that her periodic absences from performative writing and public activism made her a dabbler and dilettante, manuscript sources show that these absences were the result of her numerous pregnancies and a cycle of childbearing and nursing interspersed with cyclical liberation from reproductive labour. As a result, the book concludes with a radical view both of who utilised performance in relation to activism and of how this was possible for different kinds of individuals and in transformative ways. This challenges our understanding of what it means to dwell in the midst of spectacle, to embrace the social and intimate spheres and yet mobilise on behalf of others who seek more than mere survival.

## Notes

1 Bogad, L.M. *Tactical Performance: The Theory and Practice of Serious Play*. London: Routledge, 2016: 45.
2 See Boyd, Andrew and Oswald Mitchell, eds. *Beautiful Trouble: A Toolbox for the Revolution*. New York: O/R Books, 2012; and Sharp, Gene, *The Politics of Nonviolent Action*. Boston: Porter Sargent, 1973.
3 Rancière, Jacques. *Dissensus: On Politics and Aesthetics*. New York: Continuum, 2010: 134–51.
4 Jasper, James M. *The Art of Moral Protest: Culture, Biography, and Creativity in Social Movements*. Chicago: University of Chicago Press, 1997: 6–7.
5 Ahmed, Sara. *The Cultural Politics of Emotion*, 2nd ed. Edinburgh: Edinburgh University Press, 2014: 194.
6 Bhabha, Homi. *The Location of Culture*. Hoboken, NJ: Taylor & Francis, 2012: 284.
7 Hall, Catherine. *Macaulay and Son: Architects of Imperial Britain*. New Haven, CT: Yale University Press, 2012: 2.
8 Rothschild, Emma. *The Inner Life of Empires: An Eighteenth-Century History*. Princeton, NJ: Princeton University Press, 2011: xxi.
9 Bhabha, *Location of Culture*, 330. See also Dillon, Elizabeth Maddock. *The Gender of Freedom: Fictions of Liberalism and the Literary Public Sphere*. Stanford, CA: Stanford University Press, 2004.

# CHAPTER I

# *Forms and Increments of Performance*

> So let us welcome peaceful ev'ning in.
> Not such his ev'ning, who with shining face
> Sweats in the crowded theatre, and squeez'd
> And bor'd with elbow-points through both his sides,
> Out-scolds the ranting actor on the stage:
> Nor his, who patient stands till his feet throb,
> And his head thumps, to feed upon the breath
> Of patriots, bursting with heroic rage,
> Or placemen, all tranquility and smiles.
> . . . . . . . . . . . . . . . . . . . . . . . .
> What is it but a map of busy life,
> Its fluctuations, and its vast concerns?
> —William Cowper, 'The Winter Evening'

The Augustan poet William Cowper's (1731–1800) poem 'The Winter Evening', part of the long poem *The Task* (1784), offers a meditation on the pleasures of staying at home. The man in the crowded theatre auditorium acts out to his fellow spectators, more strenuous in his indignation than the paid actor, yet he behaves within the conventions of this paradigmatic site, jostling for space and simultaneously aware of struggles in the auditorium and onstage. Likewise, the citizen listening to the politician attends vigilantly to a lengthy speech though his feet ache, and the poet leaves it ambiguous as to who is 'bursting with heroic rage': the listener, the speaker, or perhaps both. So too, the placemen – the poet's term for sycophantic yes men – exhibit 'all tranquility and smiles' yet may have quite a different inner life of scheming discontent. Cowper's point is that performance is something regularly undertaken in the public realm (whether at a theatrical entertainment, a political meeting, or one's everyday job), that the ostensible performer will not be the only performer, and that cultivating the insight required to recognise and interpret these situations is constitutive of public life. Quietly, at home, one can reflect upon the variety and vicissitudes.

This accords with a foundational principle of performance studies, namely that performance is not exceptional but rather is as integral and constitutive of routine interactions, ritual celebrations, and social existence as it is of the theatrical stage.[1] In the theatre, but not only there, contrivances obscure or highlight how performance is invoked, made perceptible and eligible for critique. In no realm of human communication is this reducible to what is merely spoken, for performance calibrates mimetic acts and slippages of many kinds. This is sustained by speakers' and listeners' use of citational circularity – or, to use Judith Butler's most often repeated term, performativity – from refreshable cultural repertoires.[2] Performativity may surface into awareness or remain a subconscious borrowing; in either case, it consolidates as repertoires constitutive of social experience as well as theatrical performance, and it includes not only facets of presentation such as plot and character but also, *in potentia*, a full array of corporeal, proximal, vestimentary, scenographic, sonic, sociolinguistic, and figurative meanings in combination.[3] The permutations are endless yet in practise are codified into recognisable forms and genres: no one would mistake a transaction in a grocer's shop for grand opera, any more than a funeral would be confused with a funfair.

Without performance, and performance literacy, human experience would be utterly chaotic: we would not know what diverges from the usual, when to differentiate a person who shows their vulnerability and makes us worry from another who makes us exult, how to resist intimidation, whom to believe about what, where we cross a threshold from the arenas of public life to the differently fraught realms of domesticity, or why the characteristics of one culture's social field can be differentiated from another's. Without an understanding of repertoires we would not differentiate the stage actor from the scold, the politician from the citizen, or the placeman from the sincere advocate, whether in the midst of action or from a place of quiet contemplation such as Cowper's sofa. Cultural mediation happens in all cases, for assessment is integral to the 'busy life'. As a set, the scenarios are recognisable as many variants of performance (only one of which is theatre), chained together as spectatorship and action in the panorama of public and private life.

To locate these acts in history, however, engages knowledge of dramaturgy, which James Ball describes as 'the labor of connecting form and content' and thus that which 'makes an urgent question of the relationship of spectacle and its spectators'. This is both the topic and the methodology of this book. Ball's focus on twenty-first-century diplomacy is equally apt for nineteenth-century liberal advocacy: 'Dramaturgy arranges bodies, assigns them roles, authorises their speech, and directs them to act in particular styles, using certain gestures but not others.' *Liberal Lives and Activist Repertoires: Political Performance and Victorian Social Reform* explicates how rhetoric (aimed at persuasion) allies with elements of dramaturgy (which amplify a situation's intentionality) to arrange 'the contexts in which power's performance emerges and the ways it makes meaning'. For such situations to have efficacy there must be spectators to complete the scene, for 'without them the spectacle cannot signify' with its rhetoric.[4]

Finding *which* factors were perceptible – and particularly, the chaotic consequences of imperceptibility or misperception – is the quest for dramaturgical analysis. It is a practice familiar from theatregoing. There, we pay to see interhuman understanding attempted, codified into genres according to the various ways it is likely to go wrong. In Nicholas Ridout's terms, this is what is involved with learning the habitus of spectating.[5] In and out of the theatre, keen perception of when these kinds of social intelligence are invoked by various sorts of contrivance makes the code-switching of everyday performative modes a constitutive facet of both performativity and theatricality.[6] Utilising a host of linguistic and non-linguistic means, through performance we learn to calibrate empathy, as well as distanced standing aside, to negotiate our lives, contrived representations of lives like ours, and our responsibilities within communities. Performance, in other words, makes cultures 'go'.

Nevertheless, to broach a history based on these principles is challenging: which performative act can be delimited as a focus, how can the overlap between performers' and witnesses' repertoires (constituting mutual intelligibility) be recovered, and when can the circumstances be understood with reliable specificity so meaning can be attributed to an instance, or with sufficient generalisability so a trend can be established? When does aesthetic experience matter – and why – in historical accounts? Given that performance is contingent on many kinds of circulating knowledge in its formation and interpretation, and given that its combinatorial possibilities are so vast, how does it factor into cultural change and thus history? Derrick R. Spires asks a similar question in *The Practice of Citizenship: Black Politics and Print Culture in the Early United States*, focusing on how the repertoire of Black writers' 'thoughts, events, and proceedings' circulated as repertoire in 'an ongoing performance'.[7] Instead of conceiving performance as ephemerality – irrecoverably gone in the moment of its execution – we must ask how it leaves traces, both of itself and its effects. How, in other words, is it legible in its own time and to posterity?

This book is about lives spent in advocacy and judgement, and the interdependency of these functions within a performative framework.

Performance is the arena in which the people who were engaged in advocacy and judgement assessed one another: their assessments filtered into subsequent performance choices in order for people to become more effective advocates and thereby effect change within national and transnational nineteenth-century politics. Performance knowledge, in these cases and likely countless others, is what inheres to enhance understandings. But how is performance knowledge developed, where does it manifest, and how can a historian recognise it? To borrow Gary Alan Fine's terms, performance knowledge is the 'sticky culture' that unites people into a community with specific orders of interaction, links cultural knowledge to a domain via interaction protocols, and produces the persistent 'sticky memory' of its heroes' feats.[8] Likewise, in Sara Ahmed's terms, stickiness 'involves a transference of affect' as signs adhere to meanings, belying something's history, and accruing people's 'support and allegiance'.[9] Performance is the means to communicate, its repertoires delimit the contours of communities of circulating knowledge, and its trace is what historians need to recognise the filaments linking advocacy, judgement, behaviour, and variation over time. Far from being ephemeral – disappearing in the instant of its creation – performance is the sticky residue that perpetuates memory as ongoing transmission through repertoires. Thus, looking for the traces of performance in the past draws a historian's attention to how and what people in a given culture understood from one another's acts, and what adhered over time despite continuous change.

Theatre was one domain in which assessment and judgement occurred. In nineteenth-century Britain, theatre grew into a mass medium, serving people from all walks of life, and though increasing differentiation of performance products stratified the marketplace there was always a great deal of permeation of repertoires across genres, venues, and cities. Theatre was not only an institution unto itself but also a cultural technique by which artists filtered current events and evolving tastes into entertainment that refracted Britons' views of themselves, and of other times and cultures, into aesthetic forms. Though its primary purpose was to entertain, the theatre of this period also reflected a zeitgeist of cultural products widely seen and appreciated. Within the growing medium of newspapers, a cadre of professional critics arose to filter facets of this experience for readers, who consumed this and other types of performance. Given that theatre venues were pluralistically the sites for hosting other performative cultural techniques associated with the period – including trade fairs, fundraising bazaars, and evangelical religious services – this period is marked off from earlier times both by a degree of comfort about theatrical performance and by its contiguity with liberal as well as conservative trends. This helped consciousness about theatre – its diversity and appraisal – filter more fully through the nineteenth-century sensibilities. At the same time, venues emerged that were dedicated to musical performance but also used for political gatherings, such as London's Rotunda, Exeter Hall, and St James's Hall, as well as comparable spaces across the British nation and empire like the Free Trade Hall in Manchester. Their size, heterogenous fare, and scale of attendance suggest that there was a great deal of activity to leave sticky residues, and thus much for historians to trace.

This book focuses on three people who practised assessment of educational, religious, political, and artistic performance yet to whom credentialization as arbiters of excellence was not automatically granted because of their backgrounds. They accrued expertise, repeatedly demonstrated their abilities, and earned recognition through their deeds, overt agential acts that constitute and promote circulation: describing, evaluating, and facilitating performance, and advocating for opportunities to create more performance. In one case, what adheres is a reputation for delivering inspiring oratory; despite periods of withdrawal from public life, the lasting impression is of a man who held fast to his principles and helped bring about two momentous emancipation movements affecting Britain's Caribbean colonies and the United States as well as setting in motion the stirrings of independence in India. He garnered a great reputation in his heyday but is misapprehended in history. In the second case, what adheres is a man's reputation for exemplary service to liberal causes through administrative doggedness and an exceptional ability to work with people across ideological lines. This is a smaller reputation, known to his confederates but now lost to ongoing memory. In addition to the acknowledged labours, and a heavy correspondence load with interlocutors around the world, he made his living as a journalist, publishing upward of seven million unsigned words.[10] This provides ways to trace his impact on a huge variety of domestic and foreign issues, though he is hitherto but a footnote to history. Finally, a woman who was the daughter of the first figure and wife of the second has her name lightly etched in history only for once having accompanied the Black freedom-seekers William Wells Brown, William Craft, and Ellen Craft to London's Great Exhibition of 1851.[11] The life that preceded and followed this moment – meritorious of sticky memory not just by her proximity to the beating heart of the British, transatlantic, and global abolition movements – was both conventionally bound by gender and motivated to serve the great liberal causes that gave a pulse to her parents' and her marital homes.

Her thorough obscurity as an advocate and judge of performance, contributor to the political life of Great Britain, and communicant in global networks is largely a consequence of her gender.

Against the recondite nature of the man with a 'small' reputation, and his wife with none, their parent seems comparatively easy to trace. Yet from the copious manuscripts and journalistic evidence of all three figures' acts emerges a history constituted by multiple kinds of performance, adopting existing forms and helping evolve these forms into new, more efficacious ones as part of a repertoire that, many decades later, would gain the name of 'activism'. Specifically, these figures reveal how a repertoire of liberals' tactics (resistance, confrontation, networking, naming, listening, or persuading) was incrementally and better calibrated through acuity in performance to garner desired results (shifting opinion, creating legislation, manumitting the enslaved, or rupturing complacency). What would one day be called activism was for the time being known by the names of various agential forms all fully permitted by English law – letter-writing, lobbying, debate, negotiation, petitions, billboarding, leafletting, boycotts, pledging, marching, rallies, hartal, and occupation – yet also scaling up to forms of illegal protest including revolt, blockade, mutiny, uprising, mobbing, riot, and strikes. Somehow a tacit understanding emerged about what was activist (such as electioneering) and what was illegal and malevolently destabilising (such as anything on a pathway to revolution).[12] Across this spectrum, the intelligibility of lives consolidates through performance, in conjunction with print culture, into legible patterns that are both individual and emblematic. In this respect, forms (and formalist readings) significantly augment historical understanding of their dramaturgy.

## Meetings as Cultural Form

At some point before 1830, Thomas Thompson (1777–1832), 'a man of polished manners, cultivated intellect and extensive reading' who worked for the London publishing and bookselling firm of Longman,[13] wrote in his commonplace book using beautiful Spencerian cursive script:

> Lectures. Public or private are such verbal instructions as are given by a teacher while the learner attends in silence. This is the way of learning religion from the pulpit, or of philosophy or theology from the Professors [sic] Chair, or of mathematics by a teacher, shewing us various theorems or problems, i.e. speculations and practices, by demonstration and operation, with all the instruments of art necessary to those operations. Conversation is another mode of improving our minds.[14]

Though listened to in silence like the counsel of Job, lectures and even sermons were subject to performative evaluation, as Thompson indicated by writing another passage into his commonplace book a few pages later. It refers to Hugh Worthington (1752–1813), a dissenting minister little noted for what he said but much admired for the imposing way he delivered impassioned perorations:

> Mr. W's system of preaching, is the most eligible one .... While his discourses evince all the regularity of prepared compositions, they possess all the fluency of extempore eloquence. Reasoning, exhorting, animating and consoling, his intellect is all feeling, and his feeling is all intellect. While he enlightens and convinces the understanding, he attaches and captivates the affections. While he seizes the strong holds of the head, he finds the passes to the heart .... Whether his hand be laid on his heart, or raised upwards, or his finger jointed to the word it is the effect of nature and it affects by nature. Emphasis forms one of his chief excellencies; his best discourses owe much to his delivery of them .... So powerful is his eloquence that he never ended the sermon which his hearers did not wish he was about to begin.[15]

It was not Worthington's innate gifts that made him so preferred: according to the *Christian Reformer* his voice was 'hard and dry, pungent and caustic'.[16] Instead, it was his performance that suited him to his task. Thompson may have authored this passage himself, based on an observation from life, or he may have seen it elsewhere, thought it astute, and copied it. In either case, its presence in his commonplace book indicates its worthiness to be remembered, capturing the excellence of a speaker, the specificity of his technique, and the experience of his auditors.

If these passages were sufficiently on Thomas Thompson's mind that he recorded them in his commonplace book it is reasonable to surmise that he also espoused the principles of oratory – and the practice of critique – in his home. And if that is true, his third son, George Donisthorpe Thompson (1804–78), took the lessons to heart. He built upon a scant education – as he stipulated in 1847, 'I never had a quarter's schooling in my life' – and at age twelve became a city clerk.[17] He was encouraged by the prominent theologian Rev. Richard Watson (1781–1833) to pursue the Wesleyan ministry, but pivoted to train himself up to be an able debater in secular matters through lectures and classes at the London Mechanics' Institute (patronised by Lord Brougham [1778–1868] and Dr George Birkbeck [1776–1841]) and the City of London Literary and Scientific Institution (created by Lord Denman [1779–1854] and George Grote [1794–1871]), both founded in the mid-1820s.[18] He gave extemporaneous orations on behalf of electoral reform and worked to overthrow a Middlesex Tory in 1829, haranguing listeners from the top of a beer barrel on Clerkenwell Green. He spoke on behalf of the Reform Bill at St James's Church, Clerkenwell, in 1830 and 'perfectly electrified his audience', who hoisted him on their shoulders and carried him triumphantly into the street.[19] He was a Radical whose origins mitigated against fame yet who, in his twenties, cultivated a talent and overcame the odds.

Though he believed in 'perfect liberty of conscience', George Thompson responded to the 'vulgar ribaldry' with which Rev. Robert Taylor (1784–1844) preached at Hugh Worthington's old church (Salters' Hall Chapel, Cannon Street). Thompson would attract notice as a speaker by taking up Taylor's debate challenge and besting him before an audience. A former Church of England clergyman whose turn to apostatic deism led him to be dubbed 'the Devil's Chaplain', Taylor was imprisoned for blasphemy from October 1827 until February 1829. Afterward he toured the North, unsuccessfully trying to goad clergymen into debates. Essentially, in his transitions from clergyman to heretic, and from cleric to felon, Taylor went from being a preacher giving sermons to a platform speaker giving lectures. In May 1830 he presided at the London Rotunda in full clerical regalia, mocking Church of England rites. This is the most likely period when Taylor's challenge to debaters was taken up by the young layman George Thompson.[20] It was a terrific opportunity for an upstart to be noticed by pitching a performance calculated to carry a crowd.

During the waning years of English merchants' participation in the transatlantic slave trade, Thomas Thompson had been a captain's clerk on a slave-trading vessel. On his second journey, a British naval vessel stopped his ship and Thompson took the chance to be conscripted. Later, he told his son George about the conditions below decks on the slaver, the cruelty and abuse, and the sharks that dogged its wake.[21] Hearing about the slaves' suffering was one of George Thompson's earliest memories.[22] Thomas Thompson's commonplace book – likely compiled over decades – includes few direct references to slavery, though this passage stands out: 'The two greatest contrarieties of Government in the civilized world are to be found in the <u>republic</u> of North America and the absolute monarchy of Persia.' On the same page, he quotes the last two lines of this chapter's epigraph and another section of Cowper's *The Task*, one that calls for England to emancipate its colonies' enslaved, referring to Lord Mansfield's decision in *Somerset v. Stewart* (1772).

> Slaves cannot breathe in England; if their lungs
> Receive our air, that moment they are free,
> They touch our country and their shackles fall.
> That's noble, and bespeaks a nation proud
> And jealous of the blessing. Spread it then,
> And let it circulate through every vein
> Of all your empire; that where Britain's power
> Is felt, mankind may feel her mercy too.[23]

Possibly buoyed by the Liverpool abolitionist William Roscoe (1753–1831), whom he served as cashier, Thomas may have guided George toward Cowper's challenge.[24] Meanwhile, needing an income, George sought a clerkship in a London attorney's office at eighteen shillings a week, and subsequently opened a small coffee shop in Ray Street, Clerkenwell, which he operated until his speeches at a ratepayers' meeting offended the local authorities.[25] He married Anne Erskine Lorrain Spry (1807–78), the daughter of a Methodist minister in the Countess of Huntingdon's Connexion, when they were respectively twenty-six and twenty-three years of age. She immediately became pregnant, and thus securing a livelihood was urgent.

Editions of Cowper, Milton, and Shakespeare were among George Thompson's first possessions, and they played a part in making him a committed Radical.[26] In September 1831, on his wife's urging and with Lord Brougham's endorsement, the young man secured a trial as lecturer for the London Anti-Slavery Society, with the charge to develop connections in Kent and stir up support that would eventually carry the bill ending slavery in the Caribbean sugar-producing colonies through Parliament.[27] Thompson claimed to know nothing of the topic, but on his reputation of distinction in 'parochial discussions', he borrowed a pile of books and pamphlets, swotted up on the subject, and was given the opportunity to prove his mettle at the podium. After a trial, he was taken on at £200 per annum. Through 'arduous, meritorious, and most successful' labours, 'he excited attention wherever he went, and worked up Antislavery feeling with a power of tongue that, under such circumstances, was perhaps unprecedented'.[28] Six weeks into the job, during a period of anxious separation from his wife, George Thompson became a father. Within less than a year, he had graduated from the Kent circuit to the national scene, lecturing for hours at a time at meetings with three thousand auditors. He must have developed his voice appropriately for it to carry in the large halls and for such long periods, or he had this capacity beforehand, along with the power of charismatic leadership. In any case, he was a paid platform speaker and organiser and never returned to his life in either clerkship or trade.[29] Meanwhile, his father passed away, unremarked in surviving letters.

In making the transition from sparring orator to mouth-for-hire, George Thompson was launched as a professional lecturer. This was in no way a cynical or merely opportunistic move: he believed fully in his cause, taking what the oratorical guru Hugh Blair calls 'the right and true side' because it was the one to which he was most inclined.[30] Later in his career, Thompson delivered one-off and serial lectures, expounding on areas of his expertise. For example, in 1861 he gave an illustrated lecture on Hindus at the Metropolitan Tabernacle, and on other occasions he lectured at various halls on the causes of the American Civil War, the Crimean War, the 'cotton question', and of course the antislavery cause.[31] Inbetween campaigns, this enabled him to earn a modest living. But he was a political speaker, and meetings were his milieu: hold enough successful meetings and movements can accrue, linking like-minded people to increase the size and power of a cause. This happened over and over in nineteenth-century Britain: the Chartists who extended the franchise and the ACLL that established free trade as a core liberal principle may be the best-known cases, but probably every cause that came to prominence in Britain began – and was perpetuated – in this way. Britons' freedom to assemble in private or in public, especially in this era of revolutions, ensured that meetings were charged not only with political importance but also with performative frisson.

Promoting ideas through discussion and persuasion required emotional restraint and oratorical skill. At meetings, eloquence could be measured against classical precedents, style honed to be vigorous, cogent, yet austere (like Demosthenes) or gentle, agreeable, and insinuating (like Cicero). Likewise, the characteristics of auditors were gauged so that the concise eloquence that sufficed in Athens sometimes gave way to the more flowery declamation requisite for the less acute Romans, even though Demosthenes made his appeals to the common citizens and Cicero to men of the highest rank and education.[32] Thus, any meeting in Parliament, a provincial hall, or outdoors could be understood as part of a great elocutionary tradition, and any speech assessed on a continuum of extensive precedent even when seeming to flow spontaneously. Dramaturgy and rhetoric were evaluated by all present. To participate in this tradition was to exercise civil liberties and conjure the democratic polis.[33]

Many kinds of assembly have rules of order sufficiently cohesive to constitute a performative form, including weddings and funerals, festive processions, strikes and boycotts, and sporting contests. Meetings are another such cultural form, utilising a repertoire of codified actions drawing upon the affordances of public gatherings to accrue and mobilise political power.[34] Among the social practices of democratic struggle, meetings make their mark gradually. In Thompson's initial role with the London Anti-Slavery Society, and later as agent for the British and Foreign Anti-Slavery Society (BFASS) and Glasgow Anti-Slavery Society, he was deployed to towns to try to enthuse residents into creating local branches. Branch organisations functioned as nodal points for the networks through which speakers travelled and correspondence circulated. The effects of meetings were amplified in social settings and through coverage in local newspapers. Local newspaper reports were often reprinted elsewhere, reinforcing the effect through an existing or potential network of towns and cities. At whatever social stratum, meetings were the backbone of movements. Their performances are rarely as exhilarating as a Pentecostal revival or as galvanising as a riot, but they make change nevertheless. Though historiography favours revolutionary acts – theatres erupting into uproar, tumult in the streets, or upheaval of ruling orders – the humble meeting is a potent political instrument for building social change, weathering setbacks from importune developments, and keeping an issue in the public's eye.

Repertoires are drawn upon by artists, speakers, and politicians to make performance; audiences, likewise, have repertoires based on earlier experiences. What overlaps in a given performance are 'the associational, polytextual, intertheatrically citational, recombinant patterns that sustain intelligibility'.[35] To make a new, enduring, theatrical style or performance form, the constitutive repertoires of both makers and receivers must be adjusted. Likewise, to intelligibly convey new theory or political ideas to the public, repertoires of advocates and their addressees must evolve until there is overlap in intelligibility. Only where there is intelligibility can there be persuasion; only when there is persuasion can political speech grow into a social movement. Under conditions of relatively free discourse, as occurred in Great Britain from the early nineteenth century, meetings evolved a repertoire of characteristics that enabled opinions to be expressed and responded to; the single authoritative voice of the sermon or the declaration gave way to widespread dialogic free play. This is the atmosphere in which the two great principles of British liberalism (the universality of human rights and the beneficial effects of free trade) were forged.

George Thompson, among others, brought liberal principles into mainstream thought through career-long efforts to apply these principles to matters of consequence. The performative increment by which positions were advanced, changes advocated, and reform achieved was the meeting.

Meetings are a form; to understand them, formalist analysis must be done; the fruits of that analysis reveal empirical experience; empirical experience shows the stickiness of performance to culture; and this results in nuanced historical understanding of social movements and their ideological bases. Only by recognising meetings and the work of their formation, perpetuation, and repetitive replications-with-difference can we see the increments of performance, labour, argumentation, and evaluation and thereby appreciate their cumulative impact over time. As a performance form, meetings establish links between lived experience, protocols for advocacy, habits of social gathering, and the levers for political transformation that rely citationally on repertoires across times and places.[36] This marks performance as constitutive of culture and makes social formations an incremental consequence of performance.

Meetings and their sub-forms (lectures, debates, conventions, breakfasts, dinners, and soirées) were where George Thompson endeavoured to turn minds and hearts to the abolition of slavery, forge communities in common cause, and hone his own and other activists' rhetorical abilities as speakers, writers, lobbyists, and organisers so they could more skilfully impress their convictions upon those with legislative power. Newspaper accounts document meetings, turning face-to-face performances into narrated stories (or, in some cases, verbatim transcripts), their circulation proportionately amplifying the resonance of meetings' content beyond those who were present. Whereas newspapers report on meetings, manuscript letters, and diaries reveal how participants in meetings reflexively strove to become effective in their political goals by manipulating mises-en-scène to the best of their ability in service of others' liberation. In parallel to this historicising discourse, manuscripts privately document how meetings were understood as a structured yet malleable form. In his correspondence, George Thompson habitually critiqued what he saw and heard others do at meetings, and in paying attention not only to the orators but also to the mises-en-scène he treated these events as multifaceted consequential performances replete with interpersonal conflict, disagreement, deference, struggle, anxiety, and ascendance. Thompson paid attention to others' strategies and choices in making meetings and applied his observations to improve subsequent performances. The sociologist James M. Jasper calls such practices 'cultural learning because the results are changes in shared ways of thinking and acting', enabling adaptation in approaches.[37] A conscious dramaturgical process emerges from the evidence. This applies equally to routine facets of meetings, usually not warranting comment in letters or the press, including the specific casting of roles, which carried local consequence and gave less-experienced orators practice, and attendees' responses, which were recorded in (slightly edited) newspaper accounts and functioned like the stage directions in play texts.[38] Together, this gives a greater sense of orators' timing, affective facets of listeners' responses, and the details that stood out from the mundane to distinguish any given meeting.

To study meetings, a communication theorist would typically focus on rhetorical devices that were utilised, and a historian would likely view the gatherings as building blocks toward the success (or failure) of a political cause. Performance scholarship additionally emphasises how participants utilised dramaturgy: as innumerable examples will show, activists carefully calculated the implications of where meetings were held, who chaired, who else was visible on the platform, where dignitaries and women were seated, who was selected to speak on issues of heightened importance, how topics and speeches were ordered, and when and how auditors could respond.[39] Activists drew upon precedents and were conscious of the next steps in the struggle. This is a significant historiographic adjustment both to the history of rhetoric as not merely a set of formalised rules – implemented better by some, worse by others – and to the history of abolition as a moral imperative and humanitarian political struggle that peaked at certain moments but was never fully concluded. Furthermore, instead of just incidents of declamation and examples of argumentation leading to legislative change, a dramaturgical perspective reveals meetings as key to the ongoing transnational performative undertaking that connected the metropole of London to other British cities, and Britain to its colonies, trading partners, allies, and enemies. Abolition might be achieved by the stroke of a pen signing a bill into law, but the perspective offered here is that abolition movements' typical multidecade transcontinental series of meetings makes ideology evident as cultural form and shows how cultural form was legible across sectors of society and various nationalities or locations.[40] Far from emancipation being an existential rupture – chattel slavery one day, unimpeded freedom the next – the practices of abolitionism were ongoing, incremental, and discursively agonistic. Even changes in policy and practice that were effected overnight took years of preparation, implementation, and uptake. For example, the demand for an immediate, not gradual, end to slavery in British colonies first gained traction in 1824 in the West Country, the Midlands, and Ireland, spurred by a pamphlet from Elizabeth Heyrich (1769–1831).[41] The idea gained wider traction after being mentioned in Parliament in 1829, and in January 1831 the London Anti-Slavery Society hired agents (including George Thompson) to spread

Figure 1.1   'In person Mr. Thompson is tall, of a full and manly, though not robust form; the features handsome, and, when discoursing on any subject of interest, express with peculiar animation and force the various emotions of his mind. ... The position and expression are both characteristic.' (*Biographical Sketch and Portrait*, 19–20). George Thompson (by Charles Turner after George Evans), mezzotint, 1842. NPG D4367, National Portrait Gallery, London.

the word in other counties.[42] As pacifists who advocated immediate uncon-ditional abolition, Thompson and his associates were acutely aware of the social contracts that constrained belief or produced agreement, and thus what was needed to rally support, exert influence, achieve abolition, and then organise anew to assist the next cause. Newspaper circulation – which amplified meetings by stabilising or challenging hegemonic politics – plays a huge part in this, but face-to-face events constitute the substance of newspapers' incremental focus on the cause.[43]

Content filled form, and even at the outset of his career George Thompson could speak for several hours without notes (Figure 1.1). The format of meetings dictated that this was never a solo act. Even when there was a headliner like Thompson, meetings included speeches to introduce speakers, other speakers proposed and seconded resolutions (sometimes with protracted speeches), and speeches were made to thank the meeting's chairman. Thus, meetings epitomise Kirk Fuoss' concept of 'performance chaining', whereby one participant's performance leads to another participant's, then another's.[44] This is a process with identifiable links. Thus, as James Ball puts it, performance chaining situates individuals 'in space and time as a constituent part of the historical drama of world politics'.[45]

In the earliest extant transcript of one of Thompson's speeches (from Salford in 1832), Thompson is the only lecturer and yet is merely the focal point of several other men's constant activity:

> Precisely at seven o'clock he ascended the pulpit, accompanied by the Boroughreeve, William Hill, Esq.; Mr. Peter Clare, one of the Secretaries of the Anti-Slavery Society, and by Mr. James Everett, one of the members of the Committee. To the latter was assigned the office of arranging and handing to the speaker the documentary papers requisite to support the great cause of humanity.[46]

Utilising parliamentary reports, pamphlets, and possibly a transcript of an antecedent debate, Thompson quoted at length to refute and discredit arguments for retaining slavery in Britain's West Indian colonies. This was part of a series of clamorously attended debates with the Conservative upstart Peter Borthwick (1804–52).[47] Here, Thompson gave a point-by-point rebuttal of his challenger, inspiring the assembly to make frequent outbursts, as when he riffed sarcastically on one of Borthwick's comments about the purported comforts of enslaved Caribbeans' lifestyle:[48]

> Mr. Borthwick told you they [the enslaved] had wine. But I suppose this wine is to be found in the spacious habitation of the same gentleman described. (A loud laugh.) A dwelling consisting of four parlours and saloon (renewed laughter); and when instead of the destitute cabin of the slave, you find this delightful and commodious retreat, then, and not till then, will you find the negro regaling himself with wine supplied him by his most amiable master. (Great cheering.)[49]

Thus, Thompson chained his lecture to an earlier debate, and everyone present – those on the platform, James Everett, who passed up the requisite props, and the audience – took their part. Likewise, referring to the Maroon Rebellion in 1794, Thompson chained his parodic remarks to the actions of the enslaved and Borthwick's mischaracterisation of them:

> And who were the Maroons? Runaway negroes! And where had they run from! From the 'four parlours and a saloon.' What did they run from? From the light work, the beautiful clothing, and abundance of food; from the kind care and culture of the planters. And where did they run to from all this comfort and happiness? To the bleak and desolate mountains, to the fastnesses of Jamaica. Ay, to the desolate mountain, from the four parlors and a saloon.[50]

With Borthwick seated at his feet, Thompson effectively turned his opponent into an exhibit that verified the ill-considered turns of phrase that he quoted, indifference to enslaved people's plight, and thorough misapprehension of the issues, standing in for all remaining opponents to abolition. The direction of Thompson's gestures and eyeline – toward or around Borthwick and his party – and modulations of voice drew a connection this night to Borthwick's earlier speech, and this locale to Jamaica's plantation houses, slave quarters, and rebels' refuge.

Anti-slavery advocates successfully pushed through legislation but without all the provisions they desired. The Slavery Abolition Act of 1833 provided for a gradual transition from slavery to freedom through an 'apprenticeship system'. While those under six years old were freed, the enslaved over the age of six years were subjected to slavery by another name, working for low wages for up to six years while supposedly being educated (as 'apprentices') to manage future freedom. This scheme quickly proved to be a failure. By 1836, abolitionists worked to hasten the act's demise with a new bill demanding immediate liberty, which had been the preference of radicals all along. After a meeting on behalf of this effort in Birmingham Town Hall, Thompson wrote to his wife that 'It was a brilliant sight to gaze upon the magnificent Hall of this vast town (illuminated beyond the light of day, if possible) crowded with a breathless audience' of men and women.[51] The scenography was strategic: Birmingham's high bailiff (William Scholefield, 1809–67) took the chair, 'surrounded by a number of Clergymen, Dissenting Ministers of all denominations, Gentlemen, and the higher class of merchants and tradesmen'. The first resolution, citing the degeneracy caused by the apprenticeship system, unanimously carried. Joseph Sturge (1793–1859), recently returned from a fact-finding tour of the West Indies, rose to explain how complete emancipation actually served the economic interests of planters. The audience cheered his arguments for immediate emancipation and expressed strong umbrage when he cited injustices.[52] Thompson spoke in support of the third resolution, urging the Colonial Office to act against abusive planters in 'indignant terms' and appealing to Christians and the new queen 'to use their best endeavours to forward the accomplishment of so desirable a result'. He then 'sat down amidst loud and long continued cheers'.[53]

Meetings are performative formats that regulate and channel dissent. The rhetorical building blocks of meetings are speeches, but it is resolutions – and the ensuing votes on resolutions – that measure the increments of persuasion and political advances.[54] For example, during the American Civil War, while preparing to lecture in Manchester on the Southern

Confederacy, Thompson arranged with the meeting's chairman, George Wilson (1808–70), to write a resolution that would be advanced by someone, with a short speech, then seconded by someone else, with another short speech. This was engineered to give Thompson some time to rest while also determining the attitude of the assembled listeners to the topic, showing Thompson their disposition toward tension or concord so he could calibrate his approach before he resumed.[55] Unanimous outcomes of resolutions showed the persuasiveness of speakers and the gathering's likelihood of achieving unanimity in final, actionable, decisions. Approved resolutions helped determine the contours of subsequent meetings, thus giving the auditors direct input into the evolving dramaturgy as chained increments of advancing causes. As meetings begat meetings, resolutions facilitated interactive performances discursively linked to the goals and contests of other meetings (past and future) in ways that astute participants might recognise, testing the degrees of enthusiasm and filaments of allegiance.[56]

In 1831, as a novice speaker only a month into his trial with the London Anti-Slavery Society, Thompson was already attuned to the nuances of meetings' dramaturgy. He went to hear the popular preacher Rev. James Sherman (1779–1862) speak at a Bible meeting in Wye. Sherman was allied with the same Methodist splinter group as Thompson's father-in-law (the Countess of Huntingdon's Connexion), and Thompson wrote recommending this preacher to his wife. 'I was greatly delighted .... He is one of E. Parson's sort – winning – persuasive. His eloquence like soft and heavenly music, captivates you and the tear starts into your eye before you are conscious of the effect produced.'[57] This emphasises the preacher's performance acumen, his resemblance to another practitioner, and the affective outcome of his rhetoric, but Thompson also explained the casting of the paradigmatic elements of the meeting, starting with Mr Wildman taking the chair at the head of a large room in the Kings Head Inn:

> The First Resolution was moved by Mr. Bartlett [1789–1864] a very distinguished clergyman of Canterbury, and seconded by Mr. Sherman. The Speeches delivered by these gentlemen were of the first order. In fact I was enraptured with Mr. Bartlett[']s. The Second was moved by the Rev'd E.S. Lumsdaise a very excellent Clergyman with whom I went over from Canterbury & Margate some time back and seconded by G.T. [myself]. The others by clergymen – Baptists, Wesley another.[58]

Thompson's letter emphasises the ecumenical nature of the gathering's leaders: clergymen from the Church of England, at least two types of Methodists, and Baptists. He implicitly tells his wife that the gentlemen knew *how* to conduct a meeting, *what* to do to make speeches admirable, and *who* to call upon to show solidarity on issues *across* different Protestant groups. Successive resolutions built up the sense of a contest, and speakers' skill as well as the merit of the cause were always under evaluation. While speakers might be supremely skilled at manipulation, the auditors' role was to remain discerning.

Divided votes could result in more speeches, whether or not they were prompted by questions from the floor. In 1836, after speaking for three hours at Rev. Dr James Peddie's (1759–1845) Chapel in Edinburgh, Thompson wrote: 'Mr. Fraser an American Clergyman rose & endeavoured to soften down some thing I had said. This led to intensely interesting debates which kept us till nearly 1/2 past 11.' Thompson found the exchange exhilarating, 'however killing work'.[59] Several years later, after full emancipation had been secured for the enslaved in the British West Indies, Thompson turned his talents to advocating a complex set of arguments about the need to develop India, which (for a liberal) meant exploiting its agricultural potential, in particular massively increasing cotton production to undo the British textile industry's dependence on the fibre coming from forced labour camps (slave plantations) in the US South. Thompson explained that at a meeting in Doncaster a clergyman stood from the floor 'with the *Edinburgh Review* in his hand' and 'called upon me to defend myself & the [British India] Society from the charges brought against us. All went off triumphantly, my opponent confessing himself satisfied'.[60] The latest issue of the *Edinburgh Review* had cast Thompson in the centre of a misunderstanding blown up into a controversy; the opportunity to set it right in a public place was a manifestation of gentlemanly discourse adopted through the format of meetings to involve a wide swathe of social strata, chaining speech acts of meetings and quotations in newspapers to citation in the quarterly reviews.

A meeting includes speeches as well as 'business' to be decided, hence the resolutions. A soirée was a related kind of event, by invitation, less agonistic in nature, which was also chaired and featured speeches. At one such event in the Lever Street Chapel, Manchester, in 1853, Thompson gave a 'long, eloquent address' emphasising what Britons could do to overthrow US slavery, utilising both their moral institutions and commercial leverage. He then opened the floor to questions, 'and his replies gave much satisfaction, and elicited enthusiastic applause' on the comparative expense of free and enslaved labour, the choice between gradualist and immediate emancipation (the latter being the course Thompson always espoused), the agricultural development of India, the United States' Fugitive Slave

Law (which mandated people in the Northern States to cooperate in the seizure of freedom-seekers), and the United States' reasons for ending the slave trade with Africa. At some point, the Quakers gathered at the meeting were shown examples of African cotton, an illustration of a cotton-cleaning process, and an African loom. A visiting clergyman gave an address, and Thompson's future son-in-law proposed a vote of thanks, which carried by acclamation.[61]

Sometimes meetings were strictly private affairs. Anything branded a 'dinner' was likely to be an advertised yet ticketed event, usually catering to propertied men. Its heyday was the 1830s.[62] In October 1839, Thompson attended a large dinner party of wealthy Mancunian manufacturers and spinners, where he was invited to speak 'for the *special* and *specified* purpose of talking over our subject' of India, an overlooked facet of English responsibility that, according to Thompson, required education on the home front and reformed administration abroad. The meal was served at 2:00 p.m., and until 7:00 p.m. he held forth among a cordially disposed company. Thompson wrote that George Hadfield (1787–1879), the radical politician and Congregationalist, 'called upon his townsmen around him most solemnly to come forward & advocate my cause', whereupon Thompson 'took the opportunity offered ... of urging home the subject' in another speech.[63] Private meetings such as this could be especially useful for securing the allegiance of wealthy patrons and laid the groundwork for public meetings where local branches of a national organisation could be forged. Local branches facilitated lecture tours as well as the dissemination of information, gathering of petitions, and sponsorship of regional events.

Another facet of performance chaining occurred with the presentation of a petition. As Janette Lisa Martin writes, 'formulating a petition expressing political grievances was perceived to be an unalienable constitutional right and one of the few avenues for redress open to the unenfranchised'.[64] In November 1837, Thompson spoke to an overflowing house at Dr Wardlaw's Chapel in Edinburgh. In the midst of a ninety-minute speech, 'the Address to the queen with 135,000 signatures, an immense roll was brought up the platform and placed upon a table by my side. It was a glorious sight'.[65] The petition connected this meeting to many individual acts of affixing signatures to the petition, in countless previous meetings, and to the later presentation of the petition to Parliament. The roll served as a prop but also a potent speech act in all three settings, emphasising how any one meeting resists definitive closure yet makes resistant incremental engagements with political power on behalf of individuals, and individuals aggregated into movements.[66]

The act of signing a petition (often at meetings) represented the aggregated effect of presence within the system of courtly redress, connected to other modes of civic engagement – such as voting, parades, and conventions – more eligible to some people than others.[67]

## Meetings with Mobbings

Resolutions periodically registered convictions of an assembly, but throughout meetings audiences were expected to vocalise disapproval, amusement, and anything else that registered how they followed the ins and outs of the speeches: heckles, jeers, and shouts were all 'taken as evidence of a robust, democratic spirit' (Figure 1.2). Speakers were always to be given a fair hearing, and to this end 'the chair, the speakers, and the audience were collectively responsible for enforcing fair play'.[68] Generally, this all went quite well. Published protocols for how to conduct meetings were widely available, and special variants for debates were displayed on placards in advance of events.[69] It is notable, though perhaps not definitive, that illustrations of large meetings of anti-slavery, Chartist, and free trade advocates show the attendees almost universally attentive to the speaker, in contrast with illustrations of theatre audiences of the same period, which tend to show playgoers' attention on one another, and only occasionally on the stage.[70]

Dissent *about* rather than *within* a meeting entailed a separate, parallel form. For example, very rarely Chartist speakers reported being 'threatened with fire arms, assailed with brick-bats and on one occasion a dead cat', and one was even attacked by a gang.[71] This is mobbing: 'violent, riotous, or intimidatory action, in association with others, with a particular end in mind' (*OED*). Mobbings attempt to disrupt the efficacy of meetings by staging contra-performances – not merely exhibitions of disagreement within the performative parameters of a meeting – chained to the meetings themselves.[72]

In 1834, Thompson was sponsored by the Glasgow Emancipation Committee, BFASS, and New England Anti-Slavery Society to give a lecture tour in the Northeastern United States.[73] The goals were to enhance international links between abolitionists and call attention to the Presbyterian Synod's disapproval of slaveholding ministers in the US South. To many of his US supporters, Thompson was a young Lafayette, come to help liberate the enslaved. Instead of military tactics he deployed oratory and moral argument, but his heroic status was augmented by his willingness, like the Marquis de Lafayette (1757–1834), to come from abroad and face the brick-bats and tar pots of those who opposed liberty.[74] The basic

Figure 1.2 A meeting at Exeter Hall on the abolition of the slave trade, engraving by
H. Melville after T. H. Shepherd, ca. 1841. 578856i, Wellcome Collection.

protocols for meetings were observed on both sides of the Atlantic – and
Thompson's trademarked blend of erudition, impressive command of
facts, use of statistics, occasional sarcasm, and biblical exegeses in a tour
de force performance of memory and argumentation was likewise novel
on both sides of the ocean. On one side of the Atlantic, he exhorted his
countrymen to recognise their ongoing complicity in the slave trade when
buying goods made by oppressed bondsmen, and on the other side he
enjoined US citizens to recognise the contradiction of a nation founded
on liberty and freedom for all whilst millions were still in literal chains.
For his opponents in the United States, this made him more than merely
an unwelcome interloper: 'Thompson is sneeringly published here as a
"foreign emissary" – an "intermeddler in matters with which he has no
personal concern", "a foreign disturber of the peace"'.[75]

Some US abolitionists hailed Thompson as a 'young Demosthenes',
'tall, graceful and agile, his countenance fine and attractive, his voice
mellifluent', with 'eloquence … of the most commanding and winning
kind … a scholar, an orator and a gentleman'.[76] His passions seemed to
'come and go at his bidding', while he carried his hearers 'along with him,

sometimes into the solemn and sublime, then relaxing them into boister-ous laughter'. His rhetoric was complemented by tremendous 'command of language, a voice of extraordinary compass, flexibility and power, [and] strong yet graceful gesticulation'.[77] Nevertheless, he had a preponderance of detractors. The kindest of them observed that Thompson's looks were marred by 'a lurking devil about the eye and mouth, that acts as a very good index to the impudence and self-sufficiency within'. It was conceded that he was a powerful speaker, in the way that 'a trip hammer [is] a most powerful mawler of pig iron'. According to others, he had a club-room style: practised posture accompanied mere rant and a vehement sawing of the air, as he knocked 'his fist at "circumbient objects"' and intermittently 'blows his cheeks into a rotundity that would do credit to a swell fish'.[78]

There had been minor outbreaks of violence in preceding years, but dur-ing the US congressional election season of 1834 a pattern of civil unrest coalesced.[79] Thompson arrived to a nation in turmoil. During the months immediately prior to his arrival, race riots broke out from New Orleans to Philadelphia, and Boston to Cincinnati; Irish labourers building canals and railways rioted in Maryland, New York State, and outside Washington, DC; and anti-Catholic, anti-foreign tensions erupted into riots in New York City and Boston. William Ellery Channing (1780–1842), Ralph Waldo Emerson (1803–82), and John Quincy Adams (1767–1848) thought the nation was on the verge of collapse.[80] David Grimsted, who has looked at the longer pattern of discontent, sees the problem as 'ethnic hatreds; religious animosities; class tensions; racial prejudice; economic grievances; moral fears over drinking, gaming, and prostitution; political struggles' and perennially 'the albatross of slavery'.[81] The following year, out of 147 such incidents, 41 per cent were either proslavery (46) or racial (15) riots.[82]

As Harriet Martineau (1802–76) observed, merchants and ship own-ers of the North were 'exasperated into panic' fearing that the abolition-ists would get between them and Southern suppliers, and 'the panic was generously shared by those who had no ships and conducted no com-merce'.[83] Crowds assembled to break up abolition meetings, sacked the home of the abolitionist benefactor Lewis Tappan (1788–1873) and several Black churches, and went door to door looking for homes where resi-dents had failed to obey their instruction to light a candle and stand in the window, as in the book of Exodus: dwellings with Black faces or empty windows were attacked.[84] Many of these acts were planned and executed with the knowledge and guidance of civic leaders, 'gentlemen of prop-erty and standing', a phrase that Thompson and his supporters acerbically cited ever after.[85] Anti-abolitionists, frustrated that they could not stop all abolitionist publishers or prosecute their wealthy benefactors, were in many ways a proletarian force; the *Boston Chronicle*, for example, regarded mobbing as the 'property of the people'.[86] Nevertheless, mobbers were often the agents for better-heeled sponsors with direct commercial interests in perpetuating the South's economic basis. The press was complicit in inflaming unrest and blamed the targets for scaring the public 'with the sight of their burning property and demolished churches'.[87] Playing it down, Thompson wrote from Liverpool a few days before embarking: 'The riots prove nothing but the dispositions of a few thieves and ruffians to make the question of abolition a pretext for disorder that they may with impunity plunder of their property a few citizens and at the same time gratify their malicious prejudice against the colored population.'[88]

The Southern press expressed a widespread sentiment about Thompson before US auditors had heard a word from his mouth: 'The impudence, ignorance, and recklessness of such characters, deserve a severe and summary rebuke.'[89] After Thompson's arrival in New York on 20 September 1834, a gathering of nearly 100 'gentlemen' successfully urged their lodging-keeper to turn him out, along with his wife and baby daughters, who had accompanied him on the trip.

Whereas within Britain abolitionists and proslavery advocates met on the debate floor, engaged in pamphlet wars, or wrestled with one another in the press, US citizens' form of expressing dissent over slavery was not so polite. Fearing that any abolitionist advocacy would foment the enslaved to rebel, Southerners effectively intimidated Northerners into complicity. Journalists and speakers were special targets, and though violence ranged from lynchings to destruction of presses to intimidation, the most brutal and the only fatal incidents occurred in the slave states. In the North, mobs widely brought about the disruption of abolitionist meetings – escalating from unrestrained vocalisations and brute force to persecution and kidnapping – and George Thompson became an obtrusive pretext for these activities, whether they were chained as performance prequels, coincident acts, or postscripts of his meetings. An early incident, in November 1834, was mild in retrospect: Thompson's address to a meeting of women 'was disturbed by groans, hisses, and other noises, throwing candles, &c'.[90] Over the course of fourteen months he was often hidden by his colleagues, and even ran for his life, but when he could attend meetings neither disruptions nor direct intimidation kept him from striking at the heart of republican identity, citing both the US Constitution and the Christian Bible as contrary to the US slave system.[91] This foreign advocacy by a 'Wandering Insurrectionist' and 'vagabond' was considered a grievous affront, and mobbings as well as newspaper invectives intensified.[92] While abolitionists regarded Thompson's delivery at meetings as '*glorious*' and heaven-sent,[93] the proslavery mobbers sought to 'drive [out] that audacious foreigner … who is grossly abusing the rights of hospitality, to throw our country into confusion'.[94]

Thompson was a flint against which nativist mobs violently struck. He toured extensively throughout the northeastern states; lectured at and addressed over 130 meetings, soirées, and conventions; and networked with other abolitionists.[95] Even so, he was sometimes persuaded to remain silent. For example, in September 1835 he delivered three successful lectures in Plymouth, Massachusetts, and was announced for Concord. During the afternoon, 'runners were dispatched into the back parts of the town, to scour the habitations of the depraved and desperate, and stir them up to the work of outrage'. Knowing this, Thompson's sponsors cancelled the lecture, but 'excited by RUM and ready to do the deeds their more *respectable* employers were ashamed to do', mobbers crowded into the village and stoned a group of abolitionists on their way to the courthouse. Thompson was not present, yet the mob persisted 'with drums beating and clamorous shouts', degrading 'the honor of the town by yells and bonfires and the firing of cannon'.[96] In Lynn, a rather inept mob of drunken 'noisy and turbulent boys' paraded in the vicinity of the lecture hall and cried out 'fire', which produced only a brief alarm. As the meeting's closing prayers were uttered the mob rushed in, throwing eggs, even though many of the intruders were so drunk they hardly knew where they were.[97] A similar mob of 150 gathered in Abingdon in the same month, and 'At the close … as Mr. Thompson was retiring from the meeting, they cried out, "Lynch him!" "out with him!" "Hustle him out!" "Down with him!" &c. &c. and followed after him like a troop of hungry wolves – but he escaped without injury, although he was struck by a stone upon the side of his face.'[98] In Boston, a mob disrupting a women's anti-slavery meeting pretended to attack Thompson (who was elsewhere), seized William Lloyd Garrison (1805–79, his greatest US ally), and prepared to tar and feather him in Thompson's stead, while other mobs simultaneously attacked abolitionists Henry B. Stanton (1805–87) in Newport, Connecticut, and Samuel J. May (1797–1871) in Montpelier, Vermont.[99]

Garrison reflected to his wife that if Thompson 'were a murderer, or a parricide, he could not be treated more shamefully than he has been. To think of his being in danger of assassination, even in broad daylight – nay, even in the streets of Boston! Shame – infamy upon the city!'[100] Indeed, one morning Garrison and his houseguest Thompson awoke to find that a pair of gallows had been erected across the street, each rigged with a halter and the inscription 'By order of Judge Lynch' sported on the crossbar.[101] It was inconceivable that Thompson would go to the South; in Charleston $20,000 was offered for his abduction.[102] The violence in New England was neither as unchecked nor as deadly as in the slave states, but in an atmosphere where a North Carolina congressman's gift of a rope to Arthur Tappan (1786–1865) was considered hilarious – and where two Cincinnati newspapers openly recommended that the public lynch Tappan – abolitionists everywhere needed to be vigilant and even devious.[103]

Thompson stayed in the United States for over a year, but eventually he was on the run more than he was in halls addressing crowds. An October 1835 poster from Salem, Massachusetts, decrying Thompson as a fanatical 'foreign pest' expresses the openness of consensus about what Thompson represented (Figure 1.3). Less than two months later, the re-elected President Andrew Jackson 'applauded the "strong and impressive" response of Northerners "against … emissaries from foreign parts who have dared to interfere in this matter"' of slavery.[104]

From such a perspective, Thompson was a foreigner who had no right to speak, and to oppose him was to assert democracy and preserve the republic. By fall 1835, mobbings of abolitionists proved that Northerners were prepared to offer more than verbal assurance that they sided with the South on abolition.[105] Thompson was characterised in the Northern press as committing crimes against the nation, 'going about from place to place, denouncing the constitution of the United States, as at war with the rights of nature and the laws of God, thus striking at the roots of all our social relations'.[106] Preservation of pervasive racism and racist institutions was at the core of the foment, as one newspaper stated: '[we] are not disposed to yield the rights of American citizens to an army of Jim Crows and their white associates'.[107] Even opponents who would not endorse violence felt they could counter Thompson with his own weapon (rhetoric) in his trademark forum (the meeting). One wrote: 'We can make this apostle of a Black Crusade against the White population, feel and understand, that however he may gather around him crowds of foolish men and silly women, the voice of New England can speak in tones which will rival the deepest peals of thunder, in total repudiation of the slightest sympathy with his pernicious principles and worse than pernicious practice.'[108] Thompson's opponents felt that the stakes were as high as they could be.[109]

Thompson's view that as a Christian he must speak against human bondage, and that as a Briton he could give credence to US abolitionists' cause through international ties, was flatly denied by mobbers, who

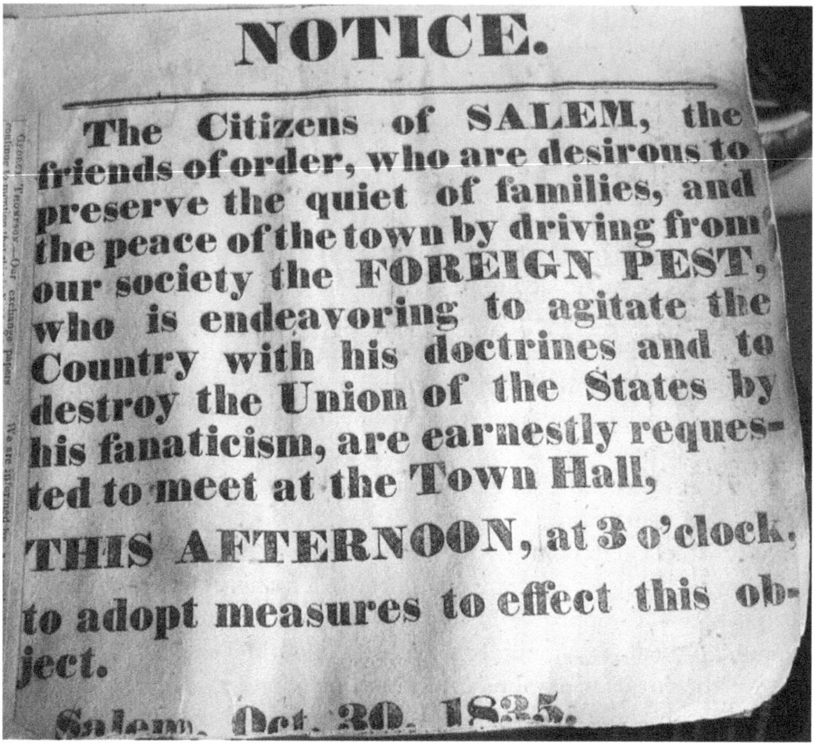

# NOTICE.

The Citizens of SALEM, the friends of order, who are desirous to preserve the quiet of families, and the peace of the town by driving from our society the FOREIGN PEST, who is endeavoring to agitate the Country with his doctrines and to destroy the Union of the States by his fanaticism, are earnestly requested to meet at the Town Hall, THIS AFTERNOON, at 3 o'clock, to adopt measures to effect this object.

Salem, Oct. 20. 1835.

Figure 1.3　George Thompson encountered this 1835 poster during his first tour of the United States and affixed it in his scrapbook. Thompson Extract Books, LC 3449.S43. Library of Congress.

took the position that all politics are national. By mobbing abolitionists, including Thompson, they sought to bring all US citizens, especially Northerners, into compliance. They were substantially successful in doing this for another three decades. From a performance perspective, what is also evident is that mobbings made ideology and social processes evident through cultural form: misrule cohered across significant variants (in action and pretext) to strengthen the social movement that preserved slavery even while its opponents continued to organise meetings and conventions to abolish it.

Reflecting on the 'mobocracy', Thompson framed the virulence and persistence of the opposition as showing how far his side had progressed in influencing the national scene and advancing the cause of abolition. He wrote to Garrison: 'yesterday the [US] abolitionists were esteemed few, mean, silly, and contemptible', but 'now they are of sufficient importance to arouse and fix the attention of the entire country, and earth and hell are ransacked for weapons and recruits, with which to fight the ignorant, imbecile, superannuated and besotted believers in the doctrines of immediate emancipation [such as himself]. This is a good sign'.[110] Garrison published this letter in his newspaper, and no wonder: it offered encouragement to abolitionists by showing how their anti-slavery meetings were chained to the nationwide foment of mobbing. In the United States, mobbing was a violent reaction to mediated critique (especially speeches and newspapers), not so much protesting liberal resistance but persistently, performatively, and forcefully intimidating opponents in forms ranging from charivari and rioting to arson and lynching. These contra-performances were not part of a counter-movement, but rather a belligerent assertion of the status quo.

Setting aside the circumstances of personal peril, Thompson deployed his rhetorical skill to name the silver lining to his travails. Even so, he brought his journey to a premature end. On 8 November 1835, his friends put him in a covered carriage and took him to a New York quay. He slunk out of port in a rowing boat and boarded a ship owned by Henry G. Chapman (1804–42, husband of abolitionist Maria Weston Chapman, 1806–85), bound for St John, New Brunswick, where he caught a British ship to Liverpool.[111] He dared not make the crossing on a US vessel. Nevertheless, abolitionism not only registered but grew: by the end of 1834 auxiliary anti-slavery societies had more than tripled in the North, even though members and their children were denied trade and turned away from schools, colleges, pulpits, and the bar.[112] Progressive advocacy and reactionary performances were, for the time being, chained.

This account of the formal characteristics and historicist interpretation of meetings and mobbings demonstrates that both forms have multiple variants yet each coheres as an epistemology with political impact.[113] Their logics were opposed rhetorically though both swelled their respective political movements performatively in consequential and durable ways, citationally referencing each other's actions; and both movements' advocacy was amplified historically by coverage in the press. Both performances and counter-performances were integral to political life and the elicitation of sympathies, and as chained events they both constituted a meaningful pattern within democracy. Knowledge economies – on which meetings were predicated – were performance opportunities for addressing and including the nation and its people. Although mobbings collided rhetorically they enmeshed with meetings performatively: as with an episodic play their locations and component parts formed a more complete impression of related episodes and opposed perspectives.

In historiography, meetings and mobbings reveal complex mappings of the challenges facing US abolitionists and their transatlantic allies. These forms were bound to and yet also repelled by each other's ideology. Not to diminish the danger experienced by the targets of some mobbings, this reveals instances of the micropolitics of reception.

## In Judgement at Meetings

Whereas Thompson's generation laboured to transform Britain's political landscape into a broad-based liberal democracy by expanding the male franchise and linking emancipation to implementation of Christian ethics at home and abroad, the next generation focused on a set of issues aimed to make the British Empire into a more economically rational system, urging a broad agenda of liberal reforms. Both sought to shift what society deemed honourable.[114] Both experienced the consciousness that Christina Sharpe characterises as being 'in the wake' of 'Black exclusion from social, political, and cultural belonging' manifest as denial of humanity.[115] Thompson's son-in-law Frederick William Chesson (1833–88) carried on the work of the elder generation while also advancing the agenda of the next, utilising his own generation's tactics (Figure 1.4). Starting in the early 1850s, Chesson organised thousands of large and small meetings, lobbied the Foreign Office on countless cases of human trafficking, and wrote about these issues for the press. Whereas Thompson was twice involved in journalism as a proprietor and occasionally as an author, Chesson worked for one of Thompson's ventures – the weekly *Empire* (1855–56) – and there found his footing. For the remainder of his life journalism was the employment that enabled him to engage so broadly in his avocations.

The eldest child and only son of a bootmaker who became a partner in an oil distillery, Frederick Chesson grew up in Gillingham, Kent. His father was killed in a manufacturing accident, and at the age of thirteen Frederick was sent to earn his living in a London office.[116] Three years later, in 1849, his mother remarried and the family relocated to Massachusetts.[117] Chesson later referred to this as 'a period of revolution, when the forces of freedom and slavery were being organised for the final struggle. It was really the beginning of the end of slavery, although it seemed, at the moment, that slavery was established on a throne that was likely to endure

Figure 1.4    Frederick Chesson, Portraits of US Abolitionists, 81.137, Massachusetts
Historical Society, 81.

for ever'. He was in the United States when the Fugitive Slave Act of 1850 came into effect, and attended a meeting with 3,000 Black protestors.[118] Chesson witnessed a man being turned over to those who hunted him, and recalled a quarter century later:

> if I lived for hundreds of years, I should never forget … the return into slavery of a fugitive slave, who had sought refuge and employment in New York. I mention this circumstance because it helped to give me that love of freedom which I have cherished ever since, and it was therefore very natural that when, some years later, the people of the Free States were involved in a tremendous struggle with slavery for their national existence, I should interest myself on behalf of the four millions of slaves in the Southern States.[119]

Nothing else is recorded about the ensuing years, until Chesson began a diary in June 1854, at age twenty-one. By this point he was enmeshed in George Thompson's networks, working in Manchester as secretary for the Peace Conference Committee (opposing the Crimean War), participating in the North of England Anti-Slavery Society and India Reform League, and writing freelance articles for the *Nonconformist*.[120] Almost certainly, Chesson met Thompson in the United States in 1850–1, when the orator was on his second US tour. In any case, they became sufficiently well acquainted that while in Manchester Chesson pined for his 'dear girl' – Thompson's second daughter, Amelia Ann Everard Thompson (1833–1902), then residing in London – whom he married in May 1855.

While in his early twenties, Chesson actively pursued self-improvement through reading as well as by attending a wide variety of lectures and political meetings. By doing so he was, in many ways, the consummate liberal subject, for he valued and sought to become the kind of person that John Stuart Mill (1806–73) advocated for in *On Liberty* (1859): someone who would 'use observation to see, reasoning and judgement to foresee, activity to gather materials for discussion, discrimination to decide, and when he has decided, firmness and self-control to hold to his deliberate decision'. Mill argued that to the extent that individuals cultivate themselves, life is enriched, diversified, and animated for all people. And just as all people – across classes, regions, and occupations – seek to improve themselves, 'politicians increasingly know they cannot resist popular will', for even as people 'now read the same things, listen to the same things, see the same things, go to the same places, have their hopes and fears directed to the same objects, have the same rights and liberties, and the same means of asserting them' they also seek differentiation from one another.[121] Most of what can be understood of Chesson's *Bildung* comes from his diary, where he describes reading historic speeches and appraising live addresses to test the resilience of arguments.[122]

Chesson's diaries show that in pursuit of self-improvement, he identified a sensorium of things seen, heard, and apprehended across the performance spectrum, explicitly engaged visual, auditory, gestural, proxemic, and aesthetic criteria, practised notating mises-en-scène, and utilised his daily diary-writing practice as aide-mémoire. Pragmatically, it helped him remember what he wrote for publication so he could ensure freelance payments; developmentally, it helped him find his unique direction amid a myriad of possibilities. For example, in September 1856 he noted purchasing an edition of Cowper's poems and throughout 1865 he read Cowper's letters and Robert Southey's biography of the poet.[123] He was interested in events that attracted large audiences, perhaps because they held the greatest capacity to influence thought yet also the greatest danger to homogenise thinkers. He was also interested in how, at small meetings, dinners, and parties, notable people conducted themselves, crafted an anecdote, and revealed their inner lives, and then what other people did in reaction. A few examples suffice to show how the parameters and criteria of his inquiry were clear from the outset yet also how he became a more astute – and concise – critic over time. This is consonant with what Jacques Rancière calls an 'emplotment of temporality': an individual seeks and finds aesthetic self-education, gives this descriptive language, and then frames 'a new collective ethos' whereby 'art and life can exchange their properties', utilising their 'polemical configuration of the common world'.[124] Bridging the thought of Mill and Rancière, Chesson exemplifies modernity and modern subjecthood-in-the-making, a proto-example of what Rosi Braidotti identifies in early twenty-first-century Europe as change, actualisation, and flux: a nomadic 'experiment in becoming' that extends creatively toward forms of public service equally connected to art and politics (though with unequal ethical impact).[125]

The first performance mentioned in Chesson's diaries took place in Manchester in 1854, while he worked for the North of England Anti-Slavery Society:

> In evening went to Queens Theatre, & saw for the first time G.V. Brooke [1818–66]. The play was Othello. Brooke was ably supported by a portion of the Drury lane Co[mpan]y. He appeared in five different magnificent costumes. His voice is rather husky, but at times it gets into a good key. His acting is good. Some of his bursts of passion are glorious, & did not appear to me to rise into rant. His great defect is one for which he is not responsible, viz, his voice. The passion of jealousy which he at times exhibited

when he supposed his wife unfaithful were acted naturally as was also the grief which he manifested after he had murdered her and when he discovered her innocence. Altogether I like him very well altho' I am still unable to tell how it is that he has won so high a position. The house was crammed in every part.[126]

In Romantic poetics, according to Rancière, the artist 'becomes a kind of symptomatologist, delving into the dark underside or the unconscious of a society to decipher the messages engraved in the very flesh of ordinary things ... making society conscious of its own secrets, by leaving the noisy stage of political claims and doctrines and delving to the depths of the social, to disclose the enigmas and fantasies hidden in the intimate realities of everyday life'. This, surely, is part of the appeal of great stories, especially when their equally great passions are acted out. Rancière argues that in the paradigm of art becoming life, 'both industrial production and artistic creation are committed to doing something on top of what they do – to creating not only objects but a sensorium, a new partition of the perceptible'.[127] For Chesson, the sensorium includes Brooke's magnificent costumes, his flawed voice, and his natural presentation of extreme emotions. Even so, at this early point, Chesson struggled to find evocative language to convey his judgement: Brooke is 'ably supported', 'his acting is good', and his passions – defined with a negative – 'did not appear to me to rise into rant'. Despite these merits, and the obvious clamour to see Brooke act, Chesson concludes 'I am still unable to tell how it is that he has won so high a position'. Chesson consistently sought to correlate performers' skill – and their singularity – to their reputation, whether he examined a great actor such as Brooke, a great political orator such as Lord Brougham, or a fashionable preacher such as Charles Spurgeon (1834–92). At this early date, in 1854, he could not reconcile his observations to the performer's reputation, nor could he very precisely differentiate why this was so.

A few months later, still only twenty-one, Chesson ventured out to hear George Holyoake (1817–1906) give an account of his 1842 trial and imprisonment for atheism. Chesson was curious about Holyoake's advocacy of secularism, yet it was not just the content of the lecture that captured his attention. The diary states that Holyoake

> is a pale, thin, young looking man with a badly grown moustache. His voice is weak but at times swells into considerable compass. His speech is of the simplest Saxon, at times he is somewhat hesitating but never embarrassed, at other times he professes a great flow of language. His logical powers are great. After he had concluded[,] an animated discussion ensued in which Johnson, Nelson, & others took part. Holyoake had the best of them.[128]

In this commentary about Holyoake's looks, vocalisation, lexicon, reasoning, and ability to handle his audience, Chesson stresses the categories laid out in Holyoake's own much-reprinted 1849 treatise *Public Speaking and Debate*, a didactic and anecdotal handbook that guides novices through Aristotle and Quintilian's basics of rhetoric, applied to the contemporaneous exigencies of platform, pulpit, juridical, and parliamentary oratory. The other great instructional text for British and US orators of this period – whether or not (like Thompson and Chesson) they lacked the advantage of university education – is Hugh Blair's 1785 treatise *Lectures on Rhetoric and Belles Lettres*, assembled from addresses he gave at the University of Edinburgh over the previous quarter century. Blair stipulates three kinds of eloquence (to please, instruct and convince, and interest and advocate) and the types of speech that typically exemplify them, in ascending order of importance and sophistication (addresses to great men by great men, the bar, and the pulpit).[129] Chesson embraced them all as an avid listener.

In 1862, a large and fashionable gathering of Eton College alumni assembled to view a silver horde worth £2,200 and to hear testimonials to the recipient, Shakespearean actor Charles Kean (1811–68).[130] The Duke of Newcastle (1811–64, secretary of state for the Colonies in Lord Palmerston's Liberal government, who had presided at a celebration of Kean a couple of years before) was meant to present the gift but was called away to Windsor by the queen. William Ewart Gladstone (1809–98), a schoolmate of Kean's, filled in for him at short notice. At the time, Gladstone was Chancellor of the Exchequer and firm ally to most liberal and radical causes; the nation's preeminent parliamentarian, he was considered worth listening to even when debating the budget.[131] Charles Kean – then the most respected actor on the British stage – received the silver engraved with Shakespearean scenes as a token of his schoolmates', friends', fellow actors', and public's esteem (Figure 1.5).

At this event, Chesson found an occasion to hear the most lauded of all living orators deliver an address (not a political speech but an encomium), then hear the British stage's most-celebrated actor deliver a speech (not a dramatic monologue but one of his own composition addressed from the oratorical platform). It was a great occasion at which to critique and to learn.[132] At this point, in 1862, Chesson had been practising this kind of evaluation in his diary for nearly a decade and was able to concisely describe the two orators' performances and their effectiveness as rhetoricians, linking his praise to the implicit commendation from the 'very numerous & brilliant assembly' gathered for the occasion. Chesson

Figure 1.5    Presentation of testimonial plate to Charles Kean at St James's Hall, London.
*Illustrated London News*, 29 March 1862, 319.

wrote two concise comments about the testimonials in his diary. The first
is this: 'Mr. Gladstone … made a very graceful & appropriate speech in
which he remarked on the fact that the drama was interwoven with the
history of every country & every age, & did justice to Kean's efforts to
elevate the stage.'[133] What Chesson refers to as 'graceful and appropriate'
in Gladstone's speech, the *Era*'s correspondent called 'one of the bright-
est pages in the history of modern Drama'. Chesson caught the essence of
individuated performance in a phrase that both characterised and evaluated the moment without pompous amplification. The *Era*, by contrast,
deployed the broad stroke of cliché.[134] Gladstone endorsed Kean's efforts
to elevate the stage by producing the work of the national poet, but it was
not just Gladstone's gracious words that impressed. The emotional display
that these words elicited from Kean and the assembled audience was just
as notable.

Upon rising to respond, Kean was so overcome that he needed several moments before he could master his mingled emotions of pride and
gratitude. Chesson simply observed in his diary: 'Charles Kean's speech in

reply was very happily expressed, poetical without grotesqueness of imagery.'[135] According to the *Era*, he succeeded through his performance of modesty amidst the recapitulation of his intentions. Kean stated:

> I had hoped, without detracting from the power of the actor, or the importance of the author, to have rendered that Stage over which I had control something more than a mere vehicle of transient amusement—an elevating and instructive recreation. (*Cheers.*) If there be any who suppose that I intended to address myself merely to the eye, my purpose has been perfectly misunderstood, for I meant but to pass through that gateway of the mind, and appeal to the understanding of my audience.[136]

Here, the *Era* notes, there was '*Great cheering*'. The newspapers document how the audience first cheered themselves (a 'brilliant and distinguished company'); then Shakespeare, a poet who, ironically, had not yet made it onto Eton's curriculum; and ultimately the public's capacity to understand Shakespeare *through Kean*, marking these productions as the supreme mid-Victorian interpretations. Kean then gave special notice of his boyhood friends, the sight of whom in the auditory recalled him to 'those loved fields, "Where once my careless childhood strayed, / A stranger yet to pain"', quoting Thomas Gray.[137] The *Era* notes: '*Here Mr. Kean was much overcome, but, after giving vent to his tears, his manly spirit soon recovered itself, while the applause and cheering lasted some minutes.*'[138] Transitioning abruptly to what Blair calls 'the pathetic part' (the penultimate section of a speech), Kean credited his wife, Ellen Kean (née Tree, 1805–80), with whom he toiled side by side, a flourish that, in his review for the *Star*, Chesson annotates with '*Loud cheers*' and the *Era* punctuates with '*Great applause, during which every eye was turned to the gallery, where Mrs. Kean was seated, who evidently experienced great difficulty to restrain her feelings.*'[139] Finally, in a succinct peroration, Kean paraphrased from *Twelfth Night* (III:3),

> I can no other answer make,
> But thanks, and thanks, and
> Ever thanks.

Whereupon 'immense applause continued for some time, and as Mr Kean retired three cheers were given for him, and then for Mrs Kean, the band playing Mendelssohn's "Wedding March"'.[140]

Oratory was Gladstone's natural element, just as emotional dramaturgy – acting allied with scenography to form a mise-en-scène – was Kean's.[141] For Chesson, Gladstone and Kean succeeded in individuating themselves through language that reflected their respective stations in life, despite this extra-professional setting: Gladstone as a statesman and Kean as a producer of Shakespeare. They came across as neither eccentric nor common, but calibrated to their stations. Gladstone's cultural ranking is shown to be appropriately calibrated to the public's esteem for Kean, just as Kean's gracious servitude to Shakespeare is rewarded proportionately by the expensive and beautiful silver.

Through constant practise over the years, Chesson learned to be succinct when he noted the dissonance between occasion, location, text, and performance. For example, he often dropped in on churches and commented upon the sermons. On holiday in Kent in 1863, he visited the garrison church within Dover Castle (St Mary in Castro), a Saxon structure whose thorough refurbishment was completed the previous year. On this occasion, he wrote in his diary: 'We went to the Gothic Church (near the heights) [re]built by [George] Gilbert Scott [1839–97]. The clergyman read the service very indifferently and preached a sermon on temptation that was scarcely removed from commonplace.'[142] To be 'commonplace' was absolute anathema. It is an obsolete term for a sermon or discourse yet also, in contemporaneous parlance, something trite. Chesson's point is that to expend the opportunity of a sermon on the trivial is to squander the opportunity to persuade the laity. To Chesson, a commonplace sermon on temptation was a dissonance between content and manner, substance and occasion. It was a performance faux pas, neither showing a suitable commitment to the subject nor aiding the auditors' moral improvement.

In his work on early modern Mexican spectacles, Leo Cabranes-Grant notes that performances are 'engines of emergence (sites for new positions, bodies, and voices) and deconstructive gestures'.[143] In other words, performances enable new constructs to emerge while also evincing the lag, or counter-pulls, within cultures; in the reception of art, the senses (perception) and sense (intelligence) confronting this lag fulfil Rancière's definition of the 'new dramaturgy of the intelligible'.[144] Together, therefore, performance and philosophy not only verify the known – such as 'tensions still at work within cultures' – but also expand on the known by encouraging intellectual, affective, and sensory perceptions conducive to new insights.[145] For example, in 1857, when Frederick and Amelia Chesson went for the first time to hear Charles Spurgeon, the Baptist preacher who had built a huge reputation since he burst upon London in 1853, they expected a lot. England spawned preaching stars from the mid-eighteenth-century, but until the 1850s there was no one like Charles Spurgeon. He became a Baptist pastor at the age of eighteen, and at a succession of venues his auditors grew to over 23,500 people at a time (Figure 1.6).[146] Everyone agreed

REV. C. H. SPURGEON PREACHING IN THE SURREY MUSIC HALL, LONDON.

Figure 1.6    Charles Spurgeon preaching at Surrey Music Hall, Kennington (Spurgeon, *Sermons Preached and Revised*, frontispiece, 1859), University of Virginia Library.

that 'his voice and elocution … are wonderful', 'very flexible and various'; but as George Eliot put it, his doctrine was a 'libel … the most superficial grocer's-back-parlor view of Calvinistic Christianity; and I was shocked to find how low the mental pitch of our society must be, judged by [the] standard of this man's celebrity'.[147]

When Frederick Chesson first heard Spurgeon he was 'sermon-tasting': exposing himself to a spectrum of theology, trying out local notables, and judging the celebrated.[148] Spurgeon's manner made a positive impression on Chesson, as did his appearance: 'the boldness of his look conveyed the idea of natural audacity'. He gave 'exceedingly lucid, intelligent, and sometimes even eloquent' commentary on the 111th Psalm, and then

> The secret of his success soon became manifest. Like his Master he speaks in parables; and there can be no more popular, animated, or successful method of communicating truth to the people. His sermon, indeed, was one series of parables, anecdotes, dialogues, and quaint sayings, each of which contained an idea, exploded an error, or proclaimed a truth. But what shall I say of his doctrine?[149]

Hugh Blair wrote that a preacher's purpose is not to inform auditors, for they have invariably heard the message before, but rather to 'make them better' people by giving 'clear views and persuasive impressions of a religious truth'.[150] To accomplish this, Spurgeon coupled a seemingly improvised style with gravity and warmth, suited to the homiletic form. However, according to Chesson, his pleasing manner was countermanded by an unyielding perspective on predestination for 'the elect', who 'might commit any sin, no matter what its magnitude, but having been fore-ordained they must be saved. Great comfort this to the sinner who believes himself to be predestined to eternal life; and poor inducement to the unfortunate reprobate to endeavour to lead a purer, and better life'.[151] For an anti-slavery advocate such as Chesson, Spurgeon's view was untenable: it gave no moral impetus for slaveholders to reform, no spiritual compass or social conscience. For Chesson, like Mill, how one chose to exercise free will was a crucial tenet of liberal subjecthood.[152] Neither Chesson nor Mill relied on religion to induce ethical action – Mill was notoriously agnostic, and Chesson, though raised a Methodist, did not join a congregation until 1864 – but the preacher's role was to guide those whose beliefs made them susceptible to the theistic checks.[153] In this first encounter with Spurgeon, Chesson approved of the performance but not the message.

Spurgeon's reputation grew steadily, as did the numbers of his fol-lowers and the size of the curious throngs who attended sermons to see for themselves what constituted the Baptist superstar's appeal. Chesson set out numerous times to attend, and was sometimes turned away from overflowing halls. As his reputation grew, Spurgeon graduated from the church at Bromley-by-Bow to Exeter Hall (3,000 seats, the chief and larg-est venue for liberal political gatherings, synonymous with anti-slavery agitation in London), Surrey Music Hall (10,000 seats), and finally the Crystal Palace in Sydenham (where up to 15,000 would gather to hear his addresses). Four years after his first encounter, Chesson heard Spurgeon at the Metropolitan Tabernacle (5,500 seats).[154]

> As viewed from its Upper Gallery the Spectacle presented by such an immense audience was a most imposing one. The acoustic arrangements are perfect. Mr. Spurgeon delivered a very forceful discourse chiefly on the punishments of the wicked, of which he drew so terrible a picture that even an unbeliever would have thrilled. He believes in the ultimate mingling of corporeal with mental anguish, but, of course, resurrection and the judge-ment must take place before this.[155]

Spurgeon's antinomianism was not calculated to please an anti-slavery activist, for he argued that *eventually*, in judgement as in earthly governance, rebellion, revelry, mirth, and ungodliness will receive their dire rewards. As a Garrisonian abolitionist, Chesson worked against exactly this sort of idea: US clergy, for example, who owned enslaved people – or even countenanced slaveholding among parishioners – were a constant sore point between British and US churches. The time until punishment on the Day of Destruction was longer than Garrisonians (including Chesson and Thompson) were prepared to wait. They advocated righteous living in the here and now – doing unto others as they would have done unto them – as the Christian's path.[156] In concert with Mill, with whom he collaborated on several campaigns, Chesson sought to put liberal culture on a moral foundation, and individual autonomy was a central tenet.[157] While they often found common cause with evangelicals, Chesson's political arguments were invariably rooted in secular thought.

Chesson's attention was not always turned to the highbrow or ennobling manifestations of performance. In October 1858, he and his father-in-law took the formerly enslaved John S. Jacobs, a friend of the family and brother of Harriet Jacobs (1813?–97),[158] to London's infamous Judge and Jury Club, across the street from Exeter Hall.[159] It was what one did with male guests from out of town. By 1858 the Judge and Jury Club had 'long been a favourite resort of country cousins, who, whilst imbibing the good things from the Chief Baron's cellar, laugh heartily at his racy and never-failing humour from the bench'.[160] The genial landlord of the Garrick's Head Hotel, 'Baron' Renton Nicholson (1809–61), decked out in silk and long peruke, ruled on cases that were tried by actors, in imitation of famous barristers, who brought forth the 'protean witness' H. G. Brooks, cross-dressed when necessary.[161] According to Joseph S. Meisel, 'Nicholson's own legal training consisted of several trials for insolvency and a few turns in jail', yet his mock courtroom entertainment lasted throughout the 1840s and 1850s.[162] J. Ewing Richie proclaimed, bluntly: 'I do not believe the audience could have stood this if it had not been for the drink …. This side [of] Pandemonium there is nothing more debasing or debased.'[163] Notwithstanding what Chesson acknowledged as 'the foulest obscenities', he still admired the defence lawyer's 'really eloquent and pathetic vindication of the prostitute class' and Nicholson's 'fine elocutionary performance' in summing up. This nocturnal resort of masculine revelry thus hosted ad hoc performances of mock debate where standards of elocution were as exacting – and as catholic – as anywhere that Chesson ventured.

Nicholson's court capitalised on the attention that courtroom argumentation had garnered in England after an 1854 law created more opportunities for counsel to give opening and closing speeches in jury trials, heightening the sense of agonistic drama.[164] From 1857, when the Matrimonial Causes Act made divorce more widely available, the Divorce Court assumed this jurisdiction from the ecclesiastical court and was invariably packed with spectators.[165] Nicholson's parody meta-juridically replicated the way that barristers played off their tripartite audience of judge, jury, and gallery: Nicholson was the judge, some of the audience were the jury, and others were more conventionally positioned as spectators. Whereas the consequentiality of an Old Bailey trial could mean life or death, the topics chosen for Nicholson's court – such as re-enactments of scandalous breach of promise or divorce cases, or, on the evening that Chesson attended, 'The Great Social Evil' (whether prostitution should be illegal) – skirted the boundaries of taste by utilising flamboyant rhetoric within the discipline of courtroom protocol.[166] The open secret of prostitution reached the heart of the cultural paradox so that even country bumpkins – or, in the case of Chesson's party, a grand seigneur of the abolitionist movement, an emancipated formerly enslaved person seasoned by experience on the abolitionist lecture circuit and the merchant marine, and a man of twenty-five who aspired to make a mark on public affairs – were entertained by what Rancière points to as something that makes 'society conscious of its own secrets, by … delving to the depths of the social, to disclose the enigmas and fantasies hidden in the intimate realities of everyday life'.[167] They were also edified by the enactors' technique. Opposing counsel at Nicholson's could utilise markedly contrasting styles, one reliant on facts and the other appealing to the emotions, but as Thompson's experience as a platform speaker showed, this would not be a problem for audiences.

Chesson was interested in what made a speaker celebrated, whatever the person's path in life. In March 1863, at a 'great meeting of the Trades Unions at St. James's hall' in support of the Union side of the American Civil War, he judged the crowded meeting 'one of the most effective I ever attended', with several speeches by working men including Messrs Howell (bricklayer), Mantz (compositor), Cremer and Petheridge (joiners), Connolly (mason), Heap (engineer), Tracey (painter), and Butler (tinplate worker) being 'admirable for their manner and their matter. Better expositions of the question I never heard, and the audience, which included such men as John Stuart Mill, Professor Goldwin Smith [1823–1910, Regius Professor of Modern History at Oxford] and Mr Stansfield [1820–98, radical MP for Halifax], was delighted'. All were there by ticket, the hall was crammed in every part, and women (including Amelia Chesson) also attended.[168] Whereas the seasoned MP John Bright (1811–89) appealed to economic arguments, the shoemaker and secretary of the London Trades Council

George Odger (1813–77), in seconding the first resolution, appealed to his listeners' sense of justice as family men:

> It was said that the Northerners had no real sympathy with the abolition of slavery. (Hear, hear.) Now, he was prepared to disprove that. (Cheers.) It was well known that people would not fraternise with a race of beings who were felt to be below them in the social scale, while they remained so. If any one present should be told that his sister or his daughter had married a negro, he would be taken aback by the tidings; but if he heard that his daughter or sister had married a black prince, he would not be taken aback at all. (Cheers.) The Northerners felt a repugnance to the negro simply because at present he was in a degraded condition. But that they really desired emancipation was proved by the proclamation of Mr. Lincoln. (Cheers.)[169]

The juxtaposition of the Quaker John Bright – a self-taught Radical, in and out of Parliament since 1843, at this time fifty-two years old and still one of the most acclaimed orators of his generation – with the working-class men is sanguine. To Chesson, 'manner and matter' are the hallmarks of a speaker, especially in a gathering such as this, where extempore skills were warranted and the community was so illustrious.

Likewise, in November 1854, Chesson critiqued a lecture on 'America in relation to Christianity' by the African American rhetoric scholar Professor William G. Allen (1820–88) because he 'evidently does not understand extemporaneous speaking'.[170] The ability to give a peroration flowingly, and with the conviction that comes from speaking one's thoughts (not merely one's text) was highly valued: a peroration was the opportunity not only to sum up the case but also to appeal to auditors' emotions. But it was not just in classical rhetoric that Chesson sought his models. At a presentation by William Howard Russell (1820–1907), the Crimean War correspondent who reported from the front and was published in the *Times* with record speed (thanks to overland telegraphy), Chesson noted, 'Russell has practiced conversation with great advantage'. Russell's poise before Sir George de Lacy Evans (1787–1870) – a general present at Crimea who had commenced his venerable career in campaigns against Napoleon – served him well in his description of the Battle of Balaklava, a blot on the British consciousness for the manifest incompetence of the Army.[171]

Well into his career, Chesson demonstrated his full maturity of observation, evaluation, and expression in a description of a House of Commons debate. On 23 February 1866, Members were set to vote on two compelling bills. The sovereign commanded that Parliament grant annuities to Princess Helena (1846–1923, third daughter to the queen) and Prince Alfred

(1844–1900, second son to the queen), and additionally Members were to vote on the creation of a national memorial to the late Lord Palmerston (1784–1865, prime minister in the late 1850s) in Westminster Abbey. This caused 'a great muster of all parties'. Chesson's report in the *Sheffield and Rotherham Independent* notes: 'Every seat was filled; every vacant place was occupied; members clustered round the door; members sat upon the raised steps of the floor between the rows of benches; members squatted on the soft cushions of the galleries. The Ministerial bench was packed with old ministers as well as new …. [Meanwhile] the ladies, whose eyes glistened through the gilded lattices behind which they are ungallantly compelled to sit', gathered in the upper reaches of the chamber. Strikingly, the report relays almost none of the speakers' words, emphasising instead their manner and impact. Gladstone, Chancellor of the Exchequer, called a motion on the question of royal annuities. From the other side of the House, Benjamin Disraeli (1804–81) seconded Gladstone's motion 'in a sepulchral voice, and with an inanimate manner'. Just as the question was to be put for a vote, Edward Playdell-Bouverie (1818–99) nit-picked from the back ministerial benches over an ambiguity in Gladstone's speech, and insisted that the House should 'settle the matter once for all' of whether the prince was to receive 'the pension for life; or provide for its extinction when, in the course of nature … [he] was elevated to the Dukedom of Saxe-Coburg Gotha'. Others then tried to speak but were inaudible in the ensuing din.[172]

The vote was called, 'the "Ayes" had it', and the House turned to the second matter. Again, Gladstone took the lead, and Chesson's report accounted for his performance and how it reflected the man whom he honoured and the impact on the chamber.

> This time it was his task to pronounce an elaborate panegyric on the veteran statesman, who only a few months ago occupied the same place as that from which he spoke. One almost looked for the broad chest, the folded arms, the sleepless eye; but a musical and penetrating voice soon recalled the fact that Palmerston has vacated his place for ever …. Need I say that Mr. Gladstone subdued all hearts by the charm of his oratory—that for a time he made men even forget their antipathies. The cheering was not loud until the end, but every finely-rounded period was followed by those murmurs of applause which it is the crowning triumph of eloquence to evoke.

Disraeli rose amidst loud cheers, yet 'he made no attempt to cope with his rival or to share his laurels – still less to bear away the palm. His words were few, his manner listless, his voice feeble and hesitating'. This was not the Disraeli who had recently bestowed 'splendid and unequalled panegyrics' on Richard Cobden (1804–65) or Abraham Lincoln (1809–65). 'The fire was gone; there only remained its smouldering embers.' The politically unpredictable Alexander Beresford Hope (1820–87), a vocal critic of architecture, followed: 'he gesticulated and raved and ranted. As he rolled about like a three-decker [ship] in a storm, one wondered what it was all about'. At last he issued aesthetic objections to 'the sculptured monstrosities' of other politicians that filled Westminster Abbey. Again, the vote was called, and as soon as this business was concluded and the topic turned to a new Constitution for Jamaica, 'the House at once thinned, and the benches became half empty'. A Scottish Member delivered a speech with an accent so thick no English person could understand him, and the matter rested. Chesson's account draws a picture of the assembly, renders the sounds and gestures of the chief speakers of both government and opposition, and enlivens descriptions of each episode with agonistic precision. This article shows his mastery of performative critique in full measure.[173]

A final example of Chesson as evaluator is drawn from the legitimate stage. In 1863, he and Amelia attended the Haymarket Theatre to see a new production, *Silken Fetters*, adapted by Leicester Buckingham (1825–67) from *Une Chaîne*, a piece by Eugène Scribe (1791–1861) seen in Paris twenty years earlier.[174] Chesson judged it

> A great success. Charles Mathews as Caleb Codicil particularly good. Marion Harris as the young lady of the piece was very natural, more so than Mrs. Mathews. A party in the royal box were somewhat noisy & chaffing a good deal, whereupon Mrs. M. (aside) exclaimed 'Charming behaviour, charming!' They were silent during the remainder of the performance. 'Cool as a Cucumber' followed—Mathews gloriously funny.[175]

Chesson's comments on Charles James Mathews (1803–78) are perfunctory, but he had rendered his judgement on this actor twice before.[176] In 1863 the attention was on the rest of the company. The anecdote about Mrs Mathews correcting the royal party is particularly interesting. A good orator knows how to compel the attention of their audience, not just by the force of personality or powerful ideas but also by the full arsenal of rhetorical devices, including veiled sarcasm. Chesson was consistently interested in audience behaviour, and here is a noteworthy instance of an actress offering a successful check on rudeness. The fact that these spectators were in the royal box is an important and economical turn in the story. They are not necessarily royalty, possibly guests of royalty, but more likely just playgoers with deep pockets, perhaps thoughtless and conspicuous in proportion. This fact makes Mrs Mathews' check on their behaviour a significant intervention whereby she asserted and was ceded her power.

## Perceptible Dramaturgies

The idea that revolutions arose from aesthetic realisations became explicit during the 1920s; however, this has a longer history of experimentation in socialist and, before that, liberal thought. Frederick Chesson exemplifies this experimentation, for his attention to art and rhetoric contributed to his political education and acumen. While this book diligently surfaces a great deal of Chesson's writing to corroborate this claim, Chesson is also a stand-in for how reception worked more broadly during his lifetime. Politics are served by better understandings of the mimetic and logistical challenges of performance (utilising rhetorical effects of the voice, body, and affect; commanding one's material; and managing spectatorial response). In Chesson's 'experiment in becoming', considerations of performance preoccupy him, personally and politically, across domestic, social, political, and artistic realms.[177] Thus, sensory experience leads to aesthetic awareness and political astuteness when the politics of aesthetics – a meta-politics – finds ways of 'proposing to politics rearrangements of its space, reconfiguring art as a political issue or asserting itself as true politics'.[178] Art does not exile Chesson from his chosen forms of activism but helps him do activism.[179]

The space (geographic site) and place (identificatory meanings of space) for politics are both important to this story. Typically, the middle-class Victorian home is thought of as a refuge from the cares and strife of the world of commerce and politics. Atypically or not, the Chessons' home fell short of this mark. Frederick often wrote at home, and early in his marriage it was where he executed many of his duties as secretary to the Aborigines' Protection Society (APS): issuing correspondence, preparing for meetings, and editing the *Colonial Intelligencer, or Aborigines' Friend*, a compendium of information and reports for members of the society. For his wife, Amelia Chesson (née Thompson), their home was the locus of private life yet also where she kept herself in busy leisure (*otium privatum*) by sewing and maintaining the family's clothing, working alongside maidservants to clean and cook, and reading. Whether reading was truly free time spent as she wished (*otium negotiosum*) or instead leisure spent in service (*otium cum seritio*) is debatable, as for a woman of her station the obligations to a household and to herself were coterminous: the guineas she earned writing book reviews brought comforts, but certainly not luxuries, into the household. According to the one extant year of her diary, her labour and daily business (*negotium*) were complicated by the on-again-off-again presence of servants, the need to tend to two infants, and visits to her mother's and grandmother Thompson's households in different parts of London, yet pleasantly punctuated by the visits of her sisters, the safe return of her father from India, and the comings and goings of female friends. Neither she nor Frederick appears to have had any wasted free time (*otium otiosum*), except when they were ill. While he had clear public responsibilities – both to the daily *Star* newspaper for which he wrote and supervised preparation of the morning editions and to the APS – at this period of her life activities centred on the home. Nevertheless, home was a place of public-oriented work: for freelance payments she wrote book reviews and compiled short notices about magazines for the *Star*, and she also took dictation for her father and laboured unremunerated (without Frederick's presence) preparing issues of the *Colonial Intelligencer*.

Just as meetings were shot through with performance chaining, connecting incidents across events, the Chessons' lives were chained by separately and conjointly experienced events. For example, on 27 October 1858 Frederick's diary notes that in the evening he went to work at the *Star*, left in time to attend the APS meeting, then returned to the *Star* office to finish preparing the morning edition. Ten days prior, he had worked on the *Colonial Intelligencer* in preparation for the APS meeting. Yet on 5 and 6 October, while Frederick consulted with a colleague about the Newfoundland Fisheries and worked into the small hours at the *Star*, Amelia was busy at home, assisting with the same APS reports. The concise entries in her diaries stipulate:

> Tues. 5 [October] Washing day. Busy directing covers for A.P.S. reports.
> Wed. 6 [October] Busy with reports still.[180]

After ongoing turmoil, Amelia had engaged a young servant girl less than three weeks before, so while keeping one eye on the washing she was largely focused on the written materials. On 10 October Frederick collected more texts from Dr Thomas Hodgkin (1798–1866, the APS' honorary secretary), and on 13 October he made the final insertions. On 17 October, while the couple and their children enjoyed a Sunday at the Thompsons' home, Frederick corrected the proofs. Without Amelia's timely involvement, competently performing certain chained duties in lieu of Frederick, deadlines would not have been met.

In their study *Everyday Ideas: Socioliterary Experience among Antebellum New Englanders*, Ronald J. Zboray and Mary Saracino Zboray describe how attendance at lectures involves complex 'social logistics': extending invitations, exchanging tickets, planning the outing, and engaging in other micro-coordination by which 'attendees acquired a communally influenced understanding'.[181] When the Chessons attended the Anti-Slavery Meeting at the Freemason's Tavern on 29 May 1858, they did so in concert with James Dailey, a Black Virginian who settled in Liberia as a merchant, was imprisoned when he attempted to flee his creditors, and, by 1857, had escaped and brought a case against corrupt Sierra Leone officials to the House of Lords;[182] and Alexander Isbister (1822–83), a Canadian Métis who distinguished himself in London as an educator. Hearing Lord Brougham speak for the first time in his life, Frederick (as usual) inserted an evaluative comment in his diary: 'The old man spoke with much of his old fire & energy, but was somewhat prolix. The other portion of the proceedings was not of special importance save & except Mr. Richard's manly protest against the American Churches.'[183] Dailey came home with the Chessons for tea, then joined Frederick and Isbister at the Olympic Theatre to see Frederick Robson (1821–64) perform in *Old Daddy Hardacre* followed by the farce *Ticklish Times*. What Frederick and Amelia note in their diaries about this day does not encompass performance chaining; rather, it includes the implied communication that enabled the convergence at the meeting, the hospitality at home half a mile away in Bloomsbury, and then the reconvergence of the men at the theatre, a little south of their earlier meeting.

These kinds of social logistics are instrumental to what Gary Alan Fine calls the 'specific orders of interaction' that link 'cultural knowledge to a domain via interaction protocols', resulting in sticky cultures. For example, on 24 June 1858, Frederick walked to Knightsbridge to attend a demonstration by John Solomon Rarey (1827–66), a US horse tamer whose gentle methods brought him international fame. In the afternoon Chesson listened to a Bow Street trial of 'Barrowes the great imposter', who was charged with bigamy. The first performance inspired a full notice in the *Star*; the second received a perfunctory mention in Chesson's diary: 'He looked very well, but rather more delicate in complexion.' During the day, Amelia was called upon by the wife of a *Star* colleague, Mrs Baxter Langley (1829–88), as well as another friend, Mrs Moore. The Chessons both sat down to tea with Mr Abington, from South Africa, and Mr Dailey. Both diaries note Abington's rendition of 'painful details' of Dutch settlers' conduct toward Kaffirs in the 1846 war. This is another instance where private life is inseparable from Frederick's daily labour (*negotium*), for over time he developed considerable expertise on South African affairs – as did Amelia, whose obituary notes that as a widow she wrote for the *Athenaeum* on this topic.[184] More than that, though, this episode shows how office colleagues' families were integrated into the Chessons' social lives, and how the Chessons' busy leisure (*otium privatum*) let them converge in wakeful conversation for a few moments of the day.

Thus, meetings could be proving grounds, flashpoints for mobbings, or steady-as-she-goes points on a long plot toward social justice. But they could also bleed across the ostensible domains of political activity and social life, sociability and domesticity, friendship and family, and even the responsibilities of a marital couple incorporating their social relationships, obligations, and pursuits. At every juncture there is performance, opportunity to gather and evaluate information, and variation that nonetheless coheres into recognisable forms.

## Advocacy, Judgement, and Play

To a large degree, the relationship between British aesthetics and politics in the mid-nineteenth century is understood through the alignment of decorative arts and poetry, for example emphasising the syncretism of William Morris (1834–96) and Jane Morris (1839–1914) in the Arts and Crafts movement or, slightly later, Oscar Wilde (1854–1900) and aestheticism. The end of the century heralds the full merging of form and function into political art, with oppositions reconciled in a series of continental experiments including symbolism, expressionism, and Bauhaus. The politics of these movements are contrasted to the totalitarian leanings of Futurism and the anarchism of Dada; in making this distinction, socialism is the measure of progressivism as well as the means to improve lives through aesthetic mediations in human development and self-actualisation (George Bernard Shaw, 1856–1950) and empowerment to choose (Bertolt Brecht, 1898–1956).

This historiography renders liberalism – the mainstream and globalised form also encompassing nineteenth-century British radicalism – largely out of the aesthetic equation.[185] Essentially, with the exception of the Great Exhibition of 1851, the formative period in the discourse of human rights is left without a theory of performative manifestations, either for individuals or for their culture. As political partisans whose multifarious engagement with performativity demonstrates how late Georgian and mid-Victorian culture was made to 'go', George Thompson and Frederick Chesson epitomise how politically active men stirred the cauldron of liberalism at its hottest moments and kept it going when public attention cooled. Aesthetic criteria were constitutive of the generative meta-politics that made things political and made art 'true politics'.[186] For Thompson and Chesson, the commonplaceness of art, exhibition, and spectacle made performance a ready-at-hand tool. Art was not something to harness to a movement redemptive of artisanship (as William Morris sought it, resistant of factory-alienated labour) or a purposeful move to put vernacular expressivity into built form (as John Ruskin [1819–1900] and George Gilbert Scott [1811–78] advocated for neo-Gothicism). Instead, performance facilitated syntheses of logos, object, and *Gestus* in forms encompassing concert music, theatre and opera, political speech and debate, applied art demonstrations, and civic ceremony, as well as a host of playful and improving activities including sport, museum-going, and the observation of natural science, and was an efficacious way to align the art of doing politics (through speaking, writing, and meeting) with its desired end.

For Amelia Chesson, performance 'stuck' differently, and so did liberal politics. The work she did in her private life (domestic, nurturing, and reproductive) was contiguous with many of the ways she engaged with public issues – editing and compiling publications, maintaining files and aiding with correspondence, and engaging socially with politically active male and female liberals in and out of her home – which demonstrates a more comprehensive aspect of liberalism and a wider dramaturgy of its enactment. Her journalism breached several gendered zones – reading and writing about books at home, seeing plays and concerts in theatres and halls, and writing about performance at the newspaper office to meet the early morning filing deadline – and extended her evaluative work in multiple vectors across the cityscape. She served on the executive committee of the National Society for Women's Suffrage in the 1870s, alongside nearly fifty MPs and feminist icons such as the interior designers Rhoda Garrett (1841–82) and Agnes Garrett (1845–1935), and the former superintendent of the Working Women's College Sarah Amos (née Bunting, 1840/41–1908). These forms of presence, meetings, and contributions to the engine of intellectual and artistic life had implications for civic, national, and transnational liberal politics that were not only on a par with her father and husband but mutually indispensable to one another's functions and success.

For Rancière, dissensus resides at the heart of politics: constantly redrawing the frame within common objects breaks a 'natural' order of ruling and being ruled, which makes the imperceptible perceptible as 'a new scenery of the visible and a new dramaturgy of the intelligible'. For Rancière, a rupture of disenchantment is necessary to dissociate 'what is seen and what is thought, and between what is thought and what is felt' in response to art, shuttling between the polarities of art and social practice. In contrast, what I find in the practices of Thompson and the Chessons, committed radicals, is a more syncretic view of art and artistry in conjunction with politics, showing how individuals, families, and communities are ordered through their protocols of interaction. Rancière's 'sensory fabric of the common' converges with the concept of performances' recognisable recombinant repertoires where 'the aesthetics of politics and the politics of aesthetics' are 'continually criss-crossed'.[187] The practice of performance enjoyment and evaluation helped British liberals selectively advocate and actively contribute toward the advancement of political agendas.

One of Rancière's framing texts is the fifteenth letter of Friedrich Schiller's (1759–1805) *Über die ästhetische Erziehung des Menschen* [The Aesthetic Education of Man, 1794], in which the central argument is that 'man only plays when in the full meaning of the word he is a man, and he is only completely a man when he plays'. The play impulse – which Schiller calls a 'communion between the formal impulse and the material impulse' – completes one's humanity by welding a passive state of receptivity with freedom, manifest as recognisable forms. Schiller writes: 'The formal impulse and the material impulse are equally earnest in their demands, because one relates in its cognition to things in their reality and the other to their necessity; because in action the first is directed to the preservation of life, the second to the preservation of dignity, and therefore both to truth and perfection.'[188] For Thompson, the stakes of rhetoric were high – his success as an orator could result in others' emancipation from slavery, ability to vote, or ability to secure affordable bread – and so to the degree that he became effective the freedoms of others could be actualised. Frederick Chesson more explicitly *played* – his experience of art (attending performances, analysing performers' techniques, and evaluating their impact) was education on a par with the moral uplift from religion and didactic learning or the satisfaction of watching cricket – and he pursued these kinds of play in order to do his life's work better. Rancière states, 'the "aesthetic revolution" produced a new idea of political revolution: the material realisation of a common humanity still only existing as an idea'. This 'idea' is accessed – and honed, over time – through play.[189] During the 1850s, Ruskin advocated something similar, and William Morris put it into effect in the aesthetics of Pre-Raphaelitism implemented through artisanship, creating an aesthetic of politics and a politics of aesthetics.[190] If we take Thompson's practices of witnessing, reflecting upon, and adopting the skills of able political performers as play, Frederick Chesson's practice of witnessing, evaluating, and critiquing the efficacy of performance, and Amelia Chesson's critical practice of witnessing and giving judgement along with her otherwise unheralded participation in the stickiness of politics or culture, these three figures

demonstrate ways to revise the historiography of political advocacy –
as oratory, organisation, and journalism – diversified into the key late
Georgian and Victorian forms of mass mediation.

The Thompson-Chesson family demonstrates, in other words, ways that
a culture with a plethora of performance and performative forms coheres as
a performance ecology actively recognised, evaluated, and utilised by liberal men and women who were self-made rather than born to the manor.
The political movements they helped forge could not be naïve about the
efficacy of performance, nor could the movements cohere without performance chaining. Countless citational acts show a consciousness that
performance was a grammar that enabled cogent expression, evaluation,
and perpetuation of political understanding; measured persuasion; and
amplified effects negotiated further afield through print and letters, both
facilitated by postal and telegraph systems that took giant leaps forward
during the Victorian period. The public sphere of debate and influence,
commerce and exchange, and national and international networks of communication registered and built upon this. Advocacy, self-advancement,
and cultural change were, quite simply, impossible without it, at least in
the liberal mould. Whereas Walter Ong shows that, with the advance of
literacy during the nineteenth century, orality gave way to reading, Joseph
Meisel counters that speech remained the means by which 'political, religious, and legal practice' flourished, for 'as never before, legislating, saving
souls, obtaining a verdict ... getting elected, filling pews, [and] acquiring
briefs necessitated speaking well'.[191] In other words, governance, politics,
spirituality, and the law remained the purview of oral expression, while
gains made by liberals, including an expanded male franchise and a global
emancipation movement, operated through the combination of meetings
with speeches and the circulation of correspondence and print. The following chapters document how this happened, bringing obscure figures
to the fore as exemplars of a general system of possibilities, and shifting
the background forward to show how organisational and familial politics
were integral to networks and circuits that advanced political causes and
cohered a repertoire of how to advocate.

## Notes

1 Goffman, Irving. The *Presentation of Self in Everyday Life*. Garden City, NY:
Doubleday, 1959.
2 Butler, Judith. *Bodies That Matter: On the Discursive Limits of 'Sex'*. New York:
Routledge, 1993.

3 This resembles what Louise George Clubb calls a theatregram: see Clubb, Louise George. *Italian Drama in Shakespeare's Time*. New Haven, CT: Yale University Press, 1989: 9–10. Robert Henke offers greater clarification on the term in his introduction to *Transnational Exchange in Early Modern Theatre*, edited by Robert Henke and Eric Nicholson. Aldershot: Ashgate, 2008: 2, 13.

4 Ball, James. *Theater of State: A Dramaturgy of the United Nations*. Evanston, IL: Northwestern University Press, 2020: 8, 13, 20, 89.

5 Ridout, Nicholas. *Scenes from Bourgeois Life.*, Ann Arbor: University of Michigan Press, 2020: 85.

6 See Davis, 'Tracy C. 'Theatricality and Civil Society'. In *Theatricality*, edited by Tracy C. Davis and Thomas Postlewait. Cambridge: Cambridge University Press, 2003: 127–55.

7 Spires, Derrick R. *The Practice of Citizenship: Black Politics and Print Culture in the Early United States*. Philadelphia: University of Pennsylvania Press, 2019: 10–11.

8 Fine, Gary Alan. 'Sticky Cultures: Memory Publics and Communal Pasts in Competitive Chess.' *Cultural Sociology* 7, no. 4 (2013): 395–414.

9 Ahmed, *Cultural Politics of Emotion*, 91, 100.

10 This can be calibrated against a fellow journalist such as Lord Robert Cecil (the future Marquess of Salisbury, 1830–1903): from 1857 to 1866, when Cecil earned his living by journalism primarily writing for the *Saturday Review* and *Quarterly Review*, he wrote about 1.5 million words. Bentley, Michael, *Lord Salisbury's World: Conservative Environments in Late-Victorian Britain*. Cambridge: Cambridge University Press, 2001: 13.

11 Merrill, Lisa. 'Exhibiting Race "Under the World's Huge Glass Case": William and Ellen Craft and William Wells Brown at the Great Exhibition in Crystal Palace, London, 1851.' *Slavery and Abolition* 33, no. 2 (2012): 321–36.

12 Clover, Joshua. *Riot. Strike. Riot. The New Era of Uprisings*. London: Verso, 2016.

13 Farmer, William. 'Letters from England. Autobiography of Geo. Thompson.' Nos. 1–7. *Liberator* 34, nos. 7–13 (12–26 February and 4–25 March 1864): 1.

14 Thomas Thompson, 'Letterbook', REAS 14, fol. 109, JRL.

15 Thompson recommends Job as the picture of a good man: 'Letterbook', REAS 14, fol. 130–1, JRL. See Job 29:21–3.

16 Worthington, Hugh. 'The Late Mr Worthington's Sermons: Extract from, on Prejudice.' *Christian Reformer, or New Evangelical Miscellany* 9 (1823): 29.

17 See Thompson's acceptance speech to his constituents: 'Tower Hamlets.' *Morning Post*, 31 July 1847, 2.

18 Farmer, 'Letters from England', 19 February 1864, 1; and Thompson, *Addresses*, 161.

19 See Farmer, 'Letters from England', 9 February 1864, 29.

20 William Farmer places this event in 1825, when Thompson was aged twenty-one, but Taylor did not hire Salters' Hall until January 1827. This casts Thompson as highly precocious, but it is more likely that he squared off against Taylor at

age twenty-six. See Morgan, Simon. 'George Donisthorpe Thompson (1804–1878).' In *Oxford Dictionary of National Biography*. Oxford: Oxford University Press, 2016 and Farmer, 'Letters from England', 9 February 1864, 26.

21  See Gifford, Ronald. 'George Thompson and Trans-Atlantic Antislavery, 1831–1865.' PhD diss., Indiana University, 1999: 15–17.

22  [Frederick Chesson], 'Public Soirée in Honour of George Thompson, Esq.' *Morning Star*, 26 February 1863, 3.

23  Cowper, William. 'The Timepiece.' In *The Task, A Poem in Six Books*. New York: M. Durell, 1796: 2: 36–7.

24  'Complimentary Breakfast to Mr. George Thompson.' *Liverpool Daily Post*, 23 January 1862, 7.

25  See 'George Thompson.' *Liverpool Mercury*, 9 September 1842, 291.

26  'Complimentary Breakfast to Mr George Thompson.' *Liverpool Daily Post*, 23 January 1862, 7.

27  *Slavery Abolition Act 1833, 3 & 4 Will IV c. 73* (28 August 1833). Brougham was an officer of the London Anti-Slavery Society. The travelling agent system dates back to the 1780s, and it combined with pressure for MPs to 'pledge' to support abolition in the early 1830s. See Gifford, 'George Thompson', 33; Turley, David. *The Culture of English Antislavery, 1780–1860*. London: Routledge, 1991: 60; and Oldfield, J.R. *The Ties That Bind: Transatlantic Abolitionism in the Age of Reform, c. 1820–1866*. Liverpool: Liverpool University Press, 2020: 48.

28  Stephen, George. *Antislavery Recollections: In a Series of Letters Addressed to Mrs. Beecher Stowe*. London: Thomas Hatchard, 1854: 150–1.

29  George Thompson to Jenny [Anne] Thompson, 19 April 1832, REAS 2/1/22, JRL.

30  Blair, Hugh. *Lectures on Rhetoric and Belles Lettres*. London: T. Tegg, 1845. Reprint, Philadelphia: Hayes and Zell, 1854: 407.

31  Frederick Chesson's diary, 19 February 1855, 4 August 1862, and 26 November 1863, REAS 11/3, 9, 10, JRL. In 1853, the Friends Meeting Hall in Manchester was the site of a series of lectures (George Thompson to Louis A. Chamerovzow, MSS Brit. Emp. S.18/C37/4, Bodleian). See also Thompson's 1857 diary for a list of lectures on Indian topics, REAS 7/4, JRL.

32  Blair, *Lectures on Rhetoric*, 289–90.

33  Here, the invocation of dramaturgy differentiates discourse (serial *énoncés* in conversation) from a much wider spectrum of statements and signs that include, but are not limited to, speech. See Franzel, Sean. *Connected by the Ear: The Media, Pedagogy, and Politics of the Romantic Lecture*. Evanston, IL: Northwestern University Press, 2013: 9.

34  Meetings were divided into three types: public, general interest, and private (whereby admission is by permission or right). Shaw, Sebag and H.A.R.J. Wilson. *The Corporation of Certified Secretaries Manual on the Law of Meetings, Their Conduct and Procedure*. London: Macdonald and Evans, 1947: 3–8.

35  Davis, Tracy C. ed. 'Introduction.' In *The Broadview Anthology of Nineteenth-Century British Performance*. Peterborough, ON: Broadview Press, 2012: 13–14.

36 Levine, Caroline. *Forms: Whole, Rhythm, Hierarchy, Network*. Princeton, NJ: Princeton University Press, 2015: 67.

37 Jasper, *Art of Moral Protest*, 309.

38 By this period, parliamentary reporters rotated in forty-five-minute shifts between taking notes (often in shorthand) and transcribing them. They edited out speakers' pauses and vocal disfluencies, and the fair copy would be ready shortly after a meeting concluded. Grant, James. *The Great Metropolis*. 2 vols. London: Saunders and Otley, 1836: 231, 236.

39 Shaw and Wilson specify that chairs could be nominated or elected at the outset of a meeting. Their duties included ensuring a quorum, being familiar with the meeting's purpose, preserving order and timeliness, keeping speakers on topic, officiating over voting, and supervising the recording of minutes. *Corporation*, 44.

40 See Brown, Christopher Leslie. *Moral Capital: Foundations of British Abolitionism*. Chapel Hill: University of North Carolina Press, 2006.

41 Heyrick, Elizabeth. *Immediate, not Gradual Abolition, or an Inquiry into the Shortest, Safest, and Most Effectual Means of Getting Rid of West Indian Slavery*. London: J. Hatchard, 1824.

42 Gifford, 'George Thompson', 32–3.

43 Rai, Shirin M. 'Political Performance: A Framework for Analysing Democratic Politics.' *Political Studies* 63 (2015): 1188–9. Habermas argues that reading newspapers constitutes a significant facet of the public sphere during this period (Habermas, Jürgen. *The Structural Transformation of the Public Sphere: An Inquiry into a Category of Bourgeois Society*. Translated by Thomas Burger with Frederick Lawrence. Cambridge: MIT Press, 1989: 181–6). In a legacy of the coffee house, at working-class as well as middle-class masculine gathering spaces (such the City of London Literary and Scientific Institution, as well as gentlemen's clubs) relatively expensive stamped papers were read by many individuals. My point extends the experience of meetings to reading reportage in newspapers, whether at clubs or at private tables, and accounts for why the interpolations of audience reactions at meetings are a significant facet of reports.

44 Fuoss, Kirk. 'Lynching Performances, Theatres of Violence.' *Text and Performance Quarterly* 19, no. 1 (1999): 1–37.

45 Ball, *Theater of State*, 12.

46 Thompson, George. *The Substance of a Speech Delivered in the Wesleyan Methodist Chapel, Irwell-Street, Salford, Manchester, on Monday, August 13th, 1832: by George Thompson, Esq. Being a Reply to Mr. Borthwick's Statements on the Subject of British Colonial Slavery*. London: J. Hatchard and Son, 1832: 3.

47 Thompson, George. *A Full Report of the Proceedings at the Meetings of Messrs. Thompson and Borthwick at Dalkeith*. Glasgow: George Gallie & W.R. M'Phun, 1833: 74.

48 See Thompson, George. *Lectures of George Thompson, with a Full Report of the Discussion between Mr. Thompson and Mr. Borthwick, the Pro-Slavery Agent, held at the Royal Amphitheatre, Liverpool, Engl., and which continued for Six*

*Evenings with Unabated Interest.* Edited by William Lloyd Garrison. Boston: I. Knapp, 1836: 94, 121.

49 Thompson, *Substance of a Speech*, 15.

50 Thompson, George. *Three Lectures on British Colonial Slavery Delivered in the Royal Amphitheatre, Liverpool, on the Evenings of Tuesday, August 28, Thursday 30, and Thursday, September 6, 1832.* Liverpool: Egerton Smith, 1832: 121.

51 George Thompson to Jenny [Anne] Thompson, 28 December 1837, REAS 2/1/41, JRL.

52 'Birmingham: Great Meeting on Negro Emancipation.' *Coventry Herald and Observer*, 5 January 1838, 3.

53 'Anti-Slavery Meeting at Birmingham.' *Aris's Birmingham Gazette*, 1 January 1838, 2.

54 Shaw and Wilson, *Corporation*, 77.

55 George Thompson to George Wilson, 11 January 1862, GB 127M20 Index 291, Manchester Central Reference Library and Archives.

56 Izzo, Gary. *The Art of Play: The New Genre of Interactive Theatre.* Portsmouth, NH: Heinemann, 1977: 26.

57 George Thompson (Tenterdon, Kent) to Jenny [Anne] Thompson, 22 October 1831, REAS 2/1/10, JRL.

58 George Thompson (Ashford) to Jenny [Anne] Thompson, 19 October 1831, REAS 2/1/9, JRL (underlining in original).

59 George Thompson (Edinburgh) to Jenny [Anne] Thompson, 6 February 1836, REAS 2/1/33, JRL.

60 George Thompson to Elizabeth Pease, 14 March 1840, 1981.M-1978, William L. Clements Library. Thompson referred to 'Article III' in the *Edinburgh Review* 70, no. 142 (1840): 391–426 (see especially 394–5), containing a notice of *Speeches Delivered at a Public Meeting for the Formation of a British India Society.* London: British India Society, 1839, and John Crawfurd's *Appeal from the Inhabitants of British India to the Justice of the People of India: A Popular Enquiry into the Operation of the System of Taxation in British India.* London: Henry Hooper, 1839.

61 'Anti-Slavery Soirée.' *Anti-Slavery Watchman*, no. 2 (December 1853), in George Thompson's anti-slavery scrapbooks, REAS 6/2, JRL.

62 Brett, Peter. 'Political Dinners in Early Nineteenth-Century Britain: Platform, Meeting Place and Battleground.' *History* 81, no. 264 (1996): 527–52.

63 George Thompson to Elizabeth Pease, 2 October 1839, 1981.M-1978, William L. Clements Library. Thompson edited, and largely wrote, the *British Indian Advocate*, which was published sporadically from January 1841 to December 1847, with sponsorship from Mancunian philanthropist industrialists.

64 Martin, Janette Lisa. 'Popular Political Oratory and Itinerant Lecturing in Yorkshire and the North East in the Age of Chartism, 1837–60.' PhD diss., York University, 2010: 82. See also Turley, *Culture of English Antislavery*, 68, 71–2.

65 George Thompson to Jenny [Anne] Thompson, 9 November 1837, REAS 2/1/39, JRL.

66 In another example invoking a prop as a stunt, Peter Borthwick said in the conclusion to his lecture on 29 August 1832: 'Mr. Thompson had said that one of them [Jamaican cart-whip] laid open the flank of a mule. He would give Mr. Thompson a challenge. He would give him liberty to lay open the calf of his (Mr. Borthwick's) leg with a Jamaica cart-whip, on condition that if he failed he should pay out of the funds of the Anti-Slavery Society, to the public charities of the town, the sum of £200. (Tremendous cheering and laughter.)' Thompson, *Lectures of George Thompson*, 105.

67 Spires, *Practice of Citizenship*, 98.

68 Martin, 'Popular Political Oratory', 97, 96. Peter Borthwick threatened to dog Thompson 'from place to place like your evil genius'. In response, Thompson told an audience, 'My cry is, "a clear stage a fair hearing," and then come on, come on, come on! (Loud cheers) With this book (the Bible) in my hand – with slavery and chains, and christians for slave's-masters, I shall never fear the issue of the contest' (Thompson, *Substance of a Speech*, 6). On 13 December 1866, Chesson observed a tumultuous, though ticketed, meeting on suffrage at the Walworth Literary Institution. The discord emanating from the gallery, then the platform, resulted in unanimous condemnatory votes, and yet 'it was all done in good humour and without any broken heads' (Frederick Chesson's diary, REAS 13/14, JRL).

69 Martin, 'Popular Political Oratory', 102.

70 In addition to Figures 1.2, 3.6, and 5.3 in this volume, compare illustrations such as Lane, Theodore. 'Snug in the Gallery.' *Theatrical Pleasures* (1821), 17.3.888-327, Metropolitan Museum of Art; Hablot Knight Browne, 'At Astley's' from 'The Old Curiosity Shop.' *Master Humphrey's Clock*, 3 October 1840; 'Meeting at Exeter Hall, London, of the Meeting of the Society for the Extinction of the Slave Trade, & for the Civilization of Africa, on 1 June 1840.' Wikimedia Commons; the daguerreotype 'The Chartist Meeting on Kennington Common', 10 April 1848, RCIN 2932484, the Royal Collection Trust; and the engraving 'Great Protectionist Demonstration in Drury Lane Theatre.' *Illustrated London News* 18, no. 483 (10 May 1851): 375.

71 Janette Lisa Martin refers to Jonathan Baristow and James Acland ('Popular Political Oratory', 219).

72 Shaw and Wilson differentiate English meetings from routs and riots (*Corporation*, 8).

73 William Lloyd Garrison, introduction to Thompson, *Lectures of George Thompson*, xxvi.

74 'Truth' and 'George Thompson', letters to the editor, in George Thompson's anti-slavery scrapbooks, REAS 6/1, JRL.

75 'George Thompson', rpt. from *Observer* (Lowell), in *Liberator*, 18 October 1834, 16.

76 Clippings from New York, Concord, and Boston, 1835, in George Thompson's anti-slavery scrapbooks, REAS 6/1, JRL.

77 'George Thompson', *Lynn Record* (MA), 4 June 1835, in George Thompson's anti-slavery scrapbooks, REAS 6/1, JRL.

78  *New York Courier & Enquirer*, 13 May 1835, in George Thompson's anti-slavery scrapbooks, REAS 6/1, JRL.

79  Cities of the North and South were awash in mob violence. In New York there were anti-abolition riots severe enough for the National Guard to be called out. Prince, Carl E. 'The Great "Riot Year": Jacksonian Democracy and Patterns of Violence in 1834.' *Journal of the Early Republic* 5, no. 1 (1985): 1–2; and Richards, Leonard L. *'Gentlemen of Property and Standing': Anti-Abolition Mobs in Jacksonian America*. Oxford: Oxford University Press, 1970: 113.

80  Prince, 'Great "Riot Year"', 3.

81  See Grimsted, David. 'Rioting in Its Jacksonian Setting.' *American Historical Review* 77, no. 2 (1972): 364.

82  Grimsted, David. *American Mobbing, 1828–1861*. Oxford: Oxford University Press, 1998: 4.

83  Martineau, Harriet. *The Martyr Age of the United States*. Boston: Weeks, Jordan, 1839: 21.

84  Evidently, this is a reading of Exodus 10:22–23: 'And Moses stretched forth his hand toward heaven; and there was a thick darkness in all the land of Egypt three days: They saw not one another, neither rose any from his place for three days: but all the children of Israel had light in their dwellings' (King James Version).

85  Richards, *Gentlemen of Property*, 116–20. The quotation derives from Boston's *Commercial Gazette*, which blessed an anti-abolition mob: 'if there is no law that will reach it, it must be reached in some other way', concluding 'the resistance will not come from rabble, but from men of property and standing'. Grimsted, *American Mobbing*, 22.

86  Qtd. in Grimsted, *American Mobbing*, 22.

87  Martineau, *Martyr Age*, 21.

88  George Thompson to Robert Purvis, 9 August 1834, MS A.9.2 vol. 7 n. 32, Weston Papers, Boston Public Library, rpt. in Taylor, *British and American Abolitionists*, 32.

89  *Alexandria Gazette* (VA), rpt. in *Raleigh Register and North-Carolina Gazette*, 7 October 1834, 1.

90  *Boston Recorder*, 28 November 1834, in George Thompson's anti-slavery scrapbooks, REAS 6/2, JRL.

91  According to David Turley, 'Within all of the religious currents sustaining antislavery, the Bible was taken as a vital revelation of God's will and a guide to right action' (*Culture of English Anti-Slavery*, 22).

92  Dateline Boston, 21 July 1835, qtd. in *Lynn Record*, 6 August 1835, in George Thompson's anti-slavery scrapbooks, REAS 6/1, JRL.

93  Ray Potter, 'Anti-Slavery in Pawtucket', letter to the editor (Pawtucket, RI), 6 July 1835, in George Thompson's anti-slavery scrapbooks, REAS 6/2, JRL.

94  'A Calm Appeal from the South to the North', Richmond, VA, 14 August [1834 or 1835], in George Thompson's anti-slavery scrapbooks, REAS 6/1, JRL.

95  Gifford, 'George Thompson', 160.

96 *Herald of Freedom* (Concord, NH), 19 September 1835, in George Thompson's anti-slavery scrapbooks, REAS 6/1, JRL.

97 'Riot in Lynn', in George Thompson's anti-slavery scrapbooks, 1833–5, REAS 6/2, JRL.

98 'Punishment of Rioters', in George Thompson's anti-slavery scrapbooks, 1833–5, REAS 6/2, JRL.

99 Martineau, *Martyr Age*, 33; and Grimsted, *American Mobbing*, 26–7.

100 William Lloyd Garrison to Helen Garrison, 9 November 1835, Boston, MS A.1.1 vol. 1, no. 80, Massachusetts Historical Society, rpt. in Taylor, Clare. *British and American Abolitionists: An Episode in Transatlantic Understanding.* Edinburgh: Edinburgh University Press, 1974: 50.

101 'Mr. George Thompson, the Anti-Slavery Advocate.' *Leeds Mercury*, 13 November 1835, 376; and *Boston Daily Advertiser*, rpt. in *Niles Weekly Register*, 3 October 1835, 74.

102 Notes for 'A Forgotten Hero', 1916, REAS 2/5/9, JRL. There is no other source for this claim.

103 Grimsted, *American Mobbing*, 29; and Richards, *Gentlemen of Property*, 93. One of Thompson's descendants wrote in 1916 of several close escapes ('A Forgotten Hero', 1916, REAS 2/5/9, JRL).

104 Richards, *Gentlemen of Property*, 63–4.

105 Grimsted, *American Mobbing*, 22.

106 *New York Courier & Enquirer*, in George Thompson's anti-slavery scrapbooks, 1834–5, REAS 6/1, JRL.

107 *Boston Commercial Gazette*, in George Thompson's anti-slavery scrapbooks, 1834–5, REAS 6/1, JRL. At this time, Jim Crow in no way connoted segregation, but rather the antic dances and catchy lyrics of blackface minstrel performances that devolved from T. D. Rice's song 'Jump Jim Crow', which debuted in 1828.

108 Unattributed clipping, in George Thompson's anti-slavery scrapbooks, 1834–5, REAS 6/1, JRL.

109 Gifford, 'George Thompson', 161; and *New York Courier*, in Thompson's anti-slavery scrapbooks, REAS 6/1, JRL. The Anglo-Canadian orator Charles Stuart (1783–1865) also toured the United States during this period.

110 George Thompson, letter to the editor (dated 22 October 1835), *Liberator*, 7 November 1835, 178.

111 William Lloyd Garrison to Helen Eliza Benson Garrison, 9 November 1835, Boston, MS A.1.1. vol. 1, Anti-Slavery Letters from Garrison, No. 80, Massachusetts Historical Society, rpt. in Taylor, *British and American Abolitionists*, 50–1; William Farmer, 'Letters from England', 26 February 1864, 36.

112 Martineau, *Martyr Age*, 22.

113 Not all mobs are the same. 'How, for example can one call "spontaneous" mobs that assembled at church meetings with bags full of rotten eggs? Or with a band? Some anti-abolition mobs, to be sure, displayed little organization. Many were disorderly. And many howled and screamed.' Richards, *Gentlemen of Property*, 83.

114  Fletcher, John. 'Denouement: Notes on the End(s) of Activism.' In *Theatre, Performance, and Activism*, edited by Stephani Etheridge Woodson and Tamara Underiner, 71–80. London: Palgrave, 2018: 75–6.

115  Sharpe, Christina. *In the Wake: On Blackness and Being*. Durham, NC: Duke University Press, 2016: 14.

116  Sergeant Lewis. 'F.W. Chesson.' *Leisure Hour: An Illustrated Magazine for Home Reading*, October 1888: 678.

117  Frederick Chesson Sr. (1810 or 1816–41) and his partner Henry Holding enlarged a herring hang on the Medway near Chatham into a manufactory to distil oil. It had been in operation about nine months when a still combusted and Chesson perished in the intense inferno. He left behind three children and his wife, Ann Chesson (1812–52), who gave birth to a fourth child three months later. 'Destruction of an Oil Manufactory by Fire, and Loss of Life.' *Standard*, 9 August 1841, 3. On 20 August 1849, the widow married Benjamin Simpson Eastwood (1825–99), a bachelor and Wesleyan minister residing in Woolwich. The new family settled first in Dennis, Massachusetts, where another son and twin girls were born. Ann Chesson was buried in Gillingham during a visit home.

118  'The Late Mr. F.W. Chesson.' *Daily News*, 7 May 1888, 5.

119  'Dinner to Mr. F.W. Chesson, at the National Liberal Club, on Friday, July 16th', in bound volume of speeches, 16 July 1886, xvi–xvii, REAS 12, JRL. According to Simon Morgan, this kind of 'conversion experience' with a 'heady mix of trauma and elation' is a common trope, belying the true nature of an extended political education. *Celebrities, Heroes and Champions: Popular Politicians in the Age of Reform*, 1810–67. Manchester: Manchester University Press, 2021: 31–2.

120  The *Nonconformist*, a weekly newspaper edited by Edward Miall, professed 'without assuming to be a religious newspaper' to take a 'political course by religious considerations, on all subjects of national interest…. Its views are those of advanced Liberalism, but in the support given to those views it is thoroughly independent.' Endpaper advertisement from *Eclectic Review*, n.s., 7 (July–December 1864).

121  Mill, John Stuart. *On Liberty*. London: John W. Parker and Son, 1859: 104–5, 109, 120.

122  Frederick Chesson's diary, 4 March 1866, REAS 11/13, JRL; and 26 and 27 April 1866, REAS 11/13, JRL.

123  Frederick Chesson's diary, 27 September 1856, and 1865 passim, REAS 11/4, 13, JRL.

124  Rancière, *Dissensus*, 119.

125  Braidotti, Rosi. 'Intensive Genre and the Demise of Gender.' *Angelaki: Journal of the Theoretical Humanities* 13, no. 2 (2008): 46.

126  Frederick Chesson's diary, 19 June 1854, REAS 11/1, JRL.

127  Rancière, *Dissensus*, 127, 122.

128  Frederick Chesson's diary, 17 September 1854, REAS 11/2, JRL.

129  Blair, *Lectures on Rhetoric*, 263.

130  See 'The Kean Testimonial.' *Illustrated London News*, no. 1137 (29 March 1862): 319.

131  Meisel, Joseph S. *Public Speech and the Culture of Public Life in the Age of Gladstone*. New York: Columbia University Press, 2001: 86–7.

132  Around this time, Chesson recorded in his diary occasions when he did more than organise and facilitate meetings. On 11 January 1862, he noted that he 'made a few remarks myself' at a meeting in Bromley-by-Bow 'to express thankfulness at the restoration of pacific relations with America.' On 25 March 1862, he lectured the APS on 'the treatment of the natives of the British colonies.' On 22 October 1862, he 'Delivered lecture for the Young Men's Society connected with Mr. Barker's chapel, at Taylor's Depository. Subject, Christianity & Colonization.' On 3 February 1863, he attended another meeting at Taylor's Repository; a great crowd assembled in the largest room and in the road below, and the event was therefore converted into an open-air meeting. Mr Thompson gave the main address and 'I said a few words at the close on the conduct of the three members for South London, who abstained from replying to the letter of invitation.' All items in REAS 11/9 and 11/10, JRL.

133  Frederick Chesson's diary, 22 March 1862, REAS 11/9, JRL.

134  'Kean Testimonial.' *Era*, 23 March 1862, 15.

135  Frederick Chesson's diary, 22 March 1862, REAS 11/9, JRL.

136  'Kean Testimonial.' *Era*, 23 March 1862, 15.

137  Gray, Thomas. 'Ode on a Distant Prospect of Eton College.' 1742. Poetry Foundation. www.poetryfoundation.org/poems/44301/ode-on-a-distant-prospect-of-eton-college.

138  'Kean Testimonial.' *Era*, 23 March 1862, 15.

139  [Frederick Chesson], 'Presentation of the Kean Testimonial.' *Morning Star*, 24 March 1862, 3; and 'Kean Testimonial.' *Era*, 23 March 1862, 15.

140  'Kean Testimonial.' *Era*, 23 March 1862, 15.

141  William Hale White, attributed in Holyoake, George Jacob. *Public Speaking and Debate: A Manual for Advocates and Agitators*. 1849. 2nd rev. ed. Boston: Ginn, 1896: 144.

142  Frederick Chesson's diary, 23 August 1863, REAS 11/10, JRL.

143  Cabranes-Grant, Leo. 'From Scenarios to Networks: Performing the Intercultural in Colonial Mexico.' *Theatre Journal* 63, no. 4 (2011): 501.

144  Rancière, *Dissensus*, 141.

145  Cull, Laura. 'Performance as Philosophy: Responding to the Problem of "Application."' *Theatre Research International* 37, no. 1 (2012): 23.

146  Meisel, *Public Speech*, 128–32.

147  Payne, Ernest A. 'Gleanings from the Correspondence of George Eliot.' *Baptist Quarterly* 17, no. 4 (1957): 180.

148  See Meisel, *Public Speech*, 113–14.

149  Frederick Chesson's diary, 17 April 1857, REAS 11/4, JRL.

150  Blair, *Lectures on Rhetoric*, 315.

151  Frederick Chesson's diary, 17 April 1857, REAS 11/4, JRL.

152 Hilton, Boyd. *The Age of Atonement: The Influence of Evangelicalism on Social and Economic Thought, 1785–1865.* Oxford: Clarendon Press, 1986: 181–2.

153 While they resided in Pimlico, the Chessons attended St Barnabas (South Kensington), where George Smith Drew (1819–80) presided over the Church of England congregation.

154 Spurgeon, Charles. 'Not Now, But Hereafter!' Sermon no. 410, Metropolitan Tabernacle, Newington, 22 September 1861. Spurgeon Gems. Accessed March 15, 2022. www.spurgeongems.org/spurgeon-sermons/.

155 Frederick Chesson's diary, 22 September 1861, REAS 11/8, JRL.

156 Spurgeon, Charles. 'High Doctrine and Broad Doctrine.' *Metropolitan Tabernacle*, 3 June 1860. The Spurgeon Center. Accessed 14 May 2022. www.spurgeon.org/resource-library/sermons/high-doctrine-2/#flipbook/.

157 Capaldi, Nicholas. *John Stuart Mill: A Biography.* Cambridge: Cambridge University Press, 2004: 272.

158 John S. Jacobs published his memoir as 'A True Tale of Slavery' in the *Leisure Hour: Magazine for Home Reading*, 1861.

159 Nicholson, Renton. *The Swell's Night Guide, or A Peep through the Great Metropolis.* London: H. Smith, 1849: 18–19. See also Jackson, Lee. *Palaces of Pleasure: From Music Halls to the Seaside to Football, How the Victorians Invented Mass Entertainment.* New Haven, CT: Yale University Press, 2019: 138–9; and McWilliam, Rohan. *London's West End: Creating the Pleasure District, 1800–1914.* Oxford: Oxford University, 2020: 53–4.

160 *Reynolds's Newspaper*, 28 March 1858, 4.

161 *Era*, 24 March 1850. 11; *Era*, 13 June 1891, 14; *Reynolds's Newspaper*, 28 November 1852, 9; and *Reynolds's Newspaper*, 22 February 1863, 4.

162 Meisel, *Public Speech*, 202.

163 Ritchie, J. Ewing. *The Night Side of London.* London: William Tweedie, 1858: 88–91.

164 Common Law Procedure Act 1854, (17 & 18 Vict. c 125). See also Meisel, *Public Speech*, 176.

165 Cohen, Deborah. *Family Secrets: Shame and Privacy in Modern Britain.* Oxford: Oxford University Press, 2013: 47.

166 See *Reynolds's Newspaper*, 28 March 1858, 4. Sergeant Valentine published a rendering of the Judge and Jury Club with the firm of Francis & Co. earlier that spring.

167 Rancière, *Dissensus*, 127.

168 Frederick Chesson's diary, 26 March 1863, REAS 11/10, JRL.

169 'Great Meeting of Trades Unionists.' *Morning Star*, 27 March 1863, 6.

170 Frederick Chesson's diary, 13 November 1854, REAS 11/2, JRL. Allen was the first Black American to be employed as a professor at a white college (New York Central College at McGrawville). He married a white woman, was compelled to flee the United States, and toured Britain starting in 1853. Blackett, R.J.M. 'William G. Allen: The Forgotten Professor.' *Civil War History* 26, no. 1 (1980): 39–52.

171 Frederick Chesson's diary, 28 May 1857, REAS 11/4, JRL.

172 [Frederick Chesson], Special Correspondent, 'The House of Commons.' *Sheffield Independent*, 24 February 1866, 6.

173 [Chesson], 'The House of Commons', 6.

174 'Haymarket Theatre.' *Morning Post*, 16 November 1863, 5; 'Haymarket Theatre.' *Daily News*, 16 November 1863, 6.

175 Frederick Chesson's diary, 14 November 1863, REAS 11/10, JRL.

176 Frederick Chesson's diary, 12 July 1855, REAS 11/2, JRL; and 11 October 1858, REAS 11/6, JRL.

177 See Braidotti, Rosi. *The Posthuman*. Cambridge: Polity, 2013.

178 Rancière, *Dissensus*, 119.

179 Debord, Guy. *Society of the Spectacle*. Detroit, MI: Black and Red, 1983: 20.

180 Amelia Chesson's diary, 5 and 6 October, 1858, REAS 10, JRL.

181 Zboray, Ronald J. and Mary Saracino Zboray. *Everyday Ideas: Socioliterary Experience among Antebellum New Englanders*. Knoxville: University of Tennessee Press, 2006: 199.

182 Pulis, John W. *Moving On: Black Loyalists in the Afro-Atlantic World*. Abingdon: Routledge, 2013: 163–4.

183 Frederick Chesson's diary, 29 May 1858, REAS 11/5, JRL.

184 'Amelia Ann Everard Chesson.' *Athenaeum*, 1 February 1902, 145.

185 See Hoock, Holger. *Empires of the Imagination: Politics, War, and the Arts in the British World, 1750–1850*. London: Profile, 2010; and Hoock, Holger. *The King's Artists: The Royal Academy of Arts and the Politics of British Culture, 1760–1840*. Oxford: Clarendon, 2003.

186 Rancière, *Dissensus*, 119.

187 Rancière, *Dissensus*, 142–3, 148.

188 Schiller, Friedrich. *Aesthetical and Philosophical Essays*. Vol. 1. Boston: Francis A. Niccolls, 1902, 53, 54–5; and see Rancière, *Dissensus*, 118.

189 Rancière, *Dissensus*, 27.

190 Weltman, Sharon Aronofsky. *Performing the Victorian: John Ruskin and Identity in Theater, Science, and Education*. Columbus: Ohio State University Press, 2007; Morris, William. *Hopes and Fears for Art: Five Lectures Delivered in Birmingham, London & Nottingham*. London: Longmans, 1902; Morris, May. *William Morris, Artist, Writer, Socialist*. Oxford: Blackwell, 1936; and Kocmanovà, Jessie and J. E. Purkyné. 'The Aesthetic Opinions of William Morris.' *Comparative Literature Studies* 4, no. 4 (1967): 409–24.

191 Ong, Walter. *Orality and Literacy: The Technologizing of the Word*. London: Routledge, 1988: 41, 109, 115, 158; and Meisel, *Public Speech*, 6.

# CHAPTER 2

# Change Making
## Incrementalism

Loud the voice of freedom spoke,
Every accent split a yoke,
Every word a fetter broke.
—James Montgomery, 'A Voyage Round the World'

Early in 1858, George Thompson watched a boatload of European survivors of the siege of Lucknow disembark in Calcutta (Kolkata). History tells us a lot about the circumstances that brought those evacuees – bedraggled, half-starved civilians and soldiers – to the Hooghly delta and the way that their homeland was forever changed by their ordeal.[1] However, history tells us nothing of how Thompson – a renowned orator, champion of manumission for enslaved Caribbeans and US residents, a proponent of free trade and electoral reform, and former member of Parliament – came to be on that riverbank or what he thought as he stood there.

## A Change Came O'er the Spirit of Our Dream

Before the Raj (the ninety-year direct rule by the British Crown over a land mass encompassing modern Pakistan, Nepal, Bangladesh, Myanmar, and the whole of the Indian subcontinent), British holdings from India to China were under administrative and military control of the East India Company. This monopolistic joint stock company, chartered by Elizabeth I in 1600, initially existed to enhance trade by securing advantage for Britain over Dutch, French, Spanish, and Portuguese competitors. During the mid-eighteenth century, the East India Company acquired control over Mughal Bengal, then successively acquired territories along the region's coastline and interior. The Company (as it was known) presided over one-sixth of the world's population, encompassing tropical and temperate zones capable of sustaining agriculture of tremendous variety. The span of its northern frontier was the equivalent distance from London

72

to Moscow, and the north-to-south axis was farther than from London to Dakar. The Company's hold was sustained by a private army twice the size of the British Army, populated by native soldiers under British command. It printed its own coinage and made its own law. Military control supported tax collection for both direct-rule states and puppet vassal states, which were legion. From its base in London's Leadenhall Street, a short distance from the Bank of England, The Company filtered the diverse wealth derived from artisanal goods and raw materials (silk cloth, raw cotton, indigo dye, tea, and opium) into British coffers, making proprietors (shareholders) fabulously rich. Proprietors elected twenty-four directors, who each had to be 'a natural-born subject of England or naturalized' with a minimum of £2,000 in stock, a mechanism to ensure white control. Some directors had served The Company in Asia and come back wealthy, while others never left British shores.[2] The Company was integral to British life, British identity, and British imperialism. Luxury goods were virtually synonymous with The Company's reach, while Indian tea was poured at every hearthside.

On the map, India was a patchwork of large and small principalities, but in reality the century between the Battle of Plassey (1757), which secured British control over Bengal, and the direct rule that followed the 1857–8 Indian Rebellion (also called the Sepoy Mutiny or First War of Independence) marked increasing consolidation of territory and power. Successive late Georgian and Victorian measures aimed to enhance laissez-faire, remove barriers to Indians' advancement based on nationality and religion, and temper the governor-general's powers; however, they failed to curb rampant abuses, maladministration, crippling taxation, and the complicity of titular rajas. Systemic abuses built up seething resentment. In May 1857, across the Northwestern Provinces and Oudh, native troops rose against their British commanders. In September, Delhi fell and the Mughal Empire was restored under Shah Bahadur II. The British public was eager for news of these events, but word travelled slowly; weeks after the events, dispatches about the heart-rending massacre at Cawnpore (Kanpur) reached Britain.[3] The rebellion was less a coordinated revolution on the part of Sepoys (spurred to indignation by rumours of animal fat on the ammunition of their new Enfield rifles) than a series of regional uprisings with symbolically collective force, yet it profoundly shook British confidence, giving rise to indignation and fervent calls for revenge.

One of the outbreaks centred on the city of Lucknow, cultural capital of Awadh, which The Company annexed in 1856. Coming under attack from 8,000 Sepoys in late June 1857, Sir Henry Lawrence (1806–57, chief commissioner of the region) retreated into the Residency, the heart of the fortified city, with a garrison of about 1,500 officers and soldiers and slightly fewer non-combatants. They endured eighty-seven days of siege before Sir Colin Campbell's (1792–1863) relief column converged with marines and sailors dispatched from Hong Kong; together they engaged the Sepoy forces that, by 14 November, numbered between 30,000 and 60,000 highly trained men bombarding what remained of Lucknow. The siege was provisionally broken, and the relief troops held position to facilitate evacuation of women, children, injured soldiers, and the sick. For nineteen days they moved 'at a foot's pace' by doolie, mule carriage, and bullock cart to Allahabad (Prayagraj), covering about 200 miles overland. Pausing in Cawnpore, Lady Inglis remarked in her diary, 'As I looked, I thought how small were the troubles and trials of Lucknow in comparison', for the valour of Cawnpore's defence against impossible odds and the agony of the captives were palpable.[4] A steamer carried the first contingent of evacuees down the Ganges, departing just before Christmas and arriving in Calcutta fifty-one days after setting out from Lucknow.

Shortly after dawn on 9 January 1858, George Thompson saddled his mare and joined the throngs of equestrians and carriages conveying natives and Europeans to greet the evacuees on the shore of the Hooghly. Calcutta's elite were present in their 'best-best clothes, conveyances, & feelings'. For miles in each direction, ships from all over the world formed 'a forest of masts ... decorated with the flags of all nations in countless profusion'.[5] The steamer *Madras* approached a specially constructed platform with a portico of scarlet cloth suspended over the ghat, and generals, colonels, secretaries, and under-secretaries lined the platform to greet survivors. A royal salute issued from Fort William, and despite the volley of guns ringing in their ears, everyone whispered as they strained to see the survivors of Lucknow – whom Thompson called 'the all enduring sufferers of an almost unprecedented Siege' – disembark. Any sense of honour was soon overcome by sympathy for those wrenched by grief and trauma. Men removed their hats at the solemn review of pallid, slow-moving evacuees.[6] Thompson observed:

> Almost every passenger wore some token of bereavement, and a countenance in which sorrow, suffering and long deferred hope had set deep marks. It was extremely affecting to behold the children—many of them orphans—they seemed as though they had just awakened from a dream.... And there were sick and wounded Soldiers, some of whom had to be borne on litters, and there were women, with ashy faces, covered with veils, whose dress and demeanor plainly shewed that they were *widows*, who had left

their earthly supporters behind them.... What a day this will be in Calcutta! What tales of horror will be told; what tears of sympathy shed; what prayers of thankfulness offered up[;] what letters to friends at home written!

The crowd wept, yet as survivors mounted the awaiting viceregal carriages they were hailed with plaudits.[7] As Lady Inglis speculated, 'no doubt this was kindly meant, but, as nearly all the passengers had lost those who were dearest to them on earth, this public demonstration must have been most painful'. Her contingent docked in Calcutta a month later, without fanfare.[8]

The Company's troops were ruthless in their attempts to suppress outbreaks. Thompson noted, 'hanging men, and blowing them from guns, is the daily and favourite amusement of the authorities ... in all parts of the disturbed districts.... The appetite for blood on the part of our countrymen appears to be insatiable'. The British showed no regard for the rule of law, even martial law; rather, the English-language press in Calcutta gloried in reporting the 'cannibal ferocity' that prevailed in the attempt to hold positions and vindicate losses.[9] The day before the Lucknow survivors arrived, Thompson mused on the irony that while the British reassured themselves with the idea that the causes of the insurrection were shrouded in mystery, the natives knew better. And yet, not one of the natives – whether lieutenant, sergeant, or private – apparently said as they faced the retributive justice of British gibbets and cannons, 'Grant me life, and I will solve the problem.'[10] It is so like George Thompson to rhetoricise the insurrection not just as a series of events, or as moments saturated in emotion, but also as a dramaturgy of multi-fold perspectives; to register how tens of millions of natives could know an answer that thousands of colonisers could not guess at; and to comprehend mute sacrifice amidst clattering bellicosity. It was not a failure of communication that led to the unfolding calamity but a fundamental withholding of empathy that made reciprocation unreachable. As Thompson wrote after the landing, thinking of the evacuees and those who greeted them with sympathetic tears,

> I could not help saying [']ah you little think that you and millions like you cause the wars which desolate the Earth, by your false ideas, yr refusal to embrace the Gospel in its true sense[,] your atheistical conduct in the practical repudiation of divine commands and your foolish and fond attachment to the miscalled honour[,] glory and patriotism by which the diabolism of carnage and murder are covered up.['][11]

This is a radical deconstruction of the conflict – a profound iteration of critical sympathy with the absent aggrieved – experienced at the very moment of the steamer's unlading.[12]

As Thompson noted in a letter to his daughter Amelia, with the rebellion 'a century of broil and battle had closed'. The Company had seemed to have no foe, but all the while discontent kindled within: 'The Native Army was believed to be loyal & true; while the nonmilitary classes exhibited an aspect of passive and resigned submission on the one hand, or of grateful devotion to British rule on the other.' Truly, he might have seen, like the narrator in Lord Byron's lyric that he paraphrases, two doomed figures: the feminised object of desire tainted by madness, and the lover of her youth exposed to horror. The repeated line, 'A change came o'er the spirit of my dream', was apt, for

> The beings which surrounded him were gone,
> Or were at war with him; he was a mark
> For blight and desolation, compass'd round
> With Hatred and Contention; Pain was mix'd
> In all which was served up to him, until,
> Like to the Pontic monarch of old days,
> He fed on poisons, and they had no power,
> But were a kind of nutriment
> … … … … … … … … …
> To him the book of Night was open'd wide,
> And voices from the deep abyss reveal'd
> A marvel and a secret—Be it so.[13]

Thompson had focused on Indian politics since the late 1830s. He had helped found an organisation intended to better inform the British public of what was being done in their name, change administrative policy, enhance more strategic and equitable trade, suppress labour abuses, empower the peasantry, foster transition to a greater measure of home rule, and, above all, demolish The Company. Like a minority of other Britons, he was neither surprised nor particularly disapproving at the turn of events.[14] The British nation, on the other hand, awoke to a living nightmare when the Sepoy army 'turned the weapons given them for our defence to our own destruction'.[15]

How did George Thompson come to be in Calcutta that day, and capable of these insights? What knowledge, forged by which tactics, enabled him to express these thoughts about the poignant moment on the Hoogly? In other words, how had his experience in advocacy – attending thousands of meetings on a plethora of topics, forging ideas at the forefront of radical thought and debating others representing every conceivable variant position – enabled him to see the wide-open book of Night and hear the warring voices emanating from the deep abyss, raging with Hatred and Contention?

## Give Me the Hurricane

Passing the Slavery Abolition Act of 1833 was Thompson's first great cause, and it cast a long shadow into his future. Twenty years after the act came into effect, he recalled the inspiration he had received as a twenty-seven-year-old hearing Henry Lord Brougham say:

> Tell me not of rights—talk not of the property of the planter in his slaves. I deny the right—I acknowledge not the property. The principles, the feelings of our common nature rise in rebellion against it…. It is in the law written by the finger of God on the heart of man; and by that law, unchangeable and eternal, while men despise fraud, and loathe rapine, and abhor blood, they will reject with indignation the wild and guilty phantasy, that man can hold property in man![16]

This 'unrivalled climax of eloquence' asserting natural law had the effect of inscribing words on Thompson's own heart. William Lloyd Garrison, who became Thompson's steadfast partner in the United States and propelled him toward a new episode of his life in the western hemisphere, likewise cited this 1830 speech, in 1859, as the principle that instigated John Brown's raid on the arsenal at Harpers Ferry.[17] A second speech from 1830 cemented Thompson's commitment to immediatism in the United States, aligning him with Garrison's views.[18] This occurred at a great public meeting in Edinburgh, where Dr Andrew Thomson (1779–1831), the leading evangelist of the Church of Scotland, sent an anti-slavery meeting into consternation by saying:

> If there must be violence, let it even come, for it will soon pass away—let it come and rage its little power, since it is to be succeeded by lasting freedom, and prosperity, and happiness. Give me the hurricane rather than the pestilence. Give me the hurricane, with its thunder, and its lightning, and its tempest;—give me the hurricane, with its partial and temporary devastations, awful though they be; give me the hurricane, with its purifying, healthful, salutary effects;—give me that hurricane, infinitely rather than the noisome pestilence, whose path is never crossed, whose silence is never disturbed, whose progress is never arrested, by one sweeping blast from the heavens.[19]

It was as if the anaphora (the repeated 'give me the hurricane') conjured a mighty force in Thompson's soul. When the opportunity came for a trial as a travelling lecturer and organiser for the London Anti-Slavery Society, Thompson – a new husband and soon-to-be father, quietly in debt from an embezzlement he would eventually repay – grasped at the chance to propel the hurricane and touch the hearts of men.[20] He was gambling with his future, venturing away from a quiet life as an obscure clerk and tradesman, but he succeeded. He never became wealthy – indeed, his income never became bountiful or secure – but he stuck with this cause and vocation.

During Thompson's initial rise to fame, there was confusion about his calling: explicitly, in discovering a major oratorical talent, his mentors wondered whether he should pursue seminary training or the law. But a married man with a small child was not in a position to pause for formal education. Instead, he became an auto-didactic star lecturer and debater whose style embraced Bible Politics (an exegetic scriptural basis for ethics, neither literalist nor cherry-picking texts, based on compassion and a sense of contemporaneity, congruent with evangelical doctrine) combined with extensive use of emergent social science (especially economic) datasets, legal precedents, first-person accounts, and anecdotal storytelling.[21] A contemporary described Thompson's use of facts as a 'peculiarity', which implies an idiosyncratic yet new style of speaking.[22] As he lectured, an assistant would pass up a text, which Thompson flourished as a prop, literally and figuratively a pretext to speak 'at a different pace and pitch, adding interest and authority to a political speech' (see Figure 1.1).[23] Thus, these facts – whether excerpts from parliamentary speeches, social science tables, royal commission reports, dispatches, or letters to editors – lent variety instead of turgidity. His baritone voice and handsome bearing were used to good effect, making auditors feel that he spoke directly to them as he held their attention for hours at a time.[24] There was no dry recitation of facts – though there were many details – but rather a seemingly impromptu 'panoramic style' marshalling data 'furnished forth by a rich elocution and lively fancy'. Whereas others might have recourse to 'a whole volume of abstract reasoning or florid declamation', Thompson's 'story charms like a well-acted tragedy or well-written novel'.[25] And so, in contrast to preaching and legal arguments, Thompson's style could embrace the energy and opposition that came from hecklers as well as vociferous concord while utilising others' words (and even numerical compilations) as persuasive evidence. In essence, his use of Biblical passages is similar, eschewing literalism and embracing historicism when apt. He used these passages to buttress, refute, and even prove what was necessary for appeals to Christian morality.

Once Thompson had proven his mettle to the London Emancipation Committee by raising support in Kent for the Emancipation Bill, he was dispatched to the North of England.[26] For another decade, almost all travel between cities was accomplished by horseback or coach, so engagements tended to be carefully calendared. By April 1832, he was delivering up to five lectures per week in a single city or nearby centres, sometimes before throngs of 4,000 auditors.[27] In other words, the Emancipation Committee deployed him as the principal speaker at meetings, where he made the case for abolition based on specific motions in chained performances involving many speakers. In Yorkshire, Thompson was on the platform along with James Silk Buckingham (1786–1855), the travel writer and East India Company critic who would soon stand for election as the first MP in the new borough of Sheffield, and James Montgomery (1771–1854), who had authored the long abolitionist poem 'The West Indies', published nearly a decade before by Longman's (Thompson's father's firm).[28] Thompson admitted to his wife:

> Your insignificant uneducated husband was quite dismayed by the circumstances in which he was placed last evening. Having to speak for the third time before Montgomery the Poet, also before Buckingham who is perhaps the most accomplished lecturer of the day, also all the four candidates for the representation of the Town and a fearful array of parsons of all denominations and critics of every grade. Yet was my success triumphant—all joined to compliment me—Montgomery moved a vote of thanks to me which was seconded by Buckingham and supported by all the candidates.[29]

In Sheffield, as elsewhere, Thompson played his part to inspire a new affiliate branch of the London Society, ensuring ongoing civic-based pressure on elected officials, who would ultimately vote on the bill to emancipate the enslaved in Britain's Caribbean sugar colonies. While it was Thompson's goal to persuade the auditory to his position, their reaction was to be instrumental in swaying the 'four candidates for representation of the town', two of whom would ultimately vote in Parliament.[30] In the absence of true Reform (giving each person a vote for their representative to Parliament), this put meetings to good use by constituents collectively enacting a polity before MPs. Single-issue campaigns frequently worked on this principle.

In meetings, Thompson drew on the advantages of his excellent memory, skilled logic, and command of language. It was not just what he said that propelled his popularity and effectiveness. A contemporary noted:

> His *forte* lay in the power of his appeals to the humanity, the sense of justice, the hatred of oppression, the innate love of liberty, of his hearers. When rapt with his theme, his frame throbbing with emotion, the perspiration dripping from his forehead and hands, his voice pealing like a trumpet, his action as graceful and impetuous as that of a blood-horse on the course, the hearer who, for the moment, could stifle the sentiment that Slavery was the most atrocious system under heaven, might be trusted to sleep quietly on his knapsack in the breach, when it spouted a torrent of fire.[31]

These characteristics, honed early on, would be evinced by Thompson the rest of his career, but after less than a year on the circuit he stretched his craft to take on a second genre of rhetorical performance, the debate. This catapulted him to national fame and secured his lifelong status as a celebrity speaker.

Debating skills were indispensable to becoming a statesman and orator, and university debating societies had made them an exclusively masculine and upper-class purview. The London Mechanics' Institute, founded in the 1820s (and which Thompson attended), was part of a proletarian movement to foster debate skills among young men who could become MPs and borough councilmen with careers launched by the Reform movement. The Archbishop of Dublin's rhetorical manual, which favoured the venerable approach to classical education, derisively noted that such societies and venues could train an insufficiently knowledgeable young man to spew 'ill-digested thoughts in well-turned phrases' without due reflection, rather than 'forming for himself, by practice in writing, a precise and truly energetic style' in extempore thought.[32] Meanwhile, popularising the techniques, George Holyoake boiled down the basic formula:

1. To state your case.
2. To clear your case.
3. To prove your case.
4. And then sit down.

This came paired with a rationale for why debate is useful:

1. It creates two-sided people.
2. It instils toleration.
3. It proves truth which may be trusted.
4. It puts into the mind the sense of reasoned truth.
5. It sows the seeds of new truth.[33]

Debating in popular assemblies, according to Hugh Blair, 'opens the most illustrious field to this species of eloquence'.[34] Thompson found his opportunity to be tested at Manchester in August 1832.

His debate opponent was a contemporary, Peter Borthwick, but there the resemblance ends. Borthwick, who erroneously styled himself of 'Borthwick Castle', was educated at Edinburgh and Cambridge Universities, contemplated ordination in the Scottish Episcopal Church, spent a period of time in Ely gaol for debt, eked out a living in Edinburgh as a tutor, and then in his late twenties turned to acting. Weeks before he signed on as advocate for the West Indian planters in 1832, he had performed Othello and Hamlet at London's minor theatres, where he received polite notices.[35] Still fishing for a vocation, he turned the notoriety gained from debating Thompson into a run for public office; he stood for Evesham at the end of the year but was not elected until 1835. As part of the 'Young England' movement, he was Thompson's polar opposite: he not only advocated slaveholders' rights and gradual abolition but opposed free trade and subsequently, as editor of the *Morning Post*, was Lord Palmerston's bellicose advocate for the Crimea lobby.[36]

Borthwick dressed as a dandy (Figure 2.1), which Thompson – who was invariably pictured, from youth to old age, in a black frock coat – thought contemptible. 'Nothing can exceed the variety and expensiveness of his apparel. Every time I see him he is drest [*sic*] in a fresh suit, and yet in his lectures he triumphantly enquires – "What have I that the slave has not?"'[37] Looking back at Borthwick's first decade in and out of Parliament, the *Illustrated London News* launched into him with uncharacteristic snidery:

> Peter Borthwick's oratory is, in matter and manner, of that style of mediocrity to which, if displayed in poetry, men, gods, and [newspaper] columns unite in denying immortality. He is fluent enough, and has a full command of words, but as to ideas and illustrations they are the most perfect commonplace.... His enunciation is particularly clear and correct, and, though savouring a little of the elocution master, his delivery of what he has to say is very commendable. It is in the matter of his discourse that Peter fails the most.[38]

If this thumbnail sketch captures Borthwick's powers at the height of his repute, there is not much about him that endorsed the advantages of university training. In 1854, he was characterised as a 'fluent speaker yet by no means scrupulously accurate in his facts. He was dull, monotonous, and wearisome'.[39] Indeed, a decade after his death he was still remembered as 'Othello Borthwick', the sort of 'stage-struck strutter, who confounds the floor of the House with the boards of a booth, till, falling into the abysm of bathos, they find themselves lost, and are lost to find wherefore, as their elocution is excellent, their attitudes accurate, and all as it ought to be, according to their ideal'.[40] This does not leave much to the imagination vis-à-vis his chances when he squared off against George Thompson.

Debate formats were mutable, the rules for each contest decided by a presiding committee. The Thompson-Borthwick debate in Manchester was no fleeting affair, compacted into an evening's meeting: instead, Borthwick led off, commanding the podium for an entire evening, and on a subsequent date it was Thompson's turn. This went on for five rounds, ten nights in total, at various venues. As Thompson stepped up to the pulpit of the

Figure 2.1    Peter Borthwick. 'Peter Borthwick's oratory is, in matter and manner, of that style of mediocrity to which, if displayed in poetry, men, gods, and columns unite in denying immortality.' *Illustrated London News*, 7 January 1843, 8. Getty Images.

Wesleyan Methodist Chapel in Salford for the last speech of the debate, he 'was again received with deafening cheers'. This was debate on a marathon timeline, a cross-class gladiatorial combat that provided superb entertainment. Thompson commenced a three-hour-and-twenty-minute speech, determined to register the plight of those across the Atlantic 'who have no[t] 60 or 70 members in the House of Commons to represent their interests, (cheers;) who have no paid agents (great cheering) in Berkely-square [*sic*], in Cavendish-square, and in Whitehall-palace; who have no one that can drive down in his carriage to Downing-street, and threaten the Minister, that if he do not do this or that he will withhold his influence and support from him (Cheers.)'.[41] This got the crowd on his side. Whereas Borthwick's speech had been 'retailed' in London multiple times, without regard to refuting what Thompson had laid out, the entirety of Thompson's tailor-made address directly and methodically took up and dismantled Borthwick's claims.

Three classic Thompsonian tactics are evident in his refutations. Halfway through, he recalled the auditory to a prior experience of their withheld empathy, implicitly complimenting them for repelling the thinly veiled racism that permeated his opponent's position: 'Mr. Borthwick talked of the planters' wives, and of the planters' daughters, and he panegyrised the ladies of England, and talked of their virtue and beauty, but his compliments fell silent to the ground.' One can imagine Thompson turning up the volume and reverberation, fuelling the assembly's energy, and then slowing the pace as he uttered a decisive hypophoric question:

> He was doing that which never will succeed—he never will flatter the women of England into an approbation of slavery. (Tremendous cheering, mingled with shouts of 'bravo.') 'There were ladies in the West Indies', he said, 'as fair as you, who have hopes, and fears, and sympathies in common with your own'. And is there not, I would ask, a negro heart, a negro's home, and a negro's wife? Has not the negro hopes, and fears, and sympathies. Women of England! I will never celebrate your beauty, your sympathy, your virtuous endearments, until you grant to me, that a negro's wife is as fair in the eyes of her husband as you are in yours. (Loud applause.)[42]

The call to cross-identify is a classic way to motivate sympathy.[43] Later, he recalled Borthwick's ploy to appeal 'to the money-getting propensities of the people of England', a ploy embedded in fears that decreased prosperity, depressed manufacturing, and shrunken markets for British goods would follow emancipation. 'What! is it come to this, that we are to continue the foul abomination, from a fear that we should spin less yarn, or weave less calico?' Thompson artfully connected this point to its antithesis – opposing freedom for the enslaved with the newly expanded right to vote among the British male middle classes – by asking 'Will you, who have just obtained the elective franchise, determine the question of liberty to others by a reference to the amount of your exports?'[44] Thompson was a genius at making economics personal, a matter of pathos, showing how one tenet of liberalism was inseparable from all others, implicating auditors in the spectrum of freedoms. But finally, in the culminating moment of the lengthy exordium, Thompson corrected Borthwick's claim that the reduction in the number of those enslaved in the thirteen British Caribbean colonies (plus Mauritius, which was also implicated in the 1833 act to eliminate slavery) was due to manumission. Instead, somehow – and exactly how is unsure because one cannot recite a table – he presented his auditors with what, in the published account, is a pair of tables extracted from Thomas Fowell Buxton's (1786–1845) official returns presented to Parliament. They demonstrate, island by island, a net falling off of the enslaved population over the past decade. In Haiti, by contrast, the population had doubled since its revolution, proving (in Thompson's estimation) that in bondage Black people died and in freedom they thrived.[45]

This was never a fair fight, but it was an entertaining combat. Press coverage enflamed Thompson's repute, and the debaters faced off again a few weeks later – this time by paid ticket – in Liverpool, Thompson's birthplace. Thompson took the opening slot and said he voiced the claims not only on behalf of 800,000 enslaved West Indians but on behalf of 'every enslaved human being in every part of the habitable globe', an early hint at his wider principles.[46] His first address emphasised that all races would face the same Judgement Day. Thus, from the perspective of salvation, slavery doomed bondsmen and their masters, for it is 'a system which degrades the body, brutalizes the mind, produces ignorance and vice in the slave; pride, arrogance, and demoralization in the master; which, in a word, debases and dehumanizes both'. In responding to his remit to explicate 'The Evils of Slavery', he baited Borthwick to refute Christian values by denying a child's right to be with its parents or turning away from the unimaginable sufferings of men and women who toil 'only not to be whipped'.[47] What propels planters' mania to extract labour in concert with the disregard for familial sanctity? Seventy-five per cent of West Indian slaves were mortgaged and subject to seizure: by what justification did planters allow this and the separation of kinfolk that ensued? Planters were consumed by '*the pride, the arrogance, the selfishness, the despotism, the irritability which the possession of arbitrary power engenders in the minds of the owners*', along with 'gross and brutal sensuality'.[48]

In rebuttal, Borthwick responded not to the foregoing speech but to one Thompson had delivered in the Manchester contest, and thus failed to reply to Thompson's catalogue of evils in the ongoing debate. Borthwick waved off immediate emancipation, giving Thompson a pretext for polysemy then mock indignation. He quoted Borthwick:

> 'By-and-by', 'by-and-by.' (*Laughter.*) At half-past six his answer was 'by-and-by'; at seven it was 'by-and-by': eight o'clock came, half-past eight, the answer was still 'by-and-by.' (*Laughter, cheers, and hisses.*) What, shall I be hissed. (*Renewed hissing.*) Gentlemen, *if* you are gentleman, (*laughter and applause,*) shall I be hissed when I quote the words of your own champion?[49]

Here is an example of Thompson 'in playful humor, throwing the galling arrow of sarcasm, scattering the *jet d'eau* of wit ... drawing the ludicrous caricature, imitating to the life any peculiarity in the tone or manner of his antagonist ... with charming grace'.[50] In this address, Thompson focused on the affective charge from testimonies of enslaved families riven apart, children forced to witness their mothers being stripped and flogged, and teenagers put under the lash, emphasising names and dates of sources, especially conservative journals. How could there be what Borthwick's party advocated – gradual abolition – when a runaway boy is hanged for stealing himself?

A week later, Thompson took the podium again in Liverpool. He brought the problem home to the Privy Council, the House of Lords, and the House of Commons, where the fifty to eighty men sent to these offices by West Indian money and influence had foregone convictions of 'religion, honour and humanity' to oppose emancipation.[51] These arguments put the perpetuation of slavery at the docksides of the Mersey, the influx point of Liverpool's wealth, making everyone in the room complicit. He riffed on the speeches given in the House of Commons advocating compensation for the planter, bounties on slave-grown sugar, and prohibitory duties on free-grown sugar. Then he conjured a dialogue to counter privilege. Imagine:

> Next morning, some lady sipping her tea, and reading the *Morning Post*, might say—'Dear me, what an amiable speech! How he pities the planter! Really, I feel inclined to pity the planter, too.' (*Laughter.*) And thus all the lady's sympathy would be on the side of the planter, and she would think nothing of the slave. But perhaps some friend by her side might just whisper—'This gentleman, who you are inclined to pity, is not in the West Indies, because he happens to be in London; he is not a planter, because he happens to be a member of the House of Commons; he is a mortgagee, and has certain parchments deposited [i.e., mortgages] with Messrs.

Drummond & Co., giving him a claim on ten or fifteen hundred slaves, and emancipation would be the annihilation of the greater part of his securities. This is the source of his eloquence, consider this, and what remains, but a piece of empty, heartless, hypocritical declamation.' (Applause.)[52]

It was a risky ploy, but Thompson parried hisses with humour and kept the auditory on his side. He appealed to their Christian morality to see through the opposition's faux arguments about economic productivity and instead grasp the root problem: those who love power must not be the jurymen for their own trial. Neither the planter, merchant, broker, nor overseer would grant emancipation – only Parliament could do that – and though he did not mention the power of the ballot box (in truth only a small proportion of householders were newly enfranchised) the implication was to choose MPs accordingly and bring them to account.

This was great theatre, and the debates were reprised again in Glasgow in February, following the general election. This time each champion spoke for an hour on the same platform, repeating the process over several nights. Thompson noted that this unaccustomed mode of debate caused him considerable effort to prepare. The clamour for entry was so great that Dr Wardlaw's Chapel was immediately filled to the rafters. Thompson reported to his wife that Borthwick's performance was abysmal. 'He floundered horribly, could not answer a word I said & sat down amidst the hootings of the great majority. My second appearance was hailed as the first & I did not fail to shew Mr B up in fine style.' For the third meeting, Borthwick's supporters attempted to get the debate moved to a small venue, with ticketing (as on the Liverpool plan). They did not succeed, which ensured a less salubrious auditory but also one disposed to favour emancipation. The capacious chapel was fortified with a sturdy barricade, and 'a very strong body of police' was in evidence to prevent the fracas of the second evening.[53]

At that point, Thompson thought Borthwick's reputation was ruined, at least in Scotland, yet another debate series – the fourth – was set for solidly Tory Edinburgh the following month. This time, they debated three times, always on the same dates, one man speaking midday and the other in the evening.[54] The most sympathetic commentator on Borthwick concluded that despite noble efforts 'he was invariably overthrown. Thompson shook him from the point of his weapon, quivering and bleeding, at every crossing of swords'.[55] Borthwick, pale and pensive, 'wandered from subject to subject', forwarded flimsy arguments, and ineffectually attempted to get the labouring classes on his side by appealing 'to their national feelings'. Thompson, who presented with 'the manly, though respectful, bearing of one who was conscious of having truth on his side, and who could not therefore be afraid of the issue', countered with 'stirring eloquence' and 'cutting sarcasm'.[56] Thompson threw every argument into the mix: economic and legal reasoning as well as testimonials and religious morality. Part of his unconventionality, therefore, was to work on his auditors' reasoning and sympathies alike. He utilised the Enlightenment model of truth along with the neoclassical debate mode of persuading through affective appeal. Until the enslaved and formerly enslaved began to address Britons in person, this was the most effective strategy. Thompson promoted identification: with the enslaved, with those who act righteously on their behalf, and most immediately with the skilled rhetorician who presented life stories, set them in a moral framework, and connected the threads of capitalism afar and at home. To be newly won over to Thompson's view was a conversion experience, akin to rebirth, just as to hear the rationale again, on multiple hearings, was to be reaffirmed in faith. This, in part, is why biblical justification worked for Thompson.[57]

In August 1833, Parliament passed the Slavery Abolition Act, a compromise on immediate emancipation. The Treasury raised over £20 million in payments for slavers (a debt not resolved until 2015) and nothing for the enslaved. The alternative was to delay further, despite the Whigs' large parliamentary majority. Under a complicated set of terms, on some islands children less than six years of age were immediately manumitted while their elders were given board and lodging as 'apprentices', without pay, until 1840, in the style of indentured labourers. Before long it was evident that the apprenticeship system was not only indefensible but also ineffectual. The date for full, immediate emancipation throughout the British West Indies was moved to 21 August 1838. Years later, John Bright admitted '*I have always considered Mr Thompson as the real liberator of the slaves in the English colonies*; for without his commanding eloquence made irresistible by the blessedness of his cause, *I do not think all the other agencies then at work would have procured their freedom*.'[58]

### Sowing the Seeds of a New Truth

Liberal networks were extensive, and evaluation of effectiveness was ongoing. The extraordinary orator Henry Lord Brougham, for example, once introduced George Thompson to listeners at Exeter Hall as 'the most persuasive speaker' he had ever heard. On another occasion, at a very late hour, when a meeting at the National Hall (Holborn) had lost much of its audience and those who remained were 'wearied … jaded, unexpectant, and longing for vacation of the chair', Thompson took the podium and, according to Holyoake, 'arrested them, inspired them, set them aflame, caps and hats rose in the air, and for years after the tale of the wonderful speech of that night was told in workshops and committee meetings'. Speaking seemed as natural to Thompson as song was to the great mezzo-soprano Maria Malibran (1808–36). He radiated honesty, marshalled his facts, and with 'grand fervour' succeeded in the one realm he thought would count most: not Parliament but the oratorical platforms of Britain, the United States, and India. Holyoake wrote that 'There was a generation of slaves who would have died for Thompson', and 'What a splendid memory is that for a deathbed!'[59]

Meanwhile, in 1831 – the year before Thompson's debates with Borthwick – a quite different type of evaluative networking centred on the floundering journalist William Lloyd Garrison, who sat in Baltimore City Jail, having called a Massachusetts merchant a murderer for taking part in the interstate slave trade. Garrison's case caught the attention of abolitionists Arthur and Lewis Tappan, who paid Garrison's fine and secured a new colleague. Garrison set up a press in Boston and began to publish the *Liberator* (1831–65), advocating immediate non-violent emancipation throughout the US slave states and condemning efforts to 'repatriate' the formerly enslaved to Liberia. In 1832, mirroring the efforts in Britain, he helped found the New England Anti-Slavery Society. Garrison also vigorously supported Prudence Crandall's (1803–90) teacher-training academy for African American women in Connecticut, an early act signalling his persistent support for both women's rights and integrated institutions. During 1833, he toured Britain to fundraise and met heroes of the 1807 campaign – Thomas Clarkson (1760–1846), William Wilberforce (1759–1833), and Thomas Fowell Buxton – but it was in the firebrand George Thompson that he found someone of his own generation, style, and convictions. When Garrison's views became more extreme, and he split from the wealthy Tappans and Joshua Leavitt's (1794–1873) Liberty Party faction in 1837, Thompson and a host of eloquent women including Lucretia Mott (1793–1880), Angelina (1805–79) and Sarah Grimké (1792–1873), Elizabeth Cady Stanton (1815–1902), and Maria Weston Chapman stood by him, for better or worse. Consistently, Garrison's supporters provided a base for Thompson to gather information, share tactics, and build a transatlantic Anglophone anti-slavery movement based on the moral imperative to end slavery.

The historian of working-class itinerant lecturers Janette Lisa Martin heralds Thompson as 'the first hired orator on the international stage', who moved between organisations and 'perhaps more than any other paid agent … made itinerant political lecturing respectable'.[60] A list of stellar jurists offered to support Thompson while he studied for a legal career at one of the inns of court, but he declined.[61] Instead, he accepted sponsorship from the Committee for the Universal Abolition of Slavery and the Slave Trade (a compendium of the Edinburgh and Glasgow Emancipation Societies, with additional financial support raised in England) to answer Garrison's invitation to visit the United States in 1834.[62] Expecting to stay three years, he scuttled the trip after thirteen months, having given 220 public lectures 'besides innumerable shorter addresses in committees, conventions, associations, &c.', and taking credit for the creation of dozens of branch Anti-Slavery Societies and the conversation of 1,000–1,200 clergymen to the cause of immediate emancipation.[63]

From the moment Thompson landed in New York, he was a flashpoint for pro-slavery interests, which ran his family out of lodgings, denounced him in the press, interrupted meetings, hanged him and Garrison in effigy, and threatened his physical safety. The State of Georgia put a $5,000 bounty on his head.[64] Thompson's enemies falsely claimed that he incited violence by saying that the enslaved ought to slit their masters' throats, which fuelled all manner of performative and printed opposition in an intense disinformation campaign.[65] US citizens 'mobbed' for many reasons during the Jacksonian period, 'ostensibly to correct problems or injustices within their society without challenging its basic structures', but African Americans took the brunt of the vigilantism.[66] Still, what Thompson deduced from mobbing was not just how virulent opposition to abolition was, but also how enmeshed pro-slavery interests and indoctrination were in all facets of white Northeasterners' private and public experience. On his return to Scotland, he told an audience about being prevented from speaking at a meeting of ladies, despite Boston's chief magistrate being in the chair. When 4,000–5,000 'well-dressed ruffians' gathered outside, the mayor came into the hall and said:

> 'Ladies, ladies, I entreat you to disperse.' One of the ladies shrewdly asked, 'Why don't you entreat the mob to disperse?' (Laughter.) 'Oh', said he, 'I can do nothing with them.' 'Well, then, call out the constables.' 'Oh! they are in the mob.' 'Call out the militia, then.' 'Oh! they are in the mob.' 'The volunteers then.' 'Oh! they are in the mob too.' (Loud laughter.) 'Oh! Well, then, go and use your personal influence.' 'Oh! I have no personal influence; ladies, ladies, you have all the reason on your side, but I entreat you to disperse.' (Great laughter, and cheering.)[67]

Exchanges were not usually so genial.[68] Thompson regarded the mobbing as a great triumph, a distinct opportunity for the abolition movement, for it brought attention to the cause (justified by the violence within US political life) and lent it a lot of momentum.[69] Whereas in the West Indian campaign he was a rearguard intellectual, in the United States (as the focus of malevolent pursuit) he experienced solidarity with others who ran for their lives. His oppression differed from that of the enslaved and freedom-seekers, yet was an empirical form of experience and discovery that complemented his erudition about slavery-based economics. It also dramatized for British abolitionists the fervour and extremism of US polarisation.[70]

Thompson's experience in Britain and the United States illustrates how essentially the same tactics (lecturing, speaking at meetings, holding conventions, and networking through social invitations) could encounter different counter-tactics in different contexts: hisses in Britain but brickbats and mobs in the US Northeast. These counter-tactics significantly contoured the kind of result that a speaker like Thompson could achieve. Calling for immediate emancipation in the United States during the 1830s was a very different matter than in the West Indies, for the means to exert political power through interwoven institutions, economies, and other ties was 'a question of extreme difficulty' in the United States, involving consent of diametrically opposed and intractable interests.[71] During the eighteenth century, the West Indies had had 'the most deadly and destructive system of chattel slavery in the New World', but after Britain banned its transatlantic slave trade (and did what it could to inhibit the traffic by other nations' ships) planters gained incentives to enhance enslaved people's longevity and fecundity. Slaveholders, many of whom lived abroad, were profit driven and thus amenable to compensation. Taxation, military enforcement, and legislation all emanated from the same source as the reparations. In the United States, there was no equivalent will, distracted interest, or leverage. Novel horrors emerged during the early nineteenth century in the new Southern territories, where systematic dehumanisation under a regime of terror was facilitated by the shift of a million enslaved people from Virginia and the mid-Atlantic states to labour camps predominantly in Louisiana and Mississippi. In the Deep South, 56 per cent of the nation's enslaved people went from producing 'no cotton to speak of in 1790 to making almost 2 billion pounds of it in 1860'.[72] Enslaved people were tyrannised to extract this from fertile land too soon made barren from monoculture.

The people who strove to propel US abolition forward on behalf of the enslaved were interconnected by ties affectively loaded by specific kinds of acts as well as geographies. When Thompson enthusiastically showed

Ann (1813–86) and Wendell Phillips (1811–84) the blue basket, green pin-cushion, and Scotch thistle he would send home with them to be sold at the fundraiser known as the National Anti-Slavery Bazaar (an annual Christmastide event staged by the Boston Female Anti-Slavery Society), the Phillipses anticipated Maria Weston Chapman's thrill at receiving objects personally handled by Thompson.[73] In 1836, the women of Clydeside sent an anti-slavery petition to US counterparts that 'unfurled over the heads of thousands' in New York. Wendell Phillips wrote to Thompson that in consequence of such moments, 'The vale of Leven [near Clydeside], Exeter Hall, Glasgow and Birmingham are consecrated spots, – the land of Scoble and Sturge, of Wardlaw & Buxton, of Clarkson & O'Connell, is Holy Land to us.'[74] Yet the cities where Thompson and Borthwick squared off represent the historical centres of cotton unlading for nearly the entire US crop (Liverpool), cotton weaving (Manchester), and tobacco and sugar processing (Glasgow), and the homeland of the overseers, lawyers, and physicians running West Indian plantations in lieu of their absentee own-ers (Scotland in general). If Britain was a Holy Land it was also beset by its own pernicious devils.

By building a transcontinental, multinational abolitionist network, activists attempted to coordinate efforts to end slavery in the United States. The idea was to closely connect people who could redirect the bases of profit. As Thompson's experience in the United States demonstrated, at this time abolition could gain ground only in the face of tremendous entrenched opposition: this was affective, structural, and economic all at once, expressed through performance, print media, and interpersonal bonds. The decade or so after Thompson returned from the United States shows him coming to terms with competing political interests, building overlapping networks of allies, and exploring forms by which to solicit new supporters, enhance allegiances, and leverage change. While Thompson did catalyse some initiatives, and holds a unique place in history, he also functioned indicatively within a system sustained by people of many tal-ents and capabilities, investments, and intensities with whom he collabo-rated. What helps Thompson stand out in the historiography is that he personally sustained networks on *three* continents, which epitomises what historian Sebastian Conrad calls 'social activity and practice' that brought into being 'the global [as] a distinct sphere of social action and of analysis'. These were constituted over time, built up on different temporalities and frameworks.[75]

Conrad asks 'when did the world become a single system?'[76] From the combined perspective of transportation and trade, a lengthy process of

bringing this transformation into being occurred across the eighteenth century. Thompson fully grasped the implications. In an 1842 speech on Corn
Law repeal that lampoons elites' use of trading networks, he conjured a
vision of dining with a protectionist member of the House of Lords who
defends the Corn Laws and thus is at odds with working people's ability to
buy bread 'at the world's value'. It is worth quoting at length.

> Alighting at his door, which, perhaps is opened by a foreign footman—
> (laughter)—you wipe your feet upon a mat made of Russian hemp (don't
> be dependent on foreigners)—loud laughter—Over your head burns a
> hall-lamp fed by oil from the polar seas, and supplied with a wick made
> from American slave-grown cotton—(don't be dependent on foreigners.)
> You are shown up stairs, and step into the drawing-room, where you tread
> upon a Turkey Carpet. (Don't be dependent on foreigners.) My Lord
> advances, dressed for dinner. A coat of the newest Parisian fashion, of Sax-
> ony wool, made by the immortal Stultz—a broach with an Indian Gem,
> set in Mexican gold. China silk stockings, Morocco pumps, and a curious
> Geneva watch, which tells him that you have been remarkably punctual.
> He introduces you to his Lady. She advances. Over her pale intellectual
> brow waves an ostrich feather. (Ostrich feathers don't grow in the tails
> of our barn-door owls.) Round her graceful neck, is a row of pearls from
> Ceylon [Sri Lanka]; over her shoulders, a profusion of Brussels lace; in her
> hand, a foreign fan; and further I might go, to prove her independence
> of foreigners, and might talk of corsets and other things as sacred; but
> will not. Let us go down to dinner. It is spread upon a table of Spanish
> Mahogany. The tureens and vegetable dishes are from Dresden. The Turtle
> is from Camanas [Cayman Islands]. (No Sliding Scale, or fixed duty for
> Turtle). The contents of the castors are all foreign. The delicious wines
> are all foreign. The side dishes are foreign, sent up by a French cook. The
> tongue, is Rein Deer. The Boar's head from Germany. The dessert comes
> on. The Olives are from Mount Lebanon. The figs are from Turkey. The
> Raisins are from Malaga. The Dates from Syria. The Apples from New
> York. The Grapes from Portugal. The preserved Ginger from Jamaica.
> The Nuts from Italy. The Pomgranates [sic] from Egypt. The Prunes from
> France. The Oranges from Lisbon. The dessert over, we go to the Ladies.
> My Lord's daughter is playing a foreign air. Singing in a foreign language.
> Has learnt under a foreign master. Has finished her education in a foreign
> country—going to be married to a foreign Count. (Dont [sic] be depen-
> dent on foreigners for your supplies.) The footman enters. Coffee from
> Mocha. Tea from Canton. Sugar from Siam. At eleven, you depart. My
> Lady is going to a Concert—*a la Musard*. My Lord, to the foreign Opera,
> to witness the debût of the admirable *figurante*, Fanny Shew-her-legs, who
> has been sent for, express from the Prussian capital, for the special enter-
> tainment of those who cannot endure the thought of seeing their country-
> men dependent on foreigners for their supplies.[77]

This convulsed the auditorium with laughter and, at the end, loud applause. Clearly, for the wealthy, the world was a single system, a global supply chain of goods and services that worked to their advantage and comfort. Meanwhile, the poor's access to flour was restricted to British produce, whatever its price.

The idea that ordinary citizens could act *upon* the system, not just exist *within* it, was countered in a series of initiatives taken during the 1830s and 1840s. This was aided by specific kinds of journalistic publicity, protective lobbying, and leverage exerted through mobilising public pressure, and took both ethical and pragmatic turns.[78] For Thompson, opposing these initiatives meant conveying how labour, prices, and commodities were linked.

As the campaign for emancipation in the West Indies ended, Buxton called for a Parliamentary Select Committee on Aboriginal Tribes (British Settlements), which reported in 1837 and sparked the formation of the APS. The APS' modern historian, James Heartfield, summarises its activities thus: 'The Society lobbied the Colonial Office, briefed governors and legislators, and gathered intelligence on the condition of aboriginal peoples for 73 years.' It took over the 'broad organisational infrastructure, geared towards humanitarian agitation' established by the emancipation movement. Its first action was to reprint the 1837 Select Committee's report, appending comments and an introduction vowing to 'assist in protecting of the defenceless, and promoting the advancements of uncivilised tribes'.[79] Paternalist and racist nomenclature notwithstanding, the APS vigorously advocated for Indigenous peoples wherever contact (and conflict) arose with white settler populations. In 1847, the APS noted 'experience has shown that this contact has almost invariably resulted in injury to and often in the extermination of the Aborigines', and it strove to address the wrongs by 'gathering intelligence from informants who were missionaries or colonial officers, liaising with native leaders, and bringing causes to the Foreign and Colonial Offices'.[80] The urgent question for many territories under British influence was how to proceed with colonial governance: not to stop the influx of European migrants who were destroying lifeways and putting land under cultivation but to acknowledge the defensible rights of native peoples, institute legal defences for them, and prevent further genocides.[81] It was a unique brief in the long history of advocating human rights.

Edward John Eyre (1815–1901, later governor of Jamaica) took up a post in 1842 as protector of Aborigines and resident magistrate to Moorrundie, the first white settlement on the Murray River, South Australia. In her study of how humanitarian obligations relate to legal regulation of Indigenous subjects under the British Empire, Amanda Nettlebec credits Eyre at this point in his career 'as someone who approached cross-cultural encounters with humanity and diplomacy. Eyre was, in truth, unusual amongst his contemporaries in his capacity to imagine colonization from the point of view of the dispossessed'. Even so, Eyre, like so many of his time and class, believed that Aboriginal people had to conform to colonisers' regulation in exchange for a dubious degree of legal and police protection.[82] Howard L. Malchow assesses the intentions of APS stalwarts such as the Quaker Tory Robert N. Fowler (1828–91) as genuine concern 'without having to address the "cupidity and rapacity" of those who might be the domestic counterparts of the evil planters and colonial employers abroad…. There is no trace of a conscious hypocrisy here, but rather the self-deception that allowed a banker and a merchant implicitly to define and accept their own world as moral by juxtaposing it to one outside that relied on cruder and more sensational disciplines'.[83] The APS' stalwarts were almost all Nonconformists, with a strong Quaker plurality. For the most part, they pursued their commercial and philanthropic interests at a great distance from any of the Indigenous peoples whom they strove to 'protect', relying on information from informants in the field, especially missionaries.

In 1838, Joseph Pease (1772–1846) persuaded the APS to hire Thompson to lecture about the society throughout the North of England.[84] As a letter to Garrison shows, Thompson felt obliged to justify this shift in his career: 'I am by no means precluded from pleading the cause of the enslaved. On the contrary, the Slavery of India, the Slave Trade of Africa, and the freedom and welfare of the Negro wherever found, are matters of special and legitimate interest.'[85] In particular, he strove to pull the APS' attention to the cause of India, where Britain presided over 150 million subjects.[86] Thompson's grand plan was to enhance the agrarian-based economy of India with free labour, increase the export of Indian cotton to supplant the United States as Britain's supplier, and keep the mills of Lancashire busy and profitable. This connected the Atlantic to the Indian Ocean as the locus of concern for the circulation and concentration of labour, commodities, and wealth. The strategy would shift trade to within the British Empire, undercut the economic basis of US slavery, and unite the liberal principles of freedom and laissez-faire in one fell swoop. Wendell Phillips grasped this new direction with enthusiasm, writing, 'It is just what we need to touch a class of men [in the Southern United States] who seem almost out of the pale of religious influence.'[87] As Phillips put it, 'Should the experiment succeed … it will give [US] slavery its deathblow.'[88] Garrison was sanguine about this strategy, for just weeks after its formation he reported 'much consternation on this side of the Atlantic, among the planters and their northern adherents.... A tocsin of alarm is sounded in the ear of the slave-holding States'.[89] This consternation resulted from rumour, not action per se. Converting the concept into action proved difficult.

Zoë Laidlaw judges that 'Thompson's brief period of APS employment is characteristic of the interconnected, contested and transnational world of British humanitarian activism in this era.'[90] Even so, connecting people and ideas did not always result in change. For structural reasons, India was something of a hot potato among philanthropists. It was administered by the India Office, not the Colonial Office, so it required different channels for lobbying than all other APS concerns. The APS – which focused on abuses inherent to the indentured labour system – left matters outside the BFASS (founded by Joseph Sturge in 1839 and merged with the APS in 1909), and was not directly involved in economic issues. Furthermore, during a period when party feeling ran high, it was difficult to recruit to an unsectarian cause.[91] Ultimately, the APS could not be swayed to care about Thompson's broader vision, and he left the APS in favour of a new organisation, this time with the critical backing of Richard Cobden, John Bright, and the Manchester School of liberal industrialists: those who stood to lose the most if cotton supplies were threatened.

The British India Society was founded in July 1839 during a meeting at Freemasons' Hall (London), and was soon bolstered by auxiliaries in Manchester and Glasgow and the support of prominent businessmen from Bombay's and Calcutta's Hindu, Muslim, and Parsi communities.[92] In addition to Lord Brougham (who presided at the first meeting), Cobden, Bright, and Thompson, its officers included Thomas Clarkson, the Irish nationalist leader Daniel O'Connell (1775–1847), the reformer William Howitt (1792–1879), Joseph Pease, General John Briggs (1785–1875, until 1827 of the Madras native infantry, an expert on the land tax and former Resident at Satara), and the recently elected free trader Dr John Bowring, MP (1792–1872). Among those on the platform that day were Nouwah Ikba-ood-doula of Oudh, Prince Shaikh Jahangir-i-Zaman Jamal ud-din Muhammad Sultan Sahib (1792?–1842, son of Tipu Sultan), and Meers Ubdool Ullee and Kureem Ullee (agents of the raja of Satara).[93] Laidlaw emphasises how this demonstrates the extent to which 'colonial lobbying organisations, and indeed reforming networks generally, overlapped', for there were members or future members of the APS, ACLL, and BFASS present.[94] The broad objectives were to bring India more into the consciousness of the British public and significantly increase the acreage of land under cultivation on the subcontinent, develop other natural resources, abolish all practices of slavery, and bring about the end of The Company 'to stay the march of famine, and quench the lust of conquest; to mitigate the land tax, and secure for the inhabitants a practical recognition of their claims to the soil'.[95] The British India Society set out to use tactics similar to those of the London Anti-Slavery Society: demand change by shifting public opinion to bring pressure upon MPs, and so (like the APS) issue a periodical to consolidate ties, communicate between London and auxiliaries, and publicise the combined cause of 'JUSTICE TO INDIA; PROSPERITY TO ENGLAND; FREEDOM TO THE SLAVE'.[96] Without question, Thompson (as 'travelling secretary' and paid lecturer) was the backbone of the organisation in all but a financial sense: he addressed meetings, lectured widely on Indian history and sociology, and contributed substantially to the society's sporadically issued journal the *British Indian Advocate* (forty-seven numbers, January 1841 through December 1847).[97] Additionally, however, Thompson undertook what would today be called 'direct action' against The Company by becoming a shareholder and then bringing business before the Court of Proprietors, using the British India Society to publicise these events.[98]

The British India Society despaired of the sabre rattling between Britain and other imperial powers that claimed the subcontinent from all sides and pulled Britain into a succession of wars and skirmishes. The solution, it argued, was to make India 'the scene of those great peaceful experiments which shall extend our influence over still wider regions' across Asia.[99] Elimination of The Company's monopoly in 1813 had not had the effect of developing India economically; the British India Society sought to spur the colony's agriculture, make its people more prosperous, and thereby create a new market for British goods under a system of reciprocal free trade.[100] The liberal twist inherent in this imperial approach shifted from a model of conquering territory and ruling politically to one of consolidating economic power within a British-based trade bloc. It offered enhanced prosperity and stability to India within a laissez-faire model while serving the interests of Britain in multiple dimensions, including reducing friction with rival empires while gradually making a more prosperous India dependent on British manufactures. In 1839, while England reaped £3 per capita taxes from New South Wales and £2/12s per capita taxes from Van Diemen's Land (Tasmania), less than 4s per head came into British coffers from India, just 6–8 per cent as much. And while the other colonies consumed £5 of English manufactures per head, Indians consumed 6d worth, just 0.5 per cent as much.[101] This calculation ignores the distinctions between settler colonies and India while emphasising the untapped land and human resources squandered by The Company's administration. The Company's administrators had long sought to make themselves, not Britain per se, wealthy. Earlier in the century, The Company had taken measures to suppress the slave trade within India (and across the Indian Ocean in multiple vectors);[102] if India could produce more commodities (such as sugar, cotton, tobacco, and indigo) cheaper than the United States or French colonies, Britain would naturally buy from its own colony instead of other sources, but the British India Society was anxious to prevent illegal labour practices of any kind from tainting Indian goods. Thus, 'European capital and foresight' combined with 'the cheap labour and persevering industry' of the Indian population twinning the liberal principles of free trade with free (waged) labour to encourage a laissez-faire economy tempered by civil and political institutions that monitor abuses.[103] From Thompson's perspective, this was 'the powerful principle of a sound and sinless political economy' freed from 'the stain of blood' inherent to US products.[104]

Letterbooks from the British India Society do not survive, but items printed in early issues of the *British Indian Advocate* give a representative showing of concerns. Christians from Tutacorin (Thoothakundi, Tamil Nadu) and Colombo (Sri Lanka) complained in a petition that a tax created in 1543 by Muslim rulers to be exacted on heathens and foreigners was still being enforced. Notably, it was collected on Sundays as Christians travelled to and from church. Payment was compelled by torturing people with whips, sticks, and thumbscrews; leaving them in the burning sun with heavy stones on their shoulders; looting their homes and belongings; and harassing womenfolk. The British land tax, which targeted certain occupations and castes but not others, was also regarded as manifestly unfair.[105] The predominance of predial (agrarian serf) labour among chamars (Dalits) of central and northern India was noted.[106] Elsewhere, kidnappers drugged men, took them aboard ships as crew, and pocketed their three months' advance with the intention of selling the men into slavery in Mauritius.[107] The Slave Emancipation Act of 1833 did not pertain to India, and while the Indian Slavery Act of 1843 was meant to address such abuses (though debt bondage and indentured labour were not outlawed), suppression of slavery proved impossible to comprehensively enforce. Abuses and inequities associated with taxation remained, and often led to bondage, inescapable servitude, and labour trafficking. India was far from the nation of 'well governed and happy people' that the British India Society envisioned fostering.[108]

Thompson did not directly agitate for the 1843 act. Instead, starting in mid-1841, he agreed to shift his attention from the British India Society

to the ACLL, having been officially seconded by the British India Society
to the League.[109] A great tea party in Thompson's honour, attended by
800 women and men, took place at the Manchester Corn Exchange to
celebrate the two organisations' kindred objectives.[110] Thompson followed this up by successfully bringing 700 Christian clergy together in
Manchester for an ecumenical meeting about the Corn Laws' so-called tax
on food, successfully appealing to the orthodox and heterodox for 'peace
and plenty' among nations. This cemented Thompson's reputation as
'common property of the church and the public'.[111] The course of six lectures Thompson delivered in Manchester, and again before the Liverpool
Mechanics' Institution, shows the linkage. He presented an overview of
India's history and its resources, its imperial history since the Moghuls,
British incursions and administration, and religious diversity, and he cul-
minated with a lecture on the 'exhaustless resources of the soil' capable
of supplying Britain with 'tropical produce' (tea, sugar, coffee, etc.) but
stunted by the land tax. India, he argued, warranted the 'benefits to be
derived from a wise and liberal policy' under a more just administration.[112]
This demonstrates his adherence to free trade principles and sets India
as a parallel case to Britain's tariffs on imported grain: Britain's agrarian
working classes suffered from high bread prices because of protective tariffs
(instead of allowing markets to self-regulate), just as the Indian peasantry
bore the brunt of reduced opportunities to labour in a globalised market
(and thus were kept in perpetual penury).

Cobden is credited with linking 'the repeal of taxes on the necessities
of life and a policy of general free trade' in the popular imagination.[113]
As J. R. Parry argues, liberals embraced free trade for both its constitutional and economic merits, for 'it demonstrated a willingness to respond
to popular grievances, showed that the State was not controlled by narrow vested interests, and might also diminish the severe divisions between
town and country. Taxation, similarly, involved questions of accountability and sectional or class favouritism'.[114] Though there was not a project to
'improve the civilization' of the North of England (as there was in India)
the interests of labourers and small property holders there were put in relation to commodity aggregation, burdensome taxation, and international
trade. This is apparent in a lecture Thompson delivered to working men
in Longtown, near Carlisle, early in 1842, where he demonstrated both a
grasp of classical economic theory and the ability to convey this in populist
terms. As a paid lecturer for the ACLL, he utilised the same criteria of analysis as for the Indian situation. For example, he pointed to the sliding scale
on grain duties (from 1s to £1/5/8 per quarter) that made grain importation

the vocation of 'gambling speculators ... who contrive to manage the averages' across seasons, bringing grain in only when domestic supplies are lowest, so they can 'reap enormous gains at the expense of a hungry and starving population'.[115] This inflated the price of bread while restricting transactions with foreign countries because they, in turn, imposed penalties on British goods, thereby ruining trade. This, Thompson insisted, was the impediment to modernisation. When a heckler suggested that instead it was machinery that ruined his prosperity, Thompson countered:

> There is a practice among sporting men of tying a red herring to a string, and trailing it along the ground, to draw the dogs off the right scent. (Laughter.) Corn Law makers are good sportsmen. (Laughter.) The people are in full cry after the Corn Laws, and the gentry who live by them want to puzzle and divide the pack. They have got the red herring of *machinery*, and the red herring of *currency*, and the red herring of *over-production*, and the red herring of *emigration*, and they are employing men in all directions to trail these herrings over the path of the people. Beware of the red herring. (Loud laughter and cheers.)[116]

Because land taxes had not been reassessed since 1694, those with high earnings were vastly under taxed. How else, Thompson posed, could the land tax yield only half of the tax on tobacco?[117] Appealing to the audience's everyday practices, he reminded them that it was manufacturers who bought their products (grain, beef, butter, and eggs), and farmers could never have too many buyers. The competitive edge faced by manufacturing and landed interests put such small producers at a disadvantage, compounding the taxation inequities. 'A far better case could be made out in favour of a bounty to increase the importation of Corn, than a duty or a sliding scale to restrain it.'[118]

The ACLL's campaign to uphold free trade as 'the pole-star of Liberalism' came to fruition in 1846, when the laws were repealed under the Tory Robert Peel's (1788–1850) premiership.[119] During this campaign, Thompson split his attention between the Anti-Corn Law agitation and the case of the raja of Satara. As peculiar as it seems for Thompson to turn to this this regal *cause célèbre*, it helped him keep Indian matters in the public eye for eight years and pointed to the need for radical reform in the administration of Britain's most populous dominion.

## The Case against the Company

At the conclusion of the Third Anglo-Maratha War in 1818, when the British usurped the Peshwa government of the Maratha Empire, virtually the entire subcontinent south of the Sutlej River was consolidated under British control. A treaty established a descendent of Shivaji, Pratap Singh (1793–1847, Purtaub Singh), as figurehead on the throne of the small principality of Satara in Maharashtra. Fifteen years later, The Company brought three charges against Raja Pratap Singh: he had conversed with subedars (native captains) to incite Sepoy soldiers to rise against the British; he had carried on treasonous correspondence with the ex-raja of Nagpore (Nagpur), trying to lure Sepoys' allegiance away from the British and to call in aid from the Russians and Turks to expel the British; and he had carried on treasonous correspondence with the Portuguese governor of Goa, encouraging the Queen of Portugal to send 30,000 troops to drive the British from India on the promise that, if this action was successful, the subcontinent would be divided between Satara and Portugal. The Bombay (Mumbai) Presidency ordered the raja to be confined in Poona, and from 12 October to 4 November 1836 he was tried in absentia by a secret commission in Satara, given no opportunity to respond to charges or see the evidence used against him, and forbidden from presenting his own evidence. When he sought advice from trusted British officials about his predicament the correspondence was intercepted. According to evidence later presented by Arthur J. Lewis (a Company proprietor), the raja displaced Sepoys' huts for stables, which created acrimony between the prince and the soldiers, but not the prince and the British.[120] Correspondence from Colonel Peter Lodwick (?–1873, the Resident at Satara) acknowledged that no one could be found to speak to the second charge and that it had been fabricated by the raja's disgruntled dewan (chief officer), who had in fact been imprisoned by Colonel Charles Ovans (1793?–1858, Lodwick's successor at Satara).[121] At the time, the ex-raja of Nagpore was 'a wretched fugitive; subsisting on the bounty of the raja of Joudpore [Jodhpur, Rajputana]' and so was in no position to excite the tsar or sultan.[122] The charge of collusion with the Portuguese, based on forged letters suspiciously bought by The Company in a Goan pawnshop, was vigorously denied by the Portuguese governor of Goa.[123] That should have been enough to end the matter, yet the raja was found guilty on all charges. His brother, Appa Sahib (?–1849, aka Raja Shahaji), a feckless puppet of the British authorities, was installed in his place.[124] When, by 1848, both brothers had died, Governor-General Lord Dalhousie (1812–60) refused to recognise either the Raja Shahaji's son, Venkoji Raje (adopted just hours before the raja expired) or the former Raja Pratap Singh's son, Durgasing (the child of his cousin, adopted in 1845) as heir.[125] This countered the Hindu practice of inheritance and set a precedent under the doctrine of lapse. Thus, the

Mahratta line was extinguished and Satara devolved to British ownership, just as Jaitpur, Sambalpur, Baghat, Chota Udaipur, Jhansi, and Nagpore would be accessioned between 1848 and 1854. Through annexation, secession, capture, or subterfuge, the British took control of Indian principalities and consolidated power and influence across the subcontinent.

What is remarkable about this case is not that foreign autocratic governors installed an Indian leader then stripped him of a voice – nor that they revoked his title, confiscated most of his wealth, and sent him into exile in Benares (Varanasi) – but that the British were almost immediately uncomfortable about their actions.[126] The secret commission generated 2,000 pages of parliamentary papers, none of which justified a charge. Wanting to 'bury in oblivion' the affair, the governor of Bombay (Sir James Carnac, 1784–1846) attempted to force a new treaty on the ex-raja in conjunction with a pardon.[127] But any reconciliatory gesture from The Company could not extend to forgiveness, for the ex-raja refused to acknowledge cause. Ex-raja Pratap Singh unfailingly protested his innocence and fully cooperated with the British in the hope that his fortune and his honour, if not his title, would be restored. As he was held in Benares under authority of the Presidency of Calcutta, his next line of appeal was The Company in London. He sent agents hence, but they were shut out of the halls of power and returned to India. In February 1840, the Court of Proprietors in London declined to hold an inquiry.[128] The most faithful of the raja's agents, Rungo Bapojee, whom B.D. Basu calls 'the first Indian agitator in England', stayed until 1 July 1841, when The Company paid off his mounting debts and bought him a ticket home.[129] This ensured he would not be present two weeks later when the Court of Proprietors in London convened a Special General Court in order to consider the entirety of evidence against the ex-raja. This was conducted in the form of a meeting, not a trial procedure or appeal to a higher court. In essence, though, the proprietors presided on their own judgement. For five days, they considered the evidence that had resulted in the raja's deposition.

It appears to have been Bapojee who entreated George Thompson to take up the cause. Thompson's friends bought stock in Thompson's name, qualifying him for a seat in the Court of Proprietors, where he joined the other shareholders to participate in the tribunal.[130] He presented himself to the assembly as someone unknown to the ex-raja and expecting nothing from him: based on Thompson's attestation, his purpose was solely to argue for justice.[131] It was unsaid, because it did not need to be said, that he was really there to undermine The Company by proving its actions unlawful.

Shortly after Thompson rose to speak, another proprietor broke in to object to Thompson reading his remarks. Thompson deftly noted the 'volume by my side' rife with printed speeches read to the court on numerous occasions and his concern that by any pretext 'the forfeiture of the power to discuss the political affairs of India, was held *in terrorem* over us, to put an end, as it seemed, to our discussion altogether'.[132] Then, setting down his prepared remarks, he established his keynote about the ex-raja's character. A series of antitheses amplified across examples pointed out that in his constancy,

> the firmness of the Raja was called obstinacy—the jealousy he had shown in defence of his honour, and his repeated protestations of innocence—all this was a mere hypocritical denial of guilt, similar to the professions of a man at the gallows. His talent was cunning, his pretended loyalty, covert treason; and, to sum up all, and justify every act committed against him, we were told he was ambitious.

Thompson then launched an extended riff on *Julius Caesar*, rousing the assembly:

> The Raja must be guilty, says one, for Mr. [Mountstuart] Elphinstone [1779–1859, governor of Bombay Province 1819–27] is a wise and prudent man. The Raja must be guilty, says another, for Lord Auckland [1784–1849, governor-general of India 1836–42], as every body admits, is a firm and sagacious statesman. The Raja must be guilty, says a third, for Sir James Carnac [chairman of the Company 1835–38 and governor of Bombay 1839–41] is kind, and generous, and forgiving. The Raja must be guilty, says a fourth, for, as you all do know, the Directors are most upright and honourable men. (Cheers and laughter).

The new raja, by contrast, was 'a debauched, abandoned profligate. A sordid and corrupt judge. An ambitious and usurping brother', a traitor to The Company and his deposed sibling.

> Now, gentlemen, 'Look on this picture—and on this'—and tell me, which you do prefer—Appa Sahib, or Purtub Sing [*sic*]? 'But Brutus says he was ambitious.' (Much applause.)

And so, he showed the raja's conviction was endorsed with as much 'evidence [as] upon which a police magistrate would not send a beggar to the treadmill. (Hear, hear, and loud cheers.)'[133] As motive, Thompson cited a minute from Sir James Carnac dated 4 September 1839, stipulating that since 'neither the ex-Raja nor his brother had children The Company would disregard the Hindu custom of appointing an heir and thereby let Satara lapse to the British government', an admission of premeditated intent to annex the kingdom. 'Here behold the history of all the past anni-hilated princes of India. (Cheers.)' Thompson then turned the case from a matter of guilt or innocence to a question of due process and the integrity of British jurisprudence. Even if the Raja was guilty, the principles of judi-cial procedure were egregiously violated and, quoting from director John Shepherd, 'THE SIMPLE PRINCIPLES OF JUSTICE CANNOT BE DESTROYED BY ANY PRECEDENT WHATEVER'.[134]

Lodwick, who refused to continue as the governor's tool, was removed from his post, and testified in London that the way the commission adju-dicated in Satara against the raja 'reminded him of the country justice who always formed his opinion from hearing only one side of a case, lest attending to the other should confuse his judgment. (A laugh.)' Colonel Ovans, who succeeded as Resident at Satara, had been one of the secret commissioners. His explicit, duplicitous charge from Bombay was to pro-voke Pratap Singh to breach the treaty of 1819. He commanded witnesses to suborn themselves and authorised forged depositions; consistently neglected to supply the raja with the documents produced for the secret Commission; and fabricated the charges that the raja had conspired with the Portuguese and the ex-raja of Nagpore.[135] Even so, at the tribunal in London these contentions were shown to be laden with prejudice. On the fifth day of debate, Thompson tried a tactical manoeuvre to oppose an amendment and declare the ex-raja innocent, but was unsuccessful. The suggestion that an impartial committee be formed to investigate was unsuccessful. A motion that the Court of Directors reconsider the ques-tion was unsuccessful. A motion to restore the raja or to restore his prop-erty was unsuccessful. The chairman's motion that 'it was inexpedient to interfere with the responsible Executive, and the amendment' carried. Not only was the decision upheld but officials in Bombay were commended for their zeal.[136]

The Court of Proprietors was not normally well attended: its business was dull, and most proprietors left the directors to get on with it. Yet for this tribunal the benches were packed with gentlemen prepared to protect their investment, including prospects of a cadetship or writership for a son or nephew ambitious to make a mark in India (Figure 2.2).[137] Thompson's accustomed success in pulling auditors to his side and turning opinion to near unanimity failed him. Records of laughter, cheering, and applause that punctuate his speeches are sympathetic *and* derisive, encouraging *and* dismissive, defensively genial *and* sneeringly negatory. He made a dull matter exciting by his wit and panache, but he was unsuccessful in garner-ing enough votes to change The Company's stance.

Figure 2.2    East India Court of Proprietors. *Illustrated London News*, 4 May 1844, 289.
Getty Images.

In July 1842, a Special Court was convened to examine some of the
papers used by the secret commission. Nevertheless, the moment the chairman took his place he declared the court adjourned. For an hour, appeals
were made to allow discussion, but to no avail. Then Thompson arrived
and determined to block the adjournment, keeping the directors from a
grand dinner at the Mansion House by speaking for four hours. After a
while, the sun set and he requested candles so he could see his documents.
This was refused, and ten minutes passed in silence as Thompson partook
of refreshments brought by his friends. 'Sir James Weir Hogg, perceiving
the physical advantage Mr. Thompson was gaining from rest … rang the
bell, and ordered in candles', whereupon another speaker launched into
a three-hour speech. It went on like this until 2:00 a.m. (twelve hours in
total). Thompson recalled 'the clamors, the epithets, the gnashing of teeth,

the threats, the insinuations, and the insults that were showered upon me. It was a day of proud triumph for the friends of the Raja. It was a day of deep humiliation and defeat for the Directors'. For exposing Colonel Ovans, Thompson was 'branded as a *liar* and a *liabeller*' but he countered by accusing the directors of a deliberate cover-up.[138]

Thompson claimed at a meeting of the Court of Proprietors on 23 September 1843 that all eleven of his charges against Ovans were proven.[139] This was in vain. The following February, another motion was put to the Court of Directors for the ex-raja to be restored, or at least heard. To avoid a vote the chairman declared an adjournment that carried forty-six to sixteen. Again, in March 1845 the same tactic was used. That July, knowing that The Company had paid out thousands of pounds for legal advice on deposing the raja, Thompson called upon the Court of Directors to 'produce the opinion of any other legal gentleman, in favor of the legality of that act'. Again, the old decision was reaffirmed. In August 1845, two days' discussion transpired respecting Ovans' actions. Rungo Bapojee, who had returned to England and qualified as a proprietor, seconded Thompson's motion and addressed the assembly in Hindi.[140] Thompson requested an impartial investigation, Mr Lewis countered with a motion that the ex-raja be heard, but yet again the old decision was affirmed. And in October 1845, Thompson tendered support of twelve charges against Ovans, moving that a select committee be struck to investigate. He was 'met by a direct negative from the Chair', who declared Ovans innocent.[141] The issue was pressed upon the Privy Council: five hours' debate ensued in Parliament, the proposition strenuously resisted by the government. Thompson reflected that 'I would have given 6 months of my life for an hour to reply' to a 'wicked speech' by Sir James Hogg (1790–1876), Liberal MP for Beverley and a Company director.[142]

Dogged and unbowed, Thompson tried again on 17 December 1845, this time calling for the directors to formally impeach Colonel Ovans on the rebuffed charges of perpetrating a series of wilful frauds, concealments, forgeries, and perjuries. Thompson was roundly abused until, finally, on 23 September 1846 he tried another stunt, saying to the Court of Proprietors: '*I agree to a sentence of self-excommunication from the society of true and honourable men, if I do not prove my charges.... I will refer to none of these, save those which have emanated from Colonel Ovans himself, and bear his own signature,* or are declared authentic, *by his own letters.*' This was a deliberate inversion, in the public eye, of the procedure used against ex-raja Pratap Singh. Thompson pointed out:

> On your side are power, boundless wealth, all the resources of law, a strong sympathy with the accused, the means of obtaining any amount of

assistance, the certainty of being heard to any extent, the assurance that you have an audience that will attach the utmost weight to whatever you can say in refutation of these charges—and here, on the other side, I stand alone, weak in body, all but exhausted in mind, deeply conscious of the responsibility I have assumed, without one friend to aid me. No matter—alone, unfriended, I challenge you to the trial, and may Heaven defend the right!

The facts that Thompson presented were neither contradicted nor disproved, yet the motion was defeated without a division. Still, he persisted 'for the sake of the people of India', whatever the cost to the reputations of The Company, to clean the 'Augean stable of corruption'.[143] Thompson took the issue to a director, Joseph Hume (1777–1855, an MP and ACLL campaigner), who took up the matter in Parliament with determination but not distinction.[144] Meanwhile, Thompson continued to use his right as a proprietor to participate in debates about the salt duty, the use of torture by tax collectors, and the building of railways in India.[145]

In 1849, Henry Brewster Stanton (1805–87) likened 'the gallant' Thompson's first appearance at the Court of Proprietors to Sir Philip Francis (1740–1818) standing up against the notorious Warren Hastings (1732–1818, Governor-General of Bengal 1772–85), 'laden with rupees and flushed with triumphs', in the 1780s.[146] If he was gallant, was he also effective? In 1967, the Indian scholar S. R. Mehrotra grudgingly conceded that 'a little good' arose from the British India Society's advancement of the ex-raja of Satara's case for 'it put the East India Company on the defensive'. He went on to stipulate what are in fact very significant shifts: 'It was partly as a result of the Society's efforts that The Company encouraged the cultivation of cotton and the investment of British capital in India, abolished slavery and mitigated the severities of the resumption laws. The most notable achievement of the Society, however, lay in the fact that it stimulated political agitation in India.'[147] The ongoing agitation at East India House in London demonstrated that The Company was under scrutiny, and singled out George Thompson as an advocate for resisting the British powerhouse. A group of young Indians eagerly took hold of Thompson's mantle.

Around the same time that Thompson had whet his appetite for debate at the London Literary and Scientific Association, the non-sectarian Hindoo College in Calcutta (founded in 1817 and admitting young men of all faiths, including scholarship students) formed a debating club, where the eponymous 'Young Bengal read Tom Paine, admired revolutionary France, hated the British Tories, wrote poems about the fallen state of his motherland and dreamt of a free and self-governing India in the future'.[148]

By the mid-1830s restrictions were loosened on the press in presidency towns, and by 1838 a Bengali weekly, *Prabodh Chandrodaya*, had 800 subscribers. Such developments were not limited to Calcutta: in many cities Indians founded newspapers, clubs, schools, missions, and societies that reflected their animosity to The Company's governance, protested in meetings, circulated petitions, and sent deputations representing popular opinion to governors. Discussion focused on sati (suttee), land and agricultural reform, rights to redress, and taxation, where by 'precept and example [they] taught their Indian fellow-subjects the art of constitutional agitation'.[149] In 1837, the Landholders' Society emerged out of this, 'with the primary object of carrying on constitutional agitation against an allegedly arbitrary, unjust and injurious measure of the British Government in India'. This functioned as a Chamber of Commerce for landed (native) interests in Calcutta, and though technically without respect to caste or country of origin, it never shook its aristocratic image.[150] The Landholders' Society organised a petition with 20,000 signatures opposing the resumption of rent-free lands, which was adopted at a public meeting with 5,000 attendees.[151] The society's heyday was short-lived, but its influence was not: Rajendralal Mitra (1824–91, president of the British Indian Association) referred to it in 1868 as 'the pioneer of freedom in this country', which gave Indians 'the first lesson in the art of fighting constitutionally for their rights, and taught them how to manfully assert their claims and give expression to their opinions'. Members sought a permanent parliamentary agent in London and, by becoming the communicating society with the British India Society in 1839, found the partnership they needed.[152]

Transcontinental knowledge exchange was crucial to activists' success. In 1842, the prominent estate holder, trader, and banker Dwarkanath Tagore (1794–1846, grandfather to Nobel laureate playwright Rabindranath Tagore) travelled to Europe (Figure 2.3).[153] While in Britain he visited hospitals and asylums, schools, dockyards, factories, breweries, printers, steelworks, engine makers, and the theatre. He witnessed a Chartist march in Scotland, which drew his awareness to the 300,000 unemployed, as well as the rough treatment that the starving in Britain endured at the hands of the military. While he was 'the urbane diplomat, emissary from the people of India, playing the "Grand Mogul", surrounded by his retainers, and exchanging gifts, courtesies, and hospitality' when he hobnobbed with royalty – even renting a barge for parties on the Thames to reciprocate hospitality – he also established strong ties with Lord Brougham and Joseph Pease.[154] Tagore was a forward-thinking entrepreneur, Calcutta's most prominent citizen, who encouraged 'interracial alliances with the

Figure 2.3    Dwarkanath Tagore (1846), steel mezzotint engraved by George Raphael
Ward after a painting by Frederick Richard Say, 1846, 1110.1.
British Museum.

non-official European community to promote an improved judicial system, local control of steam shipping between India and Europe, the abolition of the East India Company, the rights of landlords and the development of India's resources'.[155] As much as he recognised The Company's rapacity, he believed in the importance, indeed necessity, of British influence to provide government in India, for along with this came British technology, administrative order and acumen, and military strength at the frontiers.[156] Like Jamesthjee Jejeebhoy (1783–1859) in Bombay, he envisioned an 'inter-racial partnership' between Indians and the British in commerce, admin-istration, and philanthropy.[157] Thus, there was a basis for alliance with Thompson, even though Tagore also assented to receive a gold medal from the directors of the East India Company and was fêted by Queen Victoria (1819–1901) and Prince Albert (1819–61).[158]

Tagore invited Thompson to accompany him on his return journey to India, and they set out in early November 1842. After dreaming, read-ing, talking, and writing so much of India, Thompson finally had the opportunity to 'see the country for myself … mingle with its people … and through the knowledge acquired by travelling and observation, be able to be of more service to the cause of my fellow-subjects here'. While gracious, this was not mere ingratiation: during his stay, Thompson studied up to twelve hours per day and consistently sought the society of English-speaking Indians, both within organisations and for infor-mal concourse. He questioned whether published sources, which he had scoured for the past five years, accurately and completely represented India, and felt it vital to obtain the *best* information in order to inform the government and persuade Indians to the importance of 'becom-ing the narrators of their own grievances, as far as they suffered under any, that were removable by legislation', resulting in more beneficial rule.[159] During his first six months in Calcutta, Thompson continued as Tagore's guest. This show of confidence and hospitality, Thompson wrote, 'has caused all shyness to wear away from the natives. They have entire confidence in me and except that the <u>Zenana</u> [the portion of the house reserved for women] is sacred I go to their houses as one of them-selves. They flock around me at all hours, walk in and out of my rooms for all doors are open, and seem quite at home with "<u>Hindoo Thompson Sahib Bahadoor</u>" as they call me'.[160]

Thompson was sought out as a speaker, but it was his demonstration of oratorical tactics and advice on organising that ensured lasting impact. A few days after he disembarked in Calcutta, on the invitation of the self-made businessman Ramgopal Ghose (1815–68, styled the 'Indian

Demosthenes'), Thompson gave his first address to the Society for the Acquisition of General Knowledge at the Hindoo College. In another speech (the annual dinner of the Agricultural and Horticultural Society), Thompson refused to be silenced by a US guest on the topic of slavery. Defying his heckler, Thompson espoused his central idea of enhancing India as a producer of cotton, rice, tobacco, and sugar – all the tropical products Britain was dependent upon the United States to grow – and importer of manufactured English goods, a classic liberal view linking trade to peace and progress to colonialism.[161] The evidence for improvement was before him: an assembly of men educated in philosophy and English at the Hindoo College, prospering in business, strengthening ties with Asian and European commercial partners, and longing for the freedom to institute reforms in governance. As Boaventura de Sousa Santos puts it, 'there are knowledges born in the struggle and knowledges useful to the struggle', and Thompson's auditors seemed to know what to do with both, 'for the epistemologies of the South, objectivity is always intersubjectivity, indeed, self-conscious intersubjectivity. Thus, the knowledges born in or used in the struggle are always cocreations'.[162] As Thompson stated, technology annihilated distance while marking difference, escalating the rapidity of travel.[163] He marked how Young Bengal (a rising educated elite, multi-lingual and schooled in English, mathematics, history, and law) was connected to a worldwide system, for with the printing press and the steam vessel thoughts are carried with 'inconceivable rapidity … over the face of the Globe'. By embracing these technologies, Bengalis 'will learn to know England, and England will learn to know them. Knowledge will beget intimacy – intimacy will lead to friendship – and friendship will ripen into love'.[164]

The tone and message of Thompson's public speeches modulated during his first months in India, veering away from himself (or any Briton) as a source of inspiration and toward the means for individual and collective self-sufficiency. At a meeting at the home of Chunder Saikhur Deb on 30 January 1843, he urged educated Indians to pursue self-improvement and look to themselves for what they wished to obtain.[165] At weekly gatherings in the garden house of Sreekisen Singh he stressed that through sharing information in fellowship, and giving access to various strata making up the community, 'one man is able to advise, another to execute. One man may give time, another money, another labour, another influence; and thus the work proceeds'. He desired to see this brotherhood of aspiring innovators – joined together with many complexions – 'aroused to a consciousness of their own individual responsibility, capacity, and duty' in order to 'enroll themselves in the cause of their country' and assert their rights. He encouraged his associates to form a society, curate topics for discussion, and improve members' experience in literary composition through mild and friendly criticism of public speaking. Otherwise, when meetings were called at the Town Hall on weighty questions effecting Indians, all the speakers would be foreigners.[166]

There is a Realpolitik in Thompson's speeches that acknowledges grievances and the urge to find homegrown solutions. This is neither revolutionary speech nor speech contradictory to a liberal view of colonialism. Thompson urged his listeners to adopt for India 'a moral armoury' honed in Britain as an imperative counterpart to the 'physical one' of a military.[167] In other words, this is exactly the advice of using the master's tools to dismantle the master's house that Audre Lorde finds objectionable because it cannot bring about genuine change, and yet it was a tactic Young Bengal could embrace: education, self-improvement, and a greater share of their world under a British mandate.[168] If it did not examine the basis of colonialised knowledge, it was nevertheless open to being an ecology of exchanged knowledge between liberal Britons and Young Bengal, building capacity for later struggles by bringing into being a metacultural counterpublic, and reflexively engaging in discourse as a social entity.[169]

Two months into his sojourn in India, Thompson had mustered a large and loyal following, while seeking to learn at least as much as he taught. No wonder he was so unpopular with the English-language press. He claimed consistency with principles he had advocated in his British speeches, in essence promoting a process similar to Chartism: 'Make yourselves acquainted with the nature of the laws under which you live; the defects in those laws, which concern your earthly happiness and well being; learn the causes and extent of your country's grievances, and then spread your complaints in memorials and petitions before your rulers.'[170]

Thompson was emphatic – controversially so – in his opposition to the 'antagonism of race' that was the basis of British rule in India. Heedless of talents and education, the system was 'hereditary, *personal*, and inherent', and it judged Indians both unfit and ineligible to rise to the judiciary. Indeed, as subjects of 'military despotism' (epitomised by the raja of Satara) Indians had no right to self-representation and were shut out of 'every office of trust, honour, or emolument' at the disposition of the British.[171] In essence, Thompson wished to inspire Young Bengal to take power. Learning, coupled with self-awareness, enabled analysis and critique. In proposing that Young Bengal found an institution that would enable Indians to take charge of their own fate, he envisioned mentoring and advocacy roles for himself, stipulating that 'while you adhere to your original resolutions, *I will never desert you.*... I will carry your complaints before every tribunal at which I am permitted to stand. I will seek to multiply the number of your friends among the wise and generous and humane of my own country'.[172]

On 20 April 1843, the Bengal branch of the British India Society was called into being to ameliorate the condition of the Indian people and enhance the country's prosperity. It endorsed the importance of individual duty in the common cause yet put forth measures consistent with loyalty to British dominions, sovereignty, and laws. (This endorsement countered accusations that the members, though mainly Hindus, promoted a Muslim system of governance, which would have been anathema in Hindu-majority Bengal.) Any adult able to pay dues and not currently studying at a public seminary could join the society.[173]

The Bengal British India Society is credited with addressing 'almost every important question, political, social or economic affecting Bengal in particular and the country in general'. It effectively lobbied for reform in the legislative councils (including a separate council for Bengal), separation of judicial and executive functions, improvements in policing and municipal administration, and more consultation on financial decisions. Over time, it mitigated racially discriminatory practices, increasing representation of Indians in the upper echelons of the civil service. And, in keeping with reform principles of the Manchester School, its advocacy adjusted the tax burden for the Second Afghan War (1878–9); reduced duties on cotton goods; championed more liberal provisions for education, lower postage on newspapers, and disestablishment of the Anglican Church in India; brought attention to the causes of famines and epidemics; and promoted agriculture through fairs and exhibitions.[174]

Mehrotra claims that 'George Thompson's oratory cast a spell over the rising generation of Bengalis' and repeats the acknowledgement that he was the 'father of political education in India'.[175] That is not contested. His speeches were immediately collected and printed, and in 1895 seventeen of them were reprinted. In accordance with Thompson's guidance, the 170 members of the society (mostly Indians) convened no 'monster meetings' but held regular orderly meetings once a month, formed subcommittees that wrote reports, examined legislation, drafted petitions, and investigated the condition of *raiyats* (peasant tenants) in lower Bengal. These measures kept the native establishment at a distance and offended orthodox Hindus, yet worried British authorities enough for them to woo prominent members away from the society and into judicial posts.[176] The society was a locus for studying problems, not the basis for mounting significant agitation. As Thompson said, 'for the work of agitation and petitioning, as carried on in England, you are not yet prepared. You have no representative body, no *public*, in the English sense of the word. Beyond your own immediate neighbourhood, all is tame acquiescence, or sullen discontent, or interested connivance, or profound ignorance, or perfect helplessness'.[177] The actions Thompson recommended, and which the society's members took up effectively, focused on research and knowledge acquisition as the basis for advocacy, not a broad movement and certainly not sedition. They adapted the tradition of 'noisy *addas*' (in which men, including social leaders, collected for idle talk) and the *majlish* (parlour gatherings of rich men incorporating recitations, drinking, and dancing girls) into purposeful self-improvement for political aims.[178]

Instead of a holistic application of his political experience, Thompson cherry picked. In important ways this is consistent with his tactics in the United States. In both contexts, he implemented a moral campaign through which locals were to discover their own political aims and legislative agendas, but in India he did so without the additional mandate of immediatism (as in abolition), revolutionary change, or the building of a mass movement. This view was not antagonistic to the growing missionary influence (itself a locus of increasing resentment among Hindus from the 1830s), yet Thompson knew it was not the place for Bible Politics. He eschewed any sectarian or partisan allegiance in favour of pan-cultural participation, which smoothed the way for minority Muslim, Parsi, and Christian participation in Hindu-majority Calcutta. The idea was to use the Bengal British India Society as a public sphere in which ideas would emerge for making partnerships between Indians and the British, then leverage ongoing change in the judiciary and civil service, foster educational institutions with progressive curricula for young men and women, examine and reform traditional practices through legislation, and create a fairer and more sustainable basis for agricultural taxation involving both peasants and landholders. C.A. Bayly calls this 'lived life of ideas' the essential 'performative aspect of liberalism', whereby for a new generation of Indian liberals thought was 'generated out of an increasingly dense set of institutions, the law, public meetings and learned societies'.[179] Newspapers were essential to amplifying this public sphere, yet the society was to be the cauldron where ideas arose: a place for discussing ideas, honing debate and writing skills, and keeping progressive Indians and Europeans connected in common cause. Thereby, the gradualism would be organically rooted in this generation of reformers, not under British scrutiny yet devoted to radically changing the nature of colonial rule, if not the colonial ruler.[180]

Following Dwarkanath Tagore's death in 1846, the Bengal British India Society faltered. In 1851, a successor organisation emerged, the British India Association, with many of the same leaders but no Europeans. This marked the end of close cooperation between Indians and non-official Anglo-Indians in Bengali public life.[181] In 1876, the Indian Association was formed, consisting mainly of lawyers, journalists, and teachers who found inspiration in the Italian revolutionary Giuseppe Mazzini (1805–72) to work toward a united self-governing India. It failed to gain a national profile or even a regional footing in Bengal.[182]

For the remainder of Thompson's year in India he turned his attention to securing his own future, and future agenda. He travelled to Uttar Pradesh, stopping for three hours in Benares to meet with the ex-raja of Satara at the home of Governor-General Major Carpenter, then proceeded to Allahabad and Cawnpore.[183] He was en route to visit Shah Bahadur II (1775–1862), who had succeeded in 1837 as the last Mughal emperor and king of Delhi. This was nominal sovereignty, as the shah's power was restricted to Shahjahanabad, the walled city of Old Delhi, and he was pensioned by The Company. Yet he pulled out all the stops for Thompson, offering lavish hospitality: as Thompson approached Delhi on 29 July 1843, three miles outside the city 'he was met by half a dozen of the nobles of the Court with a large phalanx of attendants and was conducted to the residence allotted to him on the king's elephant, richly caparisoned, with a glittering Howday [sic] and splendid trappings. Every possible attention was shewn him' (Figure 2.4).[184] The shah sought to appoint Thompson as his agent (or ambassador) to advocate for his interests in London, and bestowed on him 'a document in Persian, handsomely engrossed and framed, in which he is styled "the wise, the high in rank, the well wisher of either side, the deputed of the Shah of Hindoostan"'.[185] During his stay, Thompson spoke frequently with the shah, the shah's sons, and nobles, remaining much occupied in sightseeing and ceremonial entertainments with 'military, civil, and clerical gentlemen' for weeks before he could get to 'the actual business which brought me to the King'.[186] The precise nature of Thompson's remit is unknown, and he does not appear to have effected anything significant on the shah's behalf once he returned to London, but

Figure 2.4    Shah of Delhi's Elephant, part of the Shah's retinue for processions
magnificently documented by Sir Thomas Metcalfe (1795–1853), Add.Or.5475, fol.59c-B.
British Library.

he was accorded a monthly 1,000 rupee allowance.[187] Thompson left Delhi
on 23 November 1843, 'having as the *Delhi Gazette* says, settled every thing
with his Majesty to his own satisfaction', stopped again in Benares to speak
with the ex-raja of Satara, and set sail from Calcutta on 14 December.[188]

## Race: Principles and Performance Strategies

Three factors contribute to game-shifting tactics that became apparent in
the latter half of the 1840s: accrued networks, internationalism, and race
politics. Carrying out activist work in this context was *personal* as well as
*social*, constituting one-on-one relationships that required cultivation and
hospitality, honed over time. In order to make networks function, there
needed to be strong ties among abolitionists within Britain and abroad,
subsuming international work into domestic life to build alliances and
consolidate support. Thus, while trying to persuade Glasgow abolitionists
to support Indian emancipation, Thompson would 'get them to my own
house to breakfast (nothing like putting our opinions into tea, & coffee
& between bread & butter when you want folks to swallow them!)'.[189]
When Nathaniel Peabody Rogers (1794–1846, editor of the Concord, New

Hampshire, newspaper *Herald of Freedom*), Charles Lenox Remond (1810–73, the first Black lecturing agent for the American Anti-Slavery Society), and John Dunlop (1789–1868, Scotland's leading temperance advocate) showed up on Thompson's Edinburgh doorstep in October 1840, they commenced a week's residence together. They had last seen one another six days earlier at an anti-slavery meeting in Newcastle-upon-Tyne. Thompson cordially welcomed them, his elder daughters Louisa (aged nine) and Amelia (aged seven), sons Herbert (aged six, 'the little one born in New England') and William Lloyd Garrison (aged four), and youngest child, Elizabeth Pease ('one little orator about a week old'), adding to the reception.[190] Across intersectional identities of race, nation, and cause, the men were fellow members of a self-organised counterpublic: mutually bound by supportive, personal, and impersonal factors.[191] Six months later, Thompson was still making introductions for Remond when they were in Manchester.[192] A lot of breakfast meetings had ensued in the meantime. When abolitionists toured, speaking at the meetings of branch societies, they were invariably hosted by key members of those localities, which created affective and pragmatic connections, strengthening transatlantic ties in ways that ongoing correspondences could not. This warmth is evident in the practice of hosting friends of friends carrying letters of introduction and, most poignantly, in that of designating namesakes: not only Thompson's two youngest children but also Caroline Garrison Bishop (1846–1929, daughter of Rev. Francis Bishop), named while Garrison made his second tour in Britain, and three of Garrison's seven children, George 'Dordie' Thompson Garrison (1836–1904, his eldest), Wendell Phillips Garrison (1840–1907), and Elizabeth Pease Garrison (1846–8).[193] Warmth was also extended to utter strangers: Unitarian minister Francis Bishop (1813–69) turned the Liverpool Town Mission into a terminus of the Underground Railroad, receiving Black freedom-seekers and fixing them up with funding and employment; likewise, Dr John Estlin (1785–1855) and his daughter, Mary Anne Estlin (1820–1902), received fugitives and found them solid footings in Bristol. In recognition, Ellen Craft and William Craft named their eldest child Charles Estlin Phillips Craft (1852–1938), honouring colleagues on both sides of the ocean.[194] Newly arrived African Americans finding temporary or permanent refuge in England, plying trades, pursuing education, and raising children 'not to work up into rice, sugar and tobacco, but to watch over, regard, and protect', may have contributed to abolitionist organisations, yet most of their names are lost to history.[195] Their counterparts who showed oratorical ability were sponsored by and often absorbed into abolitionist networks' ongoing work.[196]

Black abolitionist orators who ventured into integrated organisations and lecture circuits, particularly transnationally, show another facet of counterpublic networking. In Dwight Conquergood's terms, the ultimate form of the 'talking book' – memoir and autobiography – 'recitationally' performed oratorical acumen.[197] When auto-didacts John Sella Martin (1832–76) and Frederick Douglass published memoirs that recounted histories whose origins were in an underground Black counterpublic, having the endorsement of white abolitionists was important. For example, just before he set sail for India, Thompson wrote a brief introduction to *The Narrative of the Life of Moses Grandy*, a slave memoir that appeared in British and US editions.[198] Thompson stresses the importance of receiving a letter from a US abolitionist who vouched for Grandy's (c. 1786–?) story and worthy character. Then, hearing Grandy's 'artless tale', he appreciated the delivery of first-hand knowledge of US slavery, which, stated in Grandy's own words, could gratify his wish to raise funds to purchase any more of his children whom he was able to find 'in captivity'.[199] The text was quickly brought into print, ready for sale when Grandy spoke at the Anti-Slavery Society in Birmingham on 18 November 1842, exactly one month after Thompson signed his introduction. John Scoble (1799–1877) organised a tour and introduced Grandy at the Anti-Slavery Convention the following June.[200] This reflected the early pattern for British philanthropists interacting with African American abolitionists within Britain. Transatlantic networks were drawn upon to authenticate individuals and then to bring them to speak before anti-slavery gatherings, small and large.[201]

Whereas written memoirs benefited from white endorsements, during speeches it was both the compelling cadences, idioms, and accents from far away along with the Black speakers' presence that mattered. Like exhibits in a trial that verified the atrocities of slavery, Black Americans verbally yet also physically corroborated their *thingness* under slavery, through a limp, a back stiffened with welts, or hands formed by labour or deformed by abuse.[202] These speakers bore witness to the social death of bondage: emotions incapable of being steeled against the loss of kin, the psychic scars inflicted by capricious wickedness, and the teleological imperative of a flight toward freedom. This brought British abolitionists eye to eye with representatives of those whose suffering they sought to bring to a permanent end. The presence of Grandy's published *Narrative* not only gave him an opportunity to raise funds without charity but also allowed abolitionists to give financial endorsements – within the structure of their business meetings – by purchasing a memento that then could be more widely circulated.

The freedom-seeker Moses Roper (1815–91) commenced his first lecture tour in 1836 and published his escape narrative in 1837. Roper too carried to Britain a letter of introduction from an eminent US abolitionist who vouched for his character to a succession of British hosts, who eventually found him a place where he could acquire an education. Dr Thomas Price, a Hackney clergyman, authored the preface, recommending Roper to 'the patronage of the British public' as he embarked on a lecture tour, bundles of books at the ready.[203] By 1844, Roper had delivered over 2,000 lectures and sold 30,000 copies of his book in English and Welsh editions.[204]

Grandy and Roper set important precedents. For Black orators, the anti-slavery movement was inherently international.[205] By the time Frederick Douglass set foot in Ireland in autumn 1845, with *The Narrative of the Life of Frederick Douglass, Written by Himself* freshly printed, the pattern was set. He sold 100 copies in Dublin, his true fame still all before him.[206] Four months later, when he moved on to Britain, he had sold 5,000 copies. A cheap edition was prepared, and by the end of Douglass' twenty-month tour 11,000 copies had been sold.[207] Though moulded by the needs of white abolitionists' rhetoric, slave narratives and escape narratives offered insights into abject and liberatory experiences, and when coupled with a lecture-performance an individual's singular testament amplified a collective will, strengthening the struggle against enormous odds.[208] As Santos puts it, when meetings decentre specific 'protagonism', intercultural translation becomes a 'capacitating factor' for movements that are 'premised upon the recognition of difference'; this mobilises a movement by opening others 'up to new experiences … born not of dilettante curiosity but rather of necessity'.[209] Whereas Grandy and Roper's renown was low relative to what Douglass built up, by exposing audience after audience to their testaments, tours produced an additive effect. Furthermore, Douglass' ability to develop his presentations from personal narrative to arguments tapped into Britons' 'moral sensibilities of a public corrupted by its own unjust institutions'.[210]

From 1839, Douglass left his wife and family in Rochester, New York, in order to tell his story at anti-slavery meetings throughout the Northeastern United States. However, he was still claimed by a man named Thomas Auld (1796–1880), and while he was within the United States he could be seized and returned to bondage in Maryland. British abolitionists determined to raise the £150 to legally liberate Douglass. Some US abolitionists objected on the principle that any such payment acknowledged a master's right to hold another person as property, essentially compensating a slaveholder to replace one enslaved person with another. There were other objections, based not on natural rights but on performative grounds: paying 'the ransom took from Douglass "one of the strongest claims to the sympathy of the community"' for the testament of an eloquent man, still a bondsman, countered all claims to his inferiority that could justify his (or anyone's) chattel hood.[211] Furthermore, when Douglass was back in the United States, if he was captured and restored to Auld this would make for harrowing effects and generate sympathy for the cause. Garrison dismissed these arguments as fundamentally *not* in Douglass' interest, recognising the absurdity of subjecting someone to being 'kidnapped, tortured, perhaps killed to create an excitement'.[212] For his part, Douglass emphasised the distinction between the purchase of legal freedom and 'abstract right and natural freedom'.[213] He could not overlook – as he reminded Auld on the anniversary of his eventual manumission – that he had already had his hands bound 'and my person dragged at the pistol's mouth, fifteen miles, from the Bay side to Easton to be sold like a beast in the market, for the alleged crime of intending to escape from your possession'.[214]

Auld owned generations of Douglass' kin (four siblings remained in his thrall). How would you regard it, Douglass asked in this open letter to Auld, if I was to enter your home, make off with your daughter, Amanda, enslave her, then

> compel her to work, and I take her wages—place her name on my ledger as property—disregard her personal rights—fetter the powers of her immortal soul by denying her the right and privilege of learning to read and write—feed her coarsely—clothe her scantily, and whip her on the naked back occasionally; more and still more horrible, leave her unprotected—a degraded victim to the brutal lust of fiendish overseers, who would pollute, blight, and blast her fair soul—rob her of all dignity—destroy her virtue, and annihilate all in her person the graces that adorn the character of virtuous womanhood?

Of course Douglass would do no such thing, and even states that he would offer Auld hospitality, if he ever presented himself, to enact 'how mankind ought to treat each other'.[215] But he piles on the amplification in this open letter to recall Auld to his own deeds and to remind other readers of passages in the *Narrative*. These men were members of the same church, both adult converts – Douglass had even witnessed Auld's 'wrenching, emotional' rebirth – and yet morally they were worlds apart.[216] While abroad, Douglass leveraged his legal predicament to illustrate several points. First, the calumny of Auld – a stand-in for countless others – who, in the face of Douglass' published exposés, would like nothing better than 'to have me in his power'. Douglass highlighted the perfidy of Auld's story: 'He says

he can put his hand upon the bible, and, with a clear conscience, swear
he never struck me, or told any one else to do so!' Douglass purported
surprise that Auld would speak such an untruth, even though he robbed
Douglass of his earnings, wielded the punishment until his arm lost all
strength, and claimed a right 'to my body, soul and spirit'.[217]

During this period, Douglass regarded Thompson, who had invited him
'to make his house my home', with particularly affinity. They went everywhere together, and Douglass 'found him equal to the highest estimate
I had formed of the man' as companion and orator.[218] Having spoken
at several high-profile events, Douglass concluded that the idea of '"No
Union with Slaveholders" is becoming more and more general in London,
and throughout this country'.[219] During the campaign, the incommensurability of Auld's acts with natural law was rhetorically leveraged against
all slaveholders, with special acerbity for clergy. In a letter to Garrison,
Douglass reported:

> Scotland is in a blaze of anti-slavery agitation—The Free Church and Slavery
> are the all-engrossing topics. It is the same old question of Christian union
> with slaveholders—old with us, but new with most people here…. The
> Free Church is in a terrible stew. Its leaders thought to get the slaveholders'
> money and bring it home, and escape censure. They had no idea that they
> would be followed and exposed. Its members are leaving it, like rats escaping
> from a sinking ship…. Let slavery be hemmed in on every side by the moral
> and religious sentiments of mankind, and its death is certain.[220]

Douglass foretold that 'American slaveholders must prepare, not only to
be excluded from the communion of British Christians … [but to be]
placed beyond the pale of respectability, and, standing out separated, alone
in their infamy, let the storm gather over them.' The inaugural Congress
of the Evangelical Alliance was slated for the summer of 1846, drawing churchmen from all over the world to London. This ideally suited
Douglass' ability to denounce Southern institutions from an enslaved person's perspective and to counter Southern defenders of slavery. Sensing the
imminent Corn Law repeal (passed in the House of Lords on 25 June 1846)
as a 'brilliant success', he felt this 'has convinced the people of their power'
and he wanted to seize the moment.[221] He shifted tactics in important
regards. Instead of focusing on a book tour – telling his story as a testament – he aligned with a specific abolitionist issue, criss-crossed Britain
giving speeches, contributed to a lively pamphlet war, and saw how to create a movement from an insider's perspective. He put the onus for equal
culpability on US and Scottish Christians, and this built him into a significant figure in transatlantic abolitionist agitations.

The impetus for this went back a few years. In May 1843, after ten years of conflict, the Free Church of Scotland had broken from the established (Presbyterian) Church of Scotland, insisting on the separation of civic and spiritual power in the right of parishioners – not Scottish lairds upheld by Parliament in London – to choose their ministers. Half of the kirk's members sided with the Free Church, but they had neither land nor buildings in which to meet or house their 400 ministers, no resources to support education, and nothing with which to sustain overseas missions. Fundraising efforts during 1843–4 netted £363,871, and meanwhile five delegates were sent to North America, where the world's largest Presbyterian population dwelt, to expand the campaign. The two delegates travelled throughout the Southern United States, raising between £3,000 and £6,000. At the Presbyterian General Assembly in Louisville, Kentucky, they found much support for the Free Church but indifference over repeal of slavery.[222] When they returned home, the question was raised in Edinburgh as to whether the funds should be accepted. The General Assembly's approach was to dither, debate, and delay. Essentially, for two years it favoured retaining friendly relations with US churches, and neither condemned those churches' ties to slavery nor returned the funds.

In accepting funds from slaveholding US clergy and congregations, the Free Church's Assembly in Edinburgh was accused of having 'formed a church and ministerial alliance with "*traders in human flesh*"; and as a reward, received a portion of their profits'. To use this money precluded giving 'efficient testimony against Slavery…. For you must fellowship them as *Christians*'. The fellowship, it was argued, was bought at the expense of 3 million lives in bondage. And yet as the radical 'non-governmentalist' and non-resistance pacifist Henry Clarke Wright (1797–1870) wrote to the members and ministers of the Free Church in October 1845: 'by one act you have it in your power to make Slaveholding execrable, and to carry conviction to the conscience of every Slaveholder. How? SEND BACK THAT MONEY'.[223] This was picked up in early 1846 as the perfect pretext for abolitionists' agitation.

Send Back the Money swelled into a movement, and in March 1846 Thompson was enlisted in the effort.[224] Douglass, still enmeshed in his own manumission controversy, was another headliner. There was no possibility of direct action at the General Assembly of the Free Church, so campaigners took their message to other organisations, particularly the Glasgow Emancipation Committee (which had sponsored Thompson's first trip to the United States), the Edinburgh Ladies' Emancipation Committee, and the newly formed Free Church Anti-Slavery Society. Instead of telling

Christians not to adhere to the Free Church, they educated auditors about the issue. Speaking out against pro-slavery stances in US churches split the ecumenical accord achieved in 1841: many variants of the faithful could set aside doctrinal differences, and even accept the atheist George Holyoake, to align for free trade but not for emancipation. The most outrageous of the agitators was Wright, who, at a meeting of the Glasgow Emancipation Committee on 21 April 1846, proposed a thought experiment that recalled Douglass' proposition to Auld: what if one of the Free Church's emissaries to the United States had been seized by Presbyterian slavers and sold for £1,000, and the money sent to the Sustentation Fund?

> (Laughter.) 'We are glad to get the dollars,' says the treasurer. 'Where did you get them?' 'I happened to seize and sell Doctor [William] Cunningham [1805–61, professor of theology and church history at the Free Church College] as a slave, and he, being a strong man, and a Doctor to boot, brought a good price—(great applause,)—and I, seeing your great need and desire for money, thought it would be a comfort to me, and acceptable to you, to give you a share of the proceeds.' (Renewed applause and laughter.) 'Well,' says the treasurer, 'considering that you happened to do it, and only found yourself unhappily in the predicament of selling the Doctor, I consider it right to take it, and receive you as a good Christian.' (Immense cheering.)

But of course, the Free Church would not accept *this* money.

> If they would not build their churches and pay their ministers by the price of Doctor Cunningham, how dare they take the price of the heart-stricken slave? (Strong emotion.)[225]

In turn, the Free Church cast aspersions on abolitionists. 'Suppose I am all they represent me to be', said Wright, '"a stranger," "a foreigner," "a wandering declaimer," "a fanatic," "an ultra radical," "an infidel," "a heathen," a Jew, or Mahometan, or all these combined in one…. Does this prove they are right in "forming an alliance with manstealers?"' The character of the donors, and the judgement of those who allied with slaveholders – not their critics – was at issue.[226] Rising to speak, Thompson recalled a meeting in 1834 with Dr Cunningham, the most vigorous of the Free Church's defenders. Thompson had given him a copy of *A Picture of Slavery in the United States of America*, in which a Presbyterian minister from the Southern states recommends the excommunication of every slaveholder, whereupon Cunningham had avowed his abhorrence of the criminality of the US churches in supporting slavery and his desire to remediate this.[227] Thompson implied to the assembly that to take this money now to 'build churches and pay ministers in this country' was rank idolatry. Did Nathan or Paul or Christ or Lot or Moses so act?[228] The assembly was not prepared to brook Cunningham's hypocrisy.

The campaign had another, populist, manifestation. In Arbroath, both Douglass and Wright noted that the words 'THE SLAVE'S BLOOD' were painted in red across Free Church buildings. Slogans were blacked onto the pavement in Glasgow and Paisley, and according to Douglass, when the words could not be scrubbed off a mason chiselled them away, leaving the slogan indelibly engraved.[229] Rhetorically activating a comprehensive idea of the public sphere, the movement attempted to recruit every Scot into it. '"SEND BACK THE MONEY!" was the chorus of the popular street songs; "SEND BACK THE MONEY!" was the heading of leading editorials in the daily newspapers.'[230] Thompson encouraged women to make the slogan so commonplace – such an everyday performative – that its utterance equated to 'pass the salt' at the table. He urged parents to teach their children to shout the slogan to ministers in the street; called for it to be emblazoned in large letters on every wall in Scottish towns, written on the base of John Knox's statues, and on the tombs of covenanters; and wanted it proclaimed on a banner from the top of Arthur's Seat in letters large enough to be legible throughout Edinburgh. Douglass, along with the Quakers Eliza Wigham (1820–99) and her stepmother, Jane Wigham (1801–88), reputedly followed through by carving the slogan into the turf of Holyrood Park.[231] This was the early Victorian equivalent of a media blitz and skywriting, snowballing populist opinion.

Douglass challenged his personal detractor, the Paisley Free Church minister Rev. John Macnaughton (1807–84), to debate. The freethinker George Holyoake challenged anyone from the Free Church to debate. Neither summons was taken up.[232] While the money was never returned, Douglass admitted that it did provide the abolitionists with an opportunity to make Scottish people aware of the Free Church's connections to slavery.[233] With the potato blight ravaging crops in Scotland and Ireland, threatening crofters' and smallholders' survival, the vehemence of these tactics and support in the Highlands and major cities is noteworthy.

The Church of Scotland had condemned slaveholding as 'the highest kind of theft' and slaveholders as 'sinners of the first rank' in 1794. The United Secession Synod, Reformed Presbyterians, Relief Synod, Baptist Associated churches, and Congregational Union of Scotland all made annual remonstrances against slavery.[234] The 1846 campaign endeavoured to make the Free Church hold by this, leverage its rejection of the funds as a way to bring US brethren to righteousness, and meanwhile illustrate the incommensurability of slaveholding with Christianity (or, at the very least, Calvinism). A congregant from Mississippi countered:

> If slavery be a sin, and if advertising and apprehending slaves with a view to restore them to their masters, is a direct violation of the divine law, and if the buying, selling, and holding of a slave FOR THE SAKE OF GAIN, is a heinous sin and scandal, then verily, THREE-FOURTHS OF ALL THE EPISCOPALIANS, METHODISTS, BAPTISTS, AND PRESBYTERIANS, IN ELEVEN STATES OF THE UNION, are of the devil.[235]

Precisely. The Free Church was urged to emphatically agree. To do so would be to act against monetary self-interest to expose white power, actively refute and refuse complicity, speak back to white church members' social hypocrisy, and warn of heavenly censure in a kind of transnational gesture of repudiation. If successful in calling attention to this, and bringing Southern Presbyterians round, the Free Church of Scotland could dismantle the institution of US slavery.

The Send Back the Money campaign's tactic was to question the new church's prioritisation of disestablishment in the face of moral sin, and its effect was to raise awareness of the tendrils of US slavery reaching into a Scottish institution. In England, the effect was to revive interest in abolition among a population who thought they were done with it when they pledged £22 million to redeem Britain's enslaved from West Indian planters.[236] In both cases, it was imperative to engorge British sympathy, as Charles Lenox Remond put it, in order to carry out 'the great doctrine of human rights', for Britain's importation of cotton and other commodities gave the impetus to slavery.[237] The dialectical tactic entailed 'a pedagogy that gradually reconstructs suffering or death as ethical and political artifacts'.[238]

Objecting to the more conciliatory posture of the BFASS and wanting a strong basis for meetings to counter the Evangelical Alliance, Thompson's allies sought a national platform from which to speak. An international anti-slavery congress was mooted, yet as Richard Davis Webb argued, holding another convention was not desirable: apart from the expense, as he put it, 'I hate the speech making & splutter which such an occasion would call forth in London – mere self-display.'[239] There was already a plan afoot to bring delegates from fifty churches worldwide to the Evangelical Alliance conference in August, and another international congress seemed unwise. Due to pressure from US delegates, the Evangelical Alliance could not pass a measure precluding slaveholders from participating (even though it came down hard on Sabbath-breakers, adultery, and Catholicism) and adjourned for six weeks.[240] In the interval, abolitionists formed a new society, launched with 'a real old organized anti-slavery meeting, such as was never held before in this metropolis', followed by meetings throughout the country, pressuring the Evangelical Alliance not to admit slaveholders. Wright opened the inaugural meeting with a 'scorcher' of a speech, Garrison followed up and received 'a tempest of applause', Douglass gave 'one of his very best efforts', and the Chartist Henry Vincent (1813–78) closed the roster.[241] Thompson was in the chair for the duration of the meeting, which lasted from 6:00 p.m. to midnight.[242] This Anti-Slavery League, which addressed '*Slaveholding under all conceiveable circumstances*', did not garner unanimous support from anti-slavery organisations and individuals who cleaved to the BFASS, yet succeeded in mortifying the Evangelical Alliance into rejecting slaveholders, effectively causing it to splinter on national grounds rather than forming a multinational organisation.[243] The league held its last meeting a mere nine months later, in May 1847, but in the meantime Garrison, Douglass, and Thompson toured the nation, speaking to up to 60,000 people in total – sometimes 4,000 at a time, as in Glasgow (13 per cent of the city's population) – and distributing 25,000 tracts.[244] Additionally, they spoke at meetings of the Evangelical Alliance, National Temperance Society (also seeking worldwide organisation), and Peace Society, all chart-topping events in a season of blockbusters.

If the purpose of such meetings in the early 1830s throughout Britain was to convince the public to pressure MPs to support an abolition bill, why, in the mid-1840s, did Garrisonians embrace multifactorial movements? There was a large measure of opportunism in this decision. First, there was the advantageous coincidence of having both Garrison and Douglass as well as Thompson in Britain: superstar lecturers who, in their different ways, embodied the brunt of the United States' pro-slavery wrath. Second, this melded the format of political meetings with the fervour of evangelical revivals: swaying hearts as well as minds with Bible Politics was inherent to this trio's rhetoric, and the emotional impact of their speeches was rarely surpassed. And third, Douglass – with his eloquence and masterful use of pathos along with sarcasm and soaring language – staged what British abolitionists had sought from other Black lecturers but hitherto conjured only in theory: Black expertise, Black incontrovertibility, and Black gravitas. Douglass 'could bring out his sermon without destroying his story' of being yet a fugitive from someone who claimed to own him, body and soul.[245] When Wright proposed to a meeting in Edinburgh that Douglass should present a memorial on the Send Back the Money issue to the Free Church Assembly – 'signed by himself, presenting it for himself, and claiming to be heard by that body' – it acknowledged Douglass was able to do what no white man could.[246]

While abroad, Douglass was not free from verbal attack: the South Carolina minister Thomas Smyth, a native Irishman, who had been particularly active in helping the Free Church raise funds, spread a story that Douglass had been seen leaving a Belfast brothel (actually it was an anti-slavery meeting), which gave impetus to Smyth's pernicious counter-slogan (Send Back the N——).[247] Even so, repeatedly during this visit to Ireland and Britain, Douglass remarked to associates that he felt the British exert no 'prejudice against color'. Wherever he went – tourist attractions, art institutions, and stately homes – he witnessed that 'the white man gains nothing by being white, and the black man loses nothing by being black'. When he accompanied George and Anne Thompson to Cremorne Gardens, a leisure complex and outdoor music centre on the Thames, he felt 'every one looked as though they thought I had as much right there as themselves'. When Thompson took him to the Speaker's Gallery in the House of Commons to listen to debate on restricting the hours women and children could work in factories, he imagined the difference that would ensue if he had ventured to enter the US Congress, and wrote 'monarchical freedom is better than republican slavery – things are better than names'.[248] This sense of belonging and acceptance (paradoxical to the political system) permeated every corner of public and domestic life that he ventured into in Britain and Ireland:

> I gaze around in vain for one who will question my equal humanity, claim me as his slave, or offer me an insult. I employ a cab—I am seated beside white people—I reach the hotel—I enter the same door—I am shown into the same parlor—I dine at the same table—and no one is offended. No delicate nose grows deformed in my presence. I find no difficulty here in obtaining admission into any place of worship, instruction or amusement, on equal terms with people as white as any I ever saw in the United States. I meet nothing to remind me of my complexion. I find myself regarded and treated at every turn with the kindness and deference paid to white people. When I go to church, I am met by no upturned nose and scornful lip to tell me, 'We don't allow n——s in here'![249]

Of course Douglass' complexion mattered – this was crucial to his impact at meetings in the United States and Britain – but in Britain even where he was not performing to persuade, not known, and not on his guard, he felt noticed 'on equal terms with people as white as any I ever saw in the United States'. In meetings, his warm welcome was in part due to a perceived intersection – not so much of identity but of conviction – connecting Douglass to other causes. Thus, when he spoke alongside O'Connell in Ireland two liberation struggles were allied. Douglass, like Garrison and Thompson, successfully took the abolitionist message to a wide spectrum of society, where people felt a connection not only to the cause but also to its advocates.

For Roper, Remond, Grandy, and Douglass there was a performativity of colour involved in their reception during British tours, even if they did not experience the kinds of overt or implicit discrimination, gross or micro slights, endemic to their homeland. This suggests that at this moment Britain accorded with William Benjamin Carpenter's (1813–85) *Principles of Human Physiology* (1847) – drawing heavily from the Bristol surgeon James Cowles Prichard's (1786–1848, Dr. John Estlin's brother-in-law) ongoing antiracial ethnological research – which 'taught that black people were "not separated, by any impassable barrier, from the most civilized and cultivated nations of the globe"'.[250] For the time being, monogenism (the theory of single descent) predominated at the Ethnological Society of London, founded in 1842 as an offshoot of the APS, where members accepted that external circumstances experienced by individuals (not innate differences of race) accounted for any superficial differences in capability.[251] Estlin, Carpenter's mentor, writing the first edition of *A Brief Notice of American Slavery, and the Abolition Movement* in 1846, 'recognizes the talent of all, when given the opportunity to be cultivated', and so did the members of the Anti-Slavery League. Estlin, too, wrote that in contrast to US racism, the British class system had no 'impassable barriers' of colour marking privilege and entitlement.[252] US abolitionists, both Black and white, were engulfed in a racist system that segregated conveyances, hostelries, eateries, and places of resort throughout the North, in Britain what made the Black lecturers remarkable was not so much their skin but the stories they lived and the narratives they told, because they spoke their own truth, in plain sight.

Despotism, it turned out, was a US value and not just a monarchical one, however much the continental revolutions of 1848 – which in Britain took the milder form of Chartist demonstrations and demands – challenged this. While the picture is more complicated in Ireland, there the ideas of abolition took strong hold among English-speaking Irish. From the perspective of the British India Society, the 'love of liberty' would switch buying power from the slaveocracy of the United States to India. As Remond put it: 'Look to the confessions of slaveholders themselves', who so fear this change, 'and you will find it there avowed that the people of England, Ireland, and Scotland, have this power vested in their own hands'.[253] This, for the time being, was the complex vision of Remond, Douglass, Thompson, and their allies.

## George Thompson, MP

While the Send Back the Money campaign bloomed into a national movement, Thompson wondered what would be next for him. 'Rigorous extra-parliamentary campaigning' was the basis of his fame, and he was at the top of his powers, equally impressive in mass meetings as in a more forensic mode at East India House.[254] He talked about returning to the United States, where the issue of churches' complicity in slavery could be more directly confronted. James Buffum (1807–87, vice-president of the Massachusetts Anti-Slavery Society), who had accompanied Douglass in 1845–6, mooted the idea to Caroline Weston (1808–82, cofounder of the Boston Female Anti-Slavery Society), confidentially conveying Thompson's idea that he give his catalogue of 'twenty or thirty Lectures on British India … full of the history of that Country and People' at lyceums to cover his expenses, 'and speak in antislavery meetings as he could'.[255] Meanwhile, as early as 1839, Lord Brougham had singled out Thompson as a potential asset in the House of Commons.[256] When James Bruce (1811–63) resigned his seat in Southampton in 1842 to succeed to the Scottish peerage, a by-election was called. Thompson was one of two Liberal candidates who were advanced, styled in the local press as a Chartist and hired 'Anti-Corn Law hack', someone 'long-winded and long-eared' who had long laboured to produce a 'social war'.[257] His platform consisted of repealing the Corn Laws, extending suffrage, voting by ballot, and shortening the duration of parliaments.[258] The election day passed quietly, without the characteristic treating of electors with alcohol. Considering this was his first contest, in a constituency where he had no connections, Thompson's position at the bottom of the polls was not a disgrace.[259]

Early in 1847, with a general election pending, Thompson was mooted for at least a dozen constituencies, including Edinburgh, Plymouth, Westminster, and Lambeth, as Radicals (probably spurred by John Bright, a leading free trader elected in 1843) sought somewhere to place him.[260] It was decided that Thompson would run against two incumbents in Tower Hamlets, a district immediately east of the City of London (the largest borough in the Reformed House of Commons) that held two seats. He campaigned on a platform of promoting free trade and civil and religious liberties, including complete suffrage, vote by ballot, separation of church and state (e.g., removing bishops from the House of Lords), and his track record of anti-slavery, anti-Corn Law, and pro-Chartist agitation. Thompson's opponents were the incumbent Liberals (no other party fielded candidates). Sir William Clay (1791–1869), 'an old Whig hack', sought his fifth term; he aligned with Sir Robert Peel (1791–1869, Tory Prime Minister who split the party when he pivoted to support free trade) and campaigned on civil and religious liberty, limited expansion of suffrage, and vote by ballot.[261] The other candidate was Colonel Charles Richard Fox (1796–1873), illegitimate son of the third Baron Holland (1773–1840), 'a Whig of the old school in sturdiness' who through marriage to an illegitimate daughter of William IV (1765–1837) became son-in-law to the king and was appointed his equerry, in 1836 was given by his father a life appointment as receiver-general for the Board of Ordnance, and since 1841 had sat as MP for Tower Hamlets.[262]

Thompson held meetings nightly from 1 July, drawing large and enthusiastic crowds. Still, the night before the polls, the incumbents were expected to be returned.[263] Fox's supporters financed a smear campaign, putting out placards emblazoned with 'Who is George Thompson?'[264] Taking advantage of Thompson's refusal to hold meetings in public houses, they claimed he said 'that the trade of the licensed victuallers was "immoral, disgraceful, and wicked", and that he wished to put down all Sunday trading in the articles necessary for the comfort of the poor man' such as steamboat and railway travelling and visiting nearby Victoria Park. A letter from 'A Working Man' in the *Morning Advertiser* fanned the flames, insinuating that Thompson – whose allegiance with evangelical Dissenters aided his popularity in the district – was a prudish puritan.[265] This negative campaigning propelled Thompson's name to the fore. On polling day, masses gathered in Stepney Green to hear the candidates (Figure 2.5). When called to account for himself at the hustings, Fox simply stated that he favoured the same causes as Clay, possibly setting a record for terse speechifying. Clay and Fox were greeted with 'an outburst of hissing, groaning, and shouting', but when Thompson stepped up to the hustings 'the sound, while fully sustained in intensity, changed its character, and the applause did not cease until a new object attracted and retained attention in the person of the high constable, attired in imposing official uniform, who advanced on horseback and proclaimed silence'.[266] The crowd remained in a happy mood, one by one signing the returning officer's sheets and showing from the outset that Thompson held a two-to-one margin over either opponent.[267] At the end of the day, Thompson gave an impromptu, entirely uncharacteristic, speech acknowledging his

Figure 2.5    Tower Hamlets election, showing the hustings at Stepney Green during George Thompson's bid for re-election. *Illustrated London News*, 10 July 1852, 24. Getty Images.

loving parents' poverty and their inability to send him to a great university: indeed, he said, 'hear, ye that possess not this world's goods, and be encouraged to aspire to honours which England has to bestow – I never had a quarter's schooling in my life. (Great cheering.)'. He then rehearsed his holistic view of rights across class, creed, and nation, saying 'he had been a public man', and that 'the civil and religious freedom of man; the freedom of the food of man; the abolition of war, and universal brotherhood' were his constant objectives.[268]

Did Thompson win over the electors because he was better suited to the moment than Clay and Fox, because the strategies of discrediting him did not succeed, or because he manipulated the performative circumstances more effectively? Reaction from around the nation suggests that a populist wave carried him into office, and his track record on Reform and global vision for free trade coupled with an anti-war prosperity message played well with the idea that talented men unallied to party should get a chance to govern in the aftermath of Corn Law repeal. Lord John Russell (1792–1878, who became prime minister with a slender majority) said of Thompson: 'He will not sleep upon the opiate of a baronetcy, like Sir W. Clay, or lag and straggle in at the rear of all reform, when he must keep up with his regiment for fear of being cut off, like Major-General [*sic*] Fox.'[269] As the *Illustrated London News* summed up:

> Many shake their heads, and talk of want of 'standing,' and 'weight in society,' and other things, indicating dissatisfaction and distrust. They forget that in all free states eloquence alone is power.... There is no reason

why the unstated and talented men elected by the people in the few cases
that are exceptions to the rule should not be as honest and independent
representatives as the scores of needy scions of nobility, whom the people
choose with such alacrity, minus any talents whatever, either for speaking
or anything else.[270]

Many watched to see 'if his working are as good as his oratorical powers',
while detractors characterised him, at worst, as 'a fellow who has been in
the habit of hiring himself out as a mob-orator, and without any visible
means of living' and, at best, as one of the 'men of genius and scholars
[who] will condescend to apply themselves to business, and look at the
affairs of this world like men of this world', finding success in a constituency based on the popular vote.[271] At a public tea for 1,000 people at
the New Globe Tavern on Mile End Road, the keynote speaker, Feargus
O'Connor (1796?–1855, just elected in Nottingham as the first and only
Chartist MP), proclaimed, 'This is a great night ... because it stamps with
universal approval the man who has struggled to take the brand off the
front of universal slavery. (Tremendous applause.)' Still, the men who
ran Thompson's campaign were all too aware that only half his election
expenses had been paid.[272] He lacked, and would continue to need, cash.
British MPs were not remunerated until 1911.

As an MP, Thompson continued much as before, lending his name
to many causes and his time to a variety of nascent organisations: the
People's International League (pledged to inform the public better on foreign policy and assist the cause of universal emancipation and liberty),
National Alliance for Chartism (advocating male suffrage, vote by ballot,
and limited terms for MPs), British Anti-State Association (advocating
disestablishment of the Church of England), and Peace Society (opposing
expenditures on national fortifications in reaction to events in France, as
well as free trade between nations as a disincentive to war). He also supported a repeal of capital punishment (just enacted by French Republicans),
Hungarian freedom, and a barnstorming tour for the Parliamentary and
Financial Reform Association mounting 'demonstrations' (a.k.a. meetings)
seeking one man one vote, ballot elections, the abolition of property qualifications, pay for MPs in order that ordinary people could serve, and terms
of short, fixed durations. Meanwhile, he pursued the ex-raja of Satara's
case (and after the ex-raja's death, the cause of inheritance for his adopted
heir) with The Company's directors and in Parliament.[273] In February
1848, he was appointed to a select committee – 'one of the most mundane, routine, yet significant practices of modern society: the inquiry' –
to investigate the potential for cotton growth in India.[274] It reported

that the long-staple variety preferred by European manufacturing methods could be grown in some areas, and while the native population may be reluctant to shift to this crop, with proper encouragement – including from Indian members of mercantile firms and within the government – this could be achieved.[275]

Thompson was an active MP: present in the House, energetic with respect to his avowed causes, and called upon by ministers to speak on important matters. Even so, Holyoake's assessment is right: 'He did not exercise influence in Parliament like that which he did on the platform, but that was because he did not give his mind to that distinct kind of work.' In other words, he continued to utilise his capacity to marshal facts and put the case through oratory but did not develop into a parliamentarian. His calling was 'the wider sphere', and so 'People have talked of Thompson as a great outdoor orator who failed in the House. He did not fail – he did not seek to succeed there. That is the explanation.'[276] What Thompson did best was not calibrated to this new role: he excelled at collaborating with like-minded Radical colleagues and then swaying the people toward their view, and though he mastered several styles of debate he did not seek to modify his approaches in the House or even to work extensively with his own faction in the House to produce legislation.[277]

Just over three years into his term as an MP, Thompson sailed again for the United States, intending to be gone three months.[278] Anti-abolitionists were ready for him. At his first appearance, in Boston's Faneuil Hall, the moment he took the podium the room 'became a perfect bedlam of noise and confusion'. The voices of Abby Kelley (1811–87), the Unitarian clergymen William Henry Channing (1810–84) and Theodore Parker (1810–60), and Frederick Douglass were successively drowned in 'hisses and outcries'. The crowd was in a playful mood. Dozens of whistlers struck up a medley of 'Yankee Doodle' and 'Dandy Jim', and rings formed with dancers doing the 'Camptown hornpipe'. From the galleries, ladies looked placidly down on the charivari. The speakers quietly exited, and the meeting was broken up by order of the city marshal. Thompson later claimed that the disruptors were 'minions of the commercial interest' in Boston (i.e., cotton traders), and told his constituents that he was determined to test 'the right of a man to freedom of speech' by remaining in the United States to 'denounce inhumanity and oppression by whomsoever they were practiced'.[279] He travelled through Massachusetts, Maine, Connecticut, Pennsylvania, Ohio, and Michigan. Newspapers widely decried him as a firebrand, a Socialist, an agent of Lord Palmerston (the British foreign secretary), and most preposterous of all, 'an agent of the East India Company'.[280]

He had a warm reception in Toronto at meetings of the Anti-Slavery Society of Canada, where the focus was on reception of Black refugees and denunciations of the Liberian emigration scheme.[281] For the most part, however, in the context of President Millard Fillmore's (1800–74) proclamation against persons of colour who rescued a Black freedom-seeker named Shadrach from the custody of US marshals in Boston, Thompson was perceived as an agitator against the Fugitive Slave Law and slavery in general: a sitting member of the British Parliament regularly denouncing US citizens, *in the United States*, for not living up to their own Constitution. This was how Thompson highlighted slavery as both a moral and a federal (not just state) matter, a position that the Liberty Party had developed in the late 1840s, asserting natural rights and the law's responsibility to uphold them.[282] Thompson was hanged in effigy, along with John Bull, by a mob in front of the courthouse in Springfield, Massachusetts. Thompson spoke to an auditory of about 200 that evening, and when he left by railway he was pelted and hooted. Elsewhere, a placarding campaign accused him being 'an English serf' and 'a British spy' whose starving countrymen (the Irish) had received shiploads of food from the United States. This further convinced Thompson that Northern US citizens were under the thumb of a mere 100,000 Southern United States' slaveholders, tamely acceding to losing their rights as well as their moral compass to the 'colossal superstructure' of slavery.[283] As the sojourn lengthened, the British press began to ask why Thompson was not in Parliament, looking after his constituents' interests. There was unsubstantiated speculation that he would resign his seat in order to take up permanent residence in the United States.[284]

Thompson's experience in the United States (1850–1) exemplifies persistence amidst conflict, marking a foreigner as the (merely ostensible) provocation. As in 1834–5, abolition's opponents looked upon him as a potent threat to the nation, and various forms of agitation resulted: meetings were stormed, houses searched, noisy hunts were launched down highways and byways, and surrogates were abducted as scapegoats. As one form of political performance was interrupted, thwarted, or prevented altogether, another occurred during the near-constant transience of Thompson's tour.

Thompson returned to England on 7 July 1851, after nearly nine months abroad. The following spring, he stood for re-election, pledging jointly with Acton Smee Ayrton (1816–86) in an effort to unseat Sir William Clay.[285] Ayrton was able, but unknown: a Bombay barrister who repatriated in 1851 with a modest fortune, he joined the Financial Reform Association and aligned with most of Thompson's convictions.

The *Morning Advertiser* – Thompson's old foe – put it about that Ayrton had promised, if elected, to discharge 'the ugly incubus of certain outstanding debts since the election of 1847' and would hitherto under-write Thompson's expenses as an MP; in other words, Thompson was for sale, Ayrton bought him, and both were compromised.[286] Sceptics had a field day with Thompson's apparent hypocrisy. He rebuffed con-cern about his long absence and protested his unimpeachable integrity, amidst the crowded field of five Liberal candidates.[287] This was a closely watched contest, and the festive ceremonies at the hustings, aided by lovely weather, favoured large crowds, yet the effort was doomed.[288] The two Whigs won the ticket, and the three Radicals did not. Clay, who was assailed with groans when he addressed electors, topped the tally.[289] Exactly one year after Thompson's return from the United States, aban-doned by Dissenters, he was voted out of office, never to return.[290] In 1862 he was considered for seats in Lambeth and Southampton but did not run.[291] A *Punch* esprit offering the portraits of eminent statesmen to a pawnbroker concluded that George Thompson's visage, among 'several others better known than admired, were contemptuously refused; "he (the Pawnbroker) would be sorry to have them at any price"'.[292]

## Grant Me Life, and I Will Solve the Problem

Though his household remained in London, many of Thompson's activi-ties centred on concerns of the Manchester School. He resumed a busy schedule of attending meetings, allied explicitly with the Peace Society in the run-up to the Crimean War. He leveraged various new loans to pur-chase the *Empire*, a weekly newspaper, in order to turn it into the organ of the Peace Society. As the popular press grew in affordability, newspa-pers were poised to augment the public domain of meetings by spread-ing their news through a nationwide system of inexpensively attained information and opinion, promoting thought and critical debate with new amplitude by reaching out to working- and middle-class readers on newsstands. Unfortunately, the venture floundered then failed late in 1855, and Thompson's name was on over $1,000 of debts.[293] He liquidated all his assets, and in order to get beyond the reach of creditors, sailed to France and then to Calcutta, where he laid low until his friends could achieve 'an honourable adjustment' of his affairs.[294] He was taken in by a cousin of the late Dwarkanath Tagore, Prasanna Kumar Tagore (1801–86), a prominent member of both the Landholders' Society and the British India Association, whose father had helped found the Hindoo College.[295]

Wealthy in his own right, Tagore had practiced law and in 1854 became a clerk-assistant to the viceroy's council. Thompson was provided with separate apartments in Tagore's spacious mansion in Neptehata, with 'a noble library, society at the times when it is most agreeable, my own attendants, a profusion of servants for extra services, and a carriage without the expense of purchasing hiring or ordering!'[296]

This was markedly different from his previous sojourn in India. A few months after arriving, he asked his daughter Amelia – now a wife on the verge of motherhood – to inform the colleague handling his affairs, Louis Chamerovzow (1816–75), that

> in reference to the confidential objects of my mission, I have made important preliminary progress, that while I am operating circumspectly, and therefore slowly, I am at the same time laying the foundation of large future transactions. Tell him, I am leading a quiet, thrifty, unostentatious life, prodigal in nothing but writing paper and postage stamps, seeing little company, and courting none. Tell him that my associates are Native Hindoos, but of the first class and character. With them I eat, drink, ride, lodge, walk, talk, take counsel, and hold unreserved communication. Besides these, I have paid my respects, on his own invitation, to the late Governor General [Lord Dalhousie, remembered both as a moderniser and as a land annexer], have done the same to Lord and Lady Canning [1812–62, the current governor-general and his wife, Charlotte (1817–61)], and am a familiar guest at the house of my old friend, Mr. Halliday [1806–1901], the Lieutenant Governor of Bengal. With the European Community at large I have had nothing to do, and shall not make any effort to enlarge my acquaintances beyond the requirements of my mercantile schemes. Tell him, that three or four times in the week, I proceed at 10 am to the city, where I transact business for three or four hours.[297]

The 'mercantile schemes' involved Thompson taking on a five-year contract with a British textile manufacturer to secure quantities of a crop hitherto unknown in India; the manufacturer had patented a process capable of making 'an entirely new textile fabric, having the warmth of cotton, the durability of linen, and the beauty of the finest silk'.[298] This gave Thompson purpose and daily structure, yet he spent his fifty-second birthday 'sorrowing over a misspent life'.[299] A few days later he fell ill, vomiting bile. Seeking relief, he undertook a painful journey to Madras, then Ceylon, but the malady plagued him for three months, returning with a vengeance the following year.

Thompson's diary shows a more active social life upon his return to Calcutta. He befriended the Indian-born George Ashburner (1810–69, former editor of the *Bombay Courier*), who lavishly entertained and was head of a successful commercial house in Calcutta.[300] The deposed king of Oudh, 'a used up and feeble creature' residing in Garden Reach (Calcutta), sought Thompson's opinion about a possible restoration. For two hours Thompson 'gave him the best counsel in his power', recognising 'the injustice of his treatment by the Indian Government' and forming a sorry view of the man. Sir Radhakanta Deb Bahadur (1783–1867, a scholar and advocate of female and male education, active in the Agricultural Society and founding president of the British India Society) took Thompson under his wing, escorting him to see the Hindu festival of Durga, including nautch girls, sacrifices to idols, and musical performances. Thompson wrote letters about this and other topics including Hindu marriages and an opium sale at The Company's rooms, ethnographic and exotic in tone, which he offered to Amelia to place in a London newspaper. He renewed acquaintances with friends in the British India Society, accepted an invitation to visit the raja of Burdwan's magnificent palaces of Del Kosha and Mahtab Munezill, marvelling at this cultivated man's luxury, public works, and fascination with European art, and sent accounts to Amelia with permission to publish the correspondence.[301] He spent time with Young Bengal, and gave a lecture to the Hindu Society, another on the United States to the Bethune Society (where he claimed that 350 young men eagerly received his counsel), and a third on the native Black Act meeting at the Town Hall.[302] He extensively explored Calcutta: not just where 6,000 Europeans lived amid wide avenues and aqueducts with purified water, but also where 400,000 natives suffered from endemic cholera, dwelling alongside a river 'fetid with the excrement of a nation', open drains, and streets that flowed to the knees with rainwater.[303]

Thus, Thompson wiled away the first half of his two-and-a-half-year stay. When the rebellion erupted in May 1857, he was in an excellent position to send intelligence to his associates in England. Though he wrote intermittently for the *Star*, where his son-in-law Frederick Chesson was employed, and sent home letters on the rebellion, he did not quite step up to the opportunity.[304] Thompson had an excellent vantage from which to comment differently from all other European correspondents, yet Richard Cobden justifiably complained that 'unfortunately, owing to his desultory idle habits of mind', Thompson 'seems incapable of more than a sudden impulse, & then after a brilliant speech or letter he falls back into apathy & quiescence. But being on the spot & professing to act independently of the governing class he ought to have sent some valuable communications to the Star'.[305] When Delhi fell, Shah Bahadur II – Thompson's former sponsor – claimed his empire. Though Calcutta remained free of violence, the entire region was gripped with anxiety.

Seven months into the rebellion, Thompson wrote to Amelia that the sword drawn at 'the plains of Plass[e]y' to secure a vast inland empire and 'sheathed on the banks of the Irrawaddy', having annexed Burma (Myanmar) in the Second Anglo-Burmese War of 1852, only momentarily appeased 'the devouring appetite of the demon of Annexation'. He acknowledged that The Company's appetite for commanding the entire subcontinent did not endear Indians to British imperialism, but Britons were indifferent to this. In a short period of time, the nizams of Hyderabad formed a subsidiary alliance, effectively putting 'the richest districts of the Deccan' in British control (1798), and subsequently Jumbulpore (Jabalpur, 1818), Satara (1848), Punjab (1849), Pegu (1852), Nagpore (1853), and then Oudh (1856) were successively 'swallowed up'. Thus, 'a century of broil and battle' had transpired. He wrote, conscious of the irony, that since The Company had established rule in Bengal, 'All was tranquillity [*sic*], profound repose, and apparent security. Within the limits of the Empire, no foe was visible. Beyond our frontiers, no enemy menaced our borders; and, seated on her island throne, Victoria reigned – "the Mistress of the Seas."' A native army kept order in India, 'the nonmilitary classes exhibited an aspect of passive and resigned submission on the one hand, or of grateful devotion to British rule on the other. The friends of India', among whom he would count himself and his myriad Indian and Anglo-Indian colleagues, 'were hopeful and active, and were preparing to inaugurate the birth of a new and better era', having addressed deficiencies in 'Systems of Law, police and justice; of Education and material development', vanquishing or conciliating 'internal foe[s]'. But this was a dream.[306]

This letter was addressed to his beloved daughter Amelia, not couching anything that the public could not bear. Neither preacher nor lawyer, he dispensed with Bible Politics and eschewed the facticity of blue books. And yet this letter builds to a swift peroration, dense with meaning and powerful in effect, as if holding an auditory in supreme suspense. Bridging the close of Dalhousie's governorship (when it seemed no further conquests by the sword were warranted) to an era of peace through commerce, India found itself embroiled in 'the darkest hour of adversity and danger'. Thus peace was the British national delusion, seemingly made possible by insights of the Manchester School, efforts of transnational alliances, the success of Indian merchants and entrepreneurs, and the placement of generations of talented men – such as graduates of the Hindoo College – in positions of commerce, law, and government. At precisely this juncture, the Sepoys turned arms against the British. Why did this 'late defection and insurrection', which was 'still shrouded in unsearchable mystery', occur? As he so often did in oral harangues, here Thompson lashed his prose with pointed irony.

> No theory, yet broached, satisfies the mind that the secret of the Mutiny is known beyond the bounds of the confederacy formed for our destruction. Subadars, Havildars, Jamadars and privates have, by thousands, been suspended from gibbets, and blown from guns, yet not one has said, in the presence of the instrument prepared for his death,—'Grant me life, and I will solve the problem.'[307]

Any conqueror who could not hold power by their own rule of law – a trait so amply and protractedly demonstrated in the sad fate of Satara – is not reduced to barbarism in the face of resistance but *is* the barbarian through and through. The Sepoys, for their part, were men of might, ill-equipped to wage peace, ill-prepared to analyse and explain grievances across unbreachable cultural differences, and ill-disposed after decades of British abuse and centuries of successive foreign conquests to say it would be worth explaining this to barbarians.

Thompson continued the correspondence the following day, recalling to Amelia accounts of the 'gallant defence' mounted by Sir Henry Lawrence at Lucknow and the pathetic suffering 'of the women, dear children, and wounded men' in the Residency as they endured the siege. He reminded Amelia that she would have read about Sir Colin Campbell relieving the garrison so that the surviving 'heroes and heroines', 'that gallant band, that, hoping against hope, held out at Lucknow' could make their way overland to Allahabad. Some of them ended their slow procession that very morning on the shores of the Hooghly. Calcutta's finest showed up to greet them at the Princess Ghat, weeping freely at the sight of the so obviously bereaved survivors. As the women, children, and wounded soldiers were 'tenderly conducted' to carriages, 'there were meetings between old friends' during which they wore 'a peculiar smile not to be adequately described by my poor pen: a smile in which gratitude and joy were mingled', along with memories 'of those fearful months during which tens of thousands were raving for their lives' – *tens of thousands*, and thus Indians as well as Britons – with 'shells and round shot' raining down upon them. And then he imagined this unfolding day of deliverance, during which 'tales of horror will be told', tears would flow, 'prayers of thankfulness [would be] offered up', and 'a welcome to every house' and a 'congratulation from every heart' would issue forth.

As I looked upon the thousands greeting with tears of most genuine sympathy those who had been saved from death and horror worse than death I could not help saying ['] ah you little think that you and millions like you cause the wars which desolate the Earth, by your false ideas, yr refusal to embrace the Gospel in its true sense[,] your atheistical conduct in the practical repudiation of divine commands and your foolish and fond attachment to the miscalled honour[,] glory and patriotism by which the diabolism of carnage and murder are covered up.[']³⁰⁸

This is an allusion to what he later called 'the cannibal ferocity that now prevails', engulfing all combatants.³⁰⁹ While witnessing the distress of survivors, he named what he believed to have caused the conflict: false ideas, disregard of the Gospels, atheistical conduct, and unproductive attachment to honour, glory, and patriotism. Not intended for publication – not even in the *Star* – this insight reveals Thompson's bitterness toward his church, his nation, and the entire system of colonialism.

Layers of time (*Zeitschrichten*) connected in this moment: despite the long history of The Company, Thompson calendared the blame to 'the brief administration of one man, (Dalhousie)'.³¹⁰ Yet there were others equally culpable, such as Baron Panmure (1801–74), secretary to the War Office while Thompson was an MP. Under Palmerston's 1855 administration, Panmure rose to secretary of state for war, a post he held with record bellicosity throughout the disastrous Crimean campaign as well as the Sepoy Rebellion. Panmure was also, from its outset, a staunch supporter of the Free Church of Scotland and thus one of the Scottish noblemen who steadfastly would not 'send back the money' in 1846. Evidently, as Thompson mused on the rebellion his thoughts were peopled with many kinds of foes. As much as he aligned with Dissenters, and did not shun evangelical Anglos in Calcutta, the problem he stresses in this expression of unguarded, private thought is that 'yr refusal to embrace the Gospel in its true sense' and repudiation of 'divine commands' led to the suffering arrayed before them and the complicated affective dramaturgy that he witnessed on the riverbank and imagined transpiring over the course of the day.

The contrast between Thompson's musings and the canonical view of British character is striking. Samuel Smiles (1812–1904) memorialised the rebellion through the gallant behaviour of British officers such as Sir Colin Campbell, who escorted the survivors of Lucknow to Cawnpore despite 'the all but overpowering assault of the enemy', then persisted to see his 'precious convoy safe on the road to Allahabad', whereupon he 'then burst upon the Gailior contingent like a thunderclap'. Wounded

British soldiers, used to barracks life, stifled their expletives and, 'gentle as any children', allowed themselves to be tended by 'the ladies' and in so doing behaved as well as any gentlemen. Those who recovered – 'the rough veterans, all scarred and mutilated as they were' – treated their nurses to an entertainment in the gardens of the Taj. This perspective, read by millions in a book that modelled the mid-Victorian masculine ethos, is singularly lacking in doubt; after all, self-*help* is its keynote, not its cultural critique.[311]

Thompson did all he could to enhance his own understanding of Indian affairs – including learning from Indian colleagues in Calcutta and up country, reaching across caste and station – and in turn was respected by reformers even if deplored by the Anglo press. His allegiance to Indians could never quite equate to its obverse: Thompson would forever be an outsider to India and to the British elite. In contrast, when Dwarkanath Tagore criticised administrators he was an insider yet someone 'whose social position and fortune depended on the British'. His cousin Prasanna Kumar Tagore was likewise a man with a profession, an entrepreneur, and a civic official. Both were colonial success stories: Indians who had the ear of the governor-general and the Calcutta elite, who admired English customs, and who were loyal to the colonising power yet made way for social and commercial change and encouraged their people to follow suit.[312] Families like the Tagores were the new dynasties, accumulating wealth, enjoying splendour, courting foreign allies, and promoting the advancement of knowledge. Such people differently exemplified understanding of the world connected through empire, doing what was conducive of making more prosperity on a strategic basis. Thompson needed such powerhouses to manipulate import/export trade to promote abolition on one continent and agricultural transformation on another, and at the same time overturn the basis of apostates' wealth (fuelled by disregard for humanity as well as divine law) while creating opportunities for prosperity among a newly propertied Indian elite. In England, powerhouses like Brougham, Bright, Cobden, and Thompson strove to extend the franchise to multitudes so they could self-govern. They met to talk in small and large gatherings, forging associations of like-minded people that in turn tried to persuade more to join their causes. Even though the kinds of reforms being advocated in Britain were not yet on the horizon in India, and most of Thompson's causes were perpetually in process, only inching toward change (the exception being the end of apprenticeship in British sugar colonies in 1838), all the causes are emblematic of liberalisation, and all the efforts can be measured in the increment of meetings (debates, lectures, soirées, breakfasts, speechifying, electioneering) that eschewed civil disobedience, mobbing, and revolution in favour of discussion and consensus.

Basu acknowledges that the annexation of Satara was 'an important land mark in the History of British India, as it was the principal cause of the Indian Mutiny'. This is a strong claim indeed, and if accurate it puts Thompson's campaign against The Company in the thick of the subcontinent's liberationist historiography. At the very least, this episode brought The Company 'into disgrace and precipitated its downfall'.[313] Cobden and Bright, 'the David and Jonathan' of the free trade movement, tried to redeem the promise of the British India Society belatedly in 1853, rallying friends to oppose renewal of The Company's charter and piling on damage.[314] Their tried and true forms of redress – meetings, petitions, and deputations – were no match for what made the Sepoys swivel in their ranks and turn guns on the British. Without linking free trade to human rights through philanthropy, governance, and mutuality of interests within a colonial system – a capacious approach to mid-Victorian liberalism – reformers' efforts yielded meagre results. In retrospect, both the APS and the Peace Society regarded Indians not as mutineers but as resistors of imperial oppression.[315] It was a perspective Thompson experienced as well as thought out while standing at the Princess Ghat, where the layers of time overlapped, manifest in their strivings and failings. There were facts that exceeded argumentation – like the torments inflicted on the enslaved – whose dramaturgy could not be contained in mere talk. This is an inherent counterpoint to the tearful 'tales of horror' that Thompson expected to be relayed in Calcutta's stylish drawing rooms.

It is no wonder that when Thompson returned to London six months later he was *chétif*: wretched in spirits and depleted, unable to use his hands, and unable to sit up without assistance.[316] He had sailed by the long route, around the Cape of Good Hope, possibly to avoid the overland transfer from the Red Sea to the Mediterranean. 'Soon after his embarkation, he was stricken with a general paralysis.' 'His wife did not know him.'[317] His first evening at home, he told his son-in-law that the captain of the vessel on which he sailed did a very foolish thing. 'Taking offence at something one of the passengers said he had him put in fetters and chained to his own cabin wall for an entire week.'[318] Paralysed and declared a hopeless case by four physicians who happened to be on board, Thompson could do nothing except tell the story.

**Notes**

1 Herbert, Christopher. *War of No Pity: The Indian Mutiny and Victorian Trauma*. Princeton, NJ: Princeton University Press, 2008: 26–7, 56.

2 Philips C.H. and D. Philips. 'Alphabetical List of Directors of the East India Company from 1758 to 1858.' *Journal of the Royal Asiatic Society* 73, no. 4 (1941): 325.

3 Herbert, *War of No Pity*, 22–3.

4 See Inglis, Julia. *The Siege of Lucknow: A Diary*. London: James R. Osgood, McIlvanie, 1892, entries for 24 November and 3 December 1857, 208 and 218.

5 George Thompson (Calcutta) to Amelia Chesson, 9 January 1858, REAS 2/2/67, JRL.

6 'Arrival of Lucknow Fugitives at Calcutta.' *Reynolds's Newspaper*, 21 February 1858, 3.

7 George Thompson (Calcutta) to Amelia Chesson, 9 January 1858, REAS 2/2/67, JRL.

8 See Inglis, *Siege of Lucknow*, 227.

9 George Thompson (Calcutta) to Amelia Chesson, 22 January 1858, REAS 2/2/68, JRL.

10 George Thompson (Calcutta) to Amelia Chesson, 7 January 1858, REAS 2/2/66, JRL.

11 George Thompson (Calcutta) to Amelia Chesson, 9 January 1858, REAS 2/2/67, JRL.

12 This dual consciousness is intrinsic to narratives about the rebellion. Christopher Herbert notes of Lieutenant Vivian Dering Majendie's 1859 narrative *Up among the Pandies, or a Year's Service in India*: 'This expressly traumatic split between two states of feeling or actually two opposed selves, a humanitarian one and a callous bloodthirsty one, exemplifies just the pattern of experience – of ambivalence carried to its utmost pitch – that forms the essential thematic of Mutiny literature.' *War of No Pity*, 93.

13 Byron, George G. 'The Dream.' In *The Works of Lord Byron*. Vol. 4. London: John Murray, 1905: 40–1.

14 See 'The Indian Mutiny.' *Eclectic Review* 4 (1858): 332–46.

15 George Thompson (Calcutta) to Amelia Chesson, 7 January 1858, REAS 2/2/66, JRL.

16 Brougham, Henry. *Speeches of Henry Lord Brougham upon Questions Relating to Public Rights, Duties*. Edinburgh: Adam and Charles Black, 1838: 155–6.

17 William Lloyd Garrison, 'Speech of Wm. Lloyd Garrison, at the Meeting in Tremont Temple, Dec. 24, Relating to the Execution of John Brown.' *Liberator*, 16 December 1859, 198.

18 'Anti-Slavery Conference in Manchester.' *Manchester Times*, 2 August 1854, 9.

19 'Scotland.' *Royal Cornwall Gazette*, 23 October 1830, 4; and 'Edinburgh.' *Caledonian Mercury*, 14 October 1830, 3.

20 Thompson admitted to the charge in a letter to Elizabeth Pease, 15 June 1839: 'I have been guilty. There was <u>much of truth</u> in the report which was circulated

while I was in the United States. <u>I did act unjustly</u> towards an employer whose service I quitted in 1829. I appropriated to my own use a part of the money entrusted to my care. I need say nothing of my <u>temptations</u> or <u>intentions</u> at the time. The act was <u>a sinful one</u>. It was <u>a breach of confidence</u>. It was <u>a grievous wrong</u>. It was a <u>crime in the sight of God</u>! I sinned, <u>not</u> ignorantly <u>but willfully</u>, in despite of [*sic*] the <u>knowledge</u> the <u>goodness</u> and the <u>grace</u> of God. I was disgraced.' Wclmss002083, Box 60, William L. Clements Library.

21  See, for example, Thompson, George. *Substance of an Address to the Ladies of Glasgow and Its Vicinity upon the Present Aspect of the Great Question of Negro Emancipation, Delivered in Mr Anderson's Chapel, John-St., Glasgow, on Tuesday, March 5th, 1833.* Glasgow: David Robertson, 1833: 8–11, 14–15.

22  This is characteristic of the Enlightenment model of debate. See Smith, Kimberly K. *The Dominion of Voice: Riot, Reason, and Romance in Antebellum Politics.* Lawrence: University of Kansas Press, 1999: 132.

23  Martin, 'Popular Political Oratory', 187, 189.

24  Martin, 'Popular Political Oratory', 207.

25  Stanton, Henry Brewster. *Sketches of Reforms and Reformers of Great Britain and Ireland.* New York: John Wiley, 1849: 244–5. See also Martin, 'Popular Political Oratory', 182–3.

26  Stephen, *Antislavery Recollections*, 148–52.

27  George Thompson (Brigg, Lincolnshire) to Jenny [Anne] Thompson (Camberwell), 19 April 1832, REAS 2/1/22, JRL; and George Thompson (Manchester) to Jenny [Anne] Thompson (Camberwell), 1 August 1832, REAS 2/1/24, JRL.

28  Montgomery, James. *The West Indies, and Other Poems.* 6th ed. London: Longman, Hurst, Rees, Orme, and Brown, 1823.

29  George Thompson (Sheffield) to Jenny [Anne] Thompson (Camberwell), 8 July 1832, REAS 2/1/23.

30  'Formation of the Sheffield Anti-Slavery Society.' *Sheffield Independent*, 14 July 1832, 4. Buckingham and John Parker (1799–1881), both Liberals, were elected.

31  Stanton, *Sketches of Reform and Reformers*, 241.

32  Whately, Richard. *Elements of Rhetoric; Comprising an Analysis of the Laws of Moral Evidence and Persuasion.* New York: Harper and Brothers, 1857: 31–2.

33  Holyoake, George Jacob. *Public Speaking and Debate: A Manual for Advocates and Agitators.* 1849. 2nd rev. ed. Boston: Ginn, 1896: 50–1.

34  Blair, *Lectures on Rhetoric*, 263.

35  Frederick Chesson's diary, 14 December 1861, REAS 11/9, JRL; 'Surrey Theatre.' *Morning Advertiser*, 8 June 1832, 3; 'Coburg Theatre.' *Morning Advertiser*, 3 July 1832, 3; and 'Coburg Theatre.' *Morning Advertiser*, 7 July 1832, 3.

36  'Young England.' *Illustrated London News*, 19 August 1843, 113.

37  George Thompson (Glasgow) to Jenny [Anne] Thompson (Camberwell), 16 February 1833, REAS 2/1/26, JRL.

38  'Popular Portraits No. XXVI.' *Illustrated London News*, 7 January 1843, 8.

39  Stephen, *Antislavery Recollections*, 154.

40  *Dundee Advertiser*, 11 February 1862, 3.

41 Thompson, *Substance of a Speech*, 4.

42 Thompson, *Substance of a Speech*, 13–14.

43 Smith, *Dominion of Voice*, 199, 203.

44 Thompson, *Substance of a Speech*, 24.

45 Thompson, *Substance of a Speech*, 24–5.

46 Thompson, *Three Lectures*, 5.

47 Thompson, *Three Lectures*, 8, 14.

48 Thompson, *Three Lectures*, 18.

49 Thompson, *Three Lectures*, 27.

50 Stanton, *Sketches of Reforms and Reformers*, 245.

51 Thompson, *Three Lectures*, 66.

52 *Abolitionist*, no. 5 (1 May 1833): 67.

53 George Thompson (Glasgow) to Jenny [Anne] Thompson (Camberwell), 16 February and 19 February 1833, REAS 2/1/26 and 2/1/27, JRL.

54 George Thompson (Edinburgh) to Jenny [Anne] Thompson (Peckham), 18 March 1833, REAS 2/1/29, JRL.

55 Stanton, *Sketches of Reforms and Reformers*, 240–2.

56 *Christian Journal*, March 1833, qtd. in Thompson, *Substance of an Address*, 40–1.

57 Kimberly K. Smith makes a similar argument about slave narratives, describing them as secular conversion narratives whereby the narrator seeks admission to a polity. *Dominion of Voice*, 230.

58 John Bright, MP, to Frederick Chesson on the occasion of Thompson's farewell soirée before travelling to the United States, 14 January 1864. Published as 'Farewell to Mr. George Thompson', 22 January 1864, *Manchester Examiner and Times*, rpt. in *Liberator*, 12 February 1864, 2.

59 Holyoake, *Public Speaking*, 150–2.

60 Martin, 'Popular Political Oratory', 228.

61 Among these supporters were Lord Brougham, Sir Stephen Lushington (1782–1873), as well as Henry John Stephen (1787–1864). Lushington was a civil jurist and at that time judge of the consistory court of London, and a reformer and abolitionist closely involved in the movement leading to the 1833 Emancipation Act. He served as Tower Hamlets' first MP (1832–41), leaving Parliament to become judge of the High Court of Admiralty. Stephen came from a family of prominent abolitionists, was an expert on legal pleading, and was at this time a Serjeant-at-Law. Farmer, 'Letters from England', 19 February 1864, 1.

62 Farmer, 'Letters from England', 26 February 1864, 36. This is probably why, both in the United States and in India, George Thompson was thought to be Scottish. See 'The Fanatics', in George Thompson's anti-slavery scrapbooks, 1834/5, REAS 6/1, fol. 10, JRL; and Mehrotra, S.R. 'The Landholders' Society, 1838–44.' *Indian Economic and Social History Review* 3, no. 4 (1966): 370.

63 Thompson, George. *A Voice to the United States of America, from the Metropolis of Scotland: Being an Account of Various Meetings Held in Edinburgh on the Subject of American Slavery, upon the Return of Mr. George Thompson, from His*

*Mission to That Country*. Edinburgh: W. Oliphant, 1836: 5; and Thompson, George. *Reception of George Thompson in Great Britain (Compiled from Various British Publications)*. Boston: Isaac Knapp, 1836: 127, 135.

64 *Reception of George Thompson*, 78.

65 Thompson, George. *Letters and Addresses by George Thompson, during his Mission in the United States, from Oct. 1st, 1834, to Nov. 27, 1835*. Boston: Isaac Kent, 1837: 93–6.

66 Grimsted, *American Mobbing*, xii; and Gilje, Paul A. *Rioting in America*. Bloomington: Indiana University Press, 1996: 89.

67 Thompson, *Voice to the United States of America*, 29.

68 George Thompson (St John, New Brunswick) to William Lloyd Garrison, 25 November 1835, MS A.1.1. vol. 1, Massachusetts Historical Society, Boston, rpt. in Taylor, *British and American Abolitionists*, 52.

69 Smith, *Dominion of Voice*, 240.

70 British agitators were not free from attack. The Chartist missionary Jonathan Bairstow (fl. 1838–44) was threatened with firearms, brick-bats, and dead animals, and the ACLL lecturer James Acland (1799–1876) was mauled by toughs during a lecture in 1840. Martin, 'Popular Political Oratory', 219, based on *Northern Star*, 30 April 1842; ACLL letterbook, fol. 341, 8 May 1840, Manchester Central Reference Library; and *Bradford Observer*, 21 May 1840, 3.

71 George Thompson to Thomas Hodgkin, n.d., MSS Brit. Emp. S.18/C122/38, Bodleian Library.

72 Devine, T. M. 'Did Slavery Make Scotia Great?' *Britain and the World* 4, no. 1 (2011): 52; and Baptist, Edward E. *The Half Has Never Been Told: Slavery and the Making of American Capitalism*. New York: Basic Books, 2014: xxiii.

73 Ann and Wendell Phillips to Maria Weston Chapman, London, 30 July 1839, MS A.9.2, vol. 12, 1839 (2), Weston Papers, Boston Public Library, rpt. in Taylor, *British and American Abolitionists*, 77. See also Goddu, Teresa. *Selling Antislavery: Abolition and Mass Media in Antebellum America*. Philadelphia: University of Pennsylvania Press, 2020: 92.

74 Wendell Phillips (London) to George Thompson, 29 July 1839, MS A.1.2, vol. 8, 1839, Boston Public Library, rpt. in Taylor, *British and American Abolitionists*, 74.

75 Conrad, Sebastian. *What Is Global History?* Princeton, NJ: Princeton University Press, 2016: 116 (qtd.), 147. See also Koselleck, Reinhart and Hans-Georg Gadamer. *Zeitschichten: Studien zur Historik*. Frankfurt-am-Main: Suhrkamp, 2002.

76 Conrad. *What Is Global History?*, 96. See also Hardt, Michael and Antonio Negri. *Empire*. Cambridge, MA: Harvard University Press, 2000: 8–9.

77 Thompson, George. *Lectures on the Corn Laws*, 7 January 1842. Carlisle: J. Steel, 1842: 14–16. *À la Musard* refers to French conductor Philippe Musard's (1793–1859) promenade concerts.

78 Malchow, Howard L. *Gentlemen Capitalists: The Social and Political World of the Victorian Businessman*. Palo Alto, CA: Stanford University Press, 1992: 188.

79  Heartfield, James. *The Aborigines' Protection Society: Humanitarian Imperialism in Australia, New Zealand, Fiji, Canada, South Africa, and the Congo, 1836–1909*. London: Hurst, 2011: 23, 25.

80  *Colonial Intelligencer, or Aborigines' Friend*, vol. 1 (1847): 64–5.

81  Nettlebec, Amanda. *Indigenous Rights and Colonial Subjecthood: Protection and Reform in the Nineteenth-Century British Empire*. Cambridge: Cambridge University Press, 2019: 14.

82  Nettlebec, *Indigenous Rights*, 122.

83  Malchow, *Gentlemen Capitalists*, 188.

84  Laidlaw, Zoë. '"Justice to India—Prosperity to England—Freedom to the Slave!": Humanitarian and Moral Reform Campaigns on India, Aborigines and American Slavery.' *Journal of the Royal Asiatic Society* 22, no. 2 (2012): 309. See also George Thompson's extract books, vol. 6, 3449.S43, Library of Congress.

85  George Thompson (Edinburgh) to William Lloyd Garrison, 5 January 1839, MS A.1.2, vol. 8, 1839, Massachusetts Historical Society, rpt. in Taylor, *British and American Abolitionists*, 67–8.

86  This is the figure that Thompson cites, though by other estimates the population was as high as 247 million by mid-century. See Visaria, Leela and Pravin Visaria. 'Population (1757–1947).' In *The Cambridge Economic History of India*, edited by Dharma Kamar, vol. 2, 463–532. Cambridge: Cambridge University Press, 1983: 466.

87  Wendell Phillips to George Thompson (London), 29 July 1839, MS A.1.2, vol. 8, 1839, Boston Public Library, rpt. in Taylor, *British and American Abolitionists*, 75.

88  Ann and Wendell Phillips to Maria Weston Chapman (London), 30 July 1839, MS A.9.2, vol. 12, 1839 (2), Weston Papers, Boston Public Library, rpt. in Taylor, *British and American Abolitionists*, 78. Other US abolitionists were also keen on the scheme. See Edward M. Davis to Elizabeth Pease (Philadelphia), 28 December 1839, MS A.1.2, vol. 8, 1839, Weston Papers, Boston Public Library, rpt. in Taylor, 88.

89  William Lloyd Garrison to Joseph Pease (Boston), 1 September 1840, MS A.1.1., vol. 3, 1840, Weston Papers, Boston Public Library, rpt. in Taylor, *British and American Abolitionists*, 112.

90  Laidlaw, 'Justice to India', 310.

91  George Thompson (Attercliffe, near Sheffield) to Elizabeth Pease, 20 February 1839, Wclmss002083, Box 60, William L. Clements Library.

92  Meetings were also held in Newcastle-on-Tyne, Durham, Perth, Glasgow, Oldham, Rochdale, Leeds, Ashton-under-Lyne, Salford, and Bolton. See *British Indian Advocate*, 1 January 1841, 6–8. Cowasji Jahangir Readymoney (1812–78), Jamshedji Jijibhai (1783–1859), and Jagannath Shankarseth (1802–65) – all brokers, merchants, and philanthropists – expressed support. See also Mehrotra, S.R. *Emergence of the Indian National Congress*. Kolkata: Rupa, 2007: 18. When the British India Society was formed, Sir Charles Forbes (a Bombay merchant) pledged £500, and several members of his family contributed £20

each. The Society of Native Landowners in Bengal contributed £250. *Howitt's Journal*, 'India, the Proffered Salvation of England. Will She Have It?', no. 3, rpt. in *Liverpool Mercury*, 28 December 1847, 6.

93  *India Review*, 1843, rpt. as *Biographical Sketch*, 4.

94  Laidlaw, 'Justice to India', 312–13.

95  Stanton, *Sketches of Reforms and Reformers*, 239.

96  This is the motto on the journal's banner. The first issue had advance orders of 1,350 copies. It aspired to be weekly but at best achieved a fortnightly schedule. *Colonial Intelligencer*, no. 1 (1 January 1841).

97  The *British Indian Advocate* was edited by Mr Adam. The venture was financially precarious from the outset: days after the first issue was printed, Joseph Adshead, who backed the northern operation, unexpectedly decamped to the United States, leaving no way to pay Thompson's salary or continue the journal. See Basu, Baman Das. *Story of Satara*. Edited by Ramananda Chatterjee. Calcutta: Modern Review Office, 1922: 141; and George Thompson to Elizabeth Pease, 5 January 1840 [*sic*] [1841], Wclmss002083, Box 60, William L. Clements Library.

98  This was a deliberate, calculated move. George Thompson to Elizabeth Pease, 12 February 1839, Wclmss002083, Box 60, William L. Clements Library.

99  'The People of England and the Natives of India.' *British Indian Advocate*, 1 August 1841, 65.

100 'Objects of This Journal.' *British Indian Advocate*, 1 January 1841, 1.

101 British India. *Speeches Delivered by Major-General John Briggs and George Thompson at the Annual Meeting of the Glasgow Society for Promoting the Cause of Universal Emancipation, Protecting the Aborigines of the British Dependencies, and Bettering the Condition of the Natives of India; Held August 1, 1839*. Edinburgh: W. Oliphant, Jun., 1839: 21.

102 Allen, Richard B. *European Slave Trading in the Indian Ocean*. Athens: Ohio State University Press, 2014: 180–2.

103 *British Indian Advocate*, 1 January 1841, 1–2.

104 George Thompson, 'Correspondence. "Freedom to the Slave" Letter II.' *British Indian Advocate*, 1 April 1841, 30. See also Thompson, George. *Lectures on British India, Delivered in the Friends' Meeting-House, Manchester, England, in October 1839*. Pawtucket, RI: William and Robert Adams, 1840: 44–5.

105 'Treatment of the Princes and People of India.' *British Indian Advocate*, 1 February 1841, 9–10.

106 'Slavery in India.' *British Indian Advocate*, 1 May 1841, 35.

107 'Kidnapping Men for a Voyage to the Mauritius.' *British Indian Advocate*, 1 August 1841, 80. This report was reprinted from the *Calcutta Englishman* and corroborated in the *Bengal Hurkaru*.

108 George Thompson's speech, 'Aborigines Protection Society.' *Newcastle Courant*, 1 February 1839, 2.

109 ACLL letterbook, Manchester Central Reference Library and Archives; and 'The British India Society, and the National Anti-Corn Law League.' *British Indian Advocate*, 1 July 1841, 57–8. Thompson had been courted by the

pro-tax faction with the promise of £1,000 per year, but went with the side he personally endorsed. Farmer, 'Letters from England', 4 March 1864, 1.

110 'Tea Party to George Thompson, Esq.' *British Indian Advocate*, 1 July 1841, 58–9.

111 'Valedictory Speech of George Thompson Esq., at the Manchester Conference.' *Worcestershire Chronicle*, 1 September 1841, 4; Farmer, 'Letters from England', 11 March 1864, 1; and 'Anti-Corn Law Conference.' *Morning Chronicle* (London), 21 August 1841, 3. Attendees included Catholics, Episcopalians, and Old and New Dissenters (Presbyterians, Trinitarians, Unitarians, Baptists, Swedenborgians, Inghamites, Calvinists, and Armenians).

112 'Mr Thompson's Lectures on British India.' *British Indian Advocate*, 1 July 1841, 61. See also Thompson, George. *Six Lectures on the Condition, Resources and Prospects of British India and the Duties and Responsibilities of Great Britain to Do Justice to That Vast Empire*. London: John W. Parker, 1842.

113 Biagini, E.F. 'Radicalism and Liberty.' In *Liberty and Authority in Victorian Britain*, edited by Peter Mandler, 101–25. Oxford: Oxford University Press, 2006: 109.

114 Parry, Jonathan. 'Liberalism and Liberty.' In *Liberty and Authority in Victorian Britain*, edited by Peter Mandler, 71–101. Oxford: Oxford University Press, 2006: 72.

115 Thompson, George. *Anti-Corn Law Lecture at Longtown. Thursday January 20th, 1842*. Carlisle: James Steel, 1842: 10.

116 Thompson, *Anti-Corn Law Lecture*, 16.

117 Here Thompson (*Anti-Corn Law Lecture*, 17) cites McQueen, James. *General Statistics of the British Empire*. London: B. Fellows, 1836.

118 Thompson, *Anti-Corn Law Lecture*, 18.

119 Jenkins, T.A. *The Liberal Ascendancy, 1830–1886*. New York: St Martin's, 1994: 77, 79.

120 'The Raja of Sattara: Five Days' Debate at the India House.' *British Indian Advocate*, 1 August 1841, 66.

121 Basu, *Story of Satara*, 94.

122 *Debates at the India House: August 22nd, 23rd, and September 24th, 1845, on the Case of the Deposed Raja of Sattara, and the Impeachment of Col. C. Ovans*. London: Effingham Wilson, 1845: xv.

123 According to Bapuji Amund Rao, the conspiracy was set in motion in 1837 by himself and several members of the raja's household treasury. Haibat Rao and Atmaram Laksuman, in collusion with the Resident Colonel Ovans and the governor's man Ballajee Punt Natoo, a Brahmin, were paid handsomely to forge thirty-six documents, affixing the raja's purported seal. *The Deposed Raja of Sattara: Documents, Chiefly Official, Now for the First Time Printed*. London: W. Tyler, 1842: 54–7.

124 Kulkarni, Sumitra. *The Satara Raj, 1818–1848: A Study in History, Administration, and Culture*. New Delhi: Mittal, 1995: 31.

125 On the righteousness of succession, see Joseph Hume, letter to the editor, *Times*, 23 November 1848, 3. On Thompson's advocacy on behalf of heirs, see 'East India House.' *Morning Post*, 23 December 1847, 5.

126 Sumitra Kulkarni elaborates: 'his relatives and followers and the military escort amounted to 2,700 persons and 1,353 animals, of which 500 were horses and 600 bullocks'. *Satara Raj*, 30.

127 Basu, *Story of Satara*, 124.

128 See *Proceedings at a Special General Court of Proprietors of East India Stock, Held at the East India House, on the 12th and 13th of February, 1840, Respecting the Dethronement of His Highness the Rajah of Satara*. London: John Wilson, 1840.

129 Basu, *Story of Satara*, xxiv, 139–40, 148.

130 Farmer, 'Letters from England', 18 March 1864, 1.

131 Exactly when Thompson began to be paid for his services to the ex-raja is unclear; it was perhaps not before 1842. Undoubtedly, he and Joseph Hume are the parties whom Thornton references as 'Englishmen [who] did not hesitate to take the unhappy prince's money in payment for exertions directed against the interests of their own country, and the safety of its Indian dominions.' Thornton, Edward. *The History of the British Empire in India*. London: W.H. Allen, 1859: 428. And see Basu, *Story of Satara*, xxi, 148.

132 Thompson, George. *The Raja of Satara: Speech Delivered in the Court of Proprietors at the India House, July 15, 1841*. London: W. Tyler, 1841: 4.

133 Thompson, *Raja of Satara*, 5, 13.

134 Thompson, *Raja of Satara*, 23–4.

135 Basu, *Story of Satara*, 92–3.

136 George Thompson, speech to the general quarterly Court of Proprietors, 23 September 1846, in *British Friend of India Magazine*, October 1846, rpt. in Basu, *Story of Satara*, 462–3.

137 Thompson, in Basu, *Story of Satara*, 464.

138 'East India House.' *Morning Post*, 30 July 1842, 5; and Farmer, 'Letters from England', 18 March 1864, 1.

139 Thompson, in Basu, *Story of Satara*, 465.

140 George Thompson's diary includes a notation that he paid out £161/0/8 to Bapojee for January and February, representing his allowance and expenses. Diary, 1846, REAS 7/1, JRL.

141 Thompson, in Basu, *Story of Satara*, 468–9.

142 George Thompson (Chelsea, London) to Richard [Webb], 12 August 1845, MS A.9.2., vol. 21, 1845, Weston Papers, Boston Public Library, rpt. in Taylor, *British and American Abolitionists*, 236–7.

143 Thompson, in Basu, *Story of Satara*, 471, 472–3.

144 See 'Parliamentary Proceedings. House of Commons.' *Allen's Indian Mail*, 30 June 1847, 407–9; 3 August 1847, 466–9; and 6 December 1847, 725–7; and 'House of Commons, Monday 5 July.' *Times*, 6 July 1847, 2.

145 Farmer, 'Letters from England', 18 March 1864, 1.

146 Stanton, *Sketches of Reforms and Reformers*, 243–4.

147 Mehrotra, S.R. 'The British India Society and Its Bengal Branch, 1839–46.' *Indian Economic and Social History Review* 4, no. 2 (1967): 143.

148 Mehrotra, 'The Landholders' Society', 360.

149 Mehrotra, 'The Landholders' Society', 362.

150 Mehrotra, 'The Landholders' Society', 358 (qtd.), 367.

151 Phillips, Arthur. *The Law Relating to the Land Tenures of Lower Bengal (Tagore Law Lectures 1874–75)*. Calcutta: Thacker, Spink, 1876: 558.

152 *Englishman* (Calcutta), 3 November 1868, qtd. in Mehrotra, 'The Landholders' Society', 371; and see Mehrotra, *Emergence of the Indian National Congress*, 368.

153 Prasannakumar Tagore (1801–68, member of the governor-general's council) and William Theobold (1798–1870, barrister) served as their secretaries. Mehrotra, *Emergence of the Indian National Congress*, 369.

154 Kling, Blair B. *Partner in Empire: Dwarkanath Tagore and the Age of Enterprise in Eastern India*. Berkeley: University of California Press, 1976: 174 (qtd.), 170–2.

155 Tagore's holdings were extensive at this time: he developed his landholdings with a variety of joint-stock ventures in steam tugboats, coal, tea, and shipping by water and railway. He promoted Western-style charities such as hospitals and schools, road and sanitation improvement, and communications. Scholberg, Henry, ed. *The Biographical Dictionary of Greater India*. New Delhi: Promilla, 1998: 133.

156 Kling, *Partner in Empire*, 174.

157 Palsetia, Jesse S. *Jamsetjee Jejeebhoy of Bombay: Partnership and Public Culture in Empire*. Oxford: Oxford University Press, 2015: 8.

158 Lethbridge, Roper. *The Golden Book of India, a Genealogical and Biographical Dictionary*. New York: Macmillan, 1893: 526.

159 Thompson, George. *Speeches by Mr. George Thompson (Father of Political Education in India)*. Edited by Raj Jogeshur Mitter. Calcutta: S. K. Lahiri, 1895: 1, 7–8.

160 From Amelia Chesson's notebooks extracting Thompson's letters, mid-February and May–July, 1843, REAS 4/1–4, JRL. Thompson remarked that in May he visited Tagore's suburban mansion, which means that his residence was probably the family home in Calcutta (Letterbooks, 1837–65, REAS 4/1–4, JRL). Tagore entertained lavishly in his suburban home, Belgatchia Villa, north of the city, hosting visiting artists and dignitaries of all kinds. Kling, *Partner in Empire*, 182–3; see also 'Blair B. Kling', in Scholberg, *Biographical Dictionary*, 132–3.

161 Thompson, *Speeches*, 14.

162 Santos, Boaventura de Sousa. *The End of the Cognitive Empire: The Coming of Age of Epistemologies of the South*. Durham, NC: Duke University Press, 2018: 43–4.

163 Thompson, *Speeches*, 19; and Grindlay, Melville. *A View of the Present State of the Question as to Steam Communication*. London: Smith, Elder, 1837: 52–4.

164 Thompson, *Speeches*, 21–3.

165 Thompson, George. *Addresses; Delivered at Meetings of the Native Community of Calcutta and on Other Occasions*. Calcutta: Thacker, 1843: 12.

166 Meetings on 6, 13, and 20 February 1843, in Thompson, *Speeches*, 28 (qtd.), 46 (qtd.), and 53.

167 Speech at the opening of the Hall in the Fouzdaree Balakhana, Baboo Hurro Coomar Tagore in the chair, 6 March 1843, in Thompson, *Speeches*, 84.

168 Lorde, Audre. 'The Master's Tools Will Never Dismantle the Master's House.' In *Sister Outsider: Essays and Speeches*, 110–14. Berkeley, CA: Crossing Press, 1984.

169 Warner, Michael. *Publics and Counterpublics*. New York: Zone Books, 2002: 11–12.

170 Speech on 20 March 1843 in Thompson, *Speeches*, 124–5, and see 127.

171 Thompson, *Addresses*, 129.

172 Thompson, *Addresses*, 132.

173 'Formation of the Bengal British India Society', in Thompson, *Addresses*, 134–41.

174 Manthrirathne, Sanjeevi. 'The Reform Movements in India and Sri Lanka: A Comparative Study.' PhD diss., University of Kashmir, 2013: 162–4.

175 Mehrotra, *Emergence of the Indian National Congress*, 25.

176 Mehrotra, *Emergence of the Indian National Congress*, 29 (qtd.), 30–1.

177 Thompson, *Addresses*, 127–8.

178 Chakrabarty, Dipesh. *Provincializing Europe: Postcolonial Thought and Historical Difference*. Princeton, NJ: Princeton University Press, 2008: 151.

179 Bayly, C.A. *Recovering Liberties: Indian Thought in the Age of Liberalism and Empire*. Cambridge: Cambridge University Press, 2012: 132.

180 See Palsetia, *Jamsetjee Jejeebhoy of Bombay*, 54–8.

181 Mehrotra, *Emergence of the Indian National Congress*, 32.

182 Manthrirathne, 'Reform Movements', 175–6.

183 George Thompson (Begums Palace) to Jenny [Anne] Thompson, 29 August 1843, REAS 2/1/46, JRL.

184 *Bengal Catholic Herald* 5, no. 7 (12 August 1843): 13.

185 *Bengal Catholic Herald* 5, no. 5 (29 July 1843): 9. For an account of the visit and Thompson's defence of his choices, see letters reprinted in Glasgow Emancipation Society, *Ninth Annual Report of the Glasgow Emancipation Society*. Glasgow: D. Russell, 1843: 52–7.

186 George Thompson (Begums Palace) to Jenny [Anne] Thompson, 29 August 1843, REAS 2/1/46, JRL.

187 A parliamentary paper presented in 1848 stipulated that the king of Delhi still retained George Thompson, his 'agent in England', at this rate, which amounted to £1,200 per annum (3,500 per cent greater than the salary of an average Indian worker). 'Parliamentary Papers.' *Daily News*, 17 February 1848, 2; and Allen, Robert C. and Roman Studer. 'Prices and Wages in India, 1595–1930.' Spreadsheet. Global Price and Income History Group, University of California, Davis. Uploaded September 2009. http://gpih.ucdavis.edu/Datafilelist.htm.

188 *Bengal Catholic Herald* 5, no. 23 (2 December 1843), 45; and 5, no. 25 (16 December 1843), 49. See also *British Friend of India Magazine*, December 1843, rpt. in Basu, *Story of Satara*, 443–6.

189 George Thompson to Elizabeth Pease, 7 May 1839, Wclmss002083, Box 60, William L. Clements Library.

190   Nathaniel Peabody Rogers, letter to the editor, *Herald of Freedom* (Concord, NH), 30 October 1840, rpt. in Rogers, Nathaniel Peabody. *A Collection from the Miscellaneous Writings of Nathaniel Peabody Rogers*. Manchester, NH: William H. Fisk, 1849: 116–17.

191   Warner, *Publics and Counterpublics*, 65–124.

192   George Thompson to Elizabeth Pease, 30 April and 6 June 1841, Wclmss002083, Box 60, William L. Clements Library.

193   Stange, Douglas Charles. *British Unitarians against American Slavery, 1833–65.* Rutherford: Fairleigh Dickinson University Press, 1984: 84; see also Moran, Karen Board. 'William Lloyd Garrison.' Worcester Women's History Project, 26 March 2005. In another measure of regard, Louis Chamerovzow stood as godfather to the Chessons' eldest daughter, and at the same ceremony Frederick Chesson stood as godfather to the Thompsons' youngest daughter (Frederick Chesson's diary, 2 November 1856, REAS 11/4, JRL).

194   Stange, *British Unitarians,* 117; and Blackett, R.J.M. 'Fugitive Slaves in Britain: The Odyssey of William and Ellen Craft.' *Journal of American Studies* 12, no. 1 (1978): 52.

195   Frederick Douglass to Thomas Auld, 'To My Old Master.' *North Star* (Rochester, NY), 3 September 1848, and *Liberator*, 22 September 1848, 1–2, rpt. in Douglass, Frederick. *Frederick Douglass: Selected Speeches and Writings*. Edited by Philip Foner. Chicago: Lawrence Hill Books, 1999: 111.

196   On the commodification of minoritarian subjects, see Chambers-Letson, Joshua. *After the Party: A Manifesto for Queer of Color Life*. New York: New York University Press, 2018.

197   Conquergood, Dwight. 'Rethinking Elocution: The Trope of the Talking Book and Other Figures of Speech.' *Text and Performance Quarterly* 20, no. 4 (2000): 331.

198   Grandy, Moses. *Narrative of the Life of Moses Grandy, Late a Slave in the United States of America*. Introduction by George Thompson, iii–vi. Boston: Oliver Johnson, 1844. Thompson's introduction is dated 18 October 1842. Samantha Mitchell ('Grandy, Moses.' NCPedia, North Carolina Government and Heritage Library. 2013) writes that Grandy and Thompson met during Grandy's travels to Britain in 1843, but Thompson's itinerary definitively precluded this.

199   Thompson, introduction to Grandy, *Narrative*, iv.

200   *Anti-Slavery Reporter*, 30 November 1842, 192, 194; and 21 June 1843, 108.

201   For example, when William Craft called upon William Taylor (Church Protestant Defence) asking to lecture at Barnet Town Hall, Taylor asked: 'Before I can take him by the hand or in any way become responsible I should like to learn something about him from you[.] Will you tell me in the strictest confidence what is generally thought of him by your Society or also what you think of Ellen Craft his wife.' Letter from William Taylor to unspecified recipient, 5 May 1854, Bodleian C160/152, BFASS correspondence, Bodleian Library.

202   David W. Blight recounts Douglass' use of this tactic in 1843: '"I am one of the *things* of the South!" "Drawing himself up to his full height, and

spreading his arms wide," wrote an observer, Douglass declared, "Behold the thing!"' *Frederick Douglass: Prophet of Freedom*. New York: Simon and Schuster, 2018: 166.

203 Roper, Moses. *A Narrative of the Adventures and Escape of Moses Roper from American Slavery*. London: Darton, Harvey, and Darton, 1837: 68–70; Price, Thomas. *Slavery in America: With Notices of the Present State of Slavery and the Slave Trade throughout the World*. London: G. Wightman, 1837: vi.

204 Morgan, *Celebrities, Heroes and Champions*, 169.

205 Charles H. Nichols notes the predominance of slave narratives after 1836, edited and introduced by white abolitionists. J. R. Oldfield observes that British abolitionists' activities were avidly followed in the United States, and that after liberation in the Caribbean colonies there was a keen sense of regard and gratitude among US abolitionists. See Nichols, Charles H. 'Who Read the Slave Narratives?' *Phylon Quarterly* 20, no. 2 (1959): 149.

206 Douglass (Dublin) to William Lloyd Garrison (London), 29 September 1845, rpt. in Douglass, *Frederick Douglass*, 120.

207 Blight, *Frederick Douglass*, 179.

208 Goddu, *Selling Antislavery*, 56, 68.

209 Santos, *End of the Cognitive Empire*, 33–4.

210 Smith, *Dominion of Voice*, 233.

211 'The Ransom of Frederick Douglass.' *Liberator*, 12 February 1847, 26.

212 Kraditor, Aileen S. *Means and Ends in American Abolitionism: Garrison and His Critics on Strategy and Tactics, 1834–1850*. New York: Pantheon, 1967: 221.

213 Douglass to Henry Clarke Wright, *Liberator*, 29 January 1847, 2.

214 Douglass to Thomas Auld, 3 September 1848, rpt. in Douglass, *Frederick Douglass*, 111. The legal process to end Douglass' bondage was completed in December 1846. J. Meredith, 'Receipt for $25 Related to the Manumission of Frederick Douglass', 12 December 1846, GLC078484.05, Gilder Lehrman Collection, Gilder Lehrman Institute of American History.

215 Douglass to Thomas Auld, 3 September 1848, rpt. in Douglass, *Frederick Douglass*, 111.

216 Blight, *Frederick Douglass*, 86.

217 Frederick Douglass (Glasgow) to William Lloyd Garrison, 16 April 1846, rpt. in Douglass, *Life and Writings*, I: 149.

218 Frederick Douglass (London) to William Lloyd Garrison, 23 May 1846, rpt. in Douglass, *Life and Writings*, I: 165.

219 Frederick Douglass (London) to William Lloyd Garrison, 23 May 1846, rpt. in Douglass, Frederick. *Life and Writings of Frederick Douglass. Vol. 1, Early Years, 1817–1849*. Edited by Philip Foner. New York: International, 1950: I:165.

220 Frederick Douglass (Glasgow) to William Lloyd Garrison, 16 April 1846, rpt. in Douglass, *Life and Writings*, I: 149.

221 Frederick Douglass (London) to William Lloyd Garrison, 23 May 1846, rpt. in Douglass, *Life and Writings*, I: 165.

222 Whyte, Iain. *Send Back the Money! The Free Church of Scotland and American Slavery*. Cambridge: James Clarke, 2012.

223 Wright, Henry C. *The Dissolution of the American Union Demanded by Justice and Humanity, as the Incurable Enemy of Liberty*. Glasgow: D. Russell, 1845: 46–7.

224 Frederick Douglass (Kilmarnock, Scotland) to Maria Weston Chapman, 29 March 1846, MS A.9.2, vol. 22, 1846, Weston Papers, Boston Public Library, rpt. in Taylor, *British and American Abolitionists*, 259. Thompson came under scrutiny for what some perceived as a mercenary approach. A broadside titled 'Send Back the Money – A New Version', allegedly written by students at the Free Church College in June 1846, caught the flavour. It begins with Thompson clutching a £50 note, and in subsequent verses Douglass demands his share of the cash. Thompson reluctantly gives him £20. Whyte, *Send Back the Money!*, 84.

225 *The Free Church Alliance with Manstealers*. Glasgow: George Gallie, 1846: 13.

226 *Free Church Alliance*, 17.

227 *Free Church Alliance*, 30–1. See also Bourne, George. *A Picture of Slavery in the United States of America*. Middletown, CT: Edwin Hunt, 1834. Dr Cunningham, a theological moderate and a Tory with a compromised position on abolition that dated to 1826, had ministered in Edinburgh and Greenock. In 1846 he was appointed professor of church history and divinity in the new Free Church College. Whyte, *Send Back the Money!*, 7; and Shepperson, George. 'The Free Church and American Slavery.' *Scottish Historical Review* 30, no. 110 (1951): 132–3.

228 *Free Church Alliance*, 3.

229 Frederick Douglass in Paisley, 25 April 1846, reported in the *Renfrewshire Advertiser*, 2 May 1846, rpt. in Blassingame, John W., ed. *The Frederick Douglass Papers. Series One: Speeches, Debates, and Interviews. Vol. 1, 1841–46*. New Haven, CT: Yale University Press, 1979: 242–3.

230 Douglass, Frederick. *My Bondage and My Freedom. London: Partridge and Oakey*, 1855: 383–4. Lyrics of several of these songs are reproduced in Whyte, *Send Back the Money!*, 81–7. On Douglass' 'strategic Anglophilia', see also Rice, Alan. *Racial Narratives of the Black Atlantic*. London: Bloomsbury Academic, 2003: 172–4.

231 *Free Church Alliance*, 34–5. See also George Thompson's speech in *American Slavery: Report of a Public Meeting Held at Finsbury Chapel, Moorfields, to Receive Frederick Douglass, the American Slave, on Friday, May 22, 1846*. London: Christopher B. Christians, 1846: 24.

232 Whyte, *Send Back the Money!*, 62; and Shepperson, 'Free Church and American Slavery', 137.

233 Murray, Hannah. 'Walking Tours.' Frederick Douglass in Britain and Ireland. Accessed March 15, 2022. http://frederickdouglassinbritain.com.

234 George Thompson, speech at Mr. M'Gilchrist's Church (Rose Street, Edinburgh), 26 April 1846, in *Free Church Alliance*, 50. See also Wright, Henry C. 'Letter to the Ministers and Members of the Free Church of Scotland.' In *The Free Church and Her Accusers, the Question at Issue: A letter from George Thompson, Esq. to Henry C. Wright: And One from Henry C.*

*Wright to Ministers and Members of the Free Church of Scotland, by George Thompson and Henry C. Wright*, 6–12. Glasgow: G. Gallie, 1846: 10–11.

235 Thompson, George. *The Free Church of Scotland and American Slavery. Substance of Speeches Delivered in the Music Hall, Edinburgh, during May and June 1846, by George Thompson, Esq. and the Rev. Henry C. Wright.* Edinburgh: Scottish Anti-Slavery Society, 1846: 43.

236 Catherine Clarkson to Maria Weston Chapman, n.d., MS A.9.2, vol. 22, 1846, Weston Papers, Boston Public Library, rpt. in Taylor, *British and American Abolitionists*, 275.

237 Charles Lenox Remond, 'Slavery as It Concerns the British', lecture to the BFASS, 9 July 1841. In *Negro Orators and Their Orations*, edited by Carter G. Woodson. Washington, DC: Associated, 1925: 127–8.

238 Santos, *End of the Cognitive Empire*, 96.

239 R. D. Webb to Maria Weston Chapman (Dublin), 16 July 1846, MS A.9.2, vol. 22, no. 75, 1846, Weston Papers, rpt. in Taylor, *British and American Abolitionists*, 273.

240 Whyte, *Send Back the Money!*, 99–103.

241 Vincent, a Radical and Chartist, publisher of the *Vindicator*, stood unsuccessfully as a candidate in eight elections. He remained a popular lecturer on education, free trade, and religious tolerance, also working for the Peace Society from 1848 and repeatedly venturing to the United States after the American Civil War.

242 William Lloyd Garrison (London) to Helen Garrison, 18 August 1846, MS a.1.1, vol. 4, 1844–53, Weston Papers, Boston Public Library, rpt. in Taylor, *British and American Abolitionists*, 275–6.

243 J. B. Estlin (Bristol) to Samuel May, 12 January 1847, MS B.1.6, vol. 2, May Papers, Massachusetts Historical Society, rpt. in Taylor, *British and American Abolitionists*, 305; Samuel May (Boston) to J. B. Estlin, 26 September 1846, MS B.1.6, vol. 2, MS N-536, May Papers, Massachusetts Historical Society, rpt. in Taylor, *British and American Abolitionists*, 289–90; and Farmer, 'Letters from England', 18 March 1864, 1.

244 Stange, *British Unitarians*, 87–8.

245 Loggins, Vernon. 'Writings of the Leading Negro Antislavery Agents, 1840–1865.' In *Critical Essays on Frederick Douglass*, edited by William L. Andrews, 37–55. Boston: G. K. Hall, 1991: 45. See also *Free Church Alliance*, 56.

246 *Free Church Alliance*, 51.

247 Smyth did not abbreviate the insult. Legal action ensued, Smyth issued an apology, and Douglass was vindicated. Maclear, J.F. 'Thomas Smyth, Frederick Douglass, and the Belfast Antislavery Campaign.' *South Carolina Historical Magazine* 80, no. 4 (1979): 286–97.

248 Frederick Douglass (London) to William Lloyd Garrison, 23 May 1846, rpt. in Douglass, *Frederick Douglass*, 165.

249 Douglass did not abbreviate the insult. Frederick Douglass (Belfast) to William Lloyd Garrison, 1 January 1846, rpt. in Douglass, *Frederick Douglass*, 125. See also Charles Lenox Remond's 1842 remarks before the Legislative

Committee in the House of Representatives, where he noted that during nineteen months in England, Ireland, and Scotland, 'I was received, treated and recognized, in public and private society, without any regard to my complexion.' *Liberator*, 25 February 1842, 30, rpt. in Woodson, *Negro Orators*, 146.

250 Stange, *British Unitarians*, 176. See also Lidwell-Durnin, John. 'William Benjamin Carpenter and the Emerging Science of Heredity.' *Journal of the History of Biology* 53 (2020): 81–103.

251 Heartfield, *Aborigines' Protection Society*, 26, 75.

252 Estlin, J.B. *A Brief Notice of American Slavery, and the Abolition Movement*. London: W. Tweedie, 1853: 23, 16.

253 Charles Lenox Remond, 'Ireland.' *Liberator*, 19 November 1841, 1, rpt. in Woodson, *Negro Orators*, 137.

254 Jenkins, *Liberal Ascendancy*, 77. See also R. D. Webb (Dublin) to Maria Weston Chapman, 26 February 1846, MS A.9.2, vol. 22, 1846, Weston Papers, Boston Public Library, rpt. in Taylor, *British and American Abolitionists*, 254.

255 J. N. Buffum (Perth, Scotland) to Caroline Weston, 25 June 1846, MS A.9.2, vol. 22, 1846, Weston Papers, Boston Public Library, rpt. in Taylor, *British and American Abolitionists*, 270.

256 *Biographical Sketch and Portrait of George Thompson, Esq.* Calcutta: J.A. Gibbons, 1843: 5.

257 'The Southampton Election.' *Southampton Herald*, 7 August 1842, 2; and 'The Riots in All the Manufacturing Districts Are Suspended.' *Southampton Herald*, 27 August 1842, 2.

258 'Southampton Election.' *Morning Post*, 3 August 1842, 2.

259 Electors returned both Conservative candidates: Humphrey St John Mildmay (1825–66) with 685 votes, and George William Hope (1808–63, undersecretary for the colonies) with 682. The Rt. Hon. George Lord Nugent (1788–1850), who had been in and out of office since 1812, received 535 votes, and Thompson received 532. 'Southampton Election.' *Southampton Herald*, 13 August 1842, 4.

260 'Metropolitan News.' *Illustrated London News*, 6 February 1847, 87. 'Election Intelligence.' *Times*, 28 May 1847, 3; and 'General Election.' *Leeds Mercury*, 7 August 1847, 4.

261 'Grand Radical Demonstration in the Hamlets.' *Northern Star*, 4 September 1847, 9.

262 'The Rejected and the Elect.' *Examiner*, 7 August 1847, 1.

263 'Tower Hamlets.' *Standard*, 29 July 1847, 3.

264 Placards, which were commonly used in parliamentary contests, sometimes ran to forty lines of text, so these were especially terse. Oldfield, *Ties That Bind*, 41–4.

265 'A Working Man', letter to the editor, *Morning Advertiser*, 29 July 1847, 3. This letter was refuted by Thompson in a front-page classified

advertisement of the same day. In fact, except during his campaign, Thompson frequently attended meetings in taverns; he was not a teetotaller, though he was definitely associated with Dissenters during this campaign. The import of this is that he refused to *pay* supporters with alcohol. 'Multiple News Items.' *Standard*, 30 July 1847, 2; and 'The Elections.' *Daily News*, 30 July 1847, 3.

266 'The General Election.' *Times*, 30 July 1847, 3.

267 The final tally was Thompson 7,513, Clay 3,774, and Fox 2,718. The borough had roughly 500,000 inhabitants: this is an indication of how restrictive the franchise was even after the 1832 Reform Act.

268 'Tower Hamlets.' *Morning Post*, 31 July 1847, 2.

269 'Election News.' *Leeds Mercury*, 31 July 1847, 5.

270 Oldham elected William J. Fox (1786–1864), a popular ACLL lecturer, journalist, and Unitarian preacher with a magnificent deep voice that powerfully stirred auditors' emotions. 'The New Parliament.' *Illustrated London News*, 7 August 1847, 81.

271 'News.' *Dumfries and Galloway Standard*, 4 August 1847, 3; 'News.' *Newcastle Journal*, 7 August 1847, 2; and 'Ministerial Prospects, and the New Parliament.' *Lloyd's Weekly Newspaper*, 8 August 1847, 1.

272 'Grand Radical Demonstration in the Hamlets.' *Northern Star*, 4 September 1847, 9.

273 Laidlaw claims that 'Thompson pledged himself exclusive to Indian issues when elected for Tower Hamlets', but this claim ignores an onslaught of evidence. Furthermore, around this time there ceases to be mention of the shah of Delhi's allowance, and it is likely that this dried up, putting Thompson in desperate straits. The *British Indian Advocate* published its last four issues in 1847, all devoted to energetic pursuit of the ex-raja's case, but Thompson continued to advocate not only a wider plank of Indian issues but also a host of domestic and foreign concerns. See Laidlaw, 'Justice to India', 318; 'Metropolitan News.' *Illustrated London News*, 20 November 1847, 87; 'Free Trade with India.' *Illustrated London News*, 30 October 1847, 278; 'National Universal Suffrage Alliance.' *Morning Post*, 9 September 1847, 3; 'National Alliance for Promoting the Real Representation of the People.' *Worcestershire Chronicle*, 15 September 1847, 3; 'Summary.' *Leeds Times*, 11 September 1847, 4; 'The People's International League.' *Standard*, 16 November 1847, 4; 'The National Alliance.' *Leeds Times*, 8 January 1848, 7; 'The Great Free Trade Demonstration at Manchester.' *Leeds Times*, 29 January 1848, 8; 'Abolition of Capital Punishments.' *Morning Chronicle*, 9 March 1848, 7; 'Meeting of the British Anti-State Church Association.' *Leicestershire Mercury*, 2 December 1848, 1; 'Imperial Parliament.' *Northern Star*, 5 May 1849, 7; 'Financial and Parliamentary Reform.' *Manchester Times*, 26 May 1849, 2; 'Affairs of Hungary.' *Northern Star*, 8 December 1849, 5; and 'Proceedings in Parliament.' *Northern Star*, 9 February 1850, 6.

274 Mongia, Radhika V. 'Impartial Regimes of Truth: Indentured Indian Labour and the Status of the Inquiry.' *Cultural Studies* 18, no. 5 (2004): 749.

275 'The Growth of Cotton in India.' *Times*, 8 December 1848, 8.

276 Holyoake, *Public Speaking*, 151.

277 'The People's College.' *Norfolk News*, 23 June 1849, 5.

278 'Soirée to Mr. George Thompson, M.P.' *Standard*, 17 October 1850, 4.

279 'The Tower Hamlets and Mr. George Thompson.' *Daily News*, 24 July 1851, 3.

280 'United States.' *Daily News*, 29 November 1850, 5; and 'Mr. George Thompson in America.' *Newcastle Guardian and Tyne Mercury*, 7 December 1850, 5.

281 'A Fortnight Later from America.' *Freeman's Journal*, 11 March 1851, 2. See also Thompson, George. *Speech of George Thompson, Member of the British House of Parliament, at Toronto, May 1851*. Cincinnati: Wright, Ferris, 1851; and Davis, Tracy C. 'Oh Canaan! Following the North Star to Canada.' In *Uncle Tom's Cabins: The Transnational History of America's Most Mutable Book*, edited by Tracy C. Davis and Stefka Mihaylova, 33–58. Ann Arbor: University of Michigan Press, 2018: 48–51.

282 Kraditor, *Means and Ends in American Abolitionism*, 186–91.

283 Thompson, George. *Slavery in America: A Lecture Delivered in the Abbey-Close Church, Paisley, March 1, 1860*. London: London Emancipation Tracts, 1860: 13, 18.

284 'The United States.' *Morning Chronicle*, 23 April 1851, 7; and 'Three Days Later from America.' *Morning Post*, 19 June 1851, 6. The rumour is contradicted in 'Miscellaneous News.' *Lloyd's Weekly Newspaper*, 6 July 1851, 8.

285 'Election Intelligence.' *Morning Chronicle*, 27 March 1852, 5.

286 Rpt. from the *Advertiser*, 'Rumoured Purchase of a Seat for the Tower Hamlets.' *Lloyd's Weekly Newspaper*, 28 March 1852, 12.

287 'Elections.' *Daily News*, 7 July 1852, 2.

288 'The Elections.' *Illustrated London News*, 10 July 1852, 26.

289 'The Elections.' *Lloyd's Weekly Newspaper*, 11 July 1852, 2; and 'The Propriety of Choosing Residents as Representatives.' *Leicester Chronicle*, 17 April 1852, 4.

290 'The General Election.' *Newcastle Guardian and Tyne Mercury*, 10 July 1852, 5. The returns were: Sir William Clay 7,728, W. Butler 7,718, George Thompson 4,561, A. Ayrton 2,792, and W. Newton (secretary to the Amalgamated Engineers) 1,095.

291 Frederick Chesson's diary, 19 April and 15 November 1862, REAS 11/9, JRL.

292 Horace Mayhew, 'What I Saw at the Pawnbroker's.' *Punch*, 21 August 1852, 93.

293 Samuel Joseph May to William Lloyd Garrison, 17 January 1859, MS A.1.1, v. 2, p. 5, Boston Public Library.

294 George Thompson (Calcutta) to Amelia Chesson, 7 April 1856, REAS 2/2/55, JRL.

295 George Thompson (Calcutta) to Amelia Chesson, 23 March 1856, REAS 2/2/53, JRL.

296 George Thompson's letterbook, n.d., REAS 4/3, JRL.

297 George Thompson (Calcutta) to Amelia Chesson, 7 April 1856, REAS 2/2/55, JRL.

298 Samuel Joseph May to William Lloyd Garrison, 17 January 1859, MS A.1.2, v. 29, p. 6, Boston Public Library.

299 George Thompson's diary, 1856, REAS 7/3, JRL.

300 Travelling on a steamer from Malta in 1837, Ashburner befriended Richard Cobden and thereafter their families became close. Howe, Anthony and Simon Morgan, eds. *The Letters of Richard Cobden. Vol. 3, 1854–1859.* Oxford: Oxford University Press, 2007: 34–5.

301 Amelia Chesson's notebooks, January 1856, REAS 3/5, JRL.

302 George Thompson (Calcutta) to Amelia Chesson, 7 December 1856, REAS 2/2/61, JRL; and Basu, *Story of Satara*, 455.

303 [George Thompson], 'Our Special Correspondent', 'Calcutta as it Is and May Be.' *Morning Star*, 30 January 1857, 3. The letter was dispatched 20 December 1856.

304 See Frederick Chesson's diary, 2–15 August 1857, REAS 11/5, JRL. The letters on the outbreak of the rebellion did not arrive until August.

305 Richard Cobden to Joseph Sturge, 4 November 1857, Add MS 43722 fol. 281–2, British Library, rpt. in Howe and Morgan, *Letters of Richard Cobden*, 351–2.

306 George Thompson to Amelia Chesson, Letterbooks of George Thompson, 1839–56, REAS 4/3, JRL.

307 George Thompson to Amelia Chesson, Letterbooks of George Thompson, 1839–56, REAS 4/3, JRL.

308 George Thompson to Amelia Chesson, 9 January 1858, REAS 2/2/67, JRL.

309 George Thompson to Amelia Chesson, 22 January 1858, REAS 2/2/68, JRL.

310 George Thompson to Amelia Chesson, 7 January 1858, REAS 2/2/66, JRL.

311 The original edition was published in 1859. Smiles, Samuel. *Self-Help: With Illustrations of Character, Conduct, and Perseverance.* Edited by Peter W. Sinnema. Oxford: Oxford University Press, 2002: 331–2.

312 Kling, *Partner in Empire*, 167.

313 Basu, *Story of Satara*, 231.

314 Mehrotra, 'The British India Society', 142.

315 'As General Perronet Thompson [1783–1869, lecturer and grass-roots mobilizer for the ACLL] put it, the British public should consider Indians as fighters against imperial oppression, rather than simply mutineers.' Laidlaw, 'Justice to India', 323.

316 Frederick Chesson's diary, 11–18 July 1858, REAS 11/6, JRL; and Amelia Chesson's diary, 11–14 July 1858, REAS 10, JRL.

317 Samuel Joseph May to William Lloyd Garrison, 17 January 1859, MS A.1.2, v. 29, p. 6, Boston Public Library. Six months after Thompson's return, May

found him still partially paralysed, unable to work, and desperate for support from his friends. Thompson's rent was overdue, he could not meet his
mother's funeral expenses, the firm that had employed him in India refused
to pay salary from the day he left Calcutta, and one creditor continued to
press him for repayment of a debt.

318   Frederick Chesson's diary, 11 July 1858, REAS 11/6, JRL.

# CHAPTER 3

# Bildung

## *Leveraging Critique to Propel the Precarious into Political Life*

> Why should we not do with the middle class as we have done with
> the aristocratic class,—find in it some representative men who may
> stand for the virtuous mean of this class.... Some more ordinary
> man would be more to the purpose,—would sum up better in him-
> self, without disturbing influences, the general liberal force of the
> middle class, the force by which it has done its great works of free
> trade, Parliamentary reform, voluntaryism, and so on, and the spirit
> in which it has done them.
>
> —Matthew Arnold, *Culture and Anarchy*

As Holger Hoock notes, for an empire 'to think and act big on the global
stage required not only economic strength and military prowess, but
manifestly also intellectual, cultural, and imaginative effort'. Imaginative
entertainments were news, and news was taken up as entertainment: it
cut both ways, for to be well-versed in popular entertainment required
knowledge of current events – both foreign and domestic – because entertainment was highly topical, and thus to be truly up to date required
attendance at popular entertainments (Figure 3.1).[1] Extravaganza and its
Christmastide counterpart, pantomime, feasted on jokes and puns derived
from the foibles of politicians and celebrities and, as Jeffrey C. Cox argues,
utilised 'carnival and masking to reveal the "real" – or, at least, the mediated reality we call the "news"'.[2] As an indicative example, a succession
of the Haymarket Theatre's Easter extravaganzas during the early 1850s
exemplified how artifices about artifice emphasised the pleasure of seeing novelties recapitulated as *esprits*. Appreciating such entertainments
was a form of cultural literacy. Like others of their ilk, the Haymarket's
extravaganzas self-referentially remarked on entertainments' prominence
within the leisure market while reinforcing the process of circulation and
consumption. This is significant for all Victorians, and demonstrates the
milieu in which Frederick Chesson commenced his career as an activist,

Figure 3.1    *Voyage Round the Globe*, Haymarket Theatre, Playbill, 29 April 1854. *British Library Volume Playbills* 146 (1). Creative Commons licence.

observant of performance and edging his way into a public sphere redolent with recombinant elements of politics and entertainments.

### Recirculation

Beginning with the Haymarket Theatre's 1853 offering, J. B. Buckstone (1802–79) played a theatre manager anxious to find an appropriate novelty for his next show. He invoked his councils, the Spirit of Fashion (played by William Farren, 1825–1908, 'easy and gentlemanly') and the Spirit of

Fortune (played Mrs Fitzwilliam, 1801–54, who 'looked right regal'), and as the *Era* noted, they summoned before him a plethora of possibilities:

> The Spirits of the Corsican Brothers, of Mont Blanc, of Drury-lane, of the Lyceum, of the Royal Italian Opera, and of Uncle Tom. All these afford admirable opportunity for burlesque imitations, and the introduction of some beautiful and varied scenery. We have a slice from *Gold* at Drury-lane; a slap at the fly performance of Mr. Sands; a capital imitation of Charles Kean and Albert Smith; a fine buffo song from Mr. Corri; an elegant extract from the Lyceum; and a clever little song by Mrs. Fitzwilliam, *á propos* of Uncle Tom, winding up by the expression of a wish, most heartily responded to by the audience, that he would go 'where the other n-----'d gone.' Eventually the manager resolves to have an ascent of his own, but instead of Mont Blanc he determines to ascend the Phocian Mount of Parnassus, the favoured home of the Muses … [who] join in a fairy dance. Apollo himself is seen seated on the summit.[3]

This account of *Mr. Buckstone's Ascent of Mount Parnassus* neatly demonstrates how melodrama, travelogue, extravaganza, burlesque, and pantomime nested within other performances. Charles Kean's (1811–68) lesseeship at the Princess's Theatre was in full swing, with memorable acting in which he doubled as the indistinguishable Corsican brothers as well as appearing in Shakespeare. In 1853, Kean presented less memorable acting but impressive scenery in his Byronic adaptation *Sardanapalus*, 'a mighty picture of the antique world' displaying 'the mighty beginnings of poetry in stone', based on Austen Henry Layard's (1817–94) Assyrian excavations.[4] Journalist turned mountaineer Albert Smith (1816–60) was two-and-a-half years into his run of describing Swiss mountaineering at the Egyptian Hall, with no signs of abating (Figure 3.2).[5] The novel *Uncle Tom's Cabin* (1852) had come out in a dozen dramatic adaptations and the author, Harriet Beecher Stowe (1811–96), toured Britain and France to acclaim in 1853 (Figure 3.3).[6] But enough was enough. Mrs Fitzwilliam's song opines that the public had had their fill of *Uncle Tom* adaptations and commercial spin-offs:

> Wherever you travel, wherever you stop,
> Uncle Tom his black pole's sure to show;
> With his songs, polkas, waltzes, they fill every shop,
> Till like Topsy, 'I 'specs they must grow!'[7]

While emphasising the difference between the sentimental abolitionism of the novel and the media saturation of the eponymous hero in his stage manifestation, she seeks to banish Tom along with a raucous comic antecedent, Jim Crow, referenced with a then-common epithet in the *Era*

Figure 3.2    Mr Albert Smith's *Ascent of Mont Blanc* at the Egyptian Hall, Piccadilly. *Illustrated London News*, 25 December 1852, 565. Getty Images.

Figure 3.3    Abolition meeting held at Willis's Rooms in honour of Harriet Beecher Stowe, 1853, William Henry Fisk, watercolour. Getty Images.

FEAT OF MR. SANDS, THE "AIR-WALKER," AT DRURY-LANE THEATRE.

Figure 3.4    Feat of Mr Sands, the 'air walker', Drury Lane Theatre. *Illustrated London News*, 2 April 1853, 253. Getty Images.

review. Ellen Chaplin (1822–80) traversed the stage in *Mr. Buckstone's Ascent of Mount Parnassus* as the Spirit of Drury Lane, sporting a magnificent costume and banner inscribed with 'Gold', alluding to Charles Reade's (1814–88) play about Australian speculators then running at Drury Lane. In the olios at that theatre, a US acrobat, Richard Sands (?–1861), the 'inverted pedestrian' who had imitated Albert Smith's schtick in New York, performed an acrobatic act consisting of strolling upside down across a shiny surface, assisted by suction cups (Figure 3.4).[8] Buckstone pulled this all together in a metatheatrical tour de force of the travelogue, burlesque, and revue, referencing and succinctly imitating other high-profile entertainments.

James Wyld's (1812–87) Great Globe, installed in Leicester Square in 1851, expanded into an annex late in 1853 (Figure 3.5). It reflected a comparable approach – within an exhibition – to the nested performance at the Haymarket, utilising, as Stephan Oetterman states, a '"symbolic form" of a specifically modern bourgeois view of nature and the world'.[9] Its antecedents lay in Robert Barker's (1739–1806) panoramas, first popularised in

Figure 3.5  'Mr Wyld's Model of the Earth' (The Great Globe, cross section), Leicester
Square. *Illustrated London News*, 7 June 1851, 511. Getty Images.

1789 as a rival novelty to the waxworks, transparent paintings, models, and
magic shows around Leicester Square.[10] The Globe complex could accommodate 1,200 visitors at exhibits and lectures on geography, emigration,
and steam-powered ocean travel.[11] In them, Wyld capitalised on several
popular fixations:

> Attention was about equally divided between the globe itself, the centre of
> all the other novelties, the specimens of Australian gold [accompanied by
> Wyld's diorama of the gold fields], the model of Mont Blanc, the Vale of
> Chamouni, &c., and the views of the Arctic Regions. There are few sights
> in London where an hour or two can be more pleasantly spent, and profit-
> ably, too, than in this institution, where every knotty problem in geography
> may be solved for the visitor at once, and where the science is not drily
> taught, but illustrated in such a manner as to make a lasting impression on
> the mind.[12]

Thus, the Great Globe drew on the popularity of Albert Smith's alpine
excursion as well as the topicality of arctic exploration, boosted in 1853
by Captain Robert McClure's (1807–73) eastward-bound affirmation of
a Northwest Passage between Banks and Melville Islands.[13] And in 1853,

Wyld unveiled his new diorama of the Australian gold fields, along with impressively large nuggets (later exposed as fakes).[14] The edifying 'georama' of Wyld's Great Globe thus featured analogues traversing geography from the arctic to the antipodes.[15] During the 1853 season, London theatres also reflected the Australian gold fever in a raft of plays beyond Drury Lane's *Gold: In for a Dig* at Astley's, *Life in Australia* at the Olympic, *The Goldfields of Australia* at the Bower Theatre, and *The Golden Nugget* and *The New Tontine, or The Gold Seekers of Carpenteria* at the Queen's Theatre.[16] Just as entertainments nested within Buckstone's burlesque, entertainments, exploration, and science nested within Wyld's great panorama.

In 1854, Wyld's Great Globe became the pretext for the Haymarket's next Easter extravaganza, *Mr. Buckstone's Voyage Round the Globe*. Once again, Buckstone portrayed a manager in search of a topic. He fell asleep in an armchair at the base of the Great Globe and travelled virtually, in search of inspiration, at the behest of Cybele's four continental daughters. They were well aware that others had already appropriated what they showed Buckstone, and indeed this was their point: the Haymarket would show the public, *once again*, what everyone already knew they enjoyed. 'The stage opens at the command of *Europe*, and who should spring up but the *"Duke of Glo'ster* from Drury-Lane," and "the *Duke of Glo'ster* from the Princess's," meaning Mr. Brooke [1818–66] and Mr. C. Kean!' who accidentally flew up through the same trap. Europe also 'takes him to "the theatre of war," which he declares his utter inability to *manage'*.[17] Stagings of the Crimean conflict were yet to come (after the 'hot war' began in September 1854); while pointing out that this was not the Haymarket's kind of fare, Buckstone also alludes to the administrative debacle unfolding for the British military and government.[18] Buckstone is taken overland past the Dardanelles to see grand oriental spectacles, a Bayadere dance with Lydia Thompson (1838–1908), and a performance by 'Chinese' magicians (actually the Messrs Marshall). According to the *Morning Post*, 'in Africa he was struck with the sad appearance of its dark angel, and indulged in various ethnological reflections on the Bosjesmans, Zulu Kaffirs, Earthmen, and other unnatural [*sic*] curiosities, who would willingly come to terms with him if he would engage them. In America he has an interview with the Esquimaux from Cumberland Straits (alluding to a recent exhibition at the Adelaide Gallery), and encounters many droll adventures with the Yankees, at whom he does not fail to take a fling *à propos* of the slave trade'.[19]

The *Illustrated London News* reflected that in this performance, 'the mind is carried through the events of the year by a series of significant symbols, skilfully [*sic*] chosen, and accompanied by remarks in the dialogue – not

Figure 3.6    Scene from the tragedy of *Sardanapalus*, the Hall of Nimrod, Princess's
Theatre. *Illustrated London News*, 18 June 1853, 493.

only witty but wise, calculated to instruct as well as amuse'.[20] Buckstone
produced a third instance of J. R. Planché (1796–1880) performances in
this mode, *The New Haymarket Spring Meeting*, in which a midnight meeting of the City of London (portrayed as a Roman woman) and her sisters
Westminster and Tyburnia summon personifications of the East End's
Britannia and Grecian Theatres, followed by a scene in the grandstand
at Upsand Downs.[21] As Marty Gould put it: 'with a lilting lyric, actor
becomes traveler; performance becomes adventure'.[22]

Tragedies such as *Sardanapalus* at the Princess's Theatre traded on wide
familiarity with Layard's published illustrations of his excavations, the
exhibits at the British Museum, and the Nineveh court of plaster casts
at Crystal Palace (reconstructed in Sydenham during 1853, and opened in
June the following year) (Figure 3.6).[23] Perhaps this preoccupation was not
incidental: seventh-century BCE Assyria was the first empire that aspired
to world domination. Entertainments such as these – along with Wyld's
*Uncle Tom's Cabin* adaptations, and Albert Smith's *Ascent* – keyed into
science, exploration, geography, history, and politics as currently unfolding events. Consuming these made Victorians who they were. As Michael
Meeuwis argues, theatre was a lingua franca, 'a figure for how the human

individual functioned in society, a figure made concrete by the social scope and frequency of actual theater attendance'.[24] Looking backward to antiquity (as with Francis Talfourd's [1828–62] late 1850s burlesques at the Haymarket, which keyed into classically educated Britons' familiarity with ancient myths) or over one's shoulder to contemporary horrors (as with the *Uncle Tom* fare) involved an experience of both recognition and erudition, however ostensibly frivolous the entertainment genre.

As in Parisian year-end vaudeville reviews, such entertainments marked how, as John Dewey later put it, 'artists have always been the real purveyor of news, for it is not the outward happening in itself which is new, but the kindling of it by emotion, perception and appreciation'.[25] The turning of a new year was typically the time to etch events into memory through time-honoured social rites. Likewise, when George Cruikshank (1792–1878) summed up the year 1853 for a fold-out etching in the inaugural, January 1854, issue of *Cruikshank's Magazine*, he juxtaposed the previous year's events in dozens of tiny sketches within the body of a comet (Figure 3.7).[26] Cruikshank's 'Passing Events of 1853' was calculated to remind readers of their tastes, sensations, and inspirations.[27] Essentially, it is the visual equivalent of a quodlibet: loosely related successive quotations, light and whimsical yet also a pointed proposal for disputation.

For decades, theatre historiography has emphasised how spectacle, particularly in Shakespeare and tragedy, traded on Victorians' habit of looking at the world through pictures.[28] The insight advanced by the Haymarket extravaganzas and Cruikshank's 'Passing Events of 1853' is that the spectrum of performance lent important building blocks to popular understanding of the known world, inviting a reflexive process of knowledge-making. During the early 1850s, the referential field ranged from Australian emigration to the marvels of its gold fields; from the music of a globe-trotting conductor to the more homely ensemble of a British band; from public demonstrations against electoral corruption to judicial review of alleged malpractice; and from inebriated Christmas revellers surrounded by livestock to the rousing teetotal lectures of J. B. Gough (1817–86) and Temperance Conventions organised across Britain and the United States to launch the campaign for prohibition.[29] Entertainments inclusive of but not limited to the theatre were recirculation points for exploration, geography, ethnography, social reform, and conquest every bit as much as newspapers (and indeed, in league with them). These recirculating points for knowledge worked in one another's pockets, perpetuating both supply and demand. Art and entertainment reflected the social experience of 'interwoven human values' forming Victorians' understanding of the world, modelling citizenship and

Figure 3.7 George Cruickshank, 'Passing Events, or The Tail of the Comet of 1853', etching, *Cruikshank's Magazine*, January 1854. 2017JW5484, Theaterwissenschaftliche Sammlung, University of Cologne.

equipping citizens with an affective forum to process and connect information.[30] For example, along the comet's plasma tail atop Cruikshank's picture, the naval review at Portsmouth gives way to exploits further afield, the pinnacle being Captain Robert McClure's intercultural encounter with the Esquimeux [*sic*], who told him about 'Parry's farthest', the point on Melville Island where Sir William Edward Parry (1790–1855) had travelled in 1820.[31] This established that McClure's eastbound sailing route intersected with an earlier westbound expedition, thus confirming the existence of a Northwest Passage. This news reached England in October 1853, though McClure spent his fourth winter in the ice before completing his eastbound transit. Whereas the comet's harlequinade marked calendrical time turning, arctic exploration signified a great future of commerce, heralding unprecedented trade between Europe and East Asia, even though this speculation was to be realised on an unknown timeline.

In ancient times, comets portended great historical events, though not always the harbingers of doom seen by Marcus Manilius (fl. first century BCE).[32] In 1853, four comets were seen over Britain; from August through to October one of these benign yet 'illustrious strangers' was visible to the unaided eye, and as a metaphor this served Cruikshank's purpose well.[33] His omnibus perspective on the year covers a gamut of politics, social history, and recreation. Near the comet's head, a Black figure (possibly the character George Harris) balances an *Uncle Tom's Cabin* placard on his shoulder, standing just behind Mrs Stowe and thus commemorating her 1853 visit (Figure 3.7). At the centre, Albert Smith's *Ascent of Mont Blanc* was thought of as 'one of the institutions of the country', attracting an estimated 800,000 visitors before it closed.[34] Cruikshank illustrated this next to Drury Lane Theatre's 'air walker'.[35] The colossal winged stone lions on view at the British Museum are seen along the lower edge; this 'staging of knowledge' occurred in several burlesques as well as at the Princess's Theatre.[36] Finally, harlequinade characters, who perennially see out each year and usher in the next, mark the calendar change in the bottom right corner. Twenty-three other entertainments crowd the illustration, with political events taking up the balance of the vignettes.

Late in 1852, Lord Derby's (1799–1869) budget was overturned and power shifted from a precarious Conservative government to a coalition between the pro–free trade Peelite wing of the Tories and the Whigs, with William Gladstone as chancellor of the Exchequer. Riffing off the idea of Spiritualist table-rapping, Cruikshank shows the 'spirit of the times' turning against isolationists in January (lower left of the comet's tail). The new government's policies were inchoate: rather than reforming income tax and rationalising other forms of direct and indirect taxation, such as the stamp duty on paper and the advertising tax, it made a series of expedient adjustments concocted on the fly.[37] The flamboyant French conductor Louis-Antoine Jullien (1812–60), whose low-price 'monster concerts' with hundreds of instrumentalists were given in London and throughout the provinces, are indicated here in caricature, his audience blown back from the table (or drum) in front of him, in contrast to the enrapt spiritualists and the Whigs who look upon the toppled Conservatives.[38]

An important cluster of illustrations connects several 'ethnographic vignettes'. A troupe of Zulus – eleven men, one woman, and a child – appeared for several months at St George's Gallery. They had been brought to England by Charles Henry Caldecott (1814–79), who functioned as their manager and interpreter. Prior to each performance, he lectured on Zulu people's purported violent character. Then,

> After a supper of meal, of which the Kaffirs partake with large wooden spoons, an extraordinary song and dance are performed, in which each performer moves about on his haunches, grunting and snorting the while like a pair of asthmatic bellows ... no description can give an idea of the cries and shouts—now comic, now terrible—by which the Kaffirs express emotions. The scene illustrative of the preliminaries of marriage and the bridal festivities might leave one in doubt which was the bridegroom, did not that interesting savage announce his enviable situation by screams of ecstasy which convulse the audience.[39]

From 1850 to 1853, the Zulus and Xhosa fought the eighth of nine bitter wars in reaction to European settlers' incursions on their territory. This exhibition traded on Britons' fascination with Zulus' reputation and, as Sadiah Qureshi emphasises, 'Although the Xhosa and the Zulu were known to be distinctive peoples, Caldecott deliberately blurred the distinction whilst simultaneously acknowledging his manipulation.'[40] A second exhibit, at Regent Street, was of two San teenagers (billed as 'Earth Men', also known as 'Bushmen') who had been in England for two years. Europeans had known about the San since the sixteenth century, when the Portuguese established trade in southern Africa. By the mid-nineteenth century, the Dutch, English, and Kaffirs had brought them to the brink of extinction, believing them to be mentally inferior and not quite human.[41] The *Era* reviewer admired the Sans' clothing (made of hides) and gaudy red jewellery, and (as if to counter their reputation) noted the accomplishments of the girl, who could play the piano, and the boy, who sang 'negro melodies' from the repertoire of blackface minstrels. Their 'transformation' to European culture was featured: both could speak English and had been instructed in the catechism.[42] Another pair of performers, the 'Aztec Lilliputians', arrived from Central United States in June, en route to London's Marionette Theatre in the Strand.[43] Cruikshank depicts their command appearance at Buckingham Palace, greeting Queen Victoria, with the youngest of the royal children nearby for scale.[44] In September, the managers of all three exhibits lent them to appear together at Cremorne Gardens.[45]

Ever since Sara Baartman (1789–1815) was brought to Europe in 1810, abolitionists had objected to such exhibitions. The APS took up this cause, regarding all such people brought to Britain as non-consenting and in bondage, even if under contract.[46] Other exhibition practices corroborated the view that, notwithstanding the pretence of science, these Africans and Central Americans were exploited for racist ends. The Crystal Palace at Sydenham (pictured at the upper edge of the dust tail) featured among its many splendid halls a natural history court subsuming zoology, botany, and ethnography. Sydenham's ethnographic displays espoused a brand of scientific racism based on anatomic, physiological, and biological ideas of 'race'.[47] Wax impressions of both the Zulu and San performers were installed on a permanent basis. Thus, exhibiting the performers synecdochally with territorial and scientific conquests marks how Britons developed their sense of the world and subjected peoples, mutually changed but not equally challenged by colonialism. Soon, the impact of war and rebellion would bring this sense home even more noticeably.[48] As Howard L. Malchow argues, 'The shows were interpreted as relevant to contemporary political and military activity',[49] but the spectre of slavery was also present, as Cruikshank intimates with *Uncle Tom's Cabin*.

Two great foreign calamities are given prominence at the centre of the comet. The crisis between Russia and Turkey was pulling England and France into the disastrous Crimean conflict on the shores of the Black Sea, and in China Hong Xiuquan (1814–64, a millenarian Christian who believed himself to be the younger son of Jesus Christ) triumphed in the Battle of Nanjing, precipitating northern and western expansions in the long Taiping Civil War, which would claim 20–30 million lives and eventually, with British and French military assistance, reinstall the Manchu-led Qing dynasty in 1870. These imperial and dynastic cataclysms dominate Cruikshank's scene, at the meeting point of which is Mr Sands, upside down, and Albert Smith, climbing ever upward. November's 'Guy' (amidst the animals of the London Zoo and Aquarium and less animate chimeras from ancient Assyria) and the Lord Mayor's show, along with a host of other celebrations, ceremonies, and scandals, fill out the dust tail.

Pantomimes' dialogue utilised witty topicality to keep audiences keyed into otherwise banal plots. Buckstone's Easter extravaganzas and Cruikshank's 'Passing Events of 1853' additionally demonstrate how theatre and performance were not only parts of the annual cavalcade of events but ways to understand contemporary life, as it unfolded. Theatre and performance tested, reinforced, and calibrated an understanding of Britain's role in the world at a moment later acknowledged to be the empire's apogee; they purported to extend the understanding – if not shorten the distances – between the British and far-flung peoples; and they ironized while also cataloguing human, political, and social foibles. Just as Buckstone's choice of devices – Wyld's Great Globe and a midnight conference of London and her sisters – delighted through local recognisability, bringing the shows of London once again into view, the shows themselves were dependent upon this cavalcade of hubris, suffering, striving, pomp, posturing, exultation, and exhortation.

The British Empire's enterprises across the globe were made tangible through Cruikshank's combinatorial quodlibet of a comet. The mash-up of politics and entertainment was a metaphor of the year (and the times) but also traces how Victorians experienced their times. The shows 'created a comprehensive picture of the world and Britain's place within it', mediating how to experience imperialism and to take up roles in it. As Marty Gould explains, 'timely and topical, these various types of shows presented pieces of empire to the London spectator; collectively, they created a comprehensive picture of the world and Britain's place within it' through exhibitions of goods, peoples, artefacts, animals, art, and antiquities brought to London from abroad.[50] Marcy Norton argues that 'among the many advances in studies of colonialism and imperialism is the recognition that colonialism is no longer only something done to someone else; struggles and endeavors in the periphery changed the society and culture, as well as the economy, of the metropole'.[51] Performance, as much as newspapers or novels, brought this complex understanding to bear in Victorians' experience. As Michael Meeuwis puts it, theatre 'smoothed over the gaps between the metanarratives of the day' at precisely 'the high point of political liberalism, the post-Great Exhibition maturity of commodity culture, and the beginnings of the widest-scale period of economic (and cultural) imperial dominance by Great Britain', demonstrating the relevance that 'the individual could have ... in society'.[52] Engaging with this refracted world of play was both formative and constitutive of Victorians' paideia, for it was synonymous with a cultural education, geared toward public life constitutive of modernity and people's sense of being.[53] The panoply of spectacles, according to Erkki Huhtamo, 'blossomed within a cultural space that was crisscrossed by boundaries, and torn by ideological divisions; economic developments, social change, political ideas, and cultural trends all had an impact on them'.[54] Frederick Chesson's early years as an organiser, coming to understand how political influence could be wielded through performance and media, demonstrates how this understanding could be honed, then perpetually called upon.

## Networked Self-cultivation

Chesson's first mark in any public discussion coincides exactly with George Thompson's return from his second trip to the United States; it is likely that they met abroad and that Chesson entered Thompson's orbit through transatlantic anti-slavery circles. On 9 July 1851, the same day Thompson announced his intention to return to parliamentary duties, Chesson published a letter to the editor of the *British Banner* condemning slave-holding clergy and the 'mob law' that constrained US liberties: both were keynotes of Thompson's career. This prompted a response by a writer from Tennessee promising to 'duck you [Chesson] soundly in the horsepond reserved expressly for itinerant abolitionists' should he ever visit the region.[55]

Chesson's next mark was on behalf of the peace movement. Charles-Louis Napoléon Bonaparte's (1808–73) seizure of power and proclamation of the Second French Empire prompted a call to renew Britain's militia, in abeyance since the 1820s. Britain and her colonies' regular army was outstripped four to one by France.[56] In April 1852, a series of meetings was held in London and the provinces opposing the Militia Bill. Chesson, an eighteen-year-old novice to the political scene, was one of several little-known speakers on the topic at the Temperance Hall in Chelsea. This is the earliest trace of him at a meeting. Thompson was in the chair.[57] Chesson's views on the prospects of French aggression, and possibly a war, were set in the liberal mould, if not particularly original: he favoured promoting 'fraternal feeling' between nations in 'peaceful pursuits of an unfettered commerce, and helping forward the march of ideas'.[58] When the conflict with Russia flared and the unlikely alliance of Britain, Turkey, and France formed, fears of invasion evaporated.

Whereas in 1851 Chesson wrote to the *British Banner* from Brompton (a village adjacent to Chatham, his birthplace in Kent), and a year later he wrote to the *Sun* from New Broad Street (City of London), by September 1853 another letter to the *British Banner* (later reprinted in Garrison's newspaper the *Liberator*) shows him established in Manchester.[59] He visited with the Thompsons' eldest daughter, Louisa Nosworthy (1831–85), whose husband ran a fruit importation business, and saw Thompson whenever he came up on business. Possibly, Chesson was placed in Manchester by Thompson to prove his mettle. At the age of twenty-one, when he penned the first of his extant diary entries, Chesson was already affianced to Amelia – 'dear Millie' – the Thompsons' second daughter.[60] Chesson aligned with his intended father-in-law's interests, such as celebrations for the twentieth anniversary of West Indian emancipation, and served as honorary secretary to Manchester's newly formed North of England Anti-Slavery Society and India Reform League, a promising (yet short-lived) rapprochement between Garrisonians and the BFASS, led by Thompson and Parker Pillsbury (1809–98, manager of the American Anti-Slavery Society).[61] He successfully recruited the author and lecturer William Wells Brown (1814?–84, an African American freedom-seeker who had been fundraising in England since 1849) to the 1 August 1854 commemoration, as well as the Congregational minister Samuel Ringgold Ward (1817–66, a renowned African American orator and newspaper editor who hastily fled north in 1851 and two years later was sent on a fundraising tour of Britain by the Anti-Slavery Society of Canada). Also for that meeting, Chesson solicited letters of support from Harriet Martineau, Wilson Armistead (1819–68), J.P. Nichol (1804–59), Lord Carlisle (George W.F. Howard, 1802–64), the Bishop of Oxford (Samuel Wilberforce, 1805–73), and others whose names are less illustrious.[62]

Chesson's diary shows a fascination with the British tour of the popular Hungarian freedom fighter Lajos (Louis) Kossuth (1802–94). He was attuned to both Kossuth's performance and his potential impact on the Peace Party, a faction dedicated to arbitration with Russia that precariously straddled various positions on British responsibility for war with Russia, Christian outrage at Turkish incursions into the Balkans, and non-intervention into European freedom movements.[63] After an outdoor speech in Sheffield with 14,000 auditors, Chesson recorded: 'Pleased with the patriot's physiognomy, & still more with his oratory. I agree with G. Wilson that his democratic speeches at this juncture will do us no injury as they will serve to show upon what wildly different grounds to those of the governments, the people of this country are enthusiastic for the War.'[64] George Wilson (1808–70), who had chaired the ACLL, was 'keen to distance their liberal pacificism from Christian pacificism' (i.e., Quakerism) from early in 1853.[65] Chesson was not able to secure Kossuth or the Italian republican Giuseppe Mazzini to speak at a Peace meeting, though the attempt to do so is indicative of his collaborators' sympathies and transnationalism.

During the nineteenth century, one did not study journalism: aspirants with myriad backgrounds and educations simply wrote as freelancers and tried to get taken on somewhere as regular staff.[66] If Chesson wished to be a political organiser, he was gaining many connections in this regard. As he hoped to become a journalist, he took initiative in this direction, writing unsigned pieces for the *Nonconformist, Eclectic Review, Daily News*, and *Manchester Examiner*, showing alignment with his family background in Methodism (but not practicing teetotalism, despite his attention to the topic), and Thompson's view on social justice and anti-colonialism.[67] He continued to expand his horizons, build up credentials, evaluate everything he experienced through the pages of his diary, and hope for a permanent union with Amelia. He looked for paying opportunities, but too many friends were unlucky in business, and so it was difficult to find a staff journalist to advocate for him. However, through the autumn of 1854 his diary notes frequent contributions to the *Wesleyan*, letters that may have been commissioned from him as the Manchester correspondent.[68] He occupied himself with 'reading, writing, meditation, talking, and smoking' when in his lodgings, and visiting with Manchester's merchant committeemen when out of doors.[69]

Chesson worked under Wilson's direction on the Peace Party's campaign. Wilson was Manchester's champion of free trade, a railway promoter, exemplary political organiser, and the most popular meeting chairman of his time. Chesson already knew the free-trade politician Richard Cobden, whose essays he would later edit; the Leeds-based Quaker philanthropist and abolitionist Wilson Armistead, who had hosted the African American freedom-seekers Ellen and William Craft on census day in 1851; Parker Pillsbury, whom Chesson took to see 'some of the low haunts of Manchester' as well as the Theatre Royal when G.V. Brooke performed; and John Baxter Langley (1819–92), the ultra-radical who became editor of the *Star* in 1858 before moving on to the *Newcastle Chronicle*.[70] Thus, Chesson, who had come from a non-political family, was swiftly networked among men of Thompson's generation active in parliamentary politics, free-trade agitation, transatlantic abolitionism, and journalism.

Chesson's diaries show that talking and hearing about foreign and domestic politics was experienced conjointly with self-edification drawn from reading and discussing a wide variety of topics. He heard lectures about electricity with galvanic demonstrations by Mr Stone at the Chatham Street School of Medicine, on the United States and

Christianity by Prof. William G. Allen, African American instructor of rhetoric, Greek, and German at New York Central College (also famed for the travails he suffered in the United States as a result of his mixed-race marriage), and on the River Nile's scriptural significance and the decline of Egypt as fulfilment of Ezekiel 30:13 by Dr Halley (1796–1876). Along with a group of friends, Chesson 'beheld mortality on a dissecting table' and also visited the Royal Institution, where he especially admired Edward Matthew Ward's (1816–79) 'The Last Sleep of the Argyll', the prototype for the fresco in the House of Commons. He attended the theatre and Henry Russell's (1812–1900) concert at the Corn Exchange.[71] Russell, a ballad writer inspired by the politics and oratory of Henry Clay (1777–1852), pioneered with solo concerts and patriotic renditions in his forceful baritone. By mid-summer Chesson had heard for the third time the plain-spoken US temperance advocate J. B. Gough, a former actor, enjoying the lecture more than ever. For Chesson this was an opportunity to experience masterful performance, without susceptibility to conversion. He wrote: 'His rich humour, his soul-reaching pathos, his sublime imaginative power & his clever acting render him one of the greatest orators of the times.'[72] Gough advocated total abstinence, satirised the practice of making exceptions for 'medicinal' imbibing, and excoriated in a humorous manner parents who gave wine to their children.[73] His style was extemporaneous and he told about encounters from a first-person perspective, sprinkling in imitations and drawing into his spell 'an immense audience [that] grew hushed and still…. At his bidding, stern, strong men, as well as sensitive women, wept or laughed'. Over the course of two hours, 'he seemed to ride upon the audience,—to have mastered it completely to his will'. William Wells Brown noted that he was a pure 'theatrical mountebank', discharging tears in 'great showers' yet unequalled in getting listeners to sign the temperance pledge.[74]

Though not an abstainer himself, Chesson attended the annual meeting of the Manchester branch of the United Kingdom Alliance for the Suppression of the Liquor Traffic at the Free Trade Hall. His evocation of it in his diary alludes to the glory days of the ACLL's meetings in this venue.

> Eight thousand persons, at least, were packed together in that famous Hall. The Earl of Harrington [1784–1862] occupied the Chair, and the principal speakers were Samuel Bowly [1802–84], Dr. Burns, Sir Walter Trevelyan [1797–1879], George Cruikshank and Mr. Alderman [John] Harrison. The "great" speeches of the evening were delivered by Saml. Bowly, and Dr. [Dawson] Burns [1828–1909]. Their arguments in favour of the Maine

Liquor Law I felt I could not answer. Met Henry Wigham on the platform. Was very glad to see him. I was in the company of Mr. Parkes, & Mr. Vincent.[75]

Cruikshank was an avid teetotaller, as was the anti-slavery advocate and Quaker Henry Wigham (1822–97, brother to Eliza Wigham), a Garrisonian stalwart based in Edinburgh. Chesson's syntax and sentiment suggest he was already acquainted with the Wighams; it is also significant that he felt at ease among the luminaries seated on the platform as well as the Chartist Henry Vincent.

This suggests that during 1853–4 Chesson heard, circulated with, and entered into correspondence with a wider and wider circle of liberal advocates while he experienced a host of performance forms and styles, political issues, and strategies. Manchester was not only his trial, but also his apprenticeship and finishing school. If things went right, he could be truly launched upon a career, and seen as marriageable. The latter depended on the former.

Amelia Thompson went up to Manchester for the first of August meeting commemorating West Indian emancipation. Once his official duties concluded, Chesson noted, 'Spent the first few days with Millie doing nothing – excepting one thing.'[76] She soon returned home. On 22 August, he followed her to London, anxious of his future. While her father was in Leeds, she and Chesson went to see Albert Smith's *Ascent of Mont Blanc*, whose scenery and monologue they found 'capital'. They went to the newly opened Crystal Palace at Sydenham, which Chesson described in a letter to the *Wesleyan*.[77] Thompson returned, having tried to find backers to purchase a weekly newspaper, the intended organ of the Peace Party. Chesson's mood turned dark. 'Did nothing all the week; felt no happiness not one day.' On 4 September he went with Thompson to Fleet Street to see John Hamilton (1820–60), editor of the *Empire*, who asked for £2,000 to be bought out of the enterprise.[78] Chesson returned, feeling unwell, and talked with Amelia's parents 'about love affairs (personal) until past midnight'.[79] The next day, Thompson took him to the Reform Club, which impressed Chesson very much, and en route he spotted the retired actor Charles Kemble (1775–1854) stepping out of the Athenaeum Club. They went on to see Buckstone at the Haymarket (in *The Old Chateau* and the farce *Like as Two Peas*). Then, at supper, 'an unpleasant incident occurred' that hung between them until the end of October.[80]

Chesson remained in London two more weeks. On 9 September he met with John Hamilton and John Livesey (proprietor of the *Empire* and editor of the *Preston Guardian*) to discuss the *Empire*'s affairs.[81] Two days later, Thompson wrote to his cousin George Edmund Donisthorpe (1809–75), who, along with his partner John Croft, ran a worsted wool factory in Leeds, applying for the capital to purchase the *Empire* in partnership with John Hamilton.[82] By the middle of the month, Chesson returned to Manchester, thinking that the affair looked promising, but pining for Amelia.

Alarmingly, Chesson found the Anti-Slavery Society's account £40 overdrawn, with no means to recoup the deficit. Colleagues bickered and fired salvos at one another in the press. Chesson was struck with a prolonged bilious attack. He read books about Klemens von Metternich (1779–1859), Charles Maurice de Talleyrand (1754–1838), and Karl August von Hardenberg (1750–1822), evaluating their characters and deploring their failings. Whether this selection reflects an interest in the Congress of Vienna, diplomatic agility, political tenacity, or hypocrisy and fraud is hard to say. This was followed by reading about a series of figures, all loathed by radicals, in *The Diplomatists of Europe*.[83] Afforded a few days seaside vacation at Lytham, he varied his rather self-flagellant reading with Dickens' *American Notes* (with which he largely agreed on matters of character), the memoir of the 'Baroness' von Beck (an exiled affiliate of Kossuth), and blue books on 'the Eastern Question', detailing the status of the Ottoman Empire.

### Into the Fray

The Peace Party brought Chesson into alliance with Wilson and Thompson's former Anti-Corn Law allies, which explains the significance of Manchester as a base: industrialists, seeking uninterrupted trade, also wanted to ensure that wheat supplies from Eastern Europe were not at risk, especially at a point when supplies from the United States could be volatile if civil war broke out, the United States' aggression against Cuba escalated, or Britain actively took measures to interfere in US slavery. Keeping the industrial working class cheaply fed was of paramount importance. The Peace Party believed there was grievous cause for concern, though detractor James Martineau (1805–1900) dismissed this as wanting the public to be 'rudely tossed in the Yorkshire blanket of a peace-debate'.[84] In 1853, 30 million bushels of wheat were shipped from the five ports of the Black Sea and Sea of Azoff (lading points for the Ukrainian bread basket) to Britain and Europe. What was formerly bought for two shillings per bushel sold in the autumn of 1854 for ten shillings per bushel. Instead of prices dropping after the British harvest, when supplies were plentiful, they remained steady.[85] Crimean ports, along with the Danube, were under blockade from the new Anglo-French alliance in order to fence in Russia, which had annexed the Romanian principalities away from Turkey, signalling a form of aggression that was highly disturbing for the Austro-Hungarians.[86] Britain's other wheat supplier was also troubled. By the end of 1854, the United States had experienced a flood of forgeries that 'deranged the money market there' and led to one hundred bank failures, prostrating credit in ways not seen since 1837.[87]

With Britain concerned about its two major wheat suppliers, the Peace Party attempted to turn working-class opinion against the war by mounting a placarding campaign throughout Northern and Midland cities.[88] The initial phase focused on the 'glorious' battle of the Alma, the allies' first engagement with Russian forces, which was chaotic and under-prepared in every sense, though ultimately successful.[89] Chesson's posters, which appeared on 5 November, became infamous. A billsticker in Blackburn was arrested by order of Prime Minister Palmerston and only freed when he promised to take the placards down.[90] This was quickly followed on 14 November by the 'Dear Bread and War' and 'What Are We Fighting For?' campaign in various towns, which 'has been placarded on the walls … in tall letters; every letter helping to make out the lie as every stalwart Russian bishop helps to preach to fanatic ignorance, cruelty and falsehood'. Pro-war detractors – who dominated the press – deplored these 'flour-tub philanthropists', but they had powerful backers including Richard Cobden, George Wilson, and Joseph Sturge.[91] James Martineau, anxious that one of the placards misused a quote from his sister's writing (probably *The History of England during the Thirty Years' Peace, A.D. 1816–1846*), forwarded a copy to Harriet Martineau. She responded with a much-reprinted letter supporting the war and refuting the Peace Party's economic claims, stating that the supply problem arose from poor US harvests.[92] This was the Peace Party's most public campaign, and Chesson's first taste of being an enemy to the people. He quipped, 'How rich for one to be called "a traitor."'[93]

Joseph Sturge, a Quaker veteran of the anti-slavery movement and ACLL, complete suffragist, and zealous advocate of arbitration to avoid wars, struck back. In January 1854 he was one of a delegation sent to Russia by the Society of Friends to try to avoid conflict. He and his brother Charles (1801–88) were grain importers in Birmingham, so they not only had opportunities to monitor price and supply fluctuations but also felt the moral compulsion to warn.[94] The Sturges were ostracised by the Peace Party for trying to intercede with Tsar Nicholas I (1796–1855), but John Bright took the brunt of the public's abuse.

No stranger to controversy or pamphlet wars, Bright, it was said, 'would have been a pugilist if he had not been a Quaker'.[95] His 4 November 1854 letter to the *Manchester Examiner and Times*, later translated and printed in the *St Petersburg Journal*, put him front and centre in national attention, and he was denied the opportunity to speak when he returned to Manchester, the city he represented in Parliament. He was a veteran ACLL campaigner and ally of Thompson on Indian questions, yet Mancunians burnt him in effigy. By year's end, it was said that 'the bubble of the Peace Society has burst; the advocates of international arrangements [arbitration] have been obliged to confess that they were over-confident in the efficacy of their quack prescription, and the past has repeated itself, in the almost weekly announcement of such horrors as … must accompany a European war'.[96] British troops were decimated by disease and stymied in the field. Though the Peace Party was counter-placarded in Manchester as 'Peace Humbugs', as the year closed one of their number retorted: 'Who proved the Humbugs, time has shown, and may possibly do so again.' Scriptural quotations – 'Do good to them that hate you' from the Sermon on the Mount, and the command to love thine enemy – bolstered their case.[97]

'Cobden', Wilson told Chesson, 'is in receipt of intelligence from a distinguished officer in the fleet, which is published in the *Times*. This man said recently speaking of the battle of Alma that he hoped the people of England "were satisfied with their first butchers bill"'.[98] Richard Cobden – a free trader, not a pacifist – led the opposition to war in Parliament, aware that war frenzy diverted attention from every kind of political reform. When he returned to Leeds on 17 January 1855 to face his constituents and explain himself, West Riding electors clamouring to enter the music hall to hear him were so numerous that the meeting regrouped outdoors in the Coloured Cloth Hall yard. The texts that Chesson and Wilson had engineered for the Peace Party were pasted on every available wall in the city.

> In one of these it was declared that war caused the present high price of bread; in another, that the war had ruined the trade of the country; and in another it was put forth as a positive fact that the war spirit had been fomented, fostered, and kept alive by the newspaper press, for the sake of the profit the newspaper proprietors made out of it! On the other hand, those who were in favour of prosecuting the war with vigour, unless satisfactory terms of peace could be obtained, issued a placard on Tuesday, calling upon all opponents of Russian aggression to attend the meeting, and keep to the real question—'Are we battling for the right?'[99]

On a frosty afternoon with snow falling on his 8,000 auditors, Cobden gave one of the great speeches of his career. He reminded his constituents that the initial pretext for proposing a war with Russia (twelve to fifteen months prior) was that it would 'give freedom to struggling nationalities on the continent of Europe, and that it would have for its reference, I mean, to the invasion of Hungary, and the conquest of Circassia, or the occupation of other countries … in going to war against Russia you were going to inscribe on your banners, "the Reconstruction of Polish Nationality!"' He looked upon the war askance. 'It is a war in which we have a despot for an enemy [Russia], a despot for an ally [France], and a despot for a client [Turkey] – (hear, hear, and laughter) – and we have been for twelve months trying to make an ally of another despot [the Austrian emperor], and we have not succeeded. (Hear, hear).' Austria, Prussia, and the German confederation bordered Russia and had so much more to lose from the tsar's expansionist aggression than did Britain, yet they remained neutral. Whereas Turkey had a just cause because of incursions into its Black Sea principalities, Britain did not.[100]

Why should Britons defend Turkey? According to Cobden it was a nation with 4 million Muslims who denied all legal benefits and rights to 8 million Christians across its empire. Furthermore, from a military standpoint, the Crimean campaign was folly. He said 'We have gone 3,000 miles to attack an empire containing 60,000,000 of people and with an army of 600,000 or 700,000 men. We sent at the first an army of 20,000 or 30,000 men', thinking 'we were actually going to annihilate the Russian empire'.[101] Cobden was willing to stand against the tide of opinion. He had done so when, in 1852, fear of a French invasion of Britain – based on the idea that following Louis Napoléon's coup d'état the emperor was consumed with his destiny to avenge Waterloo and so might send 60,000 from Cherbourg in a single night – led to passage of the Militia Act. Cobden said 'I was then treated as the Utopian disciple or champion of peace, and if you want to know what was said of me, turn to the caricatures of the day, where you will find me represented as decorated with very long ears – (laughter) – looking into a cannon's mouth, and crying "Peace, peace!" ("Hear," and laughter).' Following spirited rebuttals by opponents, the opinion of the meeting was decidedly against Cobden. On a resolution that England and France were engaged in a just war against 'outrageous aggression … upon the Turkish empire' and that the tsar's 'spirit of aggrandizement … threatens the independence of other nations', Cobden's side received no more than 100 votes out of the 6,000 or 7,000 cast at the meeting.[102]

Meanwhile, negotiations to acquire the *Empire* dragged on. Supposedly, Livesey was short of cash and motivated to sell. Chesson waited anxiously, confiding to his diary that he hoped it would slip through Thompson's grasp before he had a chance to buy it.[103] On 24 October, Hamilton informed

Chesson that the post he had promised – business manager – would instead be given to another. Chesson thought it best to remain in Manchester, 'where my position is one of honour, and trust; or to accept the Editorship of the *Aylesbury News*' even though living in a Buckinghamshire backwater was far from his dream. Two days later, he discovered he had misapprehended Hamilton's intentions. He was back on the hook. Thompson's bid was accepted, and by 21 November the plan was firm, for Chesson had resigned his post in Manchester and soon began briefing his replacement, Mr Stokes. Later that day, he read 'A kind letter from my darling Millie whom I shall be right glad to see and to——.'[104] The Manchester Peace movement continued without Chesson, and on 31 March 1855 it presented a petition with 11,000 signatures to Lord Palmerston.

### Ties That Bind

On the eve of departing Manchester for his new life in London, Chesson wrote: 'Well let me hope that brighter days are dawning. I have learnt much in Manchester. I have not always been true to my own conscience in this city – let me hope that in the great metropolis I may exhibit the spectacle of a <u>true</u>, <u>brave</u>, & <u>honest</u> man.'[105] Two days later, he wrote what would be his first pseudonymous 'Defoe' letter for the weekly *Empire*, denouncing Palmerston's handling of the Crimean War, along with a eulogy of Lord Dudley Stuart, MP (1803–54), who died abroad while trying to persuade the Swedish to participate in a war against Russia on behalf of Polish independence.[106] As the next few days in London unfolded, Chesson wrote the week's summary for the *Christian News*, covered the anti-slavery conference at the London Tavern for the *Empire*, and attended a meeting at the Peace Society's office in New Broad Street, where the placard campaign formed the principal topic. The next day he returned to the anti-slavery conference and gathered notes for an article.[107] At last, aged twenty-one, Chesson was making a living as a political journalist while being involved in the liberal causes that inspired him. As a salaried journalist, he covered meetings that involved him, not merely for the sake of writing about them.

The *Empire*'s first number under the new management appeared on Friday, 1 December 1854. It did not find a large readership. By mid-February 1855, Chesson received the first warnings of the *Empire*'s difficulty from Thomas Dick, the man he had feared would supplant him as business manager. He consulted with Thompson and Wilson, resolving to get out of the situation as soon as he could, and even considered decamping to the United States.[108] Chesson spent several months in the north, attending meetings for the Peace Party, many of which Thompson headlined, trying to drum up subscribers for the *Empire*, and submitting pieces as 'Defoe' that from January through June 1855 were published on page one (a sign not of Chesson's prestige but of the lack of advertisers interested in the *Empire*; newspapers typically utilised the first page for lucrative advertising). Only two other correspondents wrote under a nom de plume: 'Voice of the People' in the last quarter of 1854 (probably Thompson), and 'Saxon' from October 1854 through June 1856 (possibly Hamilton). Despite the paper's troubles, Chesson's career and financial prospects seemed bright enough that on 7 May 1855 he and Amelia were married in Holy Trinity Church, Clapham. In September, when he resumed diary writing, he reflected: 'Suffice it to say that I do not regret the step I have taken; and that although poor in this world's goods we are rich in that mutual confidence, and affection which forms the only sure basis of permanent matrimonial happiness. Henceforth I shall live not for myself only but for another.'[109] At that moment he could not yet have known that Amelia was already pregnant for the first of fourteen times.

Chesson wrote steadily for the *Empire* while also taking up the paid secretaryship of the APS, a position vacated by Louis Chamerovzow.[110] He appears to have assumed the burden of corresponding secretary in 1857, at a point when he was more fully apprised of APS affairs. This connected him with networks of men interested in the administration of British colonies and protectorates and exposed him to information and procedures related to foreign affairs globally.

The *Empire* unsuccessfully sought a new £1,000 loan in order to become a daily. Thompson considered returning to the United States, probably intending to call upon allies to help set up a lecture tour. Life continued in this vein until mid-October 1855, when Chesson's diaries fall silent. The next two months must have been hell, for by Christmas George Thompson – on whom the debts for the troubled *Empire* fell, underwritten by the initial loan from his cousin – had fled to Boulogne, preliminary to sailing onward to India. He wrote to Amelia:

> I have not written Mr. Hamilton <u>because</u> I know not <u>how</u> to write. I want to speak to him in terms of kindness & affection, corresponding to my feelings, but should not like my words to be despised. I should like a few lines from him. Mr. Chesson will perhaps go between us, and see, if before I leave this place, we can exchange fraternal notes. I am sincere in saying that, on reflection, I make every allowance for Mr. H and forgive every threat. I enter fully into his feelings, & deeply sympathise with him.

Joyfully would I, by any sacrifice within my ability, free him, <u>at once</u>, from every weight that presses upon him…. While any burden rests upon <u>him</u> on a/c [account] of his connection with the <u>Empire</u>, that burden shall be <u>mine</u> as well as <u>his</u>, and I will take it <u>all</u>, the moment I have the power. I shall consider myself banished, until every person to whom I owe a farthing <u>is paid</u>. I am henceforth <u>abroad</u>, not to <u>avoid</u> payment of my debts, but that I <u>may</u> pay them; and have resolved, life and heath permitting, to be able to say, ere I again tread the soil of England (Oh how dear <u>now</u>) 'I owe nought but love & gratitude.'[III]

Chamerovzow was the broker between the *Empire* debtors and creditors, and spent a good deal of time with Chesson during this period. With Thompson abroad, the Chessons frequently socialised with new friends. Chesson's responsibility for making up the *Empire*'s copy increased, and he spent occasional nights sleeping in Fleet Street to facilitate compiling the paper. The price changed from sixpence to three halfpennies, nearly a year after the Stamp Act was repealed, and the paper shifted publication to Saturdays.[112]

Ironically, the *Empire*'s misfortunes brought Chesson promotion. He was appointed acting editor in March 1856, also serving on the general committee with Chamerovzow, Hamilton, Henry Richard (1812–88, former editor of the *Herald of Peace*), and the journalist Washington Wilks (1827–64).[113] By the time the *Empire* ceased publication, Chesson was its de facto editor. But meanwhile, in March, Cobden and Bright launched the daily *Morning Star* (adding an evening edition within a few months), a one-penny newspaper dedicated to advocating free trade and other principles of the Manchester School. About £9,000 was invested by men who included Salford politicians and mill owners E.R. Langworthy (1797–1874) and Elkanah Armitage (1794–1876), as well as Joseph Sturge and other Quakers.[114] By 26 April Chesson was on its weekly payroll at £1/10/6; by 6 June he was its unofficial sub-editor, working under W. Haly (editor) and Hamilton (official sub-editor). In May, when Amelia began her first confinement and Chesson's diary again went silent, he was working three jobs. When the *Empire* folded in September, Chesson wrote to Garrison '"I could a tale unfold" of the money which has been sunk in that ill-fated contemporary of your's [*sic*]',[115] drawing a contrast with the *Liberator* (1831–65). He transitioned seamlessly to writing for the *Star* at £3 per week plus a guinea for each contribution (reviews, articles, and, from September 1859, also leaders), working for the new team of John Hamilton (editor) and Henry Richard (leader editor). The *Star*'s sales started strong, at 25,000 per day, which was still short of the 30,000 circulation forecast as a break-even point (or 26,000 copies with £25 of daily advertising revenue). Sales peaked at 50,000 during a poisoning case, but fell to 17,000 in late August and 12,500 in December.[116] If the growing Chesson family spent frugally, they could live at the lower fringe of the middle class, but that depended on the *Star*'s fortunes and Chesson's supplementary incomes. It also depended on Thompson's ability to pay his debts and return from India, for otherwise responsibility for his mother, Elizabeth (1771–1859), wife, Anne, and youngest daughter, Edith (1845–1902), could fall to Chesson.

There are several reasons why the weekly *Empire* failed, politically and financially. Though its investors sunk £6,000 to £7,000 into it, this was a fraction of what was estimated to be necessary to make a new venture viable in London. It had already struggled before the takeover, and with the half-measure revisions and chaotic enforcement of the 1853 Stamp Tax on newspapers during 1855 there was neither free nor regulated trade. The firebrand working-class liberal journalist George Holyoake published a two-page supplement, the *War Fly Sheet*, distributed with the *Empire*, but this resulted in threats of fines over £600,000.[117] The *Empire*'s mandate to trumpet the Peace Party had outlived the movement's viability, and neither the politicians who backed it nor the journalists who produced it latched on to another populist cause.[118] Meanwhile, opposing papers such as the *War Telegraph* in Manchester, which reached a peak of 35,000 daily circulation, thrived.[119] Finally, with the dawning of the *Star*, a wider coalition of interests came together, although the *Star* suffered from an unclear chain of command and was seriously under financed. Initially appealing to dissenting shopkeepers and radical artisans, the *Star* grew broadly in appeal (if not in profits), reaching influence with public figures second only to the *Times*.[120]

John Bright (along with Lord Brougham) had been one of Thompson's leading promoters in the 1840s. Richard Cobden had worked with Thompson on the Corn Law repeal, and quickly grew to respect what he saw in Chesson. These multiplex, intergenerational ties served Chesson well in this phase of his career. Many observed Chesson's work for the North of England Anti-Slavery Society and India Reform League in August 1854, and even though others gave the addresses on Cuba, Brazil, and the United States, Chesson had proven himself an able organiser. During several instances when Chesson was directly or indirectly attacked in the press, or when he came to the defence of just causes and their advocates, he proved himself not just loyal but also capable of getting information and making useful arguments in print. Thus, strong ties – such as with Thompson and

Wilson – were augmented by weaker ties with others, characterised by less or intermittent time spent together, political bonds (rather than personal relationships fraught with emotional intensity), and camaraderie rather than mutual confiding on intimate matters. A 1973 study by Mark S. Granovetter on social networks demonstrates the greater importance of weak ties, such as these, for job acquisition, and Chesson's case proves the premise.[121] With Thompson away in India for an indefinite period, Chesson benefited from his existing ties, developed considerably more, and settled into lasting employment: he stayed with the *Star* until its demise in 1869, and held the administrative post with the APS until his death in 1888. On the face of it, going into journalism should have been a promising career choice – by 1880 there were over 1,834 newspapers in England, and 365 in London alone – so a person with a modicum of ability could get by.[122] Chesson wanted to flourish, but within the harmonious bounds of like-minded colleagues.

The *Star*'s editorial staff met for tea every day at 5:30 p.m. to discuss topics for leading articles. One of them recalled:

> Each topic was discussed, and finally the writer of each article was arranged. In this way each writer got help from all the others, and the result was excellent. Those were pleasant gatherings.... No restraints prevented the free expression of opinion. Differences there were, of course. Even these were useful; for they enabled a writer to understand arguments against the position he was to take up.[123]

Thus, as a young journalist Chesson learned not only from near peers such as Wilks and Edward R. Russell (1834–1920); seasoned foreign journalists such as Julius Faucher (1820–78); and veteran speakers and campaigners such as Holyoake, Edmond Beales (1803–81), and Chamerovzow; but also from staff, which over time included the Oxford economist J.E. Thorold Rogers (1823–90), art critic Henry Merritt (1822–77), dramatist and theatre critic Leicester Buckingham (1825–67), novelist William Black (1841–98), and polyglot novelist Justin McCarthy (1830–1912). McCarthy, who referred to the *Star*'s offices as 'a refuge for the denizens of ... the "Exileword of London"', helped launch the literary careers of Richard Whiteing (1840–1928), Archibald Forbes (1830–1900), and George Manville Fenn (1831–1909) within the 'Readings by Starlight' series, and furthered that of Edmund Yates (1831–94), who wrote the Flâneur gossip column in the mid-1860s.[124] Their ties with literary, artistic, and political circles augmented Chesson's opportunities to secure information as a journalist, connections as a lobbyist, and future employment in both capacities. Thus, Richard Webb – formerly sceptical about Chesson and perennially uncharitable toward the Thompsons – could assure Samuel May in 1859: 'He is I think really a good hearted young man & has got some excellent coadjutors.'[125]

Chesson accepted freelance opportunities as the London correspondent to the *Scotsman* (Edinburgh), *Independent* (Sheffield), *Guardian* (Preston), *Chronicle* (Newcastle), *Globe* (Toronto), *Hindoo Patriot* (Calcutta), and *New York Independent*, as well as editor of *The Story of a Fugitive Slave*, serialised in thirteen instalments, including his commentary, in the *Ladies' Newspaper*.[126] Throughout his career, Chesson continued to cultivate the interests of his father-in-law, as in January 1855, when he wrote a response to an attack on Thompson in the *Anti-Slavery Advocate*, even though at this same juncture Thompson was furious with Chesson, probably for incurring a small debt.[127] Despite their ongoing, overlapping, multiplex networks, from this point on Chesson advanced himself on his own merits.

Chesson's journalistic writing was not yet of uniform high quality, but his key ideas were coalescing. His October 1855 lead article for the *Empire*, 'The Uncivilised Subjects of Queen Victoria', shows his widening purview. Like the public he chides, he had been preoccupied by the war in the Crimea, yet he bade his readers to also think of conflicts on the coast of west Africa, the Bengali Santhals' revolt against British rulers, massacres of the Dyaks of Borneo, avaricious land grabs in the Cape Colony, and Australian Aboriginals experiencing appropriation of their land by white settlers. Anticipating John Stuart Mill's unequivocal stance on justice, Chesson rejects any right of subjugation by the Christian over so-called uncivilised or barbaric people, even when they resist what is imposed on them: he categorically rejects both rights of conquest and rights of discovery.[128] 'It is upon such fallacious and immoral pretexts as these that the African Slave Trade, Negro Slavery, British conquests in India, and many of the worst crimes that blacken the history of our race have been defended', he argues, likening the far flung leaders of resistance to Cromwell, Washington, and Lafayette as heroes of their people. Anyone who champions the freedom of Poles and Hungarians 'because their cause is associated with imperishable classic and historic memories' while remaining indifferent to enslaved Africans, or who believes in the white man's 'destiny … to lord it over the God-given heritage of his dark-skinned fellow-mortals', adopts a doctrine 'fit only for bandits'. Without exception, 'human rights are equal, and cannot be modified, or changed at the caprice of those who consider that they belong only to a state of civilisation'. He did not spare Christians any quarter:

> In the searching light of the sermon on the Mount, what a ghastly spectacle do our conquests in India, our Kaffir and Maori wars, and our Borneo massacres present? What oceans of human blood have been shed in

these unrighteous contests? What multitudes of agonised spirits and broken hearts have they occasioned? What mountains of slaughtered men have
they reared as monuments of the cruelty and ambition of Christian England? And what accumulated blasphemy against the Most High have they
originated? [F]or our national crimes are invariably clothed with the mantle
of religion, and are declared to have received the special benediction of
Heaven![129]

This leader, from the pen of a man not quite twenty-two, evinces strong
views yet also a cohesive perspective on the consequences of empire. This
was garnered, while within the confines of England, from broad participation in cultural life, engagement in APS correspondence, and political
work, all of which shaped his perspective as a journalist. Most of the topics mentioned became the subjects of his future columns. Thus, while this
period of Chesson's *Bildung* could not build upon the systematic formal
education afforded by a university, or even an apprenticeship within a
recognised discipline of knowledge such as law, he learned about matters
of concern across the globe, avoided the narrow prejudices of his nation
and class, and challenged parochial, xenophobic, racist, and bigoted perspectives in the wake of the liberal project while advocating for human
rights broadly.

Quakers would have balked at reading the *Star*'s sporting and theatre
columns, but the paper aimed for a broad readership. Chesson was a cricket
fan, and attended the occasional match. Early in his career, he also attended
the theatre, concerts, and opera, as economy permitted, and he reviewed
plays when his pocketbook was strained.[130] His reflections on *La Traviata*,
scandalous because of its sympathetic depiction of a prostitute, show his
growing discernment but also the limit case of his broad-mindedness. He
sat in a gallery slip and found Marietta Piccolomini (1834–99), as Violetta,
'an incomparable singer & a fascinating actress'. Meanwhile, for public
consumption he expressed regret in his *Star* review that imported French
operas such as this attract large audiences. While acknowledging that what
is '[an] immoral matter in our public journals … is successful in a pecuni-
ary point of view', he erroneously deduced 'we want neither French morals nor French politics in this country, having quite enough evil of our
own planting and culture to uproot without any fresh importations'.[131] His
diary is less judgemental and more incisive when contrasting the consummate soprano with her role: 'But there is something repulsive in the idea
of a beautiful, and pure-minded woman acting the part of a prostitute,
and of equally beautiful and pure-minded women looking on with eager
eyes, and at the close of a shocking drama, smothering the frail one with

chaplets and bouquets of flowers. Such is <u>La Traviata</u>.'[132] Whereas the public notice *advocates*, stating for example that more people should follow the queen's example and forego this opera, the private reflection *evaluates*. The following spring, he and Amelia took a cab – an unusual extravagance – to Her Majesty's Theatre to hear the opera together amid a 'large, brilliant, and, of course, appreciative' audience, and enjoyed their evening. Even so, in his diary, Frederick noted that the subsequent ballet, *La Esmeralda*, which had first been performed at the same theatre thirteen years earlier, may have provided too much insight into Carolina Pocchini's (1835–1901) legs and thighs for some spectators' taste.[133] By the time Dion Boucicault's (1820–90) sensation drama *Formosa* made a great hit in 1869, the hero's pursuit of a heroine with an unmistakeable trade struck Chesson as 'offensive' and 'commonplace', even though all the trappings of the fast life were foregone at the end: Formosa *chose* a humble life, she was not *lowered* to it.[134] This 'Girl of the Period' plot hit a nerve, but also matched the tone of the times, and courtesans not only graced the operatic stage but also the supper party in *The Corsican Brothers* 'under the moral management of Mr. Charles Kean'.[135] In art and politics, Chesson had learned to convey his views for print and retain a faithful evaluation in his private reflection.

Chesson believed that theatre – whether that of Shakespeare or Edward Bulwer Lytton (1803–73) – should 'arouse into activity the highest faculties of the mind' while evincing 'unexceptional' morals.[136] Thus, what one chose to attend, what one experienced while there, and how this reflected a communal standard for society all mattered. Entertainment was culture, as well as having the potential to positively or negatively acculture one to it. *Bildung*, like taste, was accrued through acts of judgement, not merely absorption. This reflects 'stance taking' *at and as* performance: reciprocal acts located by Richard Baumann in 'the complementary stance of audience member[s], inviting co-participants to assume an alignment to the performance that demands an evaluative response and perhaps more, such as verbal acknowledgement, commentary, encouragement, or ratification … in what amounts to co-construction of the performance'.[137] *La Traviata* is the limit case of what Chesson regarded – in 1856 – as fit matter for mixed audiences. His leisure tastes were eclectic, yet very much of the period. Whether he would still have taken that stance in the early 1870s (when he advocated for repeal of the Contagious Diseases Acts) is unlikely, for to see as he did in 1856 that 'Public morality … suffers greatly from the filthy amplitude with which these cases are reported', and to later advocate that the forced medical inspections of prostitutes in garrison towns was unconscionable, was stance taking on behalf not only of prostitutes but of all women.[138]

## Activism

At the outset of their careers, both Thompson and Chesson stepped into ongoing reform movements that had explicit tactics pursued through cogent forms of performative action. Ultimately, this enhanced how the public utilised knowledge about current events, including those cited within entertainments such as the Haymarket extravaganzas and Wyld's Globe, and mementoes of a rich performative culture such as Cruikshank's comet. As James M. Jasper argues, 'tactics represent important routines, emotionally and morally salient' in the lives of politically active people.[139] Liberals' ability to coordinate with others to organise purposeful groups, mobilise into new cohesive movements, and incrementally leverage change not only worked from a finite set of performative forms, each optimised for a tactical purpose and phase in the process, but also improvised within forms and combinations of forms to remain effective. An emphasis on incrementality is important: the proportion of effort expended to the results yielded is not favourable. To give an example of one of Chesson's causes, 'the agitation against Bulgarian atrocities achieved no more than a temporary and small-scale alteration in British foreign policy, and did not free Russia from needing to resort to arms', as Brian Harrison notes. Nevertheless, the division of labour between reformer and politician was clear: the reformer 'pushes the axis of discussion leftwards' with an uncompromising stance, then the politician effects a more moderate position through legislation.[140]

Up to the mid-nineteenth century, such work had been designated with terms such as agitation and organising. Yet as Chesson's generation replicated certain formulas it becomes apparent that – in addition to utilising critique to improve performance outcomes – liberals operated with an explicit set of assumptions about the forms through which critique would be leveraged. This is apparent not only with hindsight, but also in how Chesson's contemporaries planned and launched actions to advance successive new causes. In other words, liberals knew what they were doing and – this is hardly a shocking claim – did it over and over. This recognition goes beyond the media-based or formalist distinctions between orality and literacy, orature and journalism, or speechifying and epistolary communication. It undergirds everything Chesson learned about causes and issues that preceded his coming-of-age and continued to unfold in his maturity: settlers' encroachments on Zulu and Xhosa territories, the Treaty of Waitangi's bearing on Māori claims in successive Land Wars, or the fine line between indentured labour and slavery throughout the Indian

Ocean region. Understanding this tactically, and acting upon it overtly, constituted a repertoire, and grasping then utilising this repertoire was integral to Chesson's *Bildung*. This repertoire is still recognisable as forms constituent of activism used in the twenty-first century, whether petitioning, placarding, or speechifying.

This repertoire has a history that belies successive innovations and, ultimately, Chesson's role in history. Ever since the fifteenth century, the English lexicon has acknowledged reformers; since the sixteenth century there have been protestors and partisans; and since the seventeenth century there have been agitators and revolutionaries. The nineteenth century unleashed lobbyists, demonstrators, and boycotts upon the world, but until the twentieth century no one was called an activist. Activists may reform, protest, agitate, demonstrate, lobby, or boycott and be partisan or revolutionary, but none of these anterior terms is a true synonym. This matters for how the tactics of performance are traceable in political realms because activism has particular denotations for ascribing strategies of will and consequences of action – especially, but not exclusively – within democracies.[141] This marks a distinction relating strategists' intentionality to their choices.

Before there was a word for it, there was the cogent, argumentatively forcible, *activity* of activism. Based on mid-nineteenth-century tactics – such as confrontation, networking, listening, and pressuring – like-minded people sought change on ideological grounds utilising polemical rhetoric through written, spoken, gestural, proxemic, and scenographic expressions of solidarity and commitment to a cause, singly or within organisations. In retrospect, this is all activism, marking ways to regard repertoires – circulating and recombining forms including meetings, debates, petitions, letter writing, pamphleteering, billboarding, deputations, and conventions – as part of the history of theory-making by identifying relationships between action, intention, and outcome, and the poetics and practicalities of individuals' agency in calling for social change. Whether or not they are fully successful, social movements' leverage of repertoires strategically to obtain certain results – manumission, legislation, peace, and so forth – has political consequentiality inherent to disrupting and displacing ways of knowing and being. This points to the tactical performances of Chesson's political life (as one liberal emblematic of countless others), and the way that convictions emerged in the public sphere as discourse, oratorical practice, writing, and aesthetics in a dynamic, experimental mode in service of specific liberal-identified issues.

The term activism emerged in the blurry conceptual terrain between philosophy and psychologism.[142] In 1906 Rudolph Eucken (1846–1926), professor of philosophy at Jena, described how living, doing, and experiencing – which resembles what scholars of performance now call embodied knowledge – precedes the mind's grasp of truth. According to Eucken, rather than regarding oneself as a speck worked upon by the universe and given over to destiny (as in Romanticism), a person should undertake constant self-development to achieve a more rational world; the resulting autonomous agential activity constituted what he termed Activism.[143] As such, Eucken's Activism generatively precedes – and is something more than – cerebral comprehension.[144] From a self-generated inner life comes transformative power to change not merely perception but also the actual world.[145] Eucken's insight is the first of four steps leading to what activism has come to mean for scholars of performance, and is useful for understanding Chesson's career.

Eucken was awarded the Nobel Prize in 1908, the first philosopher laureate.[146] In his acceptance speech he likened technology (under modernism) to agency (within Activism), arguing that just as nature has been transformed by science into an intellectual concept, and technologies that ensue from scientific discovery are one additional step removed from nature, likewise, 'the social movement … reveals man as not entirely limited by a given order, but as a being that perceives and judges a given situation and is confident that it [i.e., the being] can change it essentially by its own efforts'. Thereby, humankind 'becomes a stage on which worlds meet and search for their further development'. Once humankind experiences this internality of life there can be no going back to being the gods' plaything, subject to either nature or destiny, for henceforward internality will be its own imperative to create content worth living for. Through Activism, human beings create 'movement of the world': whereas mimesis is a degraded 'copy' of the ideal, Activism is human-centric ideation that, through agency, can bring about change in the real world.[147] Thus Activism, like drama and speech acts, is a thing done and experienced that in turn calls something else into being.[148]

In his own time, Eucken was said to have 'dragged philosophy from the closet into the boudoir and the mart', connecting it to 'modern problems'.[149] The 'struggle for spiritual control of life', despite the seeming impotence against cosmic forces, laid hold of a generation: 'students worshipped him, and laymen, even, were thrilled by his oratory and carried away by his application of a vital religious inspiration to the practical problems of society as it existed'.[150] His idea is still fundamental to our faith that activism (a potential that requires continual effort) can bring about change. Despite his Nobel Prize, Eucken is said to have been 'so forgotten that even philosophers are usually surprised he was a philosopher'.[151] Nevertheless, his provision of Activism is foundational for later performance theory, participatory citizenship, and positive liberty.

Eucken had one notable follower in the Anglo world: the equally forgotten multimillionaire Henry Lane Eno (1871–1928), research associate at Princeton who in 1920 published a treatise called *Activism*. Eno's proposal to *quantify* mental Activism's amounts, range, relationship to other activities, and persistence over time was heralded in *L'Année Psychologique* as a new departure in philosophy.[152] Eno coined the word *psychon* to describe the minimum unit of awareness or activity, and thus the measurable mental basis for effecting change, refining Eucken's Activism.[153] Eno questioned what constitutes the threshold between ordinary life and Activism, which is still pertinent to the identification of politicised activity, especially the distinction between 'just being' and performance as an act with political meaning.

The pragmatist legacy of Activism is clearest amongst phenomenologists. In *Bodies That Matter*, Judith Butler posits gender as 'the forcible citation of a norm ... whose complex historicity is indissociable from relations of a discipline, regulation, punishment'. This *dispositif* became the credo for queer and feminist activists undoing the '*imaginary* logic that insistently issues forth its own unmanageability'.[154] Over the past thirty years, Butler refined her account of the constitutive processes of subjectivity and resistant discourse. In 2013, she argued that performativity 'take[s] place when the uncounted prove to be reflexive and start to count themselves, not only enumerating who they are, but "appearing" in some way, exercising in that way a "right" (extralegal, to be sure) to existence. They start to matter.... Performativity names that unauthorized exercise of a right to existence that propels the precarious into political life'.[155] Butler and her interlocutor Athena Athanasiou ruminate chiefly on the migrants, émigrés, displaced, and dispossessed, especially of Europe and Palestine. In Eucken's sense, Butler and Athanasiou are activists because their philosophical colloquy is persuasive rhetoric, but the dispossessed whom they write about also call for rights in the performativity of their dispossessed sojourn. In Eno's terms both the philosophers and the dispossessed make their activism perceptible intrinsically and extrinsically through writing, protest, and occupation, even if only on the representational or micro level. By being successively reflexive and self-affirming, appearing in/as a public, and exercising rights – all enabled by performativity – even those most marginal to society take up political consequentiality. Performativity, therefore, fills in what was vaguely unmeasurable about Eno's psychon.

James M. Jasper argues that to be motivated to take non-routine actions, to have 'the energy to march off to war or stand up to government tanks', people must experience powerful emotions. 'Powerful tropes' are condensed through abstraction, so that 'rhetoric and mobilization are inextricable' yet reliant on 'the adrenaline of emotion'.[156] In *Notes toward a Performative Theory of Assembly*, Butler seeks to clarify how the interiority experienced by the individual relates to social action. In the course of doing this, she explicitly names the importance of aesthetic discernment, alliances across groups of people, and the emergence into political life.

> Actions that are performative are irreducible to technical applications, and they are differentiated from passive and transient forms of experience. Thus, when and where there is suffering or transience, it is there to be transformed into the life of action and thought, and that action and thought has to be performative in the illocutionary sense, modeled on aesthetic judgment, bringing something new into the world. This means that the body concerned solely with the issues of survival, with the reproduction of material conditions and the satisfaction of basic needs, is not yet the 'political' body.[157]

This completes the latest step in articulating a nuanced connotation of activism. In this genealogy, impulses are sourced in emotion and concepts accrue terminology that accounts for externalised praxis. This takes seriously Eno's idea about the quantification of mental activism and the perceptibility that can accord agency in the activist's own self-awareness. It recognises, in keeping with Jasper, that things go on inside people's heads – along with 'know-how, emotional inspiration, raised expectations, shared rhetoric and images' – that have a bearing on social movements.[158] It allows for the inclusion of the non-human into rhetorics and ethics of ecology in green activism: sustained commitments that outrun the human life span or extend beyond the scope of social science. Furthermore, it emphasises the importance of physical and mental well-being, and a sense of security, in order to do political work.

In 1856, when Chesson consulted a clairvoyant who named his internal experience of 'melancholy, and lowness of spirits' as a stomach ailment, he found this 'a revelation'.[159] It is no wonder that in receiving this explanation he was energised to get on with his work. His activism took externalised forms, utilising the repertoire to try to effect social, cultural, legislative, and juridical change. Like anti-slavery organisers before him, he utilised meetings and the printed word, amplified by innovations in technology and a freer marketplace, to communicate his views. He put his case to the public not only through journalism but also, increasingly, through pamphlets such as *The Dutch Boers and Slavery in the Trans-vaal Republic* (1869), *Cuba in Revolution* (1871), *The Princes of India* (1872), *The Atlantic Cables* (1875), and *Turkey and the Slave Trade* (1877). The sale of such tracts at meetings and lectures is typical, but they were also extensively exchanged through the post, a form of information distribution among activists with strong ties, and a way to enhance weak ties through lobbying, chaining events and activists to ongoing intermittent discussion, correspondence, and newspaper coverage. Just as Thompson's generation inherited the practice of encouraging provincial auxiliaries to affiliate with London societies, organisations such as the Social Science Association (1857–84), a consistent focus of Chesson, could be formidable when gathered in one place.[160]

A key difference for Chesson's generation of activists was that with the effects of parliamentary reform they had greater likelihood than Thompson's of access to MPs. Whereas in 1831 mass meetings 'brought large numbers of men into mental and political activity' and 'laid open, as it were, a wholly new vein of political opinion and intelligence' to the public, meetings were also necessary to call MPs' attention to the public's pro-abolition majority.[161] By the mid-1850s organisations such as the APS included journalists, industrialists, barristers, and MPs: more complete and nimble sets of advocates for determining, disseminating, and lobbying for a political viewpoint. In the remainder of this chapter, three examples demonstrate how Chesson deployed his knowledge to become an adept combiner of the activist repertoires, astute observer of others utilising tactics in overtly performative ways, and lucid communicator of powerful tropes to leverage change.

## Activism across Distance

In 1857, the Toronto *Daily Globe* reported that a man gathering cranberries near Georgian Bay, on the north shore of Lake Huron, was prevented from further harvesting by an official of the Hudson's Bay Company (HBC). When this was reprinted in London's *Morning Star*, British readers, like the Canadians before them, likely knew something about what the incident meant in the geopolitics of the North American continent.[162] This cranberry picker's encounter with a company chartered in 1670 represents a multi-scalar incident – something of small magnitude yet indicative of consequential matters unfolding over time – conjoining the interests of great states and empires. 'Seeing the unimaginable' and finding 'the large in the small' was the exercise conjured by the account.[163] At the heart of it were issues of self-determination, free trade, and protection of Indigenous peoples amid an ongoing campaign about the HBC's claim to legitimacy and the disposition of its vast lands with respect to Britain and the Province of Canada. A lot was at stake in the cost-benefit analysis of trapping wild animals to near extinction and thereby destroying Indigenous people's lifeways and chances of survival, claiming virgin acreage larger than Europe for agriculture and mining, and utilising the Great Lakes as a connected waterway into the interior in lieu of the more northerly Hudson Bay watershed.

The person stooping in boggy land to harvest cranberries might have been an Ojibwe venturing beyond the Manitoulin (Wiikwemkoong) reserve, or a Métis descendant of French voyageurs and Native women. The cranberry gatherer was almost certainly not a British citizen, for farmer-settlers were unknown on the northern shore of Lake Huron, part of the Laurentian Plateau of Archean bedrock whose thin soil, where it exists, precludes tilling. The nearest settlers were 1,500 kilometres (932 miles) to the west, where in 1812 Scottish émigrés first established a community along the Red and Assiniboine Rivers, part of Lord Selkirk's (1771–1820) scheme, in a 300,000-square-kilometre (115,830-square-mile) land grant from the HBC. After initial difficulties the Red River (Assiniboia) colony expanded, mainly through retiring Anglophone 'country-born' and Francophone Métis employees of the HBC. In 1836, the colony was transferred back to the HBC and continued to be provisioned out of Fort Garry. Amidst hardships, the settlement established institutions, educated its young, and grew increasingly discontent.[164]

The HBC held a monopoly on the fur trade in Rupert's Land. During the 1840s, at its most extensive, this encompassed land as far west as the Columbia River watershed in Oregon Territory and Vancouver's Island off the Pacific coast as well as all watersheds east of the Continental Divide that flow into the Arctic Ocean, Hudson Bay all the way to Labrador on the Atlantic Ocean, and lands more or less ending at the forty-ninth parallel, a total of about 11.7 million square kilometres (4.5 million square miles). Managed by governors in London, the HBC benefited from a vast network of trapping lines and trading stations converging through York Factory on the southwest shore of Hudson Bay, a network managed by the 500 white, 10,000 mixed-race, and 50,000 Indigenous people who dwelt in Rupert's Land. The Province of Canada (1841–67), in contrast, comprised just a fraction of the southerly lands of modern Quebec and

Ontario, extending in a thin band north of the Great Lakes as far west as Grand Portage at the border with Minnesota Territory, and had 1,396,091 people at the 1861 census.[165]

By 1857, the future of the HBC's workforce of Métis and Indigenous trappers who traded manufactured goods for furs was uncertain. Six great forces were in play. (1) Minnesota was on the verge of statehood. With the prospect of a railroad to Saint Paul, the Red River Settlement had a potential new outlet for its grain and a supply source for its needs, but the HBC blocked such trade through heavy duties. Minnesota and Wisconsin's settlements pressed toward the shores of Lake Superior, which hastened the urgency to officially settle boundaries and forestall US encroachment above the forty-ninth parallel, notwithstanding the terms established by the Treaty of Paris in 1783. (2) Widespread northwestward migration of Indigenous people was imminent. This was due to encroachment of settlers and agriculture across the US plains, as well as starvation, which compressed Indigenous people's options to settle on reservations. (3) The growing role of the Arctic in geopolitics was recognised. The search for Franklin's lost 1845 expedition continued to preoccupy the British public, and in 1853 the discovery of a Northwest Passage held out the prospect of a shorter shipping route between Europe and China, yet domain over seaways was in question. During the Crimean conflict, there was concern that Russian holdings in the extreme northwestern part of North America might fall to Britain, sparking conflict with the United States along the Pacific coast. The Alaska Purchase was completed in 1867. (4) A charter extension granted to the HBC in 1849 for lands west of the Rocky Mountains would expire in 1859. Meanwhile, gold strikes on the Fraser River (and its tributary the Thompson) in 1857 brought Europeans to the region and destruction to Indigenous people. In 1858 the HBC's rights were revoked in favour of creating British Columbia as a Crown colony. In 1862 there was another gold rush on Williams Creek, in the Cariboo region. (5) Improved prospects in British Columbia renewed interest in a transcontinental railroad.[166] If travel by canoe on the continent's watersheds and by steamships to the headwaters of Lake Superior gave way to a bicoastal railway, a land conduit for goods flowing between the ports of Britain and concessions in Shanghai and Hong Kong via Montreal, Winnipeg, and Vancouver could save thousands of miles of perilous sea travel. (6) Even without the transcontinental railroad, land connections had been enhanced. Long before the Last Spike completed the transcontinental Canadian Pacific Railway on 7 November 1885, railways extended westward, connecting Toronto to Georgian Bay in 1855. This made it increasingly imaginable to export huge grain harvests from the north-western prairies to feed Britain. Of course, this involved homesteading on Indigenous lands, further exacerbating the plight of Indigenous peoples. The liberal solution – ruthlessly embraced as progress, but also softened with the language of zero-sum survival – was for nomadic Indigenous people to accommodate, abandon folkways, and farm.

And thus, in one rhetorical stroke, the cranberry gatherer near Georgian Bay 'becomes a stage on which worlds meet and search for their further development', to borrow Eucken's phrase. Instead of being characterised as a frozen repository for animal skins, from a liberal perspective Rupert's Land became a multifaceted and multiracial asset connecting Europe and Asia.[167] Thereby, the consumer in the British metropole came to see the stakes of empire, both in the prices they might pay and in the peoples with whom their fates were intertwined. This is a result of a process set in motion by discourse, and discourse enlivened by activism. On the shore of Georgian Bay, where an HBC official accosted the cranberry picker, sovereign domain existed but could not be enforced, neither for the hereditary rights of the region's First Peoples nor for the Province of Canada. Britain desperately wanted to avoid trouble, especially anything that would necessitate sending troops in the short or long term, for the Crimea and then the Indian Rebellion stretched its Army and Navy to the maximum and was costly in every way. Canada believed it had a rightful claim to the frontier but was unwilling to annex Rupert's Land if it involved paying compensation to the HBC's shareholders in Fenchurch Street. The HBC's charter – questioned though it was – would expire in 1859, and agitation to block renewal commenced in the mid-1840s. For a decade this was a hot potato that neither Britain nor Canada had the will to resolve, even though processes led by globalisation were manifest in its destiny. In Butler's terms, conjuring a vision of the cranberry picker 'propels the precarious into political life', which is to say, it is effective rhetoric that allied knowledge to performativity.

Alexander Kennedy Isbister (1822–83) was the son of an Orkney-born employee of the HBC and a Métis woman whose white father was the chief factor of Cumberland House (Waskahiganihk, on Pine Island in the Saskatchewan River). As a lad, he moved with his family to the Red River Settlement. He gained knowledge of the land and its peoples, speaking English, French, and probably Cree. Around the age of sixteen, Isbister accepted a clerkship in the HBC and was assigned to survey tributaries of the Mackenzie River. There, he communicated with Loucheaux families (Gwich'in speakers, another Athabascan language) that aided the expeditions. He learned the topography of the north to such an extent that he later predicted the area where Franklin's lost expedition could be found, on a 482-kilometre (300-mile) stretch of coastline between the Great Fish and Coppermine Rivers on King William's Island, and gathered geographic and ethnological data that he later published.[168] Nearing the age of twenty, having 'travelled through the whole country from the frontiers of the United States to the Arctic Ocean in one direction, and from Russian America to Hudson's Bay in the other', he left North America to acquire an education at Aberdeen and Edinburgh Universities, supported by a legacy from his grandfather.[169] He studied sundry topics, including medicine, while publishing in *Chambers*: 'This occasional journalism was sufficient to see him through his university career. Later it provided him with a forum from which he could criticize the Company.'[170] He moved to London, taught at the East Islington proprietary school, led the secular department at Jews' College in Finsbury Square, and then became headmaster at the Stationers' Company School. He joined the College of Preceptors, which certified teachers and developed standardised secondary school examinations, from 1861 edited its journal the *Educational Times*, and became its dean in 1872. He wrote multiple textbooks on grammar and elocution, arithmetic and geometry, bookkeeping and accounting, and commentaries on Greek and Roman classics.

This polymath, who in 1866, aged forty-four, completed his LLB (law degree) and was called to the Middle Temple, was the leading figure in the campaign against the HBC. He joined forces with the APS in 1847 to send deputations to the Colonial Office, seeking rights for native peoples and Métis, proprietary rights for landholders in the Red River Settlement, and representative government.[171] He meticulously laid out the HBC's legal history since Charles II (1630–85) granted a charter in 1670 (without the consent of Parliament and to lands that, at the time, the French king held title), convoluted and dubious charter renewals, and its disposition under successive inter-empire treaties, a theme he would return to again and again.[172] The HBC would never agree to submit to a legal test, but then the British government was not willing to insist on one. Isbister's memorial to the House of Commons in August 1848 was more explicit about the irresponsible government of the HBC, especially at Red River, and objected to the HBC's annexation of Vancouver's Island. Parliament did not prove an effective route for activism: as Barry Cooper notes, 'decisions regarding the Hudson's Bay Company seem to have been made in the Colonial Office, and in private'.[173] Meanwhile, in 1851 the trial and release of four Métis for illegally trading furs in Minnesota led to protests. Jean-Louis Riel (1817–64) assembled 500 signatures on a petition protesting against the HBC and lack of Métis representation in the Council of Assiniboia, and sent it to the APS for action. The petitioners stipulated their loyalty to the Crown – a point consistently held throughout the ensuing troubles – and desire for greater representation in public affairs, governance by the British not the HBC, and the right to use the French language in official matters.[174]

Over the years, Isbister maintained contact with his family and other informants in Red River, attempted to keep Rupert's Land before the British public, pursued regular correspondence with the Colonial Office, and published in the daily press, *Chambers*, and the APS journal the *Colonial Intelligencer, or Aborigines' Friend*.[175] In addition to his regular outlet in the *Star*, Chesson also sent articles on the matter to the Canadian press, which were published unsigned, and the *Times*.[176] Both Henry Labouchere (1798–1869) and then Edward Bulwer Lytton (1803–73), as successive Liberal and Conservative undersecretaries to the colonies, readily conceded the free trade angle: the HBC was not only the de facto governing body (it printed currency, its agents ruled on legal cases, and it set the scale for all barter) but it also held the entire right to import and sell provisions.[177] Permanent undersecretary at the Colonial Office Herman Merivale (1806–74) and Labouchere were both keen on colonisation, weighing in on the creation of Natal and compromises between Māori and settlers in New Zealand, so they were sympathetic to facets of the Red River settlers' perspective. After the election of Palmerston's government in April 1857, Isbister's efforts through official channels redoubled. By then, Chesson was the APS' corresponding secretary.

The partnership of Isbister, Chesson, and the APS is significant in numerous ways. From 1848, critics of the HBC had depicted it as

> a heartless monopoly enslaving Indians, half-breeds, and its own employees, denying them access to the civilized world [coded language for Christianity as well as secular education], debauching the Indians with liquor in order to eliminate their resistance to exploitation, and excluding from the benighted people the beneficial influences of free trade.... Employees were kept in constant debt to the Company ... and were thus unable to free themselves from a condition virtually indistinguishable from slavery.[178]

Critics needed to alter the public's view of Rupert's Land as a useless expanse, and instead bring it into the liberal imaginary as a place of untapped potential in mining and agriculture. At the same time, as Chesson put it, 'the manner in which whole tribes of Indians have melted away like snow under the company's rule is too notorious to require much observation'.[179]

With his heritage and first-hand knowledge, Isbister registered his commitment as no one else could, and endured as no one else did. By 1850, Isbister and his maternal uncle William Kennedy (1814–90) had convinced George Brown (1818–80), an abolitionist and editor of Toronto's *Globe*, to denounce the HBC, after which they worked painstakingly for the ensuing two decades to persuade Canada to annex Rupert's Land.[180] Brown supported settlement schemes, but understood that Canadians would need to be the first to take up homesteads.[181] Meanwhile, Isbister and the APS kept the fate of the Red River Settlement to the fore. The British public could conjure in their imaginations the stoic farmers (rather than adventurers and explorers), colonists far from the nearest British town who sought comity with their British motherland (never France or Turtle Island, and certainly not a heritage from both). In consistently publishing about the problem, Isbister and Chesson directed people of disparate views toward 'a shared object' that creates 'a collective force'. In Sara Ahmed's terms, such a 'glance' constitutes a social world shaped by a public that brings a distant Orient 'home' to the West. As the bodies brought 'home' were Indigenous, this interrupted the corporeal schema. They pressed questions that revealed the unevenness of the political economy, and 'that leaves its impressions, affecting the bodies that are subject to its address'.[182]

Though neither Isbister nor Chesson ever returned to North America, they coordinated the activist campaign simultaneously on two continents. In so doing, they might be said '*to touch the future on its hither side.…* in the here and now*'* as Homi Bhabha put it, whereby the 'spectacle of the social statistic, the transitive time of the body in performance' constitutes survival practices.[183] It was abundantly clear that Britain eschewed administrative and military responsibility for the territory, and would not ante up to pay the stockholders and thus buy title. Still, a stalemate presented more promising grounds for leverage than did negotiations with a unilateral power. In 1856, the APS memorialised both branches of the Canadian Parliament, asserting Canada's interest in the Northwest, the HBC's faulty legal claim, and concern about US encroachment.[184] After a decade's effort, the reformers succeeded insofar as the Liberal government struck a parliamentary select committee to gather testimony. From February through July 1857, the committee set 6,098 questions to witnesses including Isbister. Chesson and Isbister corresponded throughout these months, colluding to share information that Chesson would use in the press, including strategy for Isbister's second appearance before the committee.[185] The commission drafted a report that was replete with information but nevertheless ineffective in prompting a decision.

Two decades earlier, in 1837, another parliamentary select committee had drafted a report on Aboriginal tribes. A Quaker commentary on the report found the evidence 'lamentable and awful', for beyond the overt sufferings 'in some instances absolute extinction of the natives has already taken place – in others the work is nearly completed – whilst in most of the remainder, it is proceeding with a dreadful and accelerating rapidity'.[186] The report acknowledged how from 1810 settlers in Newfoundland so harassed the native Micmacs that by 1823 the extermination was complete. The Cree had been reduced from 8,000 or more persons to at most 300 through the effects of the HBC's quarrels with the North West Company (1780s–1821, a rival fur trading enterprise operating out of Montreal), 'in which the Indians were induced to take a bloody part, [and] furnished ... with a ruinous example of the savageness of Christians'. The HBC's peaceable trade also had injurious effects on Indigenous people, 'by encouraging them in improvident habits, which frequently bring large parties of them to utter destitution and to death by starvation'.[187] Twenty years later, Chesson regretted this 'history of desolation and death' brought about 'by the wickedness of selfish men'. Mighty nations were 'reduced to a few scattered and miserable remnants' through the effects of disease and alcohol, which the HBC offered in trade for furs, the only commodity it ever extracted.[188] Chesson failed to foresee the contrary logic of preserving the remnants of Indigenous cultures by opening the floodgates for European immigrants and missionaries, for as an ideologue he too was persuaded that free trade meant peaceful commerce, that the rule of law led to constructive institutions, and that British emigrants came willing to share their natural rights and freedoms. Yet, understanding something of the history of more easterly peoples, he saw supplanting the fur trade in Rupert's Land with settled agriculture as Indigenes' best hope of surviving the onslaught of European settlers' destruction of folkways, changes to the plain's biome, and imposition of martial and other forms of authority. Idealistically, he applied the logic of abolition – especially the British experience of emancipating West India's enslaved – as bringing economic liberties to native peoples.

Through ongoing rounds of briefing the colonial minister, writing letters and articles about foreign affairs, and attending meetings and deputations about the issues, activists personified the HBC as an antagonist to liberal principles embodied in the performativity of the Red River settlers.[189] Activists such as Chesson utilised rhetoric in two key ways to give British (and Canadian) politicians and the public the means by which to imagine the distant settlers, the Métis, and the native peoples' singularity so that they could, in turn, take agency to affect their political destinies. Whereas he wrote that the HBC ignored mineral riches and agriculture in favour of furs, no one had written the history of the HBC's treatment of Indians: indeed this is 'a blank page in the book of time' that needed to be addressed.[190] Like the story of the cranberry picker, this evocation of native people within the landscape promoted imaginary logic, cross-identification, and materiality along with the values of liberty, self-determination, and the duty to offer protection. Nevertheless, commercial initiatives also became synecdochic for the fate of Rupert's Land: not just remote outposts or farms barely managing to be self-sufficient, but proof (concurrent with the Crimean crisis) that newly cultivated fertile lands could feed 30 million Britons and (concurrent with the rebellion in India) become the bastion out of which Britain could forge a vibrant economy based on multidirectional diversified trade. The Red River settlers were a relatively known quantity, and the natives of the lands to the north and west were less so, though conjurable through the long history of exotica. By asserting the rights of both, Isbister, Chesson, and the APS brought them into discursive existence and helped propel them into British political life, calling for a constitutional Canadian government throughout the hinterlands. As people, and peoples, they started to matter, in opposition to a 'revolting and unconstitutional rule' by the HBC.[191]

Isbister testified that being governed from Toronto by a body without 'trading interest in the matter' would make all the difference. A watch post where the Saskatchewan River flows into Lake Winnipeg would suffice to surveil all traffic toward Mackenzie and Athabasca, and by this means (he asserted) a small force could maintain order over a great expanse. The trade could be taxed to pay for this.[192] Canadians sent Chief Justice William Henry Draper (1801–77) to defend their claims to the select committee of 1857, in the event of a legal tribunal on the HBC's claims arising, but Isbister bemoaned this choice: 'Mr. Draper does not even profess to represent' the views of 'the people of Canada'.[193]

As early as 1858, the APS welcomed a proposal to federate the British North American colonies. This was premature, though five years later London banks set up the International Financial Society, which agreed to purchase HBC stock at three times the nominal price, even though dividends had slid in recent years.[194] In 1867, four provinces – Ontario, Quebec, New Brunswick, and Nova Scotia – confederated as the Dominion of Canada, leaving the fate of westerly and northern lands unsettled. This went unremarked in Chesson's diary.

The following year, the new Dominion of Canada determined that the HBC's monopoly would be abolished, though it could continue the fur trade. Terms were set to sell Rupert's Land and the North-Western Territory to Canada: shareholders received compensation of £300,000. Canada appointed William McDougall (1822–1905, a proponent of westward expansion who, as commissioner of Crown lands in 1862, repossessed Manitoulin Island from its native occupants) as lieutenant-governor of Rupert's Land and the North-Western Territory, presiding over a nominated council of eight, only two of whom had connections to the area. Self-governing institutions would be forestalled for four to five years, or until the settlement's population reached 50,000. With the concurrent economic depression and high unemployment in Britain, working-class leaders urged the British government to organise emigration schemes on a large scale, but this would have significantly changed the racial and ethnic composition of the Red River Settlement, and the region as a whole.[195] Métis were concerned about an influx of Anglo-Protestant settlers, but were cut out of power. As Chesson put it, 'active disaffection' was felt by the whole Red River community, and 'moral sympathies of the entire settlement are enlisted on the side of the French half-breeds [Métis]' who had been so instrumental in building up the HBC, yet could never advance in its promotion structure beyond clerkships and were neither consulted nor compensated in the imminent transfer of domain.[196]

In advance of McDougall's arrival, a party of Canadian land surveyors set to work in the settlement. Louis Riel (1844–85), along with 120 other Métis and First Nations allies, led a rebellion at Fort Garry, refusing McDougall entry to their land and forcing him to retreat into Minnesota. They crossed the line from activism to open revolt. As Isbister noted, 'the time for memorializing has gone by'.[197] By December 1869 Riel's band declared him head of a provisional government that asserted, in part, that by repelling McDougall 'we have but acted conformably to that sacred right which commands every citizen to offer energetic opposition to prevent his country being enslaved'. They were determined 'to repel all invasions from whatsoever quarter they may come'.[198]

In the midst of the crisis, Chesson wrote a letter to the *Times* that Isbister endorsed: 'Nothing could be better, either in tone or language.'[199] Over a twenty-year period, Chesson stipulated:

> The English, the Scotch, the French elements in that population believed they were entitled to enjoy privileges similar to those which are so happily exercised by their fellow-citizens in Canada. They memorialized the Crown, they petitioned the House of Commons, their indefatigable representative in England (Mr. Isbister) made unceasing efforts on their behalf; but all in vain. The Hudson's Bay Company stood in the way, and successfully held

its own against the combined opposition of the most experienced statesmen in the United Kingdom.[200]

The settlers remained loyal to the British Crown, 'and continued to buoy themselves up with the hope that one day their just rights would be respected'. The imperial and Canadian governments were both responsible for the disaffection. Natives justly feared appropriation of their lands, for their rights sat on no 'proper footing' and the Canadian government made no overtures to them. The settlers justly reacted to the influx of surveyors and the lack of clear title to their farms. The dominion could not secure the people's confidence.[201]

In the spring of 1870, Riel's provisional government agreed to send delegates to Ottawa to negotiate for Red River's entry into confederation. A 5,600-square-kilometre (2,162-square-mile) box was drawn around the settlement to create the bilingual Province of Manitoba. That summer, soldiers were sent to seize and lynch Riel; he fled to the United States but returned covertly. In 1874, he was elected to the federal government but was banished for his part in the rebellion.

Without consultation, the HBC's wintering partners were left adrift. These fifty-three commissioned officers – men such as Isbister's maternal (late) grandfather – together held eighty-five shares that entitled them to 40 per cent of the HBC's profits. In 1871, Isbister brought their representative, member of the Manitoba Legislature Donald Smith (1820–1914), to London to contest the directors' decision to do nothing for the wintering partners while enriching their own pockets lavishly out of the agreement brokered through the International Financial Society. Isbister and Smith's starting bid was £120,000, the mention of which at the half-yearly meeting of HBC directors caused the General Court to break out into 'a perfect storm'. Isbister stated his case, whereupon he wrote 'my sitting down was the signal for a perfect tumult of disorder & confusion & Mr. Smith if he ever attempted to speak at all which I do not know was never heard'. Ten days later the shareholders agreed to an indemnity of £107,000, which yielded each chief factor about £2,500 and each chief trader about £1,250, whereupon all would retire and some would be re-engaged under new terms.[202]

Whereas Chesson and Isbister were activists in this saga, their efforts enabled the peoples of Rupert's Land to acquire performativity. These are complementary forms of agency and political engagement. Just as Isbister's rhetoric turned Rupert's Land into 'a stage on which worlds meet and search for their further development', Chesson directed his humanist vision to fight for peoples' 'more definite form' (as Eucken put it, something that must be 'discovered and realized by ourselves') and give Britons at home a way to participate in that vision.[203] Their impact over time is measured in the creation of political entities, unified governance of Canada, farms and mines across the prairies, and a railway carrying produce from sea to sea. Tragically, there is also a legacy of ongoing appropriation, disregard, and overriding of native and Métis people's self-determination. For all its talk of rights, the APS could only seek to protect.

### Advocating Activism

On 29 April 1888, after a pulmonary infection suddenly took a bad turn, Chesson's life – 'full of help and service' – ended. He was fifty-five. Though Chesson was seen and heard no more, Lewis Sergeant's (1841–1902) obituary notes 'his life remains an active force'. This is metaphoric, but also factual insofar as the repercussions of his deeds continued to be felt, and even more so because the means by which he advanced campaigns are still broadly understood and replicated. In his final days, Chesson became interested in dispossessed peoples in Madagascar and the Cape Colony, in Jubo Jubogha of Opobo (1821–91, arrested for continuing to tax British traders after his lands were appropriated), and in Samoan islanders, and in each case he approached his work systematically:

> His method was to learn all that could be known in this country [Great Britain] about the rights and wrongs of the people whose complaints had reached him, to work up his case, to inform those who were associated with him in the Aborigines['] Protection Society, or the Native Races Committee, or elsewhere; to furnish materials for questions or motions in the House of Commons; to write letters to the newspapers, full of details, but always temperate and accurate; to bring together men and women who could help the cause by speech or pen, sometimes on a public platform, sometimes at a political breakfast, sometimes in a drawing-room, at a club, or in his own office.[204]

In addition to his duties with the APS and as a journalist, he would commit himself 'instinctively, without premeditation or selfish calculation, but by force of nature and habit to any cause and any labour which appealed to his generous enthusiasm'. This sense of public duty, outside the confines of government, carried no honours. He eschewed advocating from within the confines of the state, for by remaining independent he felt he could be more powerful, as well as impartial. He was remembered for making no distinction of right and justice with respect to colour, 'and no favour was created by power and prestige.... He aided his fellows by working for them, by giving them helpful advice, by putting them in the way of helping themselves'.[205]

As a professional activist, Chesson focused energies on the liberal project of defining and instilling human rights at home and abroad. His APS correspondence, journalism, organisation of meetings and deputations, and participation on committees reflect his ability to perceive performative acts across great distances. Yet he was also involved in domestic issues, a succession of grave national crises, and unfolding liberal projects including the franchise, family law, and women's rights, which tapped optimism and anxiety. Oral and written activism are present in all, but there is a distinction between campaigns pursued through letters, small group discussions, and rule-bound meetings (descended from the abolition movement) and direct actions consisting of marches, rallies, and addresses that combined chants, singing, cheering, and sloganeering (descended from Chartism). Both forms ultimately rely on creating a locatable effect of mass support in order to leverage activism into legislative change. An example of the first demonstrates the cumulative effects of Chesson's *Bildung* applied to the biopower of exacting state-sanctioned assault for perceived sexual activity. He offered the basics of a repertoire for how to organise opposition and repeal British laws. Examples of the second show him commenting as a journalist and in his diary about the repertoires of crowds. This entails activism in moments that open up to emancipatory potential that may be foreclosed or may fundamentally transform human rights.

With hindsight, we can see how Chesson's views evolved away from questions of vice (when saw *La Traviata* in 1856) to insights about sexual rights (when he became the joint honorary secretary of the Metropolitan Association to Repeal the Contagious Diseases Acts in 1870). He liaised with an eclectic coalition of women and men (leftists, feminists, and social purity conservatives, local and national) focused on repeal of the acts that authorised compulsory, and even forcibly compelled, gynaecological examinations of any woman alleged to be a prostitute in specific garrison and naval towns.[206] For those who had failed to secure the women's franchise in recent Reform legislation, this explicit curtailment of rights was infuriating.[207] As Thompson, who came out of retirement to assist, put it: 'The existing law authorizes and requires the adoption of a process that is to the last conceivable extent indecent, degrading, brutal, and immoral, a violent outrage on female modesty, and a sentence of death upon every … womanly instinct. I[f] we can make out our case for the inviolability of the fallen and friendless, our work is done. So at least it seems to me.'[208] This conviction propelled him to the lecture circuit for a final campaign. The repeal campaign focused on the classic challenge to persuade individuals to recognise a common cause; motivate and instruct individuals to forge local organisations networked into a national movement; and use individual and organisational means to leverage pressure on MPs to change the law. In Thompson's view, 'The longer it [the campaign] lasts and the more vigorously it is conducted the better will be the education the people will receive and the clearer will be the views of those who will be called to navigate the vessel hereafter.'[209] The problem, however, was that the offending acts of inspection could not be overtly described: identificatory discomfort had to be achieved through allusion, and understanding fostered through imaginative proxy.

Josephine Butler (1828–1906), a prominent feminist leader in the repeal campaign, emphasised the gendered and classed nature of the acts: they not only associated prostitution and venereal disease wholly with women rather than men; they subjected women who had often already been abused by men to brutal, indiscreet, and degrading arrest and medical inspection by men, which could result in up to a year's involuntary confinement in venereal disease wards. Furthermore, this encroachment on liberties involved 'direct outrage on public morality and the sanctities of family life'.[210] As with the abolition movement of the early 1830s, the people recruited to get involved in this campaign and leverage pressure – notably women, whose sympathy for other women needed to be mobilised – were not enfranchised to vote their MPs in or out of office. On the face of it, this was not an ideal strategy, and yet it had worked before. As with the abolition movement, the people most affected by the legislation had absolutely no social or political standing: indeed, the voices of the women affected by the Contagious Diseases Acts were almost entirely absent from discussions, present neither at meetings nor in print. And, as for Caribbean enslaved people in the early 1830s, repeal did little to empower them.[211]

Chesson's contribution is documented in a single source. It represents his accumulated understanding of how to make a movement effective – garnered over the years of his *Bildung* and fostered by empathy across distance – to make the 'how-to' of politics accessible to new activists. He distilled it into an endlessly repeatable strategy that sets out the rhetoric and issues of reform so as to mobilise effective action. As James M. Jasper put it: 'people must articulate emerging sensibilities, judgements, and tastes, work through the implications of these, and inspire others to join them. Resources help to spread the message, and strategic action may be necessary for capturing the attention of new audiences'.[212] Chesson's contribution does just that, in support of an October 1870 determination by the National Association for Repeal of the Contagious Diseases Acts that it would oppose all known advocates of the acts at the polls. This tactic was first used in support of Baxter Langley (1819–92, Chesson's former editor at the *Star*, vice-president of the Reform League, and a qualified though non-practicing physician), who stood for election at Colchester. It was used through the general election of 1874 and a subsequent by-election where Liberals unsuccessfully stood John Delaware Lewis (1828–84) at Oxford.[213] Chesson's role was to systematically ascertain candidates' positions and lay out how to leverage pressure.

Chesson published the pamphlet *How to Influence Members of the House of Commons*, based on a text he had delivered at the national repeal meeting, in 1870. It picks up the didactic suggestions at a point when an individual has joined the cause and wants to know what to do, explaining choices within the activist repertoire.[214] The tactic is simple: impress upon your MPs that unless they vote for repeal they will lose their seats. He quotes Cobden in arguing that any failure to persuade will mean that 'the fault will lie more in the advocates than in the audience'.[215] Persistence matters. MPs will not be turned quickly, so expect that. Provide facts, but take care in presenting them in ways 'friendly' to the MP, 'for an essay or article which would convince a person of strong religious feelings or one profoundly interested in the ethics of legislation, might fail to influence a statistician or a man of the world; and therefore, in this educational work, we should endeavor to combine the results of experience with the enunciation of moral, religious and philosophical principles'.[216] Here, the remnants of Bible Politics survive well into the Victorian period, a parallel tactic with social statistics and personal testaments. In leveraging 'purely intellectual or moral influence' on an MP, constituents 'may reasonably claim to exercise perfect freedom of action ... [to] subject their representatives to any degree of pressure' that appeals to MPs' latitude for their own personal 'freedom of action'.[217]

Chesson advances two procedures 'for the conversion of enemies' to the repeal movement's position. This fascinating yet straightforward elucidation is the identical playbook for campaigns into the twenty-first century, altered only in a few details by the advent of widespread social media practices. Chesson stipulated that, first and frequently, constituents should write to their MPs, for when 'members are well aware that if a constituent feels sufficient interest in a question to write on the subject, he feels interest enough to make him remember at the next election how his member has voted'.[218] He cites Joseph Cooper (1800–1881), whose experience in getting the Act of Emancipation in the West Indies passed showed that 'no [other] method is so easily carried out, or acts so quickly and so effectively'. Chesson drew on twenty-five years of experience with politicians, writing 'I once knew a vote to be turned from the wrong side to the right one by a member receiving, on the eve of a division, five hundred letters from his constituents. All day long he was receiving and opening letters, and they produced an impression on his mind which bore fruit in the division lobby.'[219] To follow up, private interviews with MPs should be sought, especially when individuals are adept in arguing their case, know the facts, and can credibly represent the community's opinion. Then, he counselled, bide your time. Let the MP ponder the subject. After a reasonable interval, 'deputations [of several representatives] should wait upon him for the purpose of eliciting formal declaration of his sentiments, and making him feel that the question is one which distinctly affects the stability of his relations with his constituents'. This will eliminate any 'excuse for indulging in those parliamentary ambiguities with which experience has made us all familiar'. Petitions can show the strength of feeling, yet they had been over-used, with thousands presented annually to Parliament.[220] Chesson advises activists who do choose to go this route to gather signatures only within a specific constituency and present them to the local MP, otherwise MPs cannot 'judge of the extent to which those whom they represent reprobate the legislation which it is our object to repeal'.[221] Finally, public meetings' 'salutary instrumentality' is to build pressure and demonstrate that 'without distinction of party, sect, sex, class, or condition of men', hearing the exercise of free speech by earnest individuals will stir the member: 'his intellect, or if he be a man of inferior caliber, then his fears, will be quickened into greater activity; and he will be the more impressed, if, when the subject is about to be brought before Parliament' he will see its importance alongside the Corn Laws, disestablishment of the Irish Church, or any other 'great measure'.[222]

Three letters to the *Daily News* at the end of 1869 launched the Ladies' National Association for the Repeal of the Contagious Diseases Acts, with 168 signatories headed by the letters' pseudonymous author Harriet Martineau, followed by Josephine Butler and Florence Nightingale (1820–1910): at this time these reformers were, respectively, a gifted writer, galvanising speaker, and consummate yet reclusive organiser and social statistician.[223] These were compelling public figures, almost without parallel in terms of credibility and gravitas in promoting such a cause. Robert Fowler, a prominent city financier and MP for Cambridge, sponsored the

1870 bill to repeal that was anticipated in Chesson's pamphlet. William Gladstone's Liberals held a large majority, so the challenge for repealers lay within these ranks. Bright spoke eloquently against the state's role in condoning prostitution yet effectively enslaving women who worked in the trade for the benefit of standing armies.

Over the years, women campaigners were subject to some of the 'mobbing' activities more associated with US pro-slavery factions: disrupted meetings, chases, and arson. Repealers kept up the pressure through four general elections, eventually prevailing after the Third Reform Act (1884) gave the vote to most men.[224] Repeal in Britain and Ireland was achieved in 1886 through a broad coalition of persistent middle-class Nonconformists, radical working-class men, and middle-class feminists, though similar laws remained in effect in the colonies.[225] Chesson's ability for 'deep seeing' has a pale imprint on this outcome: noting the potential of every adult citizen (enfranchised or not) to become involved, stipulating what is known to be effective, and urging savvy use of the activist repertoire in consort with others. In this, as with so many causes, he played the long game.

### Observational Citizenship

Learning to put activist repertoires in motion is the hallmark of Chesson's *Bildung*. His critical practice of observation, analysis, and commentary was also deployed in watching activism instigated by others. This ascription is based not simply on actions being counter-hegemonic, but on a more complex dramaturgy attentive to different modes of *doing*, the spatiality of urbanism, and coordinated choreography. In this respect, the multitudes of people depicted by Cruikshank's 'Passing Events of 1853' provide an apt corollary. A lot is going on in the comet – technically, everything was fair game for observation – yet performative acts of many kinds are distinguishable, even if related to one another in myriad ways through theme, form, tactics, and results.

In 'Passing Events of 1853', Cruikshank depicts numerous clusters of onlookers engaged in specific participatory actions. The choices are timely and far reaching, indicatively implicating the Thompson-Chesson family. Under the banner 'Emigration to Australia' a column of figures laden with goods is led toward two ships; the previous year, Thompson's elder brother and family were among such emigrants, who helped tip the balance of Australia's European population from convicts to free settlers during the 1850s.[226] George Thompson and Chesson staged the 1853 Peace Conference, whose attendees Cruikshank depicts in a circle of onlookers. Despite the failure of the peace movement to keep Britain out of the Crimean War, Cruikshank's juxtapositions are reminiscent of the growing proximity of continents and nations' fates; after all, Frederick Chesson spent his childhood in Kent and New England, and his brother-in-law Herbert Thompson would serve as a commissioning agent in the Crimea.

As 'Passing Events of 1853' emphasises, putting oneself into a numerous company was a common facet of public life and belonging during the Victorian period. Reading journalism predicated, complemented, and reprocessed such experiences. As the Georgian republic of letters expanded from coteries to newspaper-reading masses, political organisers exploited the potential. Chesson joined the throngs and reflected on his experiences in writing, observing and documenting events' performative qualities. Across the sixteen volumes of his diaries (mid-1854 to mid-1870), a quarter-of-a-million words mark thousands of such events, showing how Chesson calibrated activism that was neither at a distance nor epistolary, but direct. He was ever attentive to dramaturgy as well as affect.

On 23 June 1860, during a period of mild conflict with France, 18,450 militiamen mustered in Hyde Park (Figure 3.8).[227] The weather was fair on this Saturday afternoon, when shop attendants and other hands had their half-holiday. Chesson found 'all the approaches to' the park 'almost blocked up by the dense masses of people, & carriages'. After gaining access, he ascertained

> the spectacle was certainly an extraordinary one, and grew in animation and interest every moment. Every housestep in the vicinity was crowded with well-dressed spectators none more so than Mr Disraeli's at Grosvenor Gate. The marble Arch, the Duke of Wellington's statue, and Hyde Park Corner were all likewise filled. Every tree in the park, commanding a view of the ground, was freighted with a burden of adventurous spirits; and the consequence was that numerous branches were lopped off, and lay scattered on the ground. The galleries stretching for a long distance from north to south almost entirely shut out the public, who had no tickets, from a view of the proceedings of the day. Seats, or rather stands consisting of planks laid upon [scaffolds] sold for five shillings and half a crown [two shillings and sixpence] a piece.

For two hours, the battalions marched by for the queen's review, and then 'upon a given signal', the volunteers 'set up an enthusiastic cheer such as is rarely heard, & is never to be forgotten when once listened to'. After the royal party drove off, 'the galleries then began to empty, and the people

THE VOLUNTEER REVIEW IN HYDE PARK.—RETURN OF VOLUNTEER CORPS DOWN CONSTITUTION HILL.—SEE PAGE 224

Figure 3.8    The Volunteer Review in Hyde Park, return of volunteer corps down Constitution Hill. *Illustrated London News*, 30 July 1860, 617. Getty Images.

to move, but it was a long time before the whole of the vast multitude had dispersed, and the park was left to solitude'.[228] These 'dense masses' and the 'vast multitude' that pressed into every corner of the park and perched on every tree limb were there for the patriotic spectacle and acted accordingly.

In 1863, London's Emancipation Committee, which planned for the support of those recently freed from enslavement by the Emancipation Proclamation, convened a meeting in Exeter Hall, London's premier political meeting venue (Figure 3.9). Chesson, the meeting's secretary and organiser, arrived to find 'the Committee room "crowded," and what was better[,] the great hall full to overflowing'. The room, which held at least 4,500, was so full that two other meetings were spontaneously convened, one in the lower hall's meeting room (capacity 1,000) and the other outside in Exeter Street (behind the hall, parallel to the Strand). The audience

Figure 3.9 'Great Anti-Slavery Demonstration at Exeter Hall.' *Illustrated London News*, 7 February 1863, 154. Getty Images.

was responsive from the first moments, and 'When Abraham Lincoln's name was mentioned the vast assemblage arose <u>en masse</u>, & continued to cheer for several minutes.... The excitement, & enthusiasm were intense. Ten thousand people, at least, must have taken part in this great and almost unprecedented demonstration.'[229] Though the event was crowded, its attendees were not a crowd. This distinction – phenomenological, not semantic – was repeatedly made by Chesson, whether describing holiday-makers at Ramsgate, depositors making a rush on failing banks, colossal outdoor political meetings for electoral Reform, or people eager to see a royal procession. At all such performative events it was important, in a liberal democracy such as mid-Victorian Britain, to notice signs of unruliness, to analyse the conduct of amassed people, and thus to distinguish between action-in-concert – behaviour calibrated to the scene and constitutive of incremental reform through activism – and signs of dissent or divergence by intractable, unlawful, or malicious reactionaries.

What did it mean to transform the populace into the dense multitude of a *mass* or *crowd* (nouns) versus the incommoding effect of a throng *pressing* or *crowding* into a space in order to *mob* (verbs)? Was amassed spectatorship at a political rally, sporting event, or demonstration such as the 1860

Voluntary Review in Hyde Park differently perceived, governed, and efficacious than the amassed spectatorship at the theatre, music halls, or concerts who stood for the national anthem, applauded jingoistic balladeers, or put a premium on the figures seated in the royal box? Understanding these distinctions was an important facet of observational and participatory citizenship, a role that Chesson strove to exemplify. As a man highly reputed for his even-tempered approach to inflammatory issues, he provides reliable and informative insights into this historical issue, giving rise to a grounded theory of assembly in a nation with a unique liberal outlook on such practices and relatively unrestrictive rights to assembly, yet a people wary of both revolution (the tyranny of the many) and despotism (the rule of the few), regardless of their views on monarchy.

The metropolitan masses are imbricated in mass culture, art, and technology. Like Karl Marx, Walter Benjamin contrasts the urban masses depicted by the literati with the 'iron mass of the proletariat'. According to Miriam Bratu Hansen, 'what is at issue is not a particular class, nor any collective however structured. At issue is nothing but the amorphous crowd of passersby, the street public', which Charles Baudelaire (1821–67) called 'the moving veil'. Benjamin sees 'the masses encoded in the architecture, fashions, events, and institutions of high-capitalist culture', and 'traces their profound impact on just about every area of cultural practice'.[230] Chesson, from his mid-Victorian vantage, also registered this 'moving veil's' impact, yet he understood it as a function not of consumer consumption but of citizen assembly. Observers bore their social markers, but what mattered for activism was how performance and commencing 'to matter' (whether imperceptibly or overtly) could 'propel the precarious into political life'. This is equally so for each figure in Cruikshank's etching (scrupulously drawn with a bonnet, mop cap, top hat, bowler, derby, or flat cap), the emancipation meeting where top hats are thrown aloft, and the 1860 militia muster, where each figure in the stands marks a man of means along the 1.7-kilometre-long (1 mile) column from Admiralty Arch to Wellington Arch. They are decorous crowds every bit as much as the working-class men whom Chesson describes weighing down the tree limbs in Hyde Park as they strained to catch a view. Their presence enacted their citizenship while specific dramaturgical locations bolstered identificatory effects. Crowds could hold multiple goals simultaneously, but each action or statement contributed.[231]

Celebrating the volunteers was indisputably a jingoistic act. Celebrating emancipation was symbolically defiant, both of the Confederacy and of the British state's official neutrality, and marked a milestone in the abolition movement transitioning to various forms of support for the emancipated. Yet what Chesson (in words) and Cruikshank (in pictures) also point to is how the process of *Bildung* – self-cultivation constitutive of internal and outward freedom – is fostered by such public forms of participation. Rather than an escape from the political into the aesthetic, Victorian *Bildung* was cultivated through varied experience and constituted through the exercise of public participation, provided that the performances were conducive to steadfast character, the cultivation of reason, and individual as well as collective advancement. There is a utilitarian streak in this, yet there is also room for whimsy, hokum, and demonstrative failure.

That said, it is notable that Chesson also described a form of crowding that did not require amassed presence yet had marked political significance. At the end of May 1863, he formed part of the APS delegation to Emperor Napoleon III that visited Paris to present a scroll commending the emperor's Algerian policy. Napoléon III had proclaimed in a letter of 6 February 1863 to his governor-general in Algeria that the Arabs' title to their lands would be respected, and that though it was a French colony, he regarded it as an Arab kingdom and was anxious that his Arab subjects not undergo the fate of North America's native peoples.[232] The emperor expressed thanks 'that his measures designed to promote the civilisation of the Arabs met with approbation in England, and had the support of those especially who were devoted to the interests of humanity'.[233] This formality complete, the emperor and the APS delegation then had a few minutes' conversation about colonial management. Chesson was impressed by the emperor but not unaware of the tumult that marred his lineage. The evening before this audience inside the Tuileries, Chesson had walked in the palace's gardens. 'At every step I was dazzled and bewildered. The scene beneath so clear and sunny a sky realized one's ideas of Elysium. Behind us the Tuilleries [*sic*] crowded with so many tragic memories – before us the long vista broken by the grand obelisk, and terminating in the distance in the Arc de Triomphe.'[234] This garden was the site par excellence of private and public oscillation – from Louis XV's (1710–74) recreation ground to Robespierre's (1758–94) revolutionary fêtes, from foreign encampments to a restored monarchy – and for Chesson its ambience was crowded with successive performances of unruly and inherently unstable history, the essence of what liberalism was intended to prevent. These tragic memories, which represented the tumultuousness of recent French history, contrasted with what Chesson was ideologically disposed to regard as progress: Napoléon III, especially in 1863, making strides toward free trade with Britain, undertaking grand public works, preparing the Suez Canal to revolutionise seaways between Europe and Asia, and making France self-sustaining in agriculture. On the sunny spring evening, this history crowded in, phantoms of the past.

The kinds of revolutionary instability that haunted the Tuileries had little purchase in Britain. This contrasts with activism as a process that solves an interior problem tied to subjectivity, expressed outwardly through performativity. In Cruikshank's comet, British unrest is signalled in two ways: Lancashire cotton spinners planning actions in a meeting (the Strike for Wages), and protesting placard bearers ('Bribery and Treating' and 'Bribery and Corruption') who are roughly jostled while the courts simultaneously review the evidence of corrupt electioneering. Whereas French tumult resulted in successive regime changes, Britain's counterpart consists of Tories knocked off their chairs and corruption tainting elections (such as allegations in Thompson's own recent contests) in the era of incremental Reform. The public, or rather the many sectors of the public who constituted the commonweal, were largely peaceful and self-determining. They sought their pleasures, to be sure, but each person's choice, taste, and discernment scaled up and aggregated in gatherings of various kinds. In Cruikshank's comet, the figures around Maestro Jullien find the concert alarming, the ale drinkers are inebriated, and two sets of boys converge with rival Guys that will ultimately blaze on bonfires, but even these vignettes built the pluralistic Victorian world. Self-cultivation – as for the 10,000 who gathered at Exeter Hall to celebrate the Emancipation Proclamation in 1863 – was a commitment to individual freedom as the route to collective advancement. As Albert Smith, who began his career as a journalist in the 1840s and nightly scaled the Alps, put it: 'We adore the streets. We know there are thousands of our fellow-men who regard them merely as the spaces included by two boundary lines of bricks and mortar, subservient only to the purposes of commerce, or the transition from one spot to another. We look upon them as cheap exhibitions – *al fresco* national galleries of the most interest[ing] kind, furnishing ever-varying pictures of character or incident.'[235] This is the ethos into which Frederick Chesson stepped in 1853, launching his as yet uncertain career. And in 1888, when he was memorialised in death, the *Daily News* noted, 'He was one of those laborious artists behind the scenes who never appear in tinsel, and who are rarely seen at the footlights, but without whom the play could not possibly go on.'[236]

## Notes

1 Hoock, *Empires of the Imagination*, 3.
2 Cox, Jeffrey C. *Romanticism in the Shadow of War: Literary Culture in the Napoleon War Years*. Cambridge: Cambridge University Press, 2014: 66.
3 'Easter Amusements.' *Era*, 3 April 1853, 10.
4 The source did not abbreviate the epithet. '"Sardanapalus" at the Princess's Theatre.' *Morning Post*, 18 June 1853, 5. See also Malley, Shawn. *From Archaeology to Spectacle in Victorian Britain: The Case of Assyria*. Farnham: Ashgate, 2012: 77–102.
5 Smith lectured in front of a moving panorama. See Huhtamo, Erkki. *Illusions in Motion: Media Archaeology of the Moving Panorama and Related Spectacles*. Cambridge: MIT Press, 2013: 215–43.
6 See McNee, Alan. *The Cockney Who Sold the Alps: Albert Smith and the Ascent of Mont Blanc*. Brighton, UK: Victorian Secrets, 2015; Smith, Albert. *The Story of Mont Blanc*. London: n.p., 1853; and Birdoff, Harry. *The World's Greatest Hit: Uncle Tom's Cabin*. New York: S.F. Vanni, 1947: 146.
7 'Easter Amusements.' *Morning Post*, 29 March 1853, 5.
8 Sands was proprietor of the Hippodrome, New York City, where he performed *Owen's Alpine Rambles*. 'Theatricals and Music in America.' *Era*, 8 May 1853, 12.
9 Oettermann, Stephan. *The Panorama: History of a Mass Medium*. Translated by Deborah Lucas Schneider. New York: Zone Books, 1997:7.
10 Oleksijczuk, Denise Blake. *The First Panoramas: Visions of British Imperialism*. Minneapolis: University of Minnesota Press, 2011.
11 'Exhibitions, etc.' *Era*, 3 April 1853, 11.
12 'Model of the Earth.' *Morning Chronicle*, 27 December 1853, 3.
13 Maclure, Robert. *The Arctic Dispatches Containing an Account of the Discovery of the North-West Passage*. London: J. D. Potter, 1854: 95, 99.
14 Lightman, Bernard. 'Spectacle in Leicester Square: James Wyld's Great Globe, 1851–61.' In *Popular Exhibitions: Science and Showmanship, 1840–1910*, edited by Joe Kember, John Plunkett, and Jill A. Sullivan, 19–40. London: Pickering and Chatto, 2012: 30. There were legitimately impressive productions brought back to England. These included a 134-pound, 11-ounce nugget that was recovered from a narrow hole near Buninyong and valued between £8,000 and £9,000. 'Monster Gold Nugget.' *Observer*, 4 July 1853, 5.
15 Wyld, J. *Map of the Gold Regions of Australia*. London: privately published, 1852. See also Huhtamo, *Illusions in Motion*, 337–42.
16 Gould, Marty. *Nineteenth-Century Theatre and the Imperial Encounter*. New York: Routledge, 2011: 139–49.
17 'Public Amusements – Theatres.' *Morning Post*, 18 April 1854, 5.
18 Davis, *Broadview Anthology*, 361–71.
19 'Public Amusements.' *Morning Post*, 18 April 1854, 5; see also Gould, *Nineteenth-century Theatre*, 25; and David, Robert G. *The Arctic in the British Imagination, 1818–1914*. Manchester: Manchester University Press, 2000: 135–7.

20 'Haymarket Theatre.' *Illustrated London News*, 29 April 1854, 393.

21 'Theatre Royal, Haymarket.' *Era*, 8 April 1855, 1.

22 Gould, *Nineteenth-Century Theatre*, 24.

23 See, for example, *The Ten Chief Courts of Sydenham Palace*. London: Routledge, 1854: 103–23; and Sir Austen Henry Layard's books *Nineveh and Its Remains*. London: John Murray, 1849; and *The Nineveh Court in the Crystal Palace*. London: Bradbury and Evans, 1854. Hoock demonstrates the popular reach of the installations in *Empires of the Imagination*, 263.

24 Meeuwis, Michael. *Everyone's Theater: Literature and Daily Life in England, 1860–1914*. Ann Arbor: University of Michigan Press, 2019: 5, 10.

25 Dewey, John. *The Public and Its Problems*. New York: Henry Holt, 1927: 184. See also Hollinshead-Strick, Cary. *The Fourth Estate at the Fourth Wall: Newspapers on Stage in July Monarchy France*. Evanston, IL: Northwestern University Press, 2019: 20–2.

26 George Cruikshank, 'Passing Events of 1853.' *Cruikshank's Magazine*, January 1854.

27 For example, see Richards, Jeffrey. *The Golden Age of Pantomime: Slapstick, Spectacle and Subversion in Victorian England*. London: I. B. Tauris, 2015, 8; and McWilliam, *London's West End*, esp. 84–103.

28 This relies on the foundation built by Booth, Michael. *Victorian Spectacular Theatre*. Cambridge: Cambridge University Press, 1981: 3, 8, 17, 29; Meisel, Martin. *Realizations: Narrative, Pictorial, and Theatrical Arts in Nineteenth-Century England*. Princeton, NJ: Princeton University Press, 1983; and Altick, Richard. *The Shows of London*. Cambridge, MA: Belknap Press, 1978.

29 In 1851, Maine became the first state to adopt prohibition. Nationwide campaigns in the United States and Britain were launched in 1853 but gained significant momentum in England only in the 1870s. Dingle, A.E. *The Campaign for Prohibition in Victorian England: The United Kingdom Alliance, 1872–1895*. London: Croom Helm, 1980.

30 Elliott, David J., Marissa Silverman, and Wayne D. Bowman. 'Introduction, Aims, and Overview.' In *Artistic Citizenship: Artistry, Social Responsibility, and Ethical Praxis*, edited by David J. Elliott, Marissa Silverman, and Wayne D. Bowman, 3–21. Oxford: Oxford University Press, 2016: 5–6.

31 Heather Davis-Fisch convincingly argues in *Loss and Cultural Remains in Performance: The Ghosts of the Franklin Expedition* (New York: Palgrave, 2012) that such encounters with arctic peoples were replete with performance.

32 Manilius authored the five-book poem *Astronomica*, circa 10–20 CE.

33 'The Comet.' *Hereford Times*, 3 September 1853, 8; Bortle, John E. 'The Bright-Comet Chronicles.' *International Comet Quarterly*, 1998. Harvard University Department of Earth and Planetary Sciences. www.icq.eps.harvard.edu/bortle .html; and Olson, Robert J.M., and Jay M. Pasachoff. *Fire in the Sky: Comets and Meteors, the Decisive Centuries, in British Art and Science*. Cambridge: Cambridge University Press, 1998: 216–17.

34 'Mr. Albert Smith's Ascent of Mount Blanc.' *Daily News*, 6 December 1853, 2; and McNee, *Cockney Who Sold the Alps*, 158.

35 'Holiday Amusements.' *Morning Chronicle*, 27 December 1853, 2.

36 Davies, Rachel Bryant. *Troy, Carthage and the Victorians: The Drama of Classical Ruins in the Nineteenth-Century Imagination*. Cambridge: Cambridge University Press, 2018: 34; and 'Adelphi Theatre.' *Observer*, 24 July 1853, 7. Michael Booth notes that Kean 'rigidly followed' the British Museum sculptures, and that Samuel Phelps' *Pericles* at Sadler's Wells that same year also utilised this source. *Victorian Spectacular Theatre*, 19–20, 53.

37 Hewitt, Martin. *The Dawn of the Cheap Press in Victorian Britain: The End of the 'Taxes on Knowledge,' 1849–1869*. London: Bloomsbury, 2014: 63.

38 The table-drum might be Distin's Monster Drum, though an illustration of this shows a vertical striking surface: 'Distin's Monster Drum at the Handel Festival.' *Illustrated London News*, 27 June 1857, 627. Jullien's flamboyance matches up well with Cruikshank's caricature. Circa 1853, Jullien composed the polka 'L'Echo du Mont Blanc' in homage to Albert Smith.

39 'The Zulu Kaffirs, at the St George's Gallery, Knightsbridge.' *Illustrated London News*, 28 May 1853, 1, qtd. in Qureshi, Sadiah. 'Meeting the Zulus: Displayed Peoples and the Shows of London, 1859–79.' In *Popular Exhibitions, Science and Showmanship, 1840–1910*, edited by Joe Kember, John Plunkett, and Jill A. Sullivan, 183–98. London: Pickering and Chatto, 2012: 192.

40 Qureshi, 'Meeting the Zulus', 185–6. Robert Gordon Latham, MD, and Edward Forbes, FRS, curators of the ethnography exhibition at Sydenham, note that Kaffir 'means, in its more limited sense, the Kaffres of Caffraria, chiefly of the Amakosa tribe, the men who have given so much trouble to the colonists. But it also has a wider or more general signification, and in this case it serves as the designation of a large family of allied populations.' Latham, Robert Gordon, and Edward Forbes. *The Natural History Department of the Crystal Palace Described: Zoology and Botany*. London: Bradbury and Evans, 1854: 55.

41 Latham and Forbes, *Natural History Department*, 57; and Engelke, Matthew. *Think Like an Anthropologist*. Milton Keynes: Penguin, 2017: 72.

42 'The Earth Men.' *Era*, 15 May 1853, 11; and 'The Drama.' *Reynolds's Newspaper*, 15 May 1853, 15.

43 'Arrival of More Wonders – the Aztecs.' *Era*, 26 June 1853, 11.

44 Bartolo and Maximo, from San Salvador, were exhibited for sixty years. See Rothfels, Nigel. 'Aztecs, Aborigines and Ape-People: Science and Freaks in Germany, 1850–1910.' In *Freakery: Cultural Spectacles of the Extraordinary Body*, edited by Rosemarie Garland Thomson, 158–73. New York: New York University Press, 1996.

45 'Cremorne Gardens.' *Observer*, 4 September 1853, 6.

46 Malchow, *Gentlemen Capitalists*, 139, 171.

47 Malchow, *Gentlemen Capitalists*, 217.

48 See Norton, Marcy. 'Tasting Empire: Chocolate and the European Internalization of Mesoamerican Aesthetics.' *American Historical Review* III, no. 3 (2006): 661.

49 Malchow, *Gentlemen Capitalists*, 169.

50 Gould, *Nineteenth-Century Theatre*, 15, 17.

51  Norton, 'Tasting Empire', 661.

52  Meeuwis, *Everyone's Theater*, 18.

53  Kaiser, Matthew. *The World in Play: Portraits of a Victorian Concept*. Stanford, CA: Stanford University Press, 2012: 1–39.

54  Huhtamo, *Illusions in Motion*, 316.

55  See F.W. Chesson, letter to the editor, *British Banner*, 9 July 1851, 11–12; and *Morning Advertiser*, 12 September 1851, 2.

56  'Standing Armies.' *Morning Advertiser*, 9 July 1851, 2.

57  'Anti-Militia Movements.' *Manchester Times*, 21 April 1852, 6. The Home Secretary, Spencer Walpole (1806–98), successfully promoted this bill as a bulwark against French invasion. By the end of the year, a Whig/Peelite coalition with Lord Aberdeen at the helm was formed when the Conservative government collapsed on the issue of tax reform. Quickly, the sense of threat shifted from France to Russia. In the summer, the Russians moved to capture Romanian principalities under Ottoman suzerainty, and Britain and France rushed troops to Varna to inhibit incursions south of the Danube. The coalition of British, French, and Ottoman forces squared up for war with Russia in the Crimean Peninsula from October 1853 to February 1856.

58  Frederick Chesson, letter to the editor, *Sun*, 31 May 1852, 7.

59  Frederick Chesson, letter to the editor, *British Banner*, rpt. in *Liberator*, 16 December 1853, 1.

60  Chesson's diaries do not indicate the date on which the engagement was formalised, but a letter from R. D. Webb to Edmund Quincy on 21 August 1854 indicates it was known that the couple was affianced: 'It is said that Chesson, a very good fellow I am sure, but I suppose very poor, is going to marry Thompson's second daughter – and this accounts to me for the active part Thompson has taken in the Manchester Conference which was got up solely by the energy of Chesson.' Rpt. in Taylor, *British and American Abolitionists*, 410.

61  Turley, *Culture of English Antislavery*, 104–5. The League published a few numbers of the *Anti-Slavery Watchman* (1853–54).

62  Frederick Chesson, letter to the editor, 'Mazzini, Kossuth and Mr Sandars.' *Daily News*, 5 July 1854, 5; Frederick Chesson's diary, 29 June and 11 July 1854, REAS 11/1, JRL; and 'Anti-Slavery Conference in Manchester.' *Manchester Times*, 2 August 1854, 9.

63  The Peace Party was originally Quaker but underwent a significant change of membership in 1849; the addition of Joseph Sturge, Samuel Bowly, Henry Vincent, Elihu Burritt, and George Thompson concerned earlier members such as Samuel Gurney. Tyrrell, Alexander. 'Making the Millennium: The Mid-Nineteenth Century Peace Movement.' *Historical Journal* 21, no. 1 (1978): 85.

64  Frederick Chesson's diary, 5 June 1854, REAS 11/1, JRL.

65  Ceadel, Martin. *Semi-Detached Idealists: The British Peace Movement and International Relations, 1854–1945*. Oxford: Oxford University Press, 2000: 34.

66  Hollinshead-Strick, *Fourth Estate*, 112.

67  Frederick Chesson's diary, 15 July 1854, REAS 11/2, JRL.

68  Frederick Chesson's diary, 10 November 1854, REAS 11/2, JRL.

69  Frederick Chesson's diary, 12 June 1854, REAS 11/1, JRL.

70  Cobden, Richard. *The Political Writings of Richard Cobden.* 2 vols. London: William Ridgway, 1867; Bennett, Bridget. 'Guerrilla Inscription: Transatlantic Abolition and the 1851 Census.' *Atlantic Studies* 17, no. 3 (2020): 375–98; and Frederick Chesson's diary, 24 and 28 June 1854, REAS 11/1, JRL.

71  Frederick Chesson's diary, 18 October 1854, REAS 11/2, JRL.

72  Frederick Chesson's diary, 18 July 1854, REAS 11/2, JRL.

73  'Total Abstinence – Oration by J. G. Gough.' *Manchester Times*, 22 July 1854, 6. See also Gough, John B. *Orations.* Rev. ed. London: Morgan and Scott, 1878.

74  Gough, John B. *Autobiography and Personal Recollections of John B. Gough, with Twenty-Six Years' Experience as a Public Speaker.* Springfield, MA: Bill, Nichols, 1869: 299–301.

75  Frederick Chesson's diary, 25 October 1854, REAS 11/2, JRL.

76  Frederick Chesson's diary, [August 1854], REAS 11/2, JRL.

77  Frederick Chesson's diary, 16 October 1854, REAS 11/2, JRL.

78  The *Empire* was formerly *London Weekly Paper, and Organ of the Middle Classes* (nos. 1–26, 15 May to 6 November 1852) and then *Tallis's London Weekly Paper* (nos. 27–77, 13 November 1852 to 29 October 1853).

79  Frederick Chesson's diary, 4 September 1854, REAS 11/2, JRL.

80  Frederick Chesson's diary, 5 and 6 September and 29 October 1854, REAS 11/2, JRL.

81  Frederick Chesson's diary, 9 September 1854, REAS 11/2, JRL.

82  Frederick Chesson's diary, 18 September 1854, REAS 11/2, JRL; see also Morgan, 'George Donisthorpe Thompson'; and George Thompson to Amelia Thompson, 27 December 1853, REAS 2/2/40, JRL. George Edmund Donisthorpe is the father of Wordsworth Donisthorpe (1847–1914), a prominent laissez-faire Liberal who opposed the Contagious Diseases Acts and other extensions of state power and who authored *Individualism: A System of Politics.* Edinburgh: Macmillan, 1889. He also participated in the repeal movement as a member of the Personal Rights Association. With his cousin William Carr Crofts (1846–94) he invented an early cinematograph-style projector in 1890. See Taylor, M.W. 'Wordsworth Donisthorpe (1847–1914).' In *Oxford Dictionary of National Biography.* Oxford: Oxford University Press, 2012.

83  Capefigue, Jean Baptiste Honoré Raymond. *The Diplomatists of Europe.* Edited by William Monteith. London: G. W. Nickisson, 1845.

84  James Martineau, 'Foreign Policy for 1856', rpt. in *Essays, Reviews, and Addresses.* London: Longmans, Green, 1890: 464.

85  'Dear Bread and the War.' *Leeds Intelligencer and Yorkshire General Advertiser*, 25 November 1854, 4.

86  'The Peace Society and the War.' *Wrexham Weekly Advertiser*, 9 December 1854, 2.

87 'Trade in 1854.' *Daily News*, 30 December 1854, 5.

88 'Dear Bread and the War.' *Leeds Intelligencer and Yorkshire General Advertiser*, 25 November 1854, 4.

89 Frederick Chesson's diary, 25 October 1854, REAS 11/2, JRL.

90 Chesson drafted the texts for all the placards. Frederick Chesson's diary, 5, 10, 18, and 20 November 1854, REAS 11/2, JRL.

91 'Dear Bread and War.' *Lloyd's Weekly Newspaper*, 3 December 1854, 6.

92 Harriet Martineau, letter to the editor, rpt. in 'The Placard, "Dear Bread and War."' *Daily News*, 27 November 1854, 5. See also 'Dear Bread and War.' *Aris's Birmingham Gazette*, 27 November 1854, 1.

93 Frederick Chesson's diary, 24 November 1854, REAS 11/2, JRL.

94 Joseph Sturge, letter to the editor, 'The Peace Society and the War.' *Wrexham Weekly Advertiser*, 9 December 1854, 2.

95 *Civil Service Gazette*, rpt. in 'Local and Other News.' *Leeds Intelligencer and Yorkshire General Advertiser*, 16 December 1854, 5.

96 'The Year 1854.' *Yorkshire Gazette*, 30 December 1854, 6.

97 A Member of the Peace Society (Sheffield), letter to the editor, 'The Peace Placards and the War.' *Sheffield Independent*, 9 December 1854, 9.

98 Frederick Chesson's diary, 21 October 1854, REAS 11/2, JRL.

99 'Mr. Cobden and His Constituents. Great Leeds Meeting: The War.' *Leeds Mercury*, 20 January 1855, supp. 1.

100 'Mr. Cobden and His Constituents', supp. 1.

101 'Mr. Cobden at Leeds.' *Bradford Observer*, 18 January 1855, 5.

102 'Mr. Cobden and His Constituents', supp. 1, supp. 3.

103 Frederick Chesson's diary, 6 October 1854, REAS 11/2, JRL.

104 Frederick Chesson's diary, 21 November 1854, REAS 11/2, JRL.

105 Frederick Chesson's diary, 24 November 1854, REAS 11/2, JRL.

106 *Empire*, 2 December 1854, 2.

107 Frederick Chesson's diary, 30 November 1854, REAS 11/2, JRL.

108 Parker Pillsbury to Samuel May, 9 March 1855, MS B.1.6, v.5, p. 66, Boston Public Library.

109 Frederick Chesson's diary, September 1855, REAS 11/2, JRL.

110 Initially, this secretaryship paid £13 per quarter, rising to £300 per annum in 1869. Frederick Chesson's diary, 15 August 1857, REAS 11/5, JRL; and 15 October 1869, REAS 11/16, JRL.

111 George Thompson (Boulogne) to Amelia Chesson (London), 25 December 1855, REAS 2/2/43, JRL.

112 Frederick Chesson's diary, 8 March 1856, REAS 11/3, JRL.

113 Frederick Chesson's diary, 1 March 1856, REAS 11/3, JRL.

114 Hewitt, *Dawn of the Cheap Press*, 130–1.

115 Frederick Chesson to William Lloyd Garrison, 12 September 1856, MS A.1.2, v.26, p. 69, Boston Public Library.

116 Hewitt, *Dawn of the Cheap Press*, 133, 136.

117 Hewitt, *Dawn of the Cheap Press*, 69, 111, 248.

118 With the loss of key donors – Joseph Price (1784–1854), Samuel Gurney (1786–1856), Joseph Eaton (1793–1858), and Joseph Sturge (1793–1859) – the Peace Party became insignificant after 1857. Tyrrell, 'Making the Millennium', 95.

119 Hewitt, *Dawn of the Cheap Press*, 68; and Tyrrell, 'Making the Millennium', 95.

120 Hewitt, *Dawn of the Cheap Press*, 130, 134–5, 137.

121 Granovetter, Mark S. 'The Strength of Weak Ties.' *American Journal of Sociology* 78, no. 6 (1973): 1361.

122 'Newspaper Press Fund.' *Observer*, 20 June 1880, 5.

123 Cooper, Charles Alfred. *An Editor's Retrospect: Fifty Years of Newspaper Work.* London: Macmillan, 1896: 100.

124 Hewitt, *Dawn of the Cheap Press*, 144; and Cooper, *An Editor's Retrospect*, 98, 145–6.

125 Richard Webb (Dublin) to Samuel May, 22 July 1859, MS B.1.6, v. 7, p. 57, Boston Public Library, rpt. in Taylor, *British and American Abolitionists*, 440–1.

126 Chesson, 'Story of a Fugitive Slave'. Chesson spent two days writing the introduction and a week editing the narrative. Frederick Chesson's diary, 8 September and 25 October 1856, REAS 11/4, JRL.

127 Frederick Chesson's diary, 6 January 1855, REAS 11/2, JRL.

128 Mill, John Stuart. *Utilitarianism.* London: Longman, Green, Longman, Roberts, and Green, 1864: 391–406, 525–34, 659–73.

129 [F.W. Chesson], 'The Uncivilised Subjects of Queen Victoria.' *Empire*, 13 October 1855, 9.

130 As Thompson's absence dragged on, the Chessons probably took responsibility for Anne Thompson's household expenses. Frederick Chesson's diary, 31 October 1857, REAS 11/5, JRL.

131 *Star*, 11 August 1856, 2.

132 Frederick Chesson's diary, 9 August 1856, REAS 11/4, JRL.

133 Frederick Chesson's diary, 18 April 1857, REAS 11/4, JRL.

134 Frederick Chesson's diary, 15 December 1869, REAS 11/16, JRL.

135 'Public Amusements: "Formosa" at Drury Lane Theatre.' *Reynolds's Newspaper*, 29 August 1869, 4. See also 'Formosa at Drury Lane.' *Suffolk and Essex Free Press*, 26 August 1869, 7; 'Drury-Lane and "Formosa."' *Era*, 29 August 1869, 10.

136 *Morning Star*, 11 August 1856, 2.

137 Bauman, Richard. 'Performance.' In *A Companion to Folklore*, edited by Regina F. Bendix and Galit Hasan-Rokem, 94–119. Oxford: Blackwell, 2012: 101.

138 *Morning Star*, 11 August 1856, 2.

139 Jasper, *Art of Moral Protest*, 237.

140 Harrison, Brian. *Peaceable Kingdom: Stability and Change in Modern Britain.* Oxford: Oxford University Press, 1982: 441, 438.

141 For variants, see, for example, Honig, Bonnie. 'Three Models of Emergency Politics.' *boundary* 2, 41, no. 2 (2014): 45–70.

142 Kusch, M. 'Psychologism.' In *International Encyclopedia of the Social & Behavioral Sciences*, edited by Neil J. Smelser and Paul B. Baltes, vol. 18, 12,388–90. Amsterdam: Elsevier, 2001. A usage in physics preceded this but has no bearing. See Robert Hunt's lecture described in 'Exeter Literary Society.' *Exeter and Plymouth Gazette*, 11 September 1852, 5.

143 Eucken, Rudolf. *Life's Basis and Life's Ideal: The Fundamentals of a New Philosophy of Life*. 1907. Translated by Alban G. Widgery. London: Adam and Charles Black, 1912: 255–61.

144 Activism was the *agon* of the psyche directed towards a god-force. Discontented with how Pragmatism shapes the world in accordance with the human condition, Eucken advocated that human beings utilise their spirituality – though not religiosity – to evaluate life. Alden, Henry Mills. 'Eucken Agonistes.' *North American Review* 201, no. 710 (1915): 57–63.

145 Such a meaning was not obvious from the start. The first people to be called activists were pro-German propagandists who advocated that Sweden forgo neutrality and 'actively' support Germany during World War I. This denotation endured through World War II (indicating German or foreign parties that cooperated with the National Socialist government) but quickly fell out of use, forgotten and irrelevant to modern parlance. See *Scotsman*, 1 December 1915, 6; Long, Robert Crozier. 'Anglo-Swedish Oppositions: A Letter from Stockholm.' *Fortnightly Review* 99, no. 590 (2016): 235–48; and 'To Put It Briefly.' *Western Daily Press*, 21 May 1949, 1. By 1950, the first contemporary connotations are evident, as in a notice of the death of Vassil Kolarov, the Bulgarian prime minister, 'one of the oldest leaders of the Bulgarian Communists, and an "illustrious activist of the International Workers' Movement"'. 'Bulgarian Premier Dies.' *Gloucestershire Echo*, 23 January 1950, 1.

146 Despite Eucken's fame and lecture tours far afield from the University of Jena, by 1914 he was judged relevant only to a few translators and 'those earnest persons who in a happier age would have combined a smattering of Matthew Arnold with a love of Samuel Smiles and a distant respect for some attenuated follower of Kant'. 'Shorter Notices: Present-Day Ethics in their Relations to the Spiritual Life; Knowledge and Life; Rudolf Eucken: His Philosophy and Influence.' *New Statesman* 2, no. 46 (1914): 636.

147 Frenz, Horst, ed. *Nobel Lectures, Literature, 1901–1967*. Amsterdam: Elsevier, 1969: 78, 81; see also Eucken, Rudolf. *Knowledge and Life*. London: Williams and Norgate, 1913; Gebauer, Gunter and Christopher Wulf. *Mimesis: Culture, Art Society*. Berkeley: University of California Press, 1996; and Taylor, Charles. *Philosophy and the Human Sciences*. Cambridge: Cambridge University Press, 1985: 207.

148 In his 1907 book *Grundlinien einer neuen Lebensanschauung* (*Life's Basis and Life's Ideal*), Eucken specifies that action unifies spirit and personality, which in turn are the root of an internally generated philosophical knowledge: 'Reality is unintelligible apart from experience.' Boyce, William Ralph. *Rudolf Eucken's Philosophy of Life*. 2nd ed. London: A. & C. Black, 1907, 275.

149 Cecil Chisholm, 'The New Ideal: Eucken's Attitude – Activism.' *Manchester Courier*, 13 February 1913, 6.

150 'A German Professor.' *Aberdeen Journal*, 17 September 1926, 6.

151 Feldman, Burton. *The Nobel Prize: A History of Genius, Controversy, and Prestige*. New York: Arcade, 2000: 56 (qtd.), 87.

152 'Analyses Bibliographiques.' *L'Année Psychologique* 22 (1920): 255–6.

153 Eno, Henry Lane. *Activism*. Princeton, NJ: Princeton University Press, 1920: 176.

154 Butler, *Bodies That Matter*, 232, 239.

155 Butler, Judith and Athena Athanasiou. *Dispossession: The Performance in the Political*. Cambridge: Polity, 2013: 101.

156 Jasper, *Art of Moral Protest*, 356.

157 Butler, Judith. *Notes toward a Performative Theory of Assembly*. Cambridge, MA: Harvard University Press, 2015: 205.

158 Jasper, *Art of Moral Protest*, xi, 39.

159 Frederick Chesson's diary, 2 August 1856, REAS 11/4, JRL. A decade later, his diary notes that he dismissed spiritualist manifestations as Satanic (31 March 1866, REAS 11/13, JRL).

160 Turley, *Culture of English Antislavery*, 56, 77.

161 Jephson, Henry. *The Platform: Its Rise and Progress*. 2 vols. New York: Macmillan, 1892: 560–1.

162 'Canada.' *Morning Star*, 3 February 1857, 2–3.

163 Santos, *End of the Cognitive Empire*, 172, 175.

164 Alexander K. Isbister, 'Suggestions for the Future Government of the Red River Territory'. In *Alexander Kennedy Isbister: A Respectable Critic of the Honourable Company*, by Barry Cooper. Ottawa: Carleton University Press, 1988: 299.

165 Statistics Canada, accessed March 15, 2022, www.statca.gc.ca.

166 Galbraith, John S. *The Hudson's Bay Company as an Imperial Factor, 1821–1869*. Berkeley: University of California Press, 1957: 359.

167 Frenz, *Nobel Lectures*, 81; [F.W. Chesson], 'Hudson's Bay Company.' *Morning Star*, 3 February 1857, 2–3.

168 Cooper, *Alexander Kennedy Isbister*, 233.

169 Isbister, testimony from 23 June 1857, in *Minutes of Evidence*, 353.

170 Cooper, *Alexander Kennedy Isbister*, 30; and see 306–9 for a bibliography of Isbister's writing.

171 Cooper, *Alexander Kennedy Isbister*, 129–30.

172 For a summary, see Cooper, *Alexander Kennedy Isbister*, 176–200.

173 Cooper, *Alexander Kennedy Isbister*, 139, 163 (qtd.).

174 Cooper, *Alexander Kennedy Isbister*, 205.

175 Cooper, *Alexander Kennedy Isbister*, 203, 211.

176 George Brown, editor of the *Globe*, signed the articles that Isbister and Chesson wrote as 'from our Special Correspondent' as if his own. Isbister complained of this to Frederick Chesson, April 1857, C/138/226, Bodleian Library; and Frederick Chesson's diary, 11 and 16 January 1870, REAS 11/16, JRL.

177 Cooper, *Alexander Kennedy Isbister*, 246, 270.

178 Galbraith, *Hudson's Bay Company*, 322–3.

179 Frederick Chesson, letter to the editor, *Morning Post*, 10 October 1856, 7.

180 Galbraith, *Hudson's Bay Company*, 334, 338–9.

181 Cooper, *Alexander Kennedy Isbister*, 259.

182 Ahmed, Sara. *Queer Phenomenology: Orientations, Objects, Others*. Durham, NC: Duke University Press, 2006: 119, 120–1, 140.

183 Bhabha, *Location of Culture*, 10–11.

184 Cooper, *Alexander Kennedy Isbister*, 240–1.

185 A.K. Isbister to Frederick Chesson, 12 May 1857, C/138/229, and 11 June 1857, C/138/231–231b, Bodleian Library.

186 *Information Respecting the Aborigines, in the British Colonies. Circulated by Direction of the Meeting for Sufferings. Being Principally Extracts from the Report Presented to the House of Commons, by the Select Committee Appointed on that Subject*. London: Darton and Harvey, 1838: iv.

187 Great Britain, House of Commons, *Report of the Parliamentary Select Committee on Aboriginal Tribes, (British Settlements): Reprinted with Comments by the Aborigines' Protection Society*. London: William Ball, 1837: 5, 7–8.

188 [F.W. Chesson], 'The Hudson's Bay Territories.' *Morning Star*, 3 November 1856, 2–3.

189 'Canada.' *Morning Post*, 3 February 1857, 2–3.

190 [F.W. Chesson], 'The Hudson's Bay Territories.' *Morning Star*, 3 November 1856, 2–3.

191 [F.W. Chesson], 'Hudson's Bay Company.' *Morning Star*, 3 February 1857, 2–3.

192 Isbister, testimony from 5 March 1857, *Minutes of Evidence Taken before the Select Committee on the Hudson's Bay Company*. London: House of Commons, 1857: 124.

193 Isbister, 129; A.K. Isbister to Frederick Chesson, 11 June 1857, C/138/231–231b, Bodleian Library.

194 Cooper, *Alexander Kennedy Isbister*, 264–5, 268, 275, 281.

195 'Important Emigration Meeting at Exeter Hall.' *Pall Mall Gazette*, 5 January 1870, 11.

196 Frederick Chesson, letter to the editor, 'The Red River Insurrection.' *Examiner and London Review*, 22 January 1870, 51–2.

197 A.K. Isbister to Frederick Chesson, 13 January 1870, C/138/233, Bodleian Library.

198 Bruce, John, and Louis Riel. 'Declaration of the People of Rupert's Land and the North-West.' *Manitoba Pageant* 9, no. 3 (April 1964). Manitoba Historical Society. Updated 1 July 2009. www.mhs.mb.ca/docs/pageant/09/rupertslanddeclaration.shtml.

199 A.K. Isbister to Frederick Chesson, 13 January 1870, C/138/233, Bodleian Library.

200 Frederick Chesson, 'The Red River Insurrection.' *Times*, 12 January 1870, 10.

201 Chesson, 'The Red River Insurrection', 10.

202 Tway, Duane C. 'The Wintering Partners and the Hudson's Bay Company, 1867–1879.' *Canadian Historical Review* 41, no. 3 (1960): 215–23; A.K. Isbister to Frederick Chesson, 5 July 1871, C/138/234, and 15 July 1871, C/138/236, Bodleian Library. This was a Pyrrhic victory for most HBC employees. Barry Cooper stresses than unless they were white and European educated, it was impossible for them to advance beyond the rank of postmaster. *Alexander Kennedy Isbister*, 30.

203 Frenz, *Nobel Lectures*, 81.

204 Sergeant, 'F.W. Chesson', 677, 679. Sergeant, a fellow journalist, had collaborated with Chesson on the Greek Committee.

205 Sergeant, 'F.W. Chesson', 679.

206 These towns included Aldershot, Canterbury, Chatham, Colchester, Deal, Devonport, Dover, Gravesend, Greenwich, Maidstone, Portsmouth, Sheerness, Shorncliffe, Winchester, Windsor, and Woolwich in England, as well as Cork/Queenstown and Curragh in Ireland. *Hansard*, HC, 20 July 1870, c. 596–601.

207 Rogers, 'Helen. 'Women and Liberty.' In *Liberty and Authority in Victorian Britain*, edited by Peter Mandler, 125–54. Oxford: Oxford University Press, 2006: 125–6.

208 George Thompson to Elizabeth Pease, 28 February 1870, REAS 2/4/29, JRL.

209 George Thompson to Elizabeth Pease, 11 April 1870, REAS 2/4/33, JRL.

210 Butler, Josephine. *Personal Reminiscences of a Great Crusade*. London: Horace Marshall and Son, 1896: 79. Mill's objections also emphasised the sexual double standard. See Jose, Jim, and Kcasey McLoughlin. 'John Stuart Mill and the Contagious Diseases Acts: Whose Law? Whose Liberty? Whose Greater Good?' *Law and History Review* 34, no. 2 (2016): 249–79.

211 The Contagious Diseases Act was passed in 1864 (27 & 28 Vict. c. 85) and extended in 1866 (29 & 30 Vict. c. 35) and 1869 (32 & 33 Vict. c. 96).

212 Jasper, *Art of Moral Protest*, 329.

213 Rogers, Helen. *Women and the People: Authority, Authorship and the Radical Tradition in Nineteenth-Century England*. Burlington: Ashgate, 2000: 202–3, 207, 214; 'Colchester Election.' *Shield*, 22 October 1870, 266–7; and 'Election Address.' *Shield*, 5 November 1870, 284–5.

214 Jasper, *Art of Moral Protest*, 331.

215 Chesson, Frederick. *Paper on How to Influence Members of the House of Commons, Read by Mr. F.W. Chesson at a Conference of Delegates from Associations and Committees Formed in Various Towns for Promoting the Repeal of the Contagious Diseases Acts, Held at the Freemasons' Tavern, 5th and 6th May, 1870*. London: National Association for Repeal of the Contagious Diseases Act, 1870: 3. The only surviving copy of this paper is at the Bodleian (with a microfilm copy at the British Library).

216 Chesson, *Paper on How to Influence Members*, 4.

217 Chesson, *Paper on How to Influence Members*, 5.

218 Chesson, *Paper on How to Influence Members*, 7.

219 Chesson, *Paper on How to Influence Members*, 6.

220 Turley, *Culture of English Antislavery*, 63–4.

221 Chesson, *Paper on How to Influence Members*, 4–5.

222 Chesson, *Paper on How to Influence Members*, 5–6.

223 See 'An Englishwoman', letters to the editor, published as 'The Contagious Diseases Acts.' *Daily News*, 28 December 1869, 6; 29 December 1869, 3; and 30 December 1869, 2; and the announcement of 'The Ladies' National Association for the Repeal of the Contagious Diseases Acts.' *Daily News*, 31 December 1869, 5. The signatories are also notable for their knowledge and experience in the anti-slavery movement, including Mary Estlin, Elizabeth Pease Nichol (1807–97), Eliza Wigham, and Jane Wigham; literary endeavours, including Elizabeth Drummond (1840–92); and radical reform, including Elizabeth Wolstenholme (1833–1918) and Ursula Bright (1835–1915).

224 *Representation of the People Act 1884, 48 & 49 Vict. c. 3* (6 December 1884).

225 See Keating, James. '"The Defection of Women": The New Zealand Contagious Diseases Act Repeal Campaign and Transnational Feminist Dialogue in the Late Nineteenth Century.' *Women's History Review* 25, no. 2 (2016): 187–206; Paul, Aparna. 'Containment of "Evil" and "Vice": The Contagious Diseases Act XIV of 1868 in Bombay Presidency.' *Indica* 48, no. 2 (2011): 127–39; and Van Heyningen, Elizabeth B. 'The Social Evil in the Cape Colony, 1868–1902: Prostitution and the Contagious Diseases Act.' *Journal of Southern African Studies* 10, no. 2 (1984): 170–97.

226 Album Book of Thomas Thompson, unbound memorandum of receipt, 7 November 1824, REAS 14, JRL. Joseph Thompson (1801–89) had gone bankrupt in 1848. His cousin Edmund Donisthorpe advanced the family £129 for the journey. They disembarked at Melbourne late in 1852, while the gold rush at Bendigo raged.

227 Hawkins, Angus. *The Forgotten Prime Minister: The 14th Earl of Derby. Vol. 2, Achievement, 1851–1869.* Oxford: Oxford University Press, 2007: 248–9.

228 Frederick Chesson's diary, 23 June 1860, REAS 11/8, JRL.

229 Frederick Chesson's diary, 29 January 1863, REAS 11/10, JRL.

230 Hansen, Miriam Bratu. 'America, Paris, the Alps: Kracauer (and Benjamin) on Cinema and Modernity.' In *Cinema and the Invention of Modern Life*, edited by Leo Charney and Vanessa R. Schwartz, 362–403. Berkeley: University of California Press, 1995: 379.

231 Jasper, *Art of Moral Protest*, 315.

232 'France.' *Daily News*, 3 June 1863, 5; and Frederick Chesson's diary, 9 March 1863, REAS 11/10, JRL.

233 Frederick Chesson's diary, 31 May 1863, REAS 11/10, JRL.

234 Frederick Chesson's diary, 30 May 1863, REAS 11/10, JRL.

235 Albert Smith, 'Physiology of the London Idler.' *Punch* 3, no. 1 (1842): 4–5.

236 'The Late Mr. F.W. Chesson.' *Daily News*, 7 May 1888, 5.

# CHAPTER 4

# *Combative Pens*

Not the men whom chance, or effort, or birth, or wealth raises to eminence, not the mere traffickers in politics, not even the politicians who carry great measures apart from origination, nor even the originators of party moves who simply float with the current or tack to catch the popular breeze, are most worthy of respect and imitation, but the men who see the need, and face prejudice, and organise victory, and convert minorities into majorities. He who does this not for reward, but in obedience to the higher law of his nature, though he seem to plough that others may reap, and though he earn obscurity whilst others acquire fame and distinction, is a genuine hero. And such was Chesson.

—Lewis Sergeant, 'F.W. Chesson'[1]

In the epigram to the previous chapter, Matthew Arnold calls for more virtuous middle-class men to take up ideas advanced by 'men of genius' and transform liberalism into the hallmark of nineteenth-century thought. The epigram for this chapter, taken from Lewis Sergeant's obituary of Frederick Chesson, portrays Chesson as an instigator who could 'see the need' and 'face prejudice' to propound progressive causes despite objections, and without reward, watching others rise to distinction while he remained in obscurity.[2] In his study of protest culture, James M. Jasper observes that shifts in moral understanding occur in tandem with shifts in tactics and organisational forms, and protestors 'help citizens think through their moral and cognitive positions'. Movements require individuals to propel them forward, yet 'research that focuses on the organizations of protest, as important as these are, loses sight of careers of protest'.[3] This chapter aims to put Chesson's career of activism into focus.

Chesson wanted a career neither as a politician nor as a civil servant; instead, he was a statesman without, who gathered evidence and articulated positions that he believed needed to be put to those in power. He was not initially what Victorians call well-connected, for neither his birthright nor his education put him into the orbit of men and women destined for distinction, but he came to know people of all ranks who relied on him and valued his judgement. Even while he was engaged with the rigours of producing a newspaper with morning and evening editions, his diaries show a steady stream of nobility, legislators, organisers, and administrators who sought his advice on the questions of the day, including colonial policy and foreign affairs, electoral reform, and the elimination of religious discrimination. In Sergeant's estimation, he was 'a genuine hero', despite obscurity, for the victories he helped organise not only shifted the zeitgeist to liberalism but enacted its principles in a myriad of ways. He got things done – through persuasive rhetoric he changed 'minorities into majorities' – yet his specific efforts can be difficult to connect to outcomes. His millions of words of journalism are largely unsigned (firm ascriptions are usually only possible through his diary notations, though his style was distinct), almost all the APS letters he penned and sent round the globe are lost (incoming letters predominate), and his contributions to meetings large and small are lightly marked. His heroism rests in quotidian activism, and even though he shows up in a multitude of ways, firm ascription of his actions is often achieved by roundabout means.

This makes it all the more remarkable that there are so many traces of his performative acts.

Though he was renowned for being approachable and respected by politicians of all persuasions, Chesson was a partisan for liberal causes, both in how he devoted his time and in how he directed his journalism. If what he wrote was a first draft for history, it was a history that favoured free trade as the route to inter-nation amity, but this was affected by fierce convictions about the responsibilities of witnessing. As Chesson wrote at the closing of the Paris Exhibition of 1867, reflecting also on the Great Exhibition of 1851,

> It was impossible that any man, however accustomed he might be to look down with an air of superiority upon the people of some other country, to retain that stupid feeling, at least in its more aggravated form, after he had seen that their intellectual and industrial progress was, in some respects, equal, and in others, perhaps, superior to his own…. We English are rapidly learning this lesson.[4]

Like these great trade fairs that helped undo prejudice, Chesson was a junction point for information that he strategically redirected into correspondence, journalism, depositions, and public meetings, all constituting civic actions of conscience. During his lifetime, the possibilities for transmitting information were revolutionised, both in kind and in speed. Diplomatic courier routes gave way to inexpensive postal systems that networked individuals, families, and businesses throughout the British Empire; cheaply printed newspapers came to carry news and opinion inflected with the gamut of political orientations to breakfast tables and parlours of all but the poorest citizens; and whereas railways constructed since 1830 carried people, letters, and newspapers from place to place, and steamships accelerated sea travel from the 1840s (by the mid-1860s, a trip from London to Dublin could be accomplished in just twelve hours), during the period of the 1850s to the 1870s the emphasis among investors and inventors was to interconnect nations and link together islands and continents on routes where railways could not go and ships were too slow.

While the telegraph abstracted and sped up information transfer, for example allowing journalists to despatch parliamentary news, diplomatic updates, and even whole speeches expeditiously to provincial cities and foreign capitals, more traditional means persisted. Chesson also continued to rely on meetings, reports, letters, tracts and pamphlets, and newspapers for information that sustained his journalism and work for the APS and other causes. As he stood against slave states, systematic annihilation of entire peoples, unjust use of force and authority, destruction and restoration of reputations, and the persistent trafficking in human beings, his countless quotidian acts mark the power of individuals coming to consciousness that adds up to activist movements. Chesson's work shows not just how the playbook of activist organising was consolidated in the mid-Victorian period – everything subsequent being variations on these forms – but how circulation of information was always key.

### Cable Knit

The first great challenge to interconnection was laying the transatlantic telegraph. The gargantuan effort to raise capital, perfect technology, and coordinate installation across the seabed was a twelve-year incremental performance of intercontinental coordination. In the wake of this technical achievement, a kind of non-epic everydayness ensued in the transmission of dots and dashes coding the information that coordinated markets, made cooperative politics a lived reality as well as a symbolic goal, and enabled insight into distant actions in unprecedented ways. A relayed message, tapped out on a land station, belied the act of its travel along copper wire at phenomenal speeds. In 1865, it took twelve days for news of President Lincoln's assassination to reach London.[5] By the autumn of 1866, news of such magnitude would have been transmitted in minutes and printed in the next edition of every British newspaper. The transatlantic cable had profound implications for how the public sphere – the realm of information and commerce – operated evermore.

The most efficient connection between Washington, DC, and London is via two islands on opposite sides of the Atlantic. In 1854, Cyrus Field (1819–92) persuaded private investors to back the New York, Newfoundland and London Telegraph Company to lay 3,300 kilometres (2,050 miles) of cable across the seabed from Valentia Bay in Ireland to Heart's Content in Newfoundland, linking Europe and North America's extant telegraphic systems. The telegraph station in Valentia would relay received messages across Ireland, under St George's Channel, thence to London, while the rustic outpost on the shore of Newfoundland would relay messages under the Cabot Strait, thence to Nova Scotia and overland systems. This was an audacious venture. How could enough wire be strung together in a single line (put out by ships in the turbulent North Atlantic), dropped to the great plateau nearly 5 kilometres (3 miles) below sea level, and join the continents for the first time since Pangea drifted apart, 175 million years before? By the time the project fully succeeded, in 1866, the North American end of the cable was already connected to a 42,000-kilometre (26,100-mile) network transmitting 2 million messages per year.[6] Whereas the earliest transatlantic cables could transmit just forty-seven to fifty-five characters per minute, once cables were duplexed messages could be sent simultaneously in each direction and transmission rates increased to 100 words per minute.[7] Britain's relationships with the United States and Canada changed irrevocably, yet there were implications worldwide. With the exchange of information, markets were instantly transformed in what Göran Therborn calls the fourth historical wave of globalisation, 'sustained by new and faster means of transport and communication', in which the first worldwide commodity market was established (in grain) as financial markets exchanged vital information about yields, prices, exchange rates, and supplies over the course of minutes, giving 'a powerful jolt to economic activity'.[8] Being able to regulate grain markets meant that remedying waste or glut was a matter of mobilising transportation to a place of undersupply. Efficiencies of exchange on a global scale portended economic and humanitarian solutions to food insecurities: theoretically, famine could be a thing of the past. Europe could be fed not only by Ukrainian but also by North American breadbaskets – a highly desirable alternative following the Crimean crisis – and the acreage under cultivation in Canada and the United States increased accordingly.

At age twenty-two, the electrical engineer Charles Bright (1832–88) empirically demonstrated that a 3,200-kilometre (1,990-mile) overland telegraph circuit was feasible. Field signed him on as chief engineer. With the dramatis personae in place, the mise-en-scène of cable-laying commenced. In the summer of 1857, one end of the line was lowered to the ocean floor, but 600 kilometres (370 miles) out from port the cable snapped. This cost £100,000 and the delay of a year.[9] They tried again the following summer: two vessels spliced ends of the cable mid-Atlantic then respectively turned toward Newfoundland and Ireland.

When Queen Victoria successfully sent a message to President Buchanan (1791–1868), the *Times* proclaimed that this concluded the 'anxious and difficult task of linking the Old World with the New, thereby annihilating space', an achievement unequalled in impact since Columbus landed in the Americas.[10] On Boston Common, 100 guns were fired and church bells pealed for an hour. New York erupted in bells, fireworks, and artillery salutes; Trinity Church held services with a procession of 200 clergymen; a huge parade with the British ambassador, representatives of the Army and Navy, and 100 veterans of the War of 1812 (signifying the end of British–American enmity) snaked through the city; and the day ended with illuminations and a firemen's torchlight parade along Broadway.[11]

All networked portions of North America received news of Europe's monarchs, Chinese negotiations, and the arrival of Asiatic shipping as soon as newspapers could pick up the relays. With tranquillity being restored to India, the British government sent word to regiments in Montreal and Halifax not to deploy back to England, saving £50,000 to £60,000 in expenses. It was clear that this technology yielded immediate financial and political benefits. Unfortunately, however, barely a month after it was landed, the very day that New York celebrated, the cable fell quiet. Only 271 messages had been sent; the cable functioned in a halting fashion for seven more weeks then was silent forever.[12]

Although engineering improvements to increase the chances of another cable's success were immediately proposed, it took a long time to raise the capital needed for the next venture. In 1865, as the American Civil War waned, Cyrus Field succeeded in finding British investors: John Bright and other free traders were vigorous supporters of the 1866 attempt. The implications of the venture were not lost on Frederick Chesson. He toured the *SS Great Eastern* – the largest ship in the world by a factor of five – as the entire cable was loaded.[13] He mused that with the imminent laying of a cable between Florida and Cuba, Britain would come into telegraphic contact with its Caribbean islands.[14] Likewise, it would link Britain to its colony on Vancouver Island, and if Western Union's scheme to lay a line up the Pacific coast to Russian America (Alaska) and Siberia succeeded, the Americas would be connected to Asia.[15] The colonial map could become a media network.

Chesson was friendly with Cyrus Field, and breakfasted with him and Professor William Thomson (1824–1907, later Lord Kelvin) to discuss the project. The polymath and anti-slavery sympathiser the Eighth Duke of Argyll (George Douglas Campbell, 1823–1900) and the physicist George Gabriel Stokes (1819–1903, Lucasian Chair at Cambridge) joined them as they sailed down the Thames to where the great ship lay at anchor. Conversation turned to Jamaica – at the time, Chesson and John Stuart Mill were embroiled in prosecuting the Eyre Affair – and they also discussed US race relations with Field and his niece, who offered positive views on the prospects for recently emancipated African Americans.[16] Two weeks later, Chesson returned to the *Great Eastern* again and voyaged upon it to Bantry Bay, Ireland.[17] The *Daily News*' special correspondent noted the range of shipboard pastimes, including the drilling of sailors and an extravaganza.[18]

While cruising, officers and families of the Atlantic Telegraph Company, the Telegraph Construction Company, and the Great Eastern Ship Company, correspondents of the London newspapers, and other celebrity passengers gathered in the saloon, 'like the drawing room of some vast house', for what Chesson termed 'an electro-biological entertainment' concocted by the journalists N. A. Woods (London *Times*) and J. C. Parkinson (*Daily News*, 1832–1908).[19] *A Cable-istic Extravaganza* was inspired, in part, by a *Punch* cartoon printed the previous summer in which a dozen mermaids tug and swing on the submerged cable; a portly Father Neptune calls out to them: 'Aho-o-o-o-oy, there! Get *off* o' that cable, can't yer – that's the way t'other one was wrecked!!!' (Figure 4.1).[20] According to the *Illustrated London News*' account of the performance, the desires of financiers, contractors, engineers, and electricians are subjected to 'the consent and goodwill of Father Neptune, the tritons, and the mermaids, who had certainly a right to be consulted about them'. G. W. Elliott (1814–93, the civil engineer and owner of coal mines) portrayed Daniel Gooch (1816–89, a director of the Great Eastern Ship Company). Captain Francis John Bolton (1831–87, East Suffolk Regiment, an expert in visual signalling) impersonated Field, and Colonel Henry de Bathe (1823–1907, commanding officer of the Scots Guard) took the role of Neptune. The mission's resident artist, Robert Charles Dudley (1826–1909), performed as Richard Atwood Glass (1820–73, Elliott's partner in the firm that manufactured the cable). Other men played a sea monster and a chorus of tritons and mermaids (observing

A WORD TO THE MERMAIDS.

Neptune. "AHO-O-O-O-OY, THERE! GET OFF O' THAT 'ERE CABLE, CAN'T YER—THAT'S THE WAY T'OTHER ONE WAS WRECKED!!!"

Figure 4.1   John Tenniel, 'A word to the mermaids.' *Punch*, 5 August 1865, 49.
Getty Images.

the schoolboy tradition of female impersonation), all accompanied by a pianist and violinist led by a Dr Ward (Figure 4.2).

> Gooch [*to the mermaids*]: My dears, beware of sitting on or tampering with the cable.
> Field: But give the messages a shove, and help them, if you're able.
> Neptune: Ev'ry time the current flies, 'twill give you delectation.
> Glass: And ev'ry separate shock will cause a curious sensation.
> Chorus: For it's here and there, and everywhere, we find the symbols flying.
>> The more they puzzle us to read, the more we keep on trying.
>> With a dot and a dash, and dash and a dot, by Bolton's numeration,[21]
>> Trying to read it is useless indeed, but it makes a new sensation!
> (*Messages on slips of paper drop from the top of the stage, and are picked up by the mermaids.*)
> First triton: Here's Mr. Jones to Mrs. Jones, 'My dear, how is poor Bobby?'
> First mermaid: Here's Mrs. J. to Mr. J., 'The child is looking nobby.'
> Glass: Here's Uncle Sam to Mistress Vic., 'I think we now may laugh, eh?'
> Field: Here's Mistress Vic. To Uncle Sam, 'Success to telegraphy!'
> (*Chorus and dance. The curtain falls.*)

Figure 4.2  'Amateur dramatic entertainment on board the Great Eastern steam-ship at sea'. *Illustrated London News*, 28 July 1866, 80. Getty Images.

Thus, the entertainment concluded with images of the cable's utility for private users as well as leaders of nations, emphasising a capacious understanding of news.[22]

Passengers on this pleasure voyage were a veritable who's who of British politics, commerce, science, and the press. Chesson was accompanied by Sir Samuel Peto (1809–89), a prominent Baptist and public works contractor who had made a fortune building railway stations, and the Quaker banker Samuel Gurney (1816–82), one of the 'weighty Friends' who had backed Field's first attempt. Gurney was a partner in the leading discount firm in London, essentially a banker to other bankers, but was over-exposed by Peto's financial obligations on the London, Chatham, and Dover Railway, and six weeks earlier was brought down with debts of £4 million. He and Chesson had worked together on the London Anti-Slavery Society from 1858, reform in the Cape since 1861, New Zealand issues, and the Freedmen's Aid Society since 1864. In 1863 they were in the APS delegation to the French emperor. As they steamed ahead, the soundness of the cable was tested scientifically with artificial

Figure 4.3   Robert Charles Dudley, 'Awaiting the reply', oil painting, ca. 1866,
Metropolitan Museum of Art, Accession number 92.10.43.

faults inserted, then gentlemen enjoyed the novelty of sending messages through it.[23]

A few weeks after the pleasure voyage, on 27 July 1866, with 3,500 kilometres (2,175 miles) of cable trailing behind it, the *Great Eastern* sailed into Trinity Bay, Newfoundland. In the days that followed, the fleet salvaged a length of cable abandoned on the sea floor in a previous attempt, connected it, and thereby duplexed the transcontinental circuit.[24] Cyrus Field retired to his cabin on the *Great Eastern*, crying like a child. It had taken a dozen years and £2.5 million investment, untold scientific experiments, priceless maritime ingenuity, and elaborate choreography to achieve the feat. In the end, the whole two-way circuit worked on a low-voltage battery: a silver thimble, a strip of zinc, and a drop of sulphuric acid emitted messages across the cold, formidable depths of the North Atlantic (Figure 4.3).[25]

Within days, Charles Bright's triumphant speech to the Liverpool Chamber of Commerce concluded with Aeneas' words, uttered when he saw images of the siege of Troy in a Carthaginian temple: 'what region of earth is not full of our calamities?' (Or, in plain English, news travels fast.)[26] Indeed, when the Atlantic line was secured, the North American Pacific coast became networked across the Euro-Asian continent to Turkey,

Persia, India, and Rangoon (Yangon). By 1871, the oceanic-overland cable network reached Australia, and communication between London and Sydney could transpire in a matter of hours.[27] On its first day of operation, the Atlantic cable reaped £1,000 in transmission fees, with instantaneous impact on market integration: a real effect that cannot be disambiguated from its symbolic significance.[28] By 1875, fifteen cables traversed the North Atlantic, and by the end of the century it was 'a planetary network' worth £1.2 million per annum.[29] What Paul Julius Reuter (1816–99) initiated in 1851, sending the closing prices on the Brussels Bourse to Aachen by carrier pigeon, had been transferred seamlessly from avian to electric means. With telegraphy, Reuter expanded his operation to Alexandria in 1865, Bombay in 1866, Melbourne and Sydney in 1874, and Cape Town in 1876. Of course, the posting of despatches and newspapers continued to be facilitated by sea and rail, but this was inherently old news by the time it was received and then printed, even if it was detailed and analytical.[30]

The 1866 transatlantic cable figuratively united siblings of the same British parent, who had been estranged by revolution and war and then increasingly reconciled through decades of amicable commerce until relations were again strained during the American Civil War. Liberal doctrine associated brotherhood with commercial interconnectedness, and international trade with diplomatic amity. From unimpeded and plentiful trade came peace, stability, and prosperity as direct causal consequences: the liberal trifecta. Roland Wenzlhuemer, following insights by Doreen Massey and Manuel Castells, complicates ideas of global transformation of space in the second half of the nineteenth century, emphasising its social and cultural production and contingency based on many kinds of relations.[31] Instead of the distance travelled by steamships and railways determining the transmission of letters and goods across the Atlantic – a factor of space, in a journey lasting a fortnight, with considerable information lag of news events – speed was newly emphasised as a condition of shortened time. Likewise, the speed at which information travelled over space fuelled the appetite for print journalism: a 'culture of precision, of rigorously scheduled time' was not just a matter of getting factory workers to their posts. A worldwide machinery of human, technical, and financial interaction that Mark Turner calls 'media time' produced morning and evening editions, weeklies, monthlies, and quarterlies for every purpose and mood.[32] This enhanced the importance of London and New York as metropoles, giving Britain and the eastern United States a premium on leveraging capital to multiply power.

The telegraph became an overt instrument of colonial control and tool of empire, sovereignty 'subordinated to communication'.[33] The Foreign

Office had its own lines, and as Benjamin Disraeli mused, 'I can't get over the feeling of magic when I receive these electronic missives'.[34] On the Asian subcontinent, telegraph lines were installed under government control following the 1857–8 uprisings, but the more typical situation was Cecil Rhodes' (1853–1902) commercial promotion of the British South Africa Company's installation of telegraph lines, proverbially from the Cape to Cairo.[35] Business and politics went hand in hand with this. The more linked up ports could become, the more information about the global traffic of ships and cargoes could be relayed from harbour to harbour; the more ports could communicate with inland centres; the more that market exchanges spoke to distant market exchanges; and the more news, information, and intelligence newspapers could provide to their readers. Thus, 'the public' became increasingly a function of print, not speech.

The French Protestant missionary Eugène Casalis (1812–91) wrote to Chesson that telegraphs from places like the Cape of Good Hope 'are like an echo which says in three or four words (understand if you can!) things which can only be explained one month or six weeks later by correspondence', by which time the explanation is no longer true.[36] This was particularly troublesome for monthly and quarterly journals, which two generations before had been the epitome of considered thought. With hindsight, Marshall McLuhan looked back on the telegraph as 'socially and psychologically corroding', ushering in 'the Age of Anxiety and of Pervasive Dread'.[37] In his view, the telegraph did not merely afford an augmentation of newspapers, intensifying the volume of news from what had previously depended upon packet despatches carried by steamships, but it weakened the impact of leaders (editorials) and thus the ability of newspapers to effectively guide the public. 'It decentralized the newspaper world so thoroughly that uniform national views were quite impossible', and the telegraph enhanced 'a discontinuous mosaic' of national groups.[38] Frederick Chesson was fully versed in the ability of this 'discontinuous mosaic' to coordinate as a result of better information, for his journalism highlighted iconoclastic stances in order to disseminate reform-oriented dissent, differentiate liberal views from the ruling government's, and pursue great consequences from quotidian activism, shifting the nation's course.

## Quotidian Activism

Logging eyewitness accounts of conflict into the historical record is an ancient practice. Thucydides (fifth century BCE) recorded the Peloponnesian War as it unfolded, and Julius Caesar (first century BCE) described his own conquest of Gaul. What the APS facilitated (perhaps not uniquely, but certainly prominently) is the reporting of acts within war, on the verge of war, and entirely separate from state conflicts to a central point, which, from 1857 to 1888, was Frederick Chesson. Correspondence flowed into his hands from every inhabited continent and many islands in between. A self-identifying network of English-speaking informants – missionaries and clergy, medics, officials of various ranks and formalities, émigrés, and residents abroad, as well as philanthropists and MPs within Britain – drew upon their knowledge to inform Chesson of their concerns, present him with credible evidence, and ask that he mobilise inquisitive, remediating, or corrective action. They wrote about individual cases, collective harm, and systemic abuse. They utilised vivid yet matter-of-fact language to describe disturbing laxity in local practices, outright breaches of law, and appalling atrocities. Chesson corroborated this information in various ways, maintaining an incessant calendar of appointments and meetings. Being kept informed about developments near and far helped him assemble excerpts for the APS' *Colonial Intelligencer, or Aborigines' Friend* (Figure 4.4), yet he also contributed to an amazing array of causes outside the APS' brief, including the Freedmen's Aid Society, which raised funds to provide formerly enslaved African Americans with basic and advanced education.[39]

Chesson wrote for the daily press (until 1869 for the *Star*, then the *Daily News*), reflecting what he learned as an activist. The *Star* was noted for its outspoken editorials and what Justin McCarthy called 'combative pens', and Chesson was assuredly one of them.[40] The *Star* is best remembered for opposing British policy during the American Civil War. It spiritedly supported President Lincoln and the North during the US crisis, opposing the London *Times*' bellicosity and support of a British alliance with the South. Additionally, an alliance with the *Dial* brought Edmond Beales onto the *Star*'s board; he was president of the Reform League and so during the 1866–67 Reform crisis the *Star* was overtly allied with the populist working-class League.[41] In a third great (but doomed) liberal cause of the decade, the *Star* promoted the work of the Jamaica Committee, chaired by John Stuart Mill and stewarded by Chesson as its indefatigable secretary; it sought to bring Governor Edward John Eyre to justice for his part in the Morant Bay Rebellion of 1865.

While Cyrus Field exerted himself to refinance his last attempts at laying the Atlantic cable, Britain and the United States became increasingly estranged. Early in 1861, Southern states began to secede, and news of the United States on the brink of war came through despatches in the US mail. With his characteristic attention to depicting a mise-en-scène, Chesson

Nº. XLVI.]       [FEBRUARY, 1852.

## THE COLONIAL INTELLIGENCER;

OR,

## ABORIGINES' FRIEND.

VOL. III.

LONDON:

PRINTED AND PUBLISHED FOR THE ABORIGINES'
PROTECTION SOCIETY;

AND SOLD BY

J. OLLIVIER, 59 PALL MALL; C. GILPIN, 5 BISHOPSGATE WITHOUT;
AND MESSRS. WARD, PATERNOSTER ROW.

Figure 4.4    Motto of the Aborigines' Protection Society, 'Ab uno sanguine' [from one blood], cover of *The Colonial Intelligencer; or, Aborigines' Friend*, 1852. University of Wisconsin Library, (public domain).

described 'an infinity of bustle in the Army and Navy Departments' and the 'commander in chief ... closeted for hours with the Cabinet. Troops move hither and thither in hot haste'. Meanwhile, 'a fleet has been despatched to the South with sealed orders' regarding the fate of Fort Sumter and Fort Moultrie, in Charleston Harbor. From Pensacola's Fort Pickens, beleaguered and cut off by 5,000 Southern troops, no further 'budget of intelligence' emerged.[42] Eight days before this was published in London, Confederates had begun the bombardment of Fort Sumter. The war had commenced.

While the American Civil War raged, Chesson and Beales formed the Emancipation Committee to plan for the freedom of the US' enslaved. By the end of 1862, the society had over 100 members, including 'some of the best known names in the country'.[43] The Emancipation Proclamation, which came into effect on 1 January 1863, occasioned a series of mass meetings across Britain. This is one indication of the strength of support for the Union cause and transnational endurance of the anti-slavery movement.[44] On 29 January, the Emancipation Committee sponsored a meeting at Exeter Hall. Distinguished speakers contained their remarks to the issue of slavery, skirting or hedging on the Union per se, even though the long game was to rally sympathy for the formerly enslaved in order to swing it for the Union.[45] The *Illustrated London News* reporter, generally sceptical of the Emancipation Committee's chances given national concerns about an uprising of out-of-work cotton millers in Lancashire, encountered 'surging crowds' in all parts of Exeter Hall, and finally, upon securing entry to the great hall, noted 'the sublime spectacle of a vast sea of upturned faces, looking up towards another sea scarcely less large that, in defiance of all the laws of gravity, has ascended and overflowed every nook and corner of the upraised expanse of the orchestra, leaving only the organ in the centre towering calmly above the excited and sloping tide of life' (see Figure 3.9). The main hall was so overcrowded that an additional meeting was convened in the lower hall, and a third in the open air of Exeter Street, which was also swarmed with well-wishers. Shouts of approbation in the lower hall rumbled like thunder in the great hall. 'These interruptions, with those arising from the constant re-echoing of the cheers from the two other meetings below and outside, gave quite a tone to the evening.' The *Illustrated London News* declared 'if we do not misread the signs then and there presented, this meeting will prove the turning-point of new and serious political issues'.[46]

The Rev. Baptist Noel (1798–1873) proposed to send a telegram to Bradford, where a meeting of 4,000 persons occurred the same evening, stating 'We are for emancipation and the Union; what are you?' The response enhanced a sense of common voice, a kind of telegraphic choral speech. Neither in London nor in Bradford, Liverpool, Bristol, Manchester, Sheffield, or Leeds, nor at any other great assemblies on this topic did the opposition attempt to divide a meeting. Naysayers were easily silenced in the face of overwhelming acclamation.[47] A few days after the Exeter Hall gathering, an assembly of at least 1,500 at the Taylor's Depository in Lambeth had so many clamouring at the doors unable to enter that organisers decided spontaneously to move the event into the open air. When mentioned, the *Times* and *Telegraph* – which had written 'scurrilous articles' about the Exeter Hall meeting – were hissed.[48] For George Thompson, who had addressed meetings on this topic for the previous eighteen months, it felt like a revival of the 1830s campaigns. He called the Emancipation Proclamation 'the Magna Charta [*sic*] of the negroes' rights. (Enthusiastic cheering.) It was written, spoken, declared, and it never could be revoked. (Cheers.) ... Jefferson Davis [1808–89] threatened with extermination four millions of people. (Sensation.)' Thompson claimed that throughout Britain the feeling was resolutely pro-emancipation, and that when votes were put to large assemblies he had never known any opponent gain more than twelve to twenty votes in favour of an amendment to an anti-slavery resolution. The *Star* reported 'he was quite familiar with these rehashes of the *Times*, the *Telegraph*, and the *Standard* – he had read all their arguments before in *John Bull*, in *Fraser*, in *Blackwood*, and in the *Quarterly* who did the work much better in their day. (Laughter and cheers.)', meaning that the counter arguments were all decades old and came from the privileged classes. What the conservative penny press failed to note was that this upsurge of support, in the capital and provinces, was based on working-class backing. 'Well-to-do gentlemen, who got up their politics during a five-minutes ride in the omnibus, might find it convenient to be set up by the articles of the *Times* – (laughter) – but the people neither read it, nor would they trust it if they did read it. (Cheers.)' Chesson, who was also on the platform, pointed out that of the four MPs for South London only Mr Layard (the archaeologist of Assyria and recently elected MP for Southwark) replied to the invitation. As a Lambeth resident, Chesson thought this was a serious consideration for the electorate as a general election neared.[49]

The meeting held at St James's Hall on 18 February 1863, where 'the floor, platform, orchestra, balconies, and highest galleries, were crowded to suffocation with a dense multitude who responded to the invitation', was altogether a tonier crowd. When an anonymous voice from the crowd called out 'Three groans for the *Times*!' it was duly answered with the requested utterances. William Evans, chair of the Emancipation Committee, presented a statement signed by 500,000 Englishwomen beseeching auditors to raise their voices against slavery. 'Who signed this remonstrance? The wife of Lord Palmerston – (cheers) – the honoured wife of the Duke of Argyll, the Duchess of Sutherland, and the Lady Mayoress. (Hear, hear.)' Evans cited the support of British working men and repeated a story from his travels in the United States where he asked a native chief what he thought of the American war. '"Sir, the black man has a soul as well as we have." (Loud cheers.)' In his speech, Thompson decried the Lord Mayor for honouring James Murray Mason (1798–1871, author of the 1850 Fugitive Slave Law, a Virginian and Confederate envoy to Britain 1862–65) with a banquet at Mansion House a week previously, calling it an insult to the government and nation.[50]

Emancipation Committee support was redirected to the Freedmen's Aid Society, focused on raising funds to educate newly liberated African Americans.[51] At a great meeting of trades unionists on 26 March 1863, John Bright's address demonstrated how support was leveraged as common cause between British workers and formerly enslaved US citizens, as well as talking up the aspirational goals of US republicanism more generally. He addressed the workers, who had sent 5.5 million of their brethren to the United States in just the previous fifteen years, nearly the population of London itself.

> There, more than in any other country, men rise to competence and independence—a career is open—and the pursuit of happiness is not at least thwarted by the law. (Cheers.) In the other section of that country labour is not only not honoured, but it is degraded. (Cheers.) Labour is made a chattel—is no more the man's own than the horse that drags the omnibus through the next street. Nor is his wife, nor is his child, nor is anything that is his, his own. (Cheers.) ... I think nothing can be more fitting for the discussion of the members of trade societies than this great question.[52]

A collapse of trade in Lancashire occasioned by minimisation of the cotton supply loomed. Even so, these working men cheered the means to end the perpetual institution of US slavery. A loan of £3 million to aid the Confederacy was condemned by London Trades Union leader George Howell (1833–1910), a bricklayer, who noted the irony that 'it was not often that working men, and particularly trades unionists, met to denounce a revolution when it had commenced'. This was seconded by George Odger (1813–77), a shoemaker and secretary to the London Trades Council, who called upon everyone to think of 'colour prejudice' in the Northern states as vincible, just as in Britain the prejudice against the Irish had, he claimed, become nearly defunct. 'It might be safely affirmed that there were not half a dozen individuals present who would not be glad to dig the graves of this pair of anomalies, and if needful sing a requiem over their graves. (Cheers.)' And, true to the pattern, he blamed the *Times*, *Telegraph*, and *Punch* for stirring irritation between the nations, the first of which, like the very devil, quoted scripture in support of slavery.[53]

Two weeks later, the African American Baptist minister John Sella
Martin wrote from Bromley-by-Bow to explain the situation in the United
States to the *Star*'s readers. Everywhere the Union army was stationed,
people of colour flocked for protection and assistance. Their needs were
great. In Kentucky, for example, Confederate forces had slayed all the
livestock and confiscated grain; the thousands of souls fleeing from such
areas were entirely bereft of belongings and a livelihood.[54] Martin had a
guaranteed sympathetic ear in Samuel Lucas (1811–65), the *Star*'s editor,
who consistently championed the Union. Lucas credited the great Exeter
Hall meeting with swinging opinion to his side: or, perhaps it would be
more accurate to say, for showing in numbers that the people had already
come to his side. At a meeting in October 1863, he credited 'those who
really influenced and guided public opinion – men like John Stuart Mill,
Professor Goldwin Smith, John Elliott Cairnes [1823–75, the leading economist of the day and close colleague of Mill], and Newman [1801–90],
and Mr. Baptist Noel. (Cheers)' with leadership of the Emancipation
Committee, which by no means considered its work finished.[55] No wonder that *Punch* quipped a month later,

> Would you see how spite infernal
> Clutches foulest mud to fling,
> Buy the London Yankee Journal—
> *Morning Star* they call the thing.[56]

This surpassed satiric irreverence to become rank insensitivity. The *Star* was,
at times, the lone voice against British neutrality, even while the government allowed a Birkenhead shipyard to surreptitiously build two iron-clad
vessels (steam rams) for the Confederacy, specifically designed for the flexibility needed in deep- and shallow-water combat along the North American
coast. This secret contract – halted by the British seizure and absorption of
the vessels into its own Navy in 1863 – violated the Foreign Enlistment Act
by earmarking weaponry for the Confederacy. John Baxter Langley investigated it in Scotland: the *Star*'s point, consistently, was that official neutrality
(especially with its Southern leaning) countenanced the 'unprovoked and
nefarious rebellion' that was a war waged as an 'extension and consolidation
of the most ruthless system of oppression the world had ever seen'.[57]

The agon of *Star*-baiting continued through President Lincoln's re-
election and assassination, then persisted after the Civil War.[58] Stephen H.
Esquith emphasises that across the press, editorial debate 'created a func-
tional equivalent to the agora, a public space that limited the boundaries
of political disagreement'. Clearly this extended beyond editorials.[59] While

newspapers purported to speak to their readers, to inform but also motivate readers to leverage influence with legislators, they also spoke of and to one another. Newspapers had personae, most famously Mr Punch, the eponymous character of the weekly satirical magazine as well as the guise of its entire staff. *Punch* quipped under the headline 'Star-Gazing Extraordinary' that 'A Tory gives as his opinion for taking in the *Morning Star*, that "it is always as well to look on the Bright side of things."'[60] *Punch* even ventured to presumptively ventriloquise verses by John Bright on the subject of the first US states' secession, poking fun at his Midlands accent.

> Yet blood! blood! blood;
> Screams the sanguinary *Times*!
> Oh God! that miscreants should (*shud*)
> Grow rich upon their crimes!

To accentuate the dialogic sense of the jest, *Punch* responded with a rejoinder to its own squib, attributing it to Richard Cobden as 'The Country Cousin's Address to Punch'.

> Have you been bitten by the *Times*,
> Or what has raised your choler?
> Now take it easy, *Punch* my boy,
> And do not rave and holler.[61]

A year later, *Punch* still referred to the *Star* as 'our Yankee friend', relentlessly adhering to an association between the paper and its political position.[62] This acidic satire would continue a few years later when *Punch* impugned the *Star* for inventing the Jamaica affair.[63]

The 'combative pens' writing for liberal newspapers such as the *Spectator* and *Daily News* in London, the *Manchester Examiner and Times*, the *Banner of Ulster* and *Northern Whig* in Belfast, *North British Daily Mail* in Glasgow, the *Scotsman* in Edinburgh, and the *Newcastle Examiner* demanded that civil and legal rights follow upon African Americans' emancipation. Bringing this to fruition was another matter. Christine Bolt reflects that 'the Freedman's Bureau was regarded cynically by the *Times* as a ruthless agency destined to supervise confiscations [of whites' land] rather than to protect the Negroes, and Radical proposals for the redistribution of land were given a chilly reception'.[64] At a moment when the British working classes conducted mass demonstrations in support of franchise reform, English liberals could not uniformly align to support giving the franchise to Black people. In Britain, the custom of using property values as the criterion for the franchise was being eroded in tandem with the provision of universal elementary education, yet there was a strong pull to traditional loci of power. The rising Liberal Sir Charles Wentworth Dilke (1843–1911) argued that 'a reading and writing basis for the suffrage in the Southern States is an absurdity', but his view did not win out.[65] The conservative press – of which *Punch* is but one example – leaned on a powerful lever against change, both in Britain and abroad. Meanwhile, the US anti-slavery movement itself failed to pivot from emancipation to full citizenship. As Teresa Goddu argues, the consolidation of the project in 'emancipation's triumph' unfortunately 'discloses white selfhood as grounded in black subjugation, a formation that has yet to be undone'.[66]

## The Jamaica Affair

Political decisions have long tails. Instead of reinvesting their compensation into the colonies in the aftermath of emancipation, planters in the British Caribbean conspicuously removed it. Fields went fallow, and the British public blissfully received goods from other markets and ignored the plight of the emancipated and unemployed Black labourers. As a report of the Edinburgh Ladies' Emancipation Committee bemoaned in 1866, after 1838 Jamaicans' troubles arose from 'the British people', who, 'thinking their work was done, left the arrangements for … [the Black] people in the hands of their former oppressors'.[67] This particular tail came to preoccupy Chesson's combative pen during the latter half of the 1860s.

Post-emancipation, Jamaican Baptists were especially active in developing a Black public sphere by imparting organisational and leadership skills to empower the peasantry. Elected church wardens gained public speaking experience and church members partook in procedural rules: they 'learned about calling a speaker to the chair, moving and seconding resolutions, raising subscriptions, forming delegations to draw up and formally present resolutions, publishing proceedings in local and metropolitan newspapers and circulating and signing petitions'.[68] These repertoires, tested in Britain by the abolition and emancipation movements, had recently become possible in Jamaica and proved adaptable in forging an advocacy movement. They were 'forms of publicly declared resistance', in James C. Scott's terminology, capable of leading to open opposition yet presumed safe.[69] In Kingston, a Mechanics' Institute was founded (corresponding to London's model) to enhance adults' access to education and literacy, and radical newspapers helped distribute information and opinion. Black advocates brought grievances to Jamaica's House of Assembly, protesting legislation, taxes, the importation of indentured labourers (primarily from India), and the privileges accorded to the established church.

These grievances went largely unheeded. Black Jamaicans' political and legal rights were consistently denied, social institutions such as alms houses and hospitals were non-existent, and community leaders who advocated for justice were ignored, sidelined, and silenced by the colonial authorities. In 1862, at a meeting of the Native Baptist chapel in Morant Bay, attendees affirmed that resolutions published in the Black newspaper *Jamaica Watchman and People's Free Press* should be forwarded abroad, to London's *Times* and Lord Brougham, Lord John Russell, John Bright, and other liberals. In response, a prominent spokesperson of the Afro-Caribbean community, George William Gordon (1825–65) – a mixed-race landholder who held a seat in the General Assembly, published the *Jamaica Watchman and People's Free Press*, and was a leader in the Baptist community – was removed by the governor from his position as commissioner of the peace. Gordon had a comprehensive view of how white-run institutions compounded Black misery, and the governor's action failed to suppress him. Early in 1865, Edward Bean Underhill (1813–1901, secretary of the Baptist Missionary Society) wrote to the secretary of state of the colonies Edward Cardwell (1813–86) acknowledging Jamaicans' widespread starvation resulting from drought and failed crops, exacerbated by low prices during the American Civil War, and recommending an inquiry into these conditions and creation of marketing associations for freeholders. The governor, in turn, blamed peasants for their own poverty and embarked on a poster campaign inveighing Blacks to stick to waged labour and remain steadfast in their habits. Gordon printed posters in a counter-campaign, and at a series of meetings across the island organisers demonstrated the effectiveness of public networks in putting speakers before large gatherings.[70]

When news of ensuing events in Jamaica reached London late in 1865, Chesson observed that 'the crashing of a shell in St Paul's, or the sudden appearance of a pirate in the Thames, could scarcely have excited more surprise' among the general public. For decades, the West Indian mails had arrived every fortnight, bringing little but weather reports and market prices. The British public was lulled into thinking that having paid out £20 million to compensate West Indian slaveholders, no further attention need be given. 'Everybody assumed that the negroes were contented, that they had no substantial grievance, and that while revolution might create its disorders in the neighbouring Republics of San Domingo [Hispaniola], the torch of revolt would never again be lighted in any portion of our West Indian possessions.'[71] Chesson, writing of this in the *Nonconformist*, countered this sardonic review of popular opinion by noting how, in fact, trouble had simmered in Jamaica on numerous fronts. Bias in selecting stipendiary magistrates from among the white governing class fed Black Jamaicans' consequent lack of confidence in the courts; low wages for plantation workers were compounded by two years of drought and crop failures; the crippling tax burden on imports (for example 88 per cent on cloth) left the poor ragged or naked; and other consequences of failing to dismantle 'the vicious effects of the slave system' were in play for Afro-Caribbean workers. Given that Black Jamaicans had been forever loyal to the British Crown, what, in all good conscience, could Britain say it had ever done for them? 'So this great "rebellion," "this great lesson for philanthropists for all time to come," resolves itself into a simple riot, the outbreak of a mob clamouring for food and doing what mobs have ever done under similar circumstances in the most civilised [*sic*] capitals of the world.'[72]

If only it had been as simple as that.

Initial intelligence about the uprising stemmed from Governor Eyre's despatch from Kingston to Consul-General Robert Bunch (1820–81) at Havana, requesting troops; this was forwarded to Consul Edward Archibald (1810–84) in New York, then to General Charles Doyle (1804–83, administrator of the government of Nova Scotia), who sent it onward by ship to London. News arrived during the first days of November, by which time the Jamaican parish of Saint Thomas in the East had been under martial law for three weeks. On 17 November, Chesson called at the Baptist Missionary Society for a list of those arrested. This disproved the *Times*' imputation upon Baptists by showing every religious denomination among the detainees.[73] By early December, Chesson and Peter Taylor (1819–91, MP for Leicester) agreed to form the 'Jamaica Committee', organising a great meeting at Exeter Hall on 12 December 1865. Meanwhile, the Colonial Office loaded a Royal West India steamer with 100 tonnes of war material, including one tonne of Colt revolvers, bound for Jamaica. This reflects the ire felt in Britain, fanned by anti-Black prejudice.[74] The *Times* broke the news first, spreading apocrypha. Though Eyre's despatch stipulated that events were confined to a single district, the *Times* magnified the sliver of news into a New York-based Afro-Fenian plot to incite Black Caribbeans to violent acts, or a Haitian-inspired attempt to create a 'Negro Republic', both rumours with external impetus.[75] Whereas the *Times* warned that if Black Jamaicans chose this moment for revolt – despite purportedly holding 'rights and immunities which other races have been too glad to acquire by centuries of struggles, of repulses, and of endurance' – the rebellion ought to be definitively crushed.[76] At this first hint of what unfolded as a gruesome, sadistic, unwarranted set of actions sanctioned by Governor Eyre, Chesson already named the British reaction as 'shameful tirades' emanating from 'the negro-hating class in this country'.[77]

> The next round of news came via a French steamer. By and large, the British press dwelt on details of torture, mutilation, and murder of white magistrates, planters, and missionaries as if this was a reprise of the Sepoy Mutiny (the 1857–8 rebellion) in India. Chesson, in contrast, likened the news to Pai Mārire, a syncretic messianic Māori cult that arose on the North Island of New Zealand and conducted a series of assaults on imperial soldiers and Pākehā missionaries in 1864–5: in other words, he assumed that there were structural causes for the violence, that people of all complexions had rights, and that philanthropists must insist on 'a full and impartial inquiry'. The truth is, that for years past the governors, legislators, and planters of Jamaica have been engaged in providing the gunpowder and laying the train for an explosion; and the only wonder is that, instead of a mob of a few hundred men and women committing murder and outrage in a single parish in the island, the conflagration has not been more general.... The crowd first attacked the Court-house at Morant Bay, where the custos [wardens] and the magistrates were in 'special' session. We should like to receive some authentic information concerning the objects of this 'special session.' ... Evils of a political and social nature, have reached their climax in a terrible outburst of popular frenzy.

Though Jamaica had the trappings of British government (a governor, Privy Council, and Legislative Assembly), these institutions were packed with yes-men and crooks. In recent times one assemblyman had been convicted of forgery, another of embezzlement, a third of defrauding widows and orphans of £40,000, and two others with purloining public funds. No wonder that the flashpoint of the Morant Bay Rebellion was a courthouse.[78] Four days before the outbreak of violence, a man was on trial at Morant Bay for trespassing on a long-abandoned plantation that had been confiscated by the state for non-payment of taxes. James Geoghegan disrupted the proceedings and was arrested, his sister Isabella Geoghegan challenged the arrest, and a mob of about 100 led by Paul Bogle (1820–65, Gordon's election agent in Saint Thomas in the East and a deacon in Gordon's Native Baptist chapel in Kingston) rescued him.[79] Four days later, during a meeting of the local vestry, Bogle led a bigger column of people from the village of Stony Gut to Morant Bay, where they were confronted by the local volunteer militia. The Geoghegans' mother, Letitia, threw the first stone, and though Bogle did his best to restore order, before the day was over the courthouse and other buildings had been burnt, twenty-five people had been killed, and thirty-one had been wounded.

News of what happened next came in through a succession of despatches, but all sides agreed on a set of facts. Black peasants took control of the parish lands. Under martial law, Eyre sent in government troops along with Maroons (descendants of Black freedom-seekers who dwelt in the mountains) to flush them out. According to Montego Bay journalist Sidney Lindo Levien (1809–95), 'Eyre the Governor sent unto them cloths of serge and shirts of blue flannel wherewith to clothe themselves, and arms and ammunition; and they went forth with blowing of horns and dressed [i.e., camouflaged] in leaves, and did battle against the rebels'.[80] The peasants, who had steeled themselves with the motto 'Cleave to the Black', fell as the troops killed indiscriminately. A thousand prisoners were brought to Morant Bay. Martial law was maintained for a full month, during which time 200 prisoners were flogged and just under 200 were executed, including Bogle. Gordon was seized in Kingston, even though the capital was not under martial law, and brought to Morant Bay. He was to be scapegoated for leading the rebellion, though no shred of evidence was produced against him. He was charged with high treason and sedition, court martialled, and hanged on Eyre's orders in the ruins of the courthouse, along with seventeen others (Figure 4.5). In the last hours of his life, Gordon passed a letter to his wife proclaiming his innocence and urging her to contact Henry Brougham and Louis Chamerovzow in London. His execution became a flashpoint for English liberals: if Gordon could be executed, what of imperialism's critic John Bright?[81]

As Chesson's *Star* colleague Justin McCarthy wrote, 'for some weeks there was hardly anything talked of, we might say hardly anything thought of, in England, but the story of the rebellion in Jamaica, and the manner in which it has been suppressed'.[82] Consistently, Chesson wrote in the *Nonconformist* and *Star* criticising the conservative press' rhetoric, hammering on coverage by the Tory *Times*, *Telegraph*, and *Standard*. He utilised not just the despatches but also private correspondence, blue books, and a structuralist view to understand how Black people's 'indignant protest' was responded to with 'bloody excesses' by 'brutal executioners' who took the lives of 439 Black Jamaicans.[83] In turn, the callousness of the conservative press can hardly be overstated. Under the banner 'Library of Fiction', *Punch* published a mock review of a tract purportedly published out of the *Morning Star* office. In 'The Reign of Terror in Jamaica', the *Star*'s writer collects information from Black Jamaicans never before known by white readers. *Punch* makes light of the atrocities, citing a woman who saw nine of her neighbours swinging then retreated to the woods, and soldiers who roused a Black family from slumber then shot the family's

Figure 4.5 'Execution of rebels at the ruins of the court house, Morant Bay.' Drawing by Alexander Dudgeon Gulland, compiler, photography album, albumen print of pen and ink drawing. Special Collections, Princeton University Library.

rebel father as he fled. 'We commend this romance of Jamaica to all the lovers of penny fiction, and we congratulate the enterprising publishers, MESSRS. BRIGHT AND SHAMMYRUMSTUFF on the spirit which induced them to engage the pen of a spicy novelist rather than to imitate the *Times*, *Daily News*, and *Telegraph*, who tamely send out gentlemen with no higher mission than to ascertain facts from credible witnesses.'[84]

Three commissioners were dispatched to Jamaica, where they spent fifty-one days examining 730 witnesses. Whereas their report was critical of the court martial, it praised Eyre for taking swift action.[85] Testimony was omitted of a person who could have corroborated that Bogle declined to fight. Gordon, for his part, was shown to have had no part in the Morant Bay massacre yet was objected to simply for being 'a dangerous and inflammatory character'. Gordon was tried and executed without any evidence of guilt – the commissioners admitted this – yet Eyre was exonerated for his juridical murder. Mill attended his first meeting on the topic on 16 February 1866, and over the ensuing year of assiduous advocacy he developed the view 'that if Mr. Eyre's conduct had been without personal malice it would have been only one degree less wicked than it was with that graver element imparted into it'.[86] Even so, the commission also extenuated the circumstances in which an Obeah man, Mr Wellington, was shot at long range then found to be still alive, shot again, and decapitated. Flogging of women by a Captain Holt was 'reprobated' on account of 'the somewhat difficult position in which he was placed', and though using wire-cats [a wire cat-o'-nine-tails] to flog men was abhorred, 'the fact that women also were flogged with this instrument of torture until one of them fainted is omitted'. Chesson wrote that this left it up to others to 'interpose, not only for the sake of the tortured living and the murdered dead, but to prevent the reign of terror which has cast so deep a stain upon the fame of England from ever repeating itself in the unwritten pages of our colonial history'.[87]

As more facts became known, letters from British perpetrators of the atrocities appeared in the Jamaican and British press. Captain Ford, a member of the cavalry, wrote that 'he and his men had taken sport in shooting black men and women in the back as they fled for their lives'. Colonel Hobbs, commander of the Sixth Royal Regiment, which ventured into the parish of Saint David and slew more than 200 people, 'openly boasted of how he had terrorized then executed the servant of one of the leaders of the uprising'.[88] Provost-Marshal Gordon Ramsay – whom Levien called 'a stern man with tiger spirit and a terror to the negroes', formerly inspector of police – coolly admitted to having 'hanged (without trial) one black prisoner merely for having made an angry face after a severe flogging'.[89] Before the end of January 1866, Chesson had received authority to begin proceedings against Ramsay.[90]

How did Chesson know to take these contrary stands as soon as the affair broke? How did Gordon know to reach out to Brougham and Chamerovzow on the verge of his execution? Answering the second of these questions is easy: Gordon was in the newspaper business, and he knew names that had been before the public for decades. Chesson's knowledge was gathered by assiduous ongoing preparation. Baptist missionary Edward Bean Underhill, whose letter sparked the 1865 meetings across Jamaica, had been in India and Ceylon from 1854 to 1857, then visited Cuba, Trinidad, Haiti, and Jamaica, where in 1859–60 he researched his book on social and religious conditions. Chesson reviewed it in the *Star* early in 1862. The book informed him broadly on the aftermath of emancipation, the structural poverty of Black people, and the retention of political supremacy among white populations.[91] Underhill's findings justify why, during a series of gatherings throughout 1865, Jamaicans engaged in classic British protest strategies – mass meetings, petitions, withdrawal of labour (hartal), and cross-class/multi-ethnic coalition building (with Black and mixed-race, urban and rural, Nonconformist and Jewish men and women) promoted through placarding – to demand civil and political rights. These were known as the Underhill meetings, even though (as he was in England) Underhill did not participate.[92] Underhill, who had been secretary of the Baptist Missionary Society, was a seasoned author and journalist with field experience in the colonies; he was just the sort of person on whom the APS relied, just the sort who would know that Brougham (in Parliament), and Chamerovzow (in anti-slavery circles) would be effective distributors of information to Radical colleagues abroad.

And so, duly, Chesson was indignant that in the flagrant disregard for *habeas corpus* the corrupt system embedded on the island should be in a position to judge anyone alleged to have instigated or suppressed a rebellion. He, along with the Manchester School, demanded full investigation, both through the fact-finding mission to Jamaica and in the select committee hearings that followed.[93] By early December 1865, Chesson was organising: sending out circulars and noting who desired to join the effort. He joined a deputation including Chamerovzow to meet with Prime Minister Lord Russell, attended a meeting at Exeter Hall organised by the BFASS, and planned another in cooperation with the City of London. Samuel Morley (1809–86) pledged £500, Charles Bright £50, and John Stuart Mill £10, and with staunch support from John Bright, Charles Buxton, MP (1822–71), Sir Thomas Fowell Buxton (a leading figure in the BFASS), Henry William Wilberforce (1807–73), Thomas Hughes (1822–96), Herbert Spencer (1820–1903), Goldwin Smith, Henry Fawcett (1833–84), and Edmond Beales, the Jamaica Committee was launched. As secretary, Chesson managed the deluge of correspondence and met privately with strategists. The Jamaica Committee engaged Edward James, MP (1807–67) and James Fitzjames Stephen (1829–94) as standing council, and prepared to 'memorialise [the] Queen against giving her assent to the bill of indemnity'.[94] Months before the commission's report was released, the Jamaica Committee's members went public, advertising the committee in newspapers and seeking denominationally specific lists of supporters in order to demonstrate non-factionalism. They contracted a pamphlet on the legislative history of Jamaica and continued to receive letters from Jamaicans, including one from an incarcerated Black minister who 'gave a shocking account of the floggings which he was brought out to witness twice a day'.[95]

Eyre was suspended and recalled to England. When the topic came up in the House of Commons, members fled from the chamber.[96] Thomas Carlyle (1795–1881) purported to know nothing of Jamaica two weeks before becoming one of the Eyre Defence Committee's most prominent members.[97] The *Times* persisted as the public voice of the Eyre Defence

Committee, insinuating with weak satire that the Jamaica Committee kept 'poor Governor Eyre' in suspense for a year until his murder charge was heard by the grand jury. But warrants needed three weeks to make their way from Southampton to Kingston, witnesses had to be found, and this took time. During this phase of the affair, the Jamaica Committee kept up pressure on the government, gathered evidence, and publicised the matter. The Radical jurist Frederic Harrison (1831–1923) investigated the questions of 'whether English citizens are amenable to a military court under martial law', and whether Conservative Prime Minister 'Lord Derby [1799–1869], the oracle of the aristocratic sphere', would present a bill to the House.[98]

Frustrated at the lack of consequences in the criminal courts, the Jamaica Committee pursued private criminal prosecutions. The workaround resembled Thompson's strategy within the British East India Company's Court of Proprietors and Alexander Kennedy Isbister's dogged undermining of the Hudson's Bay Company. Detractors turned Gordon's privileged status and well-known critique of the government against him, while, to counter this, over a period of thirty months the Jamaica Committee pursued two actions for murder against Eyre and murder charges against Colonel Abercrombie Nelson, who hunted the rebels under cover of martial law, and Lieutenant Herbert Brand (1839–1901, commander of the *Onyx*), who suppressed the revolt then presided over the court martial.[99] Foreign and domestic matters merged in tenor: suspension of the Habeas Corpus Act in Ireland, agitation for the Second Reform Bill, and the Jamaica affair 'were attempts to introduce or reinforce the accountability of political actors to law and law-makers; both [the colonies and Britain] were sites for contesting the fundamental questions of English political jurisprudence'. If martial law could be imposed capriciously in a colony as 'an essential tool of imperial statecraft', this was equally a threat to the rule of law and fundamental liberty in Britain.[100] Historians Christine Bolt, Douglas A. Lorimer, and Catherine Hall concur that in England the Jamaica affair was a turning point for humanitarian traditions that devolved from abolition, however the prominence of racist ideology undermined the fundaments of reformers' work.[101] Chesson's incremental – and ultimately unsuccessful – efforts were both historicist and juridical. He demonstrates understanding both of the complexities of racialised power in Jamaica and Britain and of the incommensurability of sanctioned acts with a liberal understanding of British law. The Jamaica Committee was neither a monolith pushed through by Mill's singular vision nor an inconsequential quaint artefact of outdated philanthropic effort. It was a bulwark against anti-Black racism at the midpoint of Victoria's reign.[102]

When, in 1850, Dr Robert Knox (1791–1862) published his *Fragment on the Races of Man*, based on lectures he had toured for several years prior, he was considered out of step with his times. He argued that the 'races' were forever poised to be at war, and however much this worried the Exeter Hall philanthropists, he asserted this as a matter of fact. In the early days of the Jamaica affair, the *Lancet* picked up this theme, lambasting Knox – who, at an earlier phase of his career had been a path-breaking anatomist (so was one of their own) – as unable even to get a rousing endorsement from ethnologists. Yet, given the fresh memory of massacres at Delhi and Cawnpore and the conflicts in Mexico, the Cape, Australia, and Ireland (where the Celts 'are concocting a *jeu d'esprit* with Fenianism and gunpowder to "hunt the Saxon from the isle"'), this view of the outbreak in Jamaica (a circumstance Knox seemed *specifically* to have foretold and which the *Times* erroneously linked to Fenians) was of a piece with Carlyle's outlook on the Eyre Defence Committee. Progressively, the *Lancet* recommended a fresh view of tropical administration, not 'as military masters lording it over a sort of serf population, and under the continual fear of whose terrible vengeance we must always live', but rather with an 'unprejudiced consideration' of the incipient violence that preoccupied Knox.[103] Chesson – an ally of both the 'broad-brimmed philanthropists' (an allusion to Quakers) and economists – and others like him were implicated by this, both in not heeding the coming tide of racism and in only feebly trying to staunch its administrative effects throughout an empire.

The problem took various forms, ranging from deadly violence to catastrophic neglect. In 1867, writing about the famine in Bengal that extended over an area of 128,750 square kilometres (49,710 square miles), affected 20 million people, and took 1.5 million lives, Chesson concluded that 'human misery has a human origin'.[104] There was irrigation in Bengal, but the system had been allowed to become dysfunctional. There was ample knowledge of the extent of food scarcity, for the calamity pressed into districts just 240 kilometres (150 miles) from Calcutta. Under such circumstances, compassion had a corollary in state action: food relief could have been sent as with the Irish Famine during the 1840s, but it was not. Reflecting on the tradition of liberal economics, Chesson wrote: 'Adam Smith and John Stuart Mill, in propounding the great truths of political science, never dreamed of enforcing them with rigid severity when society was convulsed by a great calamity, or when strict adherence to principles which, in the ordinary circumstances of human life are perfectly just and expedient, would entail widespread misery and desolation. Political economy demands no such sacrifice.' Chesson noted a spectrum of regret in the

House of Commons debate on the disaster, with the secretary of state for India (Lord Cranborne, 1830–1903, later Lord Salisbury) delivering an apt speech that 'the great evil was that English officials in India, with many very honourable exceptions, did not regard the lives of the coloured inhabitants with the same feelings of intense sympathy which they would show to those of their own race and colour'. To the unanimous approval of the House, he called this prejudice 'the curse of India and of most of our colonies'.[105] Mill crossed the floor to congratulate him.

Whereas during the 1840s and 1850s, Frederick Douglass had found few hints of a colour-based prejudice in Britain, in the mid-1860s Sarah Parker Remond (1826–94) asserted it was rife.[106] The truth all along – in Britain and throughout its empire – was in favour of Remond's view, as the vehement racialised response to the 1857–8 Indian Rebellion suggests.[107] Chesson found that the blue books on Jamaica (published by the Colonial Office), containing correspondence by clergy, magistrates, landowners, and a significant number of women, 'prove beyond doubt not only that the white people in the island originally shared Mr. Eyre's panic', but that when a full disclosure of the atrocities was made they had not 'a single compassionate thought' nor were they moved to 'one feeling of compunction'. Yet the signs of prolonged suffering had been all around them. This reflected abysmally on the Anglicans as a community, but also on Eyre, who bemoaned his treatment in the press as having 'no sympathy with … fellow-countrymen suffering under the atrocious barbarities inflicted by savages, because those savages have a black skin'. The imposition of torture and murder was justified by the British as the preservation of discipline. But to the Jamaica Committee it was clearly an exertion of power.[108]

In its efforts to bring Eyre and other officials to account, the Jamaica Committee raised, and expended, thousands of pounds to cover legal costs.[109] A little over two years into the saga, Lyulph Stanley (1839–1925, later Fourth Baron Stanley of Alderley), a young barrister, atheist, and secularist who advised on the case, questioned the propriety of continuing. Mill said he would fund it himself rather than give up. They switched tactics to prosecute under the Colonial Governors Act, yet by March 1868 even Mill's enthusiasm waned. As a final gesture, in April 1870 Chesson had Mill's protégé Dilke put a question to the House of Commons requesting compensation for Mrs Gordon, the white widow of the mixed-race legislator scapegoated by Eyre. The answer was negative. The end of the long tale came soon after, when the Jamaica Committee voted to wind up and send its remaining funds to Mrs Gordon.[110] The entire issue – a flashpoint on the powder keg of racism in the empire and Britain – traced the long tail of the 1833 emancipation decision, but essentially accomplished nothing except to show the enormity of the mechanisms ('administrative massacre, rule by terror') that resisted the committee and wielded power against Black people of all classes and faiths living in the wake of slavery.[111] The Jamaica Committee did not achieve a culture shift, though it was one of several movements that attempted to redress the exigent effects of racism and contribute to liberals' recognition of its embeddedness in Britain and colonial institutions, despite widespread knowledge of how to use the liberal playbook of performative tactics to assert rights and advocate for social justice.

## Crime Scenes: 'Doing' Activism, Conceiving Human Rights

The efforts of the British and Foreign Freedmen's Aid Society on behalf of formerly enslaved US residents and the Jamaica Committee's pursuit of executive accountability for the torture and deaths of Black Jamaicans stemmed from anti-racism and anti-imperialism. British-raised funds for the freedmen's aid movement (about US$800,000 in all, collected 1863–68) marked the peak of financial support for any such transnational cause during the Victorian period.[112] As the fate of emancipated Afro-Caribbeans shows, the transnational anti-slavery movement's attention and fundraising switched to the United States, leaving broader anti-slavery and post-emancipation initiatives with a moral mandate but little capital to back them. After the 1860s, transnational attention to what Saidiya Hartman calls African Americans' 'transition between modes of servitude and racial subjection' likewise waned.[113]

This history is relevant in thinking about the APS' approach to advocacy, especially after 1870, when it focused on leveraging networks rather than following the time-honoured anti-slavery tactics of building a broad movement through affiliated branch societies, fundraising through appeals and bazaars, and petitioning. The APS was not a large enough organisation to be called a popular movement, yet its inclusive approach to drawing in information allowed it to function globally, quite apart from its membership roll, and to try to punch way above its weight. What came across Chesson's desk as its secretary tracks the valences of the APS' work, amplified in more official channels through deputations to cabinet ministers, its publication the *Colonial Intelligencer, or Aborigines' Friend*, and meetings that frequently spawned separate, single-issue campaigns. Especially after the death of Dr Thomas Hodgkin (one of the APS' founders) in 1866 and the *Star*'s demise in 1869, when Chesson focused more on his APS secretaryship and freelance journalism rather than on producing a daily newspaper, he emerged as 'the champion of oppressed peoples all over the world'. The 'politicians of various schools ... converted his modest little room on the third floor of Broadway Chambers into a centre of activity'.[114] 'Indeed', it was said, 'when an organised movement in favour of social or political reform was urgent, his help was indispensable', and just a few minutes' walk from the Houses of Parliament and Whitehall.[115] Chesson continued to be in demand as a political advisor, for example noting in his diary that upon hearing of the *Star*'s demise Charles Buxton 'with great delicacy proposed to give me a hundred pounds for collecting and arranging materials for him on several public questions'.[116] Additionally, he and Samuel Ralph Townshend Mayer (1841–80, best known for advocating tolerance of homosexuality) were editors of the *St James's Magazine and United Empire Review* in 1872–7, and for much of 1874 Chesson edited the *Literary Monthly*.

There is ample evidence of how Chesson 'did' activism in conjunction with literary pursuits. It was never a solo endeavour. For example, in opposing the exploitive treatment of East Indian coolies in Demerara, he sought first to 'get a paper on this subject ready before the Juridical Society', so he reached out to the Social Science Association.[117] In other words, getting someone in command of facts to convey them to an interested body – in a lecture or printed form – was vital. But this could never be the only or final step: he forecast that either Buxton (long involved in West Indian affairs) or Thomas Hughes (a trades union advocate) would take up the issue in Parliament. Chesson would be on hand to help them as they prepared.

Following the Ethiopian–Egyptian War of 1874–6, England focused on conciliating the Ottoman Empire as a bulwark against Russian encroachment into Central Asia, and so steered clear of further involvement in Abyssinia. Chesson's response to Joseph Cooper's 1879 inquiry about supporting Abyssinia's King Yohannes IV (1837–89) against Muslim aggressors is indicative of how he deployed his strategic repertoire from the APS' Westminster office. With the British government's attention on the Bosphorus, Chesson told the veteran abolitionist 'there are four or five things which it occurs to me most desirable to do in this matter':

> To draw up in a connected form the facts which it is most important to bring before the public—such a pamphlet as you wrote on the African slave trade.[118]
>
> To ask Lord Selborne [Roundell Palmer (1812–95), an eminent jurist particularly interested in established religion] if he would take charge of this question in the House of Lords as he did that of Cuba.
>
> To appeal to the archbishop of Canterbury [Archibald Campbell Tait (1811–82), a liberal keenly interested in foreign politics who was most

effective in the Lords during Conservative governments] to interfere on behalf of a Christian people [the Abyssinians] who are thirsting for intercourse with the outer world, and for the means of improvement.

To ask Mr. H. Ashworth [1794–1880, Cobdenite free trader and cotton miller] to bring the subject in its commercial aspects before the Manchester Chamber of Commerce. If one [other] Chamber with that of Manchester would take the initiative much might be done.

To bring the subject before [William Edward] Forster [1818–86, MP], C. Dilke, [Sir James] Stansfeld [1820–98, MP], and other anti-slavery men who are likely to be members of the next governments. At least one can begin to look forward to a time when there will be a change of ministry and no time should be lost in instructing men.[119]

From a tactical perspective, Chesson saw the importance of putting facts before all these interests, as well as the public, in comprehensible form (point 1). In points 2, 3, and 4, Chesson considered how to mobilise people in positions of influence, while calling upon the respective powers of church (point 3) as well as state (points 2 and 5), and sought to mobilise the Lancastrian industrial elite, even after their industry's profits had begun a long decline (point 4), in order to build support across the North. He showed a canny sense of current and future political prospects in proven statesmen, both those who could be effective in the short term (point 3) and those who could lie in wait to help when their party next formed a government (point 5). These tactics show the cumulative wisdom of a quarter century's intensive networking as well as the persistent importance of leveraging Thompson's generation in emergent initiatives. Dilke, who in the coming years would be eyed as William Ewart Gladstone's successor as leader of the Liberals, is the only figure listed who was still a young man.

These tactics align with what postcolonial theorist Boaventura de Sousa Santos calls 'artisanal knowledge', which, as

> a performative kind of knowledge ... cannot be evaluated without reference to who formulates it and in what context. Being often a collective or common knowledge, its individualized mobilization always depends on the authority and effectiveness of whoever mobilizes it. In truth, there is really no knowledge but rather a cluster, a mix of knowledge/knower.

In Chesson's acumen, we can see a strategist in whom both 'know-how' and 'know-who' are mutually significant. Santos differentiates two kinds of knowledge that exist in this mixture.

> Mirror knowledge is the comforting mix that envisions the present as the ratification of the past, and the future as the present that has not yet happened. It is comforting because it constructs the reality of the struggle by

privileging answers, certainties, and confirmations. Furthermore, it tends to homogenize both times and spaces. Prism knowledge, on the contrary, assumes the incompleteness of what is already known and constructs the reality of the struggle as highly varied or faceted, thus privileging novelty, rupture, and questionings.[120]

In the steps beyond advising Cooper to write a pamphlet and name others who could bring questions before the House of Lords, House of Commons, and the nation's most powerful Chamber of Commerce, 'prism knowledge' operated. Steps 4 and 5 resemble 'the hidden transcript as practice', tactics that leave no trace, underpinned by known 'values, understandings, and popular outrage' in practical struggles.[121] Chesson's quotidian plan ensured that not only secular but also sacred realms would be addressed, rupturing the sense that Abyssinia could be a purely foreign (either exclusively temporal or religious) or merely regional (and thus unworthy) concern. Such an 'epistemology of the South' (in the sense of perspectives that challenge the hegemony of European objectivity or experience, and value the corporeality of knowledge, copresence, and struggle) both manoeuvres the empiricist's approach to describe the past and offers creative reflection on political repertoires to imagine new kinds of outcomes. In Dwight Conquergood's terms, this is 'practical knowledge (knowing how), propositional knowledge (knowing that), and political savvy (knowing who, when, and where)'.[122] This is key to Chesson's longevity and value as an advocate, even if he was too infrequently a *successful* bulwark against British indifference. His knowledge of foreign affairs was comprehensive, and from the journalist's gallery in Parliament, speakers' platforms at countless public meetings, and untold committee meetings he knew who he could work with on multiple fronts. This repertoire was long in formation and dynamically adjusted based on colleagues' shifting political commitments, availability, and reputational sway. Recognising the *social* nature of their potential to effect change in tandem with their political views resulted in an adaptable performative discourse and dramaturgy of activism.

The work had some constant imperatives: listen and network in order to shift opinions, prevent new forms of human trafficking, manumit the enslaved, and counter oppression. In many respects, performances of these ideological convictions were identical to those of earlier movements: private conversations, committee meetings, public meetings, deputations to cabinet ministers, and questions put before Parliament were daily occurrences. Yet whereas, formerly, travelling lecturers did the heavy work of persuasion, and special commissioners who were sent abroad to make enquiries returned to London as proxies for eyewitnesses, now – with the rise of mass media, rapid communication by telegraph, seaways, railroads, and the cheap post – the onus of activism and information-gathering shifted to a much more distributed and nodal model. APS records show that increasingly after mid-century, field informants – including high-ranking administrators, minor officials, private citizens, journalists, clerics, missionaries, and settlers across the world who were based in colonial outposts, entrepôts, and far-flung islands – would report observations to Chesson, the key organiser in London, who in turn took responsibility to supply sympathetic politicians and journalists with reliable knowledge. While these metropolitan influencers could rally support among the growing franchise of British male voters, and press coverage was important, the kinds of matters that came to the APS' attention from its worldwide network were more conducive to putting queries before the Foreign Office, Colonial Office, or Parliament about specific occurrences. Still, communication with the citizenry in order to leverage influence on MPs remained a vital liberal tactic.

Out of the older anti-slavery tactics developed new forms of understanding, particularly about the systematic imposition of differential restrictions on populations, the toleration of trafficking in many forms and degrees, and atrocities that occurred globally. Specifically, within the context of imperialist conquest and colonisation (and their ever-present analogue, racism), assaults upon native peoples gave the APS a unique position among activist groups. It recognised individual transgressions and aggregated experiences to issue protests against both singular incidents and patterns of offence. The combined insights and acts of anti-racism and imperial critique (not synonymous with anticolonialism) that Chesson and his network of journalists, politicians, and other activists espoused inched British liberals toward a coherent doctrine of human rights.

A recent historian of the APS concludes that by the time the society consolidated with the Anti-Slavery Society in 1909, it had no big 'wins', 'just a few cases of individual hardship alleviated and petty wrongs righted'. The APS never entirely succeeded in persuading the Colonial Office that the society's objective aligned with Britain's interests.[123] Indeed, the understanding that the APS' work helped develop the concept of human rights did not fully coalesce until the mid-twentieth century. In 1944, the Polish prosecutor Raphael Lemkin (1900–59) coined the term genocide to encompass a 'coordinated plan of different actions' to attack groups 'with the aim of annihilating them'. Whereas nineteenth-century activists used the terms extermination and elimination to refer to Indigenous population reductions under the guise of land appropriation and settlement, the APS documented what Lemkin later articulated: the APS grasped the *sense* and *particulars* of genocide without benefit of a comprehensive term. Saxe Bannister (1790–1877) – who, after a brief career in colonial service, was a contributor to the 1837 Parliamentary Select Committee on Aboriginal Tribes and helped found the APS – is indicative of nascent insights when, in 1833, he named the French government's North African policy a 'project of extermination', in opposition to native Algerians' right to self-government.[124] In 1857, Isbister wrote to Chesson expressing how biopower was wielded as an excuse for retaining the Hudson's Bay Company: some argued that ending its monopoly would mean the unbridled culling of animals. Isbister countered, 'There is more danger of the trade being put an end to by the extermination of the Indians, who are being decimated by starvation & diseases introduced by Europeans. This point has not been brought as it might before the [APS] Committee.'[125] The precarity of Indigenous peoples came about through neglect, technicalities of geopolitical posturing, and inaction in the face of belligerent opponents' actions. For example, in 1884 Robert Lester (senior member of the Natal Bar, Cradock Cape Colony) wrote to Chesson decrying England's failure to fulfil promises to assist loyal natives against the Boers. 'Pray do your best or the natives will be exterminated (they <u>are now starving</u>, the Boers <u>having stolen all their Cattle & food</u>) and Civil War will exist throughout the land.'[126] He decried the Boers as 'really and truly <u>fiends in human shape</u> and capable of anything'.[127]

Recent studies of Lemkin's unpublished manuscripts emphasise how he configured the 'total social practice' of genocide as attacking culture as well as human life.[128] In addition to the political destruction of leaders and dispossession of land and other wealth, slavery and deportation, deprivation of livelihood, habitat change, active combat, transmission of disease and withholding of medicine, imposition of religion, and curtailing of legal rights constitutive of genocides – all of which are asserted in APS correspondence – the British settlement of the Australian continent exemplified not only judicial and extra-judicial massacre but also the incremental processes of cultural genocide.[129] Deployment of mounted police in the wanton shootings of Aboriginal people in New South Wales, toleration of massacres by settlers in Victoria and the Northern Territory, and the 'blackbirding' of Pacific Islanders trafficked into Queensland made the Australian colonies a persistent target of attention decades after the natives of Tasmania, and their culture, were brought to the brink of extinction.[130] As Tom Lawson argues, Tasmania was explicitly a *British* genocide:

> Violence was carried out by British men in order to expand and then defend a British colony. The legal justification of that action was explicitly provided by the British government: indeed the instructions of the Colonial Office

stated that the colonial government was obliged to defend the colony with force against indigenous resistance. Furthermore, that resistance was itself a response to an impulse for colonial development that came from London and was sustained by massively increased emigration from Britain at the beginning of the 1820s. Throughout the period of violence the British Colonial Office maintained a commitment to the relentless pursuit of colonial development that was in many ways its cause. The new frontiers were to be defended by force.

Furthermore, the cultural dimension of the Tasmanian genocide was incontrovertible: after decades of persecution, survivors were rounded up and relocated offshore.

> Once on Flinders Island, indigenous peoples were to be transformed into a British peasantry. They were to be taught to farm the land like Europeans, to worship God like Europeans. Ultimately, the majority also died from European diseases. The campaign of transformation enacted on Flinders Island amounted to cultural genocide.[131]

As Dilke put it: 'The Saxon is the only extirpating race on earth', and this is but one example.[132] Chesson was not immune from facets of the British impulse. He passed along an idea of the Anglo-Australian journalist and reformer Edward Wilson (1813–78), recommending to the US government that native people be encouraged to cattle ranch rather than grow crops, thinking this would be a modicum more palatable to nomads, and asked for Garrison's blessing.[133]

The components of cultural genocide were catalogued in APS correspondence, if not all condemned. In 1887, Chesson drafted a summary about Aboriginal people's conditions in Western Australia. Whereas he identified Aborigines' work in the pearl fisheries as 'a downright system of slavery', inland 'the natives are gradually being exterminated' yet 'the rifle is seldom used for such purposes'. Ostensibly, he wrote, 'the great majority of settlers deal kindly with the natives' but overlook that 'something more than this is due to the original owners of the soil'. Native camps near white settlements provided seasonal labour for the men as shepherds and teamsters on sheep and cattle stations, while Aboriginal women were employed in settlers' households as nannies, laundresses, and maids.[134] A long-term observer of this practice bemoaned that these populations were the dejected remnants of those massacred in the hinterland, on whom 'syphilis and the rum bottle speedily finish the work of the Snider carbine'.[135] Meanwhile, the Bishop of Perth proposed 'to get hold of the children' of Aborigines in the Gascoyne River region, 'who, if taken at a sufficiently early age, are susceptible to civilising influences'.[136] The spectre of residential schools loomed: neither evangelical anti-slavery proponents nor more ecumenical members of the APS were disposed to counter such schemes, and the reckoning for this form of Bible Politics draws a long tail to the present.[137]

In 1862, Robert N. Fowler (a banker and Conservative politician), Isbister, and J.J. Kelley (a Mohawk) accompanied Chesson to hear his lecture 'The Treatment of Natives in Our Colonies'. Dr Hodgkin of the APS took the chair. Chesson riffed on Paul's remarks before the Areopagus that '[God] hath made of one blood all men' (Acts 17:26). This necessitated the APS' commitment 'to protect the settlers' hut or house as well as the natives' wigwam or kraal'. Chesson argued that if his auditors 'put themselves in the position of the aborigines, and saw a strong nation send men to take the most fertile of their land, and to drive them away, then they could understand the feelings of those poor people who originally inhabited our colonies'.[138] This call for radical empathy departs from the litany of facts that Quakers presented in response to the 1837 Parliamentary Select Committee on Aboriginal Tribes. They had acknowledged the 'wanton and wholesale murders', appropriation of livelihoods, fatalities among those defending their way of life, disease, and famine that 'reduced whole tribes to the lowest state of wretchedness and degradation' in order to perpetuate 'a trading system of the most fraudulent description'.[139] Yet that was empirical, not empathetic.

If the APS and a plethora of allied single-issue committees were the information gateways, what more could they do than remonstrate? Information alone was not sufficiently persuasive: it needed to translate into action. This required multi-scalar thinking involving performative acts across great distance, perhaps incremental in nature yet consequential in compass. As the repertoire of atrocities became better understood – culminating with Lemkin – the repertoire of activist redress modulated. For the most part, redress remains a post hoc repertoire (consider, for example, the work of the International Criminal Court and the UN High Commissioner for Refugees). However, prevention and amelioration can be regarded as ongoing adaptations fostered by organisations such as the UN Office on Genocide Prevention and the Responsibility to Protect, Alliance against Genocide, International Alert, Ligue Internationale Contre le Racisme et l'Antisémitisme, and organisations that promote the study and understanding of historical genocides.

Much of what came across Chesson's desk bore witness to the many inflections of genocide and sought a more consistent and effective check in Parliament over British and colonial governments' executive actions, half measures, and failures to act. As Sir Wilfrid Lawson, MP (1829–1906), put it, '"Calling attention" to these sort of things does no good – or very little': only questions that can be answered aye or no in Parliament can bring about direct censure from Britain on the colonial authorities.[140] That was a rather narrow way to approach problems, yet it resulted in a speech act that ruled out prevarication even when it did not rule in an ethical position. Chesson's roots in the Peace Party are reflected by his being a signatory to Herbert Spencer's 1881 circular for the Anti-Aggression League, which 'urged that justice shall be the fundamental principle of our dealings with other communities, whether weak or strong; and that in cases of *unavoidable* collision with what are called barbarous peoples, operations shall be carried on with the same regard for humanity and the usages of war as are observed in conflicts between civilized nations'.[141] In parallel, the international legal community began to work on similar issues but expanded its compass to consider the stance – and responsibility – of third parties, those not directly engaged in war or aggression.

At a meeting of the Association for the Reform and Codification of the Law of Nations in 1876, Joseph Parrish Thompson (1819–79) presented a paper on international law acknowledging empires' failure to act in the interest of humanity, either through territorial acquisition or through commercial exploitation. He expressed the view that Aboriginal occupants of colonies have a 'presumptive right of property in the soil' that dates back to 'the memory of man'. When 'a barbarous and despotic government' fails to care for the weak or free the oppressed, other governments have 'a settled right' to interfere. Thompson asserted on behalf of his fellow jurists: 'The time is ripe for a concerted movement in advance; for a union of Christian powers to make impossible such out-breaks of violence, rapine, and cruelty as in recent years have brought savagery into direct conflict with civilization.' Britain's suppression of the transatlantic slave trade and United States' curtailment of Mediterranean piracy provided precedents for international action against massacres in China and Dahomey, and in response to Turkish outrages during the Bulgarian revolution of 1876. The need to support freedom of conscience as 'one of the prime rights of humanity ... and religious freedom as a naked human right' applied equally whether citing Christian failures to intervene in the United States' treatment of its native peoples or the burning of Ashanti villages.[142]

Reports of attacks on Bulgarian Orthodox Christians by Ottomans rallied British sympathy to a degree achieved by few other contemporaneous causes. Deaths were estimated at 18,000 to 30,000. As Gary J. Bass notes, 'This was an age before the term *mass grave* was a staple of the news, a time when British readers might have still believed that humans did not do such things', and first-hand reportage in the *Daily News* made feelings run high.[143] Gladstone, former Liberal leader and out of government at the time, angled back into public life through his pamphlet *The Bulgarian Horrors and the Question of the East*, which promoted this cause as 'a virtuous passion' in the face of the Conservative government's inaction. The pamphlet sold a staggering 200,000 copies.[144] Gladstone's outdoor rally on 9 September 1876 (three days after the pamphlet's publication) and subsequent tour garnered outrage and positioned him as the leader of a popular front. This reaction to despotism and intolerance was the first of a series of abuses of individual rights brought to widespread attention.[145]

Gladstone's Greenwich constituents – 6,000 to 7,000 men including workers from the Arsenal and shipyards – crowded behind an area cordoned off for 2,500 ticket holders. The liberal press was disposed to be sympathetic. Indeed, the depiction of the Blackheath rally in the *Illustrated London News* shows Gladstone rousing the crowd, a row of women seated at the front of the hustings, and Chesson standing in the lower right foreground, taking notes along with the rest of the press corps (Figure 4.6).[146] Gladstone's speech followed several others, endorsing the motion for an address to the queen. The same day, meetings were held at Bridgewater, Wakefield, Norwich, and Cambridge; on the ensuing Sunday appeals were made from pulpits in London, Cambridge, Dover, and elsewhere; and at conferences of Baptists and Primitive Methodists resolutions were adopted imploring the foreign minister to 'prevent a recurrence of the barbarities'.[147] This launched the movement. Chesson, who had been reading about the 'Eastern Question' since 1854, was one of the honorary secretaries of the Eastern Question Association (formed in December 1876), which published a pamphlet series on the scope of Turkish misrule, religious and commercial facets of British policy toward Turkey and Russia, and the ethnic makeup of the Ottoman Empire. He contributed a pamphlet on Turkey's culpability that emphasises the futility of a series of proclamations from the Porte, starting in 1846, outlawing different vectors of the slave trade. Prohibition had the effect of discounting the value of some enslaved people but in no other way impeding their trafficking. Circassians who survived the genocide of 1864 (perpetrated by Russians claiming the homelands of Circassians, Abkhaz, Abazin, Chechen, and Ossetian communities in the northeastern region of the Black Sea, roughly equating to modern Georgia) flooded into Ottoman lands as refugees; many ended up as slaves, and some as slaveholders. Turks also pursued the ruthless and continuous capture of peoples from the African interior, the Upper Nile, and lands bordering the Indian Ocean, who were trafficked in Khartoum,

OPEN-AIR MEETING AT BLACKHEATH TO HEAR MR. GLADSTONE ON THE TURKISH ATROCITIES.

Figure 4.6    Open-air meeting at Blackheath to hear Mr Gladstone on the Turkish atrocities. *Illustrated London News*, 16 September 1876, 173.

ports of the Red Sea, and Tripoli. The forbidden markets were clandestine, or entirely private, and 'all visitors to Constantinople who have made inquiries into this subject will confirm me when I say that although the external signs of human servitude are only too apparent, it is extremely difficult to discover how or where the contraband trade is carried on'. African men were castrated to serve in harems, though most died from the procedure. Many women and girls were, in effect, prostitutes sold from one master to the next. Circassian girls, brought out of the settled districts at ten or twelve years of age, sold for £200 as servants, and then at age sixteen or seventeen were moved on for the price of £1,000 into polygamous marriages, without parents or brothers to advocate for them.[148]

As the regional crises intensified, public meetings on the Eastern Question decreased in frequency yet still garnered large numbers of attendees. Jingoistic mobs opposed them, but petitions for British action were ongoing: '124,657 people eventually signed one or another of the petitions opposing the government's proposal that parliament should grant a vote of credit for military preparations against Russia'.[149] The APS memorialised the foreign minister (the Marquis of Salisbury), its members exercising their combative pens, and a coalition of signatories issued a series of letters, published as *The Kidnapping of Bulgarians during the Russo-Turkish War*, 'in the hope that it will attract attention to a subject which emphatically calls for an expression of public opinion'.[150] The signatories – Chesson and Edward B. Eastwick (1814–83, linguist, diplomat with experience in Persia, former secretary to Lord Salisbury, and MP) for the APS, and Edmund Sturge and Joseph Cooper for the BFASS – urged action from Britain on behalf of thousands of kidnapped Bulgarians taken into captivity by retreating Bashi-Bazouks (Ottoman mercenaries), directing British Consuls 'throughout Turkey, Asia Minor, Arabia, Egypt, Syria, Crete, all other Turkish islands in the Levant, and also in Cyprus', to 'draw closer the bonds which ought to unite England with the Christian populations of the East'.[151]

This exchange of letters shows Salisbury, consistently immune to concern over the fates of children lost during the Turkish army's passage through Bulgaria, initially arguing that martial conditions create general confusion. His interlocutors incrementally established their case through presentation of first-hand accounts. Sir Austen Henry Layard (by January 1879 the British ambassador at Constantinople) reported that the Turkish minister of the interior ordered that all Christian children be given up, and requested names of kidnapped children and young women so that he could better facilitate their release. Lord Tenterden claimed that only three cases were validated. Meanwhile, fearful for his own security, the Greek informant to the APS, M. Spanidous (who had investigated cases in conjunction with the Bulgarian exarchate and Greek patriarchate at Constantinople), retreated to Philippopolis (Plovdiv) and requested Ambassador Layard's assurance of immunity from retribution by the Turkish secret police before returning to the Porte. Layard, who had met with Spanidous before his departure, accused him (without proof) of delusions and spurious claims. Spanidous' business associate was detained, his house was visited, and his brother's personal property was seized by the police. The sparring over facts – both Spanidous' veracity and the circumstances of the kidnappings – was only rhetorically resolved by concluding the pamphlet with Spanidous' list of eighty-two Bulgarians (aged three to twenty) taken from their homes in the Eski-Zaghra district (Stara Zagora) and another list of 226 Bulgarians (mostly aged two to eighteen) whom he rescued from Circassians, Turks, 'Gypsies', soldiers, and refugees.[152]

Both the Bulgarian and the Bosnian and Herzegovinian cases were explicit outcries about Christian enslavement in which 'white slavery' and the suffering of Christians was understood as especially worthy of action. As the preface to *The Kidnapping of Bulgarians* put it, 'It is monstrous that such a traffic should be tolerated by the civilized world.'[153] Gladstone catapulted back into popularity, opposing the Tory government's pro-Turkish policy while stoking concern about the resumption of war against Russia. As Gladstone travelled back and forth to Midlothian, thousands assembled at railway stations to see him pass through. His speeches were printed verbatim, and as many as 250,000 words were transcribed by the *Times* in a six-month period. As Jonathan Parry puts it, evangelicals, Nonconformists, and Anglicans

> gloried in the 'romantic and religious glamour' surrounding Gladstone's attack on those 'strongholds of Anti-Christ,' 'the obscene empires of Mammon and Belial.' The amount of zeal summoned up could not but give the impression that popular fervour—or 'King Mob,' as Fitzjames Stephen put it—was being summoned to overthrow, not only a government, but also the traditional style of politics, including the Liberal parliamentary leadership.[154]

Working behind the scenes, not for Gladstone per se but for some of their common causes, Chesson was less partisan in his attention. He lobbied against the trafficking of South Sea Islanders to Queensland and worked with the Social Science Congress to regulate coolie traffic from Hong Kong to Peru.[155] Subsequently, he became honorary secretary of the Society for the Suppression of the Opium Trade in 1874, Afghan Committee in 1878, Greek Committee in 1879, Madagascar Committee in 1882, and South African Committee in 1883.[156] He compassionately extended his reach to all these manifestations of human trafficking and misery and, moreover, to their frequent analogue, genocide, no matter who the victims were. In a sense, the seriality of his investments – and the repetition of his tactics, such as working with overlapping networks – marks an emphasis in how activism had evolved. The insights of the transatlantic abolition and emancipation movements were intact, and 'movement spillover' included the lesson that factionalism among liberals was to be avoided.[157] Domestic causes of free trade and Reform were intrinsic to the ideology, and the globalism of the British India Society had been indelibly absorbed.

In *The Art of Moral Protest*, James M. Jasper argues that 'protestors are not simply moral innovators, they also transform tactics and organizational forms'.[158] In relation to the high feelings generated by politicians' public speeches, Chesson's tactics emphasised presenting facts, refuting generalities, and citing those who could bear witness. Without the ability to bring eyewitnesses – freedom-seekers or the formerly enslaved – before audiences and readers to sponsor foreigners' speaking tours or endorse survivors' memoirs, this phase of anti-slavery and anti-genocide activism (imbued with anti-colonial and anti-racist convictions) sometimes traded the premium on liveness for a sense of moralised proximity vis-à-vis Europe. If Britons could envision the personal and ethnic catastrophes of fellow Christian Europeans, perhaps this could activate empathy for Zulus and Basutos in the Cape, Afghans in the Near East, and Chinese and Indian coolies in Mauritius and Demerara. Chains of reliable information deployed by key individuals remained indispensable, but the global processes of imperialism and colonialism could, perhaps, be tempered by oppositional rhetoric inspired by counter-hegemonic globalisation to 'help citizens think through their moral and cognitive practices'.[159] Short of this, as Chesson argued in a 1872 lecture about coolie labourers in Demerara, 'we may as well rub our eyes and wonder what has become of our political economy, our Bill of Rights, our supposed capacity for wise administration, our constitutional love of freedom and equality before the law, and all the other paraphernalia of free institutions and liberal ideas, which the Briton is supposed to carry with him, as part of his stock-in-trade, wherever he may go on the face of the globe'.[160]

To be a liberal in this era meant not just to have a set of beliefs but to *use them* wherever Britain had sway, even if one never left the British Isles. In Santos' sense of prism knowledge, the struggle was multifaceted, the need for questions constant, and the potential for rupture immanent. This was the essence of human rights activism: a performative ethos that called attention to itself within the activist and without, in a myriad of rhetorical outlets. In addition to grand gestures such as Gladstone's, epic topics – the jockeying of empires, and fates of whole peoples – called for non-epic actions in cooperative politics, organising, leading, asserting empirical and affective connections and synergies, fostering radical empathy, and toiling to emancipate individuals in ways that disarticulated the effects of empires, colonialism, racism, misogyny, and rapacious capitalism.

## Reputations

Activism is consistently at the conjunction of 'social context, political purpose and technological possibility'.[161] Whereas the transatlantic telegraph cable had immediate consequences for human behaviour, ameliorative and preventive organising against genocide had long delayed implementation. Even with a vast store of knowledge – about regional histories and the people who could be called upon for assistance – Chesson's 'ardour for right' could not fully prevail. Still, there were changes. Henry Fox Bourne (1837–1909), the historian of the APS who was present at Chesson's funeral, recalled Chesson's impact a decade after his demise: 'His eloquent protest shamed us out of the too common practice of laying savage settlements in ashes for every infraction of "international law." He humanised our relations with native races, and thus worked in the true interests of imperial amity in his own way.'[162] This took painstaking effort, and even resulted in a protracted illness during 1872 and 1873. Yet Chesson 'was content to perform' what another writer called 'the drudgery of public movements'.[163] This is exactly what he had always aspired to do, and it made him no less integral to others' performance.

Chesson made his mark in both political and journalistic registers. If he strove to empower others before the scenes, *Punch* caught the sense of this. Purporting to quote the *Star*'s 1868 Christmas greeting with a compliment to readers for being 'the best and most thoughtful of the active politicians throughout the empire', Mr Punch offered to join with the *Star* in being overconfident.[164] Leading with confidence, then retiring to the background, was very much Chesson's mien. This runs counter to the only uncomplimentary description of him in his portfolio of obituaries: the *York Herald* described Chesson as 'a plodding, persevering, conscientious man' but not the highest of journalists.[165] Yet at a dinner in his honour two years earlier he was lauded for having 'done more than the reading public is ever likely to know to maintain the dignity and responsibility of journalism. (Loud cheers.)'[166] It is one thing for political colleagues to assert this, and another for his fellow writers. At his death, the National Association of Journalists registered its deep sense of loss.[167] To his colleagues, such as a fellow staff member on the *Daily News*, 'He was always the same genuine, intense, energetic, unremitting, amiable friend and champion of liberty, humanity, and especially of racial justice.'[168] At the funeral, there were tributes from the APS, Rosimi Aladé on behalf of West Africans, and the Armenian Patriotic Association; representatives of the Peace Society, Liberation Society, BFASS, Anti-Opium Society, the Greek Committee, King Jaja of Opobo of Nigeria, and the Women's Suffrage Society; and prominent Liberals, including numerous MPs. And, unusually for the time, there was an attendance of nearly as many women as men at the graveside.[169] Subscribers to a fund for his widow included MPs of the Liberal, Conservative, and Home Rule parties; civil servants and colonial administrators; people who hailed from India, Africa, the United States, France, Germany, Greece, Bulgaria, and Armenia; Roman Catholics, Anglicans, Quakers, Nonconformists, and agnostics; lawyers, journalists, artists, and authors; peers and commoners, male and female; and philanthropists, businessmen, scholars, and clerics.[170]

Sir Charles and Lady Emilia Dilke's (1840–1904) carriage followed the one carrying the Chesson family (Amelia and her eight surviving children, aged thirteen to thirty-one). By this time, the Dilkes and the Chessons owed much to each other. The *Daily News* and *Athenaeum*, which published both Frederick and Amelia's writing, had been owned by Dilke's grandfather.[171] During a prior marriage, Lady Dilke was pegged as the inspiration for Dorothea Brooke, and her scholarly first husband for Casaubon, in George Eliot's (1819–80) *Middlemarch* (1871). She wrote for the *Saturday Review* beginning in the mid-1860s and was fine art editor of the *Academy*, 1873–83. She was equally accomplished as a critic of eighteenth- and nineteenth-century French art and as a public speaker for the women's trades union movement, and so, like Amelia, was a pioneering woman journalist and even more forward facing as an activist. As a prominent Chelsea Liberal, Frederick Chesson championed Charles Dilke's first run for Parliament in the newly created two-member district; in 1868, Dilke was still in his early twenties, and though from a nearly antithetical class background to Chesson the two formed a strong bond. Dilke and his fellow Liberal (Sir Henry Hoare, 1824–94) won handily, with W. H. Russell (the *Times* correspondent famously embedded during the Crimean War, and onboard the *Great Eastern* during the Atlantic Telegraph saga) in a distant third place.[172] The Dilkes and Chessons worked consistently on behalf of women's suffrage. From 1880, the Prince of Wales communicated regularly with Charles Dilke (a republican), relying on his expertise in foreign affairs backed by detailed knowledge of situations on the ground. Throughout Dilke's meteoric rise as a 'constructive radical' in the Liberal Party, then a protracted struggle after being named as a co-respondent in a divorce case, the Chessons were at his side, ardently supporting him and defending his public repute.[173] Charles Dilke endowed the high altar in Chelsea's Holy Trinity Church in memory of his loyal friend and champion, though over time the dedication became as anonymous as the dedicatee.[174]

In 1855, when Chesson worked for the struggling *Empire*, the entire print run of the British daily press was around 70,000, including 50,000 for the *Times*. With the advent of the penny press, of which the *Morning Star* and *Evening Star* were indicative, daily circulation rapidly grew to 330,000, including about 140,000 for the *Telegraph*, persistently the *Star*'s greatest rival. London papers were distributed nationwide by mail trains, supplementing the local titles with regional circulation: by the mid-1860s, for example, the trade had grown so much that Birmingham's six newspapers printed about 250,000 copies per week.[175] While it is true that the *Star* continually struggled until its demise in October 1869, Liberal-leaning papers took nearly half the nationwide market.[176] Within such a volatile market sector, there were casualties along the way. In spring 1856, the morning and evening editions of the *Star* capped at 27,000 daily sales; this gave the Manchester investors, including Bright and Cobden, short-lived gratification, however, for sales were typically 7,000 copies per day and infusions of cash were regularly needed for the operation to break even. From October 1860 through April 1862, the organ published under the conjoint banner of the *Morning Star and Dial*, absorbing the three-penny weekly *Dial* and its 8,000 subscribers, though the publications had contrasting moral and political identities. According to Martin Hewitt, historian of the penny press, even though the *Star* 'was generally more greatly valued than the *Standard* or the *Daily Telegraph* … sales stubbornly refused to reflect this'.[177] Samuel Morley, an investor in the *Star*, also invested in the *Daily News*, which, in 1868, lowered its price from three pennies to a penny. Two years later its circulation reached 150,000, the largest readership of Chesson's career.[178]

In 1865, Chesson edited Richard Cobden's works.[179] In his last two decades, his writing reached more people than ever, and though his name registered in some circles this continued to be unsigned journalism. He persevered in producing the *Colonial Intelligencer, or Aborigines' Friend*, and though his compatriots saw his hand in it all, this too was technically unsigned. The outcome of his words, not his name on them, is what mattered. In a characteristic tone, he noted in his diary: 'Amused by a juggler in a street off the Strand who prepared one of his tricks by saying that he would now show them something they had read of in Charles <u>Dixon's</u> works and in <u>the Evening Star</u>. Such is fame.'[180] Charles Dickens (1812–70), who most recently had published *Our Mutual Friend* (1865), was recognisable despite the elision. Within the *Star*, by contrast, Chesson's name was fainter even if his writerly identity was recognisable to faithful readers.

Activism was perhaps the antithesis of magic tricks. The *Daily News* characterised the work as exacting, taxing, and modest:

> The impression left on the minds of those who came in contact with Mr. Chesson was that, on the whole, he rather liked sitting up all night to write to people all over Great Britain on some great public question. It seemed equally agreeable to him to muster a deputation from the ends of the kingdom, and, then having found them a listener in the person of a Minister of State, and supplied them with arguments to lay before him, quietly to take a position in the background. So long as the facts were there, Mr. Chesson cared little for the glory of giving them their setting. They were at anybody's service who knew how to deal with them.

To be a champion of liberty, and 'especially of racial justice', took quotidian acts.[181] As one memorialist put it, 'his work was always real but unostentatious', marked by 'cooperation absolutely devoid of self-seeking show'. Nevertheless, 'he was undoubtedly a great force in the advocacy of the rights of the Native Races'.[182]

Through countless nights, in heavy seas and oppressive calms, momentous effort was actuated by the smallest gestures of a hand – scrawling across paper or tapping out its message on a silver thimble to travel the seabed – to an unseen reader. The minute performances closed distance, coordinated actions, and enhanced empathy.

## Notes

1  Sergeant, Lewis. 'F.W. Chesson.' *The Leisure Hour: An Illustrated Magazine for Home Reading*, October 1888: 677–8.

2  Sergeant was connected to Chesson through the *Athenaeum* and the Greek Committee.

3  Jasper, *Art of Moral Protest*, 373, 215 (qtd.), and see 376, 329.

4  [Frederick Chesson], 'The Close of the Paris Exhibition.' *Nonconformist*, 6 November 1867, 911.

5  Frederick Chesson's diary, 26 April 1865, REAS 11/12, JRL.

6  Field, Cyrus W. *Ocean Telegraphy: The Twenty-Fifth Anniversary of the Organization of the First Company Ever Formed to Lay an Ocean Cable*. New York: March 10, 1879. New York: privately published, 1879: 5–6, 34.

7  Bright, Charles. *The Story of the Atlantic Cable*. New York: D. Appleton, 1903: 217–18.

8  Therborn, Göran. 'Globalizations: Dimensions, Historical Waves, Regional Effects, Normative Governance.' *International Sociology* 15, no. 2 (2000): 161–2; and Marks, Steven G. *The Information Nexus: Global Capitalism from the Renaissance to the Present*. Cambridge: Cambridge University Press, 2016: 129.

9  Bright, *Story*, 46–75; and Standage, Tom. *The Victorian Internet: The Remarkable Story of the Telegraph and the Nineteenth Century's On-Line Pioneers*. New York: Walker, 1998: 78–94.

10  *Times*, 5 August 1858, qtd. in Bright, *Story*, 138.

11  Bright, *Story*, 148; Standage, *Victorian Internet*, 82; and Dibner, Bern. *The Atlantic Cable*. Norwalk, CT: Burndy Library, 1959: 39–41.

12  Dibner, *Atlantic Cable*, 43; and Bright, *The Story*, 151.

13  Frederick Chesson's diary, 15 June 1866, REAS 11/13, JRL.

14  [Frederick Chesson], *Morning Star*, 18 July 1866, 4.

15  Schwoch, James. *Wired into Nature: The Telegraph and the North American Frontier*. Urbana: University of Illinois Press, 2018: 107.

16  Frederick Chesson's diary, 15 June 1866, REAS 11/13, JRL.

17  [Frederick Chesson], *Morning Star*, 2 July 1866, 6.

18  'The Atlantic Cable.' *Daily News*, 9 July 1866, 5.

19  'The Atlantic Cable.' *Daily News*, 9 July 1866, 5; Frederick Chesson's diary, notation for 1–5 July 1866, REAS 11/13, JRL.

20  John Tenniel, 'A Word to the Mermaids.' *Punch*, 5 August 1865, 47.

21  This refers to an 'ingenious signal code', considerably more efficient than the Morse system, that could transmit in nearly any language. [Frederick Chesson], 'Departure of the Great Eastern.' *Morning Star*, 2 July 1866, 6.

22  'Illustrations of the Atlantic Telegraph Expedition.' *Illustrated London News*, 28 July 1866, 94.

23  'The Atlantic Telegraph Expedition.' *Daily News*, 29 June 1866, 3; and 'The Atlantic Cable.' *Daily News*, 9 July 1866, 5.

24  Bright, *Story*, 202; Russell, William Howard. *The Atlantic Telegraph*. London: Day and Son, 1866: 59; and 'The Atlantic Telegraph: Picking Up the 1865 Cable.' *Morning Star*, 11 September 1866, 5.

25  Dibner, *Atlantic Cable*, 83.

26  '*Quae regio in terris nostri non plena laboris?*' from Virgil's *Aeneid*, 1:460, qtd. in Bright, *Story*, 212.

27  Frederick Chesson's diary, 4 March 1868, REAS 11/15, JRL.

28  Standage, *Victorian Internet*, 89; Garbade, Kenneth D. and William L. Silber. 'Technology, Communication and the Performance of Financial Markets: 1840–1975.' *Journal of Finance* 33, no. 3 (1978): 826–8.

29  Osterhammel, Jürgen. *The Transformation of the World: A Global History of the Nineteenth Century*. Princeton, NJ: Princeton University Press, 2014: 719; and Bright, *Story*, 219–22.

30  Wenzlhuemer, Roland. *Connecting the Nineteenth-Century World: The Telegraph and Globalization*. Cambridge: Cambridge University Press, 2013: 90; and Weller, Toni and David Bawden. 'Individual Perceptions: A New Chapter on Victorian Information History.' *Library History* 22, no. 2 (2006): 145–8.

31  Wenzlhuemer, *Connecting the Nineteenth-Century World*, 41–8.

32  Turner, Mark W. 'Periodical Time in the Nineteenth Century.' *Media History* 8, no. 2 (2002): 186.

33  Hardt and Negri, *Empire*, 356.

34  Bass, Gary J. *Freedom's Battle: The Origins of Humanitarian Intervention*. New York: Alfred A. Knopf, 2008: 35.

35  Wenzlhuemer, *Connecting the Nineteenth-Century World*, 78–83; and Headrick, Daniel R. *The Tools of Empire: Technology and European Imperialism in the Nineteenth Century*. New York: Oxford University Press, 1981.

36  E. Casalis (St Jacques) [Société des Missions Évangéliques chez les Peuples non Chrétiens, Paris] to Frederick Chesson, 22 August 1880, C128/66, Bodleian Library.

37  McLuhan, Marshall. *Understanding Media: The Extensions of Man*. 1964. Reprinted, New York: McGraw-Hill, 1994: 250, 252.

38  McLuhan, *Understanding Media*, 256–7.

39  [Frederick Chesson], 'The Negro Question in Birmingham.' *Nonconformist*, 23 October 1867, 871. After the war, Britain did nothing to aid Southern reconstruction; the onus was entirely on philanthropy. See Bolt, Christine. *The Anti-Slavery Movement and Reconstruction: A Study in Anglo-American Co-Operation 1833–77*. Oxford: Oxford University Press, 1969: 33.

40  Hewitt, *Dawn of the Cheap Press*, 142.

41  Hewitt, *Dawn of the Cheap Press*, 144.

42  [Frederick Chesson], [Leader], *Manchester Guardian*, 20 April 1861, 4.

43  See Frederick Chesson's diary, 22 November to 13 December 1862, REAS 11/09, JRL. For committee members, see Eyre, John Edward. *Facts and Documents Relating to the Alleged Rebellion in Jamaica and the Measures of Repression; including Notes of the Trial of Mr. Gordon*. Jamaica Papers, no. 1. London: Jamaica Committee, 1866, 94–7. See also Bolt, *Anti-Slavery Movement*, 39–41.

44  Oldfield, *Ties That Bind*, 169.

45  Campbell, Duncan Andrew. *English Public Opinion and the American Civil War*. Woodbridge, Suffolk: Royal Historical Society, 2004: 222–3.

46  'Negro Emancipation: The Meeting in Exeter Hall.' *Illustrated London News*, 7 February 1863, 154.

47  'John to Jonathan: An Address Delivered in the Music Hall, Boston, on the 11th of October, 1870.' *Macmillan's Magazine*, December 1870: 87.

48  Frederick Chesson's diary, 31 January 1863, REAS 11/10, JRL.

49  'Negro Emancipation.' *Morning Star*, 4 February 1863, 3. See also Bolt, *Anti-Slavery Movement*, 29–30.

50  'Negro Emancipation: Another Great Demonstration.' *Morning Star*, 19 February 1863, 2.

51  Frederick Chesson's diary, 21 March 1863, REAS 11/10, JRL. See also Bolt, *Anti-Slavery Movement*, 55–7.

52  'Negro Emancipation: Great Meeting of Trades Unionists.' *Morning Star*, 27 March 1863, 6.

53  'Negro Emancipation', 6. Dilke and Mill thought highly of Odger, and Dilke supported the expenses of his Stafford by-election run in 1869 (though Odger lost this election, as well as the 1870 Southwark election). Jenkins, Roy. *Sir Charles Dilke: A Victorian Tragedy*. London: Collins, 1958: 44.

54  J. Sella Martin, letter to the editor, 'Help for the Freedmen in America.' *Daily News*, 10 April 1863, 4.

55  'Negro Emancipation.' *Morning Star*, 2 October 1863, 2. See also DuBois, W. E.B. *Black Reconstruction in America: An Essay toward a History of the Part Which Black Folk Played in the Attempt to Reconstruct Democracy in America, 1860–1880*. New York, Russell and Russell, 1935: 55–83.

56  Percival Leigh, 'The Offence is Rank.' *Punch*, 7 November 1863, 194.

57  William Evans, P.A. Taylor, W.T. Malleson, and Frederick Chesson, letter to the editor, 'Dissolution of the Emancipation Society', August 1865, rpt. in the *Anti-Slavery Reporter*, 1 September 1865, 228. See also Frederick Chesson's diary, 14 April 1863, REAS 11/10, JRL.

58  Shirley Brooks, 'A Friends' Meeting.' *Punch*, 28 April 1866, 180. See also Bolt, *Anti-Slavery Movement*, 83–113.

59 Esquith, Stephen H. *Intimacy and Spectacle: Liberal Theory as Political Education.* Ithaca, NY: Cornell University Press, 1994: 158–9.

60 'Star-Gazing Extraordinary.' *Punch*, 26 April 1862, 165.

61 '*Facit Indignatio Versum.*' *Punch*, 18 January 1862, 22.

62 'Sunday Reading.' *Punch*, 25 January 1862, 40. See also Shirley Brooks, 'A Disappointment.' *Punch*, 27 September 1862, 128.

63 Shirley Brooks, 'A Reading by Star-Light.' *Punch*, 17 March 1866, 108.

64 Bolt, *Anti-Slavery Movement*, 160–1.

65 Dilke, Charles Wentworth. *Greater Britain: A Record of Travel in English-Speaking Countries in 1866 and 1867.* 2 Vols. New York: Harper and Brothers, 1869: 1: 29–30.

66 Goddu, *Selling Antislavery*, 235.

67 *Annual Report of the Edinburgh Ladies' Emancipation Society*, 25. On the failure to protect sugar prices, see Bolt, *Anti-Slavery Movement*, 20.

68 Sheller, Mimi. *Democracy after Slavery: Black Publics and Peasant Radicalism in Haiti and Jamaica.* Gainesville: University Press of Florida, 2000: 157–8.

69 Scott, James C. *Domination and the Arts of Resistance: Hidden Transcripts.* New Haven, CT: Yale University Press, 1990: 198.

70 Sheller, *Democracy after Slavery*, 188–95, 213–19.

71 [Frederick Chesson], 'A West India "Insurrection."' *Nonconformist*, 8 November 1865, 903–4.

72 [Chesson], 'A West India "Insurrection."' *Nonconformist*, 8 November 1865, 903–4. See also Underhill, Edward Bean. *The West Indies: Their Social and Religious Condition.* London: Jackson, Walford, and Hodder, 1862: 12.

73 Frederick Chesson's diary, 17 November 1865, REAS 11/12, JRL.

74 Frederick Chesson's diary, 4 and 12 December 1865, REAS 11/12, JRL.

75 For the latter, see Sheller, *Democracy after Slavery*, 127–46.

76 [Leader], *Times*, 4 November 1865, 9. See also 'Insurrection in Jamaica.' *Times*, 3 November 1865, 10; and [Leader], *Times*, 3 November 1865, 6.

77 [Chesson], 'A West India "Insurrection"', 903–4.

78 [Frederick Chesson], 'The Negro Rebellion.' *Nonconformist*, 15 November 1865, 923.

79 Sheller, *Democracy after Slavery*, 221.

80 Levien, Sidney Levo. *A Chronicle of the Rebellion in Jamaica in the Year of Our Lord 1865.* Kingston, 1865: 11.

81 Kostal, R.W. *A Jurisprudence of Power: Victorian Empire and the Rule of Law.* Oxford: Oxford University Press, 2005: 34, 40; and Bolt, *Anti-Slavery Movement*, 38.

82 McCarthy, Justin. *A History of Our Own Times, from the Ascension of Queen Victoria to the General Election of 1880.* Vol. 3. London: Chatto and Windus, 1880: 361.

83 [Leader], *Nonconformist*, 22 November 1865, 942.

84 'Library of Fiction.' *Punch*, 24 February 1866, 77.

85 The fact-finding mission consisted of Sir Henry Storks (1811–74, briefly the colonial secretary replacing Eyre), Russell Gurney (1804–78, a Conservative MP with strong reform credentials), and J. B. Maule (1818–89, a barrister). Jamaica Royal Commission, *Report of the Jamaica Royal Commission: Minutes*

*of Evidence Taken before the Jamaica Royal commission*. London: H.M. Stationery Office, British Parliamentary Papers, 1866.

86 Frederick Chesson's diary, 12 April 1867, REAS 11/14, JRL. See also 16 February 1866, REAS 11/13.

87 [Frederick Chesson], 'The Report of the Jamaica Commission.' *Nonconformist*, 20 June 1866, 499–500.

88 Kostal, *Jurisprudence of Power*, 29.

89 Levien, *Chronicle of the Rebellion*, 9. Levien records that Colonel Hobbs seized Paul Bogle's armour-bearer, a young boy. Hobbs tied the boy to his horse, put a revolver to his head, and compelled him to identify rebels, who were then shot (16).

90 Frederick Chesson's diary, 24 January 1866, REAS 11/13, JRL.

91 Underhill, *West Indies*, 192–4. See also Frederick Chesson's diary, 9 March 1862, REAS 11/09, JRL.

92 Sheller, *Democracy after Slavery*, 190.

93 [Frederick Chesson], 'Jamaica.' *Nonconformist*, 17 January 1866, 51.

94 Frederick Chesson's diary, 21 and 30 December 1865, REAS 11/12, JRL.

95 Frederick Chesson's diary, 30 January 1866, REAS 11/13, JRL.

96 [Frederick Chesson], 'The House of Commons.' *Sheffield and Rotherham Independent*, 24 February 1866, 6.

97 Frederick Chesson's diary, 19 October 1866, REAS 11/14, JRL.

98 [Frederick Chesson], 'The Prosecution of Mr. Eyre.' *Nonconformist*, 23 January 1867, 71–2; and Harrison, Frederic. *Martial Law: Six Letters to the Daily News*. Jamaica Papers, no. 5. London: Jamaica Committee, 1867.

99 Kostal, *Jurisprudence of Power*, 16. Nelson rose to the rank of brigadier-general.

100 Kostal, *Jurisprudence of Power*, 17, 64.

101 See Lorimer, Douglas A. 'Race, Science and Culture: Historical Continuities and Discontinuities, 1850–1914.' In *The Victorians and Race*, edited by Shearer West, 12–33. Farnham, UK: Ashgate, 1996: 13.

102 On this historiography, see Kostal, *Jurisprudence of Power*, 498.

103 'The Lancet.' *Lancet* 86, no. 2205 (1865): 626–7.

104 [Frederick Chesson], 'The Famine in Orissa.' *Nonconformist*, 7 August 1867, 647–8. The figures cited in the text are Chesson's.

105 [Chesson], 'The Famine in Orissa', 647–8. See also Mohanty, Bidyut. 'Orissa Famine of 1866: Demographic and Economic Consequences.' *Economic and Political Weekly* 28, no. 1 (1993): 55–66.

106 Sarah Remond, letter, 'The Negro Race in America.' *Daily News*, 22 November 1866, 4.

107 T. Perronet Thompson (Blackheath) to Frederick Chesson, October 1857, C149/22 23, Bodleian Library.

108 [Frederick Chesson], 'Mr. Eyre in the Blue-Books.' *Nonconformist*, 12 June 1867, 487.

109 During the first three months of 1866, the Jamaica Committee expended £3,000. Frederick Chesson's diary, 18 May 1866, REAS 11/13, JRL.

110 Frederick Chesson's diary, 3 March 1868, 5 April 1870, and 27 May 1870, REAS 11/15 and 11/16, JRL.

111 Bernard Semmell, qtd. in Bolt, *Anti-Slavery Movement*, 52.

112 Bolt, *Anti-Slavery Movement*, 50–1, 113.

113 Hartman, Saidiya V. *Scenes of Subjection: Terror, Slavery, and Self-Making in Nineteenth-Century America*. New York: Oxford University Press, 1997: 6.

114 'Mr. F.W. Chesson.' *Athenaeum*, 5 May 1888, 568. See also Bourne, H.R. Fox. *The Aborigines Protection Society: Chapters in Its History*. London: P.S. King, 1899: 25.

115 'The Late Mr. F.W. Chesson.' *Nonconformist and Independent*, 3 May 1888, 411.

116 Frederick Chesson's diary, 19 October 1869, REAS 11/16, JRL.

117 Frederick Chesson to Rev. T. Phillips, 30 November 1870, C149/370, Bodleian Library.

118 Cooper translated and wrote the preface to Étienne Félix Berlioux's *The Slave Trade in Africa in 1872* (London: Edward Marsh, 1872), and subsequently wrote *The Lost Continent, or Slavery and the Slave-Trade in Africa* (London: Longmans, Green, 1875). See also Cooper, Joseph. *Observations on the Asiatic Slave-Trade*. London: Longmans, Green, 1875 and Cooper, Joseph. *Turkey and Egypt: Past and Present State in Relation to Africa*. London: Samuel Harris, 1876.

119 Frederick Chesson to Mr Cooper, 30 December 1879, C149/348, Bodleian Library.

120 Santos, *End of the Cognitive Empire*, 140.

121 Scott, *Domination*, 190.

122 Conquergood, Dwight. 'Performance Studies Interventions and Radical Research.' *TDR: The Drama Review* 46, no. 2 (2002): 152–3.

123 Swaisland, Charles. 'The Aborigines Protection Society, 1837–1909.' *Slavery and Abolition* 21, no. 2 (2000): 276.

124 Fitzmaurice, Andrew. 'Anticolonialism in Western Political Thought: The Colonial Origins of the Concept of Genocide.' In *Empire, Colony, Genocide: Conquest, Occupation, and Subaltern Resistance in World History*, edited by A. Dirk Moses, 55–80. New York: Berghahn Books, 2008: 70.

125 Alexander Isbister to F.W. Chesson, undated [filed in sequence 1857], C/138/227, Bodleian Library.

126 Robert Lester to F.W. Chesson, 27 September 1884, C/140/100, Bodleian Library.

127 Robert Lester to F.W. Chesson, 10 May 1881, C/140/88, Bodleian Library.

128 Quotations from Lemkin, 'Axis Rules in Occupied Europe', in the Introduction to Moses, Dirk, ed. *Empire, Colony, Genocide: Conquest, Occupation, and Subaltern Resistance in World History*. New York: Berghahn Books, 2008: 17, 13.

129 Docker, John. 'Are Settler-Colonies Inherently Genocidal? Rereading Lemkin.' In *Empire, Colony, Genocide*, edited by Moses, 90–4. For letters on these subjects, see Bodleian correspondence of the APS, especially MSS classes C122, 134, 135, 138, 140, 142, and 164.

130 Kiernan, Ben. *Blood and Soil: A World History of Genocide and Extermination from Sparta to Darfur*. New Haven, CT: Yale University Press, 2007: 264,

303, 308; Heartfield, *Aborigines' Protection Society*, 51–2; and F.W. Chesson to Sir Arthur Hamilton-Gordon (Governor of Fiji), 9 June 1876 and 19 January 1877, BL Add MS 49237, British Library.

131 Lawson, Tom. *The Last Man: A British Genocide in Tasmania*. London: I.B. Tauris, 2014: 203, 205.

132 Dilke, *Greater Britain*, 1:221.

133 Frederick Chesson to William Lloyd Garrison, 22 June 1877, MS A.1.2, v.39, 73A, Boston Public Library.

134 [Frederick Chesson], draft of note, 1887, C149/386, Bodleian Library. See also *Colonial Intelligencer*, April 1887, 395; and David Carly (Perth, Australia) [to Frederick Chesson], 22 October 1884, part of a series of Carly's letters dated 1883–4 and 1891 stipulating physical abuses, rapes, starvation, poisonings, and shootings, including attacks on infants in their mothers' arms, C128/82, Bodleian Library.

135 [A British citizen] to Sir Arthur Hamilton Gordon (Governor of New Zealand), forwarded to the APS, 23 September 1882, C/135/107–107a, Bodleian Library.

136 [Frederick Chesson's hand], draft of note, C149/386, Bodleian Library. See also *Colonial Intelligencer*, April 1887, 395.

137 See Tatz, Colin. 'The Destruction of Aboriginal Society in Australia.' In *Genocide of Indigenous Peoples*, edited by Samuel Totten and Robert K. Hitchcock, vol. 8, 87–116. New Brunswick, NJ: Transaction, 2011. Chesson approved of efforts to educate all colonial subjects in English, and to supplant Native folkways with English customs and beliefs. See his lecture read to the Liverpool Science Congress, 17 October 1876, rpt. as 'The Education of Native Races in British Colonies.' *Colonial Intelligencer*, 1877, 345–55.

138 'The Treatment of Natives in Our Colonies.' *South London Chronicle*, 29 March 1862, 5.

139 *Information Respecting the Aborigines*, v–vi.

140 W. Lawson to Frederick Chesson, 26 November 1880, C/140/53–54, Bodleian Library.

141 Herbert Spencer, printed circular, annotated 20 October 1881, C/149/392–392a, Bodleian Library.

142 Thompson, Joseph Parrish. *An Essay toward Principles of International Law to Govern the Intercourse of Christian with Non-Christian Peoples*. Berlin: W. Gronau, 1876: 5–6, 12, 16, 19.

143 Bass, *Freedom's Battle*, 257, 259 (qtd.).

144 Gladstone, William Ewart. *The Bulgarian Horrors and the Question of the East*. London: John Murray, 1876. See also Jenkins, *Liberal Ascendancy*, 154.

145 Biagini, 'Radicalism and Liberty', 101–24.

146 'Mr. Gladstone at Blackheath.' *Morning Post*, 11 September 1876, 6; 'Mr. Gladstone on the Turkish Atrocities.' *Sheffield Independent*, 11 September 1876, 3; and Frederick Chesson, 'The Turkish Atrocities in Bulgaria.' 11 September 1876, *Daily News*, 2.

147 [Leader], *Daily News*, 11 September 1876, 4.

148 Chesson, Frederick. *Turkey and the Slave Trade. A Statement of Facts*. Papers on the Eastern Question, no. 7. London: Cassell Petter and Galpin, 1877: 9–10 (qtd.), 14–15. Chesson relies heavily on correspondence addressed to the APS, Cooper's 1872 pamphlet (*The Slave Trade in Africa in 1872*), and diplomatic despatches. See also [Albert, F.E.], 'Domestic Slave-Dealing in Turkey' (this article is signed only F.E.A., but its authorship is confirmed in a letter from F.E. Albert to Frederick Chesson, 21 May 1878, C/123/96, Bodleian Library).

149 Jenkins, *Liberal Ascendancy*, 156.

150 Cecil, Robert. *The Kidnapping of Bulgarians during the Russo-Turkish War*. London: P.S. King and Son, 1879: 3.

151 Cecil, *Kidnapping of Bulgarians*, 8, 5.

152 Cecil, *Kidnapping of Bulgarians*, 19, 25–31.

153 Cecil, *Kidnapping of Bulgarians*, 4.

154 Parry, Jonathan. *The Rise and Fall of Liberal Government in Victoria Britain*. New Haven, CT: Yale University Press, 1993: 277.

155 Frederick Chesson's diary, 18 March 1868, REAS 11/15, and 15 December 1869, REAS 11/16, JRL.

156 Bourne, *Aborigines Protection Society*, 24–43; Brown, J.B. 'Politics of the Poppy: The Society for the Suppression of the Opium Trade, 1874–1916.' *Journal of Contemporary History*. 8, no. 3 (1973): 97–111; and Hionidis, Pandeleiumon. 'Philhellenism and Party Politics in Victorian Britain: The Greek Committee of 1879–1881.' *Historical Review/La Revue Historique* 14 (2017): 141–76.

157 Cammaerts, 'Bart. 'Social Media and Activism.' In *The International Encyclopedia of Digital Communication and Society*. Edited by R. Mansell and P. Hwa, n.p. Oxford: Wiley-Blackwell, 2015.

158 Jasper, *Art of Moral Protest*, 376.

159 Jasper, *Art of Moral Protest*, 373. If true, Chesson's efforts backdate Santos's perspective by 125 years. *End of the Cognitive Empire*, 210.

160 Bourne, *Aborigines Protection Society*, 32.

161 Gillan, Kevin, Jenny Pickerill, and Frank Webster. *Anti-War Activism: New Media and Protest in the Information Age*. Basingstoke: Palgrave Macmillan, 2008: 151.

162 Bourne, *Aborigines Protection Society*, 27.

163 *Daily News*, 7 May 1888, 5.

164 Shirley Brooks, 'Curious Coincidence.' *Punch*, 4 January 1868, 10.

165 'Obituary.' *York Herald*, 1 May 1888, 5.

166 Austin, L.F. *Dinner to Mr. Chesson, at the National Liberal Club, on Friday, July 16th, 1886*. London: National Liberal Club, 1886: xlvi.

167 'Funeral of Mr. F.W. Chesson.' *Daily News*, 7 May 1888, 3.

168 'The Late Mr. F.W. Chesson.' *Daily News*, 7 May 1888, 5.

169 'Funeral of Mr. F.W. Chesson.' *Daily News*, 7 May 1888, 3.

170 'The Chesson Memorial Fund.' *Daily News*, 5 October 1888, 5.

171 Jenkins, *Sir Charles Dilke*, 171.

172  Jenkins, *Liberal Ascendancy*, 44–6.
173  Jenkins, *Sir Charles Dilke*, 143, 169, 208; and Koditschek, Theodore. *Liberalism, Imperialism, and the Historical Imagination: Nineteenth-Century Visions of a Greater Britain*. Cambridge: Cambridge University Press, 2011: 206. For a description of the 'Chesson Defence Committee', which Chesson formed to investigate the case and put facts before the public, see Jenkins, *Sir Charles Dilke*, 330; correspondence from Lady Dilke to Frederick Chesson, BL Add MS 43907 ff 285–316b, British Library; and Nicholls, David. *The Lost Prime Minister: A Life of Sir Charles Dilke*. London: Hambledon Press, 1993: 193.
174  Gwynn, Stephen. *The Life of Rt. Hon., Sir Charles W. Dilke, Bart., M.P.* 2 vols. Completed and edited by Gertrude M. Tuckwell. New York: Macmillan, 1917: 2: 273. The cornerstone for the new church on Sloane Street was laid at the end of May 1888. The altar, carved by Harry Bates, depicts the Entombment of Christ. No marking or plaque indicating the dedication was added. Robina Canavan, email to the author, 24 June 2019.
175  Hewitt, *Dawn of the Cheap Press*, 121.
176  A merger between the *Star* and *Daily News* was posited as early as July 1868. By this time the *Star*'s circulation was about 5,000. Bright had sold out his shares, and new cash could not be raised in the depressed Lancashire economy. Hewitt, *Dawn of the Cheap Press*, 146–7.
177  Hewitt, *Dawn of the Cheap Press*, 125, 134, 138, 139 (qtd.).
178  Bass, *Freedom's Battle*, 35.
179  At the request of Cobden's widow, Chesson coordinated preparation of the editions. North Peat translated the French edition, William Cullen Bryant wrote the introduction to the US edition, and Chesson wrote the introduction to the British edition. See Frederick Chesson's diary, 7 August, 1 September, 19 September, and 24 November 1865, REAS 11/12, JRL; 30 January 1866, REAS 11/13, JRL; and 15 January 1867, REAS 11/14, JRL.
180  Frederick Chesson's diary, 2 November 1867, REAS 11/15, JRL.
181  'The Late Mr. F.W. Chesson.' *Daily News*, 7 May 1888, 5.
182  Lewis Appleton to Alexander Arthur, MP, 3 May 1888, Bodleian MSS Brit. Emp. S.18/C124/223, Bodleian Library.

CHAPTER 5

# *Experiments in Becoming*

From Mississippi and from Nile—
From Baltic, Ganges, Bosphorus,
In England's ark assembled thus
Are friend and guest.
Look down the mighty sunlit aisle,
And see the sumptuous banquet set,
The brotherhood of nations met
Around the feast!
        —William Makepeace Thackeray, 'May-Day Ode'

In his paean to the Crystal Palace, published in May 1851 on the eve of its opening, William Makepeace Thackeray (1811–63) configures it as a great banquet 'in England's ark' presided over by the enthroned 'Queen of innumerable realms'. 'The trophies of her bloodless war', transported down great rivers by 'Gaul and German, Russ and Turk', converge with 'The representatives of man / Here from the far Antipodes, / and from the subject Indian seas' in the 'rare pavilion' erected in Hyde Park.[1] The Great Exhibition – as the congress of the world's resources, products, and peoples – was the epitome of liberal ideology. It welcomed 6 million visitors, including the English working classes, who mined the iron and coal, forged the steel, built the engines, stoked the machines, worked the looms, imprinted the patterns, and sewed the cloth into the garments draped on the majority of visitors' backs.[2]

This magnificent site attracted contestatory proposals for staging counter-performances. The National Association for the Protection of Industry and Capital throughout the British Empire – the wheezing remnant of the ACLL opposition – wanted to make a show of protectionism within the Crystal Palace. Its leader, G.F. Young, MP (1791–1870), was ridiculed by *Punch* as the new Don Quixote. The Great Exhibition proved that his cause was quixotic, eccentric, and doomed.[3]

In a sardonic vein, the US abolitionist Henry Clarke Wright (1797–1870) suggested that if Britain was to show its engineering and France its artistry, the United States should exhibit its ingenuity and sources of wealth too.

> A slave-driver's whip must be there—one that has been buried deep in the flesh of American women, and that is stained with their blood. Thumb-screws, manacles, and fetters, which have encircled the limbs of American *free born* ... a slave-collar.... Representations of American women tied up to be whipped.... Above all, an American slave-auction must be there, with William and Ellen Craft on the block, Henry Clay [1777–1852] as auction-eer, and the American flag floating over it.

Wright's *esprit* went on to propose that at least 100 Black freedom-seekers should be brought from Canada and New England 'to move about among the multitude in the Fair, to be pointed out, to be known, to be welcomed and honoured by Europeans, as among the world's heroes'.[4]

Although the US' department of the palace, in the eastern apse, lacked 'the human instruments' that produced the US 'specimens of cotton, sugar and tobacco', activists created something like Wright's vision on a smaller scale.[5] They staged the impasse over US slavery, the dignity of its victims, and the amity of its transatlantic and multiracial allies at the heart of 'the mighty sunlit aisle' in Hyde Park. William Craft promoted awareness of the traf-ficking of human lives, and Ellen Craft emphasised how 'one drop' of blood stood between any free person and the spectre of shackled bondage. They inserted this tactical performance into 'the symbolic frame' of the world's fair in order to foreground dialectics and call out minoritarian positions.[6]

### Great Exhibitions

William Wells Brown, born into slavery in Kentucky (a Mayflower descen-dent on his father's side with Native American and Black heritage on his mother's), slipped away to freedom aged nineteen. He learned to read and write, became an abolitionist and agent-lecturer for the American Anti-Slavery Society (AASS), and published his autobiography in 1847.[7] The book's success brought him an invitation to the 1849 Peace Conference in Paris, after which he embarked on the British lecture circuit. George Thompson spoke at the meeting to welcome Brown to England, and the favour was returned at Thompson's farewell soirée before he left for his second trip to the United States.[8] Meanwhile, William and Ellen Craft were the first prominent abo-litionists to be targeted by the new Fugitive Slave Law. In 1850, Thompson sought them out in their Boston hiding place and urged them to travel to Britain.[9] Upon alighting in Liverpool, they joined Brown's tour.

All three Garrisonians had notable performative capacities along with activist experience in the United States. Brown's memoir of the early days of his European sojourn repeatedly demonstrates his propensity to observe character and his interest in criticism and critics; he augmented his lectures with a diorama to provide scenery along with his narration; and he later became a playwright. During their joint presentations, Brown would lead by 'giving an analysis of the development of American slavery in the South and prejudice in the North culminating in the Fugitive Slave Law', after which William Craft would take the platform and describe his escape story: his wife impersonated a youthful master while he portrayed her slave, and in these disguises they ingeniously circumvented any need for literacy or identification documents by feigning injury, deafness, and indignation over the course of their journey from bondage in Macon to freedom in Philadelphia.[10] At the end of the joint programme, William Craft would invite Ellen (billed as 'the White Slave' because of her light-toned complexion) to come up from the auditorium to the stage for a theatrical reveal. While Ellen directed her silent gaze toward each audience member – as Gay Gibson Cima astutely puts it, 'proof that race was, in fact, performative' – Brown sang abolitionist songs and passed the collection plate.[11] Cima argues that Garrisonian women 'imagined a *partisan spectator* judging them: in fact, they imagined a slave – or a more deeply committed abolitionist than themselves' judging their performance. This led to constant adjustment of 'performance strategies', whether at formal presentations or in social circumstances.[12] Thus, Ellen Craft confronted spectators' commitment to be white abolitionists dismantling structural power, whether with a witty social retort or with silence on the platform. She challenged others to be more deeply committed, along with herself.

Brown went fifteen times to the Great Exhibition. As he noted, 'In short, it is one great theatre, with thousands of performers, each playing his part.' He was acutely conscious of his own role, and described how, during his first visit, he escorted an Englishwoman on his arm, which occasioned 'jealous looks' from the Virginians in the US department.[13] Meanwhile, the 'goodly sprinkling' of other Black Americans whom Brown recognised at the exhibition was sufficient to reassure him of safety despite the 'sneering looks' of Southern gentlefolk.[14] William Craft took another performative tactic. During one of his visits to the Great Exhibition, he managed to rile a white countryman sufficiently that they verbally sparred over implications of the Fugitive Slave Act.[15] Having tested these tactics for promenading and eliciting debate, Brown and the Crafts colluded with white colleagues to expand their provocations' scope.

The Queen and Prince Consort attended the exhibition almost daily, and Saturday, 21 June, was no exception. The royal children accompanied them, along with the Queen's confidante the abolitionist Duchess of Sutherland (1806–68), peers, bishops, MPs, several of the exhibition's directors, an assortment of merchants and the prosperous middle classes, and visitors from abroad, totalling 12,732 in all.[16] Among the exhibition-goers was a party of transatlantic friends who rallied at the Thompsons' home (128 Sloane Street) then set out together for the Crystal Palace, just a kilometre (0.6 miles) away.[17] This must not be construed as one of George Thompson's schemes, for at the time he was still on his second sojourn to the United States. Instead, this was a female stratagem that reflected adjustments to the earlier performance strategies of Brown and William Craft. Anne Thompson lent her two eldest daughters, the nineteen-year-old Louisa and eighteen-year-old Amelia, to intentionally form a conspicuous multiracial and multigenerational party. They calculated their dramaturgy carefully: Anne Thompson took one arm of the British Reform advocate Mr McDonnell and Ellen Craft took the other; by her own request, Louisa Thompson took William Wells Brown's arm; and Amelia Thompson was flanked by William Craft and the chronicler of the event, William Farmer.[18] Louisa Thompson and William Brown, in particular, would raise and defy fears of stigmatised 'amalgamation', triggering Southerners.[19] The Estlins from Bristol and the Webb family from Dublin completed the party. For seven hours, they promenaded in every part of the nineteen-acre palace, taking refreshments together, and no one contested their presence. In this heterotopic space, people from all lands, with all complexions and national attire, jostled for views of the wares. Perhaps it is not surprising that a party dressed in conventional English fashions could not draw attention amidst the heterogenous crowds. They wore what L.M. Bogad terms 'social camouflage' for a calculated performance in the 'great theatre' of the Crystal Palace.[20]

The party focused their activism in the US department. In particular, they lingered around Hiram Powers' (1805–73) larger-than-life marble statue *The Greek Slave*, a head-to-toe female nude from whose delicately bound wrists hung a pair of marble chains and a cross (Figure 5.1). The title references a sale into an Ottoman harem, a slave trade as odious as the United States' but registering with distinct emotional and moral import for some viewers.[21] Phenotypically European – indeed, a classical physiognomy and physique – the woman conveys her abjection by her downward and deflected gaze. With the figure mounted on a plinth as high as an adult visitor's waist or shoulder (illustrations vary) and constantly rotating,

Figure 5.1    The US exhibits, including Hiram Powers' sculpture *The Greek Slave*, Great
Exhibition, 1851. From *Recollections of the Great Exhibition*, Library of Congress.

the angle of the slave's view could be construed to meet the viewer's or
modestly evade it.[22] The tall fringed canopy and draperies over the statue
called attention to the installation on the floor of the capacious US department, made considerably more prominent than the other example of neoclassical sculpture, Peter Stephenson's (1823–60) *The Wounded Indian*, a
few metres away.[23]

Whereas on earlier visits Brown and Craft baited Southerners to debate,
this time they hailed other visitors to bear witness to Southerners' unan-
swerability for the slave state. They spoke to each other about the abomination of slavery within a Christian republic in the hope that US visitors
would take the bait, interrupt them, and spark impromptu debates. Farmer
summarises the performative tactics:

> It would not have been prudent in us to have challenged *in words*, an anti-
> slavery discussion in the World's Convention; but every thing that we could
> with propriety *do* was done to induce them to break silence upon the sub-
> ject. We had no intention verbally of taking the initiative in such a discus-
> sion; we confined ourselves to speaking *at* them, in order that they might
> be led to speak *to* us.[24]

Though ostensibly conversing with one another, the abolitionist couples and trios addressed their remarks outward, projecting their voices and very likely opening their stances ('speaking *at* them') as actors on a proscenium stage are wont to do. They spoke 'of the wrongs of the slave', drawing a small crowd. They did not rouse an argument – Farmer claimed the visitors from the United States were 'too wary to take up' the gauntlet – but they were noticed. Then Brown escalated the provocation to put auditors in a decision dilemma.[25] He leaned across the barrier and placed a copy of John Tenniel's (1820–1914) cartoon 'The Virginian Slave: Intended as a Companion to Power's [*sic*] "Greek Slave"', which had appeared a few weeks earlier in *Punch*, within the statue's enclosure (Figure 5.2). Presumably, he then resecured Louisa Thompson's arm around his own. Tenniel's cartoon adopts a similar pose to Powers' statue, but the slave is Black, her head and lower body are draped, her marble support is sheathed in the Stars and Stripes, the pedestal is decorated with chains and crossed whips, and *E pluribus unum* is inscribed around the base. This is an *African American* slave, and her gaze is heavenward.[26] Visitors could not miss the point, and Farmer claims that contrary to British bystanders' custom of intervening at affronts to foreigners, on this occasion it was somehow clear that British visitors could not be appealed to by US bystanders, so the latter did not complain of their insult. What the multiracial party pointed out was 'the cowardice of men who evidently felt the injustice of their cause'. Juxtaposing the statue and the cartoon – a kind of micro-placarding – created a 'keenly felt' comparison, especially as Brown proclaimed 'As an American fugitive slave, I place this Virginia Slave by the side of the Greek Slave, as its most fitting companion.'[27] In so doing, Brown challenged the *dispositif* of the cartoon's equivalence between 'parody *as* critique and the parody *of* critique', rupturing the sense and sense (aesthetics and understanding) and inviting onlookers to see it in relation to his party.[28] Onlookers had the options of building solidarity or showing solidarity.

Cima stresses that the intervention's inability to spark a scene constituted failure: US visitors registered silent contempt or indifference, nothing more.[29] Lisa Merrill, another recent analyst of the performative nature of the event, concludes that the freedom-seeking US visitors' 'return and reverse [of] the gaze of their spectators' was an act of their own self-determination.[30] These views are not incommensurate, but the activists' perspective was distinct. Baz Kershaw describes how some protests can be 'the conceptual equivalent of a black hole, an infinite regress, which can in turn produce a tenuous type of hopefulness'.[31] In this vein, Farmer

### THE VIRGINIAN SLAVE.
#### INTENDED AS A COMPANION TO POWER'S "GREEK SLAVE."

Figure 5.2    John Tenneil, 'The Virginian Slave: Intended as a companion to
Power's "Greek Slave."' *Punch*, 7 June 1851, 236.

recorded that the stunt was triumphant: the party was smiled upon while passing through the palace, yet pro-slavery US visitors 'felt themselves thoroughly muzzled'.[32] The abolitionists insistently bore witness to slavery, and invoked others to understand through them. The Garrisonians' 'address to indefinite strangers', in Michael Warner's terms, showed the existence of a belief system, populated it, code-switched to suspend indifference to it, and thus hailed like-minded visitors as members of this counterpublic.[33] The outcome was that most visitors co-witnessed the party's truth while pro-slavery US visitors uncomfortably felt *too constrained to revile*.[34] The radical affiliation invited by the abolitionist party *in this place, at this moment*, through a *multi-scalar* performance, demanded the taking of sides so as to affectively isolate pro-slavery US citizens and make *them* conscious of their discordance. This differentiates between being silent and being silenced as epistemologies within the performative activism.

When the party stepped away from *The Greek Slave*, a US visitor snatched up Tenniel's cartoon; the party returned to afford him an opportunity for making remarks, but he kept silent. They moved on to the nearby display of Mathew Brady's (1822/4–96) daguerreotypes, discoursing about the images of clerics and statesmen who were pro-slavery, then to the stall of a loquacious Colt revolver demonstrator who paused his patter 'apparently to speculate as to "whose those n------ might be." He did not venture to make the inquiry'.[35] In each case, the abolitionists hailed the throngs to witness the terror of the enslaved and, scaling up the critique, the monstrous incommensurability of slavery with liberalism. What Frank Wilderson III calls 'the unthought category of the slave' became embodied in the exhibition – indeed, according to Farmer, the calm, mannerly 'fugitives' were *on exhibit*, Black, visible, voluble, defying social death – and by enjoying themselves were defiant of white supremacy's 'despotic irrationality' inherent to the United States and capitalism.[36]

Farmer stresses the significance of the 'accomplished young lady, Miss [Louisa] Thompson, becoming the promenading companion of a colored man'.[37] This could not have happened without Anne Thompson's complete cooperation. She was her daughters' chaperone and acted not in lieu of her absent husband but on her own initiative as part of an international community of committed anti-slavery activists. Little is known of her personality or actions apart from her occasional appearance at events to support her husband, but this was the second time that her husband had taken a protracted trip abroad, leaving her at home, and even when he was in Britain he was frequently on the road. She was responsible for her children's upbringing, and like other middle-class mothers she took charge of the presence and presentation of her teenage daughters in public life. Whoever thought up the action, Anne Thompson had to sanction the contours of her daughters' acts within it. What she did had a touch of genius.

Louisa and Amelia Thompson had been born and bred into the abolition movement. As babies, they accompanied their parents on Thompson's first tumultuous US tour, their parents' homes were sanctuaries to every visiting freedom-seeker and abolitionist, and during their teenage years they assisted their father with clerical work.[38] They knew both the people and the rhetoric, the tactics and the sites of Radical activism. Thus, by taking their companions' arms in parallel with Ellen Craft, they stood in solidarity with their Garrisonian friends. Moreover, given the asymmetrical marking of race as well as the notoriety of Brown and the Crafts from their lecture tours, Ellen Craft's billing as 'the White Slave' presented the commensurability of the two English roses to the Crafts' historical predicament. If British or US visitors recognised William Craft they knew to look for Ellen. *But which one of the young women was she?* While Simon Gikandi argues that the 'disquieting enigma' of slavery shaped eighteenth-century British sensibilities by existing in absentia (in Britain), this set of actions at the Great Exhibition forced attention to a pro-slavery viewpoint's 'essential condition of marginalization, exclusion, and alienation'.[39] As Simon Morgan points out, billing Ellen Craft as 'the White Slave' 'turned the trope of the exotic black body on its head' by confronting spectators with their similarity to her.[40] Just as Powers challenged the idea of slavery as debasement by elevating *The Greek Slave* through neoclassical form, Brown juxtaposed 'The Virginian Slave' while specifying his body and the Crafts' as sites where 'new identities were constructed, elaborated, and represented in an altered public sphere'.[41] By linking arms, the British and US citizens bore witness to each other's struggles, but whereas Brown's and the Crafts' blackness was defined in relation to others' whiteness – and indeed, this was the point of bringing the silent Ellen Craft to the stage at the end of her husband's escape narrative – they endeavoured to bring blackness to other visitors' attention, just as Brown juxtaposed Powers' white slave and Tenniel's Black one.

Since everyone in the party performed outward explicitly so others heard their conversations, this invited attention to voices and accents, and thus required leaning in to differentiate the women. As *Punch* noted, on a day such as this when the full fee was charged for admission, 'the high-paying portion of the public go to look at each other, and to be looked at', rather than seeking instruction from the wares.[42] On either side of McDonnell (an advocate for constitutional rights and the expansion of the male franchise in Britain), Ellen Craft and Anne Thompson represented, respectively, the freedom accorded by English soil and the opportunities newly afforded by the 1832 Reform Act, without which George Thompson would not have held a parliamentary seat yet which did not enfranchise his wife. If William Craft was recognised, was the young woman on his arm his wife, Ellen, or was she (in fact) Amelia Thompson? There is little reason to think that the Thompson girls would be recognised, but their voices would be distinct from Ellen Craft's. Speaking English amidst what Thackeray called 'the changing tongue, the various speech' of the fair, they did their utmost to be noticed in a conspicuous display and auditory of racial, gendered, generational, and international allyship. As alone and silent as *The Greek Slave* stood, this was the activists' moment to move in concert, to touch and be touched, and above all to speak and be heard.

For the three Thompson women, Ellen Craft, the Crafts' close friend and sponsor Mary Estlin (1820–1902), and Hannah Webb (1809–62), this was a seven-hour performance of social bonds referencing histories of the women's respective public constraints. None of the women could assume what Shannon Sullivan calls 'ontological expansiveness', the 'unconscious habit' arising from privilege that allows one to assume 'that all spaces are rightfully available for the person to enter comfortably'.[43] Women knew this all too well, if not all to the same degree. Infamously, at the 1840 Anti-Slavery Convention in London, white US women delegates were barred from taking their seats. While a few female lecturers were tolerated on anti-slavery circuits, they were still anomalies. By English custom, women did not speak at anti-slavery meetings except those of women's auxiliaries, they could not vote, and they certainly could not run for office. By making themselves noticeable, as Patricia Hill Collins argues, 'each individual decides the ways in which he or she will perform the social scripts suggested by controlling images'.[44] This is what the abolitionists counted on, but the scripts were multiple, intertwining, and reciprocal between activists and witnesses, and thus the responses could not be rote or easily mustered, and were not necessarily audible. As Judith Butler puts it, 'performativity functions as a chiastic relation between body and language', and hence activists could not venture forth as the embodiment of abstract rights except as reiteration, reversal, reflection, cross-reference, and circularity of the individuals' relationality to one another, depictions of the Greek and Virginian slaves, other exhibits, and other visitors.[45] This complexity explains onlookers' eloquent silence.

As a result of gendered constraints and the opportunities made (or taken), women's activism often drew on antecedents differently than did men's activism. In contrast to George Thompson and Frederick Chesson, whose work has left a mountain of evidence, women's activism requires a subtle touch to trace and attribute. Their activism resides within as well as alongside the repertoires of men and deploys artisanal knowledge particular to their gender in dynamic responses to social circumstances. Just as Quaker women used their buying power to boycott slave-grown sugar and cotton, performing activism not just at meetings but with their market baskets and at their serving tables, so too did other women remake activism utilising opportunities at hand.

## Great Inhibitions

The 1840 World Anti-Slavery Convention in London was the first meeting of its kind.[46] An international assembly of 350 answered the call, with delegates from South Africa, Jamaica, Barbados, Demerara, Guyana, France, and Ireland, though Britons and US representatives preponderated (Figure 5.3 and 5.4). On the national level, the AASS designated a multiracial contingent – William Lloyd Garrison, Rev. Nathaniel Peabody Rogers, Charles Lenox Remond, and James Mott (1788–1868) – while seven women were sent on behalf of states' anti-slavery organisations. They knew in advance of sailing that female delegates would be opposed. For the most part, Garrisonians advocated equality for women along with unconditional emancipation of the enslaved, however, the convention's host organisation, the BFASS, espoused neither. The prejudice against women delegates was compounded by religious sectarianism, especially uneasiness about some of the US Quakers' Hicksite views, but they were canny and experienced activists.[47] In addition to Lucretia Mott (founder of the Philadelphia Female Anti-Slavery Society), Sarah Pugh (1800–84, who had joined Mott's organisation after hearing George Thompson speak, and who would write the official protest to the women's unseating), Mary Grew (1813–96, whose own father argued against women speaking at the convention), Abby Kimber (1804–71), and Elizabeth Neall (1819–1907) represented the Pennsylvania Anti-Slavery Society, and Aby Southwick (1819–1904) and Emily Winslow (1822–1904) represented the Massachusetts Anti-Slavery Society.[48] This formidable group of women edited journals, taught in a school for Black pupils, founded the Free Produce Association, and organised profitable fundraising fairs to support speakers' tours. This gave them broad experience with the administrative, financial, political, and rhetorical facets of activism, including writing and speaking.[49] Anne Thompson knew them all, and preserved their

Figure 5.3    'The abolition of the slave trade' (a.k.a. 'The Anti-Slavery Society
Convention', lithograph by John Alfred Vinter, after Benjamin Robert Haydon, 1840),
lithograph, ca. 1846–64. D20516, National Portrait Gallery.

autographs in her album orné, bound between a portrait of Abraham
Lincoln and Nathaniel Rogers' description of their exclusion from the
rostrum.[50]

On the first day of the two-week convention, the assembly descended
into prolonged chaos over the US women. Rev. Alexander Harvey, representing Glasgow, argued that the rights of women had no bearing on 'the
slavery question', a position that was normative at the time with respect
to both the sexual violence inherent to slavery and broader questions of
women's social and political inequality.[51] According to Lucretia Mott,
when Samuel J. Prescod (1806–71, the delegate from Barbados) expressed
his view that 'it would lower the dignity of the Convention and bring ridi-
cule on the whole thing if ladies were admitted – he was told that similar
reasons were urged in Pennsylvania for the exclusion of colored people
from our [anti-slavery] meetings – but had we yielded on such flimsy arguments, we might as well have abandoned our enterprise'.[52] As Prescod was
Black, this was a barbed retort. George Thompson ineffectually rebutted

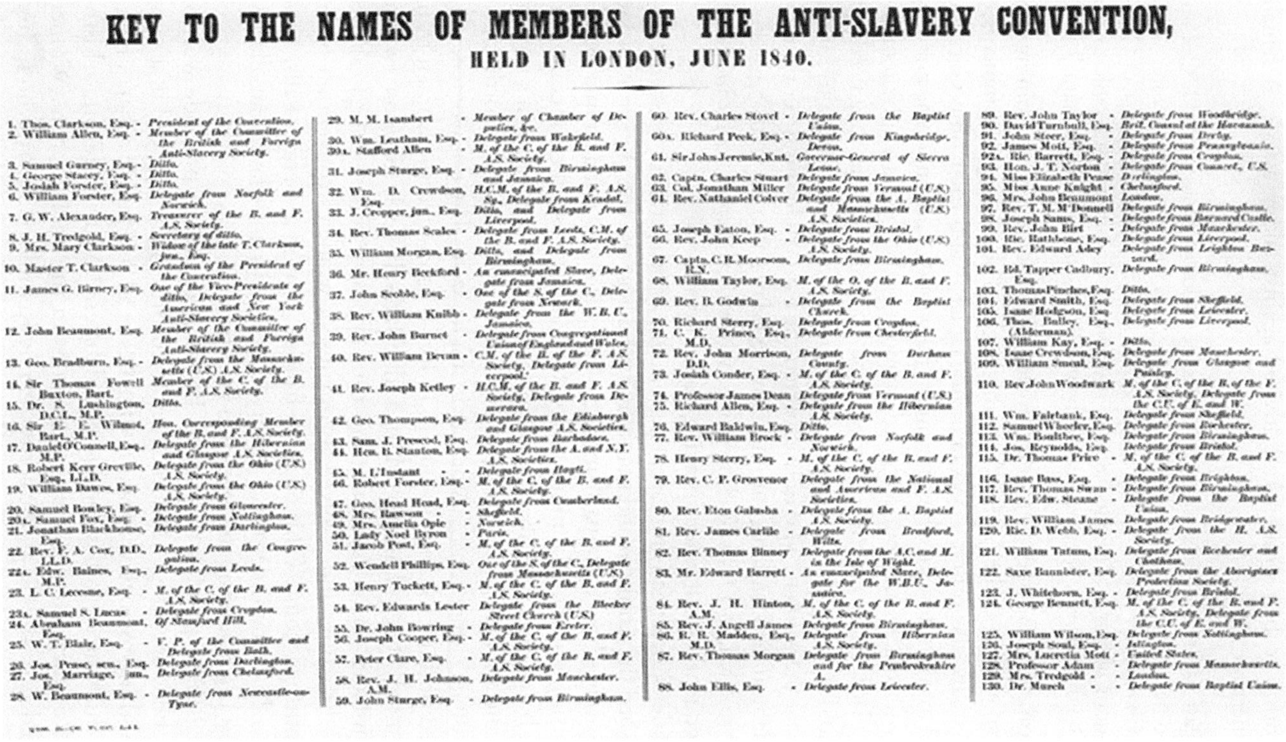

# KEY TO THE NAMES OF MEMBERS OF THE ANTI-SLAVERY CONVENTION,

## HELD IN LONDON, JUNE 1840.

1. Thos. Clarkson, Esq. - *President of the Convention.*
2. William Allen, Esq. - *Member of the Committee of the British and Foreign Anti-Slavery Society.*
3. Samuel Gurney, Esq. - *Ditto.*
4. George Stacey, Esq. - *Ditto.*
5. Josiah Forster, Esq. - *Ditto.*
6. William Forster, Esq. *Delegate from Norfolk and Norwich.*
7. G. W. Alexander, Esq. *Treasurer of the B. and F. A.S. Society.*
8. J. H. Tredgold, Esq. - *Secretary of ditto.*
9. Mrs. Mary Clarkson - *Widow of the late T. Clarkson, jun., Esq.*
10. Master T. Clarkson - *Grandson of the President of the Convention.*
11. James G. Birney, Esq. *One of the Vice-Presidents of ditto, Delegate from the American and New York Anti-Slavery Societies.*
12. John Beaumont, Esq. *Member of the Committee of the British and Foreign Anti-Slavery Society.*
13. Geo. Bradburn, Esq. - *Delegate from the Massachusetts (U.S.) A.S. Society.*
14. Sir Thomas Fowell Buxton, Bart. *Member of the C. of the B. and F. A.S. Society.*
15. Dr. S. Lushington, D.C.L., M.P. *Ditto.*
16. Sir E. E. Wilmot, Bart., M.P. *Hon. Corresponding Member of the B. and F. A.S. Society.*
17. Daniel O'Connell, Esq., M.P. *Delegate from the Hibernian and Glasgow A.S. Societies.*
18. Robert Kerr Greville, Esq., LL.D. *Delegate from the Ohio (U.S.) A.S. Society.*
19. William Dawes, Esq. *Delegate from the Ohio (U.S.) A.S. Society.*
20. Samuel Bowley, Esq. *Delegate from Gloucester.*
20A. Samuel Fox, Esq. - *Delegate from Nottingham.*
21. Jonathan Backhouse, Esq. *Delegate from Darlington.*
22. Rev. F. A. Cox, D.D., LL.D. *Delegate from the Congregation.*
22A. Edw. Baines, Esq., M.P. *Delegate from Leeds.*
23. L. C. Lecesne, Esq. - *M. of the C. of the B. and F. A.S. Society.*
23A. Samuel S. Lucas - *Delegate from Croydon.*
24. Abraham Beaumont, Esq. *Of Stamford Hill.*
25. W. T. Blair, Esq. - *V. P. of the Committee and Delegate from Bath.*
26. Jos. Pease, sen., Esq. *Delegate from Darlington.*
27. Jos. Marriage, jun., Esq. *Delegate from Chelmsford.*
28. W. Beaumont, Esq. - *Delegate from Newcastle-on-Tyne.*
29. M. M. Isambert - *Member of Chamber of Deputies, &c.*
30. Wm. Leatham, Esq. - *Delegate from Wakefield.*
30A. Stafford Allen - *M. of the C. of the B. and F. A.S. Society.*
31. Joseph Sturge, Esq. - *Delegate from Birmingham and Jamaica.*
32. Wm. D. Crewdson, Esq. *H.C.M. of the B. and F. A.S. Sy., Delegate from Kendal.*
33. J. Cropper, jun., Esq. *Ditto, and Delegate from Liverpool.*
34. Rev. Thomas Scales - *Delegate from Leeds, C.M. of the B. and F. A.S. Society.*
35. William Morgan, Esq. *Ditto, and Delegate from Birmingham.*
36. Mr. Henry Beckford - *An emancipated Slave, Delegate from Jamaica.*
37. John Scoble, Esq. - *One of the S. of the C., Delegate from Newark.*
38. Rev. William Knibb - *Delegate from the W. B. U., Jamaica.*
39. Rev. John Burnet - *Delegate from Congregational Union of England and Wales.*
40. Rev. William Bevan - *C.M. of the B. of the F. A.S. Society, Delegate from Liverpool.*
41. Rev. Joseph Ketley - *H.C.M. of the B. and F. A.S. Society, Delegate from Demerara.*
42. Geo. Thompson, Esq. *Delegate from the Edinburgh and Glasgow A.S. Societies.*
43. Sam. J. Prescod, Esq. *Delegate from Barbadoes.*
44. Hen. B. Stanton, Esq. *Delegate from the A. and N.Y. A.S. Societies.*
45. M. L'Instant - *Delegate from Hayti.*
46. Robert Forster, Esq. - *M. of the C. of the B. and F. A.S. Society.*
47. Geo. Head Head, Esq. *Delegate from Cumberland.*
48. Mrs. Rawson - *Sheffield.*
49. Mrs. Amelia Opie - *Norwich.*
50. Lady Noel Byron - *Paris.*
51. Jacob Post, Esq. - *M. of the C. of the B. and F. A.S. Society.*
52. Wendell Phillips, Esq. *One of the S. of the C., Delegate from Massachusetts (U.S.)*
53. Henry Tuckett, Esq. - *M. of the C. of the B. and F. A.S. Society.*
54. Rev. Edwards Lester *Delegate from the Blecker Street Church (U.S.)*
55. Dr. John Bowring - *Delegate from Exeter.*
56. Joseph Cooper, Esq. - *M. of the C. of the B. and F. A.S. Society.*
57. Peter Clare, Esq. - *M. of the C. of the B. and F. A.S. Society.*
58. Rev. J. H. Johnson, A.M. *Delegate from Manchester.*
59. John Sturge, Esq. - *Delegate from Birmingham.*
60. Rev. Charles Stovel - *Delegate from the Baptist Union.*
60A. Richard Peek, Esq. - *Delegate from Kingsbridge, Devon.*
61. Sir John Jeremie, Knt. *Governor-General of Sierra Leone.*
62. Captn. Charles Stuart *Delegate from Jamaica.*
63. Col. Jonathan Miller *Delegate from Vermont (U.S.)*
64. Rev. Nathaniel Colver *Delegate from the A. Baptist and Massachusetts (U.S.) A.S. Societies.*
65. Joseph Eaton, Esq. - *Delegate from Bristol.*
66. Rev. John Keep - *Delegate from the Ohio (U.S.) A.S. Society.*
67. Captn. C. R. Moorsom, R.N. *Delegate from Birmingham.*
68. William Taylor, Esq. *M. of the O. of the B. and F. A.S. Society.*
69. Rev. B. Godwin - *Delegate from the Baptist Church.*
70. Richard Sterry, Esq. *Delegate from Croydon.*
71. C. K. Prince, Esq., M.D. *Delegate from Chesterfield.*
72. Rev. John Morrison, D.D. *Delegate from Durham County.*
73. Josiah Conder, Esq. - *M. of the C. of the B. and F. A.S. Society.*
74. Professor James Dean *Delegate from Vermont (U.S.)*
75. Richard Allen, Esq. - *Delegate from the Hibernian A.S. Society.*
76. Edward Baldwin, Esq. *Ditto.*
77. Rev. William Brock - *Delegate from Norfolk and Norwich.*
78. Henry Sterry, Esq. - *M. of the C. of the B. and F. A.S. Society.*
79. Rev. C. P. Grosvenor *Delegate from the National and American and F. A.S. Societies.*
80. Rev. Eton Galusha - *Delegate from the A. Baptist A.S. Society.*
81. Rev. James Carlile - *Delegate from Bradford, Wilts.*
82. Rev. Thomas Binney *Delegate from the A.C. and M. in the Isle of Wight.*
83. Mr. Edward Barrett - *An emancipated Slave, Delegate for the W.B.U., Jamaica.*
84. Rev. J. H. Hinton, A.M. *M. of the C. of the B. and F. A.S. Society.*
85. Rev. J. Angell James *Delegate from Birmingham.*
86. R. R. Madden, Esq., M.D. *Delegate from Hibernian A.S. Society.*
87. Rev. Thomas Morgan *Delegate from Birmingham and for the Pembrokeshire A.*
88. John Ellis, Esq. - *Delegate from Leicester.*
89. Rev. John Taylor - *Delegate from Woodbridge.*
90. David Turnbull, Esq. *Brit. Consul at the Havannah.*
91. John Steer, Esq. - *Delegate from Derby.*
92. James Mott, Esq. - *Delegate from Pennsylvania.*
92A. Ric. Barrett, Esq. - *Delegate from Croydon.*
93. Hon. J. T. Norton - *Delegate from Conect., U.S.*
94. Miss Elizabeth Pease *Darlington.*
95. Miss Anne Knight - *Chelmsford.*
96. Mrs. John Beaumont *London.*
97. Rev. T. M. M'Donnell *Delegate from Birmingham.*
98. Joseph Sams, Esq. - *Delegate from Barnard Castle.*
99. Rev. John Birt - *Delegate from Manchester.*
100. Ric. Rathbone, Esq. *Delegate from Liverpool.*
101. Rev. Edward Adey *Delegate from Leighton Buzzard.*
102. Rd. Tapper Cadbury, Esq. *Delegate from Birmingham.*
103. Thomas Pinches, Esq. *Ditto.*
104. Edward Smith, Esq. *Delegate from Sheffield.*
105. Isaac Hodgson, Esq. *Delegate from Leicester.*
106. Thos. Bailey, Esq. (Alderman). *Delegate from Liverpool.*
107. William Kay, Esq. - *Ditto.*
108. Isaac Crewdson, Esq. *Delegate from Manchester.*
109. William Smeal, Esq. *Delegate from Glasgow and Paisley.*
110. Rev. John Woodwark *M. of the C. of the B. of the F. A.S. Society, Delegate from the C.U. of E. and W.*
111. Wm. Fairbank, Esq. *Delegate from Sheffield.*
112. Samuel Wheeler, Esq. *Delegate from Rochester.*
113. Wm. Boultbee, Esq. *Delegate from Birmingham.*
114. Jos. Reynolds, Esq. *Delegate from Bristol.*
115. Dr. Thomas Price - *M. of the C. of the B. and F. A.S. Society.*
116. Isaac Bass, Esq. - *Delegate from Brighton.*
117. Rev. Thomas Swan - *Delegate from Birmingham.*
118. Rev. Edw. Steane - *Delegate from the Baptist Union.*
119. Rev. William James *Delegate from Bridgewater.*
120. Ric. D. Webb, Esq. - *Delegate from the H. A.S. Society.*
121. William Tatum, Esq. *Delegate from Rochester and Chatham.*
122. Saxe Bannister, Esq. *Delegate from the Aborigines Protection Society.*
123. J. Whitehorn, Esq. - *Delegate from Bristol.*
124. George Bennett, Esq. *M. of the C. of the B. and F. A.S. Society, Delegate from the C.U. of E. and W.*
125. William Wilson, Esq. *Delegate from Nottingham.*
126. Joseph Soul, Esq. - *Islington.*
127. Mrs. Lucretia Mott - *United States.*
128. Professor Adam - *Delegate from Massachusetts.*
129. Mrs. Tredgold - - *London.*
130. Dr. Murch - - *Delegate from Baptist Union.*

Figure 5.4 'Key to the Anti-Slavery Society Convention, 1840' (list of sitters in the picture by Benjamin Robert Haydon), letterpress, 1880, PG D23547. National Portrait Gallery.

the motion to ban women and advised against taking a vote. A female
eyewitness recalled:

> Part of the time it was quite impossible to know what was said. Cries of
> 'order, order,' 'Divide, divide,' 'No, no, no, no, no,' 'Vote, vote, vote,'
> 'Chair, chair' were dinging in our ears.... It was just like a House of Com-
> mons uproar.... It ended against the women, and it was miserable to see,
> the friendly way they were after the meeting—smiling and pleasant.[53]

Garrison, Rogers, and Remond showed their solidarity by joining the
unseated women in the gallery.[54] This highlighted how being disenfranchised
was spatially allegorised – separate, not equal – and each time Garrison
refused to come down to the convention floor when called upon he not only
stood with the women but reignited memory of their exclusion by remaining in place.[55] This experience showed the US residents that they need not
be beholden to any Briton's assertion of human freedom and equality, at the
same that the women (who fully expected the ban) could misdirect through
their demeanour: 'smiling and pleasant', as Maria Waring (1818–74, sister-
in-law to Richard Davis Webb) put it, when they were actually incensed,
and eloquently silent when speaking was not permitted.

Gender difference – not race, religion, or national origin – was what distinguished the admitted and non-admitted delegates. The 1840 convention
demonstrates how extra-parliamentary liberalism was not a simple matter
of asserting rights or claiming agency, for there was insufficient consensus
on the boundedness of liberal principles. By prohibiting women's speech,
Black and white men unwittingly gave rise to what was thenceforth called
'the women's question'.[56] Whereas it might seem that the women contributed nothing to the convention, in fact it galvanised the women from
the United States: Lucretia Mott and Elizabeth Cady Stanton (whose
new husband was a Tappanite and thus opposed women delegates) met
for the first time and resolved to organise a women's convention when
they returned home. (This came to fruition in 1848 at Seneca Falls, New
York.)[57] In Britain, despite a history of women's anti-slavery auxiliaries,
feminist organisations emerged on a later timeline.

The BFASS pleaded that it was British tradition to preclude women
from public speaking.[58] Indeed, even Lord Brougham regarded it 'a most
painful thing to be thus speaking of ladies at all in a public debate', never
mind thinking of ladies speaking *in* debates.[59] Martin Hewitt, a historian of oratory, nuances this exclusion from the public sphere. Women
emerged as readers (e.g., the actress Fanny Kemble, 1809–93, who recited
Shakespeare starting in 1847) or lecturers who peppered literary topics
with elocutionary demonstrations (Mrs De Lancy and Madame Steinberg,

both at the Manchester Athenaeum in 1848). Earlier, within Radical circles, Elizabeth Sharples (1803–52) dressed as the goddess Isis to lecture
on mysticism and women's rights at the Rotunda in 1832, Emma Martin
(1811/12–51) ably debated Owenites in 1839 then eschewed Christianity and
lectured as a freethinker, garnering the admiration of George Holyoake,
and Margaret Chappellsmith (1806–83) was a salaried Owenite lecturer
during the 1840s.[60] Women's exclusion from lecterns was by custom
not mandate, though in Britain only Emma Martin can be construed
as a platform orator prior to the Anti-Slavery Convention. There was
no British counterpart to Maria W. Stewart (1803–79), a freeborn Black
woman pamphleteer who gave speeches on women's rights and abolition
in New England in 1832–3.[61] Women did not organise the equivalent
of political dinners, but more orthodox women than Sharples, Martin,
and Chappellsmith participated in discussion at teas, conversaziones,
and soirées (all invitation-only variants of meetings that grew in popularity from 1839), and masculine dinners were increasingly supplemented
by the informal mixing of the sexes. During the early Victorian period
working-class women gained increasing access to mechanics' institutes,
where, like George Thompson during the 1820s, they could be exposed
to debating. After the Reform Act of 1832, women became more prominent in elections, for example listening to candidates' open-air speeches
from their carriages and organising tea parties for female supporters of
candidates (men might be invited later in the evening). Their presence
on the hustings tacitly endorsed candidates' intention 'to behave with
civility and decorum'.[62] On the other hand, some voters' wives could be
bought: after the Second Reform Act (1867), one election agent claimed
'when he had secured the wives he cared nothing about the husbands'.
Without universal suffrage women's influence was great, if 'irresponsible
and illegitimate'.[63]

Even in liberal circles, British women struggled to get a foothold at high-
profile political gatherings. At a committee meeting to organise the 1 August
memorial celebration in 1859, Frederick and Amelia Chesson attended along
with George Thompson, Baron Linstant de Pradine (1812–83, the Haitian
chargé d'affaires in Paris), M. de Lespinasse (secretary to the Haitian delegation in London), John S. Jacobs (a freedom-seeker and former abolition speaker), William Farmer, Washington Wilks, and 'a lad of fourteen'
named Squirrell. They animatedly discussed inviting one of their female
members – the freeborn Black American Sarah Parker Remond, who had
come to England six months earlier as an experienced lecturer – to speak
at the 1 August event. Despite this heterogenous gathering, the proposition

to include Remond was unanimously rejected, a full generation after the 1840 convention. This had much to do with perceptions rather than the content of Remond's message: shortly after her arrival in England, when she followed Frederick Douglass' address to the Young Men's Anti-Slavery Society in Leeds, she spoke on 'the degradation of slavery' and gave 'painful accounts of events in slave-life'.[64] However, as Willi Coleman points out, during her two-year lecture tour she 'risked scorn by including the specifics of female enslavement', for example practices in slave markets.[65] Even so, Frederick Chesson's diary implies that her presence on 1 August would automatically entail the women's rights question as an inappropriate distraction from the main issue: 'The English public have only just learnt to tolerate women as lecturers, & they make a broad & palpable distinction between women as lecturers, & women as speakers at meetings held for the transaction of public business.'[66] Remond attended the organising committee's next meeting, where she and Thompson got into a 'great controversy … on the right of women to speak at public meetings'.[67] It was not that the Chessons or Thompson disapproved of women lecturers – in 1862 they admired Madame Marie's disquisition on Garibaldi at St James's Hall, and Frederick Chesson noted how, despite her accent, she spoke clearly, with a flow of ideas and evident self-possession – but they believed *the public* was not yet prepared to disambiguate the women's question from women speaking, and in particular, debating.[68]

In extreme circumstances, however, women were even barred from listening to debates, as when the Radical MP Edward Craufurd (1816–87) insisted that the galleries of the House of Commons be cleared of all women before discussion on repeal of the Contagious Diseases Acts could commence.[69] This repeal campaign, indisputably a women's question, brought several women speakers to the fore. At a noisy meeting in Islington to protest against extension of the acts, Helene Coote and Susanna Chapman (1807–92, wife of the publisher and physician) gave admirable speeches. Hecklers were well-handled: when 'a working man said he should be ashamed to bring his wife to such a meeting', Coote 'took up the challenge with quiet dignity, saying "I am a wife and the mother of four children and I wish to say that I am not ashamed to be here."' As Chesson noted, 'This had more effect than the most elaborate arguments.'[70] Her presentation of identity felicitously commended her cause.

The National Society for Women's Suffrage dispatched male lecturers when doing so seemed most effective.[71] However, this movement gave women much valuable experience not only by speaking at meetings but also by chairing them. During most of the 1870s, Frederick Chesson was on the General Committee, and Amelia Chesson served on the Executive Committee. In March 1870, he noted that Clementia Taylor (1810–1908, wife of his colleague on the Jamaica Committee Peter Taylor) chaired a 'numerous and brilliant assembly' at the Hanover Square Rooms. John Stuart Mill, Professor Cairnes, Lord Amberley (1842–76), Jacob Bright, MP (1821–99), and Sir Robert Anstruther, MP (1831–90), spoke, but 'the ladies had the best of the speaking' including 'Mrs. Grote, an elderly lady dressed in very bright colours [who] spoke like a bluff, hearty Englishwoman', and 'Miss Hare, who stood snuff in hand, [and] spoke in a most graceful and unaffected manner'. Frederick Chesson reserved praise for Helen Taylor (1831–1907), daughter of the late Harriet Taylor (1809–58) and step-daughter of Mill, as giving 'the speech of the day', for 'both the manner and the matter of which were perfect ... as close and incisive a piece of reasoning as any that Mill ever delivered'.[72] He added in his published notice:

> One may even go further, and assert that Miss Helen Taylor's speech was an oration—a fine intellectual performance, in which the compact and well-sustained argument was not less perfect than the admirable elocution and the womanly dignity with which it was delivered. I know people who went to hear that speech in a very skeptical frame of mind, but who came away with widely different impressions. And no wonder; they simply paid to mind the homage which is due to mind, whatever may be the sex of the individual athlete.[73]

In contrast to the United States, where declamatory training was offered to girls and boys, in Britain elocution and oratory were rarely available for women and girls until the end of the century.[74] However, Taylor had spent the late 1850s pursuing a provincial acting career, where she cultivated 'a high, clear, penetrating voice that seemed to cleave the air and reach to the remotest corner of a large hall like the high notes of a violin'.[75] Though she backed away from this career, she cultivated poise and vocal skills that assisted her political work (notably, serving three terms on the London School Board, founding the Social Democratic Federation in 1881, and attempting to run for Parliament in 1885).[76] Both Chessons got to know her through women's suffrage work and the Radical Club, which afforded liberals a friendly but vigorous platform to privately debate the issues of the day.[77]

If, for the most part, men still controlled admission to places and platforms where matters of 'public business' were discussed, there were channels for women's activism. As with the 1840 Anti-Slavery Convention and 1851 Great Exhibition, multi-scalar thinking reveals women's activism in a multitude of places and agential modes. Though the Women's Suffrage Committee used well-worn tactics, such as petitions and public meetings, its leaders also planned 'drawing-room meetings' in rural areas as well as 'office at homes' and lectures in London, welcoming women of all classes.[78] This is how activism occurred, and political insights emerged, in quotidian, incrementalist performances and protests.

For example, Louisa Thompson made a fervent foray into activism by writing a refutation of the long history of antitheatricalism that demonstrates her adult explorations of performance critique and acting. Two months after the sojourn to the Great Exhibition, she married Frederick Nosworthy (1831–99), a fruit merchant who imported 'figs, dates, currants, Malgar raisins, plums, grapes' and rice from the Mediterranean to Liverpool. Their family grew to include eight children and they lived comfortably in Manchester. George Thompson described the marriage as happy: 'She has chosen a man of average intelligence, sterling probity, first rate business habits, and irreproachable moral deportment. He is an admiring, devoted, and indulgent husband, and a fond and affectionate father.'[79] He was also a keen amateur actor who performed for various charitable causes in Manchester and London. The Chessons saw him as Claude Melnotte in Edward Bulwer-Lytton's (1803–73) *The Lady of Lyons*, and found he 'sustained his part well. He has great confidence, a good, clean, musical voice which he intones well, and can enter thoroughly into the spirit of the performance'.[80] There are *Era* notices of Frederick and Louisa Nosworthy in other amateur performances from 1855 to 1871.[81]

George Thompson was associated with evangelicalism but did not commit to a particular denomination; Anne Thompson was a Methodist.[82] Louisa Nosworthy followed her mother's example, but increasingly felt herself at odds with the suspicion of recreations and condemnation of the stage. Some Methodists countenanced recitations or readings at an athenaeum hall, but Louisa grew to enjoy fully acted plays in the leading theatres of the land.[83] To the extent that this exhilarated and edified her, she also felt troubled. In the Anglican Church, she found a way to reconcile her faith with admiration for the stage. She made a definitive move to the established church, and all her children were baptised there.[84] Over time, she not only attended plays but began to act in them. By some means, this attracted the notice of the Congregational preacher Dr Joseph Parker (1830–1902), who baited her with a theological controversy.[85] She responded by writing a threepenny pamphlet, *The Stage and Christianity Reconciled*, anonymously signed by 'An Amateur Actress of Manchester'. While Frederick Chesson critiqued her over-emphasis on the question of whether it is right to go to the theatre rather than focusing sufficiently on fulfilling one's own concept of religious duty (typical of his emphasis on conscience), he acknowledged that 'Poor Dr. Parker has, at all events, met with a plucky antagonist.'[86] She defended her choices, embraced her fate, and mock-rued that some clergy had shut actors out of the Kingdom of God.

> 'Well,' I concluded, 'I am going to hell, but it is a comfort to think how many others are going with me. I shall at least have congenial companions in my torments among the sulphurous flames. All the actors must be there, for their whole lives are spent in the service of the devil; so I shall meet the people I like most, with Garrick, Siddons, Kemble, and Kean! ... To hell have assuredly gone Addison, Colman, Congreve, and Sheridan ... surrounded by the devil and his angels, and mixed up with all the thieves, murderers, felons, and blackest villains.'[87]

This defence of playwriting and acting – likely the only example of its kind authored by an Englishwoman – reflects her struggle with doubt and the consequences of certainty. It also demonstrates solidarity with performers, including Helena Faucit (1817–98, who had retired upon her marriage in 1851 but occasionally performed at charitable benefits), while counteracting views such as the 1855 pamphlet *Appeal to the Women of England to Discourage the Stage*, authored by 'a Lady', which claims that no woman 'can so outrage her womanly feelings as to act before the public, without injuring her moral delicacy'.[88] Louisa Nosworthy took pains to remonstrate that she was entirely conscious of her nuanced moral position.

The Nosworthys were not the only members of the Thompson family to try the stage. Louisa and Amelia's brother, Herbert, had worked on the *Empire* and in an administrative capacity at the Crimean front before marrying the actress Marianne Cronin (1837–?) and taking up her profession. Apparently, the family was unaware of this latter step: Frederick Chesson learnt his brother-in-law was performing at Marylebone Theatre by a chance encounter with John Townsend (1819–92), former Liberal MP for Greenwich who returned to his earliest vocation after his enemies drove him into Chancery. Townsend had taken the lease of the Theatre Royal Leicester and engaged Herbert and Marianne Thompson for the upcoming season. Herbert worked for Townsend through the winter and spring, until his marriage crumbled. He was then briefly secretary of the Emancipation Committee, and when his health broke down, he moved in with his parents and signed over guardianship of his young son to George Thompson. Herbert lingered with consumption for several months before dying of a haemorrhage.[89] Amelia was in bed after an induced late-term miscarriage, and the news was kept from her. George Thompson was still on his third US sojourn. On discovering the body, Anne Thompson raved, distraught, in the street.[90]

Among the next generation, the Nosworthys' youngest child, Frank (1868–92), worked as a draughtsman until his sight failed, then successfully pursued a provincial acting career until his ocular complaint recurred. Desperate and depressed by his prospects, he pinned a letter to his vest, went to Macclesfield Cemetery, and shot himself in the mouth.[91]

These lives are indicative of how theatrical work was unceremoniously taken up in many families. Still, though attending stage performances of all types was a regular and welcome occurrence among the extended family, the distinction between Louisa and Frederick Nosworthy's amateurism and their brother and son's professionalism mattered. Louisa Nosworthy is notable for her spirited rebuttal of religious disapproval, finding her voice on the stage and in print. Her rather directionless and headstrong brother is notable because of how his spotty work history includes journalism, political organising, and acting, without evident training for any of these pursuits. Arguably, a path had been paved for Frank Nosworthy, though by the time of his death he had grown estranged from his family.

Rather than being 'two opposed trends', art and socially oriented practice coexisted in the same family, sometimes in the same members, and in Louisa Nosworthy's case in the conjoined action of acting and authoring her self-justification.[92] Contemporaneous views allowed for theatre and socially oriented practice to serve a common end, as George Cruikshank's 'Passing Events of 1853' suggests (see Figure 3.7). Yet, as the author Anna Jameson (1794–1860) asked in 1856, if one realm is professional and paid and the other is charitable and unpaid, and both sexes engage in both, 'why is female influence [on society] always supposed to be secret, underhand, exercised in some way which is not to appear?'[93] What chance did a woman – especially a middle-class woman – have of making an impact as a *Kulturkritik* if whatever work she could pursue was to be unpaid, unattributed, and undervalued? Against the odds, both Louisa and Amelia Thompson (and later, as the married women Louisa Nosworthy and Amelia Chesson) found novel ways to register upon art and the culture in which it was situated. Amelia even made it pay.

## Work: Relationalist Subjecthood

In *The Fantasy of Feminist History*, Joan Wallach Scott describes two Western feminist fantasies. One concerns female orators, whose wrestling with their inappropriate masculinity 'projects women into masculine public space, where they experience the pleasures and dangers of transgressing social and sexual boundaries'. The other, which she calls 'the feminist maternal fantasy', reconciles the pregnant body's difference 'in its acceptance of rules that define reproduction as women's primary role (an acceptance of the difference the equality-seeking orator refuses)'.[94] Amelia Chesson skirted both variants: she resembled men in that she was a critic yet this seems not to have roused any unease in others, and though she was maternal this did not present an ongoing barrier defined by her reproductive labour.

If this schematically accounts for Amelia Chesson's non-exceptionality vis-à-vis men, on the household level there was significant differentiation from her husband. As much as George Thompson admired and appreciated Frederick Chesson – describing him as 'self-educated, with a good endowment of intellect; holding radical opinions on almost all great subjects, and interested in every great philanthropic question of the day' – he judged his daughter Amelia as 'the superior'. Nevertheless, four years into the marriage Thompson characterised her as yielding to Frederick's lead.

> Amelia is fully capable of appreciating the labours in which he is engaged, and of affording him, not only an entire sympathy, but, often valuable counsel, and co-operation. Both have strong literary tastes. In the faculties of imagination and wit, Amelia is the superior, while, as might be expected, in the knowledge of public affairs, and the ability to discuss them, the husband takes the lead. Their married life has been one of unbroken harmony, and the shifts, and trials to which they have been subjected, have but quickened their ingenuity, and developed their resources.[95]

Thompson's own financial difficulties were a major part of these 'trials', for example his 1856–8 sojourn to India, but the 'shifts' include Frederick's need to secure employment when the *Empire* failed. In the midst of this, Amelia also stepped up to earn – contributing to 'their ingenuity' – as a freelance music, theatre, and book critic starting in January 1856, barely six months after her marriage.

Nicholas Ridout argues that the theatre's claim to be an exemplary part of the public sphere rests on its proximity to acts of criticism.[96] Even so, as with becoming an actress, writing about performance bore a special impediment for women. Like the theatre's employees and spectators, a critic must depart the theatre after the performance, but then – late at night – she must also go somewhere well-lit, heated, and respectable to write, then submit her review to her editor before travelling home in the wee hours of the morning.[97] By that hour, even actresses were long abed, and only women who made their living in the most disreputable night-time diversions were afoot. This, it is thought, was not only a disincentive for Victorian women to take up theatre criticism but utterly precluded them from doing so. Of the 241 people identified as writing theatre criticism for the Victorian and Edwardian popular press, there is just one woman. This was Pearl Craigie (1867–1906), daughter of a US millionaire and a well-connected socialite, who reviewed plays for *Life* circa 1889–90 then turned to writing novels, plays, and essays.[98]

The *Star*'s guinea-per-piece freelancer's fee granted Amelia Chesson flexibility with the household economy but not a flourishing living. Taken on as a staff writer from 1862, she received a retainer of 10s. per week in addition to the per-piece fee, and together the proceeds may have been sufficient to pay the salaries of the family's two live-in servants (a nanny and maid-of-all-work). Only with a third servant, such as a full-time cook, and a weekly laundress could Amelia be freed from housework. In essence, critical writing brought her more options but not freedom from domesticity, and certainly not leisure.

Her reviews were entirely unsigned, and so her identity was unknown to the reading public, though it was transparent to the *Star*'s staff and other critics and journalists who saw her at events.[99] To undertake all but the book reviewing (which was done at home) required resourceful stratagems involving family and friends to ensure that she could move about the city as needed, including late at night, and file her copy in time for the early-morning deadline. As theatre and music venues provided critics with two tickets, she usually invited a friend or family member to the performance, then walked with them from the West End to the *Star*'s offices. If her companion was her father, brother, or other male friends of the family, they would then turn homeward; her younger sister would wait for her; or female kin of other *Star* staff would join their relatives. Frequently, Frederick's diary indicates that he waited for Amelia before they walked home together, and sometimes this is the only indication that she had been working on a particular date.[100]

Perhaps she did not make a perceptible impact as a woman, but as the earliest discovered theatre or music critic for a daily newspaper – predating others by several decades – Amelia Chesson assuredly overcame a set of great inhibitions on women evaluating, critiquing, and giving opinions of art for the daily press. This created the potential to influence men and women, to shape (in a small way) Victorians' *Bildung*.[101] And if, when it came to discussing other kinds of public affairs, Frederick 'took the lead', as Thompson put it, this does not mean that Amelia's *Bildung* underequipped her to hold her own: her first review was of *Little Dorrit*.[102] Her reviews of fiction, biography, and nonfiction show that she was widely read and strongly inclined.[103] If she sought self-improvement from her optional course of reading biography, fiction, poetry, and political science she succeeded on an already well-established foundation for a twenty-five year old who, because of her gender, was locked out of postsecondary education, and, because of her father's chronic financial precarity, received a rather patchy preparation from music and language tutors. Despite this, one of her early submissions was a three-part review of the first part of Thomas Carlyle's *History of Frederick II of Prussia*, nearly five columns in length, replete with knowledge of German history, highly critical of Carlyle's approach, and, like the *Star*, Radical in politics and international in outlook.[104]

The familial context for this sets Amelia's individualism in relation to what Patricia S. Mann calls 'a broad spectrum of daily choices'.[105] Whereas Amelia managed the household, interacted with the extended family, and cultivated the couple's far-ranging friendship networks, Frederick's domain of journalism and politics was not his alone. After all, as her father wrote, she gave 'valuable counsel, and co-operation', which in the early years of their marriage included keeping the APS' letterbook, assisting Frederick with compiling and proofing issues of the *Colonial Intelligencer, or Aborigines' Friend*, and serving on the London Emancipation Committee. Amelia's ability to exercise her 'imagination and wit' as a critic when barely into her mid-twenties, to be appointed the regular music critic for the *Star* before the age of thirty, and to emerge as a women's suffrage organiser in her late thirties is all the more remarkable given that she weathered fourteen pregnancies and gave birth to eleven children before her forty-second birthday (Figure 5.5).

The Chessons were well-suited as a couple, differentiated not by intellectual capacity or political acumen but by physiology. Her fourteen pregnancies did not preclude her as a participant in public discourse, though they did determine the scope, intervals, and sites of her working life. His routines, in contrast, continued unaffected with barely a flicker at each new child's appearance. For example, two days after the second child was born, Frederick and his father-in-law left together for a holiday in Ramsgate.[106] Even so, the remarkable story of the Chessons is not one of separate spheres – and the forces that kept them separate, such as gender proscriptions – but the porosity of the spheres for their mutual lives as journalists and activists. Instead of a public/private distinction in which the observer and commentator on modern life is figured as male, the reproductive and nurturing cycles of Amelia Chesson's life were managed so that she too was an autonomous liberal subject.[107] If 'a woman's story is often told as part of a man's', how can a focus on performance, critique, and activism bring Amelia Chesson's distinction in the public sphere forward?[108]

The philosopher Hans Blumenberg argues that in the modern age 'all truth is earned' and henceforth 'knowledge assumes the character of labor'.[109] If this is so, knowledge kept through the labour of diary writing in turn allows insight into the routines of Amelia Chesson's personal life but also an indispensable clue as to what facilitated her work life. Only

Figure 5.5   'Looking eastward from Fleet Street (1857).' This was Amelia Chesson's route
to the *Star* office. Blanchard, *Bradshaw's Guide*, 15. Oxford University Press.

her diary for the year 1858 survives, overlapping with the 1854–70 run
of Frederick's. Whereas during that year he typically wrote about sixty
words per day in his diary, her busy life kept entries down to an average
of twenty-five words. Taken together, these eighty-five daily words document the work pattern she maintained for decades.

This is how it transpired. Three days after Amelia reviewed *Little Dorrit*, early in 1856, she and Frederick went to the Haymarket Theatre to see the Christmas pantomime *The Little Treasure, the Butterfly's Ball and the Grasshopper's Feast; or Harlequin and the Genius of the Spring*. They were young and broke, and seats could be had for a halfpenny. Frederick noted: 'Enjoyed ourselves much'.[110] During the next three months, he went to concerts, a melodrama, pantomime, and two operas, but she did not. His diary ends abruptly on 26 April and resumes six weeks later. Their first child had been born.

When this child was about six months old, Amelia and Frederick jointly authored a performance review; four months before the next child was born she had a spurt of performance reviewing. In between – unmarked in the husband's diary – the first child was weaned.[111] This pattern is made explicit in Amelia's diary when the second child's turn came to be weaned: in mid-March 1858, when this child was five months old, Amelia notes that she felt 'very poorly on account of the nursing' but began to venture out. Outings became more frequent, though on 2 July she again felt 'very poorly and began to fear that Cottie's [Constance's] Halcyon days are over as far as nursing is concerned'. In other words, a third pregnancy was suspected. Based on birth registrations this was a false alarm, yet Amelia soon began weaning anyway, using the tough love method. On 29 October 1858, the thirteen-month-old baby was dropped off at the Thompsons' home with its nanny and grandmother. The next night the Chessons and Thompsons went together to see Charles and Ellen Kean in *King John*. On Monday, Amelia took her thirteen-year-old sister Edith to see *Maritana* at Drury Lane, after which the diary notes 'home with Fred at 2 o'c[lock]'. She had written a review. A week later, Amelia checked on Constance, 'whom we found very well but not quite oblivious of what it is desirable she should forget', so instead of taking the child home she repeated the pattern of her earlier excursion and took her sister to see *Crown Diamonds* at Drury Lane. Afterward, they walked to the *Star* offices and returned home with Frederick in the early hours of the following day. She had written a review. Amelia kept her distance from her baby daughter for twenty days.

Without the obligation to nurse, Amelia embarked on a spurt of reviewing: she saw and reviewed slightly more performances in two months than she had during the previous ten. On 1 December, Amelia and Frederick went to the *Star* together in the late afternoon and both commenced their workday: he at the newspaper office while she went up Queen Victoria Street to Bishopsgate, met Mrs Baxter Langley (wife of the *Star*'s editor), and in the dusk of a winter evening progressed with her up Norton Folgate to the Standard Theatre for Madame Céleste's (1815–82) benefit night. London buses ran until 11:00 p.m. on a hail-and-ride basis; foregoing the afterpiece, Amelia could have caught either of two lines departing from Shoreditch to Bank, then any of half a dozen lines that ran from Bank toward Fleet Street, stepping off at Ludgate Circus for the short walk to the *Star* office. Amelia met Frederick at the offices a little after 11:00 p.m. and wrote her notice. The pattern varied for the Christmas pantomimes. Frederick's diary notes how he organised a fan-out to the theatres for the pantomimes: he assigned Amelia and her mother to Covent Garden, his father-in-law to the Haymarket, his brother-in-law Herbert to the East End theatres, and himself to the Lyceum. After the performances, they all congregated at the *Star* offices. Four columns of reviews were assembled, and Frederick and Amelia walked home together at 4:00 a.m.

Upon learning of the second child's birth, Thompson wrote to his daughter from Calcutta on Christmas Eve 1857, 'I was delighted with the information, that on the 27th of September you published a new and improved essay on the best means of increasing the size and beauty of the future generations of the human race. You will, of course, continue this line of authorship.' Even crediting his relief at the safe delivery and health of mother and child, Thompson conflates childbirth with writing, describing issuing a child as 'appearing before the public' – a description that is clumsily apt, for writing, pregnancy, and parturition were wrapped up in how Amelia entered uniquely into posterity.[112] In early August 1859, a third daughter was born, so during her period of greatest attendance at performances (November–December 1858) Amelia was pregnant for the third time. These two forms of sensorial experience – the pull of life and the perception of art – frame the understanding of what Amelia Chesson contended with in order to venture to performances and undertake writing. It is a reminder that in reception studies a spectator's (or critic's) absence is meaningful, as well as her presence. She regularly attended performances until 24 June 1859, and a baby came six weeks later. For the next four-and-a-half months, with three daughters under the age of four, she neither reviewed books nor ventured out to performances. This changed on Boxing Day, when all the adults of the family were again called into service to review the new pantomimes.

Amelia attended performances sporadically through October 1860. In December she submitted two book reviews, and on 10 March 1861 her fourth child was born. Six months later she ventured out, and in February 1862 she was commissioned to do the musical criticisms; henceforth, she set a brisk routine of attending performances through the spring and early summer concert season, the last on 23 July. A fifth child was born mid-October. She broke her hiatus for the Christmas pantomime, taking her eldest child to Covent Garden on its first such treat, along with Alexander Isbister. The following year-and-a-half was her busiest period to date, with several events a month, the last (a review of the Monday Popular Concert, a daytime event) on 7 June 1864. The next day, she gave birth for the sixth time. That summer, she reviewed the new poems of Alfred, Lord Tennyson (1809–92), but nothing else. Five months after the child's birth, she went to hear William Ewart Gladstone speak, and then regularly attended theatre performances and concerts for the next two years. She had a miscarriage in April 1866, took a two-month break, then was back at work. Toward the end of 1866, her attendance tapered off: she was pregnant with twins, both of whom she lost in early February 1867. This was a particularly low ebb in her health and spirits, coinciding with her brother's death, but she rallied in June and worked regularly through the end of March 1868, when she commenced a confinement, anticipating her seventh child. Frederick's diaries do not indicate that she attended a performance until a year later – she suffered another miscarriage in September 1869 – and by the time her eighth, ninth, tenth, and eleventh children were born the diaries are lost or ceased to be written.

Amelia's work followed a calendar, based on reproduction and caregiving, which as far as the evidence shows was never relieved by a wet nurse. Generally speaking, after the second child, she would nurse four to six months, then commence performance reviewing that would continue until some point in the last trimester of her next pregnancy. During these years, gender asymmetries impinge upon a distinct understanding of Amelia Chesson's work, agentially and radically as well as ingeniously, for she managed being in a masculine profession with respect to both her gender *and* her sexuality.

Amelia Chesson's chief centres of critical attention in 1858 (St Martin's Hall, Covent Garden, Exeter Hall, and Drury Lane) point to her growing specialisation in music criticism.[113] Except for one venture to the Standard Theatre, she concentrated on the West End, but particularly on venues that gave ready egress along the Strand to Fleet Street, with its plethora of buses. The Chessons greatly admired Charles Kean's productions at the Princess's Theatre, but when theatregoing in Oxford Street she did not subsequently go to the *Star*: someone else on staff reviewed those productions on different nights. Increasingly, her ambit included concerts at the Crystal Palace in Sydenham. Performances there occurred during the afternoon, and the adjoining train platforms attached to the north side of the palace in 1858 (with services to Ludgate Hill, also West Croydon,

Figure 5.6    Camille Pisarro, *Crystal Palace Sydenham*, 1871. Art Institute of Chicago.

Kensington, Victoria, London Bridge, Charing Cross, and King's Cross)
were especially felicitous to enable her to reach the *Star* office without the
need of an escort (Figure 5.7).[114] When Frederick's assignment changed
from editing the morning edition to the evening, and his hours of duty
switched from evening to daytime, he nevertheless attended at the *Star*
along with the evening shift to facilitate Amelia's writing. When she
attended Crystal Palace concerts on Saturdays, she wrote at home, and
Frederick took the review with him to be composited for the Monday
morning edition (Figure 5.6).

  This accounts for what she did, and what made it possible, but how is her
case relevant to the broader discussion about activism? Critical observation
of performance – a category including everything from social behaviour
to oratory, public spectacles, and the performing arts – was integral to
the culture of liberal activists, and Amelia Chesson practised spectatorship and citizenship as a professional critic. Granted, both her father and
husband also wrote performance criticism occasionally, and were more
prodigious authors in the political mould, but because of their gender they
did so without constrictions on their access to theatres, transportation,
or the streets, spaces that Dwight Conquergood calls 'leaky, contingent
construction[s]': locations 'that are always already constitutive of tactical

Figure 5.7 'The Great Handel Festival.' *Illustrated London News*, 27 June 1857, 640.

struggles, counter-publics, and centripetal pulls'. This matters when excavating evidence of a female theatre critic.[115]

Affecting public opinion is a 'diffuse form of instrumental political power'.[116] This qualifies as what Bruce Robbins calls 'a site of hidden, new, controversial, or otherwise interesting publicness' whereby a woman wielded power (taste and discernment over cultural affairs) in and over 'the public' in some of the most conspicuous spaces and media, namely theatres, concert halls, and the daily press.[117] Robbins' chief example is voting, but before the limited franchise was granted and women such as Helen Taylor grasped the opportunity to serve in local politics, Amelia Chesson was active both as a critic and as a political organiser. For her, culturedness was a private virtue that melded with a work function: she did not make herself the work of art (like her sister, brother, sister-in-law, brother-in-law, and nephew) or the deliverer of live speeches (like her father and occasionally her husband), but instead used critique to enhance others' culturedness and discernment about performance (and by extension understanding and advocacy of human rights). As Kate Nash emphasises, a plural view of 'differentiated social spaces in which public opinion is formed and tested' links the theatre and street for 'readers, listeners, and viewers in the mass media'.[118] Rather than contesting access to the public sphere as an orator and politician, which was Helen Taylor's tactic, Amelia Chesson linked women more equitably into the quotidian goals of participation in the public sphere by being a critic and organiser.

Mutuality within the household and extended family helped the Chessons' common goal of pursuing livelihoods that had cultural and social impacts. They experienced complementarity of pursuits: just as Frederick was sometimes Amelia's helpmeet (selecting books at the office for her to review and securing a place for her to write her performance notices late at night), she sometimes assisted with his workload. When he experienced swelling in his right thumb, she went to the office to aid him, taking dictation for two articles.[119] Reciprocal assistance took many forms. The day after their sixth child was born, he went to Exeter Hall in Amelia's stead and wrote the notice; a week later he did the same for the Crystal Palace concert.[120] After she miscarried twins, he also filled in and wrote a notice.[121] Likewise, after Frederick died, she fulfilled the literary criticism that had been commissioned of him by the *Athenaeum*.[122] This is more than reciprocal attentive kindness: they preserved each other's livelihoods as well as the household income. This also suggests that for them, the bourgeois public sphere – or, more accurately, both the '"public sphere in the world of letters" and "the political public sphere"' – was inherently mutable.[123]

In contrast to Jürgen Habermas, who separates the public sphere from the domestic sphere based on whether its places are open to debate (e.g., theatres and coffee houses versus the home),[124] the Chessons – but especially Amelia – spent time and thus located interventions across these realms. The idea of separating work from the space of home is not applicable for writers or activists, any more than separating Frederick's activity in the newspaper office from his wife's need for a rendezvous point and working space can be: she used the *Star's* office both as a *haven from* the public so she could work unmolested and as a *substitute for* the home so that she could meet tight deadlines. Quite apart from the impossibility of disambiguating workplaces from the home for many in the middle and working classes, considering how, where, and by whom liberal activism was pursued as an output of labour and a management of time casts Amelia Chesson as an innovative gender activist who consolidated women's access to culture and critique into a broader repertoire of acts than, for example, platform speakers had hitherto done.

As Seyla Benhabib argues, any spaces can become 'public spaces in that they become the "sites" of power, of common action coordinated through speech and persuasion'.[125] Through actions coordinated with others, Amelia's seat in the theatre, her desk at the *Star* office, and her reviews in the newspaper take on the force of power. Being already authorised in the public sphere is not the 'sole condition for speaking', as Judith Butler puts it, for the 'living and social conditions of agency' reside in the 'political performativity' that exceed a straightforward speech act and require interdependencies, as the female delegates to the 1840 convention showed.[126] Nancy Fraser argues that in order to deliberate as peers in the public sphere, participants must have 'rough equality' that tamps 'systematically generated relations of dominance and subordination'.[127] This has a ring of truth insofar as women were precluded from debating 'matters of consequence' at major events, but neither Victorian women's incursions into debates nor their success in bringing the women's question to the fore in multiple ways – divorce reform, child custody, property law, and of course suffrage – suggests that 'equality' was a predicate for critical speech, or that a 'vocal and coherent feminine public' wherein women could be both subordinate *and* capable of action was precluded.[128]

Despite a 'mobile repertoire of ideologies and practices' assigning women to a 'non-political private sphere' (in Geoff Eley's terms), women found ways to relocate and thus reinvent public spheres ('subaltern counter-publics', in Fraser's terms) in the domains to which they could get access, where they were automatically accorded access, and where they had near-exclusive access.[129] Theatres and concert halls, which women of all stations attended, and newspapers, which women of all classes read, are 'weak publics' conjoined through published criticism: respectively, they were influential in knowledge dissemination and opinion formation yet not decision-making. Within the British democracy, 'strong publics' such as Parliament were accountable to weak publics, hence the topicality of entertainments and the growing power of the penny press in the mid-Victorian period.[130] Some of Amelia Chesson's reviewing hints that she was aware of such vectors within the 'performative commons' at the intersection of cultural life and popular sovereignty.[131] This is especially evident in her reviews of the annual Handel Festival.

In 1857, Amelia's review of the first Handel Festival at Sydenham describes how crowds lined Queen Victoria's thirteen-kilometre (eight-mile) route from Buckingham Palace, undaunted by the 'blinding drifts' of dust stirred up from the road bed. Upon entering the Crystal Palace, she was greeted by 'deafening cheers which reverberated through the building in heavy waves and was then responded to by the multitude outside'.[132] The Queen had given birth to her ninth (and last) child two months before, and this was her first post-confinement outing, so the show of interest and sympathy was specifically maternal as well as patriotic (Figure 5.7). The combined party of

British and Prussian royals were among 11,649 auditors of *Judas Maccabaeus*, one of the lesser-known oratorios. From the second row of the royal box, Prince Albert followed the oratorio's score, marking the time and appearing thoroughly engrossed. The Queen and her attendants left immediately after the concert, while the site's architect, Sir Joseph Paxton (1803–65), led Prince Albert, the Prince of Wales (1841–1910), Crown Prince Frederick William (1831–88, recently betrothed to Victoria the Princess Royal, 1840–1901), and the Archduke Maximilian (1832–67) on a tour of the grounds. They lingered at the fountains, enjoying the views, then attempted to promenade. Amelia's review shares her specific optic and interpretation of the choreography. Despite the 'body of police' surrounding the royals:

> Their progress, seen from the point we occupied, reminded us of a real hunt. They were waylaid at every point, surrounded, stared at, cheered at, and let depart, to be again waylaid, surrounded, and gaped at by another eager crowd coming from another point of the gardens, the scene being continued until they took refuge in the carriages which conveyed them back to Buckingham Palace. It is quite true that the trio of Princes very graciously bowed to the assembled multitude; but we doubt whether, at least two of them (Prince Albert has, by this time, become accustomed to it), consider being hunted down in this indiscreet manner, stared out of countenance, and often even jostled, is [sic] a very striking mark of anything but the most vulgar and impertinent curiosity.

The review casts both the royal party and the onlookers at various points – along the route to Sydenham, in the concert hall, and on the grounds – as intrinsic facets of the spectacle of sovereignty subject to citizens' sousveillance. Instead of offering only a pro forma account of the repertoire selection and singing, Chesson describes an intricately coordinated multi-scalar event, for example noting the 120 'little fellows' who distributed the libretti as well as the royal party's escort to the refreshment area during the interval. Thereby, the social repertoires of royal-watching and management are set within the 'weak public' sphere of the streets, hall, and grounds constitutive of the performative gestalt.[133]

Two years later, in a review commissioned for the *Newcastle Chronicle*, Amelia again attempted to depict the entirety of the Handel Festival's dramaturgy and phenomenology. It begins with the early-morning crush of 20,000 gaily attired concert goers on railway platforms suffering an 'incessant struggle for places' until they disembark at Sydenham, up to 1,000 alighting every five minutes.[134] Despite the extraordinary crowding, front-of-house management was exemplary, and directions to seats were so perfect that 'to stray from the right path was impossible, even for the most helplessly erratic traveller'. For those who could not attend, as well as those who did, Amelia gives readers a perspective from the press gallery, with its 'full view of the orchestra, the transept, and indeed the entire centre of the palace' for a privileged sight of the 458 instrumentalists, 2,800 choristers, and the desk from which Maestro Costa (1808–84) conducted *The Messiah* for the centenary year of the composer's death. There was no royal party at this performance, so Costa's sovereignty prevailed: he 'succeeds in governing, with a precision that is all but incredible, a mass of performers, which, to a casual observer, seems almost too large to be at once measured by the human eye'. The gentlemen of the chorus stood in their black evening suits and 'the ladies in their filmy scarfs and bonnets of white, faint pink, and azure blue, showing at the distance, from whence we beheld them, like a polytechnic view in the act of dissolution, or like the pretty gauze tissue clouds in a "Midsummer Night's Dream", as put on at the Princess's Theatre'. Below, on the floor of the hall, numerous blocks of one-guinea seat holders were arrayed, including ladies in summery ensembles likely to 'reach home in a somewhat limp state, unless the supply of cabs at Pimlico and London Bridge was reinforced from all other parts of the metropolis' on a day when wet weather threatened. Readers who had attended the rehearsal in Exeter Hall a few days earlier were provided with a comparison of the sonority of the soloists in the two spaces. Singers were acoustically disadvantaged by so great a space, yet the tenor Sims Reeves (1821–1900) was more successful in the aria 'Thou shalt break them' than in 'Comfort ye' and 'Every Valley' because of its 'declamatory nature'. The final chorus was 'splendidly given', though accompanied by the shuffling of auditors 'too anxious to forestall one another at the refreshment tables to hear it attentively to its conclusion'.[135]

It is easy to see how, as a reviewer of music, Amelia Chesson was truly a critic of performance. Like her father, she surveiled everything, taking in the entire mise-en-scène because everything in it mattered as much as anything else. She shows how these concerts (like plays, meetings, debates, and rallies) had dramaturgies: a multitude of internal acts and forces subsumed to an experience of the whole. There were moments of grandeur and sublimity, vignettes of intimacy and tactility, matters to contest as well as acquiesce in, controlled authority in conjunction with subtleties, and things to compare as well as to hold apart. Most importantly, her reviews demonstrate she was attuned to women's experience, with a specific sensorium of femininity, including aesthetic appreciation of seeing and being part of the feminine spectacle. There were masculine spectacles too, such as the hunt of princely quarry on the palace grounds, yet as a woman, observer, and critic she demonstrated skilful documentation of women's existence in the public sphere, whether as monarch or commoner, diva or devotee, protected by a door-to-door carriage ride or subject to the elements, and lent this insight to readers. Rather than noisily clambering for her right to be a critic, or claiming her maternity in relation to the public, she *noticed* other women – extraordinary singers, amassed choristers, and spectators anxious for tea – constituting the theatre's inter-publicness of sovereignty, artistry, observation, reaction, and recreation. In this 'weak public', women performed in myriad ways, and Amelia Chesson anonymously told others about it.

From the vantage of 1870s feminism, Amelia Chesson forged a place for women in an uncharacteristic occupation; or, in the terminology of 1980s feminism, she was a 'female first'. Though she was branded 'a pioneer in lady journalism' in her 1902 obituary, she was no such thing within her extended family or social circles; for her, unconstrained by such externally derived definitions, pioneering did not matter either at home or elsewhere. From the perspective of 1990s feminism – Patricia S. Mann's *Micro-politics*, for example – a woman like Amelia Chesson is a transitional figure, incorporated into a family structure that 'provided men with the personal and psychological mooring that enabled them to perform as "autonomous" individuals in the public sphere' yet also allowed room for self-defining women outside this role.[136] Taken along with evidence of her involvement with the minutiae of domesticity – adding a puppy to the household, trimming a straw bonnet, re-dying her baby daughter's coat to get more use out of it, or making up children's clothes from fabric sent by Louisa – her work as a reviewer challenges the grand narrative of masculine claims on the discursive public sphere as well as the feminist fantasy of maternity's reconciliation of difference.[137] Pursuing self-improvement through reading political science and history, she demonstrated Friedrich Schiller's concept of the 'aesthetic education of man' (though a woman), cultivating discernment and translating this into judgement as a reviewer and a liberal advocate. Yet looking at these functions in tandem begs for a more nuanced understanding of activism in relation to her gender.

From a twenty-first-century perspective, Amelia Chesson's story is one of affective relations where actualisation results from experimentation in praxis. Rosi Braidotti provides terminology that accounts for Amelia Chesson both moving through the city and constituting her domestic, social, political, and authorial activities in forms of civic commitment as a non-unitary, relationist subject. Soyica Diggs Colbert's description of recent African American women writers is also apt, for like them

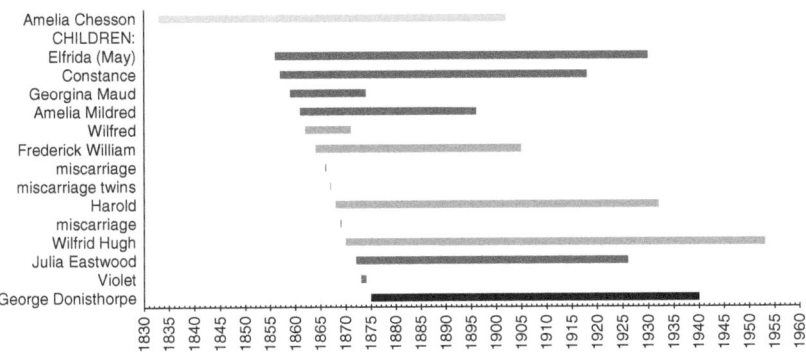

Figure 5.8   Amelia Chesson: Maternal age at parturition and children's longevity.

Amelia Chesson found 'the act of creating links across and within difference is a crucial mode of knowledge production and a way of knowing' that informed her politics and subjectivity.[138] Chesson offers a model of change, actualisation, and flux, or a nomadic 'experiment in becoming', as Braidotti puts it, that extends creatively toward forms of public service equally connected to art and politics, for 'how on earth can the distinction between the symbolic and the socio-material, the psychic and the social, the cultural and the political be kept up at all?'[139] Acknowledging the complexity of the public sphere is still inadequate to its multifactorial mediation.[140] Instead of being restrictively contained by patriarchal power or public/private conventions, Amelia Chesson demonstrates how positive and affirmative outlets coexisted and were facilitated within family networks. This gave her access to politics-in-formation; the marketplace of entertainment, musical, dramatic, and literary enrichment; and an outlet for the critical act of evaluation.

Amelia Chesson's sexuality is where the more radical aspects of relationalist subjecthood are evident. Her diary shows that sexual difference was a significant factor, the circumstances under which she could turn to writing determined by what Luce Irigaray calls the fluid mechanics of bodies, the interstitial humidity of when she was pregnant and when she did (and did not) breastfeed infants (Figure 5.8).[141] Her writing followed a biological schedule that made book reviewing feasible in one part of the calendar and theatre and concert reviewing in another. It is the contrast with Frederick Chesson's steady Sunday-to-Friday work life while he contributed to the *Morning Star* that makes Amelia Chesson's biology so evident. The Chessons naturalised the cycles arising from Amelia's reproductive and nursing encumbrances to manage their workloads, work cycles (such as the daily, quarterly, and annual production of newspapers and reports), and respective responsibilities for earning. This challenges the idea of 'structured inequality' in middle-class marriages, which Leonore Davidoff and Catherine Hall see as characteristic of family businesses, for it is the co-evolution of Amelia's writing career with Frederick's that makes the case compelling.[142]

## Sociability: The Power of Weak Publics

George Thompson and Frederick Chesson spent their time focused on the political geography of slavery, human trafficking, and genocide. Not surprisingly, their social lives were built around networks of activists engaged in resisting these practices. They did not specifically focus on women's interventions, though Frederick certainly noticed his wife's efforts and occasionally other women's.[143] Many of Amelia's friendships grew within these networks, including the wives of Frederick's political allies and newspaper colleagues as well as others whom she drew into their circle. This is typified by her relationship with Harriet Jacobs, who came to London for the second time in 1858 and immediately renewed her acquaintance with the Thompsons. Her brother John S. Jacobs, a merchant seaman, had previously befriended the Chessons and shown his fondness for them by bestowing ingenious and exotic gifts whenever he came to port. In 1858, Harriet had with her the manuscript of *Incidents in the Life of a Slave Girl*, the memoir that exposes the sexual rapacity of the slaving system and details how she lived for seven years in a confined space to evade the relentless advances of the sexual harasser who threatened to sell her children out of state. On 20 July, Amelia began to read the memoir. She and Harriet met frequently, for tea and meals, a concert, an idle afternoon, or shopping on Harriet's last day in London. Amelia anticipated Harriet's return to the United States with a mixture of support and regret.[144]

Though in relationships such as these both the Chessons enfolded freedom-seekers and abolitionists into their immediate and extended family circle – for example, hosting an evening when William Craft read his unpublished escape narrative aloud to them and the journalist and activist Passmore Edwards (1823–1911) – there is something especially tender about Amelia Chesson and Harriet Jacobs' bond.[145] Their cross-generational friendship was born of mutual fondness and a shared perspective on the invidious nature of inequality (not its effects).[146] As Jean Fagan Yellin argues, Jacobs' memoir consistently shows women responding compassionately to 'Linda Brent's' (Jacobs') sexual exploitation and desire to be a nurturing mother, and thus 'white women betraying allegiances of race and class to assert their stronger allegiance to the sisterhood of all women' by aiding the narrator.[147] Jacobs experienced this while working in the reading room and offices of Frederick Douglass' *North Star* and while living for nine months with the Hicksite Quaker Amy Post (1802–89), a participant in the 1848 Seneca Falls Convention. Post encouraged Jacobs to write the memoir, and it was Amelia Chesson (not her famous father or well-networked husband) in whose hands Jacobs entrusted the manuscript. With Jacobs having previously shown the manuscript to Maria Weston Chapman, perhaps at this point in its preparation another female reader was what she needed.[148] *Incidents in the Life of a Slave Girl* corroborated the white activist Lydia Maria Child's (1802–80) *Appeal* of 1833, showing anti-slavery activists on both sides of the Atlantic the specific repercussions of gender within slavery and the ways that sexuality – particularly through rape and reproduction along with the displacement of romantic partners and dislocation of families – was added to women's oppression and trauma as chattel property.[149] Frederick Chesson saw the book three-and-a-half years later, when the author wrote to ask him to place it with an English publisher.[150] Amelia's subsequent review in the *Star* notes the 'unceasing persecutions' that 'Dr Flint' (Dr James Norcom, 1778–1850) directed at Jacobs, driving her 'to the desperate resolution' to escape, and quotes the passage describing her hiding place. She endorsed the book as belonging in every British and US household.[151]

As Lucretia Mott's London memoir, Amelia Chesson's all-too-brief diary, and Harriet Jacobs' autobiography demonstrate, liberals enacted a civil society that defied divisibility of public and private spheres. Abolitionists' shared values and desire to effect change enhanced an ethos of hospitality and advocacy that 'blurred the lines between state, family, market, and culture' and brought matters of urgent concern inside homes.[152] The Thompsons' and then the Chessons' practice of welcoming abolitionists eschewed any inclination within the culture at large to enforce physical or social separation of races.[153] Their sense of responsibility to one another extended across nations and empires such that their private lives – which can be distinguished in various ways as time spent in sociability, leisure, the domestic life of a family, and the intimate life of a conjugal couple – imbricated public actions with private life in complex and nuanced ways. This consolidated as a recognisable repertoire of practices involving women.

Much of women's liberal activism was classified as philanthropy: fundraising bazaars, subscriptions, and ladies' sales predominate, but women also organised boycotts of slave-grown goods, blockaded shop-keepers, and participated in street protests, and thus raised consciousness of the interdependence of households and the global economy as well as their own presence in public spaces.[154] Whereas her mother may have participated in the great ACLL Bazaar of 1845, the evidence indicates other directions for Amelia Chesson.[155] Perhaps because neither her girlhood nor her marital homes were ever flush with cash, she showed no orientation to consumer activism. She did, however, show a forte for cultivating social bonds that strengthened linkages between activists. Gary Alan Fine's concept of the 'idioculture' helps account for how this functioned as 'a system of knowledge, beliefs, behaviors, and customs shared by members of an interacting group to which members can refer and that serves as the basis of further interaction'. In such a 'locally ordered and socially situated' world, the 'interaction order – a field of performance' was often attributed to externalities but in fact depended upon the 'microrealms' of coordinated participation. This turns the idea of network into a verb – networking – incorporating a flexible relation of 'linkages among recognizable groups of actors [i.e., participants] who know each other and have a shared past and a prospective future'.[156] Liberal activists collaborated in committee meetings and enacted the results of plans in public meetings, but as the Chessons' diaries consistently document, smaller groups within the idioculture also interacted in myriad ways. As George Thompson found when trying to persuade abolitionists to support the British India Society, if he could get people to his home for breakfast, there was 'nothing like putting our opinions into tea, & coffee & between bread & butter when you want folks to swallow them!'[157] It was the location as much as the repast that did the trick. Customs such as these consolidated the idioculture of reform.

Shared history often mattered, as when Amelia accompanied William Lloyd Garrison's daughter Frances Villard (1844–1928) to a concert and the next day accompanied Garrison, Villard, and Garrison's youngest son, Frank (1848–1916) to a concert at Sydenham. Garrison and Thompson had been close friends since 1833 – the year of Amelia's birth – and Garrison had known Amelia since infancy, which meant that giving this warm welcome to the sojourning family (even when she did not know them all) was more than courtesy. They had been networked her entire life, and as Fine puts it 'people are linked through what they know, and this facilitates what they do together'.[158] From 1790 through 1840 the rising middle classes exerted pressure from conjoined family, friendship, religious, and business networks to bring the Habermasian public sphere of weak influence into existence. However, until recently the view of this has been that 'this activity strictly demarcated the roles of men and women via a mobile repertoire of ideologies and practices, which consistently assigned women to a non-political private sphere, "having at most a supportive role to play in the rapidly expanding political world of their fathers, husbands and brothers"'.[59] In contrast to scrupulous historicising of family businesses by Davidoff and Hall, which contains Victorian middle-class women to a 'non-political private sphere', Amelia Chesson (and her many female and male associates) utilised domestic spaces, and family time, for deepening the bonds between activists, discussing political issues, broadening existing networks, and meeting with and without the formal connotations of conjoined business or religious ties. There was instrumentality to this, not merely women supporting the work of more public-facing men. Rather than cleaving to domestic spaces in order to maintain respectability, utilising domestic spaces in lieu of more public places (for example, salons), women in the Chessons' circles met in homes *and* in public spaces such as auditors' galleries during speeches, lecture platforms, and committee meetings. Yet the locales matter most when considered in conjunction with the categories of activity undertaken: particularly when political influence was at stake, both domestic and public spaces were infused with meaningful sociability, and when politics were advocated the boundaries of leisure time were mutable across performances of activism. This was true at the Crystal Palace in 1851 and remained so for Amelia Chesson throughout her married life.

Victorian women did not all accede to the idea of home as refuge from the world. As Mariana Ortega argues, the concept of 'hometactics' allows for women's disruption of temporal and spatial norms to intentionally forge ways of feeling at ease and have 'authentic belonging' conducive of a multiplicious identity outside domestic places. For example, hometactics can foster a sense of comfort precisely where 'familiarity and belonging in spaces that are not welcoming, safe, or familiar' prevails: which is to say, 'in worlds that "undo" us'.[160] Such 'undoing' was the objective of the Crystal Palace foray in 1851 – tactics meant to creatively unmask institutions and ideology within diverting spaces – but was also fostered by familiar genres of popular entertainment. Abolitionists' inciting of conversations at the Great Exhibition might be regarded as a tactic of the weak, but it relied explicitly on the idioculture of cross-racial abolition and hometactics of claiming the Crystal Palace as a place safe for freedom-seekers (but not the culture that enchained them) to make the invisible engine of the United States' prosperity visible in the bodies of Brown and the Crafts. Instead of celebrating settler US residents' ingenuity and dominance, the Crafts' party performatively opened up hegemonic assumptions for debate. They summoned understanding of facets of the United States not otherwise fully visible in the exhibit – the practices, laws, and ideologies of human bondage, the cultural genocides of the slave trade and unceded land appropriations, and the paradoxology of both Christianity and republicanism in such a state – of which some adamantly would not speak yet were called forth to recognise.

Labour and leisure, duty and sociability, resistance and belonging happened under many guises in Victorian diversions. Whereas Christmas was a bank holiday spent by almost everyone in domestic spaces, Boxing Day was when people emerged to conspicuously celebrate the season.[161] Every theatre wanted to capitalise on this by luring people in to see new productions, especially but not exclusively pantomimes. It gave a newspaperman like Frederick Chesson – and his family – a lot to do in a short time and epitomises the mash-up of political awareness, sociability, leisure, work, and family that characterised their lives. The brevity of this indicative diary entry encodes a huge amount of activity:

> Monday 27 Decr. [1858]
> Called on Mr. Dymond to make final arrangements for the Pantomimes &c tonight. Then went myself to the Lyceum, & wrote the following notice of the burlesque The Siege of Troy. Returned home to tea. Mrs Thompson & Edith joined Amelia, & went with her to a private box at Covent Garden. Mr. Thompson went to the Haymarket. Herbert to the East End Theatres. At Star until four A.M. chiefly revising notices. Amelia & I came home together.

Boxing Day was serious business for Frederick, Amelia, George, and Herbert, yet also social time for the two generations of women in the box at Covent Garden: whereas Amelia's mother and thirteen-year-old sister enjoyed leisure it was Amelia's work time. The next day, four full columns of the *Morning Star* were taken up by notices of these productions.[162]

In her review, Amelia Chesson describes how the opening piece, the opera *Satanella*, was truncated to end at 10:00 p.m. The pantomime followed, and when she left at midnight the harlequinade was in full swing. She then made her way from Covent Garden to the *Star*'s offices, accompanied by her mother and sister. There, she wrote a 450-word review highlighting the meta-theatricality of a theatrical insider's joke: personifications of Italian Opera and English Opera agree to divide Covent Garden Theatre between them, and Pantomime controversially claims a piece of the seasonal calendar too. Pantomimes notoriously interweave topical references, and in his review of the Haymarket piece, following a scene-by-scene plot description, George Thompson notes allusions to events of 1858: 'the Atlantic telegraph, the royal midshipman, the comet, and the abolition of the East India Company, together with the inauguration of the British empire in India, and the proclamation of Victoria as Empress of Hindostan, are among the topics which have been made available'. The personal resonances of all these events for him are apparent, but arguably they mattered to every British subject too. Comprehension was unimpaired. Frederick Chesson saw a matinee burlesquing the *Iliad*. He expressed concern that the British public was too little informed about Achilles, Hector, and Andromache to always grasp the dramatist's satire. Did they understand the joke, for example, that Cupid is 'the real author of the Siege of Troy'? The playwright counted on it; or, more precisely, he trusted that audiences would recognise the witty twist given to a commonplace of mythology and literature and enjoy snobbery's comeuppance.[163] These reviews underline how popular performances, like other facets of 'weak publics', circulate knowledge and thus are part of a year-end review of critical developments in popular culture and politics of the sort now called trending topics. Current events, sometimes via a turf war over genre, sometimes via classical knowledge, and sometimes via contemporary politics, consolidated spectators into a public.

While the others set out to see the evening performances, Frederick Chesson arrived at the office and had six hours to fill with overseeing editorial decisions for the paper. This gave sufficient time for him to author the 1,125-word article that opens the pantomimes' section. The article reflects on the contrast between the magic, fairyland, and tinsel of the Christmas entertainments and the lives of the characters in the off-season: presumably the antic, seemingly boneless acrobats of the harlequinade revert to being ordinary folk. The fantasia then takes a meta-performative turn, asserting 'Is not society itself a pantomime on the largest scale?':

> Merry clowns or pantaloons these, my friends, even when wearing the motley of a Prime Minister. No bones needed for their characters—oh no! and enormous flexibility of back-bone. Is not pantaloon often made to swallow a huge pill [i.e., a disagreeable policy]? And what wry faces he makes at the task. So is your Minister compelled to gulp many a political bolus, compounded of his own forsworn opinions, and many a grimace it must cost him. Place is his reward, as applause is the pantaloon's. Which is the honester? From Pantaloon to P------n [Viscount Palmerston], the descent is not so great.[164]

Playgoers' ability to enjoy these jests, like readers' ability to grasp the allusions in the *Star*, was commensurate with what Braidotti calls the 'grounded shared project', traversing 'social, political, ethical and aesthetic dimensions, and transversal links between them'.[165]

Private time is not necessarily separable from the work of 'weak publics'. Frederick Chesson's article ends with just such a scenario. A family prepares to head off and see the familiar characters at a panto:

> 'and eh—my dear, mind you cover yourself well up, and take care Maria's hair is nicely done so that it does not come down, and that Johnny does not forget his pocket handkerchief: and if you won't object, dear, we'll call on our way for Harry Sparkes, who met Maria at Ramsgate in the summer, you know, and brought her a nosegay on her birth-day.' 'Yes? That's right; so we can all be happy together.'[166]

This sets leisure time – a flirtation begun on vacation – and the cosy intimacy of grooming and dressing in private time into a continuous relationship with the public sphere of the theatre. Interdependencies are made explicit. This make-believe paradigmatic dramaturgy has a place on the *Star*'s page of the Boxing Day notices, replicating, by implication, the Chesson-Thompson clan's gathering on Christmas Day, which Frederick spent pleasantly 'reading, writing, smoking & pianoforte playing'; the teatime bustle at home after Frederick had written his review of the matinee and everyone prepared to set off to their evening's work; or even more so the family's gathering in the newspaper office during the wee hours of the morning to write and edit the Boxing Day notices.[167] The authors were at work though their playgoing companions were at leisure, but they mutually participated in the 'weak public' sphere, bringing family life into the theatre and the newspaper office to shape others' opinions, experience sensory pleasure, and comingle work with leisure and diversion with matters of substance.

### Domestic Life: 'But still the house-affairs would draw her thence'

In 1829, during the election for Middlesex coroner, Elizabeth Thompson (1771–1859) witnessed her precocious son George harangue the auditory from the top of a beer barrel on Clerkenwell Green.[168] She never attended another of his speeches: not as he became a rising star in the abolition movement, not when he agitated for Corn Law repeal, nor when he ran for Parliament. Yet she lived nearby in London, frequently visited by family members and supported by her son, experiencing a long widowhood.[169] Given his mother's lack of involvement in his career, it is notable that George credits his wife, who had heard him lecture at the City of London Literary and Scientific Institution, with encouraging him to apply to the

London Anti-Slavery Society in 1831.[170] When he began his first tour through Kent, Anne was heavily pregnant and unsurprisingly did not join him; nor did she do so when he attracted the limelight and criss-crossed Britain making speeches for various campaigns. Except on his first trip to the United States, when Anne travelled with their two eldest children in tow and gave birth to a third, she stayed at home (in Edinburgh, Glasgow, and Manchester before settling in London). She was not indifferent to her husband's success: Richard Davis Webb noted that she 'was always ready to make a show of him'.[171] This was not a compliment. While George recovered after returning from his second trip to India, Webb praised Frederick Chesson yet wrote of the Thompsons, 'Oh! if he had a wife worthy of him, what a man he might not [*sic*] have been. She has been a millstone to him. I suppose if I had got such a load, I should have taken to drink, or ran away to California.'[172] A few years before, Webb was in the party that accompanied the Crafts, William Wells Brown, Anne Thompson, and the Thompson sisters to the Great Exhibition. They toured the Crystal Palace together for seven hours, so while it is credible to conclude that he knew Anne Thompson well, it is also notable that he maintained such an unfavourable opinion of her impact on her husband.

Taking the intimate sphere of sociability, family, and marriage into account does more than nuance the historiography of Victorian liberal activism: it reveals interdependencies that allowed the work of reform to be done, sustained, and either optimised or compromised. If Anne Thompson really was a millstone to her husband, Amelia Chesson was a steady partner to hers. Yet with the Thompsons' frequent hosting of abolitionists, including African Americans who upon arrival in Britain had few if any networks, Anne Thompson (like the hospitable Estlins, Armisteads, Peases, Garrisons, and other abolitionists and reformers) played a big though silent part in facilitating activism from her home base. She also sufficiently admired, and possibly befriended, the unseated US women delegates to the 1840 Anti-Slavery Convention: they all signed her autograph album.[173] The children also contributed to making visitors feel at ease. Just as time spent with political and journalistic colleagues on outings to Kew, gatherings in the back garden, or tourism contiguous with activist events far from home was not purely leisure time – a bleed-over from publicness to facets of domestic life – the intimacy of marital and family life was also impinged upon by activists' inclusion in domestic circles. In her own home, as the diaries show, Amelia welcomed Frederick's colleagues to take repasts at all hours; likewise, he often returned to find her in deep discussion with a visitor. The Chessons appear equally responsible for the

social rituals of visiting, with respect to both inviting people in and carrying on conversations.[174] Sociability, friendship, and family intermixed as
hospitable gatherings often involved more than one generation and both
males and females. During parties and soirées at the homes of friends and
colleagues, Frederick clearly depicted Amelia at ease with literati, Bloomer
feminists, musical prodigies, and activists alike. Fully accounting for the
circulatory and hosting practices of abolition and reform, and recognising
their everyday manifestations, means 'there is no longer an outside', as has
been said of capitalism under modernisation. Though changes in the law,
economy, and consumerism increasingly separated work from leisure, this
'invested "family time" with symbolic significance: "togetherness" promoted a semblance of family stability and stimulated intersubjectivities'.[175]

For the Chessons, these roles and identities overlapped, though Amelia
was a more successful extrovert. Domesticity was integrated into (not antithetical to) ambitious women's identities. As Joan Perkin points out,
'Harriet Martineau bragged that she could sew shirts and make puddings'
and 'George Eliot kept careful records of the asparagus nippers and the
second-best blankets'.[176] Women were expected to manage households well.
As George Thompson impressed upon Amelia when she paid a visit to her
newly married elder sister: she was to make herself useful, 'lightening her
cares and her toils, and at the same time to acquire habits, and an education, which may be of value to yourself at some future period', taking care
to 'spare servants as much as you can, and they will the more willingly serve
you in matters where their aid is required.[177] (Evidently, she had not learned
this in her mother's household: growing up, was Amelia occupied otherwise,
or was Anne?) Though the gendering of domestic management was uncon-
tested, the ideas that arose among radical Unitarians and liberal Anglicans
in the 1830s, systematised and publicly promoted by Mill and Taylor in
*The Subjection of Women* (1869), was the milieu in which progressive marriages operated during the mid-Victorian period: 'dual responsibility and
commitment' for both spouses rather than domination by one and atomisa-
tion of allegiances.[178] Efficient household management enabled rather than
precluded women's fulfilment of responsibilities beyond the family.

This provides a context for how Amelia's marriage and activist involve-
ments diverged from her mother's. Prior to the Chessons' wedding in 1855,
while Frederick mooned over his absent fiancée and proved his mettle
as an activist in Manchester, it is difficult to imagine him visiting the
Thompsons, recounting his adventures at their fireside 'even from my boy-
ish days, / To the very moment that he bade me tell it' as Amelia listened
entranced to his 'hair-breadth scapes'. He differed from Othello not only

in that he had no danger of being taken into slavery, but Amelia differed from the gentle Desdemona even more markedly. Though Frederick had travelled to the United States and had things to tell of 'Rough quarries, rocks and hills whose heads touch heaven' in his 'travels' history', so did she. While still a teenager, Amelia had managed her father's correspondence, mastered French, read widely, and promenaded through the Great Exhibition hailing others to affirm solidarity with freedom-seekers. Even though 'the house-affairs would draw her thence', it is hard to conjecture that 'yet she wish'd / That heaven had made her such a man' as her suitor, for she was a sufficient woman unto herself, more experienced than Frederick, at this point, in the repertoire of activism (*Othello* I.3). She could not have remembered the travails during the family's 1834–5 trip to the United States, but she had heard the stories all her life. She had met the protagonists of liberalism – the Britons, Black and white from the United States, and South Asians – whereas Frederick Chesson was a newcomer to the fray. She was as much what Stephen H. Esquith calls a 'Socratic citizen' as he: critical of state and extra-state powers that define citizens' and non-citizens' rights, skilled in rallying interest groups, with a strong inclination to 'moral dialogue' responsive to conscience.[179] Rather than pushing into the public arena in order to interfere with its masculine equilibrium, she took up her place with assured dignity. Though she did not become a public speaker, her ability at speaking was acknowledged by her *Star* colleague Julius Faucher as in excess of her husband's.[180] Whereas most feminists had to prove their worthiness to take platforms alongside men, and even then struggled for the right to be heard, her father acknowledged her intellect, and in his absence her mother facilitated her stepping forth. Her husband took Faucher's comparison with equanimity.

Locating Amelia Chesson and her exploits, either as a wage earner or activist, is not a straightforward matter, but in both modes she was a history maker countering the idea of middle-class women's passivity. As Joan Wallach Scott writes of feminism's history, Amelia 'formed any number of alliances, focused on many aspects of power' to advance her ends in 'a doubly subversive critical engagement' of power and performance.[181] Yet precisely when she came most into her own – living in neither her father's nor her marital home, for the first time in her life a female head of household – further details slip from view. To surface her again after the death of her husband, it is necessary not only to rally facts but also to expose 'their structural and ideological supports and their varying and conflicting temporalities' such as the myths of female leisure, separation of public life from domestic sociability, and divorce of intimate life from matters of global consequence.[182] It is also necessary, above all, to remember her sensitivity to routine interactions and the distinctiveness of performative dramaturgies.[183]

This can be understood even at a moment of great poignancy, such as when the congregation at Frederick's funeral sang the popular hymn 'Lead, Kindly Light'.[184] When John Henry Newman (1801–90) wrote the lyrics in 1833, the year of Frederick and Amelia Chesson's births, he was an evangelical Anglican; he converted and was named a cardinal of Rome in 1879, so the choice of hymn signalled Frederick's ecumenical broad-mindedness as well as fidelity to a political ally to the very end. As the service's closing hymn, it was likely selected (or at least endorsed) by the widow Amelia. Set to Charles Henry Purday's (1799–1885) tune, the slow metre and syncopation of 'Lead, Kindly Light' ends selective lines with three successive stressed beats. While the verse is a call for guidance in troubled times, the hymn is something more. The syncopated first-person voice gives a sense of the singer hanging back despite the legato call for an unnamed saviour to 'Lead Thou me on', an accented refrain repeated in each verse. But what follows in the third verse – the last – while deployed as a funeral hymn, and how it is metrically stressed, is especially apposite:

> So long Thy power hath blest me, sure it still will lead me on,
> O'er moor and fen, o'er crag and torrent, till the night is gone;
> And with the morn those angel faces smile,
> Which I have loved long since, and lost awhile.

A solo rendition casts the singer as the departing one, but when sung in unison (as in a service's closing hymn) something entirely different is achieved: the first-person voice cannot personify the entire congregation, neither as multiple individuals nor as a collective. The effect of communal singing – solemnity and jubilance, regret giving way to acceptance, and joy anticipated at reunion with departed others – underscores that the first-person voice parts from, and leaves behind, the living, singing, congregation. This double consciousness of voicing the perspective of the departed soul while, experientially, being the bereaved unable to follow into the afterlife is an effect of performance, not evident from either the lyrics or the tune alone, requiring voices to issue forth as hearts are rent open by the emotional register of the occasion.

As a 'chief musical critic', 'a critic of singing … [who] possessed the faculty of comparison in a high degree', Amelia was primed for this experience.[185] It requires from Christians remembrance of their creed, and joy for another at the exact moment of their own anguish. After Frederick Chesson's life of striving over difficult terrain – Othello's 'rough quarries, rocks and hills' and Newman's 'moor and fen ... crag and torrent' – perhaps the congregation imagined him meeting his mother-in-law or famous father-in-law, who had slowly declined then expired peacefully a decade before, or any one of dozens of close political friends. Perhaps his family imagined him meeting his father, whom Frederick, not quite a teenager, lost to a factory conflagration, or his mother, whose cause of death Frederick never discovered. And perhaps Amelia thought of their children – Georgina (Georgy), who died aged fifteen; Wilfred (Willie), whose loss at nine years of age was acutely mourned; and Violet, who expired before her second birthday – all welcoming their father's embrace, while the eight left behind shored one another up.

During Frederick Chesson's thirty-three years of marriage, his public life touched the equivalent of Othello's cannibals, anthropophagi, and 'most disastrous chances, / Of moving accidents' (*Othello* I.3). For much of this time, when her health and obstetric condition permitted, Amelia was at his side or shoulder-to-shoulder with their colleagues at committee meetings, speeches, and social gatherings. Yet from the moment her husband's interment was concluded in 1888 until nearly fourteen years later when her own casket was laid to rest beside his – the final intimate act – the record of Amelia Chesson's life goes quiet. Of her years in widowhood we know nearly nothing, though until her youngest child finished school the family remained in the Chelsea home, 5 Tite Street, where Frederick died and she registered as a voter in parish elections from 1889. If she still had a profession she did not tell the census enumerators what it was, but then she never was recorded as anything but 'wife' while her husband was a 'journalist' or 'newspaper editor'. In widowhood, she stipulated that she 'lived on her own means'. Frederick had left her £981, and his admirers created a trust that yielded £200 per annum.[186] This allowed the youngest child, George Donisthorpe (1875–1940), to board at Emanuel School in Wandsworth. Though her grown children were able to contribute to the weekly purse, it is plausible that Amelia also earned: the *Athenaeum*'s obituary hints at what may have been a steady production of writing, and her estate was probated at £570.[187]

In her thirties Amelia secured a place at the *Star*, yet after the paper folded in 1868 and Frederick's diaries went silent in 1870 there is no way to trace her anonymous efforts in journalism: not during his prolonged illness of 1872–3 and certainly not after she was suddenly widowed in 1888. Her only obituary hints at an autobiography, her first chance to give her individuality 'free play', but it was not forthcoming.[188] What is known makes her neither definitively exceptional (can evidence of other women like her be found to compare?) nor mediocre (there is nothing amiss with workaday writing, nothing to show she is lesser than any of her male peers who filled thousands of newspaper sheets every day, organised meetings, served on committees, and advanced the incremental work of reform in myriad ways). While she fulfilled the feminine paradigm of marriage and maternity she pursued a writerly career without subterfuge or subversion; she worked within and around domestic and maternal demands and openly became a professional journalist after already being an innovative activist, networked within a wide circle of others who (unknown to history) plausibly did the same as she.

Of the Chessons' eight surviving children, only half – all the sons – married. The eldest, Elfrida May (1856–1930), taught at a school and lived with her aunt Edith and great-aunt Eliza Musgrave (née Thompson, 1808–91?). After the turn of the century, she became an independent householder and was the only daughter who lived long enough to exercise suffrage on equal terms with men. Constance (1857–1918), a teacher of English and French, lived with her mother until Amelia's death, as did the next daughter, Amelia Mildred ('Little Millie', 1861–96, a clerk at the General Post Office). Constance later moved in with her brother (Wilfrid) Hugh (1870–1953). After he was widowed in 1906, Hugh's household included his two daughters as well as his youngest sister, Julia Eastwood (1872–1926), who may have worked as a botanical artist. Frederick William (1864–1905), their father's namesake, emigrated to the United States in 1888, followed by Harold (1868–1933) and the youngest sibling, George, all three of whom settled in Massachusetts and were visited by their eldest sister in 1909. Across this generation, Hugh left the deepest mark: like his great-grandfather Thomas Thompson he clerked for a publishing house, T. Fisher Unwin, and like his parents he went on to become a critic and author. His wife, Nora Hopper (1871–1906), who published as Mrs Hugh Chesson, was a workaday novelist and poet. Hugh struggled with mental illness. He found solace in spiritualism as a widower, but suffered another blow when his eldest daughter, a new bride, took her own life after she discovered her husband's infidelity.

Over half a century of activism precedes this trailing chronicle of a transatlantic family who cleaved together across generations, struggling, striving, caring for one another, and remaining ardent for justice. Some of Anne Erskine Lorrain Thompson's (née Spry) exploits can be roused from evanescence, Louisa Eliza Spry Nosworthy's (née Thompson) advocacy for a derided profession can be credited after a century and a half, and Amelia Ann Everard Chesson's (née Thompson) exploits, corpus of anonymously published critique, work as an organiser, and repertoire of reformist activism can be lifted from obscurity.

You loved to choose and see the garish day; but now
Just as your likenesses are unpreserved and the
offspring of your maternal bodies gone,
You fade from view.
Though lost a while it was not always thus.
Keep thou my feet, remember thy past years,
And lead thou me on to see the distant scene.

# Notes

1　Thackeray, William Makepeace. 'May-Day Ode.' In *The Works of William Makepeace Thackeray*. 24 vols. London: Smith, Elder, 1869–79: 21:45. See also 'Court Circular' and 'The Great Exhibition.' *Times*, 30 April 1851, 5.

2　Ceadel, *Semi-Detached Idealists*, 33; and Needler, G.H., ed. *Letters of Anna Jameson to Ottilie von Goethe*. London: Oxford University Press, 1939: 176–7.

3　'Great Protectionist Demonstration in Drury-Lane Theatre.' *Times*, 30 April 1851, 8.

4　Henry C. Wright (Boston) to James Haughton (Dublin), rpt. in *Liberator* 21, no. 9 (28 February 1851): 4.

5　Farmer, William. 'Fugitive Slaves at the Great Exhibition (Letter to William Lloyd Garrison, 26 June 1851).' *Liberator* 21, no. 29 (18 July 1851): 116.

6　Bogad, *Tactical Performance*, 31, 26.

7　Oldfield, *Ties That Bind*, 78; and Brown, William Wells. *Narrative of William W. Brown, a Fugitive Slave. Written by Himself*. Boston: Anti-Slavery Society, 1847.

8　'Refugee from the United States.' *Daily News*, 13 October 1849, 6; and 'Soiree to Mr. George Thompson, M.P.' *Standard*, 17 October 1850, 1.

9　Thompson references this in his 1860 lecture *Slavery in America* (14). He does not name the Crafts, but they fit the description and timeline perfectly.

10　Blackett, 'Fugitive Slaves in Britain,' 47. See also Bennett, Bridget. 'Guerrilla Inscription: Transatlantic Abolition and the 1851 Census.' *Atlantic Studies* 17, no. 3 (2020): 390; and Miekle, Laura M. *Provocative Eloquence: Theater, Violence, and Antislavery Speech in the Antebellum United States*. Ann Arbor: University of Michigan Press, 2019: 1–83.

11　Cima, Gay Gibson. *Performing Anti-Slavery: Activist Women on Antebellum Stages*. Cambridge: Cambridge University Press, 2014: 201.

12　Cima, *Performing Anti-Slavery*, 3.

13　Brown, William Wells. *The American Fugitive in Europe: Sketches of Places and People Abroad*. 1852. Edited by Paul Jefferson. Edinburgh: Edinburgh University Press, 1991: 171. Farmer wrote the preface to the first edition of Brown's memoir, in 1852. The sense that people were the exhibition was widespread: see Auerbach, Jeffrey A. *The Great Exhibition of 1851: A Nation on Display*. New Haven, CT: Yale University Press, 1999: 158.

14　Brown, *American Fugitive*, 165. Brown states that he went directly from his lodgings in Cecil Street (off Drury Lane) to Hyde Park, and returned on an omnibus with the lady, espying Thomas Carlyle along the return journey. This is entirely at variance with Farmer's account and reflects a different occasion: Farmer, 'Fugitive Slaves', 116.

15 Farmer, 'Fugitive Slaves', 116.

16 'The Great Exhibition.' *Bath Chronicle and Weekly Gazette*, 26 June 1851, 4.

17 'Mr. G. Thompson, M.P., Disenfranchised.' *Reynolds's Newspaper*, 5 October 1851, 4.

18 Farmer was George Thompson's colleague in the National and Financial Reform Association. He was one of two honorary secretaries of Thompson's 1850 testimonial committee, and later worked as a journalist for the *Clerkenwell News*. *Morning Post*, 24 April 1850, 6.

19 Merrill, 'Exhibiting Race', 326.

20 Bogad, *Tactical Performance*, 58.

21 Merrill, 'Exhibiting Race', 328.

22 Droth, Marina. 'Mapping The Greek Slave.' *Nineteenth-Century Art Worldwide* 15, no. 2 (2016): n.p. http://19thc-artworldwide.org/index.php/summer16/droth-on-mapping-the-greek-slave#exhibition.

23 Holger Hoock argues that *The Wounded Indian* was another missed opportunity for critique (*Empires of the Imagination*, 392). Its failure to register as an important installation may be indicated by its contrasted placement in the *Illustrated Exhibitor: A Tribute to the World's Industrial Jubilee...* (London: Cassell, 1851) and the *Illustrated Catalog of the Universal Exhibition* (London: 1851).

24 Farmer, 'Fugitive Slaves', 116.

25 Farmer, 'Fugitive Slaves', 116; see also Boyd and Mitchell, *Beautiful Trouble*, 166–7.

26 'The Virginian Slave: Intended as a Companion to Power's "Greek Slave".' *Punch*, 7 June 1851, 4. In comparing the two versions, Jennifer DeVere Brody emphasises 'the difficulty of stabilizing what turn out to be unstable forms' rendered as Black and white (*Impossible Purities: Blackness, Femininity, and Victorian Culture*. Durham: Duke University Press, 1998: 71).

27 Farmer, 'Fugitive Slaves', 116.

28 Rancière, *Dissensus*, 144; see also Bhabha, *Location of Culture*, 105.

29 Cima, *Performing Anti-Slavery*, 222.

30 Merrill, 'Exhibiting Race', 332; see also Merrill, Lisa. '"Most Fitting Companions": Making Mixed-Race Bodies Visible in Antebellum Public Spaces.' *Theatre Survey* 56, no. 2 (2015): 138–65; and Salzer, Kenneth. 'Great Exhibitions: Ellen Craft on the British Abolitionist Stage.' In *Transatlantic Women: Nineteenth-Century American Women Writers and Great Britain*, edited by Beth L. Lueck, Brigitte Bailey, and Lucinda L. Damon-Bach, 136–52. Durham: University of New Hampshire Press, 2012.

31 Kershaw, Baz. 'Ecoactivist Performance: The Environment as Partner in Protest?' *TDR: The Drama Review* 46 no. 1 (2002): 127.

32 Farmer, 'Fugitive Slaves', 116.

33 Warner, *Publics and Counterpublics*, 120.

34 Harney, Stefano and Fred Moten. *The Undercommons: Fugitive Planning & Black Study*. Minneapolis: University of Minnesota Press, 2013: 98.

35 The epithet is not truncated in the original. Farmer, 'Fugitive Slaves', 116. Along with *The Greek Slave*, Samuel Colt's firearms exhibit was the most popular of the 600 items from the United States. Cunliffe, Marcus. 'America at the Great Exhibition of 1851.' *American Quarterly* 3 no. 2 (1951): 115–26.

36  Wilderson, Frank, III. 'Gramsci's Black Marx: Whither the Slave in Civil Society?' *Social Identities* 9, no. 2 (2003): 30–1.

37  Farmer, 'Fugitive Slaves', 116.

38  Farmer, 'Letters from England', 25 March 1864, 1. See also George Thompson to Amelia Thompson, [March/April 1849], REAS 2/2/15, JRL.

39  Gikandi, Simon. *Slavery and the Culture of Taste*. Princeton, NJ: Princeton University Press, 2001: 28–29, 33.

40  Morgan, *Celebrities, Heroes and Champions*, 173; see also Boyd and Mitchell, *Beautiful Trouble*, 180.

41  Gikandi, *Slavery and the Culture of Taste*, 207.

42  'The Shilling Days at the Crystal Palace.' *Punch*, 7 June 1851, 240.

43  Sullivan, Shannon. 'Ontological Expansiveness.' In *50 Concepts for a Critical Phenomenology*, edited by Gail Weiss, Ann V. Murphy, and Gayle Salamon, 249. Evanston, IL: Northwestern University Press, 2020.

44  Kelly Oliver, 'Witnessing', George Yancy, 'Confiscated Bodies', and Patricia Hill Collins, 'Controlling Images', in Weiss, Murphy, and Salamon, *50 Concepts*, 341, 69, 80.

45  Butler, *Notes toward a Performative Theory*, 137.

46  *Proceedings of the General Anti-Slavery Convention*. London, 1840.

47  Mott, Lucretia. '*Slavery and "the Woman Question": Lucretia Mott's Diary of her Visit to Great Britain to Attend the World's Anti-Slavery Convention of 1840.*' Suppl. 23, *Journal of the Friends' Historical Society*, edited by Frederick B. Tolles. Haverford, PA: Friends' Historical Association, 1952: 22, 27–8, 30–2; and Stange, *British Unitarians*, 52.

48  Mott, *Slavery*, 2; and Sklar, Kathryn Kish. '"Women Who Speak for an Entire Nation": American and British Women Compared at the World Anti-Slavery Convention, London, 1840.' *Pacific Historical Review* 59, no. 4 (1990): 454–5. United States anti-slavery organisations varied in their inclusiveness, even into the mid-1850s. See Spires, *Practice of Citizenship*, 108.

49  Lucy Stone (1818–93), Abby Kelley (1811–87), and Susan B. Anthony (1820–1906) all began their speaking careers as American Anti-Slavery Society agents. Oldfield, *Ties That Bind*, 81; see also Bolt, Christine. *Feminist Ferment: 'The Woman Question' in the USA and England, 1870–1940*. London: UCL Press, 1995: 47.

50  Anne Thompson, Album Orné, fols. 88–90, Oberlin College Library Special Collections.

51  Hogan, 'Time for Silence', 71.

52  Mott, *Slavery*, 29; see also Sinha, Manisha. *The Slave's Cause: A History of Abolition*. New Haven, CT: Yale University Press, 2016: 290.

53  Maria Waring to William Lloyd Garrison, No. 6 Anti-Slavery Letters, Webb MS, MS A.1.2. vol. 9 (1), Boston Public Library, rpt. in Taylor, *British and American Abolitionists*, 95–6.

54  Oldfield, *Ties That Bind*, 156–7. None of these men are listed in the key to sitters in Benjamin Robert Haydon's commemorative painting of the Anti-Slavery Society Convention. Lucretia Mott, the only US female delegate, is a mere blur (no. 127) toward the upper right corner. Inexplicably, the group portrait includes several British female delegates. See Figures 5.3 and 5.4.

55  Hogan, Lisa Shawn. 'A Time for Silence: William Lloyd Garrison and the "Woman Question" at the 1840 World Anti-Slavery Convention.' *Gender Issues* 25 (2008): 76–7.

56  McDaniel, W. Caleb. *The Problem of Democracy in the Age of Slavery*. Baton Rouge: Louisiana State University Press, 2013: 71.

57  Lucretia Mott to Maria Weston Chapman, 29 July 1840, Weston Papers. No. 112, MS A.9.2 vol. 13 pt. 1 1840, Boston Public Library, rpt. in Taylor, *British and American Abolitionists*, 104.

58  Bolt, *Feminist Ferment*, 47.

59  Qtd. in Chase, Karen and Michael Levenson. *The Spectacle of Intimacy: A Public Life for the Victorian Family*. Princeton, NJ: Princeton University Press, 2000: 47.

60  Hewitt, Martin. 'Aspects of Platform Culture in Nineteenth-Century Britain.' *Nineteenth-Century Prose* 29, no. 1 (2002): 13–14; 'The Lady Lecturers.' *Manchester Times*, 22 January 1848, 3; and Morgan, Simon. A *Victorian Woman's Place: Public Culture in the Nineteenth Century*. London: Tauris Academic Studies, 2007: 152.

61  Two of Maria Stewart's speeches are reprinted in Porter, Dorothy B., ed. *Early Negro Writing, 1760–1837*. Baltimore: Black Classic Press, 1971: 129–40. For further context on women struggling to be speakers at African American 'Colored Conventions' dating from 1837, see Woo, Jewon. 'Deleted Name but Indelible Body: Black Women at the Colored Conventions in Antebellum Ohio.' In *The Colored Conventions Movement: Black Organizing in the Nineteenth Century*, edited by P. Gabrielle Foreman, Jim Casey, and Sarah Lynn Patterson, 179–92. Chapel Hill: University of North Carolina Press, 2021.

62  Morgan, *A Victorian Woman's Place*, 179, see also 52, 132–3, 178; and Brett, 'Political Dinners', 550–1.

63  McCarthy, Justin. 'The Influence of Women in the Politics of England.' *Ladies' Treasury*, 1 February 1871, 51.

64  'The Leeds Young Men's Anti-Slavery Society.' *Leeds Intelligencer*, 24 December 1859, 5.

65  Coleman, Willi. "Like Hot Lead to Pour on the Americans…": Sarah Parker Remond—From Salem, Mass., to the British Isles.' In *Women's Rights and Transatlantic Antislavery in the Era of Emancipation*, edited by Kathryn Kish Sklar and James Brewer Stewart. New Haven, CT: Yale University Press, 2007: 180.

66  Frederick Chesson's diary, 15 July 1859, REAS 11/7, JRL.

67  Frederick Chesson's diary, 22 July 1859, REAS 11/7, JRL.

68  Frederick Chesson's diary, 22 May 1862, REAS 11/9, JRL.

69  Frederick Chesson's diary, 24 May 1870, REAS 11/16, JRL.

70  Frederick Chesson's diary, 25 April 1870, REAS 11/16, JRL.

71  Women's Suffrage Committee, Executive Committee meeting minutes, 14 January 1876, Records of the Fawcett Society, Box FL135 2LSW/A, London School of Economics.

72  Frederick Chesson's diary, 26 March 1870, REAS 11/16, JRL.

73  Clipping dated 2 April 1870, Chesson extract books, LC 3449.S43, vol. 9, Library of Congress.

74 Eastman, Carolyn. *A Nation of Speechifiers: Making an American Public after the Revolution.* Chicago: University of Chicago Press, 2009, 11, 53, 60, 74–5, 78.

75 Hyndman, Henry Mayers. *Further Reminiscences.* London: Macmillan, 1912: 433–4. For another appreciation of women's speaking voices and acumen, see 'Women's Advocacy of Women's Suffrage (by Our Male Reporter).' *Nonconformist,* 15 May 1872, 518–19.

76 Smith, Janet, and Claire Morris Stern. 'Helen Taylor Becomes Miss Trevor, Actress.' *Theatre Notebook* 71 no. 1 (2017): 21–43. Unmarried female ratepayers received the municipal franchise in 1869, enabling women to vote and serve on school boards. Taylor sought Frederick Chesson's advice on choosing a secretary for her candidature in 1876; see F.W. Chesson to Helen Taylor, 11 November 1876, Mill-Taylor/14 No. 37 (fols. 55–7), London School of Economics.

77 Frederick Chesson's diary, 27 March 1870, REAS 11/16, JRL.

78 Records of the Fawcett Society, Box FL135 2LSW/A, London School of Economics.

79 George Thompson to William Lloyd Garrison, 24 March 1859, MS A.1.2, v. 29, p. 36, Boston Public Library.

80 Frederick Chesson's diary, 7 September 1855, REAS 11/2, JRL.

81 'Theatre Royal, Manchester. Monday, 11 June, Special representation of ROMEO AND JULIET. Romeo, Friar Laurence, Peter, and the Apothecary, by GENTLEMEN AMATEURS. Juliet, by a distinguished Lady Amateur, Authoress of "The Stage and Christianity Reconciled."' Advertisement, *Manchester Courier and Lancashire General Advertiser,* 5 June 1866, 1.

82 William Farmer attributed Thompson's loss of his re-election bid to his 'want of religious membership' and lack of wealth. Farmer to Maria Weston Chapman, 27 August 1851, MS A.9.2, v. 25, p. 114, Boston Public Library.

83 [Nosworthy, Louisa]. *An Amateur Actress of Manchester. The Stage and Christianity Reconciled: The Simple Story of the Real Troubles and Experience of an Inquirer after Truth.* Manchester: Guardian Steam Printing Offices, 1866: 16.

84 In 1856, Louisa Nosworthy was on the committee raising funds for the Church of England's All Saints School, Chorlton-upon-Medlock.

85 Rev. Dr Parker, a Congregationalist, was active in the Reform League. He was in more than one controversy that year, tussling over his lectures on the *Book of Common Prayer* with Rev. J.D. Massingham and Rev. W.A. Mitton. *Manchester Courier and Lancashire General Advertiser,* 10 January 1866, 3; 27 January 1866, 5; 10 February 1866, 5; and 10 April 1866, 7.

86 Frederick Chesson's diary, 17 May and 2 June 1866, REAS 11/13, JRL. See also 29 December 1867 and 1 March 1868, REAS 11/14–15, JRL.

87 [Nosworthy], *Stage and Christianity Reconciled,* 5.

88 A Lady, *An Appeal to the Women of England to Discourage the Stage.* London: Joseph Masters, 1855: 10.

89 Frederick Chesson's diary, 27 August 1859, 7 May 1860, 9 August 1866, 26 January 1867, and 9 February 1867, REAS 11/7–8, 13, and 14, JRL. See also

*Leicester Journal*, 23 September 1859, 5; and *Leicestershire Mercury*, 10 March 1860, 5.

90 Frederick Chesson's diary, 9–14 February 1867, REAS 11/14, JRL.

91 'Tired of Life. Tragic Death of an Actor.' *Hull Daily Mail*, 9 August 1892, 3; and 'Inquests.' *Standard*, 10 August 1892, 6.

92 Rancière, *Dissensus*, 145, 133.

93 Jameson, Anna. *The Communion of Labour: A Second Lecture on the Social Employments of Women*. London: Longman, Brown, Green, Longmans, and Roberts, 1856: 123. See also Peterson, Linda H. *Becoming a Woman of Letters: Myths of Authorship and Facts of the Victorian Market*. Princeton, NJ: Princeton University Press, 2009.

94 Scott, Joan Wallach. *The Fantasy of Feminist History*. Durham, NC: Duke University Press, 2011, 66.

95 George Thompson to William Lloyd Garrison, 24 March 1859, MS A.1.2, v. 29, p. 36, Boston Public Library.

96 Ridout, *Scenes from Bourgeois Life*, 83.

97 Initially, the newspaper offices were near Somerset House; in September 1858 the *Star* moved a kilometre east to Dorset Street, Salisbury Square (near Ludgate Circus).

98 Kent, Christopher. 'Periodical Critics of Drama, Music, & Art, 1830–1914: A Preliminary List.' *Victorian Periodicals Review* 13, no. 1/2 (1980): 31–55; Davis, Tracy C. 'Theatre Critics in Late-Victorian and Edwardian Periodicals: A Supplementary List.' *Victorian Periodicals Review* 17, no. 4 (1984): 158–64; and Cima, Gay Gibson. '"To Be Public as a Genius and Private as a Woman": The Critical Framing of Nineteenth-Century British Women Playwrights.' In *Women and Playwriting in Nineteenth-Century Britain*, edited by Tracy C. Davis and Ellen Donkin, 35–53. Cambridge: Cambridge University Press, 1999.

99 In Victorian culture, unsigned journalism was associated with 'rigor and impartiality', in contrast to journalism permeated with personality and partiality. Hadley, Elaine. *Living Liberalism: Practical Citizenship in Mid-Victorian Britain*. Chicago: University of Chicago Press, 2010: 133.

100 At the start of this period the Chessons lived in Harpur Street (near Red Lion Square), a twenty-minute walk from the office. Subsequently, they dwelt at various addresses in south London, typically a thirty- to forty-minute walk from the Salisbury Square offices, before moving to Pimlico.

101 'Newspapers such as the *Leeds Mercury* and *Intelligencer* were quite aware of the importance of a female readership, carrying advertizments [*sic*] directed at women and giving increasing column space to reviews and articles on fashion with women in mind.' Morgan, *Victorian Woman's Place*, 151.

102 This review was for the *Empire*. See Frederick Chesson's diary, 15 January 1856, REAS 11/3, JRL.

103 See Amelia Chesson's diary, 1858, passim, REAS 11/10, JRL.

104 [Amelia Chesson], 'Mr. Carlyle's Frederick the Great.' *Star*, 11 September 1858, 4. See also *Star*, 18 October 1858, 4; and 25 October 1858, 4.

105 Mann, Patricia S. *Micro-Politics: Agency in a Postfeminist Era*. Minneapolis: University of Minnesota Press, 1994: 35.

106 Frederick Chesson's diary, 9 August 1859, REAS 11/7, JRL.

107 See Dillon, *Gender of Freedom*, 24–5; and Ridout, *Scenes from Bourgeois Life*, 87.

108 Fara, Patricia. 'Beyond the Double Helix.' *Times Literary Supplement*, 24 July 2020, 14.

109 Blumenberg, Hans. *Paradigms for a Metaphorology*. Ithaca, NY: Cornell University Press, 2010: 21.

110 Frederick Chesson's diary, 18 January 1856, REAS 11/3, JRL.

111 The most durable self-help book from the period recommended weaning at nine months unless the child was sickly or the mother weak. After gradual substitution of other food, 'it would be well for the mother either to send the child away, or leave the child at home, and go away herself'. Chavasse, Pye Henry. *Advice to Mothers on the Management of Their Offspring*. London: Longman, 1839: 37–8. In Maud Pember Reeves' study of London mothers, weaning generally happened towards the end of a baby's first year; see Ross, Ellen. *Love and Toil: Motherhood in Outcast London, 1870–1918*. Oxford: Oxford University Press, 1993: 141–2.

112 George Thompson to Amelia Chesson, 24 December 1857, REAS 2/2/65, JRL.

113 'Amelia Ann Everard Chesson.' *Athenaeum*, 1 February 1902, 145.

114 Musgrave, Michael. *The Music Life of the Crystal Palace*. Cambridge: Cambridge University Press, 1995: 19, 45.

115 Conquergood, Dwight. *Cultural Struggles: Performance, Ethnography, Praxis*. Ann Arbor: University of Michigan Press, 2013: 32.

116 Esquith, *Intimacy and Spectacle*, 14.

117 Robbins, Bruce, ed. 'Introduction: The Public as Phantom.' In *The Phantom Public Sphere*, vii–xxvi. Minneapolis: University of Minnesota Press, 1993: xiv.

118 Nash, Kate. 'Towards Transnational Democratization?' In *Transnationalizing the Public Sphere*, 60–78. Cambridge: Polity, 2014: 72.

119 Frederick Chesson's diary, 3 August 1865, REAS 11/12, JRL.

120 Frederick Chesson's diary, 8 and 15 June 1864, REAS 11/11, JRL. Likewise, on 2 April 1866 (REAS 11/13, JRL), he went to the opera in Amelia's stead; she was unwell and miscarried nearly three weeks later.

121 Frederick Chesson's diary, 18 January 1867, REAS 11/14, JRL.

122 'Amelia Ann Everard Chesson.' *Athenaeum*, 1 February 1902, 145.

123 Bloch, Ruth H. 'Inside and Outside the Public Sphere.' *William and Mary Quarterly* 61, no. 1 (2005): 102.

124 Fraser, Nancy. 'Rethinking the Public Sphere: A Contribution to the Critique of Actually Existing Democracy.' In *The Phantom Public Sphere*, edited by Bruce Robbins, 1–32. Minneapolis: University of Minnesota Press, 1993: 19. See also Habermas, *Structural Transformation*.

125 Benhabib, Seyla. *Situating the Self: Gender, Community, and Postmodernism in Contemporary Ethics*. New York: Routledge, 1992: 93.

126 Butler, *Notes toward a Performative Theory of Assembly*, 45, 88.

127 Fraser, 'Rethinking', 12.

128   Morgan, *Victorian Woman's Place*, 159; and Scott, *Fantasy of Feminist History*, 122.

129   Fraser 'Rethinking', 14; and Eley, Geoff. 'Nations, Publics, and Political Cultures: Placing Habermas in the Nineteenth Century.' In *Habermas and the Public Sphere*, edited by Craig Calhoun, 289–339. Cambridge: MIT Press, 1993: 312.

130   Fraser, 'Rethinking', 24–5.

131   Dillon, Elizabeth Maddock. *New World Drama: The Performative Commons in the Atlantic World*. Durham, NC: Duke University Press, 2014: 14.

132   [Amelia Chesson], 'The Handel Festival. Second Day's Performance.' *Morning Star*, 18 June 1857, 3.

133   [Chesson], 'The Handel Festival', 3.

134   Musgrave, *Music Life*, 45.

135   [Amelia Chesson], Our Own Correspondent, 'The Handel Festival: The First Day.' *Newcastle Chronicle*, 22 June 1859, 2.

136   Mann, *Micro-Politics*, 21.

137   See Amelia Chesson's diary, passim, REAS 10, JRL.

138   Colbert, Soyica Diggs. *Black Movements: Performance and Cultural Politics*. New Brunswick, NJ: Rutgers University Press, 2017: 108.

139   Braidotti, 'Intensive Genre and the Demise of Gender', 46; and Braidotti, Rosi. *Metamorphoses: Towards a Materialist Theory of Becoming*. Cambridge: Polity, 2002: 115.

140   Couldry, Nick. 'What and Where Is the Transnationalized Public Sphere?' In *Transnationalizing the Public Sphere*, edited by Kate Nash, 43–59. Cambridge: Polity, 2014: 43.

141   Irigaray, Luce. *This Sex Which Is Not One*. Translated by Catherine Porter. Ithaca, NY: Cornell University Press, 1985: 106–18.

142   Davidoff, Leonore, and Catherine Hall. *Family Fortunes: Men and Women of the English Middle Class, 1780–1850*. Chicago: University of Chicago Press, 1987.

143   See, for example, Frederick Chesson's 1875 pamphlet *The Treatment of Women in Italy*, reprinted from the *St James's Magazine*.

144   Amelia Chesson's diary, June-August 1858, REAS 10, JRL.

145   Frederick Chesson's diary, 4 February 1860, REAS 11/7, JRL. Craft read from *Running a Thousand Miles for Freedom, or The Escape of William and Ellen Craft from Slavery*. London: William Tweedie, 1860. It was published in the spring, and Frederick Chesson's notice of the book appeared in the *Star* on 15 June 1860.

146   Mohanty, Chandra. 'Under Western Eyes: Feminist Scholarship and Colonial Discourses.' *Feminist Review* 30, no. 1 (1988): 61–88.

147   Yellin, Jean Fagan. 'Introduction'. In *Incidents in the Life of a Slave Girl*, by Harriet A. Jacobs, edited by Lydia Maria Child, xix–liii. Cambridge, MA: Belknap Press, 2009: xlv.

148   Yellin, Jean Fagan. 'Incidents Abroad: Harriet Jacobs and the Transatlantic Movement.' In *Women's Rights and Transatlantic Antislavery in the Era of Emancipation*, edited by Kathryn Kish Sklar and James Brewer Stewart, 158–72. New Haven, CT: Yale University Press, 2007: 166–7.

149 See Child, Lydia Maria. *Appeal in Favor of That Class of Americans Called Africans*. Boston: Allen and Ticknor, 1833.

150 Frederick Chesson's diary, 5 January 1862, REAS 11/9, JRL.

151 [Amelia Chesson], 'Domestic Slave-Life in the Southern States.' *Morning Star*, 10 March 1862, 3. Jacobs' memoir was published as *The Deeper Wrong, or Incidents in the Life of a Slave Girl. Written by Herself* (London: Tweedie, 1860), under the pen name Linda Brent.

152 Eastman, *Nation of Speechifiers*, 12; see also Hadley, *Living Liberalism*, 20; and Oliver, Robert T. *The Influence of Rhetoric in the Shaping of Great Britain: From the Roman Invasion to the Early Nineteenth Century*. Newark: University of Delaware Press, 1986: 341.

153 Chase and Levenson, *Spectacle of Intimacy*, 143.

154 Morgan, Simon. 'Domestic Economy and Political Agitation: Women and the Anti-Corn Law League, 1839–46.' In *Women in British Politics, 1760–1860: The Power of the Petticoat*, edited by Kathryn Gleadle and Sarah Richardson, 115–33. Houndmills: Macmillan, 2000.

155 Anne Thompson preserved 'Hints to the Ladies How to Aid the League Bazaar' (May 1845), a full-page illustrated list of ways to volunteer and promote the bazaar held at Covent Garden Theatre. Anne Thompson, Album Orné, fol. 83, Oberlin College Library Special Collections.

156 Fine, Gary Alan. *Tiny Publics: A Theory of Group Action and Culture*. New York: Russell Sage Foundation, 2012: 8, 5, 24.

157 Martin, 'Popular Political Oratory', 46.

158 Frederick Chesson's diary, 21–2 June 1867, REAS 11/15, JRL; and Fine, 'Sticky Cultures', 396.

159 Eley, 'Nations, Publics, and Political Cultures', 312; see also Hall, Catherine. 'Private Persons versus Public Someones: Class, Gender, and Publics in England, 1780–1850.' In *Language, Gender, and Childhood*, edited by Carolyn Steedman, Cathy Urwin, and Valerie Walkerdine, 10–33. London: Routledge, 1985: 11.

160 Mariana Ortega, 'Hometactics', in Weiss, Murphy, and Salamon, *50 Concepts*, 169, 171.

161 Davis, Jim. 'Boxing Day.' In *The Performing Century: Nineteenth-Century Theatre's History*, edited by Tracy C. Davis and Peter Holland, 13–31. Houndmills: Palgrave, 2007.

162 'Boxing Night. The Pantomimes.' *Morning Star*, 28 December 1858, 4.

163 'Boxing Night', 4. See also Caputo, Nicoletta. '"The Farcical Tragedies of King Richard III": The Nineteenth-Century Burlesques.' *Theatre Survey* 62, no. 1 (2021): 27.

164 [Frederick Chesson], 'Boxing Night. The Pantomimes.' *Morning Star*, 28 December 1858, 4.

165 Braidotti, *Posthuman*, 92–3.

166 [Frederick Chesson], 'Boxing Night. The Pantomimes.' *Morning Star*, 28 December 1858, 4.

167 Frederick Chesson's diary, 25 December 1858, REAS 11/6, JRL.

168  Farmer, 'Letters from England', 19 February 1864, 1. The quotation in the section heading is from *Othello* I.3.

169  See, for example, Samuel Joseph May (London) to William Lloyd Garrison, 17 January 1859, MS A.1.2, v. 29, p. 6, Boston Public Library.

170  'Complimentary Breakfast to Mr. George Thompson.' *Liverpool Daily Post*, 23 January 1864, 7.

171  Richard Davis Webb (Dublin) to Anne Warren Weston, 26 September 1857, MS A.9.2, v. 29, p. 25, Boston Public Library.

172  Richard Davis Webb (Dublin) to Samuel May, 22 July 1859, MS B.1.6, v. 7, p. 57, Boston Public Library.

173  Anne Thompson, Album Orné, fol. 88, Oberlin College Library Special Collections. N.P. Rogers, editor of the *Herald of Freedom* and co-delegate with Lucretia Mott, added a testimonial to how 'This album of Mrs. George Thompson seems to me a most appropriate tablet on which to record the facts' (fol. 89).

174  Normally, 'within the domestic social space the husband was an actor, but he was not prime mover'; rather, women oversaw these social rituals. Tosh, John. *A Man's Place: Masculinity and the Middle-Class Home in Victorian England*. New Haven, CT: Yale University Press, 1999: 124.

175  Strange, Julie-Marie. *Fatherhood and the British Working Class, 1865–1914*. Cambridge: Cambridge University Press, 2015: 114.

176  Perkin, Joan. *Women and Marriage in Nineteenth-Century England*. London: Routledge, 1989: 249.

177  George Thompson to Amelia Thompson (Manchester), 2 February 1852, REAS 2/2/36, JRL.

178  Griffin, Ben. *The Politics of Gender in Victorian Britain: Masculinity, Political Culture and the Struggle for Women's Rights*. Cambridge: Cambridge University Press, 2012: 59. See also Gleadle, Kathryn. *The Early Feminists: Radical Unitarians and the Emergence of the Women's Rights Movement, 1831–1851*. New York: St Martin's Press, 1995: 113; and Mill, John Stuart. *The Subjection of Women*. London: Longmans, 1869.

179  Esquith, *Intimacy and Spectacle*, 15.

180  Frederick Chesson's diary, 21 March 1857, REAS 11/4, JRL.

181  Scott, *Fantasy of Feminist History*, 33.

182  Scott, Joan Wallach. *On the Judgment of History*. New York: Columbia University Press, 2020: 76.

183  Fine, *Tiny Publics*, 25.

184  'Funeral of Mr. F.W. Chesson.' *Daily News*, 7 May 1888, 3.

185  'Amelia Ann Everard Chesson', 145.

186  *Liverpool Mercury*, 13 December 1888, 5.

187  'Amelia Ann Everard Chesson', 145. Presumably, the capital in the memorial fund had been liquidated.

188  'Amelia Ann Everard Chesson', 145.

# Bibliography

## Manuscript Sources

Bodleian Library: Anti-Slavery Papers (Aborigines' Protection Society; British and Foreign Anti-Slavery Society)
Boston Public Library: Anti-Slavery Manuscripts
British Library: Charles Wentworth Dilke Papers; Sir Arthur Hamilton-Gordon Papers
Gilder Lehrman Institute of American History: Gilder Lehrman Collection
John Rylands Library (Manchester) (JRL): Raymond English Anti-Slavery Collection (REAS)
Library of Congress: Chesson and Thompson Extract Books
London School of Economics: Fawcett Society; Mill-Taylor Collection
Manchester Central Reference Library and Archives: George Wilson Papers; Anti-Corn Law League Letter Book
Oberlin College Library, Special Collections: Anne Thompson Album Orné
William L. Clements Library, University of Michigan Special Collections: James G. Birney Papers; Weld-Grimké Family Papers; Letters from George Thompson to Elizabeth Pease and Anne Thompson

## Newspapers

*Aberdeen Journal*
*Abolitionist* (Boston)
*Allen's Indian Mail* (London)
*Anti-Slavery Reporter* (London)
*Aris's Birmingham Gazette* (UK)
*Athenaeum* (London)
*Bath Chronicle and Weekly Gazette*
*Bengal Catholic Herald* (Calcutta)
*Boston Chronicle*
*Bradford Observer*
*British Banner* (London)
*British Indian Advocate* (London)
*Caledonian Mercury* (Edinburgh)

*Colonial Intelligencer, or Aborigines' Friend* (London)
*Coventry Herald and Observer*
*Cruikshank's Magazine* (London)
*Daily News* (London)
*Dumfries and Galloway Standard*
*Dundee Advertiser*
*Eclectic Review* (London)
*Empire* (London)
*Era* (London)
*Examiner* (London)
*Examiner and London Review*
*Exeter and Plymouth Gazette* (UK)
*Freeman's Journal* (Dublin)
*Gloucestershire Echo*
*Herald of Freedom* (Concord, MA)
*Hereford Times*
*Hull Daily Mail*
*Illustrated London News*
*Leeds Intelligencer*, a.k.a. *Leeds Intelligencer and Yorkshire General Advertiser*
*Leeds Mercury and Intelligencer*
*Leeds Times*
*Leicester Chronicle*
*Leicester Journal*
*Leicestershire Mercury*
*Liberator* (Boston)
*Liverpool Daily Post*
*Liverpool Mercury*
*Lloyd's Weekly Newspaper* (London)
*Manchester Courier and Lancashire General Advertiser*
*Manchester Examiner and Times*, a.k.a. *Manchester Times*
*Manchester Guardian*
*Morning Advertiser* (London)
*Morning Chronicle* (London)
*Morning Post* (London)
*Morning Star*
*Newcastle Chronicle*
*Newcastle Courant*
*Newcastle Guardian and Tyne Mercury*
*Newcastle Journal*
*Niles Weekly Register* (Baltimore)
*Nonconformist* (London), a.k.a. *Nonconformist and Independent*
*Norfolk News* (Norwich, UK)
*Northern Star* (Leeds)
*Observer* (London)
*Pall Mall Gazette* (London)

*Punch; or, the London Charivari* (London)
*Raleigh Register and North-Carolina Gazette*
*Reynolds's Newspaper* (London)
*Royal Cornwall Gazette*
*Scotsman* (Edinburgh)
*Sheffield and Rotherham Independent*
*Shield* (London)
*Southampton Herald*
*South London Chronicle*
*Standard* (London)
*Star* (London) in two editions: *Morning Star* and *Evening Star*
*Suffolk and Essex Free Press* (Sudbury)
*Sun* (London)
*Times* (London)
*Western Daily Press* (Yeovil)
*Worcestershire Chronicle*
*Wrexham Weekly Advertiser*
*York Herald*
*Yorkshire Gazette*

## Published Sources

Ahmed, Sara. *The Cultural Politics of Emotion.* 2nd ed. Edinburgh: Edinburgh University Press, 2014.
Ahmed, Sara. *Queer Phenomenology: Orientations, Objects, Others.* Durham, NC: Duke University Press, 2006.
[Albert, F.E.] 'Domestic Slave-Dealing in Turkey.' *Gentlemen's Magazine*, June 1878, 666–87.
Alden, Henry Mills. 'Eucken Agonistes.' *North American Review* 201, no. 710 (1915): 57–63.
Allen, Richard B. *European Slave Trading in the Indian Ocean.* Athens: Ohio State University Press, 2014.
Allen, Robert C., and Roman Studer. 'Prices and Wages in India, 1595–1930.' Spreadsheet. Global Price and Income History Group, University of California, Davis. Uploaded September 2009. http://gpih.ucdavis.edu/Datafilelist.htm.
Altick, Richard. *The Shows of London.* Cambridge, MA: Belknap Press, 1978.
'Amelia Ann Everard Chesson.' *Athenaeum*, 1 February 1902, 145.
*American Slavery: Report of a Public Meeting Held at Finsbury Chapel, Moorfields, to Receive Frederick Douglass, the American Slave, on Friday, May 22, 1846.* London: Christopher B. Christians, 1846.
'Analyses Bibliographiques.' *L'Année Psychologique* 22 (1920): 255–6.
*Annual Report of the Edinburgh Ladies' Emancipation Society, and Sketches of Anti-Slavery Events and the Condition of the Freedmen during the Year Ending 15th February 1866.* Edinburgh: H. Armour, 1866.

Auerbach, Jeffrey A. *The Great Exhibition of 1851: A Nation on Display*. New Haven, CT: Yale University Press, 1999.

Austin, L.F. *Dinner to Mr. Chesson, at the National Liberal Club, on Friday, July 16th, 1886*. London: National Liberal Club, 1886.

Ball, James. *Theater of State: A Dramaturgy of the United Nations*. Evanston, IL: Northwestern University Press, 2020.

Baptist, Edward E. *The Half Has Never Been Told: Slavery and the Making of American Capitalism*. New York: Basic Books, 2014.

Bass, Gary J. *Freedom's Battle: The Origins of Humanitarian Intervention*. New York: Alfred A. Knopf, 2008.

Basu, Baman Das. *Story of Satara*. Edited by Ramananda Chatterjee. Calcutta: Modern Review Office, 1922.

Bauman, Richard. 'Performance.' In *A Companion to Folklore*, edited by Regina F. Bendix and Galit Hasan-Rokem, 94–119. Oxford: Blackwell, 2012.

Bayly, C.A. *Recovering Liberties: Indian Thought in the Age of Liberalism and Empire*. Cambridge: Cambridge University Press, 2012.

Benhabib, Seyla. *Situating the Self: Gender, Community, and Postmodernism in Contemporary Ethics*. New York: Routledge, 1992.

Bennett, Bridget. 'Guerrilla Inscription: Transatlantic Abolition and the 1851 Census.' *Atlantic Studies* 17, no. 3 (2020): 375–98.

Bentley, Michael. *Lord Salisbury's World: Conservative Environments in Late-Victorian Britain*. Cambridge: Cambridge University Press, 2001.

Bhabha, Homi. *The Location of Culture*. Hoboken, NJ: Taylor & Francis, 2012.

Biagini, E.F. 'Radicalism and Liberty.' In *Liberty and Authority in Victorian Britain*, edited by Peter Mandler, 101–25. Oxford: Oxford University Press, 2006.

*Biographical Sketch and Portrait of George Thompson, Esq*. Calcutta: J.A. Gibbons, 1843.

Birdoff, Harry. *The World's Greatest Hit: Uncle Tom's Cabin*. New York: S.F. Vanni, 1947.

Blackett, R.J.M. 'Fugitive Slaves in Britain: The Odyssey of William and Ellen Craft.' *Journal of American Studies* 12, no. 1 (1978): 41–62.

Blackett, R.J.M. 'William G. Allen: The Forgotten Professor.' *Civil War History* 26, no. 1 (1980): 39–52.

Blair, Hugh. *Lectures on Rhetoric and Belles Lettres*. London: T. Tegg, 1845. Reprint, Philadelphia: Hayes and Zell, 1854.

Blassingame, John W., ed. *The Frederick Douglass Papers. Series One: Speeches, Debates, and Interviews*. Vol. 1, 1841–46. New Haven, CT: Yale University Press, 1979.

Blight, David W. *Frederick Douglass: Prophet of Freedom*. New York: Simon and Schuster, 2018.

Bloch, Ruth H. 'Inside and Outside the Public Sphere.' *William and Mary Quarterly* 61, no. 1 (2005): 99–106.

Blumenberg, Hans. *Paradigms for a Metaphorology*. Ithaca, NY: Cornell University Press, 2010.

Bogad, L.M. *Tactical Performance: The Theory and Practice of Serious Play*. London: Routledge, 2016.

Bolt, Christine. *The Anti-Slavery Movement and Reconstruction: A Study in Anglo-American Co-Operation 1833–77*. Oxford: Oxford University Press, 1969.

Bolt, Christine. *Feminist Ferment: 'The Woman Question' in the USA and England, 1870–1940*. London: UCL Press, 1995.

Booth, Michael. *Victorian Spectacular Theatre*. Cambridge: Cambridge University Press, 1981.

Bortle, John E. 'The Bright-Comet Chronicles.' *International Comet Quarterly*, 1998. Harvard University Department of Earth and Planetary Sciences. www .icq.eps.harvard.edu/bortle.html.

Bourne, George. *A Picture of Slavery in the United States of America*. Middletown, CT: Edwin Hunt, 1834.

Bourne, H.R. Fox. *The Aborigines Protection Society: Chapters in Its History*. London: P.S. King, 1899.

Boyce, William Ralph. *Rudolf Eucken's Philosophy of Life*. 2nd ed. London: A. and C. Black, 1907.

Boyd, Andrew, and Oswald Mitchell, eds. *Beautiful Trouble: A Toolbox for the Revolution*. New York: O/R Books, 2012.

Braidotti, Rosi. 'Intensive Genre and the Demise of Gender.' *Angelaki: Journal of the Theoretical Humanities* 13, no. 2 (2008): 45–57.

Braidotti, Rosi. *Metamorphoses: Towards a Materialist Theory of Becoming*. Cambridge: Polity, 2002.

Braidotti, Rosi. *The Posthuman*. Cambridge: Polity, 2013.

Brett, Peter. 'Political Dinners in Early Nineteenth-Century Britain: Platform, Meeting Place and Battleground.' *History* 81, no. 264 (1996): 527–52.

Bright, Charles. *The Story of the Atlantic Cable*. New York: D. Appleton, 1903.

British India. *Speeches Delivered by Major-General John Briggs and George Thompson at the Annual Meeting of the Glasgow Society for Promoting the Cause of Universal Emancipation, Protecting the Aborigines of the British Dependencies, and Bettering the Condition of the Natives of India; held August 1, 1839*. Edinburgh: W. Oliphant, Jun., 1839.

Brody, Jennifer DeVere. *Impossible Purities: Blackness, Femininity, and Victorian Culture*. Durham, NC: Duke University Press, 1998.

Brougham, Henry. *Speeches of Henry Lord Brougham upon Questions Relating to Public Rights, Duties*. Edinburgh: Adam and Charles Black, 1838.

Brown, Christopher Leslie. *Moral Capital: Foundations of British Abolitionism*. Chapel Hill: University of North Carolina Press, 2006.

Brown, J.B. 'Politics of the Poppy: The Society for the Suppression of the Opium Trade, 1874–1916.' *Journal of Contemporary History* 8, no. 3 (1973): 97–111.

Brown, William Wells. *The American Fugitive in Europe: Sketches of Places and People Abroad*. 1852. Edited by Paul Jefferson. Edinburgh: Edinburgh University Press, 1991.

Brown, William Wells. *Narrative of William W. Brown, a Fugitive Slave. Written by Himself*. Boston: Anti-Slavery Society, 1847.

Bruce, John, and Louis Riel. 'Declaration of the People of Rupert's Land and the North-West.' *Manitoba Pageant* 9, no. 3 (April 1964). Manitoba Historical Society. Updated 1 July 2009. www.mhs.mb.ca/docs/pageant/09/rupertslanddeclaration.shtml.

Butler, Josephine. *Personal Reminiscences of a Great Crusade*. London: Horace Marshall and Son, 1896.

Butler, Judith. *Bodies That Matter: On the Discursive Limits of 'Sex.'* New York: Routledge, 1993.

Butler, Judith. *Notes toward a Performative Theory of Assembly*. Cambridge, MA: Harvard University Press, 2015.

Butler, Judith, and Athena Athanasiou. *Dispossession: The Performance in the Political*. Cambridge: Polity, 2013.

Byron, George G. 'The Dream.' In *The Works of Lord Byron*. Vol. 4. London: John Murray, 1905.

Cabranes-Grant, Leo. 'From Scenarios to Networks: Performing the Intercultural in Colonial Mexico.' *Theatre Journal* 63, no. 4 (2011): 499–520.

Cammaerts, Bart. 'Social Media and Activism.' In *The International Encyclopedia of Digital Communication and Society*. Edited by R. Mansell and P. Hwa,. n.p. Oxford: Wiley-Blackwell, 2015.

Campbell, Duncan Andrew. *English Public Opinion and the American Civil War*. Woodbridge, Suffolk: Royal Historical Society, 2004.

Capaldi, Nicholas. *John Stuart Mill: A Biography*. Cambridge: Cambridge University Press, 2004.

Capefigue, Jean Baptiste Honoré Raymond. *The Diplomatists of Europe*. Edited by William Monteith. London: G.W. Nickisson, 1845.

Caputo, Nicoletta. '"The Farcical Tragedies of King Richard III": The Nineteenth-Century Burlesques.' *Theatre Survey* 62, no. 1 (2021): 25–50.

Ceadel, Martin. *Semi-Detached Idealists: The British Peace Movement and International Relations, 1854–1945*. Oxford: Oxford University Press, 2000.

Cecil, Robert. *The Kidnapping of Bulgarians during the Russo-Turkish War*. London: P.S. King and Son, 1879.

Chakrabarty, Dipesh. *Provincializing Europe: Postcolonial Thought and Historical Difference*. Princeton, NJ: Princeton University Press, 2008.

Chambers-Letson, Joshua. *After the Party: A Manifesto for Queer of Color Life*. New York: New York University Press, 2018.

Chase, Karen, and Michael Levenson. *The Spectacle of Intimacy: A Public Life for the Victorian Family*. Princeton, NJ: Princeton University Press, 2000.

Chavasse, Pye Henry. *Advice to Mothers on the Management of Their Offspring*. London: Longman, 1839.

Chesson, Frederick. *The Atlantic Cables: A Review of Recent Telegraphic Regulation in Canada*. London: Effingham Wilson, 1875.

Chesson, Frederick. *Cuba in Revolution: A Statement of Facts*. London: Head, Hole, 1871.

Chesson, Frederick. *The Dutch Boers and Slavery in the Trans-vaal Republic, in a Letter to R.N. Fowler, Esq*. London: W. Tweedie, 1869.

Chesson, Frederick. 'Paper on How to Influence Members of the House of Commons, Read by Mr. F.W. Chesson at a Conference of Delegates from Associations and Committees Formed in Various Towns for Promoting the Repeal of the Contagious Diseases Acts, Held at the Freemasons' Tavern, 5th and 6th May, 1870.' London: National Association for Repeal of the Contagious Diseases Act, 1870.

Chesson, Frederick. *The Princes of India: Their Rights and Our Duties.* London: W. Tweedie, 1872.

Chesson, Frederick, ed. and intro. 'Story of a Fugitive Slave.' *Ladies' Newspaper*, 13 September 1856–10 January 1857.

Chesson, Frederick. *The Treatment of Women in Italy.* London: Gilbert and Rivington, 1875.

Chesson, Frederick. *Turkey and the Slave Trade. A Statement of Facts. Papers on the Eastern Question*, no. 7. London: Cassell Petter and Galpin, 1877.

Child, Lydia Maria. *Appeal in Favor of That Class of Americans Called Africans.* Boston: Allen and Ticknor, 1833.

Cima, Gay Gibson. *Performing Anti-Slavery: Activist Women on Antebellum Stages.* Cambridge: Cambridge University Press, 2014.

Cima, Gay Gibson. '"To Be Public as a Genius and Private as a Woman": The Critical Framing of Nineteenth-Century British Women Playwrights.' In *Women and Playwriting in Nineteenth-Century Britain*, edited by Tracy C. Davis and Ellen Donkin, 35–53. Cambridge: Cambridge University Press, 1999.

Clover, Joshua. *Riot. Strike. Riot. The New Era of Uprisings.* London: Verso, 2016.

Clubb, Louise George. *Italian Drama in Shakespeare's Time.* New Haven, CT: Yale University Press, 1989.

Cobden, Richard. *The Political Writings of Richard Cobden.* 2 vols. London: William Ridgway, 1867.

Cohen, Deborah. *Family Secrets: Shame and Privacy in Modern Britain.* Oxford: Oxford University Press, 2013.

Colbert, Soyica Diggs. *Black Movements: Performance and Cultural Politics.* New Brunswick, NJ: Rutgers University Press, 2017.

Coleman, Willi. '"Like Hot Lead to Pour on the Americans...": Sarah Parker Remond—From Salem, Mass., to the British Isles.' In *Women's Rights and Transatlantic Antislavery in the Era of Emancipation*, edited by Kathryn Kish Sklar and James Brewer Stewart, 173–88. New Haven, CT: Yale University Press, 2007.

Conquergood, Dwight. *Cultural Struggles: Performance, Ethnography, Praxis.* Ann Arbor: University of Michigan Press, 2013.

Conquergood, Dwight. 'Performance Studies Interventions and Radical Research.' *TDR: The Drama Review* 46, no. 2 (2002). 146–56.

Conquergood, Dwight. 'Rethinking Elocution: The Trope of the Talking Book and Other Figures of Speech.' *Text and Performance Quarterly* 20, no. 4 (2000): 325–41.

Conrad, Sebastian. *What Is Global History?* Princeton, NJ: Princeton University Press, 2016.

Cooper, Barry. *Alexander Kennedy Isbister: A Respectable Critic of the Honourable Company*. Ottawa: Carleton University Press, 1988.

Cooper, Charles Alfred. *An Editor's Retrospect: Fifty Years of Newspaper Work*. London: Macmillan, 1896.

Cooper, Joseph. *The Lost Continent, or Slavery and the Slave-Trade in Africa*. London: Longmans, Green, 1875.

Cooper, Joseph. *Observations on the Asiatic Slave-Trade*. London: Longmans, Green, 1875.

Cooper, Joseph, trans. and preface. *The Slave Trade in Africa in 1872*. By Étienne Félix Berlioux. London: Edward Marsh, 1872.

Cooper, Joseph. *Turkey and Egypt: Past and Present State in Relation to Africa*. London: Samuel Harris, 1876.

Couldry, Nick. 'What and Where Is the Transnationalized Public Sphere?' In *Transnationalizing the Public Sphere*, edited by Kate Nash, 43–59. Cambridge: Polity, 2014.

Cowper, William. *The Task, A Poem in Six Books*. New York: M. Durell, 1796.

Cox, Jeffrey C. *Romanticism in the Shadow of War: Literary Culture in the Napoleon War Years*. Cambridge: Cambridge University Press, 2014.

Craft, William. *Running a Thousand Miles for Freedom, or The Escape of William and Ellen Craft from Slavery*. London: William Tweedie, 1860.

Crawfurd, John. *An Appeal from the Inhabitants of British India to the Justice of the People of India: A Popular Enquiry into the Operation of the System of Taxation in British India*. London: Henry Hooper, 1839.

Cull, Laura. 'Performance as Philosophy: Responding to the Problem of "Application."' *Theatre Research International* 37, no. 1 (2012): 20–7.

Cunliffe, Marcus. 'America at the Great Exhibition of 1851.' *American Quarterly* 3 no. 2 (1951): 115–26.

David, Robert G. *The Arctic in the British Imagination, 1818–1914*. Manchester: Manchester University Press, 2000.

Davidoff, Leonore, and Catherine Hall. *Family Fortunes: Men and Women of the English Middle Class, 1780–1850*. Chicago: University of Chicago Press, 1987.

Davies, Rachel Bryant. *Troy, Carthage and the Victorians: The Drama of Classical Ruins in the Nineteenth-Century Imagination*. Cambridge: Cambridge University Press, 2018.

Davis, Jim. 'Boxing Day.' In *The Performing Century: Nineteenth-Century Theatre's History*, edited by Tracy C. Davis and Peter Holland, 13–31. Houndmills: Palgrave, 2007.

Davis, Tracy C., ed. *The Broadview Anthology of Nineteenth-Century British Performance*. Peterborough, ON: Broadview Press, 2012.

Davis, Tracy C. 'Oh Canaan! Following the North Star to Canada.' In *Uncle Tom's Cabins: The Transnational History of America's Most Mutable Book*, edited by Tracy C. Davis and Stefka Mihaylova, 33–58. Ann Arbor: University of Michigan Press, 2018.

Davis, Tracy C. 'Theatre Critics in Late-Victorian and Edwardian Periodicals: A Supplementary List.' *Victorian Periodicals Review* 17, no. 4 (1984): 158–64.

Davis, Tracy C. 'Theatricality and Civil Society.' In *Theatricality*, edited by Tracy C. Davis and Thomas Postlewait, 127–55. Cambridge: Cambridge University Press, 2003.

Davis-Fisch, Heather. *Loss and Cultural Remains in Performance: The Ghosts of the Franklin Expedition*. New York: Palgrave, 2012.

*Debates at the India House: August 22nd, 23rd, and September 24th, 1845, on the Case of the Deposed Raja of Sattara, and the Impeachment of Col. C. Ovans*. London: Effingham Wilson, 1845.

Debord, Guy. *Society of the Spectacle*. Detroit, MI: Black and Red, 1983.

*The Deposed Raja of Sattara: Documents, Chiefly Official, Now for the First Time Printed*. London: W. Tyler, 1842.

Devine, T.M. 'Did Slavery Make Scotia Great?' *Britain and the World* 4, no. 1 (2011): 40–64.

Dewey, John. *The Public and Its Problems*. New York: Henry Holt, 1927.

Dibner, Bern. *The Atlantic Cable*. Norwalk, CT: Burndy Library, 1959.

Dilke, Charles Wentworth. *Greater Britain: A Record of Travel in English-Speaking Countries in 1866 and 1867*. 2 Vols. New York: Harper and Brothers, 1869.

Dillon, Elizabeth Maddock. *The Gender of Freedom: Fictions of Liberalism and the Literary Public Sphere*. Stanford, CA: Stanford University Press, 2004.

Dillon, Elizabeth Maddock. *New World Drama: The Performative Commons in the Atlantic World*. Durham, NC: Duke University Press, 2014.

Dingle, A.E. *The Campaign for Prohibition in Victorian England: The United Kingdom Alliance, 1872–1895*. London: Croom Helm, 1980.

Docker, John. 'Are Settler-Colonies Inherently Genocidal? Rereading Lemkin.' In *Empire, Colony, Genocide: Conquest, Occupation, and Subaltern Resistance in World History*, edited by A. Dirk Moses, 81–101. New York: Berghahn Books, 2008.

Donisthorpe, Woodsworth. *Individualism: A System of Politics*. Edinburgh: Macmillan, 1889.

Douglass, Frederick. *Frederick Douglass: Selected Speeches and Writings*. Edited by Philip Foner. Chicago: Lawrence Hill Books, 1999.

Douglass, Frederick. *Life and Writings of Frederick Douglass. Vol. 1, Early Years, 1817–1849*. Edited by Philip Foner. New York: International, 1950.

Douglass, Frederick. *My Bondage and My Freedom*. London: Partridge and Oakey, 1855.

Droth, Marina. 'Mapping The Greek Slave.' *Nineteenth-Century Art Worldwide* 15, no. 2 (2016): n.p. http://19thc-artworldwide.org/index.php/summer16/droth-on-mapping-the-greek-slave#exhibition.

DuBois, W.E.B. *Black Reconstruction in America: An Essay toward a History of the Part Which Black Folk Played in the Attempt to Reconstruct Democracy in America, 1860–1880*. New York, Russell and Russell, 1935.

Eastman, Carolyn. *A Nation of Speechifiers: Making an American Public after the Revolution*. Chicago: University of Chicago Press, 2009.

Eley, Geoff. 'Nations, Publics, and Political Cultures: Placing Habermas in the Nineteenth Century.' In *Habermas and the Public Sphere*, edited by Craig Calhoun, 289–339. Cambridge: MIT Press, 1993.

Elliott, David J., Marissa Silverman, and Wayne D. Bowman. 'Introduction, Aims, and Overview.' In *Artistic Citizenship: Artistry, Social Responsibility, and Ethical Praxis*, edited by David J. Elliott, Marissa Silverman, and Wayne D. Bowman, 3–21. Oxford: Oxford University Press, 2016.

Engelke, Matthew. *Think Like an Anthropologist*. Milton Keynes: Penguin, 2017.

Eno, Henry Lane. *Activism*. Princeton, NJ: Princeton University Press, 1920.

Esquith, Stephen H. *Intimacy and Spectacle: Liberal Theory as Political Education*. Ithaca, NY: Cornell University Press, 1994.

Estlin, J.B. *A Brief Notice of American Slavery, and the Abolition Movement*. London: W. Tweedie, 1853.

Eucken, Rudolf. *Knowledge and Life*. London: Williams and Norgate, 1913.

Eucken, Rudolf. *Life's Basis and Life's Ideal: The Fundamentals of a New Philosophy of Life*. 1907. Translated by Alban G. Widgery. London: Adam and Charles Black, 1912.

Eyre, John Edward. *Facts and Documents Relating to the Alleged Rebellion in Jamaica and the Measures of Repression; including Notes of the Trial of Mr. Gordon*. Jamaica Papers, no. 1. London: Jamaica Committee, 1866.

Fara, Patricia. 'Beyond the Double Helix.' *Times Literary Supplement*, 24 July 2020, 14.

Farmer, William. 'Fugitive Slaves at the Great Exhibition (Letter to William Lloyd Garrison, 26 June 1851).' *Liberator* 21, no. 29 (18 July 1851): 116.

Farmer, William. 'Letters from England. Autobiography of Geo. Thompson.' Nos. 1–7. *Liberator* 34, nos. 7–13 (12–26 February and 4–25 March 1864).

Feldman, Burton. *The Nobel Prize: A History of Genius, Controversy, and Prestige*. New York: Arcade, 2000.

Field, Cyrus W. *Ocean Telegraphy: The Twenty-Fifth Anniversary of the Organization of the First Company Ever Formed to Lay an Ocean Cable. New York: March 10, 1879*. New York: privately published, 1879.

Fine, Gary Alan. 'Sticky Cultures: Memory Publics and Communal Pasts in Competitive Chess.' *Cultural Sociology* 7, no. 4 (2013): 395–414.

Fine, Gary Alan. *Tiny Publics: A Theory of Group Action and Culture*. New York: Russell Sage Foundation, 2012.

Fitzmaurice, Andrew. 'Anticolonialism in Western Political Thought: The Colonial Origins of the Concept of Genocide.' In *Empire, Colony, Genocide: Conquest, Occupation, and Subaltern Resistance in World History*, edited by A. Dirk Moses, 55–80. New York: Berghahn Books, 2008.

Fletcher, John. 'Denouement: Notes on the End(s) of Activism.' In *Theatre, Performance, and Activism*, edited by Stephani Etheridge Woodson and Tamara Underiner, 71–80. London: Palgrave, 2018.

Franzel, Sean. *Connected by the Ear: The Media, Pedagogy, and Politics of the Romantic Lecture*. Evanston, IL: Northwestern University Press, 2013.

Fraser, Nancy. 'Rethinking the Public Sphere: A Contribution to the Critique of Actually Existing Democracy.' In *The Phantom Public Sphere*, edited by Bruce Robbins, 1–32. Minneapolis: University of Minnesota Press, 1993.

*The Free Church Alliance with Manstealers*. Glasgow: George Gallie, 1846.

Frenz, Horst, ed. *Nobel Lectures, Literature, 1901–1967*. Amsterdam: Elsevier, 1969.

Fuoss, Kirk. 'Lynching Performances, Theatres of Violence.' *Text and Performance Quarterly* 19, no. 1 (1999): 1–37.

Galbraith, John S. *The Hudson's Bay Company as an Imperial Factor, 1821–1869*. Berkeley: University of California Press, 1957.

Garbade, Kenneth D., and William L. Silber. 'Technology, Communication and the Performance of Financial Markets: 1840–1975.' *Journal of Finance* 33, no. 3 (1978): 819–32.

Gebauer, Gunter, and Christopher Wulf. *Mimesis: Culture, Art Society*. Berkeley: University of California Press, 1996.

Gifford, Ronald. 'George Thompson and Trans-Atlantic Antislavery, 1831–1865.' PhD diss., Indiana University, 1999.

Gikandi, Simon. *Slavery and the Culture of Taste*. Princeton, NJ: Princeton University Press, 2001.

Gilje, Paul A. *Rioting in America*. Bloomington: Indiana University Press, 1996.

Gillan, Kevin, Jenny Pickerill, and Frank Webster. *Anti-War Activism: New Media and Protest in the Information Age*. Basingstoke: Palgrave Macmillan, 2008.

Gladstone, William Ewart. *The Bulgarian Horrors and the Question of the East*. London: John Murray, 1876.

Glasgow Emancipation Society. *Ninth Annual Report of the Glasgow Emancipation Society*. Glasgow: D. Russell, 1843.

Gleadle, Kathryn. *The Early Feminists: Radical Unitarians and the Emergence of the Women's Rights Movement, 1831–1851*. New York: St. Martin's Press, 1995.

Goddu, Teresa. *Selling Antislavery: Abolition and Mass Media in Antebellum America*. Philadelphia: University of Pennsylvania Press, 2020.

Goffman, Irving. *The Presentation of Self in Everyday Life*. Garden City, NY: Doubleday, 1959.

Gough, John B. *Autobiography and Personal Recollections of John B. Gough, with Twenty-Six Years' Experience as a Public Speaker*. Springfield, MA: Bill, Nichols, 1869.

Gough, John B. *Orations*. Rev. ed. London: Morgan and Scott, 1878.

Gould, Marty. *Nineteenth-Century Theatre and the Imperial Encounter*. New York: Routledge, 2011.

Grandy, Moses. *Narrative of the Life of Moses Grandy, Late a Slave in the United States of America*. Introduction by George Thompson, iii–vi. Boston: Oliver Johnson, 1844.

Granovetter, Mark S. 'The Strength of Weak Ties.' *American Journal of Sociology* 78, no. 6 (1973): 1,360–80.

Grant, James. *The Great Metropolis*. 2 vols. London: Saunders and Otley, 1836.

Gray, Thomas. 'Ode on a Distant Prospect of Eton College.' 1742. Poetry Foundation. www.poetryfoundation.org/poems/44301/ode-on-a-distant-prospect-of-eton-college.

Great Britain, House of Commons. *Report of the Parliamentary Select Committee on Aboriginal Tribes, (British Settlements): Reprinted with Comments by the Aborigines' Protection Society*. London: William Ball, 1837.

Great Britain, Common Law Procedure Act 1854 (17 & 18 Vict. c. 125).

Great Britain. Slavery Abolition Act 1833 (3 & 4 Will. IV c. 73).

Griffin, Ben. *The Politics of Gender in Victorian Britain: Masculinity, Political Culture and the Struggle for Women's Rights*. Cambridge: Cambridge University Press, 2012.

Grimsted, David. *American Mobbing, 1828–1861*. Oxford: Oxford University Press, 1998.

Grimsted, David. 'Rioting in Its Jacksonian Setting.' *American Historical Review* 77, no. 2 (1972): 364–97.

Grindlay, Melville. *A View of the Present State of the Question as to Steam Communication*. London: Smith, Elder, 1837.

Gwynn, Stephen. *The Life of Rt. Hon., Sir Charles W. Dilke, Bart., M.P.* 2 vols. Completed and edited by Gertrude M. Tuckwell. New York: Macmillan, 1917.

Habermas, Jürgen. *The Structural Transformation of the Public Sphere: An Inquiry into a Category of Bourgeois Society*. Translated by Thomas Burger with Frederick Lawrence. Cambridge: MIT Press, 1989.

Hadley, Elaine. *Living Liberalism: Practical Citizenship in Mid-Victorian Britain*. Chicago: University of Chicago Press, 2010.

Hall, Catherine. *Macaulay and Son: Architects of Imperial Britain*. New Haven, CT: Yale University Press, 2012.

Hall, Catherine. 'Private Persons versus Public Someones: Class, Gender, and Publics in England, 1780–1850.' In *Language, Gender, and Childhood*, edited by Carolyn Steedman, Cathy Urwin, and Valerie Walkerdine, 10–33. London: Routledge, 1985.

*Hansard*. HC Deb. 20 July 1870, vol. 203, cc. 574–607. https://api.parliament.uk/historic-hansard/commons/1870/jul/20/adjourned-debate.

Hansen, Miriam Bratu. 'America, Paris, the Alps: Kracauer (and Benjamin) on Cinema and Modernity.' In *Cinema and the Invention of Modern Life*, edited by Leo Charney and Vanessa R. Schwartz, 362–403. Berkeley: University of California Press, 1995.

Hardt, Michael, and Antonio Negri. *Empire*. Cambridge, MA: Harvard University Press, 2000.

Harney, Stefano, and Fred Moten. *The Undercommons: Fugitive Planning & Black Study*. Minneapolis: University of Minnesota Press, 2013.

Harrison, Brian. *Peaceable Kingdom: Stability and Change in Modern Britain*. Oxford: Oxford University Press, 1982.

Harrison, Frederic. *Martial Law: Six Letters to the Daily News*. Jamaica Papers, no. 5. London: Jamaica Committee, 1867.

Hartman, Saidiya V. *Scenes of Subjection: Terror, Slavery, and Self-Making in Nineteenth-Century America*. New York: Oxford University Press, 1997.

Hawkins, Angus. *The Forgotten Prime Minister: The 14th Earl of Derby. Vol. 2, Achievement, 1851–1869*. Oxford: Oxford University Press, 2007.

Headrick, Daniel R. *The Tools of Empire: Technology and European Imperialism in the Nineteenth Century*. New York: Oxford University Press, 1981.

Heartfield, James. *The Aborigines' Protection Society: Humanitarian Imperialism in Australia, New Zealand, Fiji, Canada, South Africa, and the Congo, 1836–1909*. London: Hurst, 2011.

Henke, Robert. 'Introduction,' *Transnational Exchange in Early Modern Theatre*, edited by Robert Henke and Eric Nicholson, 1–19. Aldershot: Ashgate, 2008.

Herbert, Christopher. *War of No Pity: The Indian Mutiny and Victorian Trauma*. Princeton, NJ: Princeton University Press, 2008.

Hewitt, Martin. 'Aspects of Platform Culture in Nineteenth-Century Britain.' *Nineteenth-Century Prose* 29, no. 1 (2002): 1–32.

Hewitt, Martin. *The Dawn of the Cheap Press in Victorian Britain: The End of the 'Taxes on Knowledge,' 1849–1869*. London: Bloomsbury, 2014.

Heyrick, Elizabeth. *Immediate, not Gradual Abolition, or An Inquiry into the Shortest, Safest, and Most Effectual Means of Getting Rid of West Indian Slavery*. London: J. Hatchard, 1824.

Hilton, Boyd. *The Age of Atonement: The Influence of Evangelicalism on Social and Economic Thought, 1785–1865*. Oxford: Clarendon Press, 1986.

Hionidis, Pandeleiumon. 'Philhellenism and Party Politics in Victorian Britain: The Greek Committee of 1879–1881.' *Historical Review/La Revue Historique* 14 (2017): 141–76.

Hogan, Lisa Shawn. 'A Time for Silence: William Lloyd Garrison and the "Woman Question" at the 1840 World Anti-Slavery Convention.' *Gender Issues* 25 (2008): 63–79.

Hollinshead-Strick, Cary. *The Fourth Estate at the Fourth Wall: Newspapers on Stage in July Monarchy France*. Evanston, IL: Northwestern University Press, 2019.

Holyoake, George Jacob. *Public Speaking and Debate: A Manual for Advocates and Agitators*. 1849. 2nd rev. ed. Boston: Ginn, 1896.

Honig, Bonnie. 'Three Models of Emergency Politics.' *boundary 2*, 41, no. 2 (2014): 45–70.

Hoock, Holger. *Empires of the Imagination: Politics, War, and the Arts in the British World, 1750–1850*. London: Profile, 2010.

Hoock, Holger. *The King's Artists: The Royal Academy of Arts and the Politics of British Culture, 1760–1840*. Oxford: Clarendon, 2003.

Howe, Anthony, and Simon Morgan, eds. *The Letters of Richard Cobden*. Vol. 3, *1854–1859*. Oxford: Oxford University Press, 2007.

Huhtamo, Erkki. *Illusions in Motion: Media Archaeology of the Moving Panorama and Related Spectacles*. Cambridge: MIT Press, 2013.

Hyndman, Henry Mayers. *Further Reminiscences*. London: Macmillan, 1912.

*Illustrated Catalog of the Universal Exhibition*. London, 1851.

*The Illustrated Exhibitor: A Tribute to the World's Industrial Jubilee; Comprising Sketches, by Pen and Pencil, of the Principal Exhibits of the Great Exhibition of the Industry of all Nations, 1851*. London: Cassell, 1851.

*Information Respecting the Aborigines in the British Colonies. Circulated by Direction of the Meeting for Sufferings. Being Principally Extracts from the Report Presented to the House of Commons, by the Select Committee Appointed on that Subject*. London: Darton and Harvey, 1838.

Inglis, Julia. *The Siege of Lucknow: A Diary*. London: James R. Osgood, McIlvanie, 1892.

Irigaray, Luce. *This Sex Which Is Not One.* Translated by Catherine Porter. Ithaca, NY: Cornell University Press, 1985.

Izzo, Gary. *The Art of Play: The New Genre of Interactive Theatre.* Portsmouth, NH: Heinemann, 1977.

Jackson, Lee. *Palaces of Pleasure: From Music Halls to the Seaside to Football, How the Victorians Invented Mass Entertainment.* New Haven, CT: Yale University Press, 2019.

[Jacobs, Harriet]. *The Deeper Wrong, or Incidents in the Life of a Slave Girl. Written by Herself.* London: W. Tweedie, 1860.

Jacobs, John S. 'A True Tale of Slavery.' *Leisure Hour: A Family Journal of Instruction and Recreation,* 7 February 1861, 85–87; 14 February 1861, 108–10; 21 February 1861, 125–27; 28 February 1861, 139–41.

Jamaica Royal Commission. *Report of the Jamaica Royal Commission: Minutes of Evidence Taken before the Jamaica Royal Commission.* London: H.M. Stationery Office, British Parliamentary Papers, 1866.

Jameson, Anna. *The Communion of Labour: A Second Lecture on the Social Employments of Women.* London: Longman, Brown, Green, Longmans, and Roberts, 1856.

Jasper, James M. *The Art of Moral Protest: Culture, Biography, and Creativity in Social Movements.* Chicago: University of Chicago Press, 1997.

Jennifer DeVere Brody, *Impossible Purities: Blackness, Femininity, and Victorian Culture.* Durham: Duke University Press, 1998.

Jenkins, Roy. *Sir Charles Dilke: A Victorian Tragedy.* London: Collins, 1958.

Jenkins, T.A. *The Liberal Ascendancy, 1830–1886.* New York: St. Martin's, 1994.

Jephson, Henry. *The Platform: Its Rise and Progress.* 2 vols. New York: Macmillan, 1892.

'John to Jonathan: An Address Delivered in the Music Hall, Boston, on the 11th of October, 1870.' *Macmillan's Magazine,* December 1870, 81–91.

Jose, Jim, and Kcasey McLoughlin. 'John Stuart Mill and the Contagious Diseases Acts: Whose Law? Whose Liberty? Whose Greater Good?' *Law and History Review* 34, no. 2 (2016): 249–79.

Kaiser, Matthew. *The World in Play: Portraits of a Victorian Concept.* Stanford, CA: Stanford University Press, 2012.

Keating, James. '"The Defection of Women": The New Zealand Contagious Diseases Act Repeal Campaign and Transnational Feminist Dialogue in the Late Nineteenth Century.' *Women's History Review* 25, no. 2 (2016): 187–206.

Kent, Christopher. 'Periodical Critics of Drama, Music, & Art, 1830–1914: A Preliminary List.' *Victorian Periodicals Review* 13, no. 1/2 (1980): 31–55.

Kershaw, Baz. 'Ecoactivist Performance: The Environment as Partner in Protest?' *TDR: The Drama Review* 46 no. 1 (2002): 118–30.

Kiernan, Ben. *Blood and Soil: A World History of Genocide and Extermination from Sparta to Darfur.* New Haven, CT: Yale University Press, 2007.

Kling, Blair B. *Partner in Empire: Dwarkanath Tagore and the Age of Enterprise in Eastern India.* Berkeley: University of California Press, 1976.

Kocmanovà, Jessie, and J.E. Purkyné. 'The Aesthetic Opinions of William Morris.' *Comparative Literature Studies* 4, no. 4 (1967): 409–24.

Koditschek, Theodore. *Liberalism, Imperialism, and the Historical Imagination: Nineteenth-Century Visions of a Greater Britain*. Cambridge: Cambridge University Press, 2011.

Koselleck, Reinhart, and Hans-Georg Gadamer. *Zeitschichten: Studien zur Historik*. Frankfurt-am-Main: Suhrkamp, 2002.

Kostal, R.W. *A Jurisprudence of Power: Victorian Empire and the Rule of Law*. Oxford: Oxford University Press, 2005.

Kraditor, Aileen S. *Means and Ends in American Abolitionism: Garrison and His Critics on Strategy and Tactics, 1834–1850*. New York: Pantheon, 1967.

Kulkarni, Sumitra. *The Satara Raj, 1818–1848: A Study in History, Administration, and Culture*. New Delhi: Mittal, 1995.

Kusch, M. 'Psychologism.' In *International Encyclopedia of the Social & Behavioral Sciences*, edited by Neil J. Smelser and Paul B. Baltes, vol. 18, 12,388–90. Amsterdam: Elsevier, 2001.

A Lady. *An Appeal to the Women of England to Discourage the Stage*. London: Joseph Masters, 1855.

Laidlaw, Zoë. '"Justice to India—Prosperity to England—Freedom to the Slave!": Humanitarian and Moral Reform Campaigns on India, Aborigines and American Slavery.' *Journal of the Royal Asiatic Society* 22, no. 2 (2012): 299–324.

'The Lancet.' *Lancet* 86, no. 2206 (1865): 625–28.

Latham, Robert Gordon, and Edward Forbes. *The Natural History Department of the Crystal Palace Described: Zoology and Botany*. London: Bradbury and Evans, 1854.

Lawson, Tom. *The Last Man: A British Genocide in Tasmania*. London: I.B. Tauris, 2014.

Layard, Austen Henry. *Nineveh and Its Remains*. London: John Murray, 1849.

Layard, Austen Henry. *The Nineveh Court in the Crystal Palace*. London: Bradbury and Evans, 1854.

Lethbridge, Roper. *The Golden Book of India, a Genealogical and Biographical Dictionary*. New York: Macmillan, 1893.

Levien, Sidney Levo. *A Chronicle of the Rebellion in Jamaica in the Year of Our Lord 1865*. Kingston, 1865.

Levine, Caroline. *Forms: Whole, Rhythm, Hierarchy, Network*. Princeton, NJ: Princeton University Press, 2015.

Lidwell-Durnin, John. 'William Benjamin Carpenter and the Emerging Science of Heredity.' *Journal of the History of Biology* 53 (2020): 81–103.

Lightman, Bernard. 'Spectacle in Leicester Square: James Wyld's Great Globe, 1851–61.' In *Popular Exhibitions: Science and Showmanship, 1840–1910*, edited by Joe Kember, John Plunkett, and Jill A. Sullivan, 19–40. London: Pickering and Chatto, 2012.

Loggins, Vernon. 'Writings of the Leading Negro Antislavery Agents, 1840–1865.' In *Critical Essays on Frederick Douglass*, edited by William L. Andrews, 37–55. Boston: G.K. Hall, 1991.

Long, Robert Crozier. 'Anglo-Swedish Oppositions: A Letter from Stockholm.' *Fortnightly Review* 99, no. 590 (2016): 235–48.

Lorde, Audre. 'The Master's Tools Will Never Dismantle the Master's House.' In *Sister Outsider: Essays and Speeches*, 110–14. Berkeley, CA: Crossing Press, 1984.

Lorimer, Douglas A. 'Race, Science and Culture: Historical Continuities and Discontinuities, 1850–1914.' In *The Victorians and Race*, edited by Shearer West, 12–33. Farnham, UK: Ashgate, 1996.

Maclear, J.F. 'Thomas Smyth, Frederick Douglass, and the Belfast Antislavery Campaign.' *South Carolina Historical Magazine* 80, no. 4 (1979): 286–97.

Maclure, Robert. *The Arctic Dispatches Containing an Account of the Discovery of the North-West Passage*. London: J.D. Potter, 1854.

Majendie, Vivian Dering. *Up Among the Pandies, or A Year's Service in India*. London: Routledge, Warne, and Routledge, 1859.

Malchow, Howard L. *Gentlemen Capitalists: The Social and Political World of the Victorian Businessman*. Palo Alto, CA: Stanford University Press, 1992.

Malley, Shawn. *From Archaeology to Spectacle in Victorian Britain: The Case of Assyria*. Farnham: Ashgate, 2012.

Mann, Patricia S. *Micro-Politics: Agency in a Postfeminist Era*. Minneapolis: University of Minnesota Press, 1994.

Manthrirathne, Sanjeevi. 'The Reform Movements in India and Sri Lanka: A Comparative Study.' PhD diss., University of Kashmir, 2013.

Marks, Steven G. *The Information Nexus: Global Capitalism from the Renaissance to the Present*. Cambridge: Cambridge University Press, 2016.

Martin, Janette Lisa. 'Popular Political Oratory and Itinerant Lecturing in Yorkshire and the North East in the Age of Chartism, 1837–60.' PhD diss., University of York, 2010.

Martineau, Harriet. *The Martyr Age of the United States*. Boston: Weeks, Jordan, 1839.

Martineau, James. *Essays, Reviews, and Addresses*. London: Longmans, Green, 1890.

McCarthy, Justin. *A History of Our Own Times, from the Ascension of Queen Victoria to the General Election of 1880*. Vol. 3. London: Chatto and Windus, 1880.

McCarthy, Justin. 'The Influence of Women in the Politics of England.' *Ladies' Treasury*, (1 February 1871): 51–5.

McDaniel, W. Caleb. *The Problem of Democracy in the Age of Slavery*. Baton Rouge: Louisiana State University Press, 2013.

McLuhan, Marshall. *Understanding Media: The Extensions of Man*. 1964. Reprinted, New York: McGraw-Hill, 1994.

McNee, Alan. *The Cockney Who Sold the Alps: Albert Smith and the Ascent of Mont Blanc*. Brighton, UK: Victorian Secrets, 2015.

McQueen, James. *General Statistics of the British Empire*. London: B. Fellows, 1836.

McWilliam, Rohan. *London's West End: Creating the Pleasure District, 1800–1914*. Oxford: Oxford University, 2020.

Meeuwis, Michael. *Everyone's Theater: Literature and Daily Life in England, 1860–1914*. Ann Arbor: University of Michigan Press, 2019.

Mehrotra, S.R. 'The British India Society and its Bengal Branch, 1839-46.' *Indian Economic and Social History Review* 4, no. 2 (1967): 131–54.

Mehrotra, S.R. *Emergence of the Indian National Congress.* Kolkata: Rupa, 2007.

Mehrotra, S.R. 'The Landholders' Society, 1838–44.' *Indian Economic and Social History Review* 3, no. 4 (1966): 358–75.

Meisel, Joseph S. *Public Speech and the Culture of Public Life in the Age of Gladstone.* New York: Columbia University Press, 2001.

Meisel, Martin. *Realizations: Narrative, Pictorial, and Theatrical Arts in Nineteenth-Century England.* Princeton, NJ: Princeton University Press, 1983.

Merrill, Lisa. 'Exhibiting Race "Under the World's Huge Glass Case": William and Ellen Craft and William Wells Brown at the Great Exhibition in Crystal Palace, London, 1851.' *Slavery and Abolition* 33, no. 2 (2012): 321–36.

Merrill, Lisa. '"Most Fitting Companions": Making Mixed-Race Bodies Visible in Antebellum Public Spaces.' *Theatre Survey* 56, no. 2 (2015): 138–65.

Miekle, Laura M. *Provocative Eloquence: Theater, Violence, and Antislavery Speech in the Antebellum United States.* Ann Arbor: University of Michigan Press, 2019.

Mill, John Stuart. *On Liberty.* London: John W. Parker and Son, 1859.

Mill, John Stuart. *The Subjection of Women.* London: Longmans, 1869.

Mill, John Stuart. *Utilitarianism.* London: Longman, Green, Longman, Roberts, and Green, 1864.

*Minutes of Evidence Taken before the Select Committee on the Hudson's Bay Company.* London: House of Commons, 1857.

Mitchell, Samantha. 'Grandy, Moses.' NCPedia, North Carolina Government and Heritage Library. 2013. www.ncpedia.org/biography/grandy-moses.

Mohanty, Bidyut. 'Orissa Famine of 1866: Demographic and Economic Consequences.' *Economic and Political Weekly* 28, no. 1 (1993): 55–7, 59–66.

Mohanty, Chandra. 'Under Western Eyes: Feminist Scholarship and Colonial Discourses.' *Feminist Review* 30, no. 1 (1988): 61–88.

Mongia, Radhika V. 'Impartial Regimes of Truth: Indentured Indian Labour and the Status of the Inquiry.' *Cultural Studies* 18, no. 5 (2004): 749–68.

Montgomery, James. *The West Indies, and Other Poems.* 6th ed. London: Longman, Hurst, Rees, Orme, and Brown, 1823.

Moran, Karen Board. 'William Lloyd Garrison.' Worcester Women's History Project. 26 March 2005. www.wwhp.org/Resources/Biographies/williamlloydgarrison .html.

Morgan, Simon. *Celebrities, Heroes and Champions: Popular Politicians in the Age of Reform, 1810–67.* Manchester: Manchester University Press, 2021.

Morgan, Simon. 'Domestic Economy and Political Agitation: Women and the Anti-Corn Law League, 1839–46.' In *Women in British Politics, 1760–1860: The Power of the Petticoat,* edited by Kathryn Gleadle and Sarah Richardson, 115–33. Houndmills: Macmillan, 2000.

Morgan, Simon. 'George Donisthorpe Thompson (1804–1878).' In *Oxford Dictionary of National Biography.* Oxford: Oxford University Press, 2016.

Morgan, Simon. *A Victorian Woman's Place: Public Culture in the Nineteenth Century.* London: Tauris Academic Studies, 2007.

Morris, May. *William Morris, Artist, Writer, Socialist.* Oxford: Blackwell, 1936.

Morris, William. *Hopes and Fears for Art: Five Lectures Delivered in Birmingham, London & Nottingham.* London: Longmans, 1902.

Moses, Dirk, ed. *Empire, Colony, Genocide: Conquest, Occupation, and Subaltern Resistance in World History*. New York: Berghahn Books, 2008.

Mott, Lucretia. 'Slavery and "the Woman Question": Lucretia Mott's Diary of her Visit to Great Britain to Attend the World's Anti-Slavery Convention of 1840.' Edited by Frederick B. Tolles. Supplement 23 *Journal of the Friends' Historical Society*. Haverford, PA: Friends' Historical Association, 1952.

Murray, Hannah. 'Walking Tours.' Frederick Douglass in Britain and Ireland. Accessed March 15, 2022. http://frederickdouglassinbritain.com/.

Musgrave, Michael. *The Music Life of the Crystal Palace*. Cambridge: Cambridge University Press, 1995.

Nash, Kate., ed. 'Towards Transnational Democratization?' In *Transnationalizing the Public Sphere*, 60–78. Cambridge: Polity, 2014.

Needler, G. H., ed. *Letters of Anna Jameson to Ottilie von Goethe*. London: Oxford University Press, 1939.

Nettlebec, Amanda. *Indigenous Rights and Colonial Subjecthood: Protection and Reform in the Nineteenth-Century British Empire*. Cambridge: Cambridge University Press, 2019.

Nichols, Charles H. 'Who Read the Slave Narratives?' *Phylon Quarterly* 20, no. 2 (1959): 149–62.

Nicholls, David. *The Lost Prime Minister: A Life of Sir Charles Dilke*. London: Hambledon Press, 1993.

Nicholson, Renton. *The Swell's Night Guide, or A Peep through the Great Metropolis*. London: H. Smith, 1849.

Norton, Marcy. 'Tasting Empire: Chocolate and the European Internalization of Mesoamerican Aesthetics.' *American Historical Review* 111, no. 3 (2006): 660–91.

[Nosworthy, Louisa]. *An Amateur Actress of Manchester. The Stage and Christianity Reconciled: The Simple Story of the Real Troubles and Experience of an Inquirer after Truth*. Manchester: Guardian Steam Printing Offices, 1866.

Oettermann, Stephan. *The Panorama: History of a Mass Medium*. Translated by Deborah Lucas Schneider. New York: Zone Books, 1997.

Oldfield, J.R. *The Ties That Bind: Transatlantic Abolitionism in the Age of Reform, c. 1820–1866*. Liverpool: Liverpool University Press, 2020.

Oleksijczuk, Denise Blake. *The First Panoramas: Visions of British Imperialism*. Minneapolis: University of Minnesota Press, 2011.

Oliver, Robert T. *The Influence of Rhetoric in the Shaping of Great Britain: From the Roman Invasion to the Early Nineteenth Century*. Newark: University of Delaware Press, 1986.

Olson, Robert J.M., and Jay M. Pasachoff. *Fire in the Sky: Comets and Meteors, the Decisive Centuries, in British Art and Science*. Cambridge: Cambridge University Press, 1998.

Ong, Walter. *Orality and Literacy: The Technologizing of the Word*. London: Routledge, 1988.

Osterhammel, Jürgen. *The Transformation of the World: A Global History of the Nineteenth Century*. Princeton, NJ: Princeton University Press, 2014.

Palsetia, Jesse S. *Jamsetjee Jejeebhoy of Bombay: Partnership and Public Culture in Empire*. Oxford: Oxford University Press, 2015.

Parry, Jonathan. 'Liberalism and Liberty.' In *Liberty and Authority in Victorian Britain*, edited by Peter Mandler, 71–101. Oxford: Oxford University Press, 2006.

Parry, Jonathan. *The Rise and Fall of Liberal Government in Victoria Britain*. New Haven, CT: Yale University Press, 1993.

Paul, Aparna. 'Containment of "Evil" and "Vice": The Contagious Diseases Act XIV of 1868 in Bombay Presidency.' *Indica* 48, no. 2 (2011): 127–39.

Payne, Ernest A. 'Gleanings from the Correspondence of George Eliot.' *Baptist Quarterly* 17, no. 4 (1957): 179–81.

Perkin, Joan. *Women and Marriage in Nineteenth-Century England*. London: Routledge, 1989.

Peterson, Linda H. *Becoming a Woman of Letters: Myths of Authorship and Facts of the Victorian Market*. Princeton, NJ: Princeton University Press, 2009.

Philips, C.H., and D. Philips. 'Alphabetical List of Directors of the East India Company from 1758 to 1858.' *Journal of the Royal Asiatic Society* 73, no. 4 (1941): 325–36.

Phillips, Arthur. *The Law Relating to the Land Tenures of Lower Bengal (Tagore Law Lectures 1874–75)*. Calcutta: Thacker, Spink, 1876.

Porter, Dorothy B., ed. *Early Negro Writing, 1760–1837*. Baltimore: Black Classic Press, 1971.

Price, Thomas. *Slavery in America: With Notices of the Present State of Slavery and the Slave Trade throughout the World*. London: G. Wightman, 1837.

Prince, Carl E. 'The Great "Riot Year": Jacksonian Democracy and Patterns of Violence in 1834.' *Journal of the Early Republic* 5, no. 1 (1985): 1–19.

*Proceedings at a Special General Court of Proprietors of East India Stock, Held at the East India House, on the 12th and 13th of February, 1840, Respecting the Dethronement of His Highness the Rajah of Satara*. London: John Wilson, 1840.

*Proceedings of the General Anti-Slavery Convention*. London: 1840.

Pulis, John W. *Moving On: Black Loyalists in the Afro-Atlantic World*. Abingdon: Routledge, 2013.

Qureshi, Sadiah. 'Meeting the Zulus: Displayed Peoples and the Shows of London, 1859–79.' In *Popular Exhibitions, Science and Showmanship, 1840–1910*, edited by Joe Kember, John Plunkett, and Jill A. Sullivan, 183–98. London: Pickering and Chatto, 2012.

Rai, Shirin M. 'Political Performance: A Framework for Analysing Democratic Politics.' *Political Studies* 63 (2015): 1179–97.

Rancière, Jacques. *Dissensus: On Politics and Aesthetics*. New York: Continuum, 2010.

*Reception of George Thompson in Great Britain (Compiled from Various British Publications)*. Boston: Isaac Knapp, 1836.

Rice, Alan. *Racial Narratives of the Black Atlantic*. London: Bloomsbury Academic, 2003.

Richards, Jeffrey. *The Golden Age of Pantomime: Slapstick, Spectacle and Subversion in Victorian England*. London: I.B. Tauris, 2015.

Richards, Leonard L. *'Gentlemen of Property and Standing': Anti-Abolition Mobs in Jacksonian America.* Oxford: Oxford University Press, 1970.

Ridout, Nicholas. *Scenes from Bourgeois Life.* Ann Arbor: University of Michigan Press, 2020.

Ritchie, J. Ewing. *The Night Side of London.* London: William Tweedie, 1858.

Robbins, Bruce, ed. 'Introduction: The Public as Phantom.' In *The Phantom Public Sphere*, vii–xxvi. *The Phantom Public Sphere*. Minneapolis: University of Minnesota Press, 1993.

Rogers, Helen. 'Women and Liberty.' In *Liberty and Authority in Victorian Britain*, edited by Peter Mandler, 125–54. Oxford: Oxford University Press, 2006.

Rogers, Helen. *Women and the People: Authority, Authorship and the Radical Tradition in Nineteenth-Century England.* Burlington: Ashgate, 2000.

Rogers, Nathaniel Peabody. *A Collection from the Miscellaneous Writings of Nathaniel Peabody Rogers.* Manchester, NH: William H. Fisk, 1849.

Roper, Moses. *A Narrative of the Adventures and Escape of Moses Roper from American Slavery.* London: Darton, Harvey, and Darton, 1837.

Ross, Ellen. *Love and Toil: Motherhood in Outcast London, 1870–1918.* Oxford: Oxford University Press, 1993.

Rothfels, Nigel. 'Aztecs, Aborigines and Ape-People: Science and Freaks in Germany, 1850–1910.' In *Freakery: Cultural Spectacles of the Extraordinary Body*, edited by Rosemarie Garland Thomson, 158–73. New York: New York University Press, 1996.

Rothschild, Emma. *The Inner Life of Empires: An Eighteenth-Century History.* Princeton, NJ: Princeton University Press, 2011.

Russell, William Howard. *The Atlantic Telegraph.* London: Day and Son, 1866.

Salzer, Kenneth. 'Great Exhibitions: Ellen Craft on the British Abolitionist Stage.' In *Transatlantic Women: Nineteenth-Century American Women Writers and Great Britain*, edited by Beth L. Lueck, Brigitte Bailey, and Lucinda L. Damon-Bach, 136–52. Durham: University of New Hampshire Press, 2012.

Santos, Boaventura de Sousa. *The End of the Cognitive Empire: The Coming of Age of Epistemologies of the South.* Durham, NC: Duke University Press, 2018.

Schiller, Friedrich. *Aesthetical and Philosophical Essays.* Vol. 1. Boston: Francis A. Niccolls, 1902.

Scholberg, Henry, ed. *The Biographical Dictionary of Greater India.* New Delhi: Promilla, 1998.

Schwoch, James. *Wired into Nature: The Telegraph and the North American Frontier.* Urbana: University of Illinois Press, 2018.

Scott, James C. *Domination and the Arts of Resistance: Hidden Transcripts.* New Haven, CT: Yale University Press, 1990.

Scott, Joan Wallach. *The Fantasy of Feminist History.* Durham, NC: Duke University Press, 2011.

Scott, Joan Wallach. *On the Judgment of History.* New York: Columbia University Press, 2020.

Sergeant, Lewis. 'F.W. Chesson.' *Leisure Hour: An Illustrated Magazine for Home Reading* (October 1888); 677–79.

Sharp, Gene. *The Politics of Nonviolent Action.* Boston: Porter Sargent, 1973.

Sharpe, Christina. *In the Wake: On Blackness and Being*. Durham, NC: Duke University Press, 2016.

Shaw, Sebag and H.A.R.J. Wilson. *The Corporation of Certified Secretaries Manual on the Law of Meetings, Their Conduct and Procedure*. London: Macdonald and Evans, 1947.

Sheller, Mimi. *Democracy after Slavery: Black Publics and Peasant Radicalism in Haiti and Jamaica*. Gainesville: University Press of Florida, 2000.

Shepperson, George. 'The Free Church and American Slavery.' *Scottish Historical Review* 30, no. 110 (1951): 126–43.

'Shorter Notices: Present-Day Ethics in their Relations to the Spiritual Life; Knowledge and Life; Rudolf Eucken: His Philosophy and Influence.' *New Statesman* 2, no. 46 (1914): 636–7.

Sinha, Manisha. *The Slave's Cause: A History of Abolition*. New Haven, CT: Yale University Press, 2016.

Sklar, Kathryn Kish. '"Women Who Speak for an Entire Nation": American and British Women Compared at the World Anti-Slavery Convention, London, 1840.' *Pacific Historical Review* 59, no. 4 (1990): 453–99.

Smiles, Samuel. *Self-Help: With Illustrations of Character, Conduct, and Perseverance*. Edited by Peter W. Sinnema. Oxford: Oxford University Press, 2002.

Smith, Albert. *The Story of Mont Blanc*. London: n.p., 1853.

Smith, Janet, and Claire Morris Stern. 'Helen Taylor Becomes Miss Trevor, Actress.' *Theatre Notebook* 71 no. 1 (2017): 21–43.

Smith, Kimberly K. *The Dominion of Voice: Riot, Reason, and Romance in Antebellum Politics*. Lawrence: University of Kansas Press, 1999.

*Speeches Delivered at a Public Meeting for the Formation of a British India Society*. London: British India Society, 1839.

Spires, Derrick R. *The Practice of Citizenship: Black Politics and Print Culture in the Early United States*. Philadelphia: University of Pennsylvania Press, 2019.

Spurgeon, Charles. 'High Doctrine and Broad Doctrine.' Metropolitan Tabernacle, 3 June 1860. The Spurgeon Center. Accessed 14 May 2022. www.spurgeon .org/resource-library/sermons/high-doctrine-2/#flipbook/.

Spurgeon, Charles. 'Not Now, But Hereafter!' Sermon no. 410, Metropolitan Tabernacle, Newington, 22 September 1861. Spurgeon Gems. Accessed March 15, 2022. www.spurgeongems.org/spurgeon-sermons/.

Standage, Tom. *The Victorian Internet: The Remarkable Story of the Telegraph and the Nineteenth Century's On-Line Pioneers*. New York: Walker, 1998.

Stange, Douglas Charles. *British Unitarians against American Slavery, 1833–65*. Rutherford: Fairleigh Dickinson University Press, 1984.

Stanton, Henry Brewster. *Sketches of Reforms and Reformers of Great Britain and Ireland*. New York: John Wiley, 1849.

Statistics Canada. Accessed March 15, 2022. www.statcan.gc.ca.

Stephen, George. *Antislavery Recollections: In a Series of Letters Addressed to Mrs. Beecher Stowe*. London: Thomas Hatchard, 1854.

Strange, Julie-Marie. *Fatherhood and the British Working Class, 1865–1914*. Cambridge: Cambridge University Press, 2015.

Sullivan, Shannon. 'Ontological Expansiveness.' In *50 Concepts for a Critical Phenomenology*, edited by Gail Weiss, Ann V. Murphy, and Gayle Salamon, 249–54. Evanston, IL: Northwestern University Press, 2020.

Swaisland, Charles. 'The Aborigines Protection Society, 1837–1909.' *Slavery and Abolition* 21, no. 2 (2000): 265–80.

Tatz, Colin. 'The Destruction of Aboriginal Society in Australia.' In *Genocide of Indigenous Peoples*, edited by Samuel Totten and Robert K. Hitchcock, vol. 8, 87–116. New Brunswick, NJ: Transaction, 2011.

Taylor, Charles. *Philosophy and the Human Sciences.* Cambridge: Cambridge University Press, 1985.

Taylor, Clare. *British and American Abolitionists: An Episode in Transatlantic Understanding.* Edinburgh: Edinburgh University Press, 1974.

Taylor, M.W. 'Wordsworth Donisthorpe (1847–1914).' In *Oxford Dictionary of National Biography.* Oxford: Oxford University Press, 2012.

*The Ten Chief Courts of Sydenham Palace.* London: Routledge, 1854.

Thackeray, William Makepeace. *The Works of William Makepeace Thackeray.* 24 vols. London: Smith, Elder, 1869–79.

Therborn, Göran. 'Globalizations: Dimensions, Historical Waves, Regional Effects, Normative Governance.' *International Sociology* 15, no. 2 (2000): 151–79.

Thompson, George. *Addresses; Delivered at Meetings of the Native Community of Calcutta and on Other Occasions.* Calcutta: Thacker, 1843.

Thompson, George. *Anti-Corn Law Lecture at Longtown. Thursday January 20th, 1842.* Carlisle: James Steel, 1842.

Thompson, George. *The Free Church of Scotland and American Slavery. Substance of Speeches Delivered in the Music Hall, Edinburgh, during May and June 1846, by George Thompson, Esq. and the Rev. Henry C. Wright.* Edinburgh: Scottish Anti-Slavery Society, 1846.

Thompson, George. *A Full Report of the Proceedings at the Meetings of Messrs. Thompson and Borthwick at Dalkeith.* Glasgow: George Gallie & W.R. M'Phun, 1833.

Thompson, George. *Lectures of George Thompson, with a Full Report of the Discussion between Mr. Thompson and Mr. Borthwick, the Pro-slavery Agent, held at the Royal Amphitheatre, Liverpool, Engl., and which continued for Six Evenings with Unabated Interest.* Edited by William Lloyd Garrison. Boston: I. Knapp, 1836.

Thompson, George. *Lectures on British India, Delivered in the Friends' Meeting-House, Manchester, England, in October 1839.* Pawtucket, RI: William and Robert Adams, 1840.

Thompson, George. *Lectures on the Corn Laws, 7 January 1842.* Carlisle: J. Steel, 1842.

Thompson, George. *Letters and Addresses by George Thompson, during his Mission in the United States, from Oct. 1st, 1834, to Nov. 27, 1835.* Boston: Isaac Kent, 1837.

Thompson, George. *The Raja of Satara: Speech Delivered in the Court of Proprietors at the India House, July 15, 1841.* London: W. Tyler, 1841.

Thompson, George. *Six Lectures on the Condition, Resources and Prospects of British India and the Duties and Responsibilities of Great Britain to Do Justice to that Vast Empire.* London: John W. Parker, 1842.

Thompson, George. *Slavery in America: A Lecture Delivered in the Abbey-Close Church, Paisley, March 1, 1860.* London: London Emancipation Tracts, 1860.

Thompson, George. *Speech of George Thompson, Member of the British House of Parliament, at Toronto, May 1851.* Cincinnati: Wright, Ferris, 1851.

Thompson, George. *Speeches by Mr. George Thompson (Father of Political Education in India).* Edited by Raj Jogeshur Mitter. Calcutta: S.K. Lahiri, 1895.

Thompson, George. *Substance of an Address to the Ladies of Glasgow and Its Vicinity upon the Present Aspect of the Great Question of Negro Emancipation, Delivered in Mr Anderson's Chapel, John-St., Glasgow, on Tuesday, March 5th, 1833.* Glasgow: David Robertson, 1833.

Thompson, George. *The Substance of a Speech Delivered in the Wesleyan Methodist Chapel, Irwell-Street, Salford, Manchester, on Monday, August 13th, 1832: by George Thompson, Esq. Being a Reply to Mr. Borthwick's Statements on the Subject of British Colonial Slavery.* London: J. Hatchard and Son, 1832.

Thompson, George. *Three Lectures on British Colonial Slavery Delivered in the Royal Amphitheatre, Liverpool, on the Evenings of Tuesday, August 28, Thursday 30, and Thursday, September 6, 1832.* Liverpool: Egerton Smith, 1832.

Thompson, George. *A Voice to the United States of America, from the Metropolis of Scotland: Being an Account of Various Meetings Held in Edinburgh on the Subject of American Slavery, upon the Return of Mr. George Thompson, from His Mission to That Country.* Edinburgh: W. Oliphant, 1836.

Thompson, Joseph Parrish. *An Essay toward Principles of International Law to Govern the Intercourse of Christian with Non-Christian Peoples.* Berlin: W. Gronau, 1876.

Thornton, Edward. *The History of the British Empire in India.* London: W.H. Allen, 1859.

Tosh, John. *A Man's Place: Masculinity and the Middle-Class Home in Victorian England.* New Haven, CT: Yale University Press, 1999.

Turley, David. *The Culture of English Antislavery, 1780–1860.* London: Routledge, 1991.

Turner, Mark W. 'Periodical Time in the Nineteenth Century.' *Media History* 8, no. 2 (2002): 183–96.

Tway, Duane C. 'The Wintering Partners and the Hudson's Bay Company, 1867–1879.' *Canadian Historical Review* 41, no. 3 (1960): 215–23.

Tyrrell, Alexander. 'Making the Millennium: The Mid-Nineteenth Century Peace Movement.' *Historical Journal* 21, no. 1 (1978): 75–95.

Underhill, Edward Bean. *Dr. U.'s Letter. A Letter Addressed to the Rt. Hon. E. Cardwell, with Illustrative Documents on the Condition of Jamaica, and an Explanatory Statement.* London: Arthur Miall, 1866.

Underhill, Edward Bean. *The West Indies: Their Social and Religious Condition.* London: Jackson, Walford, and Hodder, 1862.

Van Heyningen, Elizabeth B. 'The Social Evil in the Cape Colony, 1868–1902: Prostitution and the Contagious Diseases Act.' *Journal of Southern African Studies* 10, no. 2 (1984): 170–97.

Visaria, Leela, and Pravin Visaria. 'Population (1757–1947).' In *The Cambridge Economic History of India*, edited by Dharma Kamar, vol. 2, 463–532. Cambridge: Cambridge University Press, 1983.

Warner, Michael. *Publics and Counterpublics*. New York: Zone Books, 2002.

Weiss, Gail, Ann V. Murphy, and Gayle Salamon, eds. *50 Concepts for a Critical Phenomenology*. Evanston, IL: Northwestern University Press, 2020.

Weller, Toni, and David Bawden. 'Individual Perceptions: A New Chapter on Victorian Information History.' *Library History* 22, no. 2 (2006): 137–56.

Weltman, Sharon Aronofsky. *Performing the Victorian: John Ruskin and Identity in Theater, Science, and Education*. Columbus: Ohio State University Press, 2007.

Wenzlhuemer, Roland. *Connecting the Nineteenth-Century World: The Telegraph and Globalization*. Cambridge: Cambridge University Press, 2013.

Whately, Richard. *Elements of Rhetoric; Comprising an Analysis of the Laws of Moral Evidence and Persuasion*. New York: Harper and Brothers, 1857.

Whyte, Iain. *Send Back the Money! The Free Church of Scotland and American Slavery*. Cambridge: James Clarke, 2012.

Wilderson, Frank, III. 'Gramsci's Black Marx: Whither the Slave in Civil Society?' *Social Identities* 9, no. 2 (2003): 225–40.

Woo, Jewon. 'Deleted Name but Indelible Body: Black Women at the Colored Conventions in Antebellum Ohio.' In *The Colored Conventions Movement: Black Organizing in the Nineteenth Century*, edited by P. Gabrielle Foreman, Jim Casey, and Sarah Lynn Patterson, 179–92. Chapel Hill: University of North Carolina Press, 2021.

Woodson, Carter G., ed. *Negro Orators and Their Orations*. Washington, DC: Associated, 1925.

Worthington, Hugh. 'The Late Mr Worthington's Sermons: Extract from, on Prejudice.' *Christian Reformer, or New Evangelical Miscellany* 9 (1823): 28–32.

Wright, Henry C. *The Dissolution of the American Union Demanded by Justice and Humanity, as the Incurable Enemy of Liberty*. Glasgow: D. Russell, 1845.

Wright, Henry C. 'Letter to the Ministers and Members of the Free Church of Scotland.' In *The Free Church and Her Accusers, the Question at Issue: A Letter from George Thompson, Esq. to Henry C. Wright: And One from Henry C. Wright to Ministers and Members of the Free Church of Scotland, by George Thompson and Henry C. Wright*, 6–12. Glasgow: G. Gallie, 1846.

Wyld, J. *Map of the Gold Regions of Australia*. London: privately published, 1852.

Yellin, Jean Fagan. 'Incidents Abroad: Harriet Jacobs and the Transatlantic Movement.' In *Women's Rights and Transatlantic Antislavery in the Era of Emancipation*, edited by Kathryn Kish Sklar and James Brewer Stewart, 158–72. New Haven, CT: Yale University Press, 2007.

Yellin, Jean Fagan. 'Introduction.' In *Incidents in the Life of a Slave Girl,* by Harriet A. Jacobs, edited by Lydia Maria Child, xix–liii. Cambridge, MA: Belknap Press, 2009.

Zboray, Ronald J., and Mary Saracino Zboray. *Everyday Ideas: Socioliterary Experience among Antebellum New Englanders.* Knoxville: University of Tennessee Press, 2006.

# Index

abolition, 209, 265, *See also* Slavery Abolition
Act, 1833
1830s campaign, 1, 5, 8, 19, 26, 77, 79
Black lecturers in Britain, 120, 125
Caribbean colonies, 15, 140, 176, 179
Trans-Atlantic Anti-Slavery Movement, 5, 6,
8, 15, 51, 78, 91, 117, 120, 177, 216, 261,
273, 297
Aborigines' Protection Society, xv, 6, 55, 95, 173,
188, 197, 201, 202, 205, 208, 209, 218,
233, 239, 243, 257, 261, 265, 272, 309
Ethnological Society of London, 127
Abyssinia, 262, 264
activism, 4, 6, 76, 197, 263, 329, *See also*
meetings
bazaars, 2, 14, 91, 261, 323
billboarding, 16, 193
boycotts, 16, 20, 193, 324
charivari, 132
crowds and masses, 217, 219
debates, 16, 22, 33, 86, 114, 193
women, 300, 302
demonstrations, 2, 131, 193
deputations, 107, 193, 264
hartal, 16, 256
leafletting, 16
letter-writing campaigns, 2, 16, 193, 209, 211
lobbying, 2, 5, 9, 16, 93, 193
marches and rallies, 3, 16, 209
mobbing, 16, 38, 57, 89, 213
pamphleting, 33, 120, 193
petitions, 2, 5, 16, 29, 91, 107, 112, 184, 193,
256, 261, 304
placarding, 8, 133, 181, 184, 257
speeches, 6, 11, 23, 26, 28, 37, 50, 60
strikes, 16, 20, 219
women's, 296, 300
zaps, 3
African American freedom seekers, 5, 9, 116, 176
Albert, Prince, 109, 290, 318
Allen, Professor William G., 51, 178
Amos, Sarah (née Bunting), 58

Anstruther, Robert, 303
Anti-Corn Law League, xv, 2, 20, 92, 95, 98, 99,
120, 128, 130, 176, 180, 181, 182, 187, 287, 324
anti-racism, 261, 265, 274, 278
Anti-Slavery Convention, 1840, 5, 296, 303,
317, 329
Anti-Slavery Convention, 1843, 117
Anti-Slavery Society of Canada, 133, 176
antitheatricalism, 3, 304
arctic exploration, 166, 171, 199, 201
Argyll, 8th Duke of, 237, 246
Armistead, Wilson, 176, 177, 329
Arnold, Matthew, 161, 232
Ashburner, George, 135
Assyrian treasures. *See* Layard, Austen Henry
Auld, Thomas, 120, 122
Australia, 94, 96, 189, 213, 241, 273
emigration, 169, 213
genocides, 5, 259, 266, 267
gold rush, 163, 165, 167, 169
Ayrton, Acton Smee, 133

Bahadur II, Shah, 73, 114, 136
Bahadur, Sir Radhakanta Deb, 136
Balkans, 5, 9, 192, 272
Bannister, Saxe, 266
Bapojee, Rungo, 101, 105
Baptists, xiv, 27, 47, 48, 123, 124, 239, 248, 256, 257
Jamaica, 250–3
Beales, Edmond, 2, 188, 243, 245, 257
Bengal British India Society, 112–14,
*See also* British India Society, est. 1839
Birkbeck, Dr. George, 17
Bishop, Caroline Garrison, 116
Bishop, Rev. Francis, 116
Blair, Hugh, 20, 43, 48, 80
Bogle, Paul, 253–5
Bonaparte, Charles-Louis Napoléon, 175, 183,
218, 239
Borthwick, Peter, 65, 81, 91
Boston Female Anti-Slavery Society, 91, 128
Boucicault, Dion, 191

Bourne, Henry Fox, 274
Braidotti, Rosi, 41, 321
Brecht, Bertolt, 57
Bright, Charles, 236, 240
Bright, Jacob, 303
Bright, John, 2, 50, 51, 87, 95, 128, 140, 181, 186, 187, 213, 236, 247, 249, 251, 254, 255, 257, 277
British and Foreign Anti-Slavery Society, xv, 21, 30, 95, 124, 176, 257, 275, 297, 300
British East India Company, xv, 8, 75, 76, 79, 96, 97, 106, 107, 109, 132, 139, 141, 258, 327
imperial expansion, 73, 101, 137
British India Society, est. 1839, 28, 76, 95–7, 106, 107, 112, 127, 136, 141, 182, 273, 324
British Indian Association, est. 1851, 107, 114, 134
Brooke, G.V., 41, 42, 167, 177
Brougham, Lord, 2, 17, 19, 42, 56, 77, 87, 95, 107, 128, 140, 187, 251, 254, 256, 257, 300
Brown, George, 203
Brown, John, 77
Brown, William Wells, 5, 15, 176, 178, 289–92, 325, 329
Buchanan, James, 236
Buckingham, James Silk, 79
Buckingham, Leicester, 53, 188
Buckstone, J.B., 162, 165, 167, 174, 179
Buffum, James, 128
Bulgaria, 9, 192, 269, 272, 275
Burdwan, Raja of, 136
Butler, Josephine, 210, 212
Butler, Judith, 196, 200, 317
Buxton, Charles, 257, 262
Buxton, Thomas Fowell, 84, 88, 91, 93, 257
Byron, Lord, 76

Cairnes, Professor John Elliott, 2, 248, 303
Campbell, Sir Colin, 74, 138, 139
Canada, 205, 207, 288, *See also* Red River Settlement
Caribbean colonies. *See* Slavery Abolition Act, 1833; abolition:1830s campaign
Carlyle, Thomas, 257, 309
Carnac, Sir James, 101, 102
Céleste, Madame, 312
Chamerovzow, Louis, 135, 185, 186, 188, 254, 256, 257
Chapman, Henry G., 37
Chapman, Maria Weston, 37, 88, 91, 323
Chapman, Susanna, 302
Chappellsmith, Margaret, 301
Chartism, xv, 2, 5, 20, 30, 38, 111, 125, 127–9, 131, 140, 179, 181, 209, *See also* women's suffrage
Chesson, Amelia (née Thompson), 2, 76, 135, 137, 176, 320, 334

activism, 331
attendance at performances, 46, 50, 179, 303, 314
diary, 323
early life, 116, 295
education, 331
gender and sexuality, 9, 185, 186, 305, 309, 313, 316, 321, 333, 334
Great Exhibition, 290, 296
and Harriet Jacobs, 323
journalism, 6, 56, 59, 276, 306–9, 311, 313, 316, 323, 326, 333
music criticism, 313, 319
marriage, 40, 177, 185, 307, 309, 316, 323, 330
meetings, 301
networking, 7, 9, 303, 309, 322, 325, 329, 331
obituary, 320, 332, 333
political work, 309, 315, 324
public/private, 7, 55, 58, 39, 315, 317
widowhood, 335
women's suffrage, 303
Chesson, Amelia Mildred ('Little Millie'), 312, 334
Chesson, Constance, 311, 334
Chesson, Elfrida May, 311, 313, 334
Chesson, Frederick, xii, 2, 7–9, 15, 39, 57, 141, 219, 276, 297, 304, 305
activism, 193, 197, 205, 208, 209, 213, 214, 233, 265, 273
anti-war placarding, 181
attendance at performances, 311
*Bildung*, 8, 41, 179, 190, 191, 193, 209, 211, 213, 218
consultant, 262
consultation with clairvoyant, 196
cricket, 190
death and funeral, 208, 219, 274, 276, 316, 332
early life, 38, 40, 161, 175, 331
Eastern Question, 270
editor
  *The Kidnapping of Bulgarians during the Russo-Turkish War*, 272
  *Literary Monthly*, 262
  *Political and Economics Works of Richard Cobden*, 277
  *St. James's* Magazine and *United Empire Review*, 262
  *The Story of a Fugitive Slave*, 189
evaluation of sermons, 47, 49
and Harriet Jacobs, 323
*How to Influence Members of the House of Commons*, 212
illness, 275, 333
Jamaica Affair, 251, 253, 254, 256, 257
journalism, 6, 9, 53, 136, 177, 184, 186, 188, 190, 202, 215, 233, 234, 242, 256, 261, 264, 311, 314, 316, 321, 326–8

Chesson, Frederick (cont.)
    lecturer, 268, 274, 315
    meetings, 29, 175, 301
    networking, 186, 187, 189, 197, 233, 242,
        263–5
    on genocides, 268, 269
    organizer, 38, 175, 177, 192, 203, 233
    performance analysis, 46, 53, 59, 162, 190, 191,
        216, 302–4
    protégé of George Thompson, 176, 263
    reading, 180
    religious orientation, 48, 177
    reputation, 232, 275, 278, 329
    Secretary APS, 6, 54, 185, 202, 243, 261, 265, 277
    Transatlantic telegraph, 236
    women's suffrage, 302
Chesson, Frederick William (Jr.), 313, 316, 334
Chesson, George Donisthorpe, 333, 334
Chesson, Georgina Maud, 312, 333
Chesson, Harold, 313, 334
Chesson, Julia Eastwood, 334
Chesson, Nora (née Hopper), 334
Chesson, Violet, 333
Chesson, Wilfred, 313
Chesson, Wilfred ('Willie'), 333
Chesson, Wilfrid Hugh, 334
China, Battle of Nanjing, 173
Church of England, xiv, 18, 124, 131, 260, 304, 330
Cicero, 20
City of London Literary and Scientific
    Institution, 17, 63, 328
Clarkson, Thomas, 88, 91, 95
Clay, Sir William, 129, 130, 133
Cobden, Richard, 2, 53, 95, 98, 136, 140, 177, 181,
    183, 186, 187, 211, 277
colonialism, 2, 7, 110, 111, 114, 139, 174, 177, 190,
    202, 237, 242, 274
Congregationalists, xiv, 29, 123, 176, 304
Contagious Diseases Acts, 5, 191, 209, 302
Cooper, Joseph, 262, 264, 272
Coote, Helene, 302
counterpublics, 116, 117, 294
Cowper, William, 11, 12, 18, 19, 41
Craft, Charles Estlin Phillips, 116
Craft, Ellen, 5, 15, 116, 288–90, 295, 296, 325
Craft, William, 5, 15, 116, 177, 288–91, 295,
    322, 325
Craigie, Pearl, 308
Crandall, Prudence, 88
Craufurd, Edward, 302
Crimean War, 20, 40, 51, 81, 134, 167, 173, 176,
    181, 183, 189, 199, 200, 205, 214, 276, 305
Cruikshank, George, 169, 178
    *Passing Events of 1853*, 169, 172, 173, 174, 192,
        210, 218, 219, 306

Crystal Palace, Sydenham, 48, 168, 173, 179, 313,
    314, 316, 324
Cuba, 187, 197, 256, 262

Dailey, James, 56
Dalhousie, Lord, 100, 135, 137, 139
De Lancy, Mrs., 300
Deb, Chunder Saikhur, 110
Demerara, 262, 274, 297
Demosthenes, 20, 31, 110
Denman, Lord, 17
Derby, Lord, 171, 258
Dickens, Charles, 180, 277
    *Little Dorrit*, 308, 311
Dilke, Charles Wentworth, 250, 260, 263, 267, 276
Dilke, Emilia, 276
Disraeli, Benjamin, 52, 53, 214, 242
Dissenters, xiv, 139, *See also* Nonconformists
Donisthorpe, George Edmund, 179
Douglass, Frederick, 5, 117, 120, 121, 123, 125–7,
    132, 260, 302, 323
Dr. Wardlaw's Chapel, Edinburgh, 29, 86
dramaturgy, 1–3, 5, 8, 12, 13, 16, 20, 23, 27, 41, 58,
    62, 75, 193, 209, 213, 217, 244, 264, 319
Draper, William Henry, 205
Dunlop, John, 116

Eastern Question. *See* Ottoman Empire
Edinburgh Emancipation Society, 89
Edinburgh Ladies' Emancipation Society, 121, 250
Edward, Prince of Wales, 276
Edwards, Passmore, 322
Eliot, George, 47, 276, 330
Emancipation Committee, 78, 215, 239, 245–8,
    305, 309
Emancipation Proclamation, 215, 219, 245, 246
Emancipation Society. *See* Emancipation
    Committee
Eno, Henry Lane, 195, 196
epistemology of the South, 264
*La Esmeralda*, 190
Estlin, Dr. John, 116, 127, 290
Estlin, Mary Anne, 116, 290, 296, 329
ethnographic exhibitions, 167, 169, 173
Eucken, Rudolph, 194, 195, 200, 207
Evangelical Alliance, 1846, 5, 120, 125
evangelicalism, 21, 129, 139
Exeter Hall, 15, 30, 48, 49, 87, 91, 215, 216, 219,
    245, 248, 252, 257, 259, 313, 316, 319
Eyre Defence Committee. *See* Jamaica Affair
Eyre, Edward John, 94, 243, 252–5, 257, 258, 260

Farmer, William, 295, 301
Farren, William, 162
Faucher, Julius, 188, 331

Faucit, Helena, 305
Fawcett, Henry, 257
Fenianism, 259
Fenn, George Manville, 188
Field, Cyrus, 235, 237, 240, 243
Fillmore, Millard, 133
Fitzwilliam, Mrs., 163
Forbes, Archibald, 188
Fowler, Robert N., 94, 212, 268
Fox, Colonel Charles Richard, 129, 130
France, 106, 131, 163, 173, 175, 183, 203, 214, 219, 275, 288, 297
Franklin, John, 199, 201
Frederick William, Prince, 318
Free Church of Scotland, 8, 120, 121, 124, 127, 139
free trade, 2, 8, 20, 21, 30, 72, 81, 92, 98, 112, 122, 128, 130, 131, 177, 182, 198, 233
Free Trade Hall, Manchester, 15, 178
Freedmen's Aid Society, 239, 247, 261

Gandhi, Mahatma, 3
Garrett, Agnes, 58
Garrett, Rhonda, 58
Garrison, Elizabeth Pease, 116
Garrison, Frank, 324
Garrison, George Thompson, 116
Garrison, Wendell Phillips, 116
Garrison, William Lloyd, 34, 35, 37, 77, 94, 116, 119, 125, 186, 267, 297, 300, 324, 329
Garrisonians, 49, 88, 125, 176, 179, 289, 294
    women, 289, 295, 297
genocides, 5, 7, 9, 202, 204, 266, 268, 269, 274, 326
Geoghegan, Isabella, 253
Geoghegan, James, 253
Geoghegan, Letitia, 253
Gladstone, William Ewart, 43–5, 52, 171, 213, 263, 270, 273, 313
Glasgow Anti-Slavery Society, 21
Glasgow Emancipation Society, 30, 89, 121, 122
globalization, 3, 7, 93, 235, 241
Gordon, George William, 251, 253–6, 258
Gordon, Mrs. George William, 260
Gough, J. B., 169, 178
Grandy, Moses, 5, 117, 118, 127
Great Exhibition, 1851, 57, 174, 233, 288, 303, 325, 329
Great Globe, Leicester Square, 165, 167, 168, 174, 192
Grew, Mary, 297
Grimké, Angelina, 88
Grimké, Sarah, 88
Grote, George, 17
Gurney, Samuel, 239

Hadfield, George, 29
Haiti, 84, 252, 256, 301
Hamilton, John, 179, 184, 185, 186
Handel Festivals, 317, 318
Handel, George Frideric
    *Judas Maccabaeus*, 318
    *The Messiah*, 319
Harrison, Frederic, 258
Hastings, Warren, 106
Haymarket Theatre, 53, 169, 174, 179, 192, 311
    *Mr. Buckstone's Ascent of Mount Parnassus*, 162
    *Mr. Buckstone's Voyage Round the Globe*, 167
    *The New Haymarket Spring Meeting*, 168
Helena, Princess, 51
Heyrich, Elizabeth, 23
Hindoo College, Calcutta, 106, 110, 134, 137
Hinduism, 20, 100, 136
Hodgkin, Dr. Thomas, 55, 261, 268
Hogg, Sir James, 105
Holyoake, George, 42, 80, 88, 122, 123, 187, 188, 301
Howitt, William, 95
Hudson's Bay Company, xv, 9, 197, 201, 206, 207, 258, 266
Hughes, Thomas, 257, 262
human rights, 2, 4, 6, 21, 95, 189, 190, 209, 270, 274, 315
Hume, Joseph, 106
Hungary, 131, 176, 183, 189

Ikba-ood-doula, Nouwah, 95
India, 5, 8, 28, 131, 189, 197, 241, 242, 251, 256, 259, *See also* British India Society, est. 1839
    1857 Rebellion, 8, 74, 76, 138, 141, 200, 236, 253, 259
    Bengal famine, 259
    Indian Slavery Act, 1843, 97
    Young Bengal, 107, 110–12, 136
India Reform League, 40, 176, 187
Indigenous peoples, 9, 93, 94, 198–206, 208, 218, 265–7, 269, 275, *See also* Aborigines' Protection Society
Inglis, Lady, 74, 75
Ireland, xiv, 23, 118, 123, 126–8, 133, 213, 235–7, 247, 258, 259, 297
Irigaray, Luce, 321
Isbister, Alexander Kennedy, 56, 205, 258, 266, 268, 313

Jackson, Andrew, 35
Jacobs, Harriet, 49, 323
    *Incidents in the Life of a Slave Girl*, 322
Jacobs, John S., 5, 49, 301, 322
Jamaica, 25, 53, 251, 254, 256, 260, 297
    Morant Bay Uprising, 253, 254

Jamaica Affair, 9, 237, 243, 252, 257, 258, 260, 261
Jamaica Committee, 243, 252, 257, 258, 260, 303
Jameson, Anna, 306
Jejeebhoy, Jamesthjee, 109
Joudpore, Raja of, 100
Judge and Jury Club, 49
Jullien, Louis-Antoine, 169, 172, 219

Kean, Charles, 43, 44, 163, 167, 191, 311, 313
Kean, Ellen (née Tree), 45, 311
Kelley, Abby, 132
Kelley, J.J., 268
Kemble, Charles, 179
Kemble, Fanny, 300
Kimber, Abby, 297
Knox, Robert, *Fragment on the Races of Man*, 259
Kossuth, Lajos (Louis), 177, 180

Labouchere, Henry, 202
Lafayette, Marquis de, 30, 189
Landholders' Society, Calcutta, 107, 134
Langley, John Baxter, 177, 211, 248
Langley, Mrs. Baxter, 56, 311
Lawrence, Sir Henry, 73, 138
Layard, Austen Henry, 168, 171, 173, 246, 272
Leavitt, Joshua, 88
lectures, 22, 90
Lemkin, Raphael, 265, 266, 268
Lespinasse, M. de, 301
Levien, Sidney Lindo, 254, 256
Lewis, Arthur J., 100, 105
Liberalism, 1, 8, 21, 38, 57, 98, 110, 141, 174, 202, 209, 233, 241, 249, 274, 300
Liberia, 56, 88, 133
Lincoln, Abraham, 51, 53, 216, 234, 243, 248, 298
Livesey, John, 179, 183
Lodwick, Peter, 100, 103
London Anti-Slavery Society, 19, 21, 23, 27, 77, 79, 96, 329
London Literary and Scientific Association, 106
London Mechanics' Institute, 17, 80, 301
Lucas, Samuel, 248
Lytton, Edward Bulwer, 191, 202

Macnaughton, Rev. John, 123
Malibran, Maria, 88
Manchester School, 95, 180, 186, 257, 263
market integration. *See* globalization
Martin, Emma, 301
Martin, John Sella, 117, 248
Martineau, Harriet, 32, 176, 330
    *The History of England during the Thirty Years' Peace*, 181

Martineau, James, 180, 181
mass communication. *See* telegraph
Mathews, Charles James, 53
Mathews, Mrs. (Lizzie Davenport, aka Lizzie Weston), 53
May, Samuel J., 34, 189
Mazzini, Giuseppe, 114, 176
McCarthy, Justin, 188, 243, 254
McClure, Captain Robert, 166, 171
McDougall, William, 205
meetings, 2, 3, 5, 6, 21, 57, 90, 101, 112, 140, 141, 193, 197, 209, 256, 264, 304, 325, *See also* activism
    breakfasts, 22, 115, 116, 324
    conventions, 22, 34, 90, 193
    dinners, 22, 29
    and dissent, 30
    India, 107
    as performance form, 26
    soirées, 22, 28, 34, 288, 330
    women, 301, 302
Merivale, Herman, 202
Merritt, Henry, 188
Methodists, xiv, 17, 27, 48, 124, 304
    Countess of Huntingdon's Connexion, 19, 27
Metropolitan Tabernacle, 20, 48
Mill, John Stuart, 2, 40, 41, 48, 50, 189, 237, 243, 248, 255, 257, 259, 260, 303
    *The Subjection of Women*, 330
mise-en-scène. *See* dramaturgy
Mitra, Rajendralal, 107
Montgomery, James, 72, 79
Morley, Samuel, 257, 277
Morris, Jane, 57
Morris, William, 57–9
Mott, James, 297
Mott, Lucretia, 88, 297, 298, 300, 323
Musgrave, Eliza (née Thompson), 334

Nagpore, Raja of, 100, 103
National Society for Women's Suffrage, 302
Neall, Elizabeth, 297
New England Anti-Slavery Society, 30, 88
New Zealand, 189, 192, 202, 239, 253
Newman, John Henry, 332
newspapers, 5, 6, 9, 63, 113, 134, 169, 214, 234, 235, 242, 249, 276
    anti-abolitionist, 33
    *British Indian Advocate*, 97
    *Daily News*, 212, 243, 249, 270, 275, 277
    *Dial*, 243, 277
    *Empire*, 38, 134, 179, 180, 183, 185, 188, 276, 307
    *Liberator*, 88, 186
    and meetings, 22, 24

*Punch,* 134, 237, 247–50, 254, 275, 287, 292, 294, 295
*Star,* 55, 56, 136, 177, 186, 187, 188, 190, 197, 202, 211, 243, 246, 248, 249, 255, 261, 275, 308, 326, 333
*Times* (London), 187, 202, 206, 243, 246, 247, 249, 251, 254, 276
Nicholas I, Tsar, 181
Nicholson, 'Baron' Renton, 49, 50
Nightingale, Florence, 212
Noel, Rev. Baptist, 245, 248
Nonconformists, xiv, 94, 212
North of England Anti-Slavery Society, 40, 41, 176, 180, 187
Northwest Passage. *See* arctic exploration
Nosworthy, Frank, 315
Nosworthy, Frederick, 304, 306, 315
Nosworthy, Louisa (née Thompson), 7, 116, 175, 290, 292, 294–6, 304, 306, 315, 330, 334
*The Stage and Christianity Reconciled,* 305

O'Connell, Daniel, 91, 95
Odger, George, 51, 247
Ottoman Empire, 180, 181, 183, 197, 262, 272
Oudh, King of, 136
Ovans, Colonel Charles, 100, 103, 105

pacifism. *See* Peace Society
Palmerston, Lord, 43, 52, 81, 132, 139, 184, 202, 246
Panmure, Baron, 139
Parliamentary and Financial Reform Association, 131
Parry, Sir William Edward, 171
Paxton, Joseph, 318
Peace Conference, 1853, 214
Peace Party. *See* newspapers: *Empire*
Peace Society, 125, 130, 131, 134, 141, 175, 177, 179, 181, 184, 185, 187, 269
Pease, Joseph, 94, 95, 107, 329
Peel, Sir Robert, 99, 129, 171
Pennsylvania Anti-Slavery Society, 297
People's International League, 131
performance, 4, 8, 12, 21, 36, 46, 86, 123, 174, 203, 219
    artisanal knowledge, 263
    and critique, 1, 23, 192, 306
    multi-scalar thinking, 268, 274, 294, 303, 318
    and performativity, 12, 13, 57, 127, 194, 195, 200, 203, 205, 207, 219, 296, 317
performance analysis, 6–9, 14, 15, 17, 20, 191
performance chaining, 24, 25, 28, 29, 33, 79
Philadelphia Female Anti-Slavery Society, 297
Phillips, Ann, 91
Phillips, Wendell, 91, 94

Piccolomini, Marietta, 190
Pillsbury, Parker, 176, 177
Planché, J.R., 168
Pocchini, Carolina, 191
Poland, 183, 189
Post, Amy, 323
Powers, Hiram
    *The Greek Slave,* 290, 294
Pradine, Baron Linstant de, 301
Presbyterian Church of Scotland, 30, 77, 121, 123
Prescod, Samuel J., 298
Price, Dr. Thomas, 118
Prince Shaikh Jahangir-i-Zaman Jamal ud-din, Muhammad Sultan Sahib, 95
Princess's Theatre, 171, 313
    *King John,* 311
    *A Midsummer Night's Dream,* 319
    *Sardanapalus,* 163, 168
prostitution, 50, 191, 211, *See also* Contagious Diseases Acts
public/private, 12, 56, 113, 193, 235, 296, 307, 317, 323
    hometactics, 325
    non-political private sphere, 325
    weak and strong public as performative commons, 317
Pugh, Sarah, 297

Quakers, xiv, 29, 51, 94, 123, 177, 181, 186, 190, 239, 259, 268, 297, 323

racism, 7, 35, 83, 111, 127, 173, 258–60, 265, 274
railways, 199, 208, 234, 239, 241, 265
Rancière, Jacques, 4, 41, 42, 46, 50, 59
Rarey, James Solomon, 56
Reade, Charles, 165
Red River Settlement, 198–207
reform, xv, 2, 6, 18, 130, 197, 243
    First Reform Act, 1832, 296, 301
    Second Reform Act, 1867, 301
    Third Reform Act, 1884, 213
Reform League, 2, 187, 211, 243
Remond, Charles Lenox, 116, 124, 127, 297, 300
Remond, Sarah Parker, 260, 301
repertoires, 2, 4, 9, 12, 13, 21, 193, 197, 250, 264, 317
Reuter, Paul Julius, 241
Richard, Henry, 186
Riel, Jean-Louis, 201
Riel, Louis, 206
riots, 32, 33
Rogers, J. E. Thorold, 188
Rogers, Nathaniel Peabody, 115, 297–9, 300
Roper, Moses, 118, 127

Roscoe, William, 19
Rotunda (The), 15, 18, 301
Roy, Raja Rammohun, 5
Rupert's Land, 198, 199, 202, 204, 205, 207
Russell, Edward R., 188
Russell, Henry, 178
Russell, Lord John, 130, 251, 257
Russell, William Howard, 6, 51, 276

Sahib, Appa, 100, 102
St. James's Hall, 15, 246, 301
Salisbury, Lord, 260, 272
Sands, Richard, 163, 165, 171, 173
Satara, Raja of, 95, 99, 101, 103, 111, 114, 131, 138
    deposition as cause of Rebellion of 1857, 141
Schiller, Friedrich, 59
Scoble, John, 91
Scott, George Gilbert, 46, 58
Scribe, Eugène, 53
Second Afghan War, 112
Select Committee on Aboriginal Tribes, 1837,
    93, 204, 266, 268
Sergeant, Lewis, 208, 232, 233
Shakespeare, William, 19, 46, 163, 169, 191, 300
    *Hamlet*, 81
    *A Midsummer Night's Dream*, 319
    *Othello*, 42, 81, 331, 333
    *Twelfth Night*, 45
Sharples, Elizabeth, 301
Shaw, George Bernard, 57
Sierra Leone, 5
Singh, Sreekisen, 110
slavery, 3, 18, 84, 85, 117, 119, 189, 192, 197, 202,
    234, 264, 265, 273, 294, 326
    coolie trafficking, 262, 273, 274
    Ottoman, 270, 272, 290
    slave narratives, 118, 322
        *The Story of a Fugitive Slave*, 189
        *Somerset v. Stewart* (1772), 18
    United States system, 28, 90, 288
Slavery Abolition Act, 1833, 26, 77, 84, 87, 97,
    212, 301
Smiles, Samuel, 139
Smith, Adam, 259
Smith, Albert, 163, 166, 168, 219
    *Ascent of Mont Blanc*, 171, 173, 179
Smith, Professor Goldwin, 50, 248, 257
Social Science Association, 197, 262
South Africa, 5, 56, 189, 192, 197, 202, 208, 239,
    241, 242, 259, 274, 297
    Natal, 266
Southwick, Abby, 297
Spencer, Herbert, 2, 257, 269
Spurgeon, Charles, 42, 47, 48
Standard Theatre, 312, 313

Stanley, Lyulph, 260
Stanton, Elizabeth Cady, 88, 300
Stanton, Henry Brewster, 34, 106
Steinberg, Madame, 301
Stephenson, Peter
    *The Wounded Indian*, 291
Stewart, Maria W., 300
Stokes, George Gabrile, 237
Stowe, Harriet Beecher, 163, 171
    *Uncle Tom's Cabin*, 163, 167, 170, 173
Sturge, Charles, 181
Sturge, Joseph, 26, 91, 95, 181, 186
suffrage. *See* Chartism
Sutherland, Duchess of, 246, 290

Tagore, Dwarkanath, 5, 104, 108, 109, 114, 134, 140
Tagore, Prasanna Kumar, 134, 140
Tagore, Rabindranath, 107
Talfourd, Francis, 169
Tappan, Arthur, 35, 88
Tappan, Lewis, 32, 88
Taylor, Clementina, 303
Taylor, Harriet, 303
    *The Subjection of Women*, 330
Taylor, Helen, 303, 316
Taylor, Peter, 252, 303
Taylor, Rev. Robert, 18
telegraph, 5, 6, 9, 197, 234, 242, 243, 265, 274, 327
    *A Cable-istic Extravaganza*, 237
Temperance Movement, 116, 125, 169, 175, 178
Thackeray, William Makepeace, 287, 296
theatre, 11
    careers, 306
    centrality to Victorian life, 3, 10, 14, 161, 171,
        174, 192, 213, 327
    and public sphere, 315
Thompson, Amelia. *See* Chesson, Amelia
Thompson, Anne, 7, 19, 26, 27, 79, 126, 187,
    290, 294, 296, 297, 304, 305, 312, 324,
    326, 328, 333, 334
Thompson, Edith, 187, 311, 326, 334
Thompson, Elizabeth (née Donisthorpe), 187,
    328
Thompson, Elizabeth Pease, 116
Thompson, George, 2, 7, 8, 21, 24, 36, 40, 57,
    126, 128, 130, 297, 330, *See also* Slavery
    Abolition Act, 1833; abolition
    Anti-Slavery Convention, 1840, 300
    Bible Politics, 78, 87, 113, 125, 137, 211, 268
    in Canada, 133
    Contagious Diseases Acts, 209
    death, 333
    debater, 18, 28, 105, 128
        Peter Borthwick, 25, 87, 91
    education, 17, 18, 130

embezzlement by, 77
and *Empire*, 134, 184, 185
ill health, 135, 141
and India, 29, 324
India first visit, 74, 114
India second visit, 141, 185, 187, 188, 307, 329
journalism, 38, 136, 314, 326, 327
lecturer, 9, 31, 78, 79, 88, 114, 125, 131, 136,
    246, 247, 288, 315
  ACLL, 98
  APS, 94
  British India Society, 97
  London Anti-Slavery Society, 20, 329
meetings, 22, 24, 109, 301, 328
MP for Tower Hamlets, 7, 131–3, 175, 296
opinion of Amelia Chesson, 307
performance analysis, 23, 27, 59
Radical, 18, 19
Raja of Satara, 99, 106
religious orientation, 304
reputation, 15, 134, 189
Send Back the Money campaign, 121, 123
sociability, 116
and the United States, 28
United States first tour, 5, 33, 38, 91, 329
United States second tour, 40, 133, 175, 288, 290
United States third tour, 305
Thompson, Herbert, 214, 305, 306, 312, 313, 315
  journalism, 326
Thompson, Louisa. *See* Nosworthy, Louisa
Thompson, Lydia, 167
Thompson, Marianne (née Cronin), 305,
    315
Thompson, Thomas, 17, 19, 79, 334
Thompson, William Lloyd Garrison, 116
Thompson-Chesson family, 4, 6, 7, 16, 58, 60,
    213, 305, 309, 312, 328
Thomson, Dr. Andrew, 77
Thomson, Profesor William, 237
Townshend, Samuel Ralph, 262
trades unions, 3, 50, 247, 262, 276
*La Traviata*, 189, 191, 209
Turkey. *See* Ottoman Empire

Ullee, Kureem, 95
Ullee, Ubdool, 95
Underhill, Edward Bean, 251, 257
Unitarians, 116, 132, 330
United States, 97, 181, 187, 217
  Civil War, 20, 26, 248, 251
    British support for Emancipation, 249
  Fugitive Slave Law, 8, 29, 40, 133, 247, 288, 289
  representation at Great Exhibition, 288, 294, 326
  settlement of Minnesota and Wisconsin, 199, 203

Victoria, Princess Royal, 318
Victoria, Queen, 29, 109, 173, 189, 214, 236, 290,
    317, 327
Villard, Frances (née Garrison), 324
Vincent, Henry, 125, 179
*Voluntary Review*, 1860, 215, 217

Ward, Samuel Ringgold, 176
Wardlaw, Dr., 91
Waring, Maria, 300
Webb, Hannah, 290, 296
Webb, Richard Davis, 124, 188, 290, 300, 329
Weston, Caroline, 128
Whiteing, Richard, 188
Wigham, Eliza, 123
Wigham, Henry, 179
Wigham, Jane, 123
Wilberforce, Henry William, 257
Wilberforce, Samuel, 176
Wilberforce, William, 88
Wilde, Oscar, 57
Wilks, Washington, 186, 188, 301
Wilson, Edward, 267
Wilson, George, 27, 176, 177, 180, 181, 184, 188
women's suffrage, 3, 6, 7, 58, 275, 276, 300, 309,
    317, 333, 334
Worthington, Hugh, 17
Wright, Henry Clarke, 121, 122, 125, 288
Wyld, James. *See* Great Globe, Leicester Square

Yates, Edmund, 188
Young, G. F., 287